The

POETRY *of*

JOHN MILTON

Gordon Teskey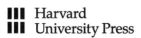

III Harvard
III University Press

Cambridge, Massachusetts
London, England
2015

First printing

Library of Congress Cataloging-in-Publication Data

Teskey, Gordon, 1953–

   The Poetry of John Milton / Gordon Teskey.

      pages cm

   Includes bibliographical references and index.

   ISBN 978-0-674-41664-2 (alk. paper)

   1. Milton, John, 1608–1674—Criticism and interpretation.

I. Title.

PR3553.T45 2015

821'.4—dc23

                                       2014040655

Annae

τὸ δὲ καλῶς κτίμενον ὦ μέγα ναίων
στόμιον, εὖ δὸς ἀνιδεῖν δόμον ἀνδρός,
καί νιν ἐλευθερίας φῶς
λαμπρὸν ἰδεῖν φιλίοις
ὄμμασιν ἐκ δνοφερᾶς καλύπτρας

"You who hold the fair-built house of the mighty cavern mouth, grant that, through the veil of gloom, with uplifted, joyful eyes, this hero's house will look upon freedom's radiant light." (Addressed to Apollo, ruling at Delphi, in the sanctuary built over the cavern in the rock, from which the vapors that inspire the priestess are exhaled.)

AESCHYLUS, *Choephori*, 458 B.C.

O Himmel! Rettung! Welch ein Glück!
O Freiheit, kehrst du zurück?

"O Heaven! Rescue! What fortune! O freedom, do you return?" (The song of prisoners emerging from a dungeon.)

BEETHOVEN, *Fidelio*, 1814; libretto by Joseph Sonnleithner from the French of Jean-Nicholas Bouilly

Ist Sehen nicht selber—Abgründe sehen?

"Is seeing itself not—to see abysses?"

FRIEDRICH NIETZSCHE, *Also sprach Zarathustra* (*Thus Spake Zarathustra*), 1883

Contents

Preface

The PRESENT BOOK is an exercise in the art of literary criticism, which I take to be the appreciation of quality, of excellence, in art made with words. Literary criticism is not science: it does not prove and discover; it persuades and reveals. But the chances of a work of literary criticism being worth reading outside expert scholarly circles are much increased if it first meets their standards, which often do involve proof and discovery. Philology, in the broad sense of the word, is where criticism starts from, but not where it ends.

That is because criticism has a higher aim, which may be described as moral and humanizing. Literary criticism is the appreciation of verbal art as a power that elevates our ordinary experience in almost every way. Literature cultivates wisdom, courage, generosity, breadth of outlook, intellectual and moral judgment, a reflective passion for justice, and, not the least of these things, pleasure, civilized pleasure as opposed to brutal or trivial pleasures. But literature also enhances our capacity for sympathizing with others, or at least for understanding them, by allowing us to travel into different moral worlds, such as that of Homer, or the authors of Genesis, or the author of *Paradise Lost*. Literary criticism strives to show why certain works of literature are good, why they have enduring quality, and, however different their values are from our own, why they are not only civilized but civilizing. I should add that I use the word *civilizing* and *civil, civilis* "of the city," with the intention of including politics, concern with the *polis*, the polity. For it seems to me—I say this as someone who cares all the arts—that literature comes first among them because it is made with our political instrument, language. Certainly John Milton put literature—which for him meant *poetry*—first among the civilizing arts, and I have written this book in agreement with his judgment on the matter.

I propose to examine the poems of a single great poet, John Milton, taking up each poem in roughly chronological order, so far as this can be determined or, in some instances, guessed. To avoid repetition and preserve clarity, I have not followed strict chronological order for the poems of the political period, or for what I call the "interstitial" Latin poems written during the Italian journey and after, including Milton's last poem in Latin, the ode to John Rouse. The book is divided according to the three well-known stages of Milton's career as a poet, the early years before the Italian journey, the middle years of political engagement, and the final years of mastery, in which the poet, now blind, composed *Paradise Lost*. For reasons I shall explain in the introduction, I call these three stages in Milton's career *transcendence, engagement*, and *transcendental engagement*.

With some regret, I have not treated the brief poetic translations in Milton's prose works, from Dante, Petrarch, Ariosto, Euripides, Sophocles, Horace, Seneca, Juvenal (in an adaptation), Geoffrey of Monmouth, and the *Flores Historiarum*. These are, of course, deft translations, although properly workmanlike. But discussion of them and of their contexts in Milton's arguments would have led too far from the concerns of this book, which is already long. A few might have merited attention to their pith, for example, the translation from Euripides that serves as an epigraph to *Areopagitica* ("This is true liberty when freeborn men / Having to advise the public may speak free"). Another, from Seneca, though it is no more than workmanlike, might have been discussed as reflecting the side of Milton's character that came to see violent revolution as a spiritual discipline, as a religious duty, and even as ritual sacrifice: "There can be slain / No sacrifice to God more acceptable / Than an unjust and wicked king." Others, such as the translation of Brutus's prayer to Diana and the goddess's reply, in Geoffrey of Monmouth's *Historia Regum Britanniae*, are agreeable but no better than their originals.

A few very minor pieces—the canceled second line of a Latin distich on Ariosto (the first line is lost); a Latin verse retraction of the Latin elegies (or of some of them), in which the poet says his breast is now encased in solid ice *("cincta rigent multo pectora nostra gelu")*; and a mocking Greek epigram, which Milton caused to be engraved on a most unflattering picture of him—are mentioned, but without discussion. Other poems perhaps deserve longer treatment than they have received here. I plead the usual excuses: time and space. *Paradise Regained* and *Samson Agonistes* no doubt deserve separate treatment, instead of being lumped together under the rubric of "late style," as they are here. My excuse is only that it interested me when I wrote this chapter to consider these works together in respect of their style, which is usually thought so contrasting.

The six chapters on *Paradise Lost* abandon the seriatim procedure and instead address what I see as the great issues raised by this great poem: its progressive view of history; its conception of history as artistically shaped, with an origin and an end; its remarkable verse (so different from any preceding blank verse, including that of Shakespeare); its sublimity and majesty; and its treatment of the central *agon*, or "struggle" of life, which is temptation. Of course, the choice of these issues is my own. There are other issues that other critics will, and do, think more important.

For example, I expect some readers may be surprised by my apparent indifference to the "problem" of Satan, though not to Satan himself, who is discussed in the chapter on Milton and the Romantics and in the chapter on temptation in *Paradise Lost*. William Hazlitt called Satan "the most heroic subject that was ever chosen for a poem" (*Lectures on the English Poets*, 1818, lecture 3; quoted in John Leonard, *Faithful Labourers: A Reception History of "Paradise Lost"* [Oxford: Oxford University Press, 2013], 2:415). Agreed. But I confess I am a little bored by discussions of Satan as a *problem*, almost as much as I am with discussions of the frigidity, or the wickedness, or the goodness of Milton's God.

So here in brief is what I think about Satan. Milton learned from the Greek tragedians, especially from the *Agamemnon* of Aeschylus, and more especially from the character of Clytemnestra—a woman, no less, and a queen—that there is much to be gained from an aesthetic point of view by making evil characters complex, glamorous, and persuasive, and to do so without changing what they are. The Greeks taught Milton to make a character majestic in evil without diminishing the evil of evil. The Latin poets taught him much, but never that. It seems to me that in nothing is Milton more Greek—that is, complex but perfectly clear in outline—than in his treatment of Satan.

As for God, Milton learned from Homer, as he did even better from Virgil, that little is lost by making the king of the gods legalistic, dull, and sententious, as people in charge generally are—and perhaps are required to be. But why must Milton's God go on for so long? In Milton's day, the thoughts of God were considered rather important, and the justification of God's ways, which is what Leibniz's new term *theodicy* meant, was also considered worthy of deep and attentive reflection. If you believe in God, and if you believe he is omnipotent, omniscient, and benevolent, then it is not uninteresting to listen to how God himself, without the mediation of theology, or of scripture, explains the problem of evil and how this problem is to be overcome. When Alexander Pope complained that Milton's God lectures like a dull theologian— "And God the Father turns a school divine" (*Epistles of Horace Imitated*, 2.1.107–8)—the age of passionate theodicy had passed, at least for the intellectual elite, if not for common people, such as Dostoevsky.

So far as I can tell—let the reader be warned I intend to speak here in somewhat formulaic terms—the immediate task of the literary criticism of poetry has three parts or, as I prefer to call them, phases. First, the task of the criticism of poetry is to explain what the intended sense of a poem is, what the poem *says*. Second, the task of the criticism of poetry is to show how the poem is also a work of art, a "made thing" that is intended to last (the Greek word, *poiêma*, means "a thing made"). Third, the task of the criticism of poetry is to reflect on why the poem is likely to last, or, as with Milton, why it has already lasted a long time and will continue to do so: why, as we say, it is *good*. (Aesthetic questions seem to me incoherent until they are detached from the analogy to the senses and put into cultural time.) These phases are philology, poetics, and aesthetics, or, to give *aesthetics* its broadest meaning, cultural endurance. There is some overlap between the three phases of the critical task, most obviously between the second and the third, between the poem at the time of its creation (poetics) and the poem's audience in time, through centuries and even millennia (aesthetics).

But there is overlap between philology and poetics, as well, the first and second phases. It seems to me no great poem can yield entirely to philological explication without interference, ambiguity, and, to use the language of information theory, noise introduced from the process of making, the underlying hum of production. The deep mystery of a poem, the sense, however illusory, of almost infinite meaning, is generated by this continual tension between philology and poetics. The dissonance, if sufficiently rich and suggestive, is passed on to the third phase, aesthetics, where it becomes resonance. So the poem endures, and is judged to be good, because of its profundity. Noise is recycled as meaning.

Yet there is something displeasingly reductive about such a formulation, as if all great poetry came down finally to error and noise, since error and noise are the rest of life and the rest of the world. These considerations suggest that the three phases of criticism—which are, to repeat, literal meaning (philology), technical arts (poetics), and enduring quality (aesthetics)—are enveloped in an atmosphere that is more primordial than they are, as perhaps we may remember from childhood, for it is the first thing we notice about poetry as children. As it happens, it is also the first thing the Greeks noticed about poetry: that it casts a spell on its audience, as if from an enchanter's wand. The term used was *thelxis*, "charm or spell," and later, *mania*, which means much the same thing as "mania" in English. Its model for Plato and others was the mania of the priestess of Apollo at Delphi, raving in the tripod of the muses, which was placed over a cleft in mount Parnassus, from which the gaseous *pneuma* of inspiration arose. (See the quotation from Aeschylus, above.) Both terms, *thelxis* and *mania*, and others like them, suggest imposing on an audience a different state of mind, one in which, as Coleridge put it, one cannot choose but hear, but in which one is also delighted and spellbound. As M. L. West has documented with philological rigor—and before him, more exuberantly, and with genius, Robert Graves—there is a rich lexical tradition in the Indo-European languages (and not, I think, only in them) in which poetic songs, *carmina*, are entertaining, challenging, and instructive, but are also magic charms.

The three phases of the criticism of poetry appear to increase in scope and, in some ways, difficulty. The first, philological explication, is much harder than is commonly supposed, especially with a poet like

Milton, and more especially with *Paradise Lost*, where syntactical difficulties abound, and also syntactical pleasures. Even advanced students can be hard-pressed to explicate the superficial meaning of a poem by Donne or of many sentences in *Paradise Lost*. As an editor of that poem I have parsed every sentence in it and cheerfully admit to having had on many occasions a hard time myself. Humility is endless, and so is philology. Beyond that, giving an account of the art with which Milton says what he says is still harder. And accounting for Milton's poetic greatness over time, his aesthetic power, is harder still. But the hardest task of all may be accounting for the quality of the spell that Milton's poetry weaves. In the following pages I have perhaps just begun on that path, or perhaps only pointed it out. My aim for the most part has been to show for each poem what Milton is saying; how he says it with consummate art; and why this art is incomparable and enduringly great.

It is a pleasure to acknowledge institutions that have with courtesy and generosity fostered my work on this project in recent years. These are the John Simon Guggenheim Memorial Foundation; the master and fellows of Massey College; the Centre for Reformation and Renaissance Studies in the University of Toronto; the warden and fellows of Merton College, Oxford; the Northeast Milton Seminar; the National University of Mexico; and the director and trustees of the National Humanities Center, where I am grateful to have held the GlaxoSmithKline Senior Fellowship, endowed by GlaxoSmithKline, Inc. I thank also my colleagues in the Department of English at Harvard for commenting on an early version of a paper on "Il Penseroso," for stimulating discussion, and for warm collegial attentions. I am grateful to the staff of the Robarts Library, University of Toronto; of the Bodleian Library, Oxford; of the Merton College Library, Oxford; of the Bibliothèque Sainte-Geniviève, Paris; of the Widener Library, Harvard; and of the Houghton Library, Harvard. Many have generously contributed conversation and criticism, often at lectures. Some, alas, are no longer among us; others, at this moment of writing, I have ungenerously forgot and can only beg their pardon for this lapse. I would mention Daniel Aaron, Sharon Achinstein, Derek Attridge, Ian Balfour, William Blissett, Piero Boitani, Elise Cavaney, Cynthia Chase, John Creaser, Eleanor Cooke, Jonathan Culler, Stuart Curran, Maria Devlin, Jeff

Dolven, the late Richard DuRocher, Philip Fisher, William Flesch, Angus Fletcher, John Fraser, David Galbraith, Louise Glück, Jamey Graham, Stephen Greenblatt, the late Marshall Grossman, Nicholas Halmi, A. C. "Bert" Hamilton, Geoffrey Harpham, Dennis Lee, Dayton Haskin, Simon Jarvis, Seth Herbst, Kenneth Hiltner, Sean Kane, the late Albert C. Labriola, Don Lavigne, Barbara Lewalski, Thomas H. Luxon, Gregory Machacek, Lynne Magnusson, Charles Mahoney, Richard McCabe, Jane Milgate, Feisal Mohammed, Mario Murgia, David Norbrook, Lady Radzinowicz, the late Balachandra Rajan, the late Stella Revard, Jason Rosenblatt, Yulia Ryzhik, Daniel Shore, James Simpson, Nigel Smith, Tiffany Stern, Paul Stevens, Roger Stoddard, Noel Sugimura, Luke Taylor, Margaret Olofson Thickstun, Ana Elena Gonzales Treviño, Marina Turchetti, Helen Vendler, Julia Walworth, Germaine Warkintin, Andrew Warren, Elizabeth Weckhurst, Leah Whittington, Joseph Anthony Wittreich, and anonymous readers for Harvard University Press. I thank Nicole Miller for her truly dedicated and excellent research assistance. I say more about my debts to Milton scholars in Appendix I and Appendix II. A finer writer listened, criticized, challenged, encouraged, and, when nothing else worked, praised as the sentences of this book came out of its author's recalcitrant head. For this and much more he is thankful to her. Of course, all errors of judgment and fact herein are my own.

Some parts of this book, since revised and expanded, have appeared in earlier publications, as follows. For Chapters 1 and 2, on the early poems and on "L'Allegro" and "Il Penseroso," *The Oxford Handbook of Milton*, ed. Nicholas McDowell and Nigel Smith (Oxford: Oxford University Press, 2009); for Chapter 5, on "Lycidas," *Milton's Rival Hermeneutics: "Reason Is but Choosing,"* ed. Richard DuRocher and Margaret Olofson Thickstun (Pittsburgh: Duquesne University Press, 2012); for Chapter 8, on Milton and the Romantics, *The Blackwell Companion to Romantic Poetry*, ed. Charles Mahoney (Malden, MA: Wiley-Blackwell, 2011); for Chapter 10, on the origin in *Paradise Lost*, *Las Hondas Regiones del Infierno*, ed. Mario Murgia (Mexico City: n.d.). I am grateful to these publishers for allowing me to redeploy this material here. Finally, my thanks to Lindsay Waters and the excellent editorial and production staff of Harvard University Press.

The Poetry of John Milton

Introduction

THIS IS A BOOK about the poetry of John Milton, which means it is a book about poetry, too, and also about being a poet. It will be observed from the title, in which the word *poetry* comes first, that this is not a book about Milton's prose or about Milton's ideas except where these are annealed in the fires of creation. Nor is it a book about Milton's life and times, about the seventeenth century or the early modern period, or even the most important series of political events in Milton's day, the English Revolution, except insofar as these things, especially the last, to which Milton was passionately committed, are of assistance in understanding his poetry and his mind, the mind of a traditionalist in aesthetics and a radical in politics.[1] Instead, this volume offers a roughly chronological appreciation of all Milton's poems from the beginning of his career to the end, from the elegant psalm adaptations he did at age fifteen, which already show Milton's insurgent temperament, to the high seriousness of the poems that formed Milton's grand meditation on history and his sharp diagnosis of the problem of history: *Paradise Lost*, *Paradise Regained*, and *Samson Agonistes*. (The date of the composition of *Samson Agonistes* remains in dispute. I hold the traditional view it is Milton's last work, whatever sketches he made for it earlier.[2])

The problem of history for Milton, to put it simply at the outset, is how to win liberty and keep it. As the idea of liberty developed in Greece and Rome (Greek *eleutheria*, Latin *libertas*), it was understood to be the restricted possession of an ethnicity, as with the Greeks, or of a citizenship, as with the Romans. All others, especially Asiatics, were slaves, even if not technically enslaved.[3] Milton radicalizes liberty by making it the defining condition of the human, originating in the Garden of Eden. But the circumstances of history, entangled as these are with our fallen moral condition, make liberty hard to win and much harder to keep. The history of Israel, as recounted in scripture, is for Milton the prime but by no means single example of this. Servitude to history is the universal condition of humanity, which is usually incapable of winning liberty and, as it appears, always incapable of keeping it. The reason, for Milton, does not have to do with large social forces but rather with what's inside us: shameful cowardice and shameless rapacity. These opposite but complementary impulses are the drivers of history. Liberty, as this idea is developed in *Paradise Lost*, is the original state of human nobility before the Fall, and true liberty is lost when Adam and Eve are banished from the Garden of Eden, having displayed in their conduct the seeds of the rapacity and cowardice that will drive history on. From this condition, that of being in history, God intends us to free ourselves, in the midst of history.

That we cannot manage to do this alone leads into the uneasy subject of Milton's Christology and his ideas on the Redeemer. To be truly free, you should be capable of freeing yourself. But how can you do so if you are not free within yourself, if your appetites and passions tyrannize over you? From a Christian point of view, which accepts the conviction of sin, to free oneself one would have to be already what one is striving to become. That is a predicament requiring aid from outside the system, aid known as grace. But this aid, once it arrives, as the incarnation of the Word in Jesus Christ, must itself become a part of the system, thus inaugurating an economy of sacrifice: Christ must become a human being and be put to the test. That is the meaning of the *Incarnation* for Milton, of God becoming flesh, at least by the time Milton reaches *Paradise Regained*. But we can see traces of this anthropic Christianity already in Milton's first masterpiece, "On the Morning of Christ's Nativity," composed shortly after his twenty-first birthday. That is, the doctrine of the Incarnation, of God becoming flesh, does not for Milton lead to a *theophany*, a "revelation of a god," but to an *anthropophany*, "a revelation of the human," such as occurs at the climax of *Paradise Re-*

gained.[4] It is a revelation of the human as having taken into itself the full authority of a transcendent God.

In traditional Christianity, the downward direction of history, typified by the degeneration of the nation of Israel (despite its periodic revivals) is suddenly reversed by the grace of Jesus Christ, who dies on the cross to redeem humanity from sin. After that sacrifice, history—at least history within the Church Militant—moves upward again, by the "work of restoration," the *opus restaurationis,* in the phrase of Hugh of Saint Victor, which progressive work is founded on Christ's sacrifice.[5] By founding the work of restoration on a different, nonsacrificial event, on Jesus's ethical and intellectual victory over Satan in the wilderness, Milton goes so far in identifying Jesus with humanity—ideal humanity—that it is not unreasonable to conclude that toward the end of his life Milton had moved out of Christianity as it had existed in Europe for a millennium and a half, even if he still believed in the divine origin of Jesus as the Son. I say this because it seems to me a Christian must in some way (whether as a victory over sin, as a penal substitution for sin, or as an example of self-sacrifice for others) believe Jesus died for the sins of humanity.[6] But Milton believed Jesus showed humanity how to win liberty and keep it.

Despite the conventional Christian soteriology—the theory of salvation—expressed in book 3 of *Paradise Lost,* I think Milton's ideas on the subject were closer to Walter Benjamin's perhaps confused but undeniably revolutionary messianism than to the ancient logic of sacrifice and satisfaction. Like Benjamin, Milton has an idea of historical time as a series of moments of opportunity, of *kairos* (the instant in battle when there is an opening in the ranks of the enemy, allowing the archer to send the arrow at a prime target) in which the possibility of radical freedom can be seized. For Benjamin, it is as if the revolution itself were the Messiah. Milton seems to have entertained a similar view in the middle period of his life, when the English Revolution held out the promise of bringing on the Second Coming of Christ, perhaps as the body of the nation in an incorporate whole. William Blake read Milton that way and his image for the displaced Christology he saw in Milton is the figure of the risen Albion, surrounded with a corona of light, his head up, his arms spread, and his hands open. The approximately cruciform image is meant to recall Jesus on the cross but to overturn its sacrificial meaning.

Enough has been said to show how Milton took a religion that from the beginning, under the Roman Empire, preached meekness and patient acceptance of the wicked condition of this world while expecting the next, and radicalized it in the new circumstances of the seventeenth century in Europe, as a political philosophy for transforming this world. (That Christianity was subversive of the supporting values of the Roman imperium in which it arose is of course another matter.[7]) Milton saw the Hebrews of the Old Testament as a revolutionary people to whom God had given a revolutionary idea: that to be obedient to Him and his law is to be freed of obedience to lesser, worldly powers—Egypt and Babylon, Hellenistic Greece, and eventually Rome—and also to be free of obsession with immoral desires. In obedience to God is liberty, especially political liberty. For a time Milton regarded the English in the 1640s as God's new Chosen People, who were ready to teach the rest of humankind how to fight for liberty. The fight would consist not only in military deeds—although there would be plenty of those—but also in the thinking on which military deeds must be based, what Blake in the proem to *Jerusalem* called "mental fight." A century after, the leaders of the American and French Revolutions would regard the English Revolution as a precedent and Milton as its prophet.

Out of this political enthusiasm in the middle period of Milton's life a new idea would emerge. The idea is to turn away from all eschatological hopes for the future, or for the present, and consider the *origins* instead—in philosophical terms, the *archai*, the determining principles standing at the beginning of history. In mythical terms, which are native to poetry, the *archê* of history is the story of Eve and Adam in the Garden of Eden. Only by returning to this biblical origin, Milton supposes, does it become possible to grasp the principles underlying history, and with them, at some uncertain time in the future, to transform the world from within.

The status of the Bible for Milton is perhaps easy to misunderstand, at the outset of the twenty-first century. For him, it was a revolutionary, not a conservative, book. The Bible was the one text that held absolute authority as political truth and could therefore be used to overturn the lies on which corruption and tyranny are based. Like his follower, William Blake, Milton seized on the Bible as an instrument for chastising the arrogance of power and exposing the weakness of its servants. The American and French revolutionaries would write their own sacred texts, though they were readers of Milton. I am pointing out what has no doubt often been commented on before: the importance in revolutionary situations of sacred texts as authorities. To what other authority can the revolutionary appeal, when the enemy holds all the worldly instruments of legitimation, an army, a government, a judiciary, a priesthood, a king? Milton seized on the Bible and drew on its incendiary power. He drew especially on its prophetic power, since the biblical prophets were themselves courageous opponents, when circumstances required, of the Temple priesthood and the king. Before *Paradise Lost* the most striking instance of Milton's turning to the Bible for revolutionary energy is "Lycidas." In the course of a decorously pagan, pastoral elegy, Saint Peter breaks in, bearing the signs of his authority, and ferociously condemns the bishops as "blind mouths" that have failed in their duty while scrambling for the benefits of power. By implication, Milton is condemning with biblical outrage the entire system of Charles I's arbitrary rule without parliament, and promising a terrible vengeance, though it is prophetically obscure: "But that two-handed engine at the door / Stands ready to smite once and smite no more" ("Lycidas," lines 130–31).[8]

What I have summarized in brief is a development in Milton's career through the three phases into which this book is divided. The three phases of Milton's career are well known: (1) the poet's idealistic youth, extending from the earliest poems to "Lycidas," *"Mansus,"* and *Epitaphium Damonis*, these last composed around his thirtieth year; (2) the poet's active middle age, during which the poems are more forcefully political, and more directly inspiring to the political idealism of the Romantics; and (3) the poet's later middle age, extending into old age, when he was at the height of his powers and composed *Paradise Lost, Paradise Regained*, and *Samson Agonistes*. These phases are not merely circumstantial developments to be explained away by where Milton was in his life and by what was happening in England at the time, so that, for example, he was an idealist when privileged and sheltered, a realist when entangled in the world, and a great author when political defeat forced his withdrawal from public affairs. We are not dealing in the first instance with a life; we are dealing with the progress of thought. Each phase overlaps untidily with the others and contains something of the others in itself. As a result, there is a development from one phase to the next in a dialectical pattern that suggests a struggle to grow, not a passive response to altering circumstances. A youthful desire to escape the world—to go to Heaven—contains in it the seed of an aggressiveness that matures into a fighting spirit directed toward the world. But this fighting spirit contains *in nuce* an inclination to detachment, so as to search for deeper principles underlying "tumultuous times" and "hoarse disputes" (*YP*, 2:807 and 821).[9] As those principles emerge, Milton attains a detachment that is also engaged. On the one hand, his detachment avoids regressing to the escapism of the first phase because his attention is now focused diagnostically on this world. On the other hand, the detachment avoids unfruitful and shortsighted pugnacity in favor of thinking about the underlying problem of history.

The first phrase is that of *transcendence*, when the problem of history is a question of how to get out of this world and into the next. It is the longing for transcendence that is staged so powerfully, and then so powerfully negated, in "On the Morning of Christ's Nativity." We are made to feel as if the coming of Christ has brought history to its end and Heaven has opened its gates to us now. In the second phase, that of *engagement*, the period chiefly occupied by works in prose, Milton is concerned to change the present world by direct action and argument. The poems of this period likewise have a mature sense of the immediate occasion and of the revolutionary possibility of making a better world now. This is often done by hitting hard, as when Milton calls down divine vengeance on the "bloody Piedmontese," who slaughtered the Waldensians—is this Europe's first poem against genocide?—or when he concludes his sonnet to Lord General Fairfax: "In vain doth valour bleed / While avarice and rapine share the land." In this period Milton's revolutionary temperament is seen at its height. He believed he was living in a moment of historical *kairos*, a time of opportunity for sudden and radical change.

The third phase, which opens with *Paradise Lost*, is that of *transcendental engagement*, when present events are pushed into the background and the problem of history returns, now as a radical exposure of the underlying moral conditions of history. The exposure lays open to view a point of departure that is outside—but only *just* outside—the system of history, on the scene of the Creation, and in the Garden of Eden. It is no longer a matter of the Son of God becoming incarnate and entering history, at its center. Instead, it is a matter of humanity, in the persons of

Eve and Adam, entering into history from an ideal state just prior to history. There, at the origin, it becomes possible to see what human nature truly is, and what it should be. For Milton, human nature is not essentially historical. In this, his youthful idealism survives into old age. To use Walter Benjamin's language—and the affinity of this language with the drama would have appealed to Milton—behind what appears to us as a series of historical events is the truth, which is that history is one single and increasing *catastrophe (eine einzige Katastrophe)*, creating a pile of the dead, such as we hear of at the conclusion of *Samson Agonistes*.[10]

The hope of undoing this catastrophe no longer lies in simple escape, that is, in transcendence, whether at the Nativity of Jesus, at the Passion, or at the Apocalypse. Nor does such hope lie any longer in a sudden and convulsive exertion of English virtue, which will bring in the Commonwealth. Instead, the hope lies in a radical separation of the mixed principles involved, of the essential nobility of human nature, on the one hand, and, on the other hand, of history as depraved human nature. The poet's conceptual orientation at this third phase is *transcendental* (note the weaker adjectival form of the word) to the extent that this orientation must stand outside the immanent conditions of history, where the principles are mixed. Transcendental engagement is an act of *diaeresis*, of separation, in order to see the principles in their originative state: (1) human nature on the scene of Creation, and (2) human history on the scene of the Fall.

Of course, the reason for such an analysis, its *telos* or fulfillment, is eventual *engagement:* to live within history while subverting its most powerful illusion; that how things are is indeed how they are, and how they must be. Like Kama Mara before Prince Gautama, Satan in *Paradise Regained* will present to Jesus this illusion of the world in its most spectacular form, a transfiguring vision of power. Jesus is shown a panorama of the known world in the first century A.D., and a march-by of the military powers of Asia and Europe: the Parthian and Roman Empires. Even Greek culture is displayed as a *picture*. Jesus can dismiss it all as "ostentation vain of fleshly arm" (*PR*, 3.387) because he cannot be confused about the difference between truth and power.[11]

The words *transcendence* and *transcendental* sound similar and indeed are; however, as I employ them, they mean quite different things. The first word, *transcendence*, is a noun and an action, a going away to Heaven, to the "palace of Eternity" (*A Masque Presented at Ludlow Castle, 1634,* line 14). The second word, *transcendental,* is an adjective modifying a noun, *engagement. Transcendental engagement* means a struggle on behalf of the good in this world by means of philosophical abstraction, isolating principles for study. In short, the phase of *transcendence* points forward in time to its *telos,* which is Heaven, and to the Apocalypse as its defining event. The phase of *transcendental engagement* points backward in time to Eden and the Creation, and to the *archai,* the "beginning principles." *Transcendence* and the *transcendental* both take us out of history and out of this world: but *transcendence* is always turned away from this world and from history, while the *transcendental* is turned toward this world and toward history. Nor is this a static orientation. In the former case it is a simple movement from here to there, from earth to Heaven. In the latter case it is a dialectical movement from here to there and back again: out of history and into myth, and then out of myth into history. This movement is progressive, not circular. History is transformed by it and is not quite the same as it was before the movement began. History is now seen in clearer, moral terms as a power acting through individuals, and ideally, ultimately, through all individuals. That is the vision of history we encounter in *Paradise Regained* and *Samson Agonistes.*

For Milton, as I have said, it is finally up to us to save ourselves, that is, to win for all humans the liberty that made us human in the first place, and to do so without relapsing into bondage again. In what sort of system does Milton imagine such a struggle taking place? It is not one in which history is all there is. It is not an immanent system. The Christian Bible provided Milton with a transcendental framework, partly mythical and partly theological, within which to imagine human being in the world as a totality and as a process of development in time. Within that frame it was possible for him to think of history as a fallen condition and as fundamentally against human liberty. *Paradise Lost* means "liberty lost." Milton's poem about the redemption of humanity by Jesus Christ, *Paradise Regained,* is startlingly not about the Crucifixion. Its subject is a mental fight in the desert between Jesus, who represents us. Jesus is an ideal human being, and one who does not have divine powers so that his moral power counts for us.[12] Against him is Satan, the orchestrator and conductor of history as continual catastrophe.

There are limitations to such a design, or so it has been alleged, because it is Christian and biblical. It is true that all Milton's poetry is inscribed within the frame of Christian ideology, although its boisterous energies threaten the integrity of that frame. Humility and charity are perhaps not among the Christian virtues most saliently exhibited by Milton. Nor was he particularly moved, as we shall see, by the two most important images in Christianity, which are images of helplessness, intended to arouse tenderness and pity. We are all of us helpless at least twice in our lives: when we are born and when we are dying. Christianity exposes this condition by means of two images: the infant in its mother's arms and the naked man hanging on the cross. Such images were not particularly stimulating to Milton, who came to Christianity and the Bible like a commander and a conqueror, not like a servant, still less a suffering servant. He took hold of the system of biblical Christianity and bent it to his will. In a real sense, as I have suggested, Milton is half-inside Christianity, which subordinates everything to a Creator and a Redeemer, and he is half-outside Christianity, asserting, instead, the originative power of humanity and its potential for saving itself. Human creative power is not therefore limited to the making of art, which is only one of its forms. It is also political, releasing the power of the human spirit to banish cowardice and overthrow corruption, including the corruption of tyranny. Milton came to see the making of poetry as a way of doing this, too. Only Dante had done as much before him.

Other epic poets before Milton—Homer, Virgil, Tasso, even Spenser—turned to exemplary moments within history, but were incapable of imagining history in its entirety, as the human condition after the Fall. After Milton, composers of long poems (Byron, despite his vivid historical imagination, may be an exception) have had difficulty conceiving of history as anything other than the defining condition of human existence. Milton created this change of perspective on history. The difference is that Milton did not think history defines what we are but rather defines what we have become and what we must overcome.

Of the twenty-one volumes of the *Columbia Edition of the Works of John Milton* on my shelf, four of the slenderer ones at the beginning contain all the poetry he wrote. In two of those volumes reposes *Paradise Lost*, one of the greatest long poems created in Europe since the first century B.C. Of these, perhaps only Dante's *Commedia* stands a little higher in the esteem of the world. Of course, the prose writings in those remaining seventeen volumes of the Columbia edition—tracts in opposition to having bishops; tracts justifying divorce on biblical grounds; defenses of the English people and of the execution of King Charles I; attacks on royalist propaganda; a theological treatise; a textbook on logic; a history of Britain and another of Muscovia; many smaller and more occasional works, including university exercises, state papers, and private correspondence—are of interest because of their author. There is also Milton's passionate plea to his countrymen to establish a free commonwealth, that is, a republic, on the model of Venice or Geneva, instead of allowing Charles II to return and take up the throne. These works are of great interest in themselves and contain some splendid writing. They are the prose of a poet burning with inspired indignation. But their relevance to our purposes here is that they helped to make Milton the creator of *Paradise Lost*.

Even in the Renaissance, when poets were often public servants, diplomats, and courtiers, the range of Milton's activities was exceptionally wide and his learning deeper than that to which even great poets attain. He was a controversialist, a political and social thinker, an educational theorist, a theologian, a logician, an historian, a moralist, a diplomatist. In his writings as well as during his years of public service, he was a participant in the first of the great revolutions of the modern world. As will be indicated by his short and appallingly erudite treatise on education for boys, Milton's learning was both deep and extensive, and always accurate. His genius for deploying that learning has been unsurpassed by any poet since antiquity except Dante and possibly Goethe. Spenser's friend Gabriel Harvey said, "It is not sufficient for poets to be superficial humanists, but they must be exquisite artists and curious universal scholars."[13] That is true of Spenser, whom Milton referred to as his "original," but Milton was far more than a flashy polymath like Harvey, and his art, although elegant and even, at times, exquisite, is also powerfully moving.

From perhaps as early as the age of ten, when John Aubrey reports he was already a poet, Milton recognized that being a poet was the most important thing about him. He shared Horace's view—although the view goes back long before Horace—that the poet is *sacer*, which means "sacred" but also "set apart" from others and devoted, almost like a sacrificial victim, to the service of God, or of the gods.

Milton combined this classical—and indeed Indo-European—idea of the poet with the Hebrew prophets of the Bible, who were dedicated to

God's service and compelled to speak the truth on his behalf, despite the grim consequences of doing so. Such a case was Jeremiah, with whom Milton identified himself on crucial occasions of danger, notably in 1642, when he published *The Reason of Church Government*: "This [the blame that falls on prophets for speaking the truth] is that which the sad Prophet Jeremiah laments, *Wo is me my mother, that thou hast born me a man of strife, and contention.* And although divine inspiration must certainly have been sweet to those ancient prophets, yet the irksomeness of that truth which they brought was so unpleasant to them that everywhere they call it a burden" (*YP*, 1:802–3). Nearly two decades later, in 1660, months before the Restoration, when he bravely published *The Ready and Easy Way to Establish a Free Commonwealth*, Milton again took up the anguished voice of Jeremiah lamenting the foolishness of the people and the imminent fall of Jerusalem: "Thus much I should perhaps have said though I were sure I should have spoken only to trees and stones and had none to cry to, but with the Prophet, *O earth, earth, earth!* to tell the very soil it self what her perverse inhabitants are deaf to."[14]

At all stages of his life, in his Latin elegies, in "Lycidas," in *Paradise Lost*, and even in *Samson Agonistes*—for Samson is a poet of the *deed*, and at supreme risk of his life—Milton regarded this condition of poetic separation as one of danger and risk. The legendary first poet, Orpheus, whom Pindar calls "the father of song," and who is the son of the muse of heroic poetry, Calliope, was torn limb from limb by the bacchantes, maddened female worshippers of Bacchus.[15] Milton refers to this event twice in his major poetry, indentifying himself with the "Thracian bard" (*PL*, 9.34), as one naturally exposed to such danger:

> What could the Muse herself that Orpheus bore,
> The Muse herself for her enchanting son
> Whom universal nature did lament
> When by the rout that made the hideous roar
> His gory visage down the stream was sent,
> Down the swift Hebrus to the Lesbian shore.
> Alas! What boots it with uncessant care
> To tend the homely slighted shepherd's trade
> And strictly meditate the thankless muse?
>
> (*"Lycidas," lines 58–66; cf.* PL, *7.32–39*)

I noted at the outset that Milton took very seriously the condition of being a poet, regarding it as a spiritual discipline and a prophetic calling. More than anything else, it was Milton's sense of poetic mission, of being called to be a poet to transact with spiritual powers, which made him a model and a sort of father figure to the English Romantics, but also to Emerson and Whitman, and later to Arnold, Tennyson, and Browning. In France, through the great translation of Chateaubriand, Milton was for Victor Hugo, Charles Baudelaire, and the most romantic of the Romantics, the painter Eugène Delacroix (who depicted Milton dictating *Paradise Lost*), the symbol of what the human spirit can achieve through the power of art. Milton is on a level with Beethoven and Michelangelo. But if I were to choose a work of art to express the Heaven-storming, world-defying character of Milton himself, it would have to be Auguste Rodin's titanic bronze sculpture of Balzac. Nothing else is sufficiently heroic. There is the same steady Roman republican defiance of tyranny and oppression, the same immovable conviction of rightness. There is also a turbulence of spirit that can hardly be contained by the spiritual system of the Christian faith, which is like the expressive robe Balzac has wrapped around himself.

Poetry is too varied a thing for one poet, even Shakespeare—officially, the greatest of the greats—to exceed all others in all things, because advantages in one direction inevitably become limitations in another. Chaucer and Shakespeare have a more robust view of human nature than Milton does; Spenser is more intellectually varied and stimulating; Donne is more witty; Jonson, Dryden, and Pope are more urbane; Byron is more worldly and fiery; Keats is more moving, possibly more wise about life and, in the odes, more exquisitely designed; Wordsworth, Milton's only major successor, unless we count democratic Whitman—and why not?—is broader in scope and more sympathetically human, and so on. But for intensity and sublimity, and for philosophical seriousness, Milton stands alone, in my judgment just above Wordsworth's exalted "philosophic song."[16] Matthew Arnold approaches the heart of the matter when he says Milton is always "a great artist in the great style" and that reading him is the closest you can come in English to the experience of reading poetry in Greek, that is, to reading Homer, Pindar, and Sophocles.[17]

What does this mean? It means, first of all, that in Milton's verse there is a sustained elevation and grandeur that is untypical of English poetry, which at its best is never far from the earthy, the worldly, the familiar, as with Shakespeare. There is also in Milton's verse an emotional compactness, as in Greek lyric poetry and tragedy, and with that compactness an intense concentration of thought such as the English language, because it is uninflected, scarcely allows. Milton cuts beneath the play of surfaces to the essential; he always purifies; he always searches for the most general, governing idea; he holds consistently to the most exalted view of his subject, as fundamentally serious and noble; and he communicates the elements of any situation, or of any complex thought, in the clearest of outlines. All of this is very Greek. Milton's periodic syntax is not invariably clear, as syntax is in Greek, in which it is impossible not to be clear.[18] But the instances of ambiguity and obscurity are surprisingly rare for a poem written in an elaborately periodic style, in English, which is not naturally suited to such a style. The resulting strain, even the occasional obscurity, is part of the aesthetic pleasure of the poem.

The description I have given so far of Milton's style, fully formed as it is in the verse of *Paradise Lost*—its clarity, its seriousness, its penetration to essentials and to ruling ideas, its stateliness and exaltation—may give the impression of aridity and the promise of little more than exhaustion. At the thought of it, perhaps, we long to be in the Boar's Head tavern with Falstaff, who is witty, never serious, and, like his body, never clear in outline. We may long for the more easygoing obscurity of thought at the opening of *Measure for Measure* and in parts of *King Lear*, for the expansive but unchallenging mysteries of *Antony and Cleopatra*, and even the dark astringencies of *Troilus and Cressida*. Surely these are preferable to Milton's stately exaltation, nobility, and seriousness, his clarity of outline, his intellectualism. But we may affirm just as surely that the qualities Milton has, and that Shakespeare does not have, afford a distinctive and very ancient aesthetic delight—and that their poet has something higher than the aesthetic in mind.[19] Nor have I have given a responsible account of the special qualities of Milton's poetry if I rest on his intellectual clarity and power. He also has qualities of the heart and soul, an exuberant joy in the living forces of nature that inspires us and sweeps us along. I have been following Matthew Arnold in comparing Milton with the Greeks—and in comparing his language with Greek. But I can give no better or shorter description of these two sides to Milton's verse, the head and the heart, than by quoting what H. D. F. Kitto says of Greek art: "The greatness of Greek art—and let us use the word in its most inclusive sense—lies in this, that it completely reconciles two principles which are often opposed: on the one hand control and clarity and fundamental seriousness; on the other, brilliance, imagination and passion."[20]

Those words, *passion, imagination,* and *brilliance,* are as well judged a description of Milton as they are of the Greeks. The passion is, of course, Milton's concern for his subject, which is the highest imaginable. Why are we in the world, and in history? Why is the experience of being in history that of a moving catastrophe? Why is there reason to hope? There is passion also in Milton's human concern for his characters, Eve and Adam, and not only because he sees them as what we could be ourselves. He has genuine, pitying concern for them as individuals.

The imagination of Milton is inspired at every moment in *Paradise Lost,* and it is unnecessary to point to his visions of Hell and of chaos, to the war in Heaven in which mountains are torn up and thrown through the air (an effect prescient of the crushing artillery barrages of the First World War), or to the sublime horror of Sin and Death shoaling the material of chaos into a "a ridge of pendent rock / Over the vexed abyss" (*PL,* 10.313–14). The Garden of Eden on its mountaintop, crowned with "Insuperable heighth of loftiest shade, / Cedar and pine and fir and branching palm" (*PL,* 4.138–39), is superbly imagined as well, in every detail; so is its destruction, "pushed by the hornèd Flood / With all his verdure spoiled and trees adrift / Down the great river to the opening gulf" (*PL,* 11.831–33). By the *brilliance* of Milton, I do not mean his intellectual clarity—power seems to me the prime quality of his intellect— but his sensuous or aesthetical clarity. Everything is brilliantly lit, even at night, and seems to shine from within:

> But neither breath of morn when she ascends
> With charm of earliest birds, nor rising sun
> On this delightful land, nor herb, fruit, flower
> Glist'ring with dew, nor fragrance after showers,
> Nor grateful evening mild, nor silent night
> With this her solemn bird, nor walk by moon
> Or glitt'ring starlight without thee is sweet.
>
> (PL, *4.650–56*)

This effect is extraordinarily sustained in *Paradise Lost.* On his title page, with quiet understatement, Milton called this great work "a poem," a fixed sort of thing, like an object on the table: a book to be got through by turning each of the pages stacked up before one, the eye traveling across every line. But Milton had been blind for a quarter century when *Paradise Lost* was published. And he was always, exquisitely, a poet of the ear and associated poetry very closely with music, as the passage quoted above shows. (Note how "Glist'ring with dew" slows the tempo slightly.) The acoustic field is organized according to time, such that everything is temporally successive, each line, and each word, holding its position until supplanted by the next. As a blind man—one who had been severely addicted to print from a young age—Milton saw more clearly than ever what the sighted were blind to: the need to restore to the experience of poetry the quality of an event unfolding in time.

That is why, when you open *Paradise Lost* and start to read from its first line, you soon care little for the sterile geometry of point, line, and plane: the visual plane of the page, or block of verse; the left-to-right sequence of lines; and the periods where the sentences officially end. (The Trinity manuscript shows Milton could be very casual about periods even when he could see.[21]) That is because you are listening; your acoustic sense is being stimulated to an exceptional degree; and the effect is to put you inside an event that will carry you on to the end. One does not look *at* sound: one is *inside* it, enveloped by its waves.

I will offer one passage of *Paradise Lost*—not perhaps one of the most famous passages, poetically speaking—that illustrates well the microtonal atmospherics of Milton's epic. By *microtonal* (a term borrowed from music) I mean subtleties of assonance that affect us unconsciously as we read because they fall beneath the level of attention at which we perceive rhyme. By *atmospherics* I mean the poet's re-creation of the subtleties of the middle voice in Greek, where what transpires is neither active nor passive but a blending of both, such that action and agent are subtly interinanimated (to use a word of Donne's) and move onward together. There are two persons on the scene of the passage I select, Adam and God, and as the passage goes forward they seem to blend with each other in the exquisite play of verbal tenses, moods, aspects, and modes. The passage is God's first reply to Adam's request for a mate different from the animals, a mate endowed with higher reason. Different and yet alike, for the animals, Adam has noticed, come in pairs:

> Whereto th'Almighty answered not displeased:
> "A nice and subtle happiness I see

> Thou to thyself proposest in the choice
> Of thy associates, Adam, and wilt taste
> No pleasure, though in pleasure, solitary.
> What thinkst thou then of Me and this My state?
> Seem I to thee sufficiently possessed
> Of happiness, or not, who am alone
> From all eternity? For none I know
> Second to me or like, equal much less.
> How have I then with whom to hold converse
> Save with the creatures which I made and those
> To me inferior, infinite descents
> Beneath what other creatures are to thee?"

> (PL, *8.398–411*)

   The passage moves like a dancer. It would take a long time to point out its verbal subtleties in detail, although it is hard to resist noting how "who can I speak to, then?" becomes the superbly reflexive and elastic, "How have I then with whom to hold converse?" There is the poised wit—imitating, as Milton often does, the ablative case—of "though *in* pleasure." The point is perhaps clear enough if we appreciate (1) how subtle and shifting the verbal atmospherics are; (2) how clear the sense is notwithstanding, how orderly its progression and sharp-edged its logic; and (3) a function of the previous two, how irresistibly the passage moves forward, like a smooth but powerful current.

Paradise Lost was begun as a drama and is a supremely dramatic poem. The word *drama* comes from a verb meaning to perform an action. Dr. Johnson picked out this energetic movement to Milton's poetry when he called *Paradise Lost*—I add the emphasis myself—a "wonderful *performance.*"[22] The dramatic character of Milton's genius reflects an affinity, however, not with the English but with the Greek tragic stage. Milton has been called a baroque poet because of this dynamism, so easily comparable to the extravagances of baroque architecture and art. But the origin of this active energy is in Milton's immersion in the Greek language, with its inner, tensile strength, and in the Latin poetry he composed, which enjoys many of the same flexible and dynamic advantages. As when one is in a broad river with islands, where topography can deceive, and where one must discern from subtle indications in the water the direction in which the main channel flows, so in Milton's verse we watch for these subtle but absorbing indications. We become accustomed to unpredictable word order; we pay attention to vestigial inflexions (*me* and *my*); and we watch relative pronouns with especial care. Without such vigilance we may be forced to work back upstream and find another way down. But we are relentlessly pushed along all the same. The artistic result in Milton's English verse—with its long periodic sentences, building clause upon clause; with its unfamiliar accusative constructions and ablative syntax, including participial phrases detached from the main body like cavalry units; with its relative and, as it first seems, subordinate clauses unexpectedly usurping the main flow of thought; with its scattered prepositions and pronouns creating an agitated rhythm; with its use of Homeric epithets and burnished, classical diction—is to effect an estrangement that augments the grandeur of the subject and confers stateliness on it. We are never quite lost, because we sense an irresistible power built up within and gradually released, until the moment for a controlled burst arrives. But when it does there is more power left, carrying the narrative onward. All these effects come from the distortion of what we think of as "natural" English. No small part of the excitement of reading Milton is watching him bend to his artistic will the otherwise brittle and unyielding English language, like a weapon taken out of the forge.

Let us now reflect upon the largest problem facing the modern reader of Milton, if we happen to know what it is. For I do not think it is his theism or his Christianity *tout court*. It is this. How can a poet who believes in the literal truth of the Bible, in the fable of Adam and Eve in the Garden of Eden, say anything true by means of that fable? To my mind, the greatest difficulty in coming to terms with Milton's *Paradise Lost* is not, as it famously was for William Empson, Milton's God. It is Milton's insistence that the Bible is true, that it is the one text that cannot be doubted, submitted to critical scrutiny, or examined in the light of the historical circumstances of its composition, which occurred over some one thousand years, in three changing languages, Hebrew, Aramaic, Greek, before it was transmitted to Milton's own time in two more languages, Latin and English. Indeed, the Bible did not become what we think of it as being, a single bound book, until nearly three centuries after the latest of the writings in it was composed. It is a much harder thing to believe the Bible is the revealed truth and word of God than it is simply to believe in God.

William Empson would have none of the pusillanimity of critics who found Milton's stern God the Father merely "embarrassing," a coy word, "with its comforting suggestion of a merely social blunder." To C. S. Lewis's statement that critics who dislike Milton's God "only mean they dislike God," Empson heartily agreed, although he found *dislike* another pusillanimous word: "I think the traditional God of Christianity very wicked." That is because at the center of Christianity is a human sacrifice, Jesus's Redemption of humankind by suffering on the cross. Empson argues, rather improbably to my mind, but with illuminating vigor, that Milton is "struggling to make his God appear less wicked," presumably by downplaying the crucifixion, which Milton does indeed do. But in the end, Empson says, honest critics feel "there is something badly wrong about it all" because of Milton's "loyalty to the sacred text."[23] That is where the greater problem lies: in Milton's loyalty to the sacred text, his acceptance of the Bible as literally true.

The question must be asked: did Milton believe literally that humanity began with two full-grown human beings, Eve and Adam, who have never been children, who find themselves in a state of bliss in the Garden of Eden, but who are cast out for eating some fruit God had forbidden, having been tempted thereto by a talking serpent, which creature would later be interpreted as Satan in disguise? Can Milton truly have rejected the subject of King Arthur for his epic poem because he doubted the historical witnesses for Arthur's existence (*YP*, 5, pt. 1:164–65; *Columbia*, 10:127–28), in comparison with Adam and Eve? Would Milton, who defended Galileo and had such a high regard for scientific knowledge, have denied or been shocked by the theory of evolution, published as Darwin's *Origin of Species*, in 1859? Richard Dawkins says it was all but impossible to be an atheist before 1859, but I do not see why not. It was easy enough, although dangerous, for Marlowe, Raleigh, and Bacon. Sir Thomas Browne, in *Religio Medici*, feels the need to defend his faith against "the general scandal of my profession," medicine, for predominating atheism; the evidence of church fathers such as Tertullian suggests belief was always harder than the alternative, agnosticism or atheism.[24] To the question whether Milton would have baulked at the theory of evolution, I think the answer must be no. He would no doubt have been stunned and surprised by it (as I was, and as you were). But simply to deny its truth would be to deny validity to the scientific method itself. Milton was on more than one occasion a defender of that method and of its greatest exponent in his day, Galileo.

Yet he would still have held his epic poem to be true, and no less true for the theory of evolution. By the *literal* truth of the Bible, Milton meant *literal* literally: that is, to the *letter*. God inspired the biblical writings in human minds—perhaps, for Milton, in the case of Genesis, the mind of Moses—to be accommodated to our understanding as light to the eye. God did not intend us to allegorize the fable of Adam and Eve in Eden, that is, to affirm with Origen and others that the elements of this fable stand for concepts that can be stated by us in other, less naive terms, terms that belong to some other system of belief, such as Neoplatonic philosophy. Instead, Milton would argue, God intended the fable to be taken exactly in the form it appears, and to be a lesson that we learn from by meditating on it. As H. R. MacCallum wrote in a classic study, "Reacting against those forms of religious speculation which delight in veiled mysteries, mysteries partially hidden by the very symbols through which they are bodied forth, Milton held that Scripture is plain and perspicuous in all things necessary to salvation and that its revelation is adapted to the mind as physical light to the eye."[25]

It is in this sense that I shall refer to the story of Eve and Adam in the Garden of Eden as a *transcendental* fiction, or myth. The myth transcends normal experience, historical witnesses, and physical possibility. But the myth is true for Milton in a deeper sense: that of being the best and indeed the only form in which to transmit back into history the moral truth of freedom.

I

TRANSCENDENCE

1

On the Early Poems

In the fourteen years between 1624 and 1637, Milton composed some fifty-two poems in four languages. The obvious watershed is "On the Morning of Christ's Nativity," the poem Milton composed little more than two weeks after his twenty-first birthday and shortly before dawn on Christmas morning, 1629. It is likely he was home in London from Cambridge, in the family home on Bread Street, which was situated on the high ground of Ludgate Hill to the west of the city center, near Saint Paul's Cathedral.[1] He would say later that the first light of dawn brought the poem to him. At the hour in which he wrote, on that particular morning, there would have been very few lights and very few sounds—no torches or candles, no carters' cries or street vendors' songs. Despite the air pollution, which was already a serious problem, the stars would have been visible and bright, especially from the hill and especially toward the east, for the city fell away in that direction onto lower ground toward London Bridge. He was waiting for dawn, which seemed, as it does when we are watching for it, to hesitate before it arrives. The stars seemed reluctant to leave and the first light of dawn hadn't touched the horizon or the dark overhead. Perhaps he began at the beginning and said to himself, "This is the month and this the happy morn."

Some days later, when he was still working on the poem, or at least polishing it, Milton described this scene in a Latin verse epistle addressed to his friend Charles Diodati:

I am singing of the peace-bearing king of Heavenly origin, of the
happy ages prophesied in Scripture, of the infant God born in a
poor stable who with his Father dwells in the Kingdom of Heaven,
of the new star born under the cosmic vault, of the hosts of angels
singing in the air, and of the pagan gods surprised in their various
shrines and banished to Hell. I gave this gift to Christ for his
birthday. The first light of dawn brought it to me.

("Sixth Elegy," lines 81–88)

"On the Morning of Christ's Nativity," or the Nativity Ode, is
Milton's first work of genius and his first contribution to the canon of
English poems that will last as long as the language is spoken. It is therefore interesting to see how Milton prepared for this achievement, which
may well have surprised him, as much as it astonishes us. But it is also
interesting to consider how the very brilliance of that achievement may
have been an obstacle to further development. Such obstacles are not
unheard of in the annals of poetry. Some poets overcome them, often
after considerable artistic and psychological struggle. Other poets do
not and are ever after in pursuit of the glory of early promise. The young
poet who finds himself or herself in these circumstances—happy to be
met by unexpected success but perhaps not fully aware how this success poses a danger—has to stop trying to repeat what has already been
done and accept the challenge of thinking about poetry in a new way.

The sudden brilliance of "On the Morning of Christ's Nativity" left
Milton supposing that the purpose of poetry is to unite heaven and earth,
the divine and the human—or, as Milton would express it almost three
decades later, "to justify the ways of God to men" (*PL*, 1.26). But this
particular purpose for poetry, entailing a vertical movement from earth
toward heaven and from heaven toward earth, is at odds with something
in the nature of poetry itself, something characterized, at the level of
figurative language, by the lateral movement of metaphorical and met-
onymic substitutions. The union of the human with the divine may be
attempted by a transcendental projection of the human in the direction of the divine, by "regaining to know God aright" (*YP*, 2:367),
whether by prayer, learning, or poetry, which Milton commonly imagines in terms of flight. Or the union of the human with the divine may
be initiated by a movement in the opposite direction, from heaven to
earth. The most important example is the Incarnation, when God, in

the person of the Son, descends into the world and experiences everything a human being experiences, except, of course, sin. (One may be forgiven for thinking that is a lot to leave out.) One of the great scenes of *Paradise Lost* is the descent from Heaven of the angel Raphael to give warning and counsel to the parents of the human race.

In biblical terms, the condescension from the divine to the human is a *covenant*, an effort by God to establish a working relationship with humanity. The first covenant was the simple command not to eat the fruit of the Tree of the Knowledge of Good and Evil. With the breaking of this covenant, however, human nature is so vitiated by sin, by the Fall, that future efforts to restore the relationship between the divine and the human are rendered ineffectual by the inability of humankind to keep its side of the covenant. Yet God is determined that his relationship shall be restored. History, biblical history, is the story of his efforts to do so. Up to the time of the Incarnation, God's method of doing so is synecdochical: he lets one part of humankind stand for the whole, Noah and his family for the rest of humankind; Abraham and his descendants for the rest of humankind; Moses and the keepers of the Law, the Hebrews (later, the Jews), for the rest of humankind; David and his kingdom for the rest of humankind. As descendants of the tribes of Judah and Benjamin, the Jews are themselves a part or, to use the prophetic word, a remnant of the Hebrews, the ten tribes of the northern kingdom of Israel having been lost. There is a suggestion in the prophets that with the coming of the Messiah and the establishment of his kingdom on earth, the Jews will be a priestly people, ministering to the rest of humankind, so that it is not only the Jews who will be saved.

But for Christians this promise is never fulfilled—or at least not in this way. The Incarnation of the Son of God in the person of Jesus Christ is therefore the next, and the most extreme, effort at making one part of humanity stand for the whole. Jesus stands for all. As the Son says in *Paradise Lost* when proposing to atone for the sins of mankind: "Account me Man" (*PL*, 3.138). Jesus is for a time the only human being about whom God cares and thus the only human being who stands condemned of original sin and under a sentence of death: "Account me Man." But once Jesus has undergone the sentence and died on the cross, atoning for original sin on behalf of humanity, humanity is included in this atonement. What was formerly the tactic of the separated part, of the remnant, has become something like the figure of synecdoche, where the part stands for the whole, a figure otherwise known as the *symbol*. No longer does "Account me Man" mean "forget the rest of mankind and focus your wrath on me." The phrase now means "include the rest of mankind in me, and impute my merit to them." That is the meaning of the Incarnation. The downward motion of the Son from Heaven to Earth is repeated in the figures of Truth, Justice, and Mercy, who return to earth because he does:

> Yea, Truth and Justice then
> Will down return to men,
> Th'enameled arras of the rainbow wearing,
> And Mercy set between,
> Throned in celestial sheen,
> With radiant feet the tissued clouds down steering,
> And Heaven, as at some festival,
> Will open wide the gates of her high palace hall.
>
> ("*On the Morning of Christ's Nativity*," lines 141–48)

Making poetry becomes for Milton a shamanistic art involving movement up and down on a vertical axis, or ladder, between Earth and Heaven and between the Earth and Hell or, as he called them in the Latin poems, Olympus and Tartarus. In keeping with this view, he continually associates poetry with flying. But a great imaginative turning point in Milton's career is the moment, at the beginning of book 7 of *Paradise Lost*, when he relinquishes soaring and says he will now speak "Standing on Earth, not rapt above the pole." (For Milton, the *pole* is not one of the terrestrial poles, our North and South Poles. The pole is the highest point on the orb of the universe. To be "*rapt* above the pole" is to soar above the stars into Heaven.) To the extent that poetry is concerned with the world that is spread out around us horizontally, our environment, this world is for Milton not the natural world but rather the world God created. All relations between beings in the natural world—competitive, cooperative, and metamorphic relations—are reinscribed by Milton onto the relation between the Creator and his creatures. Poetry itself is inspired not from springs in the earth but from above: the proximate cause of poetry is the poet, but its ultimate cause is the Creator. For the Christian poet who claims inspiration from God, the poem is a secondary revelation of what God has created—or of what

God has done, especially at the Creation. This makes it difficult for the poet to be a creator in his own right, which he does by drawing inspiration—material inspiration—from outside Christian culture: from the classical pagan tradition.

A figure of poetic vision is offered to us at the beginning of the twelfth book of *Paradise Lost*, when Adam stands with the angel Michael on the mountain above Paradise, learning what is to come in the future. Whereas poetic vision is comparable with flight, with transcending the earth, the most frequent image of poetry in Milton's later verse is associated with articulate sound, with narrative. Adam has already learned of this future as it extends from the moment, shortly to come, when he and Eve will be led out of the garden and human history will begin. In an astonishing series of pageants, with much anthropological speculation on primitive humans, Adam actually sees this history up to the time of the great deluge, which covers the entire earth with water and then, like an aging face, wrinkles as it is blown upon by the north wind and dried by the sun. Michael pauses here, "betwixt the world destroyed and world restored" (*PL*, 12.3). Up to this moment, that is, through most of the second half of book 11, Adam has not merely heard but seen, in visions, what is to come in the future. How does he see them? Milton tells us three things Michael did: he removed the cataract-like film from Adam's eyes that had grown on them since he ate the fruit; he cleansed the visual nerves extending back from the eyes; and he instilled in the eyes themselves drops of water from the Well of Life:

> But to nobler sights
> Michael from Adam's eyes the film removed
> Which that false fruit that promised clearer sight
> Had bred, then purged with euphrasy and rue
> The visual nerve (for he had much to see)
> And from the Well of Life three drops instilled.
>
> (PL, *11.411–16*)

His spirits overcome by these attentions, Adam sinks down, unconscious and entranced, as he sank down before, dazzled and overpowered by God's presence, "as with an object that excels the sense" (*PL*, 8.456), in the moment before God created Eve by taking a rib from his side. But he is soon raised and told to open his eyes to the visions of the future, visions he is to be shown by the angel Michael, whom he calls, "True opener of mine eyes" (*PL*, 11.598). It is important that all these things be seen, until they are swept from Adam's sight by the great Flood, or "Deluge," from which Noah and his household are saved in the ark. The rainbow is set in the heavens as a covenant that the earth shall continue to the end of time through the course of its cycles, of sewing and harvest, summer's heat and winter's frost, until the Apocalypse—"till fire purge all things new" (*PL*, 11.900). It is important that Adam himself see the rainbow that Noah and his family—"the ancient sire . . . with all his train" (*PL*, 11.862)—shall see: "over his head beholds / A dewy cloud and in the cloud a bow / Conspicuous with three listed colors gay / Betok'ning peace from God and cov'nant new / Whereat the heart of Adam erst so sad / Greatly rejoiced" (*PL*, 11.864–69).

What Milton had to learn after "On the Morning of Christ's Nativity," and despite that poem's success, is that while poetry would remain for him oriented to the divine, poetry is fundamentally, and in the broadest sense of the term, an ethical art, one that concerns itself with lateral relations between the proper self and the other. With empathy, poetry crosses the boundary of our seemingly irreducible difference, body to body and mind to mind. It is like what I hear of quantum entanglement or action at a distance. We sympathize with something or someone far off and not present before us, although the poem is present in front of us. Metaphor, the living heart of poetry, is not an anagogical but a lateral movement; it is not a "going up" but a "carrying across."

We have thus two periods in Milton's early career up to "Lycidas," one before and one after "On the Morning of Christ's Nativity" (1629). The most immediately noticeable change is that in the first period Milton writes poetry mostly in Latin and in the second period mostly in English. Before "On the Morning of Christ's Nativity," Milton wrote one poem in Greek, six poems in Italian, and nineteen poems in Latin ranging in length from four-line epigrams to a mini-epic of 226 lines. He wrote only seven poems in English, and three of these—or two, if one of them was in fact written later—are translations: the two psalm adaptations, which he wrote when he was fifteen, and a word-for-word rendering of a brief ode by Horace, ending with the fine phrase, "To the stern god of sea." (This last poem is all but impossible to date, but it is usually given to this period.)² Of the four remaining, original compositions in English, only two—"On the Death of a Fair Infant Dying of a Cough" and "At a Vacation Exercise in the College"—give any indication of the greatness that Milton would attain.

In the second period, by contrast, that is, after "On the Morning of Christ's Nativity" and up to "Lycidas," Milton wrote only two significant poems in Latin. (I exclude the verse postscript to his love poems, "Haec ego mente . . . ," which seems to me likely to have been written after "Lycidas," and the unpublished, nugatory couplet on Ariosto's exemplary renunciation of the legal profession, one line of which has been lost. For both, see the chronology.) In this second period Milton wrote one more poem in Greek—another adaptation of Psalm 114, imitating the archaic style—and no further poems in Italian. But he wrote twelve poems in English. One of them, *Comus,* or *A Masque Presented at Ludlow Castle, 1634,* is more than four times longer than anything Milton had written hitherto. Its central concern is vital today: the ethics of the human use of nature. The other major achievements of this second period between "On the Morning of Christ's Nativity" and "Lycidas" are Sonnet 7, "How Soon Hath Time," and the twinned poems, "L'Allegro" and "Il Penseroso" (that is, "The Happy, or Lively Man" and "The Reflective, or Pensive Man"). These are concerned with the ethical organization of the self.

The two psalm adaptations, which were done—the point bears repeating—when the poet was only fifteen years old, are interesting for how his mature manner can occasionally be heard, for example, when designating biblical figures in classical terms. In the paraphrase of Psalm 114, which is in heroic couplets, the parting of the Red Sea is personified as a classical god hiding his "froth-becurlèd head" (line 8) and the children of Abraham are "the blest seed of Terah's faithful son." The version of Psalm 136, which is done in tetrameter couplets interspersed with the refrain, "For his mercies aye endure, / Ever faithful, ever sure," is meant to be sung and probably was, at least in Milton's family. But the classical influence is strong: the sun is "golden-tressèd" (line 29); God's hand is "thunder-clasping" and quells "wrathful tyrants" (lines 38 and 10), one of whom is called "large-limbed Og" and another— Pharaoh himself—"the tawny king with all his power" (lines 69 and 54). The Red Sea is delightfully hellenized as "the Erythraean main" (line 46). In both poems, the mighty organ tone of the poet's mature style breaks through: "Shake earth, and at the presence be aghast / Of him that ever was, and ay shall last" ("Paraphrase on Psalm 114," lines 15–16).

Milton wrote an epigram in Greek, probably as a school exercise, which bears a Latin title indicating that the verses are spoken by a philosopher to a king, *"Philosophus ad Regem."* The king is urged, for his own benefit, to spare the unjustly condemned philosopher's "most wise head" *(sophôtaton karênon)*. This is not the last time Milton would evoke the perilous role of the intellectual as the rightful counselor to power, but also, not infrequently, as a victim of power.

In Italian, Milton wrote five skillful sonnets and a fifteen-line "song," or canzone, in which the poet is asked why he writes in the Italian language when *altri lidi*, "other shores"—by which he means Latin and English—await him. His answer is that he writes in Italian because he is in love; as the beloved herself says, Italian is the language of which Love is most proud: *"Questa è la lingua di cui si vanta Amore"* (line 15). Milton goes on, however, in a different mood (and in a phrasal anticipation of "Lycidas," line 73), to say that on one of those other shores, whether Latin or English, he will win the immortal reward of an eternal garland: *"l'immortal guiderdon d'eterne frondi"* (line 11). The *eterne frondi* and *altri lidi* anticipate the "laurels" and "other groves" of "Lycidas," as the *"immortal guiderdon"* does the "fair guerdon."

Of the four original creations in English before "On the Morning of Christ's Nativity," two—a conventional, Petrarchan love sonnet asking the nightingale to sing before the cuckoo, thus bringing the poet some hoped-for success in love, and an elegant song in the style of Jonson, welcoming "the flowery May, who from her green lap throws / The yellow cowslip, and the pale primrose" ("On May Morning," lines 3–4)— show no more ambition in the poet than to be a gentleman versifier. The remaining two poems do show ambition, the specifically Miltonic ambition to go soaring through the universe and, by the power of poetry, to unite the heavens with the earth—and even to control the dark realms under the earth. It is an ambition that would culminate in *Paradise Lost*.

The first of the two ambitious poems is a funeral elegy addressed to the poet's niece ("O fairest flower, no sooner blown [bloomed] but blasted"), entitled "On the Death of a Fair Infant Dying of a Cough."

It is written in seven-line rhyme royal stanzas, which, thanks chiefly to Chaucer's *Troilus and Criseyde* and Spenser's *Faerie Queene* (Spenser adds another two lines to the stanza), were associated with heroic verse. Milton would use the rhyme royal stanza in the proem, or "introduction," to "On the Morning of Christ's Nativity" and also in the self-confessed failure of "The Passion," which is all proem, until the poet gives up, never making it into the poem itself. (A *proem* is literally that which comes before [*pro+*] the "path of song," *oîmos aoidês*.)

In the Fair Infant elegy the poet asks the child whether she was in fact human, as she seemed, or whether she was an angel who took on the appearance of a human being (as the Bible tells us other angels have done) during her brief visit to earth:

> Or wert thou of the golden-wingèd host
> Who having clad thyself in human weed
> To earth from thy prefixèd seat didst post
> And after short abode fly back with speed
> As if to show what creatures Heaven doth breed,
> Thereby to set the hearts of men on fire
> To scorn the sordid world and unto Heaven aspire?
>
> *("On the Death of a Fair Infant Dying of a Cough,"*
> *lines 57–63)*

That is certainly what Milton's heart is on fire to do. The verse is breathless and not always perfectly grammatical—faults Milton would soon correct—but it shows his classical training, and the last line of the stanza, "to scorn the sordid world, and unto Heaven aspire," evokes the haughtiness that will be a touchstone of Milton's art.

Milton concludes the poem with a prophecy that if his sister, Anne, "the mother of so sweet a child," will wisely learn "to curb [her] sorrows wild," God will give her another child, one who will make her name famous until the end of time. He is of course right that wild sorrows are extravagant and must be given up. But the prospect of having in compensation another child who will make her name famous may not have had as soothing an effect on the bereaved mother's anguish as the poet expected.

Lastly, to make an end of Milton's apprentice poems in English, there is the remarkable passage of verse in heroic couplets, which, when he had it printed with his other poems in 1645, Milton entitled "At a Vacation Exercise in the College, Part Latin, Part English." In the final year of his BA degree at Cambridge (he would remain another three years to take his MA), Milton was chosen by his classmates to deliver a speech celebrating the coming vacation. After a spirited holiday discourse in Latin prose that contained, as expected on such occasions, crude jokes to please his audience, Milton unexpectedly broke into verse, English verse, and greeted the English language thus: "Hail native language, that by sinews weak / Didst move my first endeavouring tongue to speak!" (lines 1–2). He then startlingly declared his soaring ambition:

> Yet had I rather, if I were to choose,
> Thy service in some graver subject use,
> Such as may make thee search thy coffers round
> Before thou clothe my fancy in fit sound:
> Such where the deep transported mind may soar
> Above the wheeling poles, and at Heaven's door
> Look in and see each blissful deity,
> How he before the thunderous throne doth lie,
> Listening to what unshorn Apollo sings
> To the touch of golden wires while Hebe brings
> Immortal nectar to her kingly sire.
>
> ("*At a Vacation Exercise in the College*," lines 29–39)

We see again and more fully in these verses Milton's half-unconscious and continually expressed desire, which would remain with him until at least the middle of *Paradise Lost:* to take flight on the wings of song, to soar into the heavens and look in on the counsels of the gods, or of God (compare "Elegy 5 *In Adventum Veris*," lines 15–20, and *"Ad Patrem,"* lines 35–40). As the passage continues, Milton imagines himself plunging downward from the heavens first through the sphere of fire (which at the time was believed to encircle the earth above the atmosphere), next through the atmosphere itself—the "misty regions of wide air next under"—and, finally, continuing his rapid descent, through the snow-white, cumulous clouds and the dark thunderheads until the stormy waves of the sea (agitated by "green-eyed Neptune") flash into sight:

> Then passing through the spheres of watchful fire
> And misty regions of wide air next under

> And hills of snow and lofts of pilèd thunder,
> May tell at length how green-eyed Neptune raves
> In Heav'n's defiance, mustering all his waves.
>
> *("At a Vacation Exercise in the College," lines 40–44)*

How much of this Milton succeeded in reciting on the occasion to an audience of not-entirely-sober undergraduates is unknown, but it must have caused some astonishment. With its description of reentering the atmosphere from space, it astonishes us. Yet within three to five months of his launching this defiant promise, Milton would make good on his claim to be a poet of genius, one whose visionary imagination soars into the heavens and descends not only into the depths of the sea, where the "wakeful trump of doom must thunder through the deep" ("On the Morning of Christ's Nativity," line 156), but also into Hell itself, whose "dolorous mansions" will be opened to the "peering day" ("On the Morning of Christ's Nativity," line 140).

In Milton's day, and indeed up to the twentieth century, the first poetry any European poet was likely to hear—and to learn to pronounce—was in Latin, at school, especially at the elite classical schools or gymnasia such as Milton's Saint Paul's. The first verses a poet was likely to compose were also in Latin, also at school, where boys learned to adore the formulae of classical Latin poetry by composing Latin verses of their own. The practice of imitative versifying continued at university, where students and fellows regularly produced Latin, English, and, more rarely, Greek funeral elegies honoring eminent persons. Milton wrote fine Latin elegies to commemorate Cambridge University officials—for example, the university beadle and the vice-chancellor—as he did also for the neighboring bishops of Ely and Winchester, the latter being the famous preacher, Lancelot Andrewes. Both bishops, incidentally, were translators of the Authorized Version of the Bible, which had appeared in 1611.

The elements of Latin poetry are different from those of English poetry and are more difficult to learn. The labor of acquiring those elements gave poets and their audiences in the age of Elizabeth and James certain underlying assumptions about what poetry in English should be like: more subtly musical, or *cantabile*, which means more precise in the management of vowels, accent, and syllable count than medieval English poetry was thought to be at the time. (Textual obfuscation and

philological ignorance made Chaucer's and especially Langland's great
poems appear in the sixteenth and seventeenth centuries more crude
in versification than they actually were.) From the middle Tudor period on—roughly, that is, from the earlier half of the century before
Milton's birth—the syntax of English poetry, disciplined by Latin, became at once more complicated and more regular. Although the quantitative meter of Latin poetry was never successfully adapted to English
(not for lack of trying), its example created higher standards for subtlety and precision in English syllabic-accentual verse.

The culture of Latin poetry reached beyond technical effects. People
grew accustomed to the idea that poetry should be otherworldly, difficult, and strange. The chief means for achieving this strangeness was
by continual allusion to classical myths and especially to the classical
gods—often, and in Milton's case especially, in indirect, recondite ways.
In a deep sense, the language of poetry and the structures of myth were
supposed to be one and the same, constituting a higher-order language
by which poetic truth speaks to us in its native tongue. A rough sea may
be a rough sea to a writer in prose; to a poet it is a rough sea as well, but
it also green-eyed Neptune, raving.

Needless to say, such notions had ambivalent consequences for Christian poets, and especially for Milton. From the beginning to the end
of Milton's career there is tension between, on the one hand, the ideological unity and transcendental verticality of Christian belief and, on
the other hand, the tolerant multiplicity of classical myth. Milton's Latin
poetry shows us this tension at one of its extremes, the pagan extreme
of metamorphic verse, where nothing is quite what it is because everything is turning into something else, as if striving forever to recapture
the lost presence of a full earthly being. The scene, so to speak, of Milton's Latin poetry is therefore one of perpetual, polymorphous transformation, of metaphor unbound. How could such a scene, such a terrain, ever take the print of Christian truth?

Milton rejoiced in the richness of classical myth and in the technical
challenges of using it for his own rhetorical ends. A good example of
his learning to do so, of his mastering what we might call *mythopoeic
supercondensation*, is the workmanlike poem written on the death of the
vice-chancellor of Cambridge University, one John Gostlin, a medical
doctor. This poem is not untypical of such performances, which were
important to Milton's later growth as a poet.

If we put the bare statements of *"In Obitum Procancellarii Medici"* beside the number of allusions to classical myth by which each statement is supported, the skeletal structure of the elegy looks like this:

1. Accept that you must die (four classical allusions).
2. If strength could beat death (three classical allusions),
3. If magic could beat death (three classical allusions),
4. If medicine, the vice-chancellor's specialty, could beat death (three classical allusions),
5. You, vice-chancellor (three classical allusions),
6. Would not have died (two classical allusions).
7. But you did die (one classical allusion).
8. May you rest peacefully (six classical allusions).

The proportion of classical allusion to substance is by no means so consistently extreme as this in *Paradise Lost*, or even in "Lycidas." But Milton practiced the art of mythopoeic supercondensation in the more than one thousand lines (1,078) of Latin verse he composed before the age of twenty-one. The experience gave him the technical foundation for the densely allusive but subtler productions of his maturity.

The nineteen Latin poems Milton wrote before "On the Morning of Christ's Nativity" are therefore the major artistic effort of this earlier period. Of these, two, which Milton never published, are obvious school exercises in praise of rising early, a subject more congenial to the schoolmaster than the schoolboy, unless the schoolboy is Milton. A more impressive poem, but also an obvious school exercise, *"Apologus de Rustico et Hero,"* is a brief moral fable about a peasant, a landlord, and, interestingly from the future author of *Paradise Lost*, an apple tree. (C. S. Lewis was also influenced by this very minor tale of Milton's). Every year the peasant troubled to bring the landlord delicious fruit from the aged tree until the landlord greedily replanted the tree in his garden in the city, where it withered. Appropriately, the landlord himself states what he has learned from his greedy behavior: that it is best to enjoy fruits generously offered instead of seeking the fruits for themselves. Now both the fruit and its parent tree are lost to him: *"Nunc periere mihi et foetus et ipsa parens"* (line 12). Considering this fable too slight for publication with his other poems in 1645, Milton added it to his collected poems in 1673, near the end of his life. Perhaps he concluded (he would not be the first aged master to do so) that the simple moral lesson of such a fable has more power to make us better than all the glories of a masterpiece like *Paradise Lost.*

Five of the Latin poems are light epigrams for Guy Fawkes Day, which is still celebrated in England, in commemoration of the famous Gunpowder Plot, a conspiracy to blow up Parliament when King James I was present to open Parliament and deliver the speech from the throne. The plot was laid for November 5, 1605—the psychological 9/11 of Milton's day—with the important difference that this plot was foiled. These poems are nugatory efforts: it's not easy to see why Milton published them in 1645 instead of *"Apologus de Rustico et Hero."* But they gave rise to an ambitious poem on the same subject—it is Milton's longest performance in Latin—entitled *In Quintum Novembris,* "On the Fifth of November."

In Quintum Novembris is 226 lines of heroic hexameter verse, the meter Milton deemed suitable for rejoicing at God's favoring the English Protestant religion enough to prevent the king and Parliament from being blown sky-high by a conjuration of the pope and the devil. The most brilliant passage in the poem describes Satan's journey to the pope to arrange this explosion, flying on greasy wings of pitch over the frozen Alps and down the Italian peninsula to Rome, keeping the cloud-bearing Apennine Mountains on his left wing and, on his right, the lowlands of ancient Etruria (Tuscany), infamous for sorcery and witchcraft (lines 45–51). With its geographical and anthropological preoccupations, not to mention the obvious pleasure the poet takes in imagining flight, this passage gives a foretaste of *Paradise Lost.* Of course, Milton would one day see Tuscany—ancient Etruria—and the Apennine Mountains that run down Italy's spine, with their soaring heights and deep, shady valleys. In *Paradise Lost* he would mention Vallombrosa, which means "shady valley." The fallen angels lie entranced on the lake of Hell, "Thick as autumnal leaves that strew the brooks / In Vallombrosa where th'Etrurian shades / High overarched embow'r" (*PL,* 1.302–4). There is a long tradition, much favored by the Romantic poets, that Milton visited the monastery of Vallombrosa to the east and south of Florence, high on a mountain, not far from one of the roads leading south to Rome. There is a commemorative plaque there in his honor. Such a visit is improbable, but Milton passed through the Apennine landscape, where he seems to have been less impressed by the barren mountain heights than by the densely wooded, shady valleys. I will add that on my way up the steep, winding road to the monastery, where there was a conference of Miltonists in 1988, at a small hamlet on one of the hairpin turns in the road, I spotted a sign, "Bar Giovanni Milton." The tradition survives.

Two of the Latin poems appear to be related to university assignments and show greater intellectual powers than any of the poems mentioned so far: *"De Idea Platonica quemadmodum Aristoteles intellexit"* and *"Naturam non pati senium."* The first is an ironical reflection on how a literal-minded Aristotle understood Plato's doctrine of the ideas, and especially the idea of Man (which is not, actually, a Platonic doctrine). The second is a meditation on the question—a serious one in Milton's day—whether nature suffers decay.

The core of the nineteen Latin poems written before "On the Morning of Christ's Nativity" consists of the six Latin elegies, which range in length from 24 to 140 lines. Not all of these, despite the generic term *elegy*, are funeral poems: only two are. An elegy such as "Lycidas" is a funeral poem, as is the elegy commemorating the Cambridge University beadle *("Elegia Secunda. In Obitum Praeconis Academici Cantabrigiensis").* Milton personifies "plaintive Elegy herself"—*ipsa querebunda Elegëia* (line 23)—whose sad harmonies will resound throughout the university.

But Milton follows the ancient Greeks and Romans in using the term *elegiacs* to designate poems written in couplets, or distichs, of alternating six- and five-foot dactylic lines. In the strict sense, an elegy can be written only in Greek or Latin, languages that are adapted to quantitative meter. (Rilke writes the *Duino Elegies* in German, loosely and occasionally imitating the classical verse form.) Because "Lycidas" was not written in elegiac measure, Milton does not call the poem an *elegy*, as we do, but a *monody*, which means a poem or song sung by one singer, in contrast with a choral ode or hymn, like the Nativity Ode.[3] The elegiac meter was considered suitable for wide-ranging and informal subjects—among them, notably, love (as in Elegy 7)—and was sometimes used in epistles, as Milton does in the epistles addressed to his school friend Charles Diodati and to his former tutor, Thomas Young (Elegies 1, 4, and 6). More than in any of the other poems of his youth, Milton expresses himself personally in the elegies, revealing his cerebral temperament, his love of ancient Greek and Roman civilization, his passionate idealism, and his noble ambition, not to mention his gift for friendship. Nor, as we see in Elegy 7, to our relief, does Milton altogether omit the pleasure of seeing pretty girls in the street and of going to the theater. He has a sense of humor and uses it—occasionally, if moderately, at his own expense.

Milton would write more poems in Latin. Between "On the Morning of Christ's Nativity" and "Lycidas" he wrote two considerable ones (they are 90 and 120 lines, respectively): Elegy 6, to Charles Diodati, and *"Ad Patrem,"* Milton's poem of thanks to his father for his superb—and expensive—education. He goes flying in this poem, too, and he explains something of his reason for associating poetry with flight. In classical myth, Prometheus, to Jove's annoyance, stole fire from the gods above and gave it to humans, thus allowing humans to rise above the condition of beasts. The story is about literal fire and fire's usefulness to humans in becoming human. But Promethean fire was regularly interpreted allegorically as the spark of divine intelligence from the heavens, a spark that is most visible in poetry, retaining, as poetry does, the traces of the sacred Promethean fire: *"Sancta Prometheae retinens vestigia flammae"* (line 20). As a poet, Milton's "fiery spirit" is naturally drawn upward toward this original fire. His spirit travels with the rapidly whirling spheres, soaring and singing, in harmony with the choir of the stars, an immortal and ineffable song:

> Spiritus et rapidos qui circinat igneus orbes,
> Nunc quoque sydereis intercinit ipse choreis
> Immortale melos et inenarrabile carmen.
>
> ("Ad Patrem," *lines 35–37*)

Milton's rhetorical purpose in *"Ad Patrem"* was to excuse himself for dedicating his life to poetry rather than pursuing, as his father expected, a lucrative career in the law or in one of the other professions. But Milton had some leverage, of which he makes full use in this poem. His wealthy father, who was a scrivener (a profession that combined the roles of financier and lawyer), was also a composer of note. John Milton Senior still has a place in the roster of seventeenth-century English composers. But we can only wonder what the Puritan dedicatee of *"Ad Patrem"* made of some of the statements in it: that poetry pleases the (plural) gods above—*"Carmen amant superi"*—and binds the lower deities of Hell (not devils: deities); that through poetry the future is revealed to the priestesses of Apollo at Delphi and to the Cumaean sibyl, also a priestess of Apollo; and that it is while uttering poetry that the priest at the altar eviscerates the sacrificial bull to read the future in its steaming entrails (lines 21–29).

The calmer sixth elegy, addressed to Charles Diodati, was written before this, in December 1629, very soon after the completion of "On the Morning of Christ's Nativity." In it, Milton gives his first more or less open statement of what, at this particular moment, he thinks poetry is for: to join humanity with the divine, though not by eviscerating bulls. To Diodati's explanation that excessive holiday cheer has prevented his sending Milton any verses, Milton replies that that is no excuse: song loves Bacchus, the god of wine, and Bacchus loves songs, *"Carmen amat Bacchum, carmina Bacchus amat"* (line 14). Six classical examples follow, including that of the sublime Pindar, whose mighty verses are swollen by the god of wine, inspiring rhapsodies on the thrilling Olympian contests and the brief, but divine, splendor of victory (lines 23–26). Many gods, Milton assures Diodati, care for and inspire the light-stepping elegiac verses, which are stimulated into being not only by Bacchus, the god of wine, but also by Ceres, the goddess of grain, and by Erato, the titillating muse, who is aided by Venus and Cupid. All of this means that banquets and wine, and their allied pleasures, are no impediment to the composition of elegiac verses (lines 49–54).

"But," says Milton, or, in Latin, *"At"* (line 55)—*but* is his favorite adversative in either language and a word always to watch for in Milton's verse—there is the kind of poet who would write of wars, of the Heavenly counsels of Jove, of great and pious heroes and semidivine captains. This poet sings of the sacred counsels of the gods above and equally of the infernal realm where the savage dog Cerberus barks:

> At qui bella refert, et adulto sub Iove caelum,
> Heroasque pios, semideosque duces,
> Et nunc sancta canit superum consulta deorum,
> Nunc latrata fero regna profunda cane . . .
>
> *(Elegy 6, lines 55–58)*

The poet who aspires to sing of these things must not eat and drink liberally: he must live an ascetic life instead, tempering his diet and drinking pure water from a simple beech-wood bowl. He is like the priest who goes forth to confront the offended gods (note again the unchristian plural). There follow five elaborate examples of classical poets in this vein, concluding with a description of Homer's *Odyssey*. For the poet, Milton says, is sacred to the gods and is their priest, breathing from deep in his breast and from his lips the very words of Jove: *"Diis etenim sacer est vates divûmque sacerdos, / Spirat et occultum pectus et ora Iovem"* (lines 77–78).

That Milton aspires to be a poet of this second, higher kind is clear enough when he turns abruptly to his recent composition, "On the Morning of Christ's Nativity." He has been singing, he confides to Diodati, the peace-bearing king of Heavenly seed—*"Paciferum canimus caelisti semine regem"* (line 81)—the coming of the happy ages promised in holy scripture, the child born in a lowly stable who with his father rules the Heavens above, the new star appearing in the night sky, the army of angels singing in the air, and the sudden castigation of every pagan god in his or her particular shrine—*"Et subitò elisos ad sua fana deos"* (lines 81–86). These events in "On the Morning of Christ's Nativity" are the "gifts" Milton has presented to Christ for his birthday: *"Dona quidem dedimus Christi natalibus illa"* (line 87).

From the evidence of this epistle and of "On the Morning of Christ's Nativity" itself, it is reasonable to conclude that in December 1629 Milton underwent his artistic conversion, dedicating his life to serving God as a poet. But he would do so as a poet writing in English, not in Latin, a language too entangled with the worship of the very pagan gods who are, at the end of "On the Morning of Christ's Nativity," so dramatically rooted out of their shrines. The plural gods of Latin poetry have been banished. The course has been set for the writing of *Paradise Lost*. But Milton would not arrive at the beginning of that great task for many years yet.

The one poem from this second period, that between "On the Morning of Christ's Nativity" and "Lycidas," that was composed in Greek—it is perhaps better called an "exercise" than a poem—does show Milton working to attain a plausible synthesis of Christianity with classical culture. It is a translation of Psalm 114, the same psalm Milton rendered in English when he was fifteen years old, beginning "When the blest seed of Terah's faithful son / After long toil their liberty had won." By this time Milton knew Hebrew and was translating from Hebrew into Greek, skillfully marrying the heroic hexameter verse and the largely formulaic diction of Homer to the theme that would fire his imagination for all his life: God's miraculous liberation of "the children of Israel, the shining race of Jacob," from bondage in Egypt. Milton adds with a classical flourish, although the basis for it is there in the psalm, that this is bondage to masters who are "barbarous in speech," *barbarophônon* (lines 1–2). Egypt and its Pharaoh were symbols of tyranny and would remain so for the rest of Milton's life. Indeed, as we see in the novels of Faulkner, in Negro spirituals, and in the imagery of reggae music, Egypt and Pharaoh, and of course Babylon, the later city of bondage, have remained symbols of tyranny and slavery ever since.

The Greeks loved freedom—*eleutheria*—which was their greatest moral discovery, and Milton loved Psalm 114 because it illustrates what he most deeply believed: that what God wants for us all is our original but lost freedom.[4] This teaching would be the central idea of Milton's poetic maturity, in *Paradise Lost, Paradise Regained*, and *Samson Agonistes*. In the years during which he wrote polemical prose, the exodus from Egypt would be Milton's symbol of the English Revolution.

The best of the elegies is the longest, Elegy 5, entitled "On the Coming of Spring," or, to give it its Latin title, *In Adventum Veris*. The fifth elegy is a pagan romp celebrating new life returning to the world as the rising sun returns from the south to the north, bringing a revival of poetic inspiration in the speaker, as well. The sun is personified as the god Phoebus Apollo, who drives a burning chariot across the sky, carrying the orb of the sun. The old Ptolemaic cosmology, which makes the sun orbit the earth on a weaving or serpentine course along the equator, crossing the equator going south at the beginning of winter and going north at the beginning of spring, was more suitable for poetry than the newer Copernican system, in which the earth orbits the sun, although Milton would brilliantly and wholeheartedly adopt the Copernican system in *Paradise Lost*.[5] Milton was of course familiar with the Copernican system, and he was interested in it enough to take the trouble, when he was in Florence, to meet the man who proved and vastly extended Copernicus's hypothesis, Galileo, then under house arrest in the hills outside the city.

In the older poetical version of how the seasons occur, winter comes when Phoebus Apollo drives the chariot of the sun below the equator as far as to the Tropic of Capricorn, whence he turns and starts north again. (The word *tropic* means "a turning.") As he drives his team north, Phoebus crosses the equator again at spring equinox, when the hours of night are equal to those of the day—which is what the word *equinox* means. After spring equinox, the days will continue to lengthen in relation to the hours of night until summer solstice, when the sun has reached its farthest point north, the Tropic of Cancer. The sun seems to stand there for a moment (whence the word *solstice*) before turning south toward the equator again, which it crosses at the autumn equinox. As Phoebus drives his chariot south, cold weather will return and the days will grow shorter. The evening shadow, as Milton says in the last line of the poem, will intrude upon our northern sky, beneath our northern pole. Milton's verse captures both movements of the sun as we perceive it from earth: its daily rising in the east and its annual return from the south in the spring. The sun leaves the Ethiopians in the south (*Ethiopians* is originally a Homeric word and means, literally, "the scorched-faced ones") and the fields of the old man Tithonus, in the east: Africa and Asia. Bending the golden reins of his fiery chariot, Phoebus drives his team toward the northern constellation of the bear, Arcturus: *"Iam sol Aethiopas fugiens Tithoniaque arva, / Flectit ad Arctoas aurea lora plagas"* (lines 31–32). Why do the "Tithonian fields" mean the east? Tithonus, a mortal, was beloved of the goddess of the dawn, Aurora, and of course the dawn comes up in the east, where the sun rises. The gods gave Tithonus immortality, but not eternal youth, so that he became with time appallingly decrepit. The story is alluded to by Milton later, for Phoebus, the sun, must persuade Aurora, the dawn, to get out of bed, where she lies with old Tithonus, and take to the sky before him: "arise"—*Surge*—and leave "the bedchamber of that old man!" says Phoebus. What good is it for her to lie in an "impotent bed" when the man she now loves, Cephalus, the son of Aeolus (god of the winds), awaits her in a grassy meadow of Mount Hymettus, the soaring heights of which are already touched by her fires?

> Desere, Phoebus ait, thalamos Aurora seniles,
> Quid iuvat effoeto procubuisse toro?
> Te manet Aeolides viridi venator in herba,
> Surge, tuos ignes altus Hymettus habet.
>
> (*Elegy 5, lines 49–52*)

Aurora blushes with shame at this exposure of her crime, but even as she does so she urges her horses of dawn to speed toward her lover. (For the glowing hoofprints of the horses of dawn, see "On the Morning of Christ's Nativity," lines 19–20: "Now while the heaven by the sun's team untrod / Hath took no print of the approaching light.")

Still another heavenly motion is imagined: that of the moon retreating before the rising sun, whom Milton now calls *Lucifer*, which means "the light-bearer," a name he will use again in "On the Morning of Christ's Nativity" (line 74). Cynthia, who is the goddess of the moon and the sister of Phoebus, is also Diana, or Artemis, the huntress. When Cynthia discerns the fiery wheels of her brother's chariot soaring above the horizon, she seems glad to put away her weaker rays of moonlight. Taking up her bow and quiver again, she makes for her woods:

> Laeta suas repetit sylvas, pharetramque resumit
> Cynthia, Luciferas ut videt alta rotas,
> Et tenues ponens radios gaudere videtur.
>
> *(Elegy 5, lines 45–47)*

Thus far in the poem, Milton has skillfully associated the pagan gods with the motions of the heavenly bodies, that is, with celestial geometry, an allegorizing rationalization of the Olympians that goes back to classical antiquity itself—to the age of Pericles, in fact, and the building of the temple of the Parthenon. Up to this point, only Aurora's assignation on the grassy slopes of Hymettus gives an indication of what is to come: an orgy of satyrs and nymphs in the forest, the May rites of young men and virgins spilling out of the cities at dawn and running to meet in the fields, and an exuberant convocation of the Olympian gods, who, as the golden age seems to return, have come down from the heavens to feast in the woods. One thinks of Bellini and Titian's great painting, *Feast of the Gods*, in its woodland setting.

Although the system of vague allegorization remains in force, an energy that is more exuberantly pagan breaks through at the moment earth, Tellus, casts off hated old age and revives her youth: *"Exuit invisam Tellus rediviva senectam"* (line 55). At the sight of Phoebus, Tellus yearns for the sun god's embrace. Milton addresses Phoebus in an apostrophe to transmit the good news: *"Et cupit amplexus Phoebe subire tuos"* (line 56). She bares her luxurious, life-giving breasts and cries out her lascivious passion, urging Phoebus to lie down beside her in a grassy forest glade and put his fires—once unwisely employed by Phaeton, who crashed the sun's chariot on the earth—to the "wiser use"—*tuo sapientius uteris igni*—(line 93) of making love. She isn't afraid, says she, of being carbonized, like the unfortunate Semele, when *she* lay with Phoebus, nor does she fear being scorched by the burning axle-tree of the solar chariot when Phaeton crashed (the "burning axle-tree" appears in "On the Morning of Christ's Nativity," line 84). No, she implores Phoebus twice (lines 88 and 94), "come hither, and lay your radiant head [*lumina*, 'beams'] on my breast": *"Huc ades et gremio lumina pone meo"* (lines 91–94).[6]

Thus, says Milton, Tellus breathes out her passion in words that carry with them the aroma of spices from Arabia and tincture of Paphian roses, which are sacred to Venus, the goddess of love, and all other creatures are likewise inflamed (lines 59–60 and 96). For Cupid, lighting his torch from the sun, speeds through the world, loosing his arrows upon mortals and gods, including his mother, Venus, whose beauty is restored as she seems to rise once again from the sea. The young men sing a marriage song to the god Hymen—*io Hymen!*—and, as the song echoes through the woods, Hymen himself appears in his yellow gown, redolent of saffron (lines 105–7). Young virgins, their lovely breasts bound up with gold, run out to the woods—to the *amoeni* (line 109), or idealized natural locations—each praying to Venus to give her the man of her dreams. As evening falls, we see in the crepuscular light the satyrs and nymphs flitting through the trees and the meadows with the goatgods Sylvanus, Faunus, and Pan. No nymph or dryad, not even the venerable goddess of plenty, Cybele, and her matronly daughter, Ceres, the goddess of grain, are safe from the lust of these wood-gods (lines 119–30).

Even on high, on soaring Olympus, Jupiter is at play with his wife, and, in a scene again reminiscent of Bellini and Titian's *Feast of the Gods*, he convokes the Olympians to a feast in the woods: *"Iupiter ipse alto cum coniuge ludit Olympo, / Convocat et famulos ad sua festa deos"* (lines 117–18). The gods unhesitatingly prefer the woods to the sky, and every grove is inhabited by its own deities: *"Dii quoque non dubitant caelo praeponere sylvas, / Et sua quisque sibi numina lucus habet"* (lines 131–32).

If we were in doubt that the purpose of poetry, as Milton sees it, is to unite the earthly with the divine, he repeats this last phrase in the optative mood: *"Et sua quisque diu sibi numina lucus habeto"* (line 133), "And long may each grove have its own gods." He beseeches the gods not to desert their woody haunts, and he wishes for the return of the ages of gold, the *aurea saecla*. For when the golden age returns, Jove himself (and not only Justice) will come down to this miserable earth and make all well again.

In this descent of Jove to earth, we cannot fail to see the similarity to the principle of Incarnation; nor can we fail to sense the difference. For Milton, as for many Renaissance authors, classical myth is an anticipatory distortion, a "recollecting forward," to use Kierkegaard's phrase, of Christian truth. There were various explanations for this. For example, the Greek myths were supposed to have been acquired from the Egyptians, whose own analogous myths were encodings of an oral tradition going back to Moses and having an authority equal to or higher than the authority of scripture. Alternatively, to mention the theory Milton illustrates so brilliantly in the first book of *Paradise Lost*, the Greek myths were inspired by the Greek gods themselves, who were in truth fallen angels—devils—who had set themselves up in the world as local gods to draw worship away from the true God. The myths bore a resemblance to Christian truth—the return of the golden age, for example, is an analogy of the return of the Son and the Kingdom of God on earth, prophesied in the Book of Revelation—because Christian truth was, so to speak, psychologically buried in the human mind, and so analogous versions of that truth would have spontaneous, psychological appeal. The Greeks worshipped Apollo, Zeus, and Diana because they were similar to Christ, God the Father, and the Virgin Mary, although the Greeks didn't know of this resemblance, even as it drew them nearer to truth. On the one hand, Greek myths were thought to be derivative distortions of an original truth (as in the game "Telephone"); on the other hand, Greek myths were thought to be demonic parodies of that original truth. Early in his career—notably in "On the Morning of Christ's Nativity"—Milton inclines to the former, derivative view; later—in *Paradise Lost* and *Paradise Regained*—he inclines to the latter, parodic view.

These ideas and vague notions about the epistemological status of classical myth lie behind the entanglement of classical myth with Christian truth in all Milton's verse. For poets in Milton's day, and indeed well into the eighteenth century, it was impossible to dispense with the classical myths because they constituted, as I said at the outset, the ground of the possibility of poetic speech. But how did Milton understand the status of classical myth? Generally speaking, Milton's conscious purpose in using classical myth is not, like the allegorical interpreters of such myths, to see through the myths all the way back to their original truths, as Bacon tried to do in *De Sapientia Veterum*, "On the Wisdom of the Ancients." That would be looking backward, and Milton's instinct with respect to myth is always to look forward, to ask not "what does it mean in its original context?" but rather "how can it be used toward a better end in the future?"[7] Milton's conscious purpose is what may be called *capture:* the reappropriation of the beauty and psychological appeal of classical myth for the promotion of Christian truth. Milton intends to use everything to hand in justifying the ways of God to men.

The work of entanglement and capture is evident throughout "On the Morning of Christ's Nativity," which exerts a complex but firm grip on the whole of classical culture—and indeed of human, religious culture—or what Milton would call *idolatry.* When he describes the pagan gods in the fifth elegy, however, the poet has more difficulty keeping his own imagination disentangled from the insidious allure of an idolatrous and fertility-worshipping culture.

The Incarnation of the god who with his father rules the poles, as Milton says it in the sixth elegy, when describing "On the Morning of Christ's Nativity," does not bring about a return of the classical golden age, as the speaker of "On the Morning of Christ's Nativity" expects at one moment: "Time will run back and fetch the age of gold" (line 135). Instead, time will run forward to the Apocalypse. For the Incarnation effects a radical transformation of time, which is no longer a perpetually spinning gyre or circuit. Simple, repetitive time becomes history, Christian history, descending, after the Fall of Man, to the point of Incarnation, and then reascending gradually, after the Crucifixion and Resurrection of Christ, to the Apocalypse, which is the end of time: "And then at last our bliss / Full and perfect is" (lines 165–66).

But the ideal pagan consummation, which the poet imagines in the fifth elegy, the return of Jove to earth and the renewal of the golden age, is unattainable within the bounds of classical time. We see what pagan temporality is in the opening lines of the fifth elegy, where time is forever turning back on itself (and into itself) through the seasonal cycle, even as it calls back the fresh breezes of spring and makes the weather grow warm: *"In se perpetuo Tempus revolubile gyro / Iam revocat zephyros vere tepente novos"* (lines 1–2). Unable to stop, or even to slow, time's perpetually rotating gyre, the speaker lamely asks Phoebus to drive his rapid team as slowly as he can, so that the spring will seem to last a long time. Just as futile is the speaker's closing wish that freezing winter will be late when he, winter, brings us long nights, and when the bright evening skies under our northern pole are assailed by shadow— *"Brumaque productas tarde ferat hispida noctes, / Ingruat et nostro serior umbra polo"* (lines 139–40). Such wishes are futile, of course, and show how this system of belief, which celebrates desire as fertility, is finally incompatible with desire. It won't take a long time for winter to return; it won't take a short time for winter to return: it will take exactly as long as it takes.

The speaker's request may be futile, but in some form we all entertain such a wish when nature is momentarily kind to us: that this glorious moment will last. As indeed it does. Time as it is experienced, not chronological but existential time, slides past at different speeds, as we are reminded in Philip Larkin's "Cut Grass": "Lost lanes of Queen Anne's lace, / And that high-builded cloud / Moving at summer's pace."[8] Summer has its own pace, though only on its very best days. It may be illogical to wish that Phoebus drive his swift team as slowly as he can: *"Tu saltem lente rapidos age Phoebe iugales / Qua potes"* (lines 137–38). But wishing time to go slowly is very close to the center of what it means to be human, when pleasure is entangled with awareness of mortality. We watch the fleeting beauty of the slowly moving, slowly changing cloud. Not to feel the pain of this beauty, the pain of wishing it to stay and knowing it can't, is to miss the beauty altogether, for the pain is a part of the beauty. Across the tranquil scene with which the fifth elegy concludes, when the summer sky is still bright overhead, falls the shadow that the speaker wishes away. The shadow belongs to this beauty, framing it and deepening it.

If we entertain this thought as a complete statement of the case, it must leave us where we are left at the conclusion of one of Virgil's eclogues, among the lengthening shadows, passing by a tomb near the road, as the rain begins to fall and a song is taken up. That moment, the culmination of what pagan art can achieve, is gloriously recaptured at the conclusion of *Paradise Lost:* Adam and Eve descend the hill at evening; the rain becomes their tears; and the tomb becomes their place of rest. But this Virgilian moment also marks the beginning of history. Milton loved the Roman historian Sallust for his moral sense and for his style. But for Milton, history in its essence, as *radical* change, is what classical culture is unable to think about. The return of temporality in the closing lines of the fifth elegy indicates—as surely as if the shadow lengthening in the sky were a finger pointing to the truth— that the woodland feast of the gods is not the union of the earthly with the divine: it is a reduction of the divine to the earthly. The gods may come down to us, improving our lives by warding off ill and enlarging our capacity for pleasure, but we do not ascend to the gods. An earth inhabited by gods becomes the classical *locus amoenus*, where we can lie down openly with one another like the innocent beasts, in the shameless security of the peaceable kingdom. But we can never take flight to the stars. In the laterally reticulating, metaphorically polyvalent system of Milton's fifth elegy, poetry is a power of the earth, not of the sky. Indeed, the sky itself is drawn down to the earth, as Phoebus is to the earth's breasts.

In the deepest sense, therefore, the fifth elegy is a poem not about the coming of spring, not about sexual potency and sexual desire, and not even about the pagan gods and their return to the earth with the golden age. It is a poem about poetry, which is at once its strength and its weakness. This is a weakness because in the fifth elegy poetry is trying to exist for itself, which it can never do long and stay healthy. *"In Adventum Veris"* is a poem about poetry that tries to be sufficient to itself—not as art for art's sake, but as art for earth's sake. *Art* corresponds with what Heidegger meant by "world." Art and the powers of the earth strive in this poem to be one and the same, but only because art is striving to surrender to earth. Or does perhaps earth become visible to us through art, which is therefore responsible for it?[9]

To answer that question we need to consider more closely what is said about poetry in the fifth elegy. We hear at the outset of Philomel, that "light-wingèd dryad of the trees," as Keats calls her in "Ode to a Nightingale" (line 7), a traditional symbol of poetry. Philomel begins her song in the woods when the woods themselves are still silent—*"dum silet omne nemus"* (line 26). It is as if the capacity for sound resident in those silent woods, which are soon to echo with hymns to Hymen, the cries of the nymphs, and even the panting of the gods, were conferred on those woods, or at least were awakened in them, by Philomel's song. Poetry—metamorphic variability—isn't merely song, *carmen:* it is the ground of the possibility of song, the earth out of which these woods grow.

Other figures of poetry in the fifth elegy—aside from the speaker himself—are a shepherd, a shepherdess, and a sailor, this last being a figure that is closer to the speaker than we might at first suppose. Milton shows us the shepherd recumbent on a soaring crag—"*Forte aliquis scopuli recubans in vertice pastor*" (line 41)—watching the light rise and addressing Phoebus, accusing the god of having little care for the girl in his bed, so swiftly has he taken up his horses (lines 43–44). So speak the powers of earth to the heavens: you belong to us. It is uncertain to me where the shepherd's apostrophe to Phoebus ends, that is, whether it ends with this jesting remark or continues through the description of Cynthia returning to her woods and of Phoebus crying out to Aurora to leave the bed of Tithonus and seek out her lover Cephalus (lines 43–52). (In that case, the speaker of the poem would resume at line 53, with the description of Aurora blushing for shame even as she hurries off to her lover.) The shepherd is certainly more of a poet if these mythopoeic variations on the heavenly motions—the setting of the moon and the rising of the dawn—are attributable to him, and I will admit I am inclined to give him these lines for that reason. The shepherd reappears—I presume he's the same shepherd—playing on his pipe with seven reeds to accompany a shepherdess, Phyllis, who joins the words of her own songs to the tunes that the shepherd plays: "*Nunc quoque septenâ modulatur arundine pastor, / Et sua quae iungat carmina Phyllis habet*" (lines 113–14). These lines evince Milton's usual fascination—it is a major theme of "*Ad Patrem*" and central to "At a Solemn Music"—with an ideal poetry that marries words to song. But these songs are not the music of the spheres, nor do they harmonize with the music of the spheres. They are the songs Phyllis happens to have—*sua quae habet Phyllis*. This is music within nature, not the music of nature.

The last figure of the poet, appearing in the two lines immediately following, also makes a music that is in nature, but this music has a magical power to move nature from within, a power that is not implied in Phyllis's songs, nor is it in the shepherd's music. He is a sailor, who with his nocturnal song placates his stars (so they will not bring evil weather) and summons the dolphins from the depths of the ocean to the surface, where they leap joyfully among the waves: *"Navita nocturno placat sua sidera cantu, / Delphinasque leves ad vada summa vocat"* (lines 115–16). The shepherd who greets Phoebus at dawn, the shepherdess who has her own songs to sing, and even the sailor whose song has power to placate the stars and to summon the dolphins, are figures of a poetry that is immersed in nature. It is a pagan voice that will likewise summon the dolphins, or at least invoke them, in "Lycidas," to "waft the hapless youth" (line 164). The shepherd, the shepherdess, and the sailor are transformations of Philomel—or, rather, Philomel, whose name means "lover of song," is their mythic distillation. Song, and with it myth, is generated within the system about which it sings.

What about the speaker? In keeping with Renaissance Neoplatonic tradition, he says he is inspired by a sacred madness, a *furor*, which affords him a vision of the secrets of nature and of the gods ruling on Olympus.[10] But his Olympian moments are rare and unconvincing because he is chiefly preoccupied with nature. He says he feels his own poetic powers being revived by the spring and that he will make the subject of his song the very power that inspires it: *"Ver mihi, quod dedit ingenium, cantabitur illo"* (line 23).

This too is song that is generated within the system of nature and belongs to the system it sings. There is something suffocating about it. In *Paradise Lost*, Milton will celebrate the divine creative power, the power that created the world and is now inspiring *Paradise Lost*. The song of *Paradise Lost* is empowered to look back on its own source, the Creation of the world, evincing the same creative power as this power is extended through the song. The structure is the same as that of *"In Adventum Veris,"* where the reviving power of spring gives the poet the power to celebrate. But the circuit is larger in *Paradise Lost* and takes in much more in its arc (Heaven and Hell and, eventually, history), whereas in *"In Adventum Veris"* the song remains trapped within nature. Even as the speaker soars above nature, he is not looking beyond nature; he is looking down into it. He says that his soul, freed from his body, is rapt into the heights of the clear smooth skies (*"Iam mihi mens liquidi raptatur in ardua coeli,"* line 15) to soar among the clouds. But no sooner does he ascend to this height than he peers down into the enclosed haunts of the poets and soothsayers, and the hidden resorts of the gods: the *penetralia vatum* and the *interiora deum* (lines 17–18). His soul has knowledge of what is done everywhere on Olympus, nor does his inspired sight fail to pierce the "blind" places of Tartarus, the classical Hell, which is far under the earth:

> . . . Et mihi fana patent interiora deum.
> Intuiturque animus toto quid agatur Olympo,
> Nec fugiunt oculos Tartara caeca meos.
>
> *(Lines 18–20)*

Clearly, the speaker's powers reach higher and lower than those of the sailor, who sings to the stars above him and summons the dolphins from the depths of the sea. But even the apparently transcendental movement of the speaker's poetic power remains submerged, like the Olympians in their forest glades, in the earthbound, metamorphic world of pagan myth, where poetry can never soar for long without having to return to the earth from which its nourishment comes. Like the perpetual gyre of time, it is of the nature of poetry always to turn back on itself and to turn into itself, which is why the turning of the line—the *versus*—and the turning of the figure, the *trope* (which also means "a turning"), are essential to poetry, or at least to the poetry of earth. Unlike history, or theology, poetry seems to offer no escape—no escape that belongs to itself—from this condition of involuted self-reference, from the chambered nautilus of its echoing and reechoing song.

The exuberance of Milton's imagination is fully displayed in the fifth elegy—more so than in "On the Morning of Christ's Nativity," which with its monosyllabic diction and exact meter exhibits an imposing self-control. The beauty of the Latin language, which is exposed by the high artifice of Latin poetry, is like marble that has been quarried from the earth and polished to stand in the light. But for Milton the beauty of Latin poetry cannot be disentangled from the moral chaos of pagan religion, the song of the earth. As a Christian poet, Milton would have to write in English.

Milton composed "On the Morning of Christ's Nativity" rapidly and, as it seemed to him then, effortlessly. It came in a single breath of inspiration that left the poet feeling he had stepped out of time into a place where the harmony of Creation was all around him and the movement of history—by which I mean the revolutionary reversal of history effected by the birth of Christ—could be surveyed from a higher coign of vantage. The dominant aesthetic mood of the poem is of ecstatic arrest, as when the stars hesitate to leave the sky at dawn: "The stars with deep amaze / Stand fixed in stedfast gaze" (lines 69–70). But beneath the ecstasy (*ek+stasis*, "to stand apart" from time), we feel a deep resonance, which is the slow inevitability of historical time. In an instant, we find ourselves transported to a place where the possibilities are vaster than those experienced in *"In Adventum Veris,"* where everything is ruled by the earthly cycles of time. The third stanza of the poem, which follows the beautifully compressed account of the Incarnation in the previous two, captures the breathless magic by which we are made to feel we have stepped out of our moment of time to be in another. The interrogative mode of the stanza—"Say, Heaven'ly Muse, shall not thy sacred vein / Afford a present to the infant god?" (lines 15–16)—heightens the mood of expectancy. We suppose that the gift the poet will receive from the muse and offer to Jesus is to be transmitted now, that is, at the time of the composition of the poem, on Christmas morning, 1629. But by the fifth line of this stanza, which opens with the word *now*, we find ourselves transported back in time to the actual morning of Jesus's birth: "Now while the heaven, by the sun's team untrod, / Hath took no print of the approaching light" (lines 19–20). The pinkish dappling in the sky that we see just before dawn is imagined by the poet as the hoofprints from horses drawing the chariot of Phoebus, god of the sun. He is saying it is still completely dark.

There is, therefore, no sign of dawn and the stars are still out, brilliantly shining. They are the "spangled host" (a *host* is an army) that Milton refers to as drawn up in military *squadrons*, keeping watch. Milton shows us real stars. But at a higher level of poetic truth, those stars are an army of angels guarding the world and waiting to burst into song. The squadrons are a military image (the greater part of this poem is martial in tone), but that image is joined to universal peace, a theme to be sounded later on:

> No war or battle's sound
> Was heard the world around;
> The idle spear and shield were high uphung.
> The hookèd chariot stood
> Unstained with hostile blood;
> The trumpet spake not to the armèd throng,

> And kings sat still with awful eye,
> As if they surely knew their sovran Lord was by.
>
> *("On the Morning of Christ's Nativity," lines 53–60)*

We may note that, as with those hoofprints of light, the imagery is saying the opposite of what the poet means. He affirms that the world is at peace, but he does so with stirring martial imagery.

In the third stanza of the proem, the poet, looking eastward, descries the three wise men of the gospels—whom he pleasingly calls "wizards"—hastening to Jesus's cradle with their gifts. They are "star-led wizards" because they are led along the road to Bethlehem by the new star that has appeared in the heavens. There, they will worship the newborn king and give him gifts of gold, frankincense, and myrrh. But, to mild comic effect, Milton commands himself, or his muse, to "run" to get there ahead of the wizards (to "*prevent* them," as he says, using the etymological sense of the word, which means to "come before," *prae+venire*). He wishes to have the honor of being the first to give the new king a gift and the first to worship this king. The gift he will give is the very poem we are reading. Why shouldn't he come first? As a Christian from sixteen hundred years in the future, he knows more than the wizards do: that the child has come into the world to redeem it; that the child will save us from our sins; and that this child also created the world in the beginning. The excitement of the stanza is ignited by the first word, "See!":

> See how from far upon the eastern road
> The star-led wizards haste with odors sweet.
> O run, prevent them with thy humble ode
> And lay it lowly at his blessed feet.
> Have thou the honor first thy Lord to greet,
> And join thy voice unto the angel choir
> From out his secret altar, touched with hallowed fire.
>
> *("On the Morning of Christ's Nativity," lines 22–28)*

What follows in "The Hymn" itself is a complete biblical vision of history, from the Creation of the world to the Apocalypse, with Christ's birth at the center of time.

Formally, the poem is divided into a four-stanza proem in modified rhyme royal and the twenty-seven stanzas of "The Hymn," proper. (At line 24 the poem as a whole is referred to as a "humble ode," which means a pastoral song, in keeping with the scene of the shepherds that is shortly to be described.) The rhyme royal stanza is a seven-line stanza like the one above, **ababbcc**, with two more syllables in the final line (twelve, instead of ten). This twelve-syllable line is sometimes called an *alexandrine*, after the twelve-syllable French poetic line. But for Milton and his audience, the twelve-syllable line would recall the final line in the stanza of Spenser's *Faerie Queene*, which is better referred to as a *hexameter*, having six feet or (normally) twelve syllables. The effect of the elongated termination is to make each stanza a pronouncedly integral unit, nor is this separating effect confined to the introductory stanzas. Milton sustains the effect through the hymn, giving the poem that articulate stateliness from one spectacular stanza to the next, like floats in a parade. This is so in even in the hymn's seventeenth stanza, which is grammatically dependent on its predecessor; "with such a horrid clang / As on Mount Sinai rang" (lines 157–58).

The four stanzas of the introduction divide neatly in two; two stanzas on the occasion and subject of the poem, two stanzas on the poet's desire to offer his poem to the Christ-child. The opening stanza gives us the occasion:

> This is the month and this the happy morn
> Wherein the Son of Heav'n's eternal King,
> Of wedded maid and virgin mother born,
> Our great redemption from above did bring,
> For so the holy sages once did sing
> That he our deadly forfeit should release
> And with his Father work us a perpetual peace.
>
> ("*On the Morning of Christ's Nativity*," lines 1–7)

The subject of the poem is thus stated abstractly and in brief. The atonement, or Redemption for our "deadly forfeit," original sin, is brought to us by God's Son, who was born of the Virgin on this day, December 25. This New Testament event was predicted by the Old Testament "holy sages," the Hebrew prophets, who are inspired, according to Christians, by the third person of the Trinity, the Holy Ghost. Already, the perspective of time has been opened. In the next two stanzas the poet brings us into the present moment, invoking the Heavenly Muse—this is the

Holy Ghost, again—to give him a gift for the "infant God." The scene is now refocalized in the present time, shortly before dawn on December 25, 1629.

The twenty-seven stanzas of the "Hymn" are in a more complex eight-line stanza with lines of varying length, suggesting the odes composed by classical poets, especially Pindar and Horace. (Imperfect Renaissance texts, especially of Pindar, made these poets' stanzas seem even more complex than they are.) As you can see in the example below, the rhyme scheme of the stanza of the hymn proper is **aabccbdd,** with **a** and **c** lines, trimeters, of six syllables each: "it was the winter wild / While the Heaven-born child" (lines 29–30); and "Nature in awe to him / had doffed her gaudy trim" (lines 32–33). The **b** lines have ten syllables (plus an extra syllable when there is a double syllable, or "feminine" rhyme). The **d** rhymes, which make the final couplet of the stanza, have eight and twelve syllables, respectively: "It was no season then for her / To wanton with the sun, her lusty paramour" (lines 35–36). The three rhyming couplets of the stanza are divided, as two fence posts divide three sections of fence, by rhyming decasyllabic iambic pentameter lines: "All meanly wrapped in the rude manger lies" and "With her great master so to sympathize" (lines 31, 34). The stateliness of the poem owes not a little to the rigor with which Milton adheres to his metrical scheme. Put all together, the stanza looks and sounds like this:

> It was the winter wild
> While the Heaven-born child
> All meanly wrapped in the rude manger lies.
> Nature in awe to him
> Hath doffed her gaudy trim
> With her great master so to sympathize:
> It was no season then for her
> To wanton with the sun, her lusty paramour.
> *("On the Morning of Christ's Nativity," lines 28–35)*

What genre or kind of poem this is has much to do with the person to whom it is addressed. In ancient Greek poetry, *hymns* are addressed to gods—there are hymns to Apollo, to Dionysus, and so on—and *odes* are addressed to mortals who have achieved something godlike, usually a victory in the athletic games.[11] By titling the main body of his poem a *hymn*, Milton is suggesting that his hero is a god—or, rather, God. Even so, "On the Morning of Christ's Nativity" closes quietly and intimately, in a beautiful stanza that fully emphasizes the humanity of the child, while the signs of his divinity—the star overhead and the angels guarding the stable—stand at a distance.

At the poem's conclusion, Mary has laid her child to sleep in the manger. The new star in the heavens, prophesying peace, is imagined as a lamp-bearing handmaid who has brought her chariot to a halt over the stable, around which a guard of angels in brilliantly polished armor is placed. With the possible exception of that armor ("harness"), which betrays Milton's martial temperament, the final tableau is an altogether conventional Christmas pageant picture:

> But see, the Virgin blest
> Hath laid her babe to rest.
> Time is our tedious song should here have ending.
> Heav'n's youngest-teemèd star
> Hath fixed her polished car [chariot],
> Her sleeping lord with handmaid lamp attending.
> And all about the courtly stable
> Bright-harnessed angels sit in order serviceable.
>
> *("On the Morning of Christ's Nativity," lines 237–44)*

Although there are no marked internal divisions to "The Hymn," it is divided in four parts. These are of twelve, six, and eight stanzas, plus the single-stanza conclusion just quoted, repeating the word *see* from the proem. The first part of the hymn (stanzas 1–12) describes the scene on earth at the coming of Christ, with the pastoral scene of the shepherds, who hear music in the Heavens and then see the angels who make it. This part concludes with a vision of the Creation of the world, when this music was first heard, sung by "the sons of morning" (line 119). In the second part (stanzas 13–18), which has the poem's crucial turning point, the narrator enthusiastically hopes that the angels' music will purify the earth, destroy Hell, and open the gates of Heaven for us all to enter into at the present time, by which he means the time of the birth of Christ. The narrator then says that this cannot happen—"But wisest Fate says 'no' / This must not yet be so" (lines 149–50)—because Jesus has still to die on the cross and history must continue on its long course to the Apocalypse and the Last Judgment, when "The dreadfull Judge in middle air shall spread his throne" (line 164). Only after that will our bliss be "full and perfect" (line 166) as we enter Heaven. Even so, our assurance of that bliss begins now, because Satan—"The old dragon under ground" (line 168)—is no longer Prince of the Air and will be chained up in Hell: "And wroth to see his kingdom fail, / Swinges the scaly horror of his folded tail" (lines 171–72). The third part (stanzas 19–26) develops this last point through eight stanzas describing Satan's associates—that is, all the other devils, disguised as pagan gods—being cast down into Hell with him. The final stanza, as we saw, takes us back to the scene of virgin and child, inviting us to look once again, although not at the traveling wizards but at the child laid to sleep by his mother. That calls for silence: "Time is our tedious song should here have ending" (line 239).

Although the poem takes us back to the time of the birth of Christ, we are made to feel as if widely separated moments in time are drawn together and can nearly be seen all at once: the time of the Creation of the world and of the apocalyptic end of the world; the time of the entry of the Creator himself, as the baby Jesus, into the world he created; the time of the salvation of the world when Jesus will die on the cross—"the bitter cross," as Milton calls it, garnering the phrase from Shakespeare (1 *Henry IV*, 1.1.27)—and the time of the composition of "On the Morning of Christ's Nativity," on Christmas morning, 1629. There is also the time—whatever time it happens to be—in which we are reading the poem: "See!"

In the opening seven stanzas, Nature is abashed at the coming of her Creator, who calms her by sending to earth the goddess Peace, who with her wand "strikes a universal peace through sea and land" (line 52). The whole earth is at peace and waiting, as it seems, in breathless expectancy: "While birds of calm sit brooding on the charmèd wave" (line 68). The stars do not want to leave the sky because they would lose the sight of the coming of their lord into their world. The sun does not want to rise because he is ashamed to be compared with the "Son": "He saw a greater sun appear / Than his bright throne or burning axel-tree could bear" (lines 83–84). At this moment of expectancy, time stands still, or seems to.

We then hear the music made at the birth of Christ, when the angels in the skies sang to the shepherds at night as they were watching their flocks: "such music sweet / Their hearts and ears did greet, / As never was by mortal finger strook . . . all their souls in blissful rapture took" (lines 93–98). The music lasts for a time before the shepherds see its source.

> The helmèd cherubim
> And swordèd seraphim
> Are seen in glittering ranks with wings displayed,
> Harping in loud and solemn choir
> With unexpressive notes to Heaven's new-born heir.
>
> *("On the Morning of Christ's Nativity," lines 112–16)*

Unexpressive means "inexpressibly beautiful."

The rapture that this music creates in the shepherds' souls is then compared to the music that sounded at the creation of the world—no, it is *identified* with that music. This is one of the finest moments in the poem. The angelic song referred to in the Gospel according to Luke is the same music sung by the angels, those "sons of morning," when God made the world. We should recall that the "Creator great" of this stanza is the same person as the baby in the manger. He has been born into the world he made:

> Such music (as 'tis said)
> Before was never made,
> But when of old the sons of morning sung,
> While the Creator great
> His constellations set,
> And the well-balanced world on hinges hung,
> And cast the dark foundations deep,
> And bid the welt'ring waves their oozy channel keep.
>
> *("On the Morning of Christ's Nativity," lines 117–24)*

Milton was never much interested in the images of helplessness that are central to Christianity: the baby in its mother's arms and the man on the cross, but here, that baby is also the Creator who "cast the dark foundations" of the world. Each line of this stanza is strongly end-stopped, and the beauty of the whole is increased when we lengthen the time of the pause between lines.

Although the angels' song appears to be being performed for the occasion, what the shepherds have been hearing is also, at a different poetic intensity, the music of the spheres, a classical idea picked up by Christianity. It is the music that the universe makes as a result of the harmonious interaction of its moving parts, those rotating, invisible, crystalline spheres. The reason we can't hear this music is because we are fallen: Adam and Eve heard it, but since their fall sin has made our ears dull. The speaker of the poem allows himself to imagine that if we could hear that music now, the Edenic golden age will be brought back out of the deep past. All the problems we know on this earth will disappear: "Time will run back and fetch the age of gold" (line 135). So complete will be this moral transformation that Heaven itself will appear before us in the sky, beckoning us to enter: "And Heav'n as at some festival / Will open wide the gates of her high palace hall" (lines 147–48).

This is the moment of intense hope. Milton loves to create such moments of ecstasy (a similar one is the catalogue of flowers in "Lycidas"), in order to break them. This fantasy, too, is about to be broken. The feeling captured in this moment is not unrelated to hopes actually expressed at the time of Christ: that the Savior's coming into the world means the end of history is near and we will soon be in Heaven. But the Christian who writes some sixteen centuries later knows better: Jesus will have to die on the cross and, down the long centuries, the Christian Church will have to struggle to win souls for an unimaginably distant salvation. This turning point is marked with that Miltonic adversative, "But":

> But wisest fate says no,
> This must not yet be so:
> The babe lies yet in smiling infancy,
> That on the bitter cross
> Must redeem our loss,
> So both himself and us to glorify.
> Yet first to those ychained in sleep,
> The wakeful trump of doom must thunder through
> the deep.
>
> ("*On the Morning of Christ's Nativity*," lines 149–56)

The Crucifixion, more than three decades in the future, has yet to come, since Christ is still—*yet*—in "smiling infancy." The word *yet* (which has the advantage over *but* of incorporating time) is picked up again five lines later. For emphasis, it is at the beginning of the line, launching us far into the future, to the end of the world. At that time, the dead, hearing the trumpet of the Apocalypse, will rise out of their tombs and even out of the depths of the sea: "Yet first to those ychained in sleep, / The wakeful trump of doom must thunder through the deep" (lines 155–56). Even as he imagines that time, the poet compares the sound of the trumpet, its *clang* (a Greek word for *noise* Milton is fond of), to another crucial historical moment, long before the birth of Christ: the giving of the Law to Moses on the summit of Mount Sinai, when the Hebrews were wandering in the wilderness, the wilderness itself being for Milton a symbol of history:

> The wakeful trump of doom must thunder through the
>   deep
>
> With such a horrid clang
> As on Mount Sinai rang
> While the red fire and smould'ring clouds out brake:
> The aged earth aghast
> With terror of that blast
> Shall from the surface to the center shake,
> When at the world's last sessïon
> The dreadful judge in middle air shall spread his throne.
>
> ("*On the Morning of Christ's Nativity," lines 156–64*)

That "dreadful judge" is *also* the child-king who came into the world, the man who was crucified to save the world, and the "Creator great" (line 120) who made the world in the first place. Even as Christ transcends the world, he is everywhere involved in it, creating, saving, and judging. Of course, in judging he is sending to Hell some of the dead who have been raised, where they will be punished eternally in the same bodies with which they sinned in life. Still, the poet assumes that he and his audience, having accepted that Christ died to save them from Hell, will be among those who go to Heaven instead: "And then at last our bliss / Full and perfect is" (lines 165–66).

Although this event is far in the future, the Incarnation of Jesus Christ has one immediately positive effect: from this point forward

Satan and his troops of devils will not be free to range in the world among us, and in the air above us. For from this happy day, the Nativity of Jesus,

> The old dragon under ground
> In straiter limits bound,
> Not half so far casts his usurped sway,
> And wroth to see his kingdom fail
> Swinges the scaly horror of his folded tail.
>
> *("On the Morning of Christ's Nativity,"*
> *lines 168–72)*

With this picturesque image of Satan—it is not unlike the one from Milton's boyish Latin narrative poem of some four years previous, *In Quintum Novembris*—the poet leads us into his poem's spectacular third part. It is a virtuosic display of classical and Near-Eastern erudition, an anthropology of pagan religions. In it, the classical gods—not only the Greek and Roman classical gods but also the brutish gods of Egypt and the brutal gods of Palestine—are driven out of the world.

In this militantly Christian poem the classical gods are not a second-order language for poetry but devils who have escaped Hell and set themselves up as gods on earth to draw worship away from the true God, thus damning more souls. With the appearance of the Christ-child on earth, they are driven back to Hell. Apollo is the god of poetry and the leader of the muses. But he is not spared amidst this *Götterdämmerung* of Olympians. His oracles, prophecies, and mighty songs—even the epics of Homer—are reduced to a single hollow shriek:

> The oracles are dumb,
> No voice or hideous hum
> Runs through the arched roof in words deceiving.
> Apollo from his shrine
> Can no more divine,
> With hollow shriek the steep of Delphos leaving.
> No nightly trance or breathèd spell,
> Inspires the pale-eyed priest from the prophetic cell.
>
> *("On the Morning of Christ's Nativity," lines 173–180)*

Milton is driving out the entire classical tradition, so he can reabsorb it on his own terms. In the years leading from "On the Morning of Christ's Nativity" to "Lycidas," Milton's English poems would undertake to define what these new terms might be.

As I mentioned, the gods are the angels who fell with Satan to become devils like him. They got into the world when Adam and Eve sinned. They became Apollo and the other Olympians; the Greek wood-gods; the Latin lars and lemurs; the obscene Peor; the innumerable Baalim of the Canaanites; Ashtaroth (another plural); Ammon, the dying god; Moloch, inside whose idol babies were roasted; and the animal gods of Egypt. All these "Troop to th'infernal jail" (line 233). The last of them, Egyptian Osiris, feels the power of "the dreaded infant's hand" (line 222), an image that is no less impressive or consistent for its alluding to the infant Heracles strangling the great serpents that were sent to kill him in the cradle. "Our babe," says Milton, "to show his Godhead *true*"—for Jesus is no fake, like the classical gods—"can in his swaddling bands control the damnèd crew" (lines 227–28). With that powerful image, the fleeing gods are at once reduced to "flocking shadows" and "fettered ghosts" rushing downward, like Homer's gibbering souls, to the underworld. These gods are Greek, Roman, Palestinian, and Egyptian. They are associated with the Mediterranean world and with the numerous sacred sites around the Mediterranean Sea. Milton thinks geographically. So that England and the north of Europe will not be excused from this purgation, Milton says that the fairies, who dance in their grassy mazes by moonlight, fly away, too: "And the yellow-skirted fays / Fly after the night-steeds, leaving their moon-loved maze" (lines 235–36). Even the word *skirt*, which Milton knew to be of Old Norse origin, and which did not necessarily designate a female garment, is an indicator of "north."

We are then given the final stanza, with its beautiful and, as I said, highly conventional cameo of virgin and child. But the martial atmosphere returns with those angels in bright order guarding the stable. They are a sign to us that Milton's Christianity will not be fugitive and cloistered, retiring and contemplative. It will be a militant Christianity, ready to fight in the world.

I mentioned that a poet is unlikely to overcome the creative obstacle of an early success without psychological and artistic struggle. There is evidence of artistic struggle in the weaker poems Milton wrote after "On the Morning of Christ's Nativity," largely as a consequence of his trying to extend the success of this poem into other areas of religious vision. These are "The Passion," "At a Solemn Music," "On Time," and "Upon the Circumcision." *Weaker* must be understood comparatively, of course: these are weak poems for Milton. "At a Solemn Music" and "On Time" would have survived four centuries even if their author never wrote "On the Morning of Christ's Nativity." The least of them, "Upon the Circumcision," has eight lines out of its twenty-eight that are well formed (1–5 and 20–23).

The self-confessed failure of "The Passion," which consists of eight seven-line stanzas of rhyme royal and never gets beyond frantic gestures, is the most obvious example of Milton's attempt to extend the success of "On the Morning of Christ's Nativity" into other areas of religious vision. He has the right instinct, however: that choosing the correct form and sticking to it will often carry one through, and bring inspiration. In this poem, that doesn't happen. The brief mention Milton gives of himself in the proem to "On the Morning of Christ's Nativity" and perfunctorily at the end of the poem is here expanded to fill all eight stanzas. Taking flight as usual, but this time with aid, as Chaucer was carried by the eagle, Milton imagines his spirit being carried to Jerusalem by "some transporting cherub" ("The Passion," line 38) and let down on the rock of the Holy Sepulcher. There, he says, his hot tears will inscribe his poem on the rock as they fall from his eyes in regular poetic meter: "for sure so well instructed are my tears / That they would fitly fall in ordered characters" (lines 48–49). *Instructed tears?* Although his instinct with respect to form is correct, Milton naively imagines his poem will spring also from the spontaneous overflow of powerful feeling, as in fact it did in the case of "On the Morning of Christ's Nativity." So perhaps the expectancy of success does not so much evince naivety on Milton's part as it does reasonable but unjustified hope. In any event, the magic has fled, leaving in its place the absurdity and strain of metrical tears. In a note he attached to "The Passion" when he published it in 1645, after an interval of fifteen years, Milton says, "This subject the author finding to be above the years he had when he wrote it, and nothing satisfied with what was begun, left it unfinished." Why did he publish it at all? There is good writing in it, for example, "See, see the chariot, and those rushing wheels / That whirled the prophet up at Chebar flood" (lines 36–37). But I suspect there was another reason, as well. Milton tended to see his life as a spiritual adventure and to see his poems as illustrations of his progress.

After the achievements of the years that would follow "The Passion," achievements that include "L'Allegro," "Il Penseroso," *A Masque Presented at Ludlow Castle, 1634*, and "Lycidas," Milton wanted to show what we may call (in Hegelian language) the work of the negative in the life of poetic inspiration. Inspiration isn't always direct, something to be had for the asking. Sometimes, inspiration comes when delving into something else, such as one's own unworthiness and fear of death, as in "Lycidas"; or when adopting a dramatic form where inspiration has no traditional place, as in *A Masque Presented at Ludlow Castle, 1634*; or even when trying to push inspiration away, as in the apotropaic openings ("Hence, loathed Melancholy!") of "L'Allegro" and "Il Penseroso." Spurn inspiration and it will come.

The best of the three devotional poems, "At a Solemn Music," is a beautiful expression of an idea that was dear to Milton's heart throughout his life: that music brings us closer to God—not instrumental music alone, but music that is sung. God's entire Creation, the universe and all the creatures in it, is a vast musical composition. At the fall of Adam and Eve, human beings introduced dissonance—"disproportioned sin" (line 19)—into this cosmic composition, thus breaking the music (line 21) or making it impossible to hear. (One thinks of Soviet condemnation of musical dissonance as counterrevolutionary.) The components of human song, melodious voice and rhythmical verse (line 2), therefore originate in the structure of the universe itself: they are "sphereborn" (line 2) and, in allusion to the cosmic music described at the end of Plato's *Republic*, they are "sirens" (line 1). (In the myth of Er, Plato imagines a creature called a *siren*—the word had previously designated the tempting singers of Homer's *Odyssey*—perched on each of the eight concentric spheres of the universe, each siren chanting a single note contributing to the harmony of the whole.) The human counterpart of this harmony is the joining together of the singing human voice with articulate, rhythmical language, as in Milton's own adaptation of Psalm 136:

> Let us therefore warble forth
> His mighty majesty and worth.

> For his mercies ay endure,
> Ever faithful, ever sure.
>
> *(Lines 89–90, plus chorus)*

Thus do we praise the Creator, as all creatures must do. What is important for Milton, therefore, is not where the song comes from but where the song is going.

When we sing solemn religious music, our minds are briefly raised to Heaven, where we seem to hear the hymns sung by the angels and the saints (exemplary humans who have already died and gone to Heaven) before the throne of God:

> And to our high-raised phantasy present
> That undisturbèd song of pure consent
> Ay sung before the sapphire-coloured throne
> To him that sits thereon.
>
> *("At a Solemn Music," lines 5–8)*

In fact, the poem is not a statement of the case but a prayer that the case may be so. It is a prayer to Voice and Verse themselves. Would they please join, or "wed" their powers in us, so that we may in turn join in with those Heavenly songs of the angels and saints with our own, "undiscording voice" (line 17)? For if we do so, we will be innocent again. This is the delirious hope expressed with sustained irony in "On the Morning of Christ's Nativity": that if such music "enwrap our fancy long" all will be well on the earth (line 134). In its political form, it is the anarchic expectation that by seizing the moment of enforced ideological conformity history may be transcended and utopia attained. (Let counterrevolutionaries learn to sing with undiscording voice or be shot.) This is where the poet adds, arrestingly, at the poem's turning point, "As once we did" (line 19). We were once in a state of innocence, until we sinned, and when we lost that state of innocence we fell into disharmony, as did all creatures with us. But before that Fall occurred, we (and all other creatures) were "swayed" (line 22)—that is, totally controlled—by God's love. For God's love was like a conductor before the orchestra of his creatures, whether those creatures were humans in their "first obedience" or animals and plants in their original "state of good" (line 24). Let us hope that we will soon "keep in tune with Heaven" (line 26) until God unites us with his choir. Despite this theological correction of course—God alone can reverse the consequences of the Fall, and not by singing. The mistake is the denial of the agony of Christ's sacrifice, a sacrifice that is real in itself, but that is also a figure for the agony of history. In "On the Morning of Christ's Nativity," there is a turn toward suffering, struggle, and work. Here, God will merely take charge of events "ere long," and then let us join the choir (lines 26–28).

Music is treated with perhaps greater inspiration (if less thoroughly and less theoretically) in "On the Morning of Christ's Nativity" in "L'Allegro" and "Il Penseroso," and in "Arcades," a small masque, or courtly entertainment, with a splendid wood-god—a *daemon* or *genius*— who cares for the plants and trees of the forest:

> But else in deep of night when drowsiness
> Hath locked up mortal sense then listen I
> To the celestial sirens' harmony
> That sit upon the nine enfolded spheres
> And sing to those that hold the vital shears
> And turn the adamantine spindle round
> On which the fate of gods and men is wound.
> Such sweet compulsion doth in music lie
> To lull the daughters of Necessity
> And keep unsteady Nature to her law
> And the low world in measured motion draw
> After the Heavenly tune which none can hear
> Of human mould with gross unpurgèd ear.
>
>   ("*Arcades*," lines 61–73)

What is said in these lines up to "Necessity" comes from the tenth book of Plato's *Republic*, adding an extra sphere to correspond more nearly with medieval tradition, and introducing the idea that human beings cannot hear the music that the cosmos makes because human hearing lost its acuteness at the Fall, becoming "gross." Milton refers often to the theme of cosmic music, as early as the Second Prolusion, which is on the music of the spheres, "*De Spaerarum concentu*," where he calls it a "symphony of the stars," *astrorum symphonia* (*YP*, 1:234–39), and says if we cannot hear this harmony, instead of denying its existence, we should instead blame our feeble ears, which are unable or unworthy to catch such songs and such sweet sounds: *"Quinimo aures nostras incusemus debiles, quae cantus et tam dulces sonos excipere aut non possunt, aut non dignae sunt"* (*Columbia*, 12:154). In "On the Morning of Christ's Nativity," the spheres do not make music perpetually and of their own accord, like a machine, as they do in the Second Prolusion. They are addressed personally and are *exhorted* to make music: "Ring out, ye crystal spheres!" (line 125). This exhortation makes all the difference.

In Christian tradition the celestial music of the spheres can become audible to us only when we are "purged" of sin, which in effect means only when we are in Heaven. As John Carey notes of these verses from "Arcades," Milton probably recalls the delightful passage on cosmic music from *The Merchant of Venice*, when Jessica and Lorenzo are lying on a bank at night, looking at the stars and thinking of the music that they make: "But whilst this muddy vesture of decay [the body] / Doth grossly close it in, we cannot hear it" (5.1.64–65).

Perhaps the most remarkable feature of "At a Solemn Music" is its syntax: the first twenty-four of its twenty-eight lines are comprised by a single sentence winding down through its variations like a long musical phrase. Through the dance of prepositions and participles, we see Milton experimenting with lengthening that musical phrase, building a rhythmical system above that of the shorter poetic line, while heightening the articulation of its parts. For the first time in Milton's English poetry, the technical foundations of the art of *Paradise Lost*—its elaborately vehement syntax—are being explored: "Wed your divine sounds, and mixed power employ / Dead things with inbreathed sense able to pierce" (lines 3–4). That entire splendid second line modifies *power.*

So far as its content is concerned, "On Time" is a theological windup toy, suitably destined, as an earlier, canceled title indicates, for inscription on a clock case. But this poem carries on the syntactical experiment of "At a Solemn Music" and may be read (ignoring the unreliable punctuation) as a single sentence turning on the complementary prepositions *when* (lines 9, 14, and 19) and *then* (lines 11 and 20). (One could put a period after *gain* in line 8, making the poem two sentences, as one could after *flood* in line 13. But the opening of the following phrase with the preposition *for*—"For when as each thing bad thou hast consumed" (line 9)—diminishes grammatical separation and feels like the opening of a long subordinate clause. This seems still more true of the clause opening with *when* in line 14.)

In this poem, Milton is also experimenting with the pulsatile effects he can achieve by interspersing short six-syllable lines among ten-syllable lines—something he will do in the proems to "L'Allegro" and "Il Penseroso" and, most impressively, in "Lycidas." For this, the influence of the Italian canzone has been remarked on by scholars, and Milton certainly knew and used that form.[12] But if (after the rhythmical brilliance of "On the Morning of Christ's Nativity") Milton needed any precedent for so simple but effective an innovation, Spenser's "Epithalamion" is the most likely source for it.

As to the syntactical experiment, it is impressive for the way it shows Milton learning to build long rhythms above and beyond the intricate ones that are restricted to the interior of the single verse line or, at most (with the help of enjambment), to one and a half lines. This technique of building rhythms above the verse line lengthens and complicates the musical phrase beyond the expected frame of the ten-syllable row—or tone row. The later plays of Shakespeare give some precedent for this. But Milton hardly needed permission to explore something so natural to his mind and to his experience of Latin prose. His rhythms above the level of the line are more carefully organized than in Shakespeare's later verse, in which the integrity of individual lines is sometimes lost. In Milton the regular beat of the individual line is preserved in a manner recalling the *ostinato* in music. The short lines of "On Time" actually complement this effect because they punctually draw our attention back to the rhythms of the individual lines. In "On Time" we have another of the early architectural sketches for the organlike contrapuntal rhythms of *Paradise Lost*.

The sentence, for I shall treat the poem as a single sentence, begins with three imperative verbs—*fly*, *call*, and *glut* (lines 1–4)—in which Time is asked to run faster than he already does, to call upon the hours to keep up with his accelerated pace, and finally to devour, as he does, everything that falls into the past: "And glut thyself with what thy womb [stomach] devours" (line 4). That *what* is the whole physical universe, which Time will devour. It seems large to us, but it is actually "false and vain [empty]" (line 5). The universe is therefore reduced to near nonexistence as soon as Time devours it, so that Time's gain is as trivial as our loss. Once Time has eaten everything (an important qualification is now added: "each thing *bad*"), he will eat himself and disappear, like the snake swallowing itself by the tail, a popular Renaissance image of eternity in relation to time.[13] This is the image Milton intends to conjure up for us. But we cannot fail to be reminded of the much more terrifying, autophagic hunger of Death in *Paradise Lost*, who grows hungrier with everything he devours. In his torment he seems to feed on his own ravenous being. Here, by devouring himself, Time gives way to *eternity:*

> Fly envious Time . . .
> And glut thyself with what thy womb devours
> Which is no more than what is false and vain
> And merely mortal dross,
> So little is our loss,
> So little is thy gain,
> For when as each thing bad thou hast entombed,
> And last of all thy greedy self consumed,
> Then long eternity shall greet our bliss.
>
> *("On Time," lines 1–11)*

If Time eats "each thing *bad*," then each thing that is *good* all the way through (a popular etymology of *sincerely* was "unmixed with wax") will escape Time's maw and have a place in eternity: "When every thing that is sincerely good / And perfectly divine . . . shall ever shine" (lines 14–16). Good things will be preserved for eternity together with *truth, peace,* and *love,* which are already there, in eternity, because they are universals unaffected by time and have always been, and always will be, established in Heaven, "about the supreme throne" (line 17).

This is God's throne, as God exists in relation to us. It is the throne, as we are told in a difficult relative clause, "Of Him, t'whose happy-making sight alone . . . we shall forever sit" (lines 18–21). In Milton's somewhat antiquated use of the dative, we sit *to* the sight of God as we might sit *to* a dinner. God is him whose sight we sit to. When? The answer is, "when once our Heav'nly-guided soul[s] shall climb" (line 19) to Heaven and we are rid ("quit") of our "earthly grossness"—rid, that is, of our weighty corporeality (line 20). Then, our spiritual bodies will be, in a beautiful phrase, "attired with stars" (line 21). Moreover, from the vantage point of eternity—and this is something Milton often liked to imagine (see, for example, the conclusion to *"Mansus"*)—we will be able to look down upon all events and all things in time, including our own being in time, as if they were still going on. But the things that make being in time terrible—the unexpected evils that come to us by chance, the expected evil of death, and the quotidian evil of time—will not be altogether annihilated. They will still be there, although no longer as our masters. They will be under our feet, like chained prisoners in a Roman triumph:

> Then, all this earthly grossness quit,
> Attired with stars we shall forever sit
> Triumphing over Death and Chance and thee, O Time.
>
> *("On Time," lines 20–22)*

"Upon the Circumcision" refers to "On the Morning of Christ's Nativity" in its opening lines and proposes, logically enough, to celebrate the next important event in Jesus's life. After the Feast of the Nativity, the next in the Christian calendar is that of the Circumcision, which is celebrated on January 1. It is Milton's worst published poem—far worse than "The Passion"—partly, no doubt, because it explores a side of Christianity (sacrificial blood mysticism) that is inimical to Milton's essentially ethical temperament and his commitment to Christian liberty. What Saint Paul calls Jesus's *obedience* "becoming obedient unto death, yea, even the death of the cross" (Philippians 2:8), is the courageous decision of a mature man, fully aware of what he would suffer and why. In "Upon the Circumcision," that obedience is assured ("seal[ed]"), not by any act of courage on Jesus's part, for he is still an infant, but by his suffering pain (and spilling a little blood) when his foreskin is removed, which "seals obedience first with wounding smart" (line 25). What is being said here is that the wound inflicted on a child, without its consent, of course, is the mystical sign of that child's later consent to die on the cross, obediently. Milton didn't believe in this nonsense, and it shows. Yet even in this unworthy poem there are lines worthy of Milton: the Son "Emptied his glory, even to nakedness; / And that great covenant which we still transgress / Entirely satisfied" (lines 20–22). I can't think of a more concentrated summary of Christian theology.

In the three devotional poems Milton was looking to continue composing religious verse in the manner of "On the Morning of Christ's Nativity," but he didn't find his way. Nor would he, until "Lycidas." In

"L'Allegro," "Il Penseroso," and *A Masque Presented at Ludlow Castle, 1634*, Milton thinks about poetry in a broader frame: not as a religious art but as an ethical one. Sonnet 7 is the bridge across which Milton travels from the religious to the moral.

Milton composed Sonnet 7, "How Soon Hath Time," when he turned twenty-four, in December 1631, by which date "Time, the subtle thief of youth" had "Stol'n on his wing [his] three and twentieth year" (lines 1–2). The sonnet sets the mood for this period in Milton's life, a mood that finds its fullest expression in "Lycidas." But the sonnet is the channel from "On the Morning of Christ's Nativity" to "Lycidas," that is, from a brilliant and effortless achievement in Christian devotional verse to an agonizing struggle for faith—faith in art as well as in God. Now he has devoted his life to the art of poetry, an art he will pursue not for its own sake but for the good of humanity and the service of God.

How well has Milton used his time? How much has he already achieved? How soon will his careful preparation be realized in a substantial achievement, one worthy to follow "On the Morning of Christ's Nativity"? His "hasting days," he says, "fly on with full career," but he has nothing to show for them. (Presumably, he is forgetting "On the Morning of Christ's Nativity.") Nor does he have anything splendid in progress, neither blossom nor bud: "my late spring no bud or blossom shew'th."

To those of us who passed the age of twenty-four some time ago, it may be amusing that a young man of that age, having written a large number of poems in four languages, some of them very long, and one undoubted masterpiece, should be downcast at how little he has achieved. But the feeling is perfectly in tune with the psychology of an ambitious young person, especially one as ambitious and brilliant as Milton. He concludes, however, by expressing another sentiment altogether, taking advantage of the form of the sonnet to turn the thought back on itself. He acknowledges that God does not urgently need poetry by Milton, and that when the time comes, if it comes at all, for Milton to serve God, the decision and the timing will be God's alone: "All is, if I have grace to use it so, / As ever in my great Taskmaster's eye" (lines 13–14). These famous lines resound with a firm faith in God's providence, but it is a faith matured by the poet's modest diffidence of God's accepting service from him. He has come some distance from "On the Morning of Christ's Nativity," when he proposed to run with his poem to Christ's cradle—or to have his muse do the running for him, which is much the same—in order to get there ahead of the wise men. His gift will be first. Now his gift can be last, or never delivered at all. Mere readiness is all.

We have seen how, after the failure of "The Passion," Milton went on to think about poetry in a new way. Not all his efforts were brilliant successes. But most were creditable, even for him. He then took a new direction and began to take poetry less seriously. The result, unexpectedly, was a string of minor masterpieces: "L'Allegro" and "Il Penseroso," and, if we can speak of it as minor, *A Masque Presented at Ludlow Castle, 1634.*

"On Shakespeare" is a tribute published anonymously in the second folio (1632) of Shakespeare's works. It has a striking final line: "That kings for such a tomb would wish to die." What sort of tomb is that? Milton says we will be so absorbed in Shakespeare's writings that we will seem to turn into marble statues as we read: "Then thou our fancy of itself bereaving / Dost make us marble with too much conceiving" (lines 13–14). Elaborate tombs are decorated with full-size marble statues. Hence, when we read Shakespeare, we will be immobilized, like marble statues on a tomb, by too much thinking, "too much conceiving." That is what Milton means by a "live-long monument" (line 8). Shakespeare's monument will last forever because there will always be new readers to take up the spaces in the niches of the text. Being entombed among them, Shakespeare's resting place is one that even the greatest kings could envy and give their own lives to have: "And so sepulchered in such pomp dost lie / That kings for such a tomb would wish to die" (lines 15–16). This poem is much admired and anthologized, perhaps because of the meeting in it of Shakespeare and Milton. The poem can be praised as a good piece of work for its purpose: to provide an extravagant encomium to set before Shakespeare's plays, in dedication to him. The contrivance of a living tomb of readers is a clever one, and Milton brings it off suavely. That the poem has no feeling, and that its praise is forced, should not much lessen our cool esteem.

However, I much prefer the two comic and yet sincere funeral elegies to Thomas Hobson, the university carrier, especially the first: "On the University Carrier, who sickened in the time of his vacancy, being forbid to go to London, by reason of the plague." Despite his great age,

Hobson has been for many years escaping Death, because every time Death looks for the carrier at Cambridge, he is on his way to London; and every time Death looks for him in London, Hobson is on his way back to Cambridge. (An Arabian tale involving Mecca and Medina has the same structure, but in it the man is trying to avoid Death. Hobson seems to do so unconsciously.) When the plague caused traffic to cease, however, Death caught up with his man at last. The scene is an affectionate one. Death relieves Hobson from his Sisyphean toil, and acts with the deference of a considerate servant:

> [Death] in the kind office of a chamberlain,
> Showed him his room where he must lodge that night,
> Pulled off his boots and took away the light.
> If any ask for him it shall be said,
> Hobson has supped, and's newly gone to bed.
>
> *("On the University Carrier," lines 14–18)*

Also from this period is "Arcades," with its tutelary genius of the wood: "For know by lot from Jove I am the power / Of this fair wood, and live in oaken bower" (lines 44–45). At night the wood-god—a figure of raw poetical talent—listens to the music of the cosmic spheres. In the Christian tradition this night music is mechanical and deterministic. It will not be in *Paradise Lost* (*PL* 4. 680–88). But the passage anticipates the majesty of Milton's epic cosmos:

> But else in deep of night when drowsiness
> Hath locked up mortal sense, then listen I
> To the celestial sirens' harmony,
> That sit upon the nine enfolded spheres,
> And sing to those that hold the vital shears,
> And turn the adamantine spindle round,
> On which the fate of gods and men is wound.
>
> *("Arcades," lines 61–67)*

I have yet not mentioned a favorite among the lesser English poems of Milton's twenties: the graceful "Epitaph on the Marchioness of

Winchester," which stands in my estimation somewhere between the minor and the major poems of this period. While it is not perhaps the most interesting poem from a philosophical or theological point of view, it is the most genuinely moving, arousing our sympathy for the noblewoman whose child died in the womb shortly before she died herself: "the languished mother's womb / Was not long a living tomb" (lines 33–34). Instead of the rhetorical splendors and mythopoeic supercondensation we are accustomed to seeing in Milton, the "Epitaph on the Marchioness of Winchester" exhibits the elegantly understated, aristocratic grace we associate with the best poems of Ben Jonson, as in the touchingly simple couplet, often singled out: "Gentle lady may thy grave / Peace and quiet ever have" (lines 47–48). It must be said also that the eminent figures Milton lamented in his Latin elegies died full of honors and years, in full expectation of Heaven. Their deaths are not tragic, and there hangs about the extravagant sorrow expressed in Milton's Latin elegies more than a trace of irony.[14] But the death of a young woman in childbirth is another matter. We cannot help thinking of the physical pain in detail, of infection and blood. The poet's task is to place a decent and beautiful screen in front of such thoughts, not only for our sake but hers. There is therefore considerable relief in her beautiful apotheosis, "Far within the bosom bright / Of blazing majesty and light" (lines 69–70). There, she is "clad in radiant sheen, / No Marchioness, but now a Queen" (lines 73–74).

Three years after "On the Morning of Christ's Nativity," Milton at last reached the point where he knew he should stop trying to force the issue and simply write poetry when he could, on whatever subject inspired him. He had to stop trying to be a Very Important Christian and return to concentrating on his art. It was a question of entrusting that ambition to hands other than his own, and perhaps also to the surprising resources of craft. That was the only solution possible, and it was a difficult one to find because it is a paradoxical solution. For Milton, relaxation itself can appear to be an act of iron resolve:

> Yet be it less or more or soon or slow
> It shall be still in strictest measure even
> To that same lot, however mean or high,
> Toward which time leads me, and the will of Heaven.

> All is, if I have grace to use it so,
> As ever in my great Taskmaster's eye.
>
> *(Sonnet 7, lines 9–14)*

While his Taskmaster is silent, Milton is free to write for pleasure. Writing for pleasure meant thinking *about* pleasure. Is pleasure fundamentally a mood? In the next two poems Milton will explore this possibility.

~ 2

On "L'Allegro" and
"Il Penseroso"

THE PAIRED POEMS, "L'Allegro" and "Il Penseroso" ("The Lively Man" and "The Reflective Man"), are unique in English literature. Yet the representation of opposite possibilities in the self is common enough in poetry, and Milton had already done something like it in Elegy 6, "*Ad Carolum Diodatum,*" when he introduced the two contrasting kinds of poet: the poet of eros, whose songs are beloved of Bacchus, the god of wine ("*carmina Bacchus amat,*" line 14), and the abstemious *vates,* from whose inner breast and lips are heard the voice of Jove himself ("*Spirat et occultum pectus et ora Iovem,*" line 78). William Blake's *Songs of Innocence and Experience* are perhaps the deepest example of the oppositional and analytic impulse in the poetic imagination—although all Blake's prophecies are inspired by the muse of contradiction. Analysis of the self into distinct voices articulating the poet's "inner quarrel," as Helen Vendler calls it,[1] is a creative principle in Yeats from the early poem "The Two Trees"—the one bearing trembling flowers and fruit, the other "the ravens of unresting thought"—to the late, discursive poems expressing ambivalent political and personal judgments. The inner quarrel is formally evident in Yeats's "Dialogue of Self and Soul," inspired by Marvell's two dialogue poems—"Dialogue between the Resolved Soul and Created Pleasure" and "Dialogue between Soul and Body." Indeed, almost all Marvell's poems up to the "Horatian Ode"—for example, "To His Coy Mistress" and "The Mower against Gardens"—express one side of a debate in which the other is implied: "Half the world shall be thy slave," says Pleasure to the Soul, "the other half thy friend."

Contradiction is fundamental to the way poetry thinks—metaphor itself is a kind of contradiction—and when Yeats's soul enjoins his self to "Fix every wandering thought upon / The quarter where all thought is done," he, the soul, would silence verse itself. For verse, the "turning" of words, effectuates the delirious movement of poetry between opposite ideas and opposite moods: on the one hand, revulsion at "the frogspawn of a blind man's ditch"; on the other hand, the acceptance (and, no doubt, the detachment) by which we have the strength to say, "Everything we look upon is blest."

But separating the elements of the dialogue into two distinct personae speaking two distinct poems, each persona, or "mask" (per+sonare, "to sound through"), holding the other in horror and contempt, is unique. I refer especially to those symmetrically opposed introductions to "L'Allegro" and "Il Penseroso," the apotropaic proemia wherein the opposing character is formally banished—"Hence, loathèd Melancholy!" "Hence, vain, deluding joys!" Nor do we find in other poems built on explicitly oppositional terms, such as the poems I have mentioned by Marvell, Blake, and Yeats, what we do find in Milton's "L'Allegro" and "Il Penseroso": the feeling of a magic incantation. More broadly, the poems are distinguished for their elaborate artifice, their mythopoeic learnedness, their psychological range, as they are for the stunning clarity of the many *genre* scenes they offer, and for the profound suggestiveness of what is said in them about the power of art. Assuming "L'Allegro" to have been written first, it is wonderful to contemplate how Milton managed to preserve and reproduce the original inspiration in its opposite mood, while adhering faithfully to the structure of the earlier poem.

It is uncertain when Milton composed "L'Allegro" and "Il Penseroso." Most scholars believe they were written after he took his MA degree at Cambridge and had embarked on some five years of private study, first at Hammersmith and then at Horton. The delineation of "characters," originally an ancient literary form, became fashionable in Milton's day, just before the rise of the novel. But Milton's elegant, playful poems bear little resemblance to the prose character studies of the period. Instead these poems reflect a preoccupation with what it means to be a "persona" in a fully individuated way, rather than a social person bound to others by the ties of family or class, or even by the need to make a living: "retirèd Leisure" is in Melancholy's train; an active aesthetic leisure is, so to speak, the condition of the possibility of Mirth.

Milton was a mature man in his twenties when he wrote these poems, but they reflect a younger state of mind—that of what we would now call "the young adult"—an age when one can seriously put to oneself the question: "What kind of a self shall I choose to be?" as if such a choice can be made. (To an extent it can, and to a greater extent it can't, as one discovers when one is no longer a teenager.) That is why each poem ends with the sort of contractual bargain teenagers at one time or another will imagine they can strike with their fates: "These delights, if thou canst give, / Mirth with thee, I mean to live" ("L'Allegro," line 151–52); "These pleasures, Melancholy, give, / And I with thee will choose to live" ("Il Penseroso," lines 175–76). Such propositions reflect the absurdly naive but unavoidable question (unavoidable when you are sixteen) of what mood one should choose to be in for the rest of one's life.

The Lively Man and the Reflective Man are recognizable in our own jargon as "extroverted" and "introverted" personality types. But because the poems concentrate on the self apart from the ties of family and society, the extroversion of L'Allegro, the Vivacious Man, is a "turning-outward" toward others that remains a private experience, the experience of observing others at work and at play and especially (when the poem concludes) the experience of music, music made without any musicians we can see. So it is, too, *mutatis mutandis*, with Il Penseroso, the Reflective Man, whose introversion is made easier by his preferring night to day, the forest to the open fields, and to the lecture hall or the sociable university quadrangle, his lonely study in a tower. The Reflective Man's introversion does not, however, resolve itself into a hard core like Milton's heart in Sonnet 6, which "arms itself within itself, a perfect diamond" ("[il] mio cuor . . . S'arma di sè, d'intero diamante," line 8). Instead, the Reflective Man's self is perfected in the ecstatic dissolution it experiences through music:

> There let the pealing organ blow
> To the full-voiced choir below
> In service high and anthems clear,
> As may with sweetness through mine ear
> Dissolve me into ecstasies.
>
> *(Lines 161–65)*

When we consider the representations of music that come near the end of both "L'Allegro" and "Il Penseroso," each evoking Orpheus, the archetypal musician and poet, the poems seem to be less about the opposition of two personae than they are about the emotional possibilities of art, from the "wanton heed and giddy cunning" (L'Allegro," line 141) of subjective, aesthetic experience, which always turns back on itself, to the "service high and anthems clear" of Christian worship, which is directed to the transcendent other.

"L'Allegro" begins with a proem intended to drive off its threatening opposite, Melancholy, a monster born in the underworld, by the river Styx. In the realm of primitive magic and Hesiodic daemons, to know the true name and genealogy of something is to control it. How and by whom was Melancholy conceived? The answer is, by an ugly copulation of the triple-headed hound of Hell, Cerberus, with a vestigially personified Midnight, a Midnight having none of the particularity of Spenser's half-blind, wicked, scheming, crook-backed crone. Since Melancholy is no longer in Hell but in the world, threatening the mood of the Lively Man, the *allegrezza* of L'Allegro, he must be banished before the speaker may safely invoke its opposite, Euphrosyne or Mirth, lest open war break out between the two. The monster is banished, however, not to the Hell in which it was born but to an unknown ("uncouth") cave in the land of the Cimmerians, a strange, remote people who live in perpetual twilight in the wilderness ("desert") at the edge of the world. The monster Melancholy is banished, that is, to the periphery, and what is banished to the periphery will of course return—as a "pensive nun." The apotropaic proemium is a temporary gesture, a clearing for contemplative reflection on the mirthfulness that understands itself (mistakenly? provisionally?) to be opposed to contemplative reflection:

> Hence, loathèd Melancholy,
> Of Cerberus and blackest Midnight born,
> In Stygian cave forlorn,
> 'Mongst horrid shapes and shrieks and sights unholy.
> Find out some uncouth cell
> Where brooding Darkness spreads his jealous wings
> And the night-raven sings.
> There, under ebon shades and low-browed rocks,

As ragged as thy locks,
In dark Cimmerian desert ever dwell.

                    ("L'Allegro," lines 1–10)

The complicated rhyme scheme (**abbacddeec**) and alternating line lengths show the influence of Italian lyric poetry, now thoroughly absorbed (Milton wrote no more poems in Italian after Sonnet 6, even when he was in Italy), and of Spenser's Italianate "Epithalamion." As in Spenser, a mood of enchantment is created by the suspended rhymes, which chime in upon us unexpectedly, notably the "c" rhyme on "cell," which remains unmated with "dwell" until the last word of the introduction: "In dark Cimmerian desert ever dwell." The surprise of that final rhyme is increased by our having already heard and been satisfied by the internal rhyme, *desert / ever.* The enchanting effect is enhanced by the syncopated rhythms of the shorter lines, for example, the line, "as ragged as thy locks," which follows the ponderous, open vowels of the preceding verse: "There, under ebon shades and low-browed rocks / As ragged as thy locks." The phonic slowness in both lines is overlaid by the rhythmical rapidity of the second, shorter line.

By "a mood of enchantment" I do not mean just an aesthetic effect. I mean the feeling that we are in the presence of real incantatory power that has the force of a magic spell, banishing a malign spirit from our presence. The apotropaic magic may then be assumed when the poet changes to the more regular tetrameter meter that governs the rest of the poem and immediately accelerates it, a trick Milton picked up from the opening of the second act of *A Midsummer Night's Dream*, where the fairies are introduced in exotic measures, indicating their existence on a different plane of reality. But as their discussion proceeds the meter modulates insensibly into regular iambic pentameter couplets. In this poem, the change occurs abruptly with Milton's favorite telltale word, *but*. With that *but*, he turns on his heel from the vicious genealogy of Melancholy to the propitious one of Mirth:

But come thou goddess fair and free,
In Heav'n yclept Euphrosyne
And by men, heart-easing Mirth,
Whom lovely Venus at a birth

With two sister graces more
To ivy-crownèd Bacchus bore.

("L'Allegro," lines 11–16)

When she wakes the speaker at dawn, Mirth is instructed to bring with her a lengthy train of attendants, among whom is "the mountain nymph, sweet Liberty":

Haste thee nymph, and bring with thee
Jest and youthful Jollity . . .
And in thy right hand lead with thee
The Mountain nymph, sweet Liberty . . .
And at my window bid good morrow . . .
While the cock with lively din
Scatters the rear of darkness thin.

*("L'Allegro," lines 25–26, 35–36, 46,
and 49–50)*

Liberty is a mountain nymph because in Milton's view inhabitants of the mountains live harder lives and are sternly independent, like the ancient Hebrews or the Greeks, in contrast with peoples who live on coastal plains or in great river valleys, like the ancient Philistines on the Canaanite, Mediterranean plain, or the Egyptians and Babylonians beside the Nile and the Euphrates, who being given to their pleasures are easy prey to tyrants. But here, in "L'Allegro," *liberty* means little more than freedom from the hard physical labor of the kind the plowman, the shepherd, the milkmaid, and the mower must do, although the plowman whistles as he works and the milkmaid sings (lines 63–68).

With the wonderful, martial image of the cockcrow "scattering the rear of darkness thin," as if darkness were a retreating army, the poet draws the curtain back from the "landscape" (line 70), a new, fashionable term imported from Holland, where landscape painting had just begun. The landscape is disclosed beneath the rising sun, "Robed in flames and amber light" (line 61). Through it the Lively Man will briskly walk, his eye catching its "pleasures" (line 69)—they are not to him objective *things* in themselves so much as they are subjective *pleasures*—one by one: fields darkly furrowed from being newly turned; boles of huge elms rising from the hedges bordering those fields; green hills under the rosy clouds; ruddy, burned-over grasslands beside the gray fallows; late-summer meadows spangled with daisies; shallow, rushing brooks flowing into wide, slow-moving rivers; and, in the distance, "Mountains on whose barren breast / The laboring clouds do often rest" (lines 73–74; lines 70–76 paraphrased). One may at first think such a list, such a panorama, is charming enough but otherwise unremarkable. It is in fact a startling technical and imaginative leap from the somewhat airless biblical world of the English poems up to now and the robust opening outward, in "L'Allegro," to the physical world. This is the awakened imagination that will give us the rich earth and cosmic splendors—all of them intensely physical—of *Paradise Lost*.

That this is an autumn or late-summer landscape is confirmed when Phyllis and Thestylis bind the sheaves. Or, if the hay is still drying in a great conical heap in the field—"the tanned haycock in the mead" (line 90)—Thestylis and Phyllis resort thither, for what purpose we remain uninformed, and one suspects this epicene speaker doesn't care. There are people in this landscape, busy with their work and with their pleasures: the hunter who sounds his horn, the plowman, the milkmaid, the mower pausing to sharpen his scythe, Thestylis and Phyllis on their way to the haycock, and the shepherd in the dale, under a hawthorn's ragged bark, anxiously counting his sheep at first light. The speaker takes them all in with delight, and he wants nothing more.

The speaker's objective presence is so vague that he at first lacks any clear grammatical subject, being introduced into the landscape by the participial phrases, "Oft list'ning how the hounds and horn" (line 53) and "Sometime walking not unseen" (line 57). He can wander on the periphery of life and, though he is "not unseen," he is not much remarked. Yet he sees much. He sees the simple country folk not only when they are outdoors making music, sawing on their "jocund rebecks" (line 94), and dancing "in the chequered shade" (line 96)—a fine image of the pleasure we take in the afternoon light that falls through overhanging boughs—but also when they are at supper in their cottages, and when they spin their fairy tales by the cheerful hearth, over "the spicy nut-brown ale" (line 100). He doesn't take his eyes off them until they are in bed, lulled to sleep by the "whispering winds" of the evening (line 116). Is sex deliberately left out, to tell us something about the speaker, or is it merely for the sake of decorum? Even if the reason is the latter, the effect is to make the speaker interestingly uninterested in that side of life.

Country people go to bed early and rise with the dawn. Once they have turned in, the Lively Man appears to be instantly transported to the city, merely by the recollection of its pleasures: "Towered cities please us then / And the busy hum of men" (lines 117–18). These pleasures seem to be as much literary as they are social, bringing before the speaker's eyes knights and ladies in their halls or on the tilting yard, or at ceremonies graced with revelry and pageants (lines 125–28). The dreamlike character of this urban interlude in a medieval past is made explicit in verses that take us back into the country: "Such sights as youthful poets dream / On summer eves, by haunted stream" (lines 129–30). *Haunted* stream? We are reminded of the magic spell under which the poem is supposed to unfold, although the literary quality of the spell is suggested by the one contemporary urban pleasure Milton names, the theater:

> Then to the well-trod stage anon,
> If Jonson's learned sock be on
> Or sweetest Shakespeare, fancy's child,
> Warble his native wood-notes wild.
>
> *("L'Allegro," lines 131–34)*

For a brief moment, lasting through these four rapid lines, we are in a real, public world, that of the London stage in the 1630s: Milton could have attended such plays. He had written an epitaph for Shakespeare, which was published with the second folio, and Ben Jonson was still alive in London when Milton wrote these lines. No longer are we in the imaginary world of the speaker's fantasies, its warm cottages and nut-brown ale as unfamiliar to him as "Fairy Mab" and the "drudging goblin" (lines 102 and 105). He has read about these in books, among them, incidentally, Ben Jonson's masques. The "well-trod stage" belongs to a material world, but one in which Jonson's learning and Shakespeare's imagination are more real than anything else.

Even so, the Lively Man's Shakespeare is not writing or mounting a play: he is "warbling," that is, singing. The singing is still in our ears when the speaker is "lapped," that is, submerged in and caressed by "Lydian airs" (line 136), the music of the effeminate and sensual East.

(Milton's musical taste for once follows Plato's.) After we are given a brief opening into the objective world of the theater, and of social discussion about theater—Jonson is learned, Shakespeare's is a natural talent—subjectivity overwhelms us again. The speaker's soul is "pierced" (line 138) by music that is "Married to immortal verse" (line 137). But the music is soon a force of its own, making the self "wanton" and "giddy" with its counterpoint:

> Married to immortal verse
> Such as the meeting soul may pierce
> In notes with many a winding bout
> Of linked sweetness long drawn out,
> With wanton heed and giddy cunning,
> The melting voice through mazes running,
> Untwisting all the chains that tie
> The hidden soul of harmony.

> ("L'Allegro," lines 137–44)

What kind of music is this? It sounds to us like the music of extreme subjectivity, music we will love for the ecstasy it induces in our souls, which are now deliciously lost in that larger hidden soul of harmony. Such music is what it was in the beginning: an incantation, a magic spell. Formerly this spell had the power to drive Melancholy off to the edge of the world, the Cimmerian land. The incantation then had the power to call the Spirit of Mirth from whatever place she inhabits, bringing with her "Quips and cranks and wanton wiles, / Nods and becks and wreathed smiles" (lines 27–28), a well-stocked repertoire of cheerful social tics. There is also a parade of very minor Greek and Roman gods, from the spirit of youth, Hebe, to "Sport that wrinkled Care derides / And Laughter"—in the classic pose of that god whom the Romans took seriously indeed—"holding both his sides" (lines 31–32).

Now the power of the incantation, transmitted through music, reaches past these minor deities far into the underworld, to Elysium, where Orpheus raises his head from its pillow of somniferous blooms. He does so to better hear those strains. The music penetrates as far into the underworld as to the Elysian fields but not, it would seem, to the throne of Pluto. Had the strains penetrated that far they would have been equal to Orpheus's song, with which he won Eurydice back. They would have "quite" (that is, "entirely") set Eurydice free:

> That Orpheus' self may heave his head
> From golden slumber on a bed
> Of heaped Elysian flowers, and hear
> Such strains as would have won the ear
> Of Pluto to have quite set free
> His half-regained Eurydice.
>
> *("L'Allegro," lines 145–50)*

Is there a suggestion in Eurydice's name that such music is not quite serious enough for real life? Her name means "wide-ruling justice," as Milton knows. The question is not answered. It hangs in the air for a short time, like that music.

On this splendid note, by which the original sense of the poem as an incantation is recaptured, the speaker abruptly concludes with his impossible proposal: "These delights if thou canst give, / Mirth with thee I mean to live" (lines 151–52). What delights is he speaking of? That of seeing Orpheus heaving his head from off those Elysian flowers (the very head the maenads severed from his body)? Or of watching Corydon and Thyrsis dine on herbs and country messes and drink their nut-brown ale? These are not delights but their shadows: fantasies, half-formed images and pictures fleeting in rapid sequence through the mind. The poet has captured pure poetry, that is, the core of the experience of reading poetry, which is this rapid flow of bright images only partly seen.

"Il Penseroso" follows the same structure as "L'Allegro" and was un-doubtedly composed later. What is remarkable about "Il Penseroso" in the first instance is simply the unlikelihood of its peculiar achievement, which is to imitate the form of the earlier poem with content diametri-cally opposed, and to do so with undiminished inspiration.

"Il Penseroso" opens with an apotropaic proem in the same form as that of "L'Allegro," although this one has no genealogy to parallel the birth of Melancholy from Cerberus and Midnight: "vain deluding joys," in the plural, are banished. The enemy lineage, that of the god-dess of Mirth, and indeed the goddess herself, remain disdainfully unacknowledged. All that the speaker will acknowledge is a crowd of lightweight "deluding joys," the children of who knows whom. We seem to be talking about the pure experience of poetry again. As the regular tetrameter measure of the body of the poem begins, the speaker hails the goddess Melancholy and tells us she is black like two legendary black beauties, Prince Memnon's sister and Cassiopeia, who became a constellation. We then learn her ancient and staid genealogy: Melancholy was born of Vesta, the Roman goddess of the hearth (and hence of the household), and Saturn, the father of the Olympian gods, including Jove, who overthrew him. By reaching back before the Olympian gods of Greek and Roman mythology, Milton is emphasizing the extreme antiquity of Melancholy's line, making her fundamental to human existence (in a way that Mirth is not) and even to the metaphysical order of the world: she is "higher far descended" (line 22), he says, when comparing her with Memnon's sister and Cassiopeia. The remark is aimed at the parents of Mirth, who are the lightest of the Olympians, Venus and Bacchus. Melancholy is invoked as a "pensive nun"—though nuns had not been seen in England for a hundred years— who is "devout and pure, / Sober, steadfast, and demure" (lines 31–32). She is described in a long passage of lines that run on breathlessly, with increasing speed. Yet even as the lines speed up, Melancholy's pace slows to a standstill. She seems to turn into a marble statue, so rapt is she in the contemplation of God:

> Come, pensive nun, devout and pure,
> Sober, steadfast, and demure,
> All in a robe of darkest grain,
> Flowing with majestic train,
> And sable stole of cypress lawn
> Over thy decent shoulders drawn,
> Come, but keep thy wonted state
> With even step and musing gait
> And looks commercing with the skies,
> Thy rapt soul sitting in thine eyes,
> There, held in holy passion still,
> Forget thyself to marble, till
> With a leaden downward cast,
> Thou fix them on the earth as fast.

("Il Penseroso," lines 31–44)

Simply drawing this scene out in all its detail, so that we see the nun clearly and sense the diminishing of liveliness in her body, is a virtuosic performance. In slow motion, we see her demure carriage; her dark, sumptuous garments; her even, stately pace; her rapturous eyes turned Heavenward; her sudden pause, overcome with sacred emotion; her extension of this pause into a trance; and finally her breaking of the trance with her eyes only, when she turns them on the earth, with a "sad leaden" look. All this magnificence is magnificently slow, even as we feel we are running out of breath reading the words. Of particular interest is Melancholy's "forget[ting] herself to marble" (line 42). That is how Milton had earlier imagined the readers of Shakespeare, as marble figures on a tomb, immobilized by thought: "Then thou our fancy of itself bereaving, / Dost make us marble with too much conceiving" ("On Shakespeare," lines 13–14). Milton has fetched back the image here and improved it immeasurably, even in this briefer use of it. In the Shakespeare poem, the image is a "conceit," in the sense that term is used of metaphysical poetry. Milton rejected such ornaments as too fanciful and ostentatiously clever. Elsewhere, he asks the English language to bring him something from her wardrobe to clothe his thoughts in:

> Not those new-fangled toys and trimming slight
> Which takes our late fantastics with delight,
> But cull those richest robes and gay'st attire
> Which deepest spirits and choicest wits desire
>
> *("At a Vacation Exercise," lines 19–22)*

The conceit of Shakespeare's readers being turned to marble as they read him, and so forming an elaborate tomb with sculptures on it, is such a "toy." But the image of Melancholy's pace slowing down as she contemplates the heavens, until she *briefly* forgets herself to marble reflects a deep spirit in the poet. Unlike the image from the poem on Shakespeare, it is also in excellent taste, or what Milton calls *choicest wit*.

Attending Melancholy is a long train of vestigial personifications favoring reflection: Peace, Quiet, Fasting, Leisure (for reflection requires leisure, that is, wealth), and Contemplation, the climax of the series, followed by Silence. The word *contemplation* implies inclusive visual inspection and modeling within a cleared mental space, like that of the Roman temple, which is, as of course Milton knew, etymologically present in the word *contemplation*. Contemplation is represented as prophetic vision, in particular the prophetic vision of Ezekiel, a notion of the prophetic that is far beyond that with which the poem concludes, in "something like prophetic strain" (line 174).

The following figure of Silence is "hist" along for the sake of contemplation unless, of course, the nightingale sings, which instantly puts us back in the forest. It is like Milton to emphasize, first, the visual character of reflective thinking as inclusive inspection and then, as a musician and a poet, to correct that visual bias by introducing the nightingale, Philomel, smoothing with her song "the rugged brow of night" (line 58; cf. *Comus*, lines 250–51, where the Lady's song smoothed "the raven down / Of darkness till it smiled"). With masterly art, Milton contrasts the alacrity of "L'Allegro" with the wonderful effects of spaciousness and distance in "Il Penseroso," as when the moon at her height is "Like one that hath been led astray / Through the heaven's wide pathless way" (lines 69–70). Note how the double rhyme, *hath . . . astray / path . . . way*, opens up twice from a short *a* to a long: everything is sonorously lengthened.

Another such splendid moment is when the speaker wanders in the forest at night and hears across a body of water, from a neighboring town, the distant curfew bell calling its citizens (but not the speaker) indoors, enjoining them to cover their fires and go to bed for the night. Milton has caught how the sound of a bell is louder when it crosses water while still seeming to come from afar. We are not sure the curfew bell is objectively "far off," if *objectively* can mean anything in this connection; it is *subjectively* far off, it sounds so:

> Oft on a plat of rising ground
> I hear the far-off curfew sound
> Over some wide-watered shore
> Swinging slow with sullen roar.
>
> *("Il Penseroso," lines 73–76)*

Roar had a wider sense in Milton's day than it does in ours. It could refer to any loud sustained noise, like the roar of a crowd, but the splendid phrase *sullen roar* is typical of the greater degree of phenomenological distortion in this poem, as compared with its predecessor. We do well to remember that the speaker's is a mind that, altering, alters all, as moonlight breaking through a cloud alters not only the external forms but the very moods that irradiate from things we see in the night. The curfew bell isn't peaceful and calm: it is sullen, and it roars.

Almost immediately, we are in a room beside a dying fire in the very town we have just seen from a distance, across water, and it is curfew time again, as the bellman drowsily blesses the doors of each house. This is a small country town, not London. The quick change of scene, for which the pretext is bad weather ("Or if the air will not permit," line 77), is the poet's way of showing us what youthful would-be philosophers discover, time after time, imagining they have found a great thing. To be reflective, they discover, is continually to change one's point of view on all things, and to do so rapidly, because nothing is quite solid or real: everything is in motion, everything flows, as Heraclitus said, and the same stream cannot be stepped into twice. The confusion of thought with reality is gently mocked by Socrates, in the *Cratylus*, as laughable but plausible: he quotes Heraclitus and says the oldest of gods were named after streams, because their names sound like streams.[2] Snapping up impressions from the spume of things, we are situated in this room only long enough to hear the bellman's drowsy charm and that last poignant vestige of Mirth, the lonely cricket on the hearth (line 82).

As in "L'Allegro," we are transported from the rustic cottage to a more exalted scene, although not, on this occasion, the "towered cities" of "L'Allegro" (line 117) but a solitary "high, lonely tower" (line 87), where our reflective speaker studies. Instead of poring over his books, he calls up the learned spirits at home, out of office hours:

> Or let my lamp at midnight hour
> Be seen in some high lonely tower
> Where I may oft outwatch the Bear
> With thrice-great Hermes or unsphere
> The spirit of Plato to unfold
> What worlds or what vast regions hold
> Th'immortal mind that hath forsook
> Her mansion in this fleshly nook.
>
> *("Il Penseroso," lines 85–92)*

The tower may remind us of the towers of "L'Allegro," "Bosomed high in tufted trees" (line 78), but this tower is solitary: it is not part of a college, or a monastery, still less of a court. It is what Yeats calls "the far tower where Milton's Platonist / Sat late," seeking "an image of mysterious wisdom."[3] But our Reflective Man's desire to be disembodied, and so to gaze upon a plurality of "worlds" and "regions," suggests a more unstable and flitting intelligence. His tower is more like the strand before the Martello tower of *Ulysses*, the place of impotent reflection on the ineluctable modality of all visible—which is to say, all appearing, all phenomenal—things.[4]

Here, however, we see the first signs of exuberance in our Reflective Man, for he does not present himself with his back bent and his spectacles on, poring over the weighty folio of Hermes Trismegistus and the volumes of Plato. Milton would not have regarded the works attributed to the pseudo-author, "thrice-great Hermes," a fraud exposed by the great Isaac Casaubon, as even once-great. Milton is telegraphing a certain naivety in his tower Platonist. Like a magician, the Reflective Man boldly calls down the spirits of these hoary names from the heavenly spheres and questions them. He likewise presents himself as watching, not reading, the tragedies of ancient Greece and of later ages, presented by "gorgeous Tragedy" herself (line 97), as if he were Shakespeare's Prospero. He calls on Melancholy again ("But, O sad virgin," line 103)—lest we forget the poem is addressed to her—wishing she could also give him access to legendary authors who don't exist in books, Musaeus, and Orpheus, whose lament for Eurydice "Drew iron tears down Pluto's cheek / And made Hell grant what love did seek" (lines 107–8). What Orpheus sought was of course the return of his wife.[5] The speaker wishes that Melancholy might call up Chaucer, as well, to finish "The Squire's Tale," the most mysterious of the *Canterbury Tales*. The speaker wishes also to hear—though from what source is unclear ("great bards beside")—more medieval tales of magic and romance: "Of forests and enchantments drear / Where more is meant than meets the ear" (line 119).

After these night scenes, Milton imagines the speaker in the morning, as he has imagined his Lively Man being wakened at dawn by the spirit of Mirth at his window. Now he is greeted by Morn herself, in civil suit, as befits the speaker's mood. Morn brings with her gusts of wind and showers—are those showers her civil suit or the overcast? The Reflective Man's morning walk is brief, however, and has none of the brio of the Lively Man's peregrinations. He is soon in the woods again, and in silence, except for the droning of bees and the murmuring of the brook. These sounds put him to sleep so that he may be visited by a strange, mysterious dream. Not the least of what is strange about the dream is its hovering, like a hummingbird, over a pool. The pool is so still it reflects the sky and also the wings of this dream, so that the dream greets its own reflection: "And let some strange, mysterious dream, / Wave at his wings in airy stream" (lines 147–48).

This is the strangest and most difficult moment in "Il Penseroso." It is nearly unintelligible, like Freud's "navel" of the dream. The personified dream sees itself reflected in the stream and waves with its wings at its own wings. But the content of what the dreamer dreams is not this winged figure, which merely delivers the content. This content is a moving picture of some kind, a "lively portraiture" (line 149); the dreamer sees it, but we never do. This "lively portraiture," occurring in the sleeper's mind, bears no resemblance whatever to the hovering spirit that has laid it softly on the sleeper's eyelids. When the sleeper wakes from this dream, he has no reason to cry to dream again, for he is now in a supernatural world where Nordic fairy spirits make music that surrounds him in the woods:

> And as I wake, sweet music breathe
> Above, about, or underneath,
> Sent by some spirit to mortals good,
> Or the unseen genius of the wood.
>
> *("Il Penseroso," lines 151–54)*

Here the poem might end, only adding the final couplet, "These pleasures Melancholy give, / And I with thee will choose to live" (lines 175–76), leaving out everything in between. If lines 155–74 were cut out of it, "Il Penseroso" would be only four lines longer than "L'Allegro" and would keep closer symmetry with its partner. It would be an ending very close in spirit to the forest scenes of Marvell's *Upon Appleton House*, with their spooky evocation of a speaker communing with the spirits of nature and slowly, inadvertently, disclosing to us a mind overstepping the boundaries of normal common sense and of educated common sense—a mind hermetically enclosing itself in its fancy. Marvell's speaker is a little like that hovering dream, waving at the reflection of its own gorgeous wings. Marvell studied "Il Penseroso" with care and much of his poetry—not just its meter—is indebted to it. If any poet of the seventeenth century was willing to portray through his or her speakers the

Reflective Man in the fully reflective sense of that waving dream in "Il Penseroso," it was Marvell.

But Marvell would have been as disinclined as Milton was impelled to what follows in the poem. What follows is a retreat from this scene of imaginative excess, with a churching of its visionary offspring. The pagan visions of the forest are now subordinated to Christian worship:

> But let my due feet never fail
> To walk the studious cloister's pale
> And love the high embowèd roof
> With antique pillars' massy proof
> And storied windows richly dight
> Casting a dim religious light.
>
> ("Il Penseroso," lines 155–60)

I noted earlier how fond Milton is of making a transition at a critical moment by a strongly adversative *But* at the beginning of a line. With such a *But*, both "L'Allegro" and "Il Penseroso" modulate in the eleventh line from their proems to the main body of the poems: "But come thou goddess fair and free"; "But hail thou goddess, sage and holy." Generally, "L'Allegro" introduces scene transitions with the smoother, less wrenching words *Oft*, *There*, and *That* (one time each), *Then* (two times), *Or* (four times), and the paratactic *And*, which is used for this purpose eleven times, and on one occasion, in three successive lines: "And the milkmaid singeth blithe, / And the mower whets his scythe, / And every shepherd tells his tale" (lines 65–67). *But* is used in "Il Penseroso" for a strong transition three times before the poem's turning point. (The *But* beginning line 125 is grammatical rather than rhetorical.)

The peripatetic *But*—"But let my due feet never fail" (line 155)—is much more strongly marked rhetorically than the two that are in the middle of the poem. To paraphrase: "Bring Peace and Quiet, *but* most of all bring Contemplation" and "Let me see gorgeous tragedies, *but* most of all let me see and hear Musaeus and Orpheus." This new *But*, however, "But let my due feet never fail," takes the Reflective Man into church and there dissolves him in the music of the pealing organ and the choir. Extreme subjectivity is always seeking to dissolve itself in ecstatic union with an "other" that only a moment before it has tried to deny. When subjectivity arranges its own dissolution, it invariably reconstitutes itself again at a distance, as an observer of what it has just done: "Dissolve me into ecstasies, / And bring all Heaven before mine eyes" (lines 165–66). There should not be any eyes left before which to bring all Heaven.

Once again, we might expect the poem to end here with its concluding couplet: "These pleasures, Melancholy, give, / And I with thee will choose to live" (lines 175–76). What could be better? It seems the perfect place to end, with the glorious vision of Heaven, like the vision of Heaven in "On the Morning of Christ's Nativity," but a vision that is timely here and not falsely anticipatory. For ending here would have suggested, as Milton did in the sixth elegy, that there are higher things than the poetry of merriment. Milton seems deliberately to avoid what he normally does as unselfconsciously as breathing, which is to put all things in hierarchical relation to one another. Ending the poem with Heaven before our eyes would have radically subordinated the earlier poem, "L'Allegro," and all the delights of Mirth. Doing so would not be inconsistent with Milton's character. It would have subordinated all the pleasures of "Il Penseroso" except this last pleasure, if it is a pleasure: Heaven.

At this time in his life, Milton was seeking how to be a Christian poet, and he had sought out the kind of poetic expression that can transcend this world and bring Heaven before our eyes—and then put us inside it. But in these paired poems he begins to become a poet of this world. He was also a poet of decorum, which he would call "the grand masterpiece to observe" (YP, 2:405). Decorum—the organizing of all parts of a poem into a consistent and harmonious whole—demanded two things at the conclusion of "Il Penseroso": (1) that the two poems, "L'Allegro" and "Il Penseroso," remain equally matched as moral possibilities; and (2) that the speakers of the two poems remain distinct personalities that will not be confused either with each other or, more important, with the poet. We have seen already how the poems would not remain equally matched as moral possibilities if "Il Penseroso" ended in an apotheosis. "L'Allegro" would be firmly subordinated. In such a case we would also lose sight of the speaker, Il Penseroso, who would dissolve not into Heavenly ecstasies but into Milton, his author, rendering the final couplet discordant and perhaps requiring its abandonment.

Milton does not wish us to suppose he is striking any such bargain as these poems strike in their final couplets. Unlike the Lively Man, the Reflective Man has to be brought back into view for us, solidified and placed at a distance, so that he may become for us a picture—a "lively portraiture." He becomes a picture even to himself, imagining himself in "weary age" (line 167) as a hermit in a "mossy cell." He has learned the secret correspondences and cosmic affinities between the stars and the plants. This is a more modest version of the knowledge he had sought in his tower, which was to trace all the patterns of "true consent" (line 95) between, on the one hand, the daemons in the terrestrial elements of fire, air, water, and earth and, on the other hand, the planets and stars overhead.

The Reflective Man hasn't changed essentially from the narcissist we saw in his tower—or, rather, who saw himself in his tower—although he has grown more subtle with age. He hopes to attain, from the "old experience" that has made him thus, "something like" (much virtue in that *like*) "prophetic strain." What is meant here by the word *prophet?* We are tempted at this moment to identify the speaker of "Il Penseroso" with Milton, supposing *prophet* to mean "something like" Hebrew *nabi* and to denote the Old Testament prophets—courageous, visionary speakers of the word of God. It is more likely, however, that the Greek sense of the word *prophet* is meant, "a speaker forth" of the hidden will of the gods. A Hebrew prophet, as the story of Jonah teaches, doesn't have a choice whether to speak: he, and sometimes she, as in the case of Deborah, is compelled to do so, despite the bitter consequences. Milton in the prose identifies his own circumstances with this compulsion. The Greek *prophetes,* as we meet him in Homer, notably at the outset of the *Iliad,* in the figure of Chalcas, also speaks with reluctance. He asks Achilles for assurances that what he says, should it offend a great king—Agamemnon is present—will not lead to his being punished. Even so, the Greek prophet is very far from being an unwilling speaker through whom the gods *insist* on speaking. He is a searcher of the jealously guarded secrets of the gods, which are wrenched from the organs of sacrificed animals and captured in the patterns of bird flight.

That is something like the "prophetic strain" foreseen at the end of "Il Penseroso," a knowledge to be arrived at by going up an inclined slope from knowledge of the natural world to knowledge of the will of the gods. We call that inclined slope *experience* and, when we have got up some distance on that slope, *old experience:* "Till old experience do attain / To something like prophetic strain" (lines 173–74). But prophecy is about flight and inspiration, not about climbing.

For a long time I rather disliked those verses without quite knowing why: they seemed to jar with the following couplet, which ends the poem: "These pleasures, Melancholy, give, / And I with thee will choose to live" (lines 175–76). The lines about old experience jar especially with the word *pleasures*. It may be a pleasure to read Plato and Hermes Trismegistus, or to hear the far-off curfew bell and the song of the nightingale. It is even a pleasure—although more than pleasure is intended by it—to hear "service high and anthems clear" (line 163). But is it a pleasure to prophesy? Like the "high service" with its music, there is something more to prophecy than subjective pleasure. Indeed, prophecy has nothing to do with pleasure: prophecy is beyond the self and its pleasures or its sorrows. That is because prophecy is a particular kind of social act. It is at this boundary between personal pleasure and social action where the horizon of the Reflective Man's intelligence is seen.

Part of growing up is discovering there are two distinct kinds of pleasure around which prudent people try to organize their lives: that of cheerful society and that of reflective solitude. These are the two states Milton personifies in his twinned poems, "L'Allegro" and "Il Penseroso." Ideally, the two kinds of pleasure come together in what we call *work*. Children know the pleasures of the senses and are taught intellectual pleasures. Adults who devote themselves only to the pleasures afforded by the senses, as the followers of Comus do in Milton's masque, are, as Milton says, "perfect" in their misery. That they would not agree with this judgment is of course a philosophical problem, but one on which Milton has firmly taken sides, as Mill would do: it is better to be a dissatisfied human than a satisfied pig. Besides, if they agreed with this judgment, that agreement would perhaps be the beginning of the end of their misery. For Milton, the perfect misery that follows upon accepting to drink from Comus's enchanted cup is not regression to libidinal childishness. It is regression to the state of a beast:

> Soon as the potion works, their human countenance,
> T'express resemblance of the gods, is changed
> Into some brutish form . . .
> And they, so perfect is their misery,
> Not once perceive their foul disfigurement,
> But boast themselves more comely than before

And all their friends and native home forget
To roll with pleasure in a sensual sty.

(A Masque Presented at Ludlow Castle,
1634, *lines 68–77*)

In the mature person, sensual pleasures are neither rejected nor indulged in unreasonably. Sensual pleasures are refined in two ways, first by being drawn up into cheerful society, of which love is the highest expression; second, by being drawn up into reflective contemplation, of which worship and wonder are the highest expressions. Contentment and melancholy are lower manifestations of this cheerfulness and this reflection. One of the great questions of life, therefore, is how the two mature forms of pleasure may be brought to complement each other, instead of being in conflict with each other. A more personally urgent question is to which form of pleasure, cheerfulness or reflection, one inclines. The pleasure of cheerfulness, which in its upper register shades into joyful ecstasy, is not always or even mostly sexual. An experience closer to the essence of the mirthful man of Milton's poem is an experience of polyphonic music that Milton calls "giddy." The soul is "pierced" by rapid, overlapping chains of musical notes (as in a canon), "With linkèd sweetness long drawn out":

With wanton heed and giddy cunning,
The melting voice through mazes running,
Untwisting all the chains that tie
The hidden soul of harmony.

("*L'Allegro*," *lines 141–44*)

The pleasure of reflection in solitude shades in its upper register, as I said, into worship, or religious ecstasy. For that experience, Milton's musical symbol is not contrapuntal harmony but music sung in unison, so that what was formerly "The *hidden* soul of harmony" now is revealed to us by the "full-voiced choir," which sings above the "pealing organ":

There let the pealing organ blow
To the full-voiced choir below
In service high and anthems clear
As may with sweetness through mine ear

> Dissolve me into ecstasies
> And bring all Heaven before mine eyes.
>
> *("Il Penseroso," lines 161–66)*

Milton was not a worshipper of poetry as a final good: to be serious, poetry had to be *for* something greater than itself. In middle age, Milton stated that it is the responsibility of the poet "to imbreed and cherish in a great people the seeds of virtue and public civility" (*YP*, 1:816). When Milton was at the height of his powers, when he was composing *Paradise Lost*, he declared his aim was to "justify the ways of God to men" (1:26). In his twenties, however, Milton was still too young to take himself so seriously without danger to his art. The experience and wisdom would come, as they do, with time—the time that is needed for living and for serious reflection on life.

The speakers of "L'Allegro" and "Il Penseroso" confront life as a series of choices between different moods and the pleasures and delights these moods bring. The Lively Man and the Reflective Man wander through their landscapes observing, listening, delighting, reflecting, and choosing. They do not speak with others, except for those spirits that the Reflective Man "unspheres" or hopes to unsphere. The Lively Man walks "not unseen" (line 57), a litotes indicating he is indeed observed; even so, we sense he is little remarked. The Reflective Man walks "unseen" (line 65) except by himself. His habit is to seek places of resort "Where no profaner eye may look" (line 140). Each of these solitary speakers faces a choice. Shall I live with Mirth? Shall I live with Melancholy? Each comes to a conditional conclusion at the end: *if . . . then*. The answer is in each case provisional but clear: if the "delights" (line 151) this poem called "L'Allegro" enumerates are given me, then I will live with heart-easing Mirth (line 13). If the "pleasures" (line 175) this poem called "Il Penseroso" enumerates are given me, then I will live with "divinest Melancholy" (line 12).

But life is not like that. We have to deal with others most of the time, as these speakers do not, and the choices we face with respect to these others, and with respect to our own fates, are neither so simple nor so unthreatening as those contemplated by Milton's speakers at the end of their poems. They are not tempted. They are not solicited. They are not asked to join something or to agree to anything. They are not given orders, nor do they give any. They are not placed in danger. The speakers are detached from the choices they make—they seem to stand above themselves—in a way that does not accord with how life is lived, in the thick of it. But their detachment does accord, eerily and truthfully, with how we imagine we govern our lives, especially when we are young. Milton in his twenties had already acquired a habit of disciplined self-observation and self-criticism. The choices his speakers are considering are of course very shallow in comparison with the choices Milton was considering at this time: how to devote himself to God's service and how to compose poetry worthy of that service. To understand big choices, think about little ones first. By miniaturizing choice in the theater of his mind, that is, by considering choice in the comparatively trivial circumstances in which the Lively Man and the Reflective Man find themselves, Milton is able to position the phenomenon of choice at an aesthetic distance for detached contemplation and control. Philosophers abstract; poets miniaturize. Milton was perhaps, by means of these poems, teaching himself that life choices are often not made by standing above one's own life and considering it from a distance, aesthetically, as if the judging self could be separate from and superior to the life being judged.

Where do life choices meet with social obligations and social encounters? What is the social context of decisions such as the Lively Man and the Reflective Man place before themselves? For Milton, long before he was reasoning on church government or household liberty or the way tyrants degrade the morals of their subjects, the social context of decision remained personal, in the face-to-face encounter.

The most dramatically interesting of such encounters—one that was surely not unfamiliar to the virginal and temperate postgraduate, who had roomed for years with fellow students who were neither—is temptation. Milton appears to have been mocked for his fastidiousness. What is temptation? Milton would have been familiar with the Greek word *peirasmos*, which means "a testing," as when one tests the silver content of a coin. (It is one of the things the money changers at the temple were doing when Jesus overturned their tables.) Temptation is a testing, to see if one is true metal and not an alloy, not a mixture. But the testing works by proposing a choice, which is to accept or to reject something offered as a gift. This is the most basic of human situations. One of the signal events of modern sociological and anthropological thinking is

Marcel Mauss's *The Gift: Forms and Functions of Exchange in Archaic Societies*, or *Essai sur le don. Forme et raison de l'échange dans les sociétés ar-
chaïques.* Temptation confronts one with the choice whether to accept
or refuse something offered. One misunderstands the situation entirely,
however, if one's attention is focused on the gift. The gift is of no value
in itself. It is the medium of value. It is a channel of communication,
like a fiber-optic cable or a frequency. The gift offered is the medium
of a relationship, and also of a bond with the giver. In *Paradise Regained*,
Jesus says he counts Satan's "specious gifts no gifts but guiles" (2.391).
A gift is a bond. What is offered is therefore less important than who
is doing the offering and what bond will be forged with the offerer,
should the offer be accepted. In "L'Allegro" and "Il Penseroso," the gifts
seem more important than those not unattractive goddesses who offer
them, Mirth and Melancholy.

But in life, the offerer is always more significant than what is offered.
Whether one accepts or refuses the offer tests one's ability to see through
the screen of the offered thing to the character of the one who offers.
In the narcissistic fantasy worlds of "L'Allegro" and "Il Penseroso," gifts
come for free, out of nowhere, and in profusion, as they should, and as
is natural—or so the speakers suppose, like children. But in life every
gift accepted is a bond with the giver. This moral insight into the gift
would be lodged at the center of Milton's greatest works, *Paradise Lost,
Paradise Regained*, and *Samson Agonistes.* The great givers in the first two
are God and Satan. As created beings, we have already, without having
any choice in the matter, accepted a gift from God, the gift of our very
being. This is the strongest of all bonds and is indissoluble. Satan's goal
is to loosen the bond that exists between receiving creature and giving
Creator, and if possible to destroy the bond, by temptation—offering
something else. Eve is offered the chance to become a goddess; Adam
is offered (by Eve) the chance to keep Eve. *Paradise Regained* is a series
of offered gifts that are refused. In *Samson Agonistes*, Samson has abused
the gift of strength given him by God: "God, when he gave me strength,
to show withal / How slight the gift was, hung it in my hair" (*SA*, lines
58–59). Samson will be offered help by his father and also by Dalila,
whose gift is the most alluring of all for a prisoner grinding at the mill
with other slaves: a life with her of freedom, ease, and sexual pleasure.
Even Harapha, the "tongue-doughty giant" (*SA*, line 1181), comes bearing
a gift, which is the gift of recognition: "thou know'st me now / If thou

at all art known" (*SA*, lines 1081–82). The Philistine officer offers Samson food, a wash, and fresh clothes—"I will see thee heartened and fresh clad" (*SA*, line 1317)—and more subtly, the possibility of freedom: "doff these links. / By this compliance thou wilt win the lords / To favor, and perhaps to set thee free" (*SA*, lines 1410–12). The moral bond forged by the gift, whether a well- or an ill-meaning gift, is to become a central theme of Milton's career and the vital, structuring element of the drama of his great works. The drama of which I speak is of course that of *temptation*. Milton introduces this drama for the first time in *Comus*, or to give its full and irreducibly occasional title, *A Masque Presented at Ludlow Castle, 1634.*

3

On the Work Not Called Comus

Lᴵᴋᴇ ᴛʜᴇ Aᴛᴛᴇɴᴅᴀɴᴛ Sᴘɪʀɪᴛ at its conclusion, who seems to fly off in all directions at once, or like the title it has never quite had, the poetical event commonly referred to as *Comus*, and by scholars as *A Masque Presented at Ludlow Castle, 1634* (or by some shortening of this designation), is an evanescent thing. We hardly know what it is, or what exactly it means, or even what it is properly called. It is also a big thing. The text we have is more than four times longer than anything Milton had composed previously, and by the same proportion longer than anything he would compose in verse before *Paradise Lost* three decades later.[1] Passages of it are inspired beyond anything Milton had written before. This imaginative freedom may remind us of Milton's Latin poems, with their higher density of mythological allusion, in contrast with the stately progress of "On the Morning of Christ's Nativity" or the temperate, methodical hedonism of "L'Allegro" and "Il Penseroso." As in the Latin verse, the same quiet humor, the spirit of parody ("By . . . the Carpathian wizard's hook," lines 871–72), lightly grazes the surfaces of more serious moods. This trace of an authorial smile is present throughout, but it is more evident behind the feverish imaginings of Comus—as when, in a passage I shall quote from later, the enchanter argues ingeniously and ludicrously for immoderate indulgence in pleasure, to keep nature in proper ecological balance. Milton is a morally serious poet, and he makes direct, ethical, and political demands on us in a way Shakespeare, for example, does not. But he is always entertaining, often playful, and never more so than when contemplating the fatuous deliberations of venality, as with Belial in *Paradise Lost* and *Paradise Regained* ("fleshliest incubus" [*PR*, 2.152]), and as with Comus here. When Comus first hears the Lady sing, he indulges in rapturous praise ("smoothing the raven down / Of darkness till it smiled," lines 251–52), and then abruptly concludes, "I'll speak to her, / And she shall be my queen" (lines 264–65), as if it will be as easy as that. Part of his charm is his never losing hope that seducing the Lady will be as simple as speaking, as long as he can do so without being interrupted by her "moral babble" (line 807). He just needs to speak *more*. He has the se-ducer's faith that if he is being listened to at all, he will prevail. Comus is an enchanter, and he trusts in his personal charm as much as in his magical charms.

Milton's masque is a stunning poetic achievement, one that may even provoke us to reevaluate the higher reputation that "Lycidas," written three years later, is routinely accorded over all Milton's early works, in-cluding *A Masque*. When he arranged his poems for publication in *Poems 1645*, Milton positioned *A Masque* last among the English poems, in the place of honor, with "Lycidas" preceding rather than following it. It is true that "Lycidas" would have been lost if sandwiched between *A Masque* and the Latin *Poemata*, which are both treated as separate books within the larger book, having their own title pages and front matter.[2] It is also true that "Lycidas" is unequaled for its stark contrasts and its sudden changes of mood, in depicting the "wily subtleties and refluxes" of thought in the contemplation of ambition and loss (*YP*, 1:817). There is nothing in *A Masque* to equal the strong mood contrasts in "Lycidas," for example, the transition from the gorgeous unreality of the catalogue of flowers to the stern vision delivered by the real terrors of the sea. *A Masque* is suppleness itself, *ipsa mollities*, as Sir Henry Wotton said, referring to its lyrical part, agreeably blurring the contrast between the fantastical and the real (*Poems 1645*, p. 72). "Lycidas" forces them apart. But at very least we may venture to affirm that the compressed power of "Lycidas" achieves a mythical range—the sudden apostrophe to the nymphs, for example, and the reference to the Dee's "wizard stream" (line 55)—that was prepared for by more extensive mythopoeic explorations in *A Masque*.

The unprecedented size of this work alone gave the poet reason to hope he would compose "something so written to aftertimes, as they should not willingly let it die" (*YP*, 1:810). We should never underestimate the significance of length in a poet's ambition to be great. Milton would have completed this work with his confidence renewed, after the low point recorded three years earlier in Sonnet 7, when he felt he had little to show for so many years of hard study and earnest effort in poetry.

A Masque is almost the length of a Greek tragedy, a comparison that would certainly have occurred to the author, for whom Greek tragedy, emerging from what Nietzsche called the spirit of music, would have seemed to the poet to be closer to the masque form, which includes music and dance, than to any play from the Elizabethan, Jacobean, or Caroline stage. This analogy is doubtless what Sir Henry Wotton meant when referring to the "tragical part" of Milton's *Masque*, which displays many of the incidental characteristics of Greek tragedy. These include a substantial introduction by a supernatural being (the Attendant Spirit); a deus ex machina, or "god from the machine" (in the person of Sabrina)—saving from without a situation that cannot be resolved from within; a sharp verbal contest over moral ideas (in the two debates, that between the two brothers, and that between Comus and the Lady); a dialogue in stichomythia, or rapid-fire exchange (when the Lady and Comus first meet); a variety of meters to create choral and lyric effects within the frame of a dramatic narrative; an extensive and familiarly evoked mythological universe, especially at the beginning and the end; and, in the Attendant Spirit's commentary, a choral digression from the immediate theme to universal truth.

Milton appears to have been trying to borrow something of the rigorous structure and serious purpose of tragic form to lend stability to a work that could never find stability as an opus, because of the self-escaping nature of the masque genre and its ineluctable status as an unrepeatable event. That is why, despite its size, Milton's masque telegraphs a feeling of lightness in comparison with "Lycidas." Samuel Johnson was right to praise the quite extraordinary writing in *A Masque:* "a work more truly poetical is rarely found." But he admires it as "a series of lines" while observing its deficiency as drama.[3] The deficiency is not, however, on the technical level, as Johnson supposes. The problem lies deeper: in what we must speak of as the ontological ground of this work in an event. Yet the festive and impermanent character of the masque affords its author a certain freedom, allowing him to write for the moment instead of for the ages. But it leaves the work curiously hanging in the air.

Perhaps never again would Milton permit himself the freedoms he takes in this work, not even in *Paradise Lost*, where great exuberance is under sterner control, or in *Paradise Regained*, with its iron control. The unprecedentedly large scale of the masque, and perhaps also the relinquishing of control that allowed the poet to write at such length, afforded an imaginative freedom barely hinted at in earlier works, although the references to Orpheus from "L'Allegro" and "Il Penseroso" are in a similarly wild, Dionysian vein (see lines 145–49 in "L'Allegro" and lines 105–8 in "Il Penseroso"). But the wider range and greater fluency come at a price. As Angus Fletcher remarked, "There is a sublime empty-headedness about this whole enterprise," as contrasted with "restricted, wittier, sharper, more modest aims."[4]

The imaginative background to this work is continually changing and vast in extent. The rapid alteration of frames of reference (most prevalent in the prologue and epilogue) suggests aerial perspective in baroque ceiling painting. The reader experiences a dizzying uncertainty with respect to direction of movement and determination of place. The meaning at the center—the main composition, so to speak, to continue the comparison with painting—is clearly drawn, in the central opposed figures of Comus and the Lady. Comus, the Attendant Spirit, the two brothers, and those briefly but distinctly seen goddesses, Faith, Hope, and Chastity—all seem to be borne upward on billowing clouds, into the sunlight and blue air beyond. The Hesperides are whirled up alongside them, while Sabrina, goddess of the mighty River Severn, glides away on the stream to disappear at last under the waves of the ocean.

Behind these bright figures all is uncertain, such that we lose our orientation with respect to what is "up" and what is "down." We cannot tell where everything is tending. Being clearly depicted themselves, the characters' shifting contexts render them obscure. The Lady's chastity has been vindicated, but where does that take us, and where does it take her? To Heaven or to the marriage bed? Above the chiming spheres? To the Garden of the Hesperides, in the extreme west of the world? Such questions refer us to the work's implicit cosmological surround, its mythopoeic environment, and its ideological form. But the environment itself is unstable.

At the outset we are presented with a simple, vertical cosmology inherited from medieval Christianity. There is a bright and good Heaven above and a dark, sinful earth below, a "sin-worn mold" (line 17). Hell is still farther down, inside the earth, as we may imagine Comus's palace to be. There are also the underwater palaces of the sea-gods, situated in the western ocean and suggesting Atlantis. The chiming spheres of the cosmos are in between the earth and Heaven, so that getting to Heaven means being taught by Virtue to climb above the "sphery chime" (1021):

> Mortals that would follow me
> Love Virtue: she alone is free.
> She can teach ye how to climb
> Higher than the sphery chime,
> Or, if Virtue feeble were,
> Heav'n itself would stoop to her.
>
> (A Masque Presented at Ludlow
> Castle, 1634, *lines 1018–23*)

There is a clearly Protestant sense that some are chosen or *elect* to lead a virtuous life. Not everyone—indeed very few—will want to follow the Spirit. "Mortals *that would* follow me" is restrictive: "those few, elect mortals who are inclined to follow me." It is to their aid, not to just anyone's, that the Attendant Spirit descends to this vile earth:

> Yet some there be that by due steps aspire
> To lay their just hands on that golden key
> That opes the palace of Eternity:
> To such my errand is, and but for such,
> I would not soil these pure ambrosial weeds
> With the rank vapours of this sin-worn mould.
>
> (A Masque Presented at Ludlow Castle, 1634,
>
> *lines 12–17*)

We who are on earth should "aspire" (12)—that is, we should ascend by continually turning and rising, as in Dante's *Purgatorio*—to get from the lower world into the higher. The final step cannot be taken in this life, however, but only after death, "after this mortal change" (line 10). At the outset, the point of virtue is not to make this world a better one but to get out of this world into the next—and only after death.

We might speak of this opening idea—the point of virtue is to get out of this world into the next, after death—as establishing the tonic key of the work, to which it will return at the end. The dominant key is how virtue can improve the present world, transforming it as a whole or transforming certain elect persons in it—and doing so before death, not after. For example, the Elder Brother speaks of chastity as a militant force in the world that repels evil "where very desolation dwells" (line 428). Chastity turns "brute violence" to "sudden adoration and blank awe" (line 452). The Lady herself refutes Comus not with the promise of the blessings of the next world, but with the possibility of more even distribution of nature's blessings in this world:

> If every just man that now pines with want
> Had but a moderate and beseeming share
> Of that which lewdly-pampered Luxury
> Now heaps upon some few with vast excess
> Nature's full blessings would be well dispensed
> In unsuperfluous even proportïon.
>
> (A Masque Presented at Ludlow Castle, 1634,
> *lines 768–73*)

The stately dance with which the masque concludes suggests the attainment of virtual order in this world; the western paradise, the Hesperides, mentioned in the Attendant Spirit's epilogue, suggests an ideal of virtuous marriage, also in this world. Only in the final lines do we return to the tonic key when the Attendant Spirit exhorts us to "love Virtue," who will teach us how to get out of the world, "to climb / Higher than the sphery chime" (*A Masque Presented at Ludlow Castle, 1634*, lines 1019–21).

This tension between tonic and dominant keys, or between, on the one hand, a strictly vertical cosmology and, on the other hand, a horizontal one promoting a virtue that is active in this world, will be felt in the larger trajectory of Milton's career. In the prose works he will compose after 1641, he will become fully engaged with the world. And a synthesis, or a higher resolution of transcendentalism and engagement, will be achieved in *Paradise Lost* and *Paradise Regained*. We shall see something of this development, though we shall see it indistinctly, in the epilogue of Milton's masque.

The vertical cosmology, sketched out for us by the Attendant Spirit in his opening lines, soon modulates as his speech goes on to a pagan, horizontal cosmology, full of seascapes and sea sounds from the Mediterranean Sea and the "wide Atlantic." The latter becomes "the unadornèd bosom of the deep" (line 23) stretching to the west, over the horizon.[5] On this latter plan, ultimate value turns out not to be high above but far outward, where the sky meets the sea—"where the bowed welkin slow doth bend" (line 1015)—or just over the horizon, in the western paradise of the island of the Hesperides. In this horizontal system happiness is attained not in the next world, "after this mortal change" (line 10), but in this world, where Venus and Adonis symbolize natural generation and Cupid and Psyche symbolize marriage. In these figures we are shown the marriage, in this life, of desire and the soul. But what has that to do with virtue?

As is to be expected, there is considerable interference between these two systems and the ideals they promote. We could complain about this dissonance, as Dr. Johnson was inclined to do, and about the mounting absurdities that result from the conflict—in this work, and in "Lycidas," too—or we could excuse the dissonance as the inevitable result of having to write out Christian values within a pagan system of decorum. (The Attendant Spirit, for example, is not an angel but a classical *daemon*, as he is called in the manuscripts, which fact allows him his western journey. The Hesperides is of scant interest to angels, despite "many a cherub" Milton imagines reposing in the flowers there, before he replaces them with "young Adonis" [line 999]). The supreme God is "Jove" (line 1011), not Jehovah. "Manna dew" is changed to "Sabaean dew," which recalls spices brought to Solomon by the queen of Sheba, and then to "Elysian dew" (line 996).[6]

But we need not either condemn or excuse what is in truth an aesthetic effect in which a certain amount of noise in the signal is to be experienced as richness of background, like a complex wine. We reinterpret the cosmological and ideological incoherence as profound—and it is. It is a way of thinking about the order of the world, instead of accepting one total system or another as true and rejecting the loser as wicked and false. Milton's masque is more open to the productive clash of heterogeneous systems.

The mythopoeic background to this work is therefore continually shifting and vast in extent. We are transported from the heavenly spheres, the "regions mild of calm and serene air" (line 4), inhabited by "bright aerial spirits" (line 3), to the trident-wielding sea-gods of the ocean, especially the western approaches to the British Isles. From thence we are conducted to the Tyrrhenian Sea in the Mediterranean—north of Sicily and west of the Italian mainland—where Bacchus transforms the Etruscan pirates into dolphins before he falls upon Circe's isle, and upon Circe herself, thus fathering Comus, who becomes another maker of monsters. The main action puts us in a dark and tangled "ominous wood" (line 61), its bristling pine boughs a "nodding horror" (line 38) in the dark. Because boys like to imagine horrible things in the dark, we hear of souls lingering foully in churchyards, longing to reinhabit their corpses, so as to copulate and feast in the grave:

> Such are those thick and gloomy shadows damp
> Oft seen in charnel vaults and sepulchers
> Ling'ring and sitting by a new-made grave
> As loath to leave the body that it loved
> And linked itself by carnal sensualty
> To a degenerate and degraded state.
>
> (A Masque Presented at Ludlow Castle, 1634,
> *lines 470–75*)

But we have already had the cleansing sight of the heavenly personifications—Faith, Hope, and Chastity (we expect Charity, but Chastity comes in her stead)—in crisp white linen, as we may imagine them, sailing over the tops of those pines, in the moonlit air (lines 213–15). We hear the "barbarous dissonance" and "wonted roar" (lines 549–50) of Comus's rout, howling "like stabled wolves or tigers at their prey" (line 534), and we hear Circe and the "flowery-kirtled Naiades," who with their song cause pitiless Scylla to weep and voracious Charybdis to mutter—or rather, "murmur"—soft applause (lines 253–59). We hear pure strains of music that invoke the nymph Echo in her "airy shell / By slow Meander's margent green / And in the violet-embroidered vale" (lines 231–33). These are strains, as the Attendant Spirit says, that are capable of creating a soul under the ribs of death (lines 561–62). During Comus's discourse in favor of indulging the senses to the limit of their capacity and beyond (it was Bacon's thought that science should extend our capacity for pleasure), we are invited to listen for the low hum of silkworms in their cocoons, and we are overwhelmed by the clamor of birds filling the sky to cause an eclipse of the sun, "the winged air darked with plumes" (line 730). We see Chastity again in the heavens, now in daylight, attired with the beams of the sun, scorching anyone who would "arm his profane tongue with contemptuous words" against her (line 781). In the other direction, ascending from below, we see monsters of the deep rising to the surface of the ocean to gaze on that sun—and that would be terrible—should ladies, "in a pet of temperance" (line 721), fail to cover their bodies with fabulous jewels. As Comus explains, the monsters would come to the surface and gaze on the sun because the brightness of the diamonds left ungathered on the floor of the ocean will have accustomed the monsters' eyes to the light:

> The sea o'erfraught would swell and th'unsought
>   diamonds
> Would so emblaze the forehead of the deep
> And so bestud with stars that they below
> Would grow inured to light and come at last
> To gaze upon the sun with shameless brows.
>
>   (A Masque Presented at Ludlow Castle, 1634,
>   *lines 732–36*)

With such wealth before him, indulging the very excess he must also condemn, and doing so with virtuosic skill, Milton evidently felt he could afford to cut out lines like the following, which describe the stream of ocean as it reaches its farthest point in the west to flow around the island of the Hesperides, thence dividing its flood so that, as it returns, half flows back into the Atlantic Ocean and half flows down into the abyss of Hell:

> The jealous ocean that old river winds
> His far-extended arms till with steep fall

Half his flood the wide Atlantic fills
And half the slow unfathomed Stygian pool.[7]

We are observing the pagan system of the world with the ocean flowing around its rim, as in a chariot race, with the Hesperides as the distant mark around which the ocean turns. Some three decades later, evoking a still larger system, Milton would find a place for that final epithet, when the narrator of *Paradise Lost* returns from Hell across the abyss of Chaos, having "escaped the *Stygian pool* though long detained / In that obscure sojourn" (*PL*, 3.14–15).

As the foregoing passages show—and many more examples could be cited—there is a wild and almost uncontrolled energy to the writing in this work, crackling and sparking throughout, occasionally breaking into flame. The unsettled inspiration has much to do with the work's failure to accomplish a complete transition from occasional entertainment to poem, in the fullest sense of the word—a "made thing" or *poiema*—with an autonomous existence that is no longer grounded in an originative event. The lack of any convincing, legitimate title to replace, on the one hand, the pallid designation most in favor now, *A Maske*, or, on the other hand, the usurping title, *Comus*, is the most obvious symptom of the work's continuing dependence on its original occasion. Criticism of this work has not addressed the way its onto-poetic foundation is uncertainly distributed between being a poem and being an event. There are so many other things to speak of. Such as the Castlehaven scandal, or the political significance of masques in the 1630s, which were the Stuart court's fabulously expensive, targeted instruments of propaganda, or, behind all the mere poetry, the promotion in this work of Laudian Arminianism and conformity with the archbishop's new regulations for worship.[8] The onto-theological status of Milton's masque as a work of art may appear too remote and too abstract an issue to be as important as empirically verifiable matters of *context*. Such suspicions of the relevance of philosophical concerns, dressed in positivist historicizing, dismiss fundamental questions as mere distractions from the hard stuff of politics. In that light, the question this work puts before us continually—what is a poem?—seems unimportant by comparison, mere philosophical babble little better than the Lady's moral babble. Such dismissive rhetoric is part of the ideological self-stabilizing of an unexamined metaphysics in which history is real and poems are not. Taking poetry seriously means dismissing such dismissals, and also their own suppositions about the grounds of the literary real.

Perhaps there will be some benefit for our understanding of this text if we grasp it at the point of decision where it is either the remainder of a past *event* or a substantial *thing*, a poem. The question posed at this point of decision becomes more interesting still when we reflect that Milton was aware of it and strove, with only partial success, to free the masque from its originative ground in a spoken event and to give it the autonomy of a made thing, to put the written text before the spoken event, instead of the other way around.[9] The metaphysical question of *the event* has been of considerable interest of late in philosophy, from Heidegger's *Das Ereignis*, "the event, the coming into being and into appearance," to recent discussion by Alain Badiou and others. In particle physics, events are more fundamental than things, which are temporary—exceedingly temporary—constructs of events. It seems to me every work of art strives to make the transition from an event to a thing, ultimately a preserved thing. Milton strove to do this with *A Masque* so as to ground the work in the realm of art that endures and is serious and has weight—thus making it a poem. That such an extraordinary work, a work that is on an unprecedented scale for this poet, should be regarded as lightweight in comparison with "Lycidas" is a symptom of the problem Milton faced in trying to ground *A Masque Presented at Ludlow Castle, 1634*, on something more enduring than an event. He was never able to name this work after something other than a castle or an earl.

The event in question is the performance of this masque on Michaelmas night, September 29, 1634, at Ludlow Castle (now a ruin), in Shropshire, near the Welsh border, on the occasion of the first Earl of Bridgewater John Egerton's installation as Lord President of Wales and the Marches (roughly, counties adjacent to Wales). Michaelmas is an important administrative date in the year, when university term begins, rents fall due, and offices change. The angel Michael is the Christian Janus. Egerton had been traveling with his family, performing the duties of his new office, and arrived at Ludlow Castle late in August.[10] The festivities, which took place a month later, marked the official beginning of Egerton's service as Lord President, or Lord Lieutenant (as the

office is also called). This *incipit nunc* is the point of the long complimentary passage in the prologue to the masque, spoken by the Attendant Spirit. The Attendant Spirit bows to the noble peer he describes,
who is present at this event:

> And all this tract that fronts the falling Sun [Wales and
>   the Marches]
> A noble peer of mickle trust and power
> Has in his charge with tempered awe to guide
> An old and haughty nation proud in arms [the Welsh]
> Where his fair offspring, nursed in princely lore,
> Are coming to attend their father's state
> And new-entrusted scepter. But their way
> Lies through the perplexed paths of this drear wood.
>
> (A Masque Presented at Ludlow Castle, 1634, *lines 30–37*)

The earl and his lady, the Countess of Bridgewater, were seated in
state on the occasion, watching three of their children perform, the "fair
offspring" referred to in the prologue: John, the Lord Brackley, age
eleven, playing Elder Brother; Thomas, age nine, Second Brother; and
Alice, age fifteen, the Lady, whose solo song to Echo is one of the set
pieces of this entertainment. The Attendant Spirit or, as he is called in
the manuscripts, the *Daemon*, was played by Henry Lawes, the composer of the music, including the five songs that have survived. In the
narrative, the Attendant Spirit speaks the prologue, guides the children
through their trials, and generally manages the action from the stage.
It is he who presents the children at the end to their parents in a stately
dance. It is perhaps noteworthy that in the actual speeches the *Daemon*
is never referred to as such, nor is he called *Attendant Spirit*. Instead,
he is called *Thyrsis*. In the prologue, his sky-robes with their wings are
shed to reveal the shepherd's weeds beneath (the sky-robes would be
resumed for the epilogue):

> Therefore, when any favored of high Jove
> Chances to pass through this adven'trous glade
> Swift as the sparkle of a glancing star
> I shoot from Heav'n to give him safe convoy,
> As now I do. But first I must put off

> These my sky-robes spun out of Iris' woof
> And take the weeds and likeness of a swain
> That to the service of this house belongs.
>
> *(A Masque Presented at Ludlow Castle, lines 78–85)*

At the end, the Attendant Spirit sings a song that presents the children, as it says in the stage direction, *"to their father and mother,"* who are watching from their state among their guests:

> Noble Lord and Lady bright
> I have brought ye new delight.
> Here behold so goodly grown
> Three fair branches of your own.
>
> *(A Masque Presented at Ludlow Castle, 1634, lines 966–69)*

In the dangers they have faced, the children have been tried by Heaven and they have come through the trial with glory, "to triumph in victorious dance / O'er sensual Folly and Intemperance" (lines 974–75). In this manner is introduced the culminating formal dance, in which the parents almost certainly joined with their children. (The pronoun in the stage direction from the Trinity and Bridgewater manuscripts, *"they daunce,"* is not firmly decisive on this point, but the dance of honored persons with performers, especially after a direct address of this kind, is conventional to the masque form.)[11]

Milton wrote the text, which was probably cut for performance; but he almost certainly did not travel the 150-plus miles to Ludlow, and he had nothing further to do with the production. It was left to Lawes, who was a court musician, a probable acquaintance of Milton's musician father, a retainer in the household of the Earl of Bridgewater, and music master to the Bridgewater children, to attend to the innumerable concerns of a theatrical production, in addition to composing, rehearsing, and conducting the music, and perhaps choreographing and rehearsing the dances. Lawes also played the challenging part of the Attendant Spirit, having to sing some of his own declamatory airs. These show his unparalleled skill at fitting music to words "with just note and accent," as Milton said in Sonnet 13, in praise of Lawes. Moreover, Lawes had a great number of spoken lines, which were probably delivered in the singing or *Sprechstimme* style typical of masques.[12] The point in the sonnet appears to be that Lawes figured out how to fit music to the correct accents and vowel quantities of English, rather than doing it the other way round, as was usual, making the words lie down on the Procrustian bed of the musical phrase. Doing so would have allowed Lawes, outside the formal songs, for example, in the invocation of Sabrina, to employ a style of speech resembling singing.

Although it is not generally thought Lawes played the part of Comus, as well, which would have been a considerable feat, it should be noted the script was written to make this possible: the Attendant Spirit and Comus are never onstage at the same time, and the Spirit's late arrival (at line 814), when the boys assault the palace of Comus, is telling. Furthermore, doubling the part of Comus would have allowed Lawes to be on stage as conductor for all the dances, including the wild *antimasque* performed by Comus's rout. (The nineteenth-century rumor that Milton himself played Comus is a temptation to be firmly resisted.) Even if he did not perform the part of Comus, Lawes's role in the production, as co-creator of the event, is clearly very large. We do not know who played the major part of Sabrina, goddess of the River Severn, who makes an otherworldly appearance and dances with her nymphs before freeing the Lady from the enchanted chair. John Creaser argues convincingly she was a member of the local gentry, in keeping with the local symbolism associated with her part and with subtle indications of social equality between her and Alice Egerton.[13] The music for Sabrina's song has not survived, but the part would have required a grown woman with near-professional attainments in singing and dancing.

The presentation of the children to their parents, at the end, follows the masque convention of merging audience with players and has strong ritual overtones. The masque in performance is not so much a detached aesthetic object, intended for contemplation, as it is a social action that flows directly into the world to which it is presented. Hence the word *presented* in the title. The presentation and formal dance would have been followed by general dancing, the "revels," as they are termed, after which the *Daemon* delivers what was at the time a brief epilogue, closing the festivities: *"They daunce, the daunces all ended the Daemon singes or sayes."*[14] This is the stage direction in the Bridgewater manuscript, the closest version to the original performance. The epilogue consists (approximately) of the last twelve lines of the present text:

> Now my task is smoothly done
> I can fly or I can run
> Quickly to the earth's green end[15]
> Where the bowed welkin slow both bend,
> And from thence can soar as soon
> To the corners of the moon.
> Mortals that would follow me,
> Love virtue, she alone is free,
> She can teach ye how to climb
> Higher than the sphery chime
> Or, if virtue feeble were,
> Heav'n itself would stoop to her.[16]

That is the performance version. What about the poem, the literary opus or work? In 1637, when Lawes published this work, two major passages had been added to Bridgewater: a twenty-seven-line expansion of the climactic confrontation between Comus and the Lady (lines 779–806), and a thirty-six-line description of a fabulous western paradise on the island of Hesperides, containing the following items: a golden tree with its golden apples; Hesperus, the evening star; the three daughters of Hesperus; the Graces; the "rosy-bosomed Hours" (line 986); alleys of aromatic cedar trees; west winds carrying the aromas of Nard and Cassia (lines 989–91); flower beds of hyacinths and roses; and the end of the rainbow with its goddess, Iris, who employs the rainbow like a garden hose to water the flowers. The flowers are of more various hue than Iris's own rainbow, now called her "purfled scarf" (line 995):

> Iris there with humid bow
> Waters the odorous banks that blow
> Flowers of more mingled hue
> Than her purfled scarf can show
> And drenches with Elysian dew
> (List, mortals, if your ears be true)
> Beds of hyacinth and roses
> Where young Adonis oft reposes
> Waxing well of his deep wound.
>
> (A Masque Presented at Ludlow Castle,
>   1634, *lines 992–1000*[17])

Two mythological couples are now introduced. The first, as we have begun to see, is Adonis and Venus, the "Assyrian Queen" (line 1002). Adonis lies slumbering in those beds of hyacinth and roses, "waxing well of his deep wound" (line 1000), which he received from the boar, allegorically interpreted as the killing power of winter. The scene is adopted from the Garden of Adonis in book 3 of Spenser's *Faerie Queene* (canto 6), a myth fulsomely allegorized before and after Spenser, in works Milton knew, for example, by Natalis Comes and by George Sandys. We are invited to interpret the myth of Adonis along the same lines, as an allegory of the cycles of sexual generation that must pass through the "annual wound" of Adonis or, to use his Near-Eastern name, Thammuz. The phrase *annual wound* is from *Paradise Lost* (1.447).[18]

The second couple, adopted from the late Roman author Apuleius, but more immediately from Spenser, is Cupid and Psyche, or desire and the soul, who are not situated, like Venus and Adonis, in the garden itself but directly above it in the heavens, among the stars and the classical gods, who have at last consented to their marriage, after Psyche's "wandering labors long" (line 1006), parodying the labors of Hercules (one of which was to visit the garden of the Hesperides to steal the golden apples on the tree). Spenser places Cupid and Psyche in the Garden of Adonis, which confirms that Milton paid close attention to this episode in *The Faerie Queene* for his purposes here. It also confirms that Cupid and Psyche, though "far above" the Hesperides, belong to that place and not to a Christian Heaven. Their location is not, therefore, above the "sphery chime" (line 1021)—the rotating spheres of the cosmos—but rather in a classical paradise in the western sky, far out instead of way up.

But we may say more truly still that Cupid and Psyche are situated in what Coleridge, speaking of *The Faerie Queene*, called "mental space."[19] For the phrase "Far above, in spangled sheen" (line 1003) is less a spatial than a dialectical indication, that is, an indication of the next stage of thought. I shall return to this thought later.

There is a prophecy in this heaven, for "so Jove hath sworn" (line 1011), that Psyche will give birth "from her fair unspotted side" (line 1009) to the twins, Youth and Joy (line 1011). Only then, on this note, do we pass to the old epilogue that was spoken on Michaelmas night, 1634: "But now my task is smoothly done" (line 1012).

The Trinity manuscript shows Milton began thinking about this Hesperian scene at an early stage of composition, developing a wilder

version of it in the prologue and at a later stage moving it to the conclusion, to keep the Christian orientation of the prologue unambiguously so. Interestingly, the younger brother uses the image of the
Hesperian tree as a symbol of the Lady's body and the golden blos-
soms and fruit as a symbol of her genitals, which might be assaulted
by violence:

> But Beauty like the fair Hesperian tree
> Laden with blooming gold had need the guard
> Of dragon-watch with unenchanted eye
> To save her blossoms and defend her fruit
> From the rash hand of bold Incontinence.
>
> (A Masque Presented at Ludlow Castle, 1634,
> *lines 393–97)*

The genital aspect of married love will become important in the
Hesperian passage of the epilogue.

The Bridgewater manuscript still has the Hesperides passage at
the beginning, its flowers drenched with "Manna dew" (line 21), a
phrase deleted in the Trinity manuscript.[20] In the Trinity manuscript,
the passage containing "Manna dew" is deleted entirely and when the
passage is rewritten. "Sabaean dew" (from the tip of Arabia) takes its
place and is then deleted in favor of "Elysian dew." The change is confirmed in the published text of 1637 and later, of course, 1645.[21] This
passage is next transferred to the epilogue in the Trinity manuscript,
struck out, and then rewritten in the form it will appear in the text of
1637, with Venus and Adonis and Cupid and Psyche. This final touch
in the Trinity manuscript indicates the general direction in which this
passage has been revised, from a biblical to a classical context: *Manna*
dew, associated with the Israelites in the wilderness, and *Sabaean* dew,
associated with the queen of Sheba, become *Elysian* dew, associated with
the classical gods. The Eastern spices associated with Eden, nard and
cassia, are still there, and of course Venus is given her Near-Eastern
appellation, "the Assyrian Queen" (line 1002). This is a very Eastern
western paradise, increasing our uncertainty where the Attendant Spirit
is really going. Perhaps he is going anywhere on the horizon, that is,
anywhere on the rim of the great circle of the world, which rests on the
ocean like a shield.

Anything seems possible at the limit of such a world. The phrase *to the ocean* recalls the Homeric phrase *es ôkeanon*, which describes a limit or a boundary to the earth. Homer's gods journey to the limits of the earth, to feast with the "blameless Ethiopians" *(amumonas Aithiopêas)*. In the *Odyssey* the Ethiopians are called "the remotest of men" *(eschatatoi andrôn)* because they live on the edges of the earth.[22] The blameless-ness and remoteness of the Ethiopians appear to have been recalled by Milton as another pagan adumbration of Paradise. The Ethiopians' faces are burned (that is the meaning of their name) because they live where the sun never sets but travels around the circumference of the earth in a great circle. This is the most likely meaning of the phrase "where day never shuts his eye" (line 978). It is certainly not a reference to the moon, as some learned editors have supposed. If there are blameless Ethiopians beyond the Hesperides, intoning through the smoke of their sacrificed bulls, they are over the horizon of this text. But, as we noted, this poem has such porous mythological boundaries we are not mistaken to feel that such scenes might at any moment heave into sight.

There is an obvious tension between the transcendent Christian Heaven we hear of in the final twelve lines—and which we have heard of in the prologue—and the earthly paradise so lavishly described here, with the two couples representing different phases of earthly love, culminating in the issue of Cupid and Psyche, emerging from her "unspotted side" (line 1009): the twins Youth and Joy. (Apuleius gives *Voluptas*—in context, "sexual pleasure"—as the child of Cupid and Psyche.) In what sense are either youth or joy the issue of the soul? We are left wondering how to resolve this tension between immanent, virtuous pleasure and tran-scendental virtue—virtue that gets you into Heaven. We are also left to wonder how to resolve that tension with the main action's theme, which is chastity.

Even when the work was finally in print, the poet appears to be un-satisfied and to be reflecting on how to resolve these tensions. That would explain the anonymousness of the 1637 publication and the epi-graph from Virgil's second eclogue. It suggests the poet's dismay at exposing his work prematurely to the world: *"Eheu! quid volui misero mihi! Floribus Austrum / Perditus. . . ."* ("Alas! What did I wish for, poor me, I have let in the south wind upon my flowers, to their destruction.") The ellipsis with the suspended verb completes the thought: *"et liquidis immisi fontibut apros"* ("and I have let in wild boars [to trample] my crystalline streams") (*Eclogues*, 2.58–59). This appears to say the text published in 1637 is in the poet's judgment not quite ready to be a *poem*, although a *"Poem"* is what Henry Lawes pointedly called this text when he published it, saying that the "oft copying" of it at the request of his friends had "tired his pen." Exposure to the fixed form of print may destroy its potential to be the mature and finished poem it is becoming. So too will exposure of it to those unclean wild boars, which we meet when we consult the rest of the passage in Virgil, and which are us.

The plot unfolds across three set scenes or, since they are scenes for dancing, three tableaux. (I assume the second tableau, in Comus's palace, presents a dance of Sabrina and her water nymphs.) The first tableau presents a wild Bacchic *antimasque* by Comus and his followers, preceded by Comus's song. The second tableau presents a contrasting, elegant, and otherworldly dance of Sabrina and her water nymphs. The third tableau has two principal dances, of contrasting texture: the boisterous but innocent country jigs of the swains and the stately dance of the children with their parents.

The scene of the first tableau is a dark wood through which the children must pass to attend the ceremonies at Ludlow Castle celebrating their father's "new-entrusted sceptre" (line 36). It is before this forest the Attendant Spirit delivers the prologue, removes his sky-robes to reveal the pastoral weeds underneath, and retires or is "viewless" at the sound of "hateful steps" (line 92).

Comus and his rout of beast-headed monsters, wearing fine sparkling clothes, bearing torches, and making a *"riotous and unruly noise"* (stage direction after line 92), perform the wild Bacchic dance technically known as the *antimasque*, performed with the studious barbarism of Stravinsky's *Rite of Spring*: "Come, knit hands and beat the ground / In a light fantastic round. *The Measure*" (lines 143–44). Before the dance begins, however, Comus has a long speech to deliver in *Sprechstimme*, indicating that night has arrived in the forest and anticipating the sensuous pleasures and obscene religious rites that are to ensue, beginning with that dance.

Comus's first words are a beautiful evocation of the changing of the light in the skies and a still more beautiful evocation of the natural world. Only gradually does this world begin to merge with and descend into

the infernal. This occurs at the point the dance of all things together
in nature, including the fish in the sea, gives way to the celebration of
actual pagan rites. As if it were a natural event, like the sudden drop of
temperature in the forest at night, we are led from the picturesque to
something more alarming, from pert fairies and dapper elves to the
horrible goddesses Hecate and Cotytto overhead, in a magic chariot,
up to no good.

Comus says the evening star Hesperus, "the star that bids the shepherd fold" (line 93), has risen from the horizon to the zenith: "Now the
top of Heav'n doth hold" (line 94):

> And the gilded car of Day
> His glowing axle doth allay
> In the steep Atlantic stream
> And the slope Sun his upward beam
> Shoots against the dusky pole
> Pacing toward the other goal
> Of his chamber in the East.
> Meanwhile, welcome Joy and Feast,
> Midnight Shout and Revelry,
> Tipsy Dance and Jollity. . . .
>
> (A Masque Presented at Ludlow Castle,
> 1634, *lines 95–104)*

("Steep" is a Latinism, *altus,* an epithet of the sea, meaning "deep." It
survives in English in the phrase *the high seas.)* The sun cooling the
burning axle of his chariot in the "steep Atlantic stream" to the west is
a wonderful and not unpleasing image, as the temperature drops. And
of course we will see something like it again at the conclusion of the
masque, when we too are taken in imagination to the horizon of the
ocean in the west. All of nature dances with Comus:

> The sounds and seas with all their finny drove
> Now to the Moon in wavering morris move
> And on the tawny sands and shelves
> Trip the pert fairies and the dapper elves.
>
> (A Masque Presented at Ludlow Castle, 1634, *lines*
> *115–18)*

From schools of fish and scampering elves we meet, suddenly and alarm-
ingly, the goddess of "nocturnal sport" (line 128), Cotytto. Nor, when
we look at her, do we look down, as at those fish and fairies; we look up.
For Cotytto is provided, like the sun, with a chariot, one suitable for
the nighttime sky—a "cloudy ebon chair"—which she shares with another and better-known goddess of hidden Hellish rites, Hecate—lust
hard by hate, as Milton will say in *Paradise Lost*:

> Hail goddess of nocturnal sport,
> Dark-veiled Cotytto, t'whom the secret flame
> Of mid-night torches burns. Mysterious Dame—
> That ne'er art called but when the dragon womb
> Of Stygian darkness spits her thickest gloom
> And makes one blot of all the air—
> Stay thy cloudy, ebon chair,
> Wherein thou ride'st with Hecat', and befriend
> Us thy vowed priests, till utmost end
> Of all thy dues be done, and none left out.
>
> (A Masque Presented at Ludlow Castle, 1634, *lines*
> *128–37)*

The idea-image—that the darkness of night, when the moon is obscured by the clouds, is expectorant from the stomach ("womb") of a
dragon inhabiting Styx—is spectacular. So too is its sound. Using enjambment, Milton continues to develop the technique of constructing
in blank verse rhythmical units above the level of the ten-syllable line,
as in that parenthetical qualification of opportune occasions for invoking
Cotytto: "that n'er art called but when the dragon womb of Stygian darkness spits her thickest gloom and makes one blot of all the air" (lines
130–33). We can say the line in a single breath because it rushes forward with impulsive, trochaic rhythms: "That **N'ER** art **CALLED**
but **WHEN** the **DRA**gon **WOMB** of **STY**gian **DARK**ness **SPITS**
her **THICK**est **GLOOM** and **MAKES** one **BLOT** of **ALL** the
AIR." The effect is locked in and confirmed—something Milton will
do repeatedly in "Lycidas"—by a short line rhyming with its predecessor
and also containing a change of tone, in this case a change from mood
music to a sharp command, almost the single word "Halt!": "**STAY**
thy **CLOU**dy, **E**bon **CHAIR**!" (line 134). There is a sense of urgency

to the command. Cotytto and Hecate have to stop flying about and get down to business. All their vile solemnities must be accomplished before dawn—"Ere the blabbing Eastern Scout" (line 138) reports them to the sun.

But the Lady enters instead, disturbing the plans for the evening but presenting new opportunities. Comus and his rout hide so he can overhear what she says. She has become separated from her brothers in the wood and drawn to this spot by the sound of "ill-managed merriment" (line 172). Being too refined to yell, she proposes to indicate her location to her brothers by singing a song to the nymph Echo. Comus goes into raptures at her music and, after resolving to make her his queen, throws a powder in her eyes that causes her to mistake him for a humble shepherd. He addresses her as a "foreign wonder" (line 265)—the entire passage is startlingly similar to Satan's first address to Eve in *Paradise Lost*—and immediately overplays his hand with extravagant praise, suggesting she is too good for this place, which is what Satan will say. Of course, Comus also outright lies, claiming to have seen the Lady's missing brothers and even to have worshipped them for their beauty—an act redolent of the superstitious behavior of Spenser's Archimago: "I was awe-struck, / And as I passed I worshipped" (lines 301–2). He offers to fetch her brothers for her while she waits in his hovel—actually his palace, in the "navel" (line 520) of the wood. There, he will tempt the Lady to drink from his magic glass, which the Attendant Spirit refers to at the outset as "His orient liquor in a crystal glass" (line 65), the effect of which is to turn one's head into that of a beast, "all other parts remaining as they were" (line 72). The other effect of the magic drink is that it makes the drinker join Comus's rout, forgetting family and friends.

> Soon as the potion works their human count'nance,
> Th'express resemblance of the gods, is changed
> Into some brutish form of wolf or bear,
> Or ounce or tiger, hog or bearded goat,
> All other parts remaining as they were
> And they, so perfect is their misery,
> Not once perceive their foul disfigurement
> But boast themselves more comely than before

> And all their friends and native home forget,
> To roll with pleasure in a sensual sty.
>
> > (A Masque Presented at Ludlow Castle, 1634, *lines*
> > *68–77)*

And so they depart, as the Lady innocently accepts his proposal, repeating the pastoral thought from the sixth book of Spenser's *Faerie Queene*, the Legend of Courtesy:

> Shepherd, I take thy word
> And trust thy honest offered courtesy
> Which oft is sooner found in lowly sheds
> With smoky rafters than in tap'stry halls
> And courts of princes where it first was named
> And yet is most pretended.
>
> > (A Masque Presented at Ludlow Castle, 1634,
> > *lines 321–26)*

As the two of them leave, the Lady utters a prayer to Providence: "Eye me, blest Providence, and square my trial / To my proportioned strength" (lines 329–30). She is of course asking for what Providence already ensures: that no one will be tempted beyond his or her power to resist any temptation that person will meet. But the prayer is a moving one, and is appropriate at this moment of her departure, just before her brothers' arrival on the scene.

Meanwhile, in another part of the wood, the brothers discuss their sister's danger and the philosophical problem whether virtue has any power in this world or is under any protection. This continues until they are rallied by the Attendant Spirit, disguised, as I have mentioned, as the shepherd Thyrsis, a family servant known to them. Directed by Thyrsis, and also armed by him with a plant, *Haemony*, which we noted has the power to repel enchantments, the brothers hasten to the rescue of their sister.

The second tableau opens in the palace of Comus, where the Lady is imprisoned by enchantment in a chair and urged by Comus to drink the magic potion in his cup, a "cordial julep" (line 672) signifying abandonment to pleasure:

> Behold this cordial julep here
> That flames and dances in his crystal bounds
> With spirits of balm and fragrant syrops mixed.
> Not that Nepenthes which the wife of Thone
> In Egypt gave to Jove-born Helena
> Is of such power to stir up joy as this . . .
> Why should you be so cruel to your self
> And to those dainty limbs which nature lent
> For gentle usage and soft delicacy?
>
> (A Masque Presented at Ludlow Castle, 1634, *lines*
> 672–81)

After Comus's long discourse on pleasure as a thing naturally belonging to beauty, the Lady refutes him and threatens—this Milton added in 1637—to bring his palace down around his ears by the power of her rhetoric, which would cause the earth to shake in sympathy as she defends "the sun-clad power of Chastity" (line 782) and "the sage and serious doctrine of Virginity" (line 786):

> Yet should I try, the uncontroulèd worth
> Of this pure cause would kindle my rapt spirits
> To such a flame of sacred vehemence
> That dumb things would be moved to sympathize
> And the brute Earth would lend her nerves and shake
> Till all thy magic structures reared so high
> Were shattered into heaps o'er thy false head.
>
> (A Masque Presented at Ludlow Castle, 1634, *lines 793–99*)

Thrown into panic by this threat—"She fables not, I feel that I do fear" (line 800)—Comus mutters to himself some terrific verses that also belong, like the Lady's climax, to the passage added in 1637. They are in the tone of *Paradise Lost:*

> She fables not. I feel that I do fear
> Her words set off by some superior power;
> And though not mortal, yet a cold shudd'ring dew
> Dips me all o're as when the wrath of Jove

> Speaks thunder and the chains of Erebus
> To some of Saturn's crew.
>
> (A Masque Presented at Ludlow Castle, 1634,
lines 800–805)

We now return from the added passage to the text that was there from the beginning, in the two manuscripts. Comus seems about to use force: "Come, no more, / This is mere moral babble, and direct / Against the canon laws of our foundation; / I must not suffer this" (lines 806–9).

At this moment the two brothers burst in with drawn swords (recall that their ages are eleven and nine) and drive him and his followers off, shattering his magic glass but failing to capture him or his wand, and so leaving the Lady imprisoned in the chair. These shortcomings are observed by Thyrsis, when at last he arrives. (Either he is slow for a Heavenly spirit, or he needs to let the boys exercise their virtue alone, or Lawes has been playing Comus and needs time to change costumes between leaving and returning.)

In this quandary, Thyrsis proposes they appeal (in song, of course) to the goddess of the River Severn, Sabrina—Ludlow is on the Teme, a tributary of the Severn. They do so in splendidly lyrical song that is positioned to contrast with the dark effusions of Comus. There is something purifying about these invocations. A hush of wonder attends Sabrina's appearance with her nymphs, dancing. Her first words, "By the rushy-fringèd bank, / Where grows the willow and the osier dank / My sliding chariot stays" (lines 890–92), show us how reluctant she is to be there. Her chariot waits for her in an eddy of the river, and her mind is still on it, as if she is uncomfortable straying too far from the water. But there is something she must do, and she has come to do it. She is unaccustomed to treading the earth, her ancient home, and having become weightless she never bends the velvet cowslips over which she walks with "printless feet": "Thus I set my printless feet / O'er the cowslips velvet head, / That bends not as I tread" (lines 897–99). She commands the Lady to look on her and then administers a few drops of "precious cure" (line 913) and a few charmed words. These interventions free the Lady, who rises from the chair. Whereupon Sabrina hastens back to the river, on which she will glide in her chariot to the sea: "I must haste ere morning hour / To wait in Amphitrite's bower" (lines

920–21). In the performance, the crisis is not the confrontation of Comus and the Lady, although Milton made sure that *would* be the crisis in the version we read. The crisis is instead the apparition of Sabrina, a magical presence who is normally retired and withdrawing. Sabrina's appearance is like the breathless moment in a Noh drama when the spirit from the past suddenly appears to tell his or her story in dance and in song. Sabrina does not need to tell her story, because the Attendant Spirit already has.

Let us pause for a moment over Sabrina, that mysterious figure. To do so is to digress from our purpose, but Sabrina herself is a digression, and a remarkable one. We come to see the episode Milton creates for her as a turning aside that takes us into the center of what the masque is trying to see: the depths of hidden openness in the natural world and the clearing at the heart of this world. Sabrina is the goddess of the great River Severn, the longest river in England (in the British Isles, only the Shannon in Ireland is longer). The Severn flows down from the Welsh mountains to the northwest of Ludlow, flowing in an easterly direction into England and Shropshire, past many important towns, and describing a great circle as it turns slowly southeast. The Spirit speaks of the "thousand petty rills, / That tumble down the snowy hills" (lines 926–27), and those hills are in Wales. By the time the river is a great moving flood, it is in England, flowing by the Shropshire towns: "May thy lofty head be crowned / With many a tower and terrace round" (934–35). The river then turns west and runs for the Bristol Channel, debouching into the Irish Sea and eventually the "wide Atlantic." Although most of the river's course was in Milton's day in England, as it still is, it was anciently the boundary between England and Wales. Ludlow is on the Teme, a tributary of the Severn, and so in the vast Severn watershed, inside the circle it describes. We recognize the Severn as the source of life for the entire region, and also as its historical destiny, not unlike Friedrich Hölderlin's Rhine, which rushes eastward in the Alps toward the Caucasus before being turned abruptly west, to flow by great cities in Europe. Sabrina's mystery comes from her evocation of a geographical place but also from something deeper than mere place, something that underlies all places and supports them, while at the same time drawing away from them, secluding itself. Like nature, which loves to hide, as Heraclitus said, Sabrina is unwilling to appear, preferring the cool and dark depths of her river, where the weeds are thickest, to the human world the river supports and makes possible. But the human world, as it activates itself in art, is interested in making this hidden realm, on which it depends, come into appearance. The human world coaxes the physical world that supports it into rising up from below. The song calling Sabrina to the Lady's aid is a calling to art from within art—a calling, that is, to appearance, to presencing. With its appeal, "Listen and save!," the song is an invocation of powers concealed from the very world they nourish and support: "the world grounds itself on the earth, and earth juts through world" ("*Die Welt grüdet sich auf die Erde, und Erde durchragt Welt*").[23] So it is with Sabrina, who lives in the hidden depths of the great River Severn, reluctant ever to appear, although she is brilliant and graceful beyond human comprehension, and when she appears she strikes all with wonder. But when she retires, another vision rises up, which is that of the earthly world, of the waves of the river, of the streams that run into it, and of the snowy Welsh hills from which these descend. The seasons of a river are brought into view, placid in summer, torrential in October, and even the terraces and towers of her cities, which are seen for a moment from an earthly point of view, as if they grew out of nature, which of course they do.

Yet such a vision is fleeting. Even as Sabrina dances before us she wants to retire. She is eager to help the Lady, however, because the Lady is her kind, a modest virgin, bearing in her the secrets of the earth and appearing in the world not with joy but reluctance. The Lady appears to us first in a clearing, a dancing space, although she does not dance. She sings. But later the singing and the dancing of Sabrina are the prelude to the Lady's release. This moment is just as much a loosening of bonds for Sabrina as it is for the Lady.

Sabrina fled the world and sought to live under the current, in the mud and the reeds and in the dark main channel under the surface, where a river flows fastest and most exerts its power. We can be certain her "sliding chariot" (line 892) is on the surface only at night, when she cannot be seen; she keeps to the middle of the stream, where it is swiftest and deepest, far from the banks. Not only is it painful for Sabrina to leave the river; it is painful for her chariot, too, which waits in an eddy of the stream, close to the bank, in unaccustomed shallows. She is anxious about that chariot among the rushes and the willows the entire time she is before us.

Her story is that she was a princess in the Trojan line, a descendant of Anchises, and the daughter of King Locrine. Fleeing her wicked step-dame, Gwendolen, she threw herself into the river:

> The water nymphs that in the bottom played
> Held up their pearled wrists and took her in,
> Bearing her straight to aged Nereus' hall
> Who, piteous of her woes, reared her lank head
> And gave her to his daughters to imbathe
> In nectared lavers strewed with asphodel
> And through the porch and inlet of each sense
> Dropped in ambrosial oil till she revived
> And underwent a quick immortal change,
> Made goddess of the river.
>
> (A Masque Presented at Ludlow Castle, 1634,
> *lines 833–42)*

I remarked on the mildly disorientating perspectival effects of this work and these are splendidly on view in this passage, though on a smaller scale. Sabrina sinks down in the stream and the nymphs below hold up their wrists, their pearl bracelets catching the light from above, to take hold of the drowning maiden and draw her down farther, into the weeds. But the vertical direction is changed as they conduct her sideways, down-stream, in a westerly direction toward the sea and, presumably, along the bottom of the river. Leaving the brackish estuary for the salty depths, still bearing the maiden, they descend to the ancient sea-god Nereus's fabulous hall in the deep. There, the god and his daughters revive her, making her the goddess of the river—to which, presumably, she then returns and in which she now resides, "Under the glassy, cool, translu-cent wave" (line 861).

The baroque effects of bodily movement in aerial perspective—of weightlessly floating, of slowly rotating, of ascending and descending, of advancing into the foreground and retreating into the background, and above all of being borne by others—are reproduced in this passage in the description of the maiden's body underwater being conducted by nymphs to the sea. The special effects that were achieved by means of flying machines and the like in the Stuart court masques are captured instead in Milton's verse. Like an allegorical figure seen against the sky, by Rubens, for example, in the Banqueting House at Whitehall, Sabrina flies, she soars, she is borne weightlessly off into the distance, and she undergoes an apotheosis, becoming immortal, shining in pearls—but all underwater.

Once Sabrina has freed the Lady and retired, the children and Thyrsis flee the palace of Comus before the enchanter can assault them "with some other new device" (line 941). Besides, as Thyrsis reminds them, there are country dances to be seen if they arrive in time.

The third tableau opens showing Ludlow town with the castle in the background and young swains performing the dances, with much leaping. These are the same dancers, having changed costumes, who performed the *antimasque*, as Comus's rout. As Lady Alix Egerton speculates, they were likely the local Morris dancers.[24] Thyrsis, in a song, orders these dancers to retire so another dance can take place, the orderly and stately dance to which all have been tending, in which the children and (as is probable) their parents participate. As Thyrsis sings in the concluding lines of his final song, the children "triumph in victorious dance / O'er sensual Folly and Intemperance" (lines 974–75). The stage direction in *1637* and *Poems 1645* reads, "*The dances ended, the Spirit epiloguizes.*"

I mentioned that the history of criticism of this work shows how difficult it is to stop thinking of the text, much altered as it was after the performance, as secondary with respect to the occasion, as if the essence of this work were that occasion and the text incoherent without it. Because this is to some extent a true judgment, limited as this truth is, it is hard to think of Milton's masque with respect to where it is going—which is in the direction of becoming an autonomous poem—rather than with respect to where it came from, its originative occasion. An *event* is a "coming forth" (*e+venire*), an emergence, which because of this "eventual" character (*OED* definition one) must also recede and disappear. Disappearance is a part of its meaning.[25] As an "emergence" the event belongs more intimately to its circumstances, and for this reason the event cannot be resolved, as a work of art can be, into a thing. You cannot put an event into a museum (although this is often attempted), or into a library, or into an anthology, or into a musical or theatrical repertoire. That is not to say works of art do not capture or celebrate events, but for this capturing to occur they must reduce events to things upon which preservation, reproduction, and cultural transmission can work.

Works of art can deliberately interrogate this process, as with, for example, Marcel Duchamp's "readymades," or Joseph Beuys's "actions," such as *Ausfegen* (Sweeping Up), in which the artist's sweepings of the street after a May Day protest are put in a case in a museum, with the red broom with which they were swept, or when the blackboard left over from the event of a lecture is sprayed with a preservative and placed in a museum. A musical composition written out in a score can be said to be a captured event, and a similar observation can be made of plays, which unlike masques are meant to be repeatedly performed and are successful to the degree to which this repetition occurs. One can cite many examples, but in every case, preservation, fixing, rendering the *event* into a *thing*, a relic of its occasion, belongs to the reduction of the event to the status of a work of art. A work of art is intended to endure as a thing in an unchanging state, for future contemplation and cultural transmission.

Let us consider, in this light, the title *A Masque Presented at Ludlow Castle, 1634*. It names first a genre, the *masque*, which might as well be "fireworks"; it then names the coordinates of an event that occurred at one place and at one time and is not intended to occur again, for masques are onetime events dependent on the actual persons being celebrated and presented. So far as the eventual character of this work is concerned—that is, the circumstances of its occasion and the ritual and social purposes served by the masque—disappearance, not endurance, is essential to its meaning.

The cultural presence of any work of art—that is, what presence or "being" a work may be said to have in a culture—has three phases or "appearances." The first is its appearance as a *treasure*, which is something secreted or hidden away for protection (*secretum* is the Latin translation of Greek *thesaurus*). But this putting away of the thing is also a "positing" (*thesis*) of the work as a work of art. The work is secreted because of its value as art. Corresponding roughly to this phase are the Trinity and Bridgewater manuscripts.

The second phase of the work is its *reproduction*, a second "leading forth," or a second positing, *thesis*. The 1637 text of *A Masque* best corresponds to this phase. The treasure is now being preserved, partly hidden away and partly brought forth before the world, negating its tendency to withdraw into its disappearance, and thus affirming its presence as a *Poem*. Lawes does not speak of preserving the work for the future but only of making it available to those who want to read it now. It has become a *monumentum*, a "monument," a thing to be shown others (L. *monere*), but it is not yet a thing to be transmitted in time.

The third phase of the work is its entering into *tradition*, a word that means "handing on," transmission. This phase enters into a kind of cultural reproduction that goes beyond that previous monumental reproduction. It is a dissemination, a scattering of seed that will grow in the future: the element of temporality has entered into account. We see the process beginning in the publication of *A Masque* in *Poems 1645*, where it is included with Milton's other poems to date—those he wished to preserve—as in a time capsule. Cheaper editions of Milton today may have the monumental purpose of "showing" the work to the widest possible number of readers at the present time, in the same way Lawes printed the work so that he would not have to "tire his pen" further in answer to requests. But every new scholarly edition of this work is an attempt not only to make it widely available to readers now but also to transmit it forward in time.

Let us consider a remote example, so as to strengthen our understanding of how *A Masque* relates to these three phases of the work of art. The Paleolithic paintings in the Lascaux caves are preserved as a treasure and are now closed to all but a very few preservers and scholars. They are placed beyond reach and secreted away. But this placing of the caves out of reach is also a placing of them up, a positing, or *thesis (Setzung)*, which affirms their existence as works of art, whatever their original use was. They are at once hidden away and set up, as a proposition. It is this removal from sight—for which of course there are very sensible, practical reasons—that elevates the paintings in the cave to the status of art. They are precious; they are worth preserving; they are posited as "art."

The monumental phase of representation comes next. A reproduction of the caves—or of one of the galleries—has been manufactured with great skill and care and now stands near the site. It can be visited. This monumental re-creation is where the work has been made available to all who would see it now, as Lawes's 1637 edition was intended to make the work available to his contemporaries—but not to the future.

In the manufacturing of a reproduction of the cave with its paintings, the original that has been posited or "set up" as unique—and for this reason secreted away—is now brought forth again so that it may be present to us as a thesis. The thesis says, "This is art." The paintings say, "We are here and not here." The cave paintings have entered into aesthetics, that is, into the perceptual experience of art as a subject-object relation. The artworks may be contemplated in the light, for all to see, instead of being preserved in darkness, and treasured.

When the work of art passes into the third phase, that of the artwork in a tradition, the subject-object relationship of its earlier phase, that of aesthetic perception, is now a mediated relation. This mediated relation may be referred to as *transmission* and *teaching*. The work that was present to itself alone and then present to the other is now present to others, in the plural, through the mediated process of teaching, which is didactic transmission. Didactic transmission does not give a direct experience of the work, as in aesthetics, but an experience of the work in terms of its margins, its commentaries, its historical circumstances, and its connections with other works in the same canon or grouping. The most obvious manifestation of this mediated, pedagogical relation to the work is the concept of *approaches*, of ways of "coming toward" the work without ever quite arriving in its presence. (We may note the frequency of the locution *approaches to* in pedagogical texts.)

The temporality that asserted itself in the first phase as the imperative to preserve was negated in the second phase by the imperative to experience the work now, in the now. Temporality returns in the third phase as the negation of the value and even the possibility of this experience of the work in the now, which in this pedagogical phase of transmission seems naive. You cannot simply go to the reproduced Lascaux cave and look at the paintings on the wall, experiencing them for yourself. You need to know about Paleolithic Europe, Paleolithic anthropology, sociology, religion, and ecology. You need to know the theories, all of them, if possible, and form your own opinion—ultimately by means of publication. Temporality has returned at this phase. Formerly, temporality's purpose and name was preservation; now its name is progress, the idea that our understanding of the work increases over time and with labor.

It is perhaps because we live in an age of expanded education and multiple editions, in which the fear of losing touch with the original presence of the works is correspondingly increased, that modern editions of Milton are preoccupied—as eighteenth- and nineteenth-century editions were not—with recapturing so-called original spelling and punctuation. These belong in large measure to the second, monumental phase and are largely artifacts of printing. For Milton, the being or presence of his poem as a treasure, a thing secreted and precious, is not fundamentally textual or visual (as it is for modern poets) but is rather acoustical and musical—and spiritual. The treasured poem is like those precious *fontes* in Virgil, sources that remain hidden, except from poets and the gods. Until, that is, their streams are trampled in and muddied by wild rooting boars. By those beasts, Milton may mean vulgarians such as ourselves. But the way to reach us vulgarians is through the medium of print. That, perhaps, is what is suggested to his mind by those rooting snouts, by those stamping hooves, and by the inky mess to which they reduce the muse's crystal stream.

4

On Engagement in A Masque

On Karl Marx's tomb in Highgate Cemetery is inscribed the final and most famous of his *Theses on Feuerbach* (1845), number 11: "The philosophers have only *interpreted* the world in various ways; what's necessary is to *change* it" ("Die Philosophen haben die Welt nur verschieden *interpretiert*; es kommt aber darauf an, sie zu *verändern*.") He would have approved of the Lady in Milton's *A Masque Presented at Ludlow Castle, 1634.* She thought the same way, perhaps with more clear resolve than her creator. The turnaround in philosophy envisioned by Marx—from theoretical interpretation to practical change—is part of a larger European event that began well before him, as of course he understood. It began in Renaissance utopian thought, which expressed itself not only in the literary genre of the utopia but in architecture and town planning, in political philosophy, and in the new science. A similar turnaround, from transcendence to engagement, began in Milton's poetic career with this new work, stimulated, perhaps, by a virtuous, haut bourgeois distaste for the vulgar luxury in which his social betters lived, including his employer, the Earl of Bridgewater, whom the masque honors. This was the second time—"Arcades" was the first—Milton brought his poetry into a mercantile transaction with the world. It was an experience different from transacting with the muses. Masques of the period were conspicuously wasteful and, to puritans and to the people at large, the genre had become the symbol of vulgar waste and immoral self-display by an absolutist regime.

But a more proximate cause for the first motions, in *A Masque Presented at Ludlow Castle, 1634*, of Milton's turn from transcendence to engagement may well have been his lingering dissatisfaction with the concluding tableau of "Il Penseroso." Our last sight of the Reflective Man is of an aged, cunning pedant, one who can "rightly spell"—that is, name over, by heart—every herb and every star. After a lifetime of study and reflection, what good has he been to anyone? What good has he been to himself? Milton is imagining his own old age after a life without commitment—he places himself before himself in everything he writes, as Coleridge said—and he doesn't like what he sees.

The opening verses of *A Masque Presented at Ludlow Castle, 1634*, are spoken by the Attendant Spirit, newly arrived from Heaven. In them Milton sets forth brilliantly the orthodox Christian view on the abject condition of this world, and on the need to exercise virtue in order to leave this world for a better place. In Marx's terms, that is an interpretation of the world. Unexpectedly, however, Milton now began to think how this world might be changed for the better, and made not only more virtuous but more holy. His answer is not Marx's. Although we are less than a decade away from the opening of hostilities in the English Revolution, class hostility isn't class struggle. Milton's answer is a traditional, humanist one: more virtue and better distribution. Even so, Milton's tendency is to the radical end of Renaissance humanism and is not discordant with the republicanism of Machiavelli and the scientific spirit of Bacon. It is not unreasonable to think that Milton's later republicanism and materialism are extensions of what we begin to see in *A Masque Presented at Ludlow Castle, 1634:* the intention to change the world by means of active virtue.

This incipient alteration of perspective, from transcendence to engagement, is seen first in the Lady. Unlike the Attendant Spirit, who cares for nothing but Heaven and for all who are trying to get there, the Lady shows little interest in Heaven except as an authority for validating her arguments. Her arguments are directed at this world. Heaven is her authority for the claim that the freedom of her mind is inviolate, that her judgment is not subject to tyrannical power, although her body is. Heaven will bear witness, she promises, to her affirmation of the power of chastity as a force for good here. And Heaven is the ultimate justification for her claim—we have heard nothing remotely like this in Milton before—that Nature's bounty should be distributed fairly, "in unsuperfluous, even proportïon" (line 773). Indeed, the real issue of the Lady's debate with Comus is an ecological one. In what way should humans comport themselves with respect to the natural world? The answer is moderation, which opens an awareness of nature that is very different from Comus's ravenous appetite for it.

The Lady comes to her views on social justice and ecological wisdom by dialectical means, that is, by countering earlier positions taken by Comus and, as a result, finding herself in a new place, as well. The first of Comus's positions is that nature should be used up as fast as possible, to feed luxury, which is a thing good in itself, and the more extravagantly excessive the luxury, the better. (Milton's famously fastidious but sparing taste in food is a political statement.) Comus's position on nature provokes the Lady's counterargument on social justice: there is enough for all, and for elegant luxury, if distribution were fair. Comus's second position is that without our intervention in nature, in the pursuit of luxury, nature is dangerously out of balance with itself. We must counter nature's runaway productiveness. Otherwise nature will be, as Milton has Comus put it, in a wondrously compressed phrase, "strangled with her waste fertility" (line 729). The solution to this second point is the premise of the first: nature should be used up as quickly as possible, to feed luxury. Rapacious greed is not only good in itself but also good for nature.

In the next phase of his career, in *Areopagitica*, Milton will say, "I cannot praise a fugitive and cloistered virtue, unexercised and unbreathed, that never sallies out and sees her adversary, but slinks out of the race where that immortal garland is to be run for, not without dust and heat . . . that which purifies us is trial, and trial is by what is contrary" (*YP*, 2:515). By "trial" he means a "contest" or *agon* in the arena or stadium of this world, and in the dust and heat of struggle. Formerly, Milton's attitude to the present world was one of pious disgust, as if the earth were infected with what in the Nativity Ode he calls "leprous sin" (line 138). One does not struggle with the world in the contest for justice and truth. One does what one can, what one must, to leave this world for a better one.

This attitude is carried over into the opening lines of *A Masque*, in which the Attendant Spirit, a *daemon*, speaking the prologue, tells us he has descended from his home in the celestial regions, "Above the smoke and stir of this dim spot / Which men call earth" (lines 5–6).

The greater part of these men, "with low-thoughted care," are crowded together, like ignorant beasts to the slaughter, preoccupied only with how to survive, how to "keep up a frail and feverish being," although survival itself in such a world is of no value. The only thing to be valued is that crown of glory to be won after death—"this mortal change"— when we are out of this world and above it, in Heaven, "amongst the ènthroned gods on sainted seats" (lines 6–11). These opening lines are like a strong major chord, announcing the key signature of the work as a whole and mapping its universe:

> Before the starry threshold of Jove's court
> My mansion is where those immortal shapes
> Of bright aerial spirits live ensphered
> In regions mild of calm and serene air
> Above the smoke and stir of this dim spot
> Which men call earth and with low-thoughted care,
> Confined and pestered in this pinfold here,
> Strive to keep up a frail and feverish being
> Unmindful of the crown that virtue gives,
> After this mortal change, to her true servants
> Amongst the ènthroned gods on sainted seats.

(*A Masque Presented at Ludlow Castle, 1634, lines 1–11*)

Those true servants are the chosen ones among us who perform virtuous deeds, not for any good the deeds do in this world but for the prize that they win in the next. Such virtuous deeds lead the elect spiritually upward, by "due steps," as in an upward-turning, unicursal labyrinth (like the one portrayed in the allegorical *Tablet of Cebes*, which Milton mentions in *Of Education* as an "easy and delightful book of education" [*YP*, 2:383–4]), to seize a golden key that will open Heaven's gate. The Attendant Spirit tells us he has descended to help these persons alone, who are already aspiring; and he concludes with a final expression of disgust at this rank and stinking world:

> Yet some there be that by due steps aspire
> To lay their just hands on that golden key
> That opes the palace of eternity.
> To such my errand is and but for such

> I would not soil these pure ambrosial weeds
> With the rank vapors of this sin-worn mold.
>
> (A Masque Presented at Ludlow Castle, 1634,
> *lines 12–17*)

In Milton's career this conventional disgust with an unredeemable world will be supplanted by the more positively engaged and aggressive attitude we have witnessed in *Areopagitica*. The change is evident enough in the prose works Milton will write in the next decade, the 1640s, and in the poems he wrote in defense of those works. But the transition begins to make its appearance in *A Masque* as the possibility of liberating the potential for redeeming pleasure and uniting pleasure with virtue. That potential will be converted to a revolutionary energy, so at least the poet will suppose, capable of changing the world. Its realization will be symbolized at the end of *A Masque* by the paradisal garden of the Hesperides (sacred to Juno, goddess of childbirth), which is on an island in the extreme west, at the limit of the stream of ocean, where the sun sets and the rainbow ends.[1]

To his garden of the Hesperides, Milton has appropriated the Garden of Adonis in *The Faerie Queene*, which in Spenser's allegory is the source of generated bodies in time. In an articulation for which there is no mythological precedent, Milton has also translated Spenser's dying god, Adonis, to the western paradise, "waxing well of his deep wound / In slumber soft" (lines 1000–1001), while Venus is seated nearby, in pensive mood: "and on the ground / Sadly sits the Assyrian queen" (lines 1001–2). Suppressing the sexual explicitness of Spenser's account, Milton's intention is to draw upon the powerful, organic resonances of Spenser's allegory. Indeed, all Spenser's poetic thinking in this great episode of *The Faerie Queene* is implied and furthered in Milton's Hesperian paradise. In Spenser, Adonis is perpetually enjoyed by the goddess Venus, "when ever that she will," and is protected by her from annihilation at the hands of the Stygian gods, "which doe her love envy" (*The Faerie Queene*, 3.6.46). He is the "Father of all formes"— that is, of all organic life forms—and he is therefore "subject to mortalitie," like all living things. But as the origin "that living gives to all," Adonis cannot ever wholly die himself. That is why he is perpetually "waxing well," as Milton says, of his death wound. Here is the corresponding passage in Spenser, in which Adonis is "by succession made perpetuall":

> But she herselfe, when ever that she will,
> Possesseth him, and of his sweetnesse takes her fill.

> And sooth it seemes they say: for he may not
> For ever die, and ever buried bee
> In baleful night, where all things are forgot;
> All be he subject to mortalitie,
> Yet is eterne in mutabilitie,
> And by succession made perpetuall,
> Transformed oft, and changed diverslie:
> For him the Father of all formes they call;
> Therefore needs mote he live, that living gives to all.
>
> (The Faerie Queene, *3.6.46–47*)

Spenser goes on to say Venus has imprisoned the savage boar—the one that in the myth fatally wounded Adonis—in a rocky cave under the mount on which the garden is situated. Meanwhile, safe in the garden, Adonis keeps company with Venus's son, Cupid, who resorts thither after ransacking the world with cruel wars like that at Troy, setting up his trophies in "woful harts / Of many wretches" (*Faerie Queene*, 3.6.49). So far, in Spenser's account, the eroticism that assures the renewal of living forms in the world is a decidedly mixed affair: Adonis is "eterne in mutability," and Cupid or *eros*, "desire" (L. *cupio* "to desire"), causes terrible wars and heart-struck agony, reducing us to "wretches."

As a poet, Spenser must give us in a vision a realization of the perfect joy to which all these agonies tend. He therefore draws from Apuleius the tale of Cupid and Psyche, desire and the soul, the parents of *Voluptas* or "Pleasure." But instead of showing them together among the Olympian gods, he places them here in the Garden of Adonis, "after long troubles and unmeet upbrayes":

> But now in stedfast love and happy state
> She with him lives, and hath him borne a chylde,
> *Pleasure*, that doth both gods and men aggrate,
> *Pleasure*, the daughter of *Cupid* and *Psyche* late.
>
> (The Faerie Queene, *3.6.50*)

In the epilogue to *A Masque*, Milton adopts Spenser's allegorical sequence, from Venus and Adonis to Cupid and Psyche. His final vision

of Cupid and Psyche is the culminating symbol—and the culminating
thought—to which he turns after showing us Venus and Adonis. Milton's doing so confirms—though of course he knew Spenser's source,
Apuleius—that he is following the track of the allegorical poet of *The
Faerie Queene* and absorbing Spenser's meaning into his own. The transition from organic love, symbolized by Venus and the wounded Adonis,
to ideal love, symbolized by Cupid and Psyche, is marked by one of
Milton's telltale "buts":

> Sadly sits the Assyrian queen.
> *But* far above in spangled sheen
> Celestial Cupid, her famed son advanced,
> Holds his dear Psyche sweet entranced
> After her wandering labours long
> Till free consent the gods among
> Make her his eternal bride
> And from her fair unspotted side
> Two blissful twins are to be born,
> Youth and Joy, so Jove hath sworn.
>
> (A Masque Presented at Ludlow Castle,
> 1634, *lines 1002–11*)

We see them embracing in the western sky above the horizon, with
the "spangled sheen" of the stars behind them—and the garden of the
Hesperides below. They are not a vision of the joys of Heaven to be
experienced after death; they are a vision of the future, of a possibility, and of a hope to be developed out of conditions existing in this
world.

It is true that Milton does not leave us with this mysterious vision of
the future but returns, as I said, to the tonic key with which he began.
He does so, moreover, by recapitulating the image with which he began,
that of the virtuous climbing up through the chiming, celestial spheres
and getting above them, into Heaven:

> Mortals that would follow me,
> Love Virtue, she alone is free.
> She can teach ye how to climb
> Higher than the sphery chime.

> Or, if Virtue feeble were,
> Heaven itself would stoop to her.
>
> *(A Masque Presented at Ludlow*
> *Castle, 1634, lines 1018–23)*

A Masque concludes juxtaposing, without any mediation or transition, the vision of the garden of the Hesperides in the west, including Cupid and Psyche, with this final vision of ascent through the celestial spheres. There is an unresolved tension between these two systems of value. The one places the fullest realization of value in the natural world, at a horizontal distance, as something to be reached in the future. The other places ultimate value overhead, in Heaven, as something to be reached after death. The first is historical and collective; the second is apocalyptic and individual. The humanistic redemption of nature and pleasure, and of a virtue meant for service in this world, is canceled by the apparent return of what the Attendant Spirit described at the outset: a puritanical model of the natural world as abject but as capable of being transcended—left behind—by virtuous deeds, although only after death. But there is a difference. What the Attendant Spirit now describes is not the earth as the "sin-worn mold" (line 17), which is below the sphere of the moon, but rather the "sphery chime" above the moon: the part of creation that is not subject to the effects of the Fall. The recapitulated, vertical system of value is brought back improved, having been modified by the Hesperian vision. That these contrasting but juxtaposed systems are incompatible is not in itself of great interest. What is of interest is the energy in this work that tends away from the theological orientation we see at its beginning toward a humanist redemption of worldly pleasure as virtue. This change is not completed, yet there is in this work a tendency in another direction, a stretching and a bending toward it: that of the future. As we saw in the previous chapter, this work is never quite self-identical because it is always becoming something else. It is becoming engaged. The work never arrives at its inchoate, prophetic, and visionary goal—the meaning of that dance—because the goal changes even as it moves.

What then is the change that is being shadowed in *A Masque?* In the simplest terms, it may be envisioned as a shift from an ethical system that is vertically arranged in space, with good above and evil below, to one that is arranged horizontally in time, with the promise of greater liberty to be enjoyed in the future. In *A Masque*, however, what Milton will eventually understand in universal and discursive terms as human liberty is the mysterious union of virtue and pleasure in love, attended by the arts. Our power to achieve this state is with us even now, as potential, or *dynamis*, but this power can be liberated only by moral effort in time.[2] That is what Milton almost says in *A Masque*.

In Marx's thesis—that the philosophers in the past have interpreted the world in various ways when the point is to change it—the various interpretations of the world all assume the stability and invariance of what they interpret. If what passed for the truth changed fundamentally, the philosophers have assumed, it would not be true. Another interpretation would therefore be required, a better one, a more comprehensive one, to save the phenomena. This new interpretation would get beneath that recent change and reveal it to be the superficial manifestation of a deeper invariance. To be knowable—so these philosophers with their various interpretations have assumed—the world must not change. But that the world can change of its own accord is not Marx's point, which would be another interpretation. His point is that *we* have to change it.

In contrast with this new ideal of commitment to change, the various interpretations of the world require that the philosophical interpreter be detached from what is interpreted and not engage in any such transformative work. Detachment is the condition of understanding.

In calling for us to abandon this cherished, philosophical detachment from the world in favor of active engagement, what Marx means by *world* is insensibly changed, as at the stroke of an enchanter's wand. No longer does *world* mean nature, the cosmos, in which human beings are secondary actors; *world* means human society, which is now at the center of nature, as is human action. This reorientation from nature to society is as radical as Socrates's reorientation of philosophy from nature to ethics. For Marx, human society is the instrument for changing itself, through class struggle, and human society is also the instrument for changing the natural world, through technology.

What are the roots of Milton's view of the world? Christianity carries forward from its earliest days as an oppressed sect under the all-powerful Roman Empire a sense of the world as fundamentally subject to change, in contrast with all ancient philosophical worldviews. For early Christianity, the world is merely a *saeculum*, a period of time. Indeed, Christianity would subvert Rome at last by attacking it on its only undefended frontier, that of time. But Christianity also carries forward from its earliest days an inheritance from stoicism: a contempt of the world that derives from an unacknowledged powerlessness over it. Early Christianity gives up on the world and does not try to change it. Instead, it saves souls for the next world, which will come after this world has exhausted its remaining time. As time went on and the millennium passed, however, the world Christianity had long since inherited from Rome seemed enduring enough to be worthy of philosophical attention, of lasting architecture, and of stable institutions, especially the church, which fights in this world to win souls for the next.[3]

In broad terms, the early poetry of Milton inherits this traditional Christian view of this world as solid and enduring but sinful. The point is to get out of it as soon as possible, as we see at the moment in "On the Morning of Christ's Nativity" when, supposedly, at the birth of Christ, the music of the spheres will cause Heaven to appear and open her gates, inviting us to enter Heaven now, instead of at the Apocalypse: "For if such holy song / Enwrap our fancy long . . . Heaven as at some festival / Will open wide the gates of her high palace hall" (lines 133–34 and 147–48). Everything of value in this world longs for and tends toward eternity, which is another world and another kingdom, the Kingdom of God.

Before he wrote *A Masque Presented at Ludlow Castle, 1634*, Milton understood his poetic and prophetic task as seeing the world *sub specie aeternitatis*, that is, from the unchanging point of view of Heaven, and to inspire us to see it as he does. But there is little sense of wanting to change the present world, from which the poet remains coolly detached. Even in "On the Morning of Christ's Nativity," where he is emotionally engaged, the poet remains intellectually detached from the scene and entirely conventional in outlook. He gives us nothing but orthodox Christian ideas.

In comparison to the acts of the Son of God—who creates the world, who comes into it as a child, who defeats the pagan gods, who will die on the cross, who will defeat Satan and lead us to Heaven—the actions of all humanity are passive, much more so than in the introduction to *A Masque Presented at Ludlow Castle, 1634*. The poet's task is to understand and communicate God's plan for history, while waiting for the world to end. "On the Morning of Christ's Nativity" is thus an interpretation of the world according to a system that is given in advance. Milton's vague plans to become a Christian poet-prophet—as witnessed in "The Passion," in "At a Solemn Music," in "On Time," and in "Upon the Circumcision," the last three composed the year before *A Masque Presented at Ludlow Castle, 1634*—amounted to little more than persuading people to be good and joyous Christians. What that is is already known, and so is the world, until it is destroyed.

"L'Allegro" and "Il Penseroso" give us secular speakers who are likewise passively disengaged from the world, viewing it theoretically. The cheerful man observes the landscape, eavesdrops on the stories country people tell, goes to the theater, and is sent into raptures by music, although, as I noted, he doesn't make any music himself. The pensive man is still more detached. In the lonely tower of theory, he calls down from their spheres in the Heavens the spirits of the philosophers of old, to question them. His love of philosophy is an aesthetic and sensuous passion for the movements of thought, not a passion for truth. The pensive man doesn't do philosophy. Beyond reckoning up the correspondences between things on earth and stars in the heavens, he has no conception of thinking.

A Masque opens, in the prologue of the Attendant Spirit, with much the same outlook, adjusted to Christianity. Moral effort is important, not for the sake of changing the world but only for the sake of getting out of it. The slightly comical image of the virtuous in this world aspiring, as in purgatory, to that higher place where they can seize a golden key and open the gates of Heaven, is one that does not alter the world in the least. It is a kind of thinking that calculates how to get to Heaven and acts duly on those calculations, in a system wherein all the calculations have already been made. What passes for thinking is no more than a proper calculation of how the system works, and a proper representation of the whole in relation to the parts. The purpose of poetry is to exhort others to play the game well and climb above the spheres in order to be free.

To be *free*, it appears, is to be free *of* something: to escape from this world. *World* in its seventeenth-century sense, before the Copernican system was imaginatively as well as scientifically accepted, means the largely poetical system of nested, crystalline spheres that by their turning make the "music of the world," the *musica mundana*. To go above those spheres is to go to Heaven. Hence the world is a thing to escape, and Christianity will tell you how to do so: love virtue, and practice it. And of course believe Christ died for your sins—although this is left out to keep the pagan decorum. So long as this system predominated in Milton's mind, he could not think of other possibilities because other possibilities are exactly what a tight system is built to exclude.

For new thinking to occur, the system must be opened and disturbed, its rules broken so that unexpected questions can be asked, such as the following: (1) "Is there any goodness whatever latent in this world?"; (2) "Is this latent goodness, if it exists, a power that can be brought to virtue's aid—in this world?"; and, finally, (3) "Can the world itself be changed?" These questions begin to make their shadowy appearance in Milton's masque. They do so partly because the greater length of this work forced the poet to surrender the control he formerly exercised over his writing. The paganism that was always kept down—at least in English poetry—began seriously to undermine the monolithic structure of the poet's ideology, especially, as we see, at the end. In "On the Morning of Christ's Nativity," the pagan spirits, which were so strictly expelled from the system—like all systems, this one is constructed by violent exclusion—have drifted back into sight, like those "yellow-skirted fays" in "On the Morning of Christ's Nativity" who "fly after the night-steeds, leaving their moon-loved maze" (lines 235–36). If the fays disappear over the western horizon with the steeds of night, they have not been banished to Hell, like the other gods, but are part of the natural cycles of this world.

At the most wondrous moment of Milton's masque, Sabrina, a Briton princess who is metamorphosed by Milton into a classical goddess, rises from the stream as a new and unexpected act of thinking, in answer to the question: what benevolence exists within the order of the natural world? Sabrina does not belong to the mythological universe outlined by the Attendant Spirit in the prologue, even when he speaks of Neptune's "tributary gods" ruling the "sea-girt isles / That like to rich and various gems inlay / The unadorned bosom of the deep" (lines 21–23). For us, at least, Sabrina is the unexpected guest, invoked at the unexpected impasse, when the Lady remains fixed in her chair and the Attendant Spirit, in his disguise as Thyrsis, is unable to free her. Sabrina rises out of the waters as the children of Prometheus rise out of the earth. She is a new thought called up by a spirit from Heaven (the disguised Thyrsis) who may well have been surprised at himself. Milton's poetic thinking begins in such spontaneous moments of relaxed mental control over his mythological universe, and in the allowing of such disallowed thoughts. We are seeing revolutionary value emerging from below instead of theological value being imposed from above. What begins in *A Masque*, though very dimly, is the kind of thinking that would lead, in the second phase of Milton's career, to engagement with this world and to fighting for liberty.

The civil war would sweep away the old regime of which the Stuart masque was the symbol. The king himself—Marvell's "royal actor"— would be executed in 1649 on the "tragic scaffold" in front of the Banqueting House, where the most sumptuous masques were performed.[4] It is true that in *A Masque Presented at Ludlow Castle, 1634*, the theme of temptation looks forward to *Paradise Lost* and finds precocious treatment here, although more than the theme of temptation is taken in hand. Yet for many of its critics in the past, the meaning and relevance of *A Masque Presented at Ludlow Castle, 1634*, are to be found in widening circles of context that are increasingly remote from the text: the circumstances of its occasion and performance first of all; the council of Wales and the Marches; the lurid Castlehaven scandal; and the politics, if they can be called that, of the antebellum period during the years of Charles I's personal government. The truth is, none of these things has any relevance whatever to the poetic art of this work. That is why the poetry—that "dainty entertainment" with its aberrant mythology—is so often and so sadly regarded as the lyrically decorative remainder of more serious matters.

Milton would have held that there is one thing and only one thing to be taken seriously about this work, and that is its series of moral ideas, which are summarized at the end: "Love Virtue, she alone is free" (line 1019). These ideas can be stated simply. Milton teaches that virtue is good (lines 9 and 703) and that virtue is free (line 1019). He teaches that pleasure—also known as *vice*—is alluring but bad (lines 760–61), and also that vice is disfiguring (lines 68–77), addictive (lines 474–75), and unfree (line 384). He teaches that the point of virtue is to get out of this world into the next (lines 12–14 and 1020–21) and that temperance is good for whomever has the discipline to practice it (lines 763–66). He teaches that temperance does good for others, as well, because it dispenses the blessings of nature "In unsuperfluous, even proportïon" (line 773). That is a lesson that applies to this world and not to the next, and it is certainly not conventionally Christian. Milton teaches that Heaven assists virtue (lines 13–14 and 1022) and that nature does, too: "dumb things" are "moved to sympathize" when virtue is oppressed and calls for justice (line 796).

This mood of speculative inquiry becomes more intense at three moments. The first is the question mooted in the debate between the brothers on whether there is a moral force latent in the world. The second is the question raised in the contest between Comus and the Lady: what is the right use of nature? The third is the question—implicit in the Attendant Spirit's mythological epilogue—in which these two earlier questions are put together in time. Is there a future time when moral goodness will be crowned by innocent joy?

It was observed in the previous chapter that in *A Masque Presented at Ludlow Castle, 1634*, Milton composed a poetic work four times longer than anything he had previously composed and by the same proportion longer than anything he would compose until *Paradise Lost*. *Paradise Lost* is more than ten times longer than *A Masque*; *Paradise Regained* is about twice as long as *A Masque*; and *Samson Agonistes* is about three quarters again as long as *A Masque*. At more than two thousand lines, the scale of *A Masque Presented at Ludlow Castle, 1634*, makes it unlike anything Milton had composed before. On the smaller poetic scales—the sonnet, the elegy, the ode, the hymn, the monody—Milton was already a master of form. But the large scale of this work presented a new challenge based on dramatic instead of purely formal exigencies. The sequence of scenes and tableaus is well planned and well fitted together. It is in the places where thinking is required that there are signs of struggle. For example, the lines concerning the pagan western paradise of the Hesperides were much rewritten, and were transposed from the prologue to the epilogue, with considerable adjustment in both places, but with the purpose of taming the extravagance of the prologue so it would work with what follows.[5] Indeed, in its final form the prologue is conventional in thought and purely dramatic in purpose, like the prologue before an ancient play, spoken by a god (the *Bacchae* comes to mind). It is beautifully organized into four parts, each well defined, and each beginning with the mention of an Olympian god: "Before the starry threshold of Jove's court" (line 1); "But to my task. Neptune" (line 18); "Bacchus, that first

from out the purple grape" (line 46); and "Therefore, when any favored of high Jove" (line 78). The conclusions to each of these parts are
definitive, too: "I would not soil these pure ambrosial weeds / With the
rank vapors of this sin-worn mold" (lines 16–17); "And listen why, for
I will tell ye now / What never yet was heard in tale or song / From
old or modern bard in hall, or bower" (lines 43–45); "And all their
friends and native home forget / To roll with pleasure in a sensual sty"
(lines 76–77); and "But I hear the tread / Of hateful steps; I must be
viewless now" (lines 91–92). The somewhat formulaic orderliness of the
structure of the prologue reflects the skillful, dramatic architectonics
of the work as a whole.

In adjusting to the larger scale of this work, therefore, dramatic structure presented no problem, even as the poet strained the form by far
exceeding the length of any other masque known to us today. But Milton
was less certain than he ever had been in his earlier, more religious poems
what his real concerns were—transcendent or earthly—and where he
was going creatively. What was he doing as a poet, and why? What kind
of work must poetry do in the world? What worldly work is Milton's
poetic talent worthy of? He didn't quite know. He was finding out. These
problems are not structural but conceptual, involving a new engagement with thinking originally in verse.

A natural early reaction to the discovery of such problems—
collectively, the problem of thinking—is the low-level panic that accompanies the loss of direction:

> What might this be? A thousand fantasies
> Begin to throng into my memory
> Of calling shapes and beckoning shadows dire
> And airy tongues that syllable men's names
> On sands and shores and desert wildernesses.
>
> (A Masque Presented at Ludlow Castle, 1634,
> *lines 205–9)*

Understandably, Milton tries to write himself out of trouble, to be brilliant when something deeper—he hardly knew what—than his habitual
Christian transcendentalism was required. The brilliance of the writing
was a way of covering up the uncertainty while pressing onward and,
as he hoped, of blindly hitting upon stability at last. An example, one
among many, is the breathless logorrhea of the Elder Brother's discourse

on chastity and vice, concluding with the vision of damp souls in churchyards:

> Such are those thick and gloomy shadows damp
> Oft seen in charnel vaults and sepulchers
> Ling'ring and sitting by a new-made grave
> As loath to leave the body that it loved
> And linked itself by carnal sensuality
> To a degenerate and degraded state.
>
> > (A Masque Presented at Ludlow Castle, 1634,
> > *lines 470–75*)

For breathlessness, note the enjambments in the second and penultimate lines ("sepulchers / Ling'ring"; "sensuality / To" [*sensuality* having three syllables—sen-sul-tee]); the metrically awkward linking of polysyllables in the first of these examples; the clustering of consonants (especially **t**) in the second example; and the ungrammaticality of singular pronouns *(it, itself)* with a plural antecedent, *shadows*. Even the vehemence of the closing phrase, "To a de**GEN**'rate and de**GRA**ded **STATE**" sounds as if it ends with relief, expelling the last breath remaining in the lungs.

These words of the Elder Brother's are the conclusion to a very long harangue of fully sixty-one lines, in truly older-brother style. The Second Brother's response, "How charming is divine philosophy!" (line 476), is amusing because for an instant we seem to see Milton at work, tying off the hemorrhage with "philosophy." But even now he is unable to move on. For the Second Brother, true to character in second brothers, catches the contagion of prolixity from the first. It's his turn to speak now, and he would have gone on just as long, we suspect, but for a timely interruption:

> Not harsh and crabbèd as dull fools suppose
> But musical as is Apollo's lute
> And a perpetual feast of nectared sweets
> Where no crude surfeit reigns . . .
> *ELDER BROTHER:* List, list, I hear
> Some far-off hallo break the silent air.
>
> > (A Masque Presented at Ludlow Castle, 1634,
> > *lines 477–81*)

The occasional excesses, and the moments of somewhat aimless writing, are not to be censured, however. The surprise is that they give us so much pleasure, at least on the page, which is the only place they count anymore—as Milton knew. They enrich the harmonic environment of the poem and increase its dynamic range, from sober commonplace to shrill speculation, if there can be such a thing—and the Elder Brother proves there can be. We wander with him in the dark on these paths that appear to lead nowhere; we are in danger of walking in circles; we are always worrying we are. How much easier it would be for the brothers to look evil in the face and defy it!

Before this work, as I have suggested, and also at its beginning and end, Milton appeared to have all the answers: thank God and praise Him; be good in this life, but only so you will go to Heaven in the next. It is the wholly traditional, conservative Christian view of life as a means to an end. This is not original thinking but the expression of thought that has already been done, and not by Milton. To think is to deal in uncertainties and open questions. Thinking leads into and even requires the excesses of the Elder Brother's speech, and of Comus's inventive and futile seduction. Thinking for the poet is questioning and questing, where questing is the narrative counterpart of the adventure of thought. We feel in *A Masque*, as we do not in any of Milton's poems before, that the work is unfolding for the poet as an adventure the end of which is as unknown to him as to us, until we arrive there, astonished, first at Sabrina and then at the sight of Cupid and Psyche.

This vision of Cupid and Psyche, "sweet entranced" (line 1005) in their marriage embrace, having the "free consent" (line 1007) of the gods and giving birth to twins, Youth and Joy, is the conceptual end point of the masque's thinking. In this vision pleasure is not ennobled by virtue, or excused by it—our usual puritan outlook—but rather virtue is ennobled by pleasure. This is a suitable idea for the arts, which are present in Apuleius and may be assumed to be implied here. In Apuleius's extended fairy tale, in books 4–6 of his *Metamorphoses*, the final scene with the banquet of the Olympians is clearly an allegory of the arts. With the newly immortalized Psyche between his arms, Cupid reclines in the seat of honor, the gods celebrate, the Hours scatter roses and other sweet flowers, the Graces spray balm over the assembly, while Apollo sings and plays the cithara, the Muses sing, satyrs play pipes—and Pleasure, *Voluptas*, is born (as we are told will occur in the fullness of time) from the union of erotic desire and the soul, with all the arts in attendance: "By this rite Psyche came into Cupid's hands and there was born to them in the fullness of time a daughter, whom we name 'Pleasure.'"[6] Apuleius's fable ends by subsuming sexual joy into the higher pleasures of the arts. But Milton gives us a vision of something he regards as even higher than the arts because it is what the arts are always pointing to, which is ideal life. The arts ennoble and crown a life of virtue with pleasure, which is the fulfillment of virtue.

The virtue of patience that Psyche has shown in her labors—in Apuleius, they are a parody of Heracles's labors, and Heracles is the Renaissance symbol of virtue—is now being ennobled by Pleasure. The issue of Cupid and Psyche is not the joy of eternity or Heavenly halleluiahs—"saintly shout and solemn jubilee" ("At a Solemn Music," 9)—but the earthly pleasures of youth and joy. What can it mean to say virtue is ennobled by pleasure? How, for a Christian poet, can the pleasures of this world be a *telos*?

We may not be able to answer such questions with words like *politics* and *engagement*, which take earthly bliss as a legitimate goal. Nor can we forget that in the masque's final lines Milton prudently withdraws from this vision and corrects his course, reorienting us away from the western horizon to Heaven, which is far above the stars and planets of that "sphery chime" (line 1021). He also puts virtue back in pride of place, as the power that teaches us to "climb" to Heaven, and to which Heaven, if there is need, will "stoop" with prevenient grace to lend aid.

In the two debates in *A Masque*, Milton grapples with the metaphysics and the ecology of morals. The first debate is between the two brothers and the second between Comus and the Lady. Their subjects are, respectively, whether virtue is its own defense and what is the right use of nature. From a dramatic point of view it could be said with Johnson that the first debate is too long—and, in the circumstances, absurd. The brothers have lost their sister in a dark wood and instead of thinking how to find her they think whether the cosmos is so organized that virtue in its highest form, virgin majesty, symbolized by Diana, is its own defense. In the length of these debates, in the careful marshaling of positions and in their poetic elaborations, we see Milton grappling for the first time in his English poetry (we see it sooner in the Latin poems) with fundamental moral questions.

Is it metaphysically possible for virtue ever to be defeated by evil force? Can virtue be overwhelmed by superior power? That is what the Second

Brother fears will happen to his virtuous sister, who is alone and defenseless in the forest at night and liable to be the victim "of savage hunger or of savage heat" (line 358). In a moment of startling mythological power, anticipating the epilogue—the Second Brother affirms the Lady is like the golden tree in the garden of the Hesperides, which must be guarded by a dragon:

> But beauty, like the fair Hesperian tree,
> Laden with blooming gold, had need the guard
> Of dragon watch with unenchanted eye
> To save her blossoms and defend her fruit
> From the rash hand of bold Incontinence.
> You may as well spread out the unsunned heaps
> Of miser's treasure by an outlaw's den
> And tell me it is safe as bid me hope
> Danger will wink on Opportunity
> And let a single helpless maiden pass
> Uninjured in this wild surrounding waste.
>
> (A Masque Presented at Ludlow Castle, 1634, *lines*
> *393–403)*

Opposing this view, the Elder Brother affirms his sister has her own supernal defense, a "hidden strength," chastity, which is given by Heaven but is still proper to her and creditable to her: "a hidden strength / Which if Heaven gave it may be termed her own" (lines 418–19). He too reverts to mythological example, drawn, as he tells us, from the learning of the classical world, from "the old schools of Greece" (line 439), although the example may be traced more directly to Spenser's Belphoebe, who represents the perfection of nature within the natural world. For natural idealists like the Elder Brother—he is a Platonist who sees goodness as latent in nature instead of beyond—it remains almost impossible not to believe that moments of visionary ecstasy are intuitions of moral truth. Spenser's Belphoebe is one of the great poetic thoughts of this truth. Belphoebe's virgin power is what the Elder Brother sees in his sister, and calls *chastity:*

> 'Tis chastity, my brother, chastity:
> She that has that, is clad in complete steel
> And like a quivered nymph with arrows keen

> May trace huge forests and unharbored heaths
> Infamous hills and sandy perilous wilds
> Where through the sacred rays of chastity
> No savage fierce, bandit or mountaineer
> Will dare to soil her virgin purity,
> Yea there where very desolation dwells
> By grots and caverns shagged with horrid shades
> She may pass on with unblenched majesty.
>
>   (A Masque Presented at Ludlow Castle, 1634,
>   *lines 420–30)*

Chastity can disarm evil by "sudden adoration and blank awe" (line 452), and these are just the emotions we have seen Comus express when he first discerns the Lady and hears her song. But he does not respect his own spontaneous admiration, and the awe he feels is not sustained. Instead, his awe becomes his goad, urging him on to disfigure her and make her his own. Milton's Satan will likewise be struck dumb for a moment and "stupidly good" before the majesty of Eve (*PL*, 9.465). But not for long.

The Elder Brother's confidence in the metaphysical power of chastity is not an appeal to Heaven—even if Heaven "gave it"—but to a positive magic immanent in the Lady and in nature. His image for it is that "quivered nymph" (line 422)—that is, she carries a bow, and in a quiver, arrows—who is "clad in complete steel" (line 421), her moral armor, and may pass unharmed through all the dangers of the world. The nymph represents the perfection of nature, its *telos*, which is to say everything that nature is trying to be, in order to accomplish its perfection. But it is a perfection that does not transcend nature, any more than Diana or Belphoebe do, and it is not quite a human perfection because it does not include marriage. Instead of privileging escape from the world, as the Attendant Spirit does in the prologue, the poet sets forth invulnerability as the outward sign of a quality that is immanent in the world. This is an important moment. We are seeing in this work, for the first time—and perhaps this, too, is a consequence of the poet's striving for length—an effort to define goodness as fully realizable in this world, instead of in the next. Chastity will become liberty.

When the Attendant Spirit, in the person of the shepherd Thyrsis, informs the brothers that their sister has been led away by Comus, the younger brother is confirmed in his view of the malice of nature and of his sister's helplessness:

> O night and shades,
> How are ye joined with Hell in triple knot
> Against th'unarmèd weakness of one virgin
> Alone and helpless! Is this the confidence
> You gave me, brother?

Completing the line, the Elder Brother replies,

> Yes, and keep it still;
> Lean on it safely; not a period
> Shall be unsaid for me. Against the threats
> Of malice or of sorcery or that power
> Which erring men call Chance, this I hold firm:
> Virtue may be assailed but never hurt,
> Surprized by unjust force but not enthralled,
> Yea, even that which mischief meant most harm
> Shall in the happy trial prove most glory.
>
> (A Masque Presented at Ludlow Castle, 1634,
> *lines 580–92*)

The Elder Brother says that even where most harm is done by evil, there, too, and there especially, virtue shall be vindicated and win glory in the trial. These are brave words. However, they ignore the portion of truth in the Second Brother's argument: the need for active defense. Of more interest is the Elder Brother's final assertion that evil is a pure substance that is mixed in the world with another pure substance, goodness. Evil can be separated out from good, at least in principle, and it will be separated indeed at the end of time. But before the end the process of separation can begin, and this process we may call moral struggle:

> But evil on itself shall back recoil
> And mix no more with goodness, when at last,
> Gathered like scum and settled to itself,
> It shall be in eternal restless change

> Self-fed and self-consumed. If this fail,
> The pillared firmament is rottenness
> And earth's base built on stubble. But come, let's on.
>
> > *(A Masque Presented at Ludlow Castle, 1634,*
> > *lines 593–99)*

This means that the world is not entirely abject, as the Attendant Spirit told us at the outset, and that struggle in this world will contribute to the victory of goodness—in this world. The Elder Brother will express this in militant terms, promising to drag Comus "by the curls to a foul death":

> But for that damned magician, let him be girt
> With all the grisly legïons that troop
> Under the sooty flag of Acheron,
> Harpies and Hyrdras, or all the monstrous forms
> 'Twixt Africa and Ind, I'll find him out
> And force him to restore his purchase back
> Or drag him by the curls to a foul death,
> Cursed as his life.
>
> > *(A Masque Presented at Ludlow Castle, 1634,*
> > *lines 602–9)*

The Attendant Spirit is the agent of goodness, now mixed with the world in the disguise of the shepherd Thyrsis. Thyrsis points out that the Elder Brother's courage—"I love thy courage yet, and bold emprise" (line 610)—will not be sufficient to overcome the powers of the enchanter: "He with his bare wand can unthread thy joints / And crumble all thy sinews" (lines 614–15). Militant action alone cannot save the Lady, unless it draws on a hidden power in nature. If Heaven saves the Lady, then the Elder Brother's claim about that power that is "her own," chastity, falls to the ground. That is the reason the Attendant Spirit lags behind when the brothers break in on Comus; that is also the reason the Attendant Spirit seems unable to get the Lady out of the chair. Heaven alone cannot save the Lady, nor can unaided virtue or "bold emprize." A third power is needed that is neither transcendent nor merely virtuous. There must be magic in it. Magic is what Sabrina brings and what Sabrina means.

To repeat, direct Heavenly intervention cannot save the Lady. Nor can unaided militant action by the brothers save the Lady. Moreover, despite the Elder Brother's confidence in the power of chastity, the Lady cannot save herself. She is imprisoned in the chair, though in no further danger. For Comus cannot defeat her, either. There is no reason to think Comus's resolution to "try her yet more strongly" (line 806) will succeed, any more than Satan could have taken Eve by force. Comus himself says he must "dissemble" (line 805). The *trying* that Comus refers to is a trial, a testing, not a forcing. The greater strength he refers to is peremptory command, to startle and frighten the Lady into drinking the orient liquor, because of what Comus supposes is a habit of obedience. She will not do so, of course, because she is obedient to herself. He cannot touch the freedom of her mind.

The point is a simple one, but it is always well to remember what the Lady is being saved *from*. She is not being saved from the fate of Comus's rout: being transformed into a monster. She is being saved from an impasse not unlike that in which the Son will stand in *Paradise Regained*. It is the impasse between evil and good, and it may seem to us as if the world is looking on, waiting for the result. Evil does not rule the world entirely, because virtue fights against it, with Heaven on its side. But Heaven does not rule the world or we would be puppets with no virtue of our own, "such an Adam as he is in the motions" (*YP*, 2:527). Yet virtue cannot win on its own, or Heaven would have no purpose. Goodness would collapse into relativism, with the result, as Ulysses implies in *Troilus and Cressida*, that nothing is good: "Then every thing includes itself in power" (1.3.119).

The Attendant Spirit has descended from Heaven to give aid to virtue, which is always weak against the full onslaught of evil, and especially the first onslaught. Heaven therefore "stoops" (line 1023) and gives aid—but not too much. A latent, potential power that is a pure substance, opposite to evil, must rise up out of nature and give aid to virtue. In politics, it is struggle. In poetry it is magic.

In *A Masque*, the first magic that saves is in the neglected plant *Haemony*—it is trodden on daily, but its power is always there. The second saving magic is wielded by the water nymph, Sabrina. She is always there, in the River Severn, and makes her appearance, when she has been rightly invoked, only to work her countermagic against the enchantment of the chair. Neither the plant *Haemony* nor the river goddess Sabrina belong totally to nature—they transcend it—but all the same they are latent powers of goodness in nature. It is this immanent but also transcendent power of goodness that will break the impasse.

The magic plant Thyrsis gives the brothers, *Haemony*, is named after Thessaly, *Haemonia*, where magic abounds, but it is also named after marriage. The name of the Roman god of marriage is *Haemon*, and it is a surprising name to be introduced at this moment, although marriage is a protection against the promiscuity Comus incites in his followers.[7] The Lady is mature and unmarried, a dangerous state, and the masque is probably an announcement of her readiness for marriage. It is appropriate *Haemony* protect her. Even so, we have heard nothing of marriage before and will not again until the final vision of the masque.

Haemony grows in this world but flowers in "another country"—and the "other" is at one and the same time native to this place and alien to it, present and not present. The plant is rooted here and puts forth, close to the ground, a darkish leaf with prickles on it (line 631), but it is disesteemed and trodden down by the "dull swain." In "another country," however, it bears a golden flower:

> Amongst the rest a small unsightly root,
> But of divine effect, he culled me out.
> The leaf was darkish and had prickles on it
> But in another country, as he said,
> Bore a bright golden flow'r, but not in this soil,
> Unknown, and like esteemed, and the dull swain
> Treads on it daily with his clouted shoon
> And yet more med'cinal is it than that Moly
> That Hermes once to wise Ulysses gave.
> He called it *Haemony* and gave it me
> And bad me keep it as of sovran use
> 'Gainst all enchantments, mildew blast, or damp
> Or ghastly furies' apparition.
>
> (A Masque Presented at Ludlow Castle, 1634,
> *lines 629–41)*

We note that *Haemony* is effective as a medicine against natural ills, mildews, and damps, as well as supernatural ones, enchantments and ghastly furies. It has natural and supernatural powers. So far as the latter are concerned, it has even more virtue than the prophylactic *moly* Odysseus conceals on his person when he goes to bed with Circe. As to the flower of *Haemony*, the speaker Thyrsis's literal meaning is that if you plant it here, it puts forth only the leaf with prickles, but if you plant it there, in that other country, it puts forth a bright golden flower. Even so, we have noted it has natural and supernatural powers at once, not in two respective worlds. It is rooted here and grows up to there, uniting our present world and that other country where it blooms. Like Sabrina, it smoothly slides from one place to another, without leaving the first.

The other country *Haemony* flowers in seems at first to be Heaven as the *other country* is usually glossed. On this reading the golden flower signifies the reward of virtue after death, according to the vertical Christian cosmology set forth at the beginning of the masque. But Heaven is not continuous with nature, as *Haemony* is. The best interpretation of the flowering *Haemony* is that it stands not for Heaven but for the future, when the goodness that is now merely latent in nature, as potential, will bloom in full sight. We would be taking the matter one step further than Milton does to say that the garden of the Hesperides we see in the epilogue is the bloom of *Haemony*, or that the garden of the Hesperides is the other country in which *Haemony* blooms. But in the poetic thinking of this masque both of them—the bloom and the garden—stand for the future.

That is why *Haemony* is essential to breaking the standoff between the powers of evil and good. Its virtue is not Heavenly but earthly. It represents a power for good that is latent in nature and that can be brought to the aid of virtuous agents, who cannot win alone. Through the figure of *Haemony*, the possibility of improving this present world begins to emerge.

The second debate is more dramatic than the first because one of the debaters has been bound to a chair and is understandably indignant at such treatment. It is a test of wills, and that is what every powerful drama comes down to, from *Antigone* to *Tartuffe*. There is also dramatic irony. The magician seems to have the upper hand. But we soon discern his predicament and feel his desperation, and if we miss it, the Lady points it out right away: he cannot touch the freedom of her mind (line 663). Up to this point, Comus has used force and fraud to try and make the

Lady his queen. But he has won nothing and can win nothing without gaining her consent to drink from his glass. His deceiving her and immobilizing her has only made success more unlikely, deepening his predicament. His arguments are imaginative rhetorical displays, but as with his magic, there is desperation in their very brilliance. We know the Lady knows he cannot win, and he knows it, too, because she tells him, and his magical powers tell against him. The paradoxical nature of the struggle of wills between the Lady and Comus—in his strength is his weakness—gives this debate its dramatic interest and sharpens its dramatic irony.

The debate is further enriched by the extraordinary arguments Comus musters, in which the vast resources of the natural world are placed in the service of beauty and pleasure:

> Wherefore did Nature pour her bounties forth
> With such a full and unwithdrawing hand
> Covering the earth with odors, fruits and flocks,
> Thronging the seas with spawn innumerable
> But all to please and sate the curious taste?
> And set to work millions of spinning worms
> That in their green shops weave the smooth-haired silk
> To deck her sons; and that no corner might
> Be vacant of her plenty, in her own loins
> She hutched th'all-worshipped ore and precious gems
> To store her children with.
>
> (A Masque Presented at Ludlow Castle, 1634, *lines 710–20)*

But beauty, he further insinuates, only appears to be the superior recipient of nature's profusion because it is up to beauty to serve the natural world by keeping it within bounds, and by thankfully consuming what the "All-Giver" gives. God would be insulted by a temperance that implies that He is—the phrase is especially good—"a penurious niggard of his wealth":

>   if all the world
> Should in a pet of temperance feed on pulse,
> Drink the clear stream and nothing wear but frieze

> The All-Giver would be unthanked, would be unpraised,
> Not half his riches known and yet despised,
> And we should serve Him as a grudging master,
> As a penurious niggard of his wealth
> And live like Nature's bastards, not her sons.
>
>   (A Masque Presented at Ludlow Castle, 1634, *lines 720–27*)

What is more, if beauty fails to use up nature's surcharge, nature will be "cumbered," "o'erfraught," and even—to single out another splendid phrase—"strangled with her waste fertility":

> Who would be quite surcharged with her own weight
> And strangled with her waste fertility:
> The earth cumbered and the winged air darked with
>   plumes;
> The herds would over-multitude their lords;
> The sea o'erfraught would swell and th'unsought
>   diamonds
> Would so emblaze the forehead of the deep
> And so bestud with stars that they below
> Would grow inured to light and come at last
> To gaze upon the sun with shameless brows.
> List, Lady, be not coy.
>
>   (A Masque Presented at Ludlow Castle, 1634,
>   *lines 728–37)*

The right use of nature's bounty, says Comus, is frenetic consumption, for two reasons: gratitude and ecology. The Lady has an answer to each of these reasons. Frenetic consumption leads to the opposite of gratitude. It leads to blasphemy, and is itself a kind of blasphemy, since nature—here, we have the Protestant ethic in a nutshell—"means her provision only to the good" (line 765). Of still more interest is the psychological insight that being given plenty breeds ingratitude and blasphemy, whereas being given little does not. This seeming paradox is physically expressed by the contradiction, as it were, of the gullet being crammed downward with food as it explodes upward with blasphemies:

> for swinish gluttony
> N'er looks to Heav'n amidst his gorgeous feast
> But with besotted base ingratitude
> Crams and blasphemes his feeder.
>   (A Masque Presented at Ludlow Castle, 1634,
>   *lines 776–79)*

To Comus's other argument, the ecological one—that exploiting nature's gifts as fast as we can is a kind of husbandry and is good for nature—the Lady points to the social consequences of such a view. Rapid exploitation of nature does not result in more for everyone: it creates haves and have-nots, the former pining with want and the latter overwhelmed with heaps of "vast excess":

> If every just man that now pines with want
> Had but a moderate and beseeming share
> Of that which lewdly-pampered luxury
> Now heaps upon some few with vast excess
> Nature's full blessings would be well-dispensed
> In unsuperfluous, even proportion
> And she no whit encumbered with her store.
> And *then* the Giver would be better thanked,
> His praise due paid.
>   (A Masque Presented at Ludlow Castle, 1634,
>   *lines 768–76)*

The Lady affirms that the right use of nature—and the best way of thanking God—is the proper and fair distribution of her gifts, "in unsuperfluous, even proportion." She also suggests something important about pleasure that Milton continued to promote and to practice all his life: that the secret of pleasure is in the practice of restraint. One enjoys more by taking less, and allowing that less to rise above the senses and stimulate the heart and the mind—and even the soul.

Beneath these arguments on the right use of nature's gifts, and on the right way of thanking God for them, is another argument about autonomy and power, as we should expect in a situation where one character wants to enslave the other and the other intends to remain free.

Nothing is at stake dramatically in the arguments about the right use of nature; much is at stake in this, the real argument, which remains largely subterranean. Comus says that indulgence in pleasure will give the Lady autonomy, which her virginity is presently a bar to: "be not cozened / With that same vaunted name 'virginity'" (lines 737–38). In a manner that strikingly resembles the arguments Satan will address to the Son in *Paradise Regained,* three decades later, Comus subjects the Lady's autonomy to the contingencies of economics, one of which is time—"Beauty is Nature's coin, must not be hoarded" (line 739); "If you let slip time, like a neglected rose, / It [beauty] withers on the stalk with languished head" (lines 743–44). These of course are arguments that seek to have the Lady compromise her autonomy out of the very fear of losing her autonomy.

But Comus's real meaning, which may be partly concealed even from himself, is that beauty is the prize of whomever has the power to take it, as is suggested by the passive voice of "must be shown": "Beauty is Nature's brag and must be shown / In courts, at feasts, and high solemnities / Where most may wonder at the workmanship" (lines 745–47).

Opposed to this view is that beauty is self-knowing and autonomous. The name for this self-knowing, autonomous beauty is *chastity,* which governs the world but does not exploit it. Its key terms of defense are *governance* and *wisdom,* "a well-governed and wise appetite" (line 705). From Comus's point of view, beauty is material for use by a superior force, and this superior force must exploit nature and beauty as much as possible to keep them from self-knowledge and self-rule, or autonomy, and to keep down insurgency: "The herds would overmultitude their lords" (line 730). The trick in Comus's temptation is his suggesting that the power to use beauty will be the Lady's as she converts her own beauty to others' pleasure and use. Comus tries to convince her she will be the subject of beauty, the one who puts beauty to use: "Why should you be so cruel to your self / And to those dainty limbs which nature lent / For gentle usage and soft delicacy?" (lines 679–81). But in truth she is to be used by another, perhaps not very gently, one who intends between sessions to make her his drugged and ornamental queen. The debate would be of little interest in itself if there were not at stake in it two opposing views of how one should be in the world: self-possessed or exploitative.

In its own way, the debate is as interesting as that between Mutabilitie and Jove, in the incomplete seventh book of Spenser's *Faerie Queene*.
There, we have a contest between Mutabilitie's legitimacy and Jove's
power, although legitimacy asserts its rights using power and power asserts its rights by claiming legitimacy. In Spenser's allegory, the issue
can be decided by an intellectual judgment delivered from above, by
the Goddess of Nature, although this judgment has force behind it:
Mutabilitie is "put downe and whist [silenced]" (7.7.59).

In this work, however, because it is dramatic, the issue must be decided by an exertion of force, when the brothers drive off Comus with
his rout and break his glass. The Lady herself threatens to use force, as
we shall see, but this in no way undermines her representing opposition to the will to power. There is a difference between the will to power
for its own sake and the use of power to safeguard what the will to
power would destroy.

So important is this distinction that Milton made a large addition of
fully twenty-seven lines, in which the "dumb things" in nature and the
"brute Earth" herself (lines 796–97) stand ready to intervene, the former
to sympathize with the Lady's pleading the pure cause of "the sage /
And serious doctrine of virginity" (lines 786–87), the latter to "lend her
nerves and shake" (line 797). (The theory that the poet is distinguishing
systematically between *chastity* and *virginity* seems to me illusory.)

Milton made this addition after there was any thought of the work's
ever again being performed. Absent from the Trinity and Bridgewater
manuscripts, the passage in question appears for the first time in Lawes's
published text of 1637. The twenty-seven lines are an extension of the
Lady's last words in the performance, with their splendid vehemence:
"Crams and blasphemes his feeder" (line 779). Immediately following
this, the new addition begins with her words, "Shall I go on / Or have
I said enough?" (lines 779–80), a question the poet asked himself ("Shall
I make her go on?") and answered in the affirmative. In the performance
version, the line beginning "Crams and blasphemes his feeder" is completed with Comus's answer: "Come, no more" (line 806), which is more
suitable, dramatically. He is putting a stop to her abuse. Yet there is
something wonderful in the taunting aggression of the question she puts
to him, "Shall I go on?" Have you had enough thrashing yet?

She thinks he has not. He is irredeemably vile. Because of that, nothing
she can say could convince him; even if she could convince him, so that

he actually agreed with her, he would be unworthy of the favor of being convinced. Even so, should she deign to teach him of the sublime mystery and "sage and serious doctrine" of virginity, the earth herself would join her in vehement protest, and shake:

> Thou art not fit to hear thyself convinced.
> Yet should I try, the uncontrollèd worth
> Of this pure cause would kindle my rapt spirits
> To such a flame of sacred vehemence
> That dumb things would be moved to sympathize
> And the brute Earth would lend her nerves and shake
> Till all thy magic structures reared so high
> Were shattered into heaps o'er thy false head.
> COMUS: She fables not, I feel that I do fear
> Her words set off by some superior power.
>
> (A Masque Presented at Ludlow Castle, 1634, *lines*
> *792–801)*

Speaking to himself, Comus understands the threat is real, "She fables not," and in verses that look forward to *Paradise Lost*, he feels the chains of Erebus and Hell:

> And though not mortal, yet a cold shuddering dew
> Dips me all o'er as when the wrath of Jove
> Speaks thunder and the chairs of Erebus
> To some of Saturn's crew. I must dissemble
> And try her yet more strongly. Come, no more,
> This is mere moral babble, and direct
> Against the canon law of our foundation;
> I must not suffer this.
>
> (A Masque Presented at Ludlow Castle, 1634,
> *lines 802–9)*

At "Come, no more," the added passage ends and we resume what was there in the original version. But what we see just before this, in a passage written as many as three years after the original, is a new and more aggressive appreciation of divine wrath as morally active in the world. No longer is the world a prison that virtue helps us escape; the world has become a place in which and for which virtue fights against evil, and truth fights against error.

The Attendant Spirit says the world is altogether bad, because it is sinful. Comus says the world is altogether good, because it is pleasurable: "welcome joy and feast, / Midnight shout and revelry, / Tipsy dance and jollity" (lines 102–4). The Lady says that although the world is a free field of action for wickedness, giving up on this world and aspiring only to Heaven is not permissible. Because we have a duty to improve the world while we are here, the world must have potential for good in it, and must be made such that it will give what Milton in *Paradise Lost* will call "respiration to the just / And vengeance to the wicked" (12.540–41).

But that is to go further than Milton's thinking goes in this work, even if this work tends in that direction. His subject is the redemption and elevation of pleasure, which leads us to the uncomfortable suspicion there may be something good in what Comus says. With Milton, it is with arguments as it is with gifts: it depends on who is doing the giving or the arguing, not (altogether) on what is being given or argued.[8] Perhaps the thought closest to Milton's heart which is expressed in this work—or found in this work—is the Lady's response to Comus's "treasonous offer": "none / But such as are good men can give good things" (lines 702–3). The question is no longer whether pleasure in itself can be redeemed, as a thing purely good or evil. Instead, the question looks beyond pleasure to what we may call its relations of exchange: who gives pleasure to whom, why, and for what in return? With this development we reach Milton's major theme, which is temptation.

5

On "Lycidas" as Primitive Art

Since the nineteenth century, when Mark Pattison, suiting the image to the thing, called this stream-filled poem "the high-water mark of English Poesy," Milton's "Lycidas" has had more votes than any other as the greatest short poem in English—or, at 193 lines, the greatest shorter poem in English. The time is past when one could say, as John Ruskin did of this poem, that "no English words are more familiar to us." But at least among Miltonists, and perhaps a few others, the high estimation of "Lycidas" survives to this day. Although Barbara Lewalski begins her analysis with more moderate language than Pattison's, she goes on to call "Lycidas" "a stunning fusion of intense feeling and consummate art," and she affirms that no previous or subsequent funeral poem "has the scope, dimension, poignancy and power of 'Lycidas.' "[1]

Each word of this statement bears reflecting on—*scope, dimension, poignancy,* and *power:* "Lycidas" is far wider ranging in scope—in cultural as well as in geographical scope—than any other funeral poem, or, indeed, than any other poem of its length. Its sources lead us back to, and then take us forward from the Mediterranean world of Greco-Roman antiquity—the sea-lanes on which Theocritus traveled between Syracuse, Alexandria, and Cos; the mountains of Arcadia and Sicily; and, under the Alps, the broad valley of the Po through which Virgil's Mincius flows into the Adriatic (it now flows into the Po itself). We pass on to Renaissance Florence, Urbino, and Naples, and then to the political and religious landscape of sixteenth- and seventeenth-century Protestant England. But we have scarcely arrived there when we are whirled unexpectedly outward to the Celtic fringe of the British archipelago, with its druidical rites and wizard streams, a culture of immemorial antiquity faintly glimpsed through North Atlantic fogs.

Following these song lines from the Tyrrhenian to the North Sea, "Lycidas" is the poem of Europe, not only in space but in time.[2] It enfolds several temporal dimensions, each one representing a strand of thought in the European mind: natural time and work time, with the alternating rhythm of day and night, of sun and star; tenacious, persisting demonic time, the time of cursed ships, gaping shears, and grimly predatory wolves; retrospective, or memorial, time, belonging to rites of burial and to ceremonies of remembrance, but also to art, the muses being daughters of Memory, that is, of funeral; historical, or progressive, time, which is linked with institutions such as the church and the university, well or badly run; prehistoric or magical time, with its haunted mountains, sacred groves, desert caves, and prescient streams; prophetic and apocalyptic time, which is captured from the Bible and replayed through the liturgical year; and underlying these times, bearing them up like a rope bridge slung over an abyss, performative time: time as it is experienced in the interior of song. Because the performance of "Lycidas" staggers and halts and must be started up again several times, we seem to look through the ropes of the bridge into the abyss underneath us.

This cubist juxtaposition of asynchronous time frames chiefly accounts for the difficulty of "Lycidas": we seem to see too many surfaces at once. There is too much information for any single point of view to prevail and arrange the others in due proportion with one another. Who is singing and to whom, and by what or by whom is the song inspired? Are we present at a song, at a funeral, a series of hallucinations, a vision, or a coroner's inquest? Who or what exactly are we mourning under the name "Lycidas," and how many of them are there? Is he a shepherd, a divinity student, the author John Milton, "man in his creative capacity, as Christian humanist poet-priest," as David Daiches said, or is he in his archetype the dying god Adonis, though Adonis isn't mentioned in the poem? Is he all of us or only the creative among us, or is he no one, is he anonymous, or nearly so, a collocation of voices, a convergence of streams? What other mourning poem ends by so fragmenting its object as to place it—that is, *him*, though he is both a thing and a person, a corpse and a soul—in three different locations representing three different time frames: in the sea, in Heaven, on the shore; in the present, in the future, and in the dreamtime of a mythic past?

"Lycidas" moves us to pity and fear, emotions that are highly aestheticised in the poem and yet only more intense for this beauty. There is the pathos of the memory of songs shared under the opening eyelids of the morn and under the fresh dews of night; there is the pathos of the stilled leaves of the hazel copses and of the abject weeping willows. There is gorgeous pathos in the cascade of flowers strewn on the bier from the hands of those vestigially personified valleys, and there is thrilling poignancy in the vision of the dolphins on the smooth hyaline, making an arch with their backs and bearing a body to land. As to the terror in "Lycidas," it grows in intensity as the poem goes forward, from the disturbing image of the taint-worm in the herds, putting us in mind of the worms that will devour us from within, to the shock of a bloody face streaming past underwater—and then the menace of the Fury's fatal shears. The terror returns with the nightmare vision of a ship rigged with curses and "built in th'eclipse"; it returns again at the sight of human bones cast against a rocky shore by "sounding"—that is, booming—seas.[3] (The "two-handed engine at the door" perplexes more than frightens, unless you happen to be a Laudian bishop, though that "grim wolf" is alarming enough.)

As to the sublimity of "Lycidas," it overwhelms our capacity to imagine. This power builds to a climax in the evocation of oceanic magnitude in two directions, the vertical and the horizontal. These are the depth of the ocean—extending from storm-tossed surface to monstrous deep—and the expanse of the ocean. Yet we see only a portion of that expanse—a *frith*, as Milton will say of a portion of chaos—which stretches from the distant coast of northwest Spain to the near-arctic Hebrides islands. The vision of Heaven that follows is also sublime, but familiar, too, for this Heaven is at once transcendentally other and the same, opening for Lycidas on "other groves and other streams" not unlike the ones he has left. He is enraptured by a music no shepherd of Arcady ever made or heard, the song from the fourteenth chapter of Revelation, "a voice from Heaven, as the voice of many waters" (14:2). Yet at the end of "Lycidas" (for sublimity must round on its sources—if possible, unexpectedly—and reduce them to one), the source of this vision appears before our eyes for the first time: an "uncouth swain" in a blue cloak, singing in a burring, rustic dialect of Greek with "eager thought," that is, with unrefined but powerful inspiration. He sings all day and doesn't rise until evening, no doubt twitching himself as well as his cloak, intending to depart somewhere tomorrow. That qualification—"tomorrow"—is important for the closure of "Lycidas." In an earthly anticipation of those "other groves and other streams," the singer rises at evening intending to depart on the morrow for fresh woods and pastures new and, we may suppose, other streams. What will he do until then? Sleep, or listen to the owls.

It is not surprising that for these reasons—its vast scope, its temporal complexity, its poignancy and power, and, to add another factor to its magic, its irregular but virtuosic technique, blending Greek, Italian, and English models but soaring free of them all—"Lycidas" was long regarded as the work against which anyone seeking to make a mark on the criticism of English poetry must come to terms, impossible as it is to do so in terms that remain stable.[4] The poem gives us too much information for one explanation to encompass them all, and it delivers this information through too many impossible-to-coordinate dimensions of time.

Suddenly, however, and not long after what one critic called, with only some exaggeration, "an explosion of scholarship,"[5] the obsession with "Lycidas" stopped. Critical attention migrated to the Romantics, leaving Milton's great elegy abandoned, like a wreck on the shore. Nowadays, it is not much loved, however much it is coldly admired. Contemporary poets I have spoken to regard "Lycidas" with distaste as artificial, confused, and confusing, and above all as too Christian. Fashionable theory might be rushed to the scene of the emergency. There is a case to be made for the heterological energies surging in this polyglot text, for the place of "Lycidas" in mobility studies and transhumance and for cultural studies' analysis of the uses of performance and role-playing for self-identification in elite groups. Students at Cambridge in Milton's day spoke Latin to one another (in keeping with university rules) while pretending, at least in this poem, to be Arcadian shepherds—"and old Damoetus loved to hear our song" (line 36). This was while real shepherds to the north and northwest, in Cumberland, Yorkshire, and the borders, leading very different lives, were a pillar of England's material wealth, paying for those Cambridge festivities.

Say what we will of its antiquated style, the concerns of this poem are hardly irrelevant today. In grim illustration of the phrase *ubique nau-fragium est*, "shipwreck is everywhere" (the inscription to *Justa Eduardo King*), people still drown in the Mediterranean Sea, crossing from Africa to Europe. Doubtless they are mourned by someone in some-place, perhaps in the Sudan, and the mourners wonder where they are floating. Shepherds on the "high lawns" (line 25) of rugged Albania and the Caucasus are armed with Kalashnikovs instead of flintlock weapons, as in Byron's day, or Lermontov's and Tolstoy's ("The Wild Albanian kirtled to his knee, / With shawl-girt head and ornamental gun").[6] In a May-time snow flurry, I halted in the road before a shepherd and his dog, high in the mountains of Sicily's central ridge in sight of Mount Etna. The sheep were crossing the road in the whirling snow, swarming around their guide as his ear was bent to his cell phone. At the sight, I heard the phrase "to shepherd's ear."

We are speaking of marginal but not unsuccessful people; like the Gypsies or Roma, these pastoralists whom we know from Virgil's first eclogue are subject to continual displacement. They are therefore tough and resourceful, not entirely law-abiding survivors. Bedouin goatherds with Land Rovers and camels bought with drug profits (especially that most intoxicating of drugs, information) still play a curiously ambiguous role in the Middle East, in the Sinai, and in the Judean desert, crossing regularly and secretly between Israel and the West Bank. The United States and its allies are withdrawing from a war with and among a shep-herding and goat-herding people in the highest mountain region in the world. The conflict is over what it always has been for mountain people: guns, drugs, control, and information. You can read about it in yesterday's news, or in Churchill's classic account from the 1880s, *The Malakand Field Force*, a British expedition into many of the same valleys. Death, with its bedeviling counterpart, war, is always present to these people, and so is mourning and, with mourning, song. In the mountains of the Caucasus and in the Carpathians, in Crete and in Sicily, songs commemorating bandit shepherds go back centuries and in some cases to antiquity.

"Lycidas" may still appear, as it has appeared in the past, to open ques-tions while unfolding along its uncertain, interrupted, wandering, and passionate course. Or at least "Lycidas" appears to be finding new ways of asking the old question about death: what is life worth, since we die? How should we live our lives, since we die? What compensation or "meed" is attainable in life, since we die? Does the natural world care for us—and especially for poets, the creators of art—more than it does for anything else living in the natural world, since we die? Finally, a question peculiar to "Lycidas" for the intensity with which it is asked, what significance, treatment, and care should be given to the dead human body, and what is the point, since we all die? The Christian apotheosis of "Lycidas" appears to silence these questions at once. The classicism of the poem appears to translate serious questions into an elaborate, competitive game.

The last question I mentioned—why should we care for the dead human body?—is shockingly introduced with the first of the poem's unexpected images: "He must not float upon his wat'ry bier / Unwept, and welter to the parching wind / Without the meed of some melodious tear" (lines 13–14). "*Wat'ry bier*"? Exact information about saltwater drowning is deployed in this startling composite image, which yokes a funeral bier—an image that elevates and dignifies the body, stabilizing it for contemplation—to the restless violence of the sea, rolling the body over wave crests and down into troughs. Only after it has been submerged some days, having absorbed seawater and become bloated with gases from decomposition, does the drowned body become buoyant enough to float on the surface, *weltering* or rolling in the waves (OE *weltan*, "to roll"). The corpse is then exposed to the wind and sun, which exposure dries and hardens the skin to a black shell with suppurating exudations through the cracks. It is in this condition that drowned bodies sometimes come ashore in the surf, as people who live near the sea know, and as Synge's *Riders to the Sea*, Joyce's *Ulysses*, and Edward Bond's *The Sea* instance. Walking near Sandymount Strand, Stephen Dedalus meditates on the ineluctable modality of the visible, recalling "Lycidas" as he does so: "a corpse rising saltwhite from the undertow, bobbing landward, a pace a pace a porpoise. There he is. Hook it quick. Sunk though he be beneath the watery floor. We have him. Easy now. Bag of corpsegas sopping in foul brine . . . Hauled stark over the gunwale he breathes upward the stench of his green grave, his leprous nosehole snoring to the sun."[7]

In *Riders to the Sea*, as in "Lycidas," there is quite a lot of speculation—taking into account tides, current, and winds—where a body is floating now and where it, or rather "he," will come ashore. Milton's shocking image of the body "welter[ing] to the parching wind" as it drifts toward shore is joined by violence—so Johnson describes the technique of metaphysical poetry—to what is heterogeneous to it: the image of a body on a funeral bier, beside which, instead of howling winds, mourners eulogize the departed and weep for their loss.

The eulogizers at the bier will appear later in this poem, among them (for we are to suppose there are more), the River Cam and "the pilot of the Galilean lake" (line 109), and so will the flowers to strew that "laureate hearse" (line 151): the "rathe primrose," the "tufted crowtoe," the "white pink," the "pansy freaked with jet," the "glowing violet," the "musk-rose," the "well-attired woodbine," cowslips, amaranths, daffodils—this last a distortion of Greek *asphodelos*, common in the southern Mediterranean, that is, in ancient Magna Graecia, especially Apulia, and, as Theocritus tells us, or rather, as his goatherd Lycidas tells us, put into mattresses to aid sleeping (lines 142–46). A common flower whose bulbs afforded food to the poor, seasoned with mallows, asphodel is also, according to Homer, the flower that grows in meadows near the Elysian fields, which are reserved for heroes.[8]

I cannot read this passage without thinking of Neanderthal burial sites where the dead have been interred in caves with, it is alleged, flowers strewn over them. I like to think they're asphodels. The placing of flowers on the dead human body is one of the first recognizably human acts, and it is recognizable as human because it is futile—like art. We now know animals—at least the higher mammals—are not merely survival machines. Animals engage to some extent in social play and mourning. But if knowledge of death is the beginning of culture, strewing the dead with flowers is the sign of that knowledge and of that beginning, and the strewing is futile, from the point of view of survival. To beautify the dead body, not the living one, is the purest statement of our defiance of the inevitable truth of our death. It is a lost cause from the outset, and yet for some reason worth it. So, too, is seeing the ruffled waves of the ocean as a funeral bier. We try to force the image to work in our minds, calming the waters a little and hushing the winds. But we fail, and try once again, until we read on, only to find more disturbances like this one. It comes upon us that the aesthetic force of the poem—may we call it its pleasure?—is in these disturbances and the effort they demand, but not for any resolution on the other side of them, though the poem pretends to give one at last. It is most likely this rhythm of trying and failing that is behind the reluctance of the muses to sing, their "denial vain and coy excuse" (line 18). Culture is hard work for little or no gain, and the muses need coaxing.

We know that however much care we show for the body, however much we dignify and beautify the body, it will in the end lie in the grave—or roll in the sea—and undergo hideous transformation until the bones are bare. Skeletization, as it is called in the religious world of shamanism, is a condition to be wished for—as we see in the Mexican Day of the Dead—because it represents the end of decay. The Greek word from which we take *skeleton* indicates dryness, or a drying, the removal of the moisture of life that at once frees the moist *psyche* from attachment to the body and confers on the body the power of endurance.[9] We cannot look at a body on a funeral bier, or in a funeral home, washed and dressed, embalmed, adorned or surrounded with flowers, without there floating before the eye of mind, juxtaposed to the scene before us, the faintest transparency of what this body will become. We interpose decay. The poet has a reason to afford us the briefest image of another poet's disarticulated bones ("where'er thy bones are hurled," line 155): there is grim comfort in the thought that they are at last bare.

The forced compositeness of the "watery bier" gives two images pressed unnaturally together and may be psychologically interpreted as the speaker's inability to accept the un-Arcadian circumstances of the shepherd's death. Lycidas should be on a bier in the Arcadia of "high lawns" (line 25) and soaring peaks, and shepherds should be standing by that bier, weeping and singing. He should not be floating on the sea. It hurts to think that whatever care and respect we may show a dead body, all care in the end fails. At least in the end that is nature, which is the only end we know. Perhaps then every form of bodily care, caring for the sick, for example, and for the poor, is futile. Still, the question remains: why do we care for dead bodies, knowing what we do? What point can there be in "interposing" ("For so to interpose a little ease / Let our frail thoughts dally with false surmise," lines 152–53) care and respect for the dead human body? That is the question of "Lycidas," and the key to it is in the word *human*. But the key proves as elusive as that lost, drowned poet's body, which the singer imagines being "hurled" to uncertain destinations, as the "whether . . . whether" construction suggests, its answer depending on conditions of *weather*. The singer cannot tell if the body has been swept far to the north, to the "stormy Hebrides," or southward to Saint Michael's Mount and the great rocks of the Cornish coast, or still farther south, out into the open sea, toward the distant shores of Spain and France, "Namancos and Bayona's hold" (lines 156 and 192). As with this elusively floating body, so too with the question of the human in "Lycidas": it is swept away and lost.

I suggested that the wealth of unhappy questioning in "Lycidas" is dismissed at its peroration, its Christian *consolatio*, which begins with the words "Weep no more." But perhaps this too is an unsuccessful effort, like the "wat'ry bier" (line 12), such that the early image teaches us how to read the consolation as a trying, an effort, an *essai*. In any event, its opening words, "Weep no more," give good advice: weeping has to have a period. "*Ecquis erit modus*?" "Will there be any end to this?" asks Pan, the god of Arcady, in Virgil's *Eclogues* (10.28). His appearance in a train of other visitors to Gallus, who for love of Lycoris is lying in his death-agony, prefigures those of Camus and Saint Peter in "Lycidas": "*Pan deus Arcadiae venit*" (10.26). The god is impatient with his shepherds' incessant weeping for Gallus. The god Love, *Amor*, cares nothing for such appeals to mercy. Far from being moved to mercy, *Amor* is never sated with tears, no more than grass is sated with streams, or bees with clover, or goats with leaves. Tears are nourishment to *Amor*. The only cure is to draw a line or *modus* and make an arbitrary end, to "weep no more." The same is true for mourning as for love. It is Virgil's peculiar genius in this poem to make the lamentation for Gallus in his love-agony indistinguishable from a funeral elegy, but with the advantage that we get to hear from Gallus, the cause of all this lamentation, who wishes he were a shepherd, not a soldier, supposing that as a shepherd he'd have had a truer love. Or, if he should die of love anyway, he would wish to be commemorated in Arcadian songs, for only the Arcadians are expert in song: "*soli cantare periti / Arcades*" (10.32–33). How softly his bones would rest in the grave if in the future the Arcadian shepherds' pipes would tell his loves: "*o mihi tum quam molliter ossa quiescant, / vestra meos olim si fistula dicat amores*" (10.33–34).

The hard but necessary truth spoken by Pan and implied at the turning point of "Lycidas"—you have to move on—is complicated by the statement in the line following: "Lycidas . . . is *not* dead" (line 166). Yes, he is, we object. If the poem is not to be merely paradoxical—"Lycidas is dead . . . Lycidas is not dead"—then there has to be a different sense in which the second statement is true. There has to be a different meaning of the predicate *dead*, splitting its subject into two parts, one part physically dead, the other part spiritually alive. Or, as it happens, *dead* but resurrected from death later, at the end of time: dead now, alive later. The strain of this futile strewing of hope is betrayed—it almost seems to me, deliberately so—by the most facile of analogies. As the sun (for that is what is meant by "the day-star," line 168) sinks in the western ocean but rises again in the east, so Lycidas's body has sunk "beneath the wat'ry floor" (line 167) but has risen again in another place:

> So sinks the day-star in the ocean bed
> But yet anon repairs his drooping head
> And tricks his beams and with new-spangled ore
> Flames in the forehead of the morning sky,
> So Lycidas sunk low, but mounted high.
>
> *("Lycidas," lines 168–72)*

We might suppose the analogy is justified, however, as an imperfect premonition of the truth in the line immediately following. It is the first openly Christian statement after the turn to consolation that occurs with the words "weep no more": "Through the dear might of him that walked the waves" (line 173).

What part of Lycidas rose up by the might of him that walked the waves, his soul or his body? And when exactly did he rise? A great question of Christianity is what happens to the souls of those who have "fallen asleep" until the Last Judgment, when the bodily resurrection of the dead transpires in an instant, in the twinkling of an eye (1 Corinthians 15:6 and 51). Do the souls in the mean time go to purgatory, which Protestants must condemn as an invention of what Claudio in *Measure for Measure* calls "lawless and incertain thought"?[10] Do they rest in the bosom of Abraham, whatever that means? That question is avoided by the vision of an apocalyptic Heaven, the Heaven of the book of Revelation, to which the dead shepherd is raised. Lycidas joins the elite troupe of those who died virgins and are married to the Lamb, singing the "un-expressive," that is, the inexpressibly beautiful "nuptial song":

> There entertain him all the saints above
> In solemn troops and sweet societies
> That sing and singing in their glory move
> And wipe the tears forever from his eyes.
>
> *("Lycidas," lines 178–81)*

The presence of the "saints" (that is, of all who are admitted to Heaven at the Last Judgment), of the mystic nuptial song of the Lamb, of our glorified bodies, mentioned by Saint Paul (for that is the meaning of "singing in their *glory*"), and of the wiping of tears from the eyes, make it clear that this is the Heaven at the end of history, not any Heaven that might be thought to exist now, concurrently with the time of our mourning.[11] Such Heavens are more commonly the object of Roman Catholic, Counter-Reformation painting, in which the martyred saint or hero is welcomed into Heaven at the moment of being martyred or buried on earth. For the Roman Catholic saint, Heaven is always there, now, just above: the saint's soul enters Heaven immediately on being released from the body. In the Protestant point of view, by contrast, Heaven is reserved until after the end of time, when the heavenly Jerusalem descends. Of course, eternity can't come after or before any stretch of time. Therefore, eternity and the end of time are not quite the same thing, but the end of time is for us the only gateway to eternity. This means that the vision of Lycidas in Heaven is a prophecy of the future, not a vision of what has happened already to Lycidas's body, which we must understand as still being lost in the sea, despite the past tense: "So Lycidas sunk low, but mounted high" (line 172).

Milton has left us with a religious question: if the dead are not raised until the end of time, in that general resurrection Paul describes in the great fifteenth chapter of 1 Corinthians, what happens to the soul immediately after death? From a cerebral standpoint, this is an interesting question to ponder. But it was a question of visceral urgency to Milton's audience, especially to the grieving family of the poet's "learned friend," Edward King (headnote to "Lycidas," added in 1645). We can hear his mother's anguished questions: Where is he? Where is my son now? Where does my Christian faith tell me my son is, since nobody around me knows? Milton shows considerable artistic courage in not providing one of the anodyne solutions to be found in the elegies preceding "Lycidas" in the obsequies for Edward King, many of them ludicrous. But for us the hard question—how do we use art to make life worth it, since we die?—comes earlier in the poem. The theological question, what happens to the soul after death but before the Last Judgment, feels like an avoidance of the more urgent one: How may art may justify life in the face of death?

So much for the problem of the Christianity of "Lycidas," which, as we have seen, does not afford an easy answer to the old questions of death and life. It circumvents the old questions with what seems to us a theological technicality. But let us return now to the poem's allusive, learned style, its baroque classicism. Contemporary students feel much the same way as do contemporary poets about "Lycidas," with the exception of those who have studied themselves into a liking for such encrypted strings as "O fountain Arethuse and thou honored flood / Smooth-sliding Mincius crowned with vocal reeds," or "meed of some melodious tear," in which *meed* is already an antiquated word and *melodious tear* is an affected way of saying "poetical song," which is also affected. We do not think of poetry as song, although it might be better for us if we did. Nor do we imagine contemporary poetry being half-spoken or sung to a stringed instrument such as the singer of "Lycidas" is shown playing at the end. But when the literary history of our time is written surely a large place in the story will be occupied by artists who plugged in electric guitars. In an age of radio and amplified sound that has turned solitude and solitary reflection into subversive activities—even humanities professors are urged to collaborate, to speak on panels and think in sound bites—we persist in regarding poetry as primarily textual, assuming the orality of verse to be, like shepherds, a thing of the past. But there are shepherds today, and they sing, although they are unknown: "Thus sang th'uncouth swain" (line 186). Poets shouldn't sing, and they shouldn't be shepherds. And when did shepherds ever sing like this:

> Yet once more, O ye laurels, and once more
> Ye myrtles brown with ivy never sere,
> I come to pluck your berries harsh and crude
> And with forced fingers rude

> Shatter your leaves before the mellowing year.
> Bitter constraint, and sad occasion dear
> Compels me to disturb your season due,
> For Lycidas is dead, dead ere his prime,
> Young Lycidas, and hath not left his peer.
> Who would not sing for Lycidas?
>
> *("Lycidas," lines 1–10)*

Who *would* sing for Lycidas? And who is singing now? The question is compelling only because we are supposed to have heard it before, in a classical poet—*neget quis carmina Gallo?* "Who would deny a song to Gallus?" (*Eclogues*, 10.3). The first definite statement comes in the eighth line: "Lycidas is dead." The rest seems like learned nonsense with nothing real in it, although if you have harvested grapes in a bad year, or too early, you know what it means to shatter leaves and cut your hands. Even so, this harvest of laurel and myrtle berries is just one more of the learned allusions stacked up from the outset of this poem. They do transport us into another place, but that place appears to be the work-shop of learned poets' inchoate materials. The opening of "Lycidas" reads like something earlier than a first draft, the noise that starts to echo in your head and that you write down automatically but not well and so discard. These opening lines are not inspired, or are cunningly meant to seem uninspired. They read like a necessary evacuation, not an intake of breath. Learning has been marshaled, but the muses have not come.

Already in 1637, when Milton composed "Lycidas," Sicilian and Arcadian literary shepherds with their flocks and pipes had been around for almost nineteen hundred years—ever since Theocritus introduced them into poetry, or united them in poetry, and with them the name *Lycidas*, Λυκίδας—its final syllable to be pronounced in the Doric manner with a long open *a* and a pronounced final sibilant: *daawsss*. Theocritus was the first, as the scholiast Artemidorus said, to unite the Bucolic muses, "formerly scattered" around the Doric cultural fringe, into one troop (the phrase is *sporades poka*, whence our "sporadic," and is reminiscent of the Doric Sporades islands, the scattered ones). A rough equivalence forms in Milton's mind between Doric and Celtic cultures, both of them pushed out to the periphery, both retaining older, even primitive cultural forms, such as magic and divination, and the worship of rustic country gods. The term *idylls*, "little songs" *(eidullia)*, is not used by Theocritus but by his commentators and is a diminutive of heroic odes.[12] Although Theocritus's verse is in hexameters, the meter of epic—which would have been impossible two generations before him[13]—the aesthetic range of this poetry is displayed between rough and smooth and between bitter and sweet. There is the bitterness of unrequited love and the bitterness of death, corresponding inexactly with the roughness of pine trees, rocks, wolves, and thorns. There is the sweetness of running water, of flowers, herbs, honey, tree shade, and song. The last is symbolized by poets being protected by and sacred to bees which can also sting.[14] The forested, mountainous regions in which these songs are sung are overseen by rough and smooth gods in the isolated, land-locked, rustic province of Arcadia in the northeastern Peloponnesian peninsula, in Greece, in the mountainous interior of the island of Cos, and in the southeastern region of Sicily, in the Hyblaean Mountains stretching northward from Syracuse to Etna's slopes. On the one hand, there is hairy and horny Pan, and the still rougher Priapus—that bitter, mocking god with his never-satisfied erection, a rough symbol of what unrequited passion really means. On the other hand, there are the nymphs and the muses, who are as smooth as the streams they tend and as sweet as the songs they inspire.

The opening words of the first idyll of Theocritus are "something sweet" *hadu ti*, which is how the shepherd Thyrsis refers to the whispering of the breeze in the branches of a rough pine beside a smooth stream. This onomatopoeic whispering breeze is a *psithurisma* (psee-thoor-eeez-ma). Virgil recognizes this sounding of a tonic chord and in his first eclogue mentions rough pines and smooth fountains. But he does so with a difference in the famous bittersweet opening lines, juxtaposing the sting of being driven away from one's home—an exile due to forces beyond the pastoral world—and the sweetness of making music in the beech tree's shade. One shepherd is heading out on the road, homeless, displaced by the victorious Augustus's expropriation of land for his soldiers. The other is teaching the woods to reecho the name of his love, fair Amaryllis: *"formosam resonare doces Amaryllida silvas."* Virgil's pastoral world has an inside and an outside. From the inside, it looks natural, but we know a god—Augustus—has created the ease that is enjoyed there. Theocritus does not have this inside and outside. That is what makes him look less sophisticated, less literary, more authentic and primitive—which is of course the poet's sophisticated, literary aim.

In Theocritus's first idyll, Thyrsis mentions the sweetness of whispering pine and pure spring, and compares these to the sweetness of the music of the unnamed goatherd he addresses, whose singing is inferior only to Pan's. (I imagine this goatherd is Lycidas, whom we meet later.) But just as sweetly, the goatherd replies, is the music Thyrsis makes—this is the third use of the word *sweet* in seven lines—which flows forth and falls like the spring water cascading from that rock high above them: "*hadion, ô poimên, to teon melos hê to kataches / tên apo tas petras kataleibetai hypsothen hydôr*" (Theocritus 1.7–8).

Milton sees how the contrast of rough and smooth, of bitter and sweet, is essential to pastoral poetry from the beginning, and he builds it into his poem, for example, in the transition from Saint Peter's stern language to the almost saccharine floral passage (lines 113–51). Another sensuous contrast pervading the poem is between fresh flowing water and salt wave, for example, the rolling, "wat'ry bier" of line 12 and the "sacred well" of line 15. The watery contrast is plucked from Virgil's tenth eclogue, where the sweet spring, Arethusa, passes unsullied through the bitter *(amara)* salt waters of the sea (*Eclogues*, 10.4–6). The contrast of rough and smooth, of bitter and sweet, modulates into something stronger in "Lycidas," an alternation between comforting pastoral beauty and oceanic horror. It is a poem of emotional extremes, and is much less well tempered than Virgil's *Eclogues*, in which sadness is qualified by beauty and beauty by sadness. In "Lycidas," the intense moments of sweetness are associated with the repetition compulsion and with neurotic delusion, the "false surmise" that Lycidas can be properly buried and properly mourned (line 154). The moments of horror are eruptions of a lacerating truth, with salt in the wound: Lycidas has drowned in the sea and his body, bloated and torn, will not be recovered.

In consequence, the style of Milton's "Lycidas" is allied more closely to the archaic country language of Theocritus's goatherds (goatherds inhabit the wilder mountain uplands) than it is with Virgil's silver-tongued hayseeds. The rough Doric dialect of Theocritus's characters is a deliberate literary effect, one Milton immediately spotted, and which he regarded as distinct from, and perhaps superior to, the fine-spun suavity of Virgil. That first word in Theocritus, *sweet (hadu)*, with its aspirated, broad open vowel sounded far back in the mouth, is the Doric form of Attic *hêdu*. The repetition of this sound in the opening lines announces a rough, unsophisticated, countrified verse.

Theocritus's goatherd Lycidas is originally from Crete, which has higher mountains and wilder country than Cos, where we meet him, and he is a mysterious, somewhat sinister fellow. (It is no accident he turns to the left as he departs, having with a careless laugh awarded his crook of wild olive—another indication he comes from higher, more mountainous country—to Simichidas, his competitor in song—and the narrator of Theocritus 7.) Lycidas's name associates him at once with wolves *(lykos)* and perhaps with Apollo, one of whose epithets means "wolf-slayer," something Lycidas, as a goatherd in remoter regions, has probably been. With a rank and shaggy goat hide on his shoulders, an ancient shirt and heavy belt, a glinting eye and ready laugh, Theocritus' Lycidas is rougher than the pretty fellow (he is called *formosus*) of the same name in Virgil's *Eclogues* (7.67). He is certainly more modest about his own singing (cf. *Eclogues*, 9.32–34). He is ironically modest, referring to his song as a "little ditty" *(meludrion)* that he made the other day in the mountains. He awards Simichidas the victory, as we noted, with a merry, or rather a "sweet" laugh (Theocritus 7.128)—there's sweetness again—perhaps because Simichidas boasts his songs are carried by Fame *(fama)* up to Zeus's throne (Theocritus 7.91–93). The throne of Jove features in "Lycidas" (line 16), and Milton seized on the word *fama* to make it resonate at a crucial dramatic moment of his poem: "Fame is no plant that grows on moral soil . . . Of so much fame in Heav'n, expect thy meed" (lines 78–84).

For all his modesty and savage mountain roughness, Theocritus's Lycidas has high literary standards. He despises the highfalutin and prizes what is elegant and subtle. He says that even as he hates the builder who would rear his house-roof as high as the peak of Mount Oromedon—the highest mountain on Cos—so too does he hate the loud crowing cocks (the epic poet Apollonius of Rhodes is probably meant) who would contend with the Chian nightingale, by whom Lycidas means Homer (Theocritus 7.47–48).[15] The word *nightingale* is lovely in itself, but still lovelier in Greek because it means "songstress." The bird's name is formed from song: *aeidô* "I sing" and *aêdô* "nightingale."

Simichidas, the narrator, is pleased with the victory accorded to him by his opponent. The outcome seems only right to him, but not to us—such is Theocritus's irony. I imagine Lycidas is Theocritus's slanted self-portrait, like Milton's "uncouth swain" (line 186).

I shall return to this poem, Theocritus 7, for its astonishing climax, which comes only after Lycidas has departed for his mountains. But for the present I return to Theocritus's first idyll to indicate how Milton's debt to Theocritus is greater even than his considerable debt to Virgil. Virgil gave him phrases but no landscape, and perhaps no dominating sound. Theocritus gave him a particular, strained tone and a unified vision of the pastoral world of Sicily. It is a world of contrasts, of shaggy pines and delicate flowers, of weathered mountain heights looking down on summer meadows—"high lawns" (line 25) as Milton calls them—and steep-sided valleys where those flowers grow among light breezes and gushing brooks, protected from the gales overhead and the full glare of the summer sun, the "swart star" (line 138). We recall that what impressed Milton about the Apennine Mountains in Italy was not the height of the peaks but the depths of the shadowy valleys, captured in the name *Vallombrosa*. Theocritus's shepherds and especially his goatherds are a rougher lot; they are not disguised Roman aristocrats. They live closer to nature and closer, in every sense, to the edge. They also live closer to the gods and to local divinities, to the water nymphs that inspire them to song, to Pan, and to the remoter Olympians. Their lives are primitive, and part of primitivism is belief in the gods as numerous and omnipresent. Even here, among these things, are gods, said Heraclitus. When Pan appears in Virgil's tenth eclogue, we are told he is the god of Arcadia, *deus Arcadiae*, as if he were wearing a sign. He is a purely literary invention. He brings in another voice, another point of view. But one does not feel a numinous presence.

Characteristically, Milton's imagination thrusts back through intermediaries such as Virgil to what seems to him older, more primal, and nearer to the source of inspiration. Milton's somewhat imaginary relation to Theocritus—himself an urbane and highly artificial primitive—characterizes what I mean by *primitive art*: not an art that is itself authentically primitive, whatever that would mean, but an art that sees other art as closer to bare life in nature and draws inspiration from this felt authenticity. In this sense, Picasso's *Demoiselles d'Avignon*, which started the modern movement of primitivism in the visual arts, is a work of primitive art, even if it happens to be inaccurate to characterize the African and Oceanic masks that inspired the painting as primitive.

"Lycidas" is primitive art because it is inspired by what is seen as the authentically primitive elsewhere, and it draws inspiration especially from that primal quality. Virgil's eclogues are not quite primitive in this sense because they refine Theocritus and make him urbane.

Theocritus's own art is of course also "primitive" in the sense I have defined: that is, its primitivism, its rustic setting and themes, even its dialect, is the invention of a sophisticated and urbane artist, like Picasso. What Paris was to artists in the early twentieth century, Alexandria was to poets in the third century B.C. I expect Milton knew this, but knowing it did not serve his purposes so well as treating Theocritus as at least *more primitive* and *more authentic* than Virgil, and certainly more authentic than Virgil's successors in pastoral up to Sannazaro, Buchanan, Spenser, and William Browne, all of them more Virgilian than Theocritan, and so cut off from any true connection with the inspiring original stream. The famous words of Artemidorus I have mentioned, that before Theocritus the bucolic muses were scattered, indicate Theocritus is at some distance from the primitive source; however, he was at least *closer* to the source, as close as any one poet could be, and in Milton's eyes that was enough to make him archaic and authentic.

Virgil, in contrast, is far from this source, and that is where he wants to be. Virgil's country shepherds are not rustic, and their shepherd's costumes only partly disguise the sleek Augustan courtiers that wear them. Part of the game of Virgil's *Eclogues* is to represent the simple life—so alluring to those who don't live it—with real emotional sweetness and poignancy, but in language of the highest refinement, language such as one would be likely to hear only in literary circles in Rome. Virgil has little if any interest in being authentic, in capturing the old. But that is Milton's interest, which was perhaps born when he first looked into Theocritus. It must have seemed a revelation, like Keats first looking into Chapman's Homer. Here were real shepherds and goatherds. Here was authentic country life from the third century B.C., and authentic paganism, not the pallid Augustan deities. Instead of a pretty backdrop of copses and hills, as in Virgil, whose eclogues are set in the broad northern valley of the Po, here was rugged landscape, with "valleys low" (line 136), "high lawns" (line 25), or meadows for summer pasturage, and heavily wooded mountains rising straight from the sea, like "the shaggy top of Mona high" (line 54). In "L'Allegro" and "Il Penseroso," we have already observed Milton's passion for landscape. As a supereducated artistic genius whose creativity relied on his ability again and again to break out of his encyclopedic knowledge of the tradition, Milton was an authentic primitive artist. He was highly inauthentic in his passion for authenticity, and he knew it.

I imagine that when Milton agreed to contribute to the volume for Edward King—he had left Cambridge years before—he opened Theocritus and was again seized by what he saw and heard, right from those opening words, *hadu ti to psithurisma:* "Something sweet is in the whisper of the pine tree, goatherd, which makes her melody by these streams, and sweet also is your pipe. In that, you are second in contest only to Pan" (Theocritus 1.1–3). This is different in every way from the weary-sounding opening of "Lycidas"—"Yet once more . . . and once more . . . I come to pluck your berries harsh and crude" (lines 1–3). But both of them have an allure that is partly metrical, partly imaginative, partly pure magic. One cannot wait to read on.

This first idyll of Theocritus, and especially Thyrsis of Etna's song, will give Milton's "Lycidas" its designation of the poem as a "song" and its repeated invocation of the muses (Theocritus 1.64, etc.). The first idyll also supplies Milton with its keyword commands—"begin" (Theocritus 1.64, etc.; "Lycidas," lines 15 and 17) and "return" ("return" is how Milton appropriates, "begin again the song" *palin archet' aoidas* [Theocritus 1.104, etc.; "Lycidas," line 132]). Also fetched from Theocritus's first idyll are the questioning of the nymphs (Theocritus 1.66; "Lycidas," lines 50–55); the description of nature lamenting, together with the overturning of the natural order (Theocritus 1.71–75 and 132–36; "Lycidas," lines 39–48); the eminent visitors ([Hermes, Priapus, and Aphrodite] Theocritus 1.77, 81, and 95; "Lycidas," lines 74–75 [Apollo], line 96 [Hippotades], line 103 [Camus], line 109 [Saint Peter]); the Sicilian hills and vales (Theocritus 1.67–69; "Lycidas," lines 25–31, 133); purple flowers and hyacinths (Theocritus 1.132–33; "Lycidas," lines 141 and 150); and one mention of the stream Arethusa, the famous fountain of Syracuse, to whom the dying Daphnis sadly bids farewell, as he does also the more rustic streams in the vale of Thymbris (Theocritus 1.117–18). Arethusa is important to Virgil, who invokes her in his final eclogue, asking her to aid him with his final labor—*Extremum hunc, Arethusa, mihi concede laborem* (*Eclogues* 10. 1), thus suggesting she has aided him all along. In return for her aid, Virgil wishes that Arethusa's sweet waters, as they pass beneath the Sicilian waves, shall not be mingled with the salt sea. With that, he commands her to begin: *incipe* (*Eclogues*, 10.1–6), a command Milton will repeat (lines 15 and 17).

The "fountain Arethuse" is invoked in "Lycidas," together with Virgil's river, the Mincius, after the wandering course of the poem has been interrupted by the classical god Apollo—the sun god, who dries up the waters:

> O fountain Arethuse, and thou honored flood,
> Smooth-sliding Mincius crowned with vocal reeds,
> That strain I heard was of a higher mood,
> But now my oat proceeds.
>
> *("Lycidas," lines 85–88)*

The poem is again interrupted, some 23 lines later, by the Christian "god," Saint Peter, with his savage condemnation of the corrupt shepherds of the church. This second interruption requires another invocation of the waters of pastoral song, which have been frightened off by the dreaded voice, as earlier the waters were frightened by the "higher mood" imposed by Phoebus: "Return Alpheus, the dread voice is past / That shrunk thy streams; return, Sicilian muse" (lines 132–33). Who is the fountain Arethusa, who is Alpheus, and what is the connection between them?

The fullest account of Arethusa is given by Arethusa herself, in the fifth book of Ovid's *Metamorphoses* (5.572–641). She was a wild nymph of Arcadia, devoted to Artemis-Diana. One day, to escape the heat, Arethusa swam naked in the river Alpheus, the largest river in Arcadia, and in the entire Peloponnesus. The river became enamored of her and took human form to pursue her, naked, through the entire region of Arcadia. The poor girl's clothes were left on the opposite bank of the river, and the urgent Alpheus was between her and them. They ran all day, until she was at last on the point of being overtaken, at which she prayed to Diana for aid. Diana hid her in a cloud, but the river-god waited patiently, calling Arethusa's name, for he did not descry any tracks leading out of the cloud to either side. At this impasse, Diana transformed Arethusa into a stream. But Alpheus, not to be foiled, resumed his fluid form, intending to mingle with Arethusa one way or the other.

Diana therefore opened the earth as a route of escape, and Arethusa, now a stream, passed through the caverns until she came to the sea—as

Virgil thought—or else she passed entirely under the sea, keeping her course for Sicily. In either case, she rose up out of the ground, though still very close to the sea, on the island of Ortygia, which bounds one side of the harbor of the ancient city of Syracuse. She is still there today.

There is an uncertainty at the end of Ovid's tale that is not carelessness but the reflection of an ancient debate. It is whether Alpheus does or does not succeed in mingling his waters with Arethusa's, to travel with her to Ortygia and rise up with her there as a fountain. Or does Arethusa escape? Ovid seems to indicate Arethusa escapes. Pausanias acknowledges the dispute: some are of the opinion Arethusa escaped Alpheus, some not. Pausanias says she did not escape. The river Alpheus, he says, continued his course to the sea and there, in its depths, met Arethusa and mixed with her, and together they kept on their course through the sea to Sicily and Ortygia. Pausanias cites verses from the oracle at Delphi, when Apollo sent Archias the Corinthian to found Syracuse, designating Ortygia, off Trinacria (Sicily), "where Alpheus's mouth bubbles / As he mingles with the springs of the fair-flowing Arethusa." Further legends mention that when the offal of sacrificed animal victims at Olympia were thrown into the nearby course of the river Alpheus, the spring of Arethusa at Syracuse was discolored, and that a cup thrown into Alpheus in Arcadia would reappear at Syracuse.[16]

If mingling with the bitter waves of the sea is a figure for oblivion and loss, then Arethusa was granted what Virgil wished for her: immortality, or something very close to it. Silver coins from Syracuse, minted long before Virgil wrote, show Arethusa. Indeed, to this day in Syracuse, Arethusa is still a name to conjure with and to trade with. She has been appropriated by countless businesses, from coin laundries to auto repair shops and hotels. On the island of Ortygia in Syracuse's harbor this powerful fountain still rises with great force, and miraculously close to the sea. She was strong enough for Nelson to water his entire fleet from her on his way to victory at the Battle of the Nile. Gazing at her, I wondered if Alpheus was remembered, or if local opinion held he was not successful in mingling his waters with Arethusa's. Then I saw a sign on a nearby terrace overlooking the harbor: "Bar Alpheo." So there he is, offering something stronger than Arethusa's virgin stream.

The famous seventh idyll of Theocritus, which is set on Cos and usually called "The Harvest Home," is interestingly titled for the reader of "Lycidas," "First Fruits," or more literally, "Fruiting Forth" or "Swelling Up" (*thalusia*, from *thallo*, "to bloom, flourish, shoot out, swell"). In addition to the name "Lycidas," this poem supplies Milton with the Hebrus river; the halcyons (which appear in "On the Morning of Christ's Nativity"); the asphodels, which become, as was noted, Milton's rustically named "daffadillies"; the word *fame (fama)* applied to a song that rises to the throne of Jove; and of course a song commemorating a poet, Comatas. Comatas is now a divinity, but he wasted away for love like snow on the rough Caucasus mountains (the imagined fate also of Virgil's Gallus). Comatas was lamented by the mountain oaks and was once miraculously fed by bees because the sweet nectar of the muses flowed from his mouth (lines 80–82).

Theocritus's seventh idyll, "Fruiting Forth," ends gorgeously in a *locus amoenus* where the shepherds who were on their way to the feast, just after Lycidas parts from them "on the left," sit down in the shade of aspens and elms. They were transporting jars of wine for the feast but seem unconcerned with that duty. Near them is a cave sacred to the nymphs, where the bees are humming, and from which a pure stream gushes forth. The smell of ripe fruit is all around them, as are the songs of crickets in the grass, of tree frogs above them, and of larks and goldfinches still higher up. The shepherds open the jars of four-year-old wine, such wine, we are told, as the centaur Chiron never served to Heracles, and such wine as that Sicilian mountain man, great Polyphemus, never drank when Odysseus got him drunk.

The purpose of these odd comparisons to Heracles and Polyphemus is to suggest a momentary elevation of the tone, a raising of sights from the rough–smooth, bitter–sweet country world of pastoral to the world of high heroic myth. The change of register is indicated as soon as the jars have been opened and the wine mixed with water from the stream. The song is to be inspired by the Castalian nymphs of Parnassus. These are higher muses on a higher mountain. They are announced in an archaizing, heroic hexameter as the nymphs who hold the steep side of Parnassus: *Nymphai Kastalides Parnassion aipos echoisai!* (line 148). As the poem concludes, a nearby altar to Demeter appears—an appropriate goddess for harvest and fruits, and of course for Sicily, where Persephone was seized. The goddess is the last thing we see, smiling on these shepherds, and holding in either hand nourishing wheat sheaves and somniferous opium poppies. The opium poppies are there not for their obvious use but because they added a sense of immemorial antiquity, being sacred to goddesses of the Mediterranean islands since Minoan times, long before Demeter was heard of.

I draw out this description to show how the poem has been carefully contrived at the end to effect a gradual ascent from the pastoral world in its ideal state, a *locus amoenus*; to the higher world of myth, overseen by the Castalian muses; and finally to a vision of the divine, of the goddess herself, with opium and wheat. It seems to me just the kind of scene that would fascinate Milton, exciting his historical imagination with a vision of the pagan world. In that world, ascent from the natural to the divine is gradual and continuous, not, as in the Hebrew and Christian worldview, sudden and discontinuous. This pagan worldview, the scene of natural idolatry—gods are everywhere—and of gradual, mystical ascent, limns a form of life that is gone forever, or so Milton supposed.

We have seen it go in "On the Morning of Christ's Nativity," where the nymphs "in twilight shade of tangled thickets mourn" (line 188). Such is the world we see at the beautiful, mystical conclusion of Theocritus's seventh idyll, in which the humble, natural world of elm trees and aspens, of bees, crickets, tree frogs, and goldfinches, of running stream and treasured wine, swells up and fruits forth as high as to the gods. Milton has been here. He didn't go through these poems with a shopping basket, picking up images and words where he found them: he read these poems with sympathetic intensity. In Theocritus, there is no rupture in the continuum, as there must be in "Lycidas"—or for that matter in any Christian poem—in which the word *other* is key: "Where other groves and other streams along / With nectar pure his oozy locks he laves" (lines 174–75).

Sannazaro uses *other*, as do others, all of them paganizing and eroticizing Christians: "*Altri monti, altri piani, / altri boschetti e rivi / vedi nel cielo, e più novelli fiori; / altri fauni e silvani / per luoghi dolci estivi / seguir le Ninfe in più felici amori*" ("other mountains, other meadows, other copses and streams, you will see in Heaven, and fresher flowers than here; other fauns and sylvanuses, in sweet summer landscapes, will pursue nymphs to happier fulfillments").[17] This otherness to Christian consolation, the promise of salvation in another life, another world, gives the lie to the initial, organic, and continuous pastoral world that Theocritus shows us so beautifully in the seventh idyll. After three centuries of hard use in Renaissance neo-Latin verse, which Johnson knew well from an early age (as a youth, he knew a considerable amount of Politian and other Renaissance Latin poets by heart), the tedious lamentations of swains could no longer give pleasure, which is what Johnson means by "disgusting," and also what he means by "vulgar."[18] Even the diction of "Lycidas" is for him "easy." Virgil's *Eclogues* begin with two singsong verses that were among the first hexameters learned in school— "*Tityre tu patulae recumbans sub tegmine fagi / Silvestrem tenui musam meditaris avena*" ("Tityrus, as you lie under the shade of a spreading beech tree, with your slender reed you practice the woodland muse"). In the sixth eclogue, after Phoebus has plucked Tityrus by the ear and admonished him not to aspire to higher strains, that is, to chant of kings and battles, the poet says he will meditate the rustic muse with a slender reed: *agrestem tenui meditabor harundine Musam* (6.8). Virgil's careful distinction of objective registers of song—the high heroic and the lowly pastoral—is taken up into "Lycidas" subjectively as a distinction between high and low points of view on the song: on the one hand, fame as it may or may not be attained to on earth, whether deserved or not, and bandied about like the winds in Chaucer's *Hous of Fame*; on the other hand, fame that "lives," that is, lasts and "spreads aloft by those pure eyes / And perfect witness of all-judging Jove" (lines 64–66).

Johnson also thinks "Lycidas" defiles the most awful sacred truths with the decorative machinery of pagan religion, and the objection can hardly be dismissed with Hazlitt's madcap picture of a bewigged Johnson borne by dolphins on the sea. One of the ways Enlightenment criticism, beginning in France with the Abbé du Bos, saw itself as having reached a higher degree of civilization, or *politeness*, was in its refusal to approve the incoherent mixture of pagan deities with Christian truth, so common in the art of the seventeenth century. Rubens's great cycle of paintings on Marie de' Medici, especially her arrival in France, where she is greeted by priests, angels, and tritons, was commonplace for describing this transgression, as was Spenser's *Faerie Queene* for English critics such as Joseph Spence. We have seen already that Milton is more careful about this than Johnson supposed, and that this care is exercised in "Lycidas," too. Although its motivation is different—being at once Christian and critical—Johnson's objection boils down to much the same objection held by modern readers: distaste for the conspicuous learning. "Lycidas" is a narrow valley of echoes, in which almost every line alludes to another line in Greek, Latin, Italian, and English poetry (and perhaps some

French, if what has been detected in Du Bellay and Ronsard isn't already in the Italian), which the ideal reader is intended to detect, or at least to feel. This resulting acoustic composite, a collage made out of timeworn poetic phrases from other languages, gives the poem resonance, as if what it says has been reverberating down the ages and now finds complete expression here.

That at least is the intention. But perhaps the great lexicographer's ear could discern too accurately the source of every echo and every echo's context. The disgust with pedantry can be even more intense among those who are profoundly learned in books, such as Johnson, than it is among those who are not, and who despise or distrust learning, such as Wordsworth. We live in the shadow of Wordsworth and believe poetry is an affair of passion, of direct experience of nature and of life, and of personal memory. We do not envision poetry as something put together out of books: "Up! Up! my friend, and quit your books . . . Come, hear the woodland linnet" ("The Tables Turned," lines 3 and 10). In "Lycidas," there is too much that smells of lamp and the library, as befits a university volume of the kind in which the poem first appeared.

In the very difficulty of "Lycidas" there is an implicit spiritual claim that reflects the changing role of poetry in the modern world. The center of the creative process has shifted from *ethos* to *pathos*, from the poet as an authority, the archetype of which would be Virgil as he was seen in the Middle Ages, to the poet as a suffering shaman, mediating voices and powers beyond the poet's own voice and power, and even undergoing a species of sympathetic transformation into what the poet sees and hears. Instead of being crowned with laurels, as Petrarch was in Rome, the modern poet dons a series of masks, like the *personae* of Pound and of Yeats—masks of animal as well as human forms, as when Yeats assumes the mask of a swan and also of a girl. The poet doesn't soar upward, as Milton soared above the wheeling poles, observing the metaphysical movements of heavens and descending to report what he has seen. The poet now begins with a descent into the turbulent forms of the world, entering the rag and bone shop of the heart out of which they come. The poet descends farther, into the formless substance beneath them, of which Parmenides spoke. Baudelaire resigns his poetic *auréole*—its substance is the light of the heavens—to the mud of the Paris street, so that he may be disguised and anonymous, like "simple mortals," because dignity bores him ("la dignité m'ennuie").[19] He reappears as a panicked swan escaped its market cage, its webbed feet slapping the dry and unfamiliar stones, trailing its dusty plumage over the uneven pavement and then beating its wings frantically in the dust of an empty drain. Then, with its heart full, recalling the lake where it was born and lived, it cries, "Water, when will you fall? Lightning, when will you thunder?":

> Un cygne qui s'était évadé de sa cage,
> Et, de ses pieds palmés frottant le pavé sec,
> Sur le sol raboteux traînait son blanc plumage.
> Près d'un ruisseau sans eau la bête ouvrant le bec
>
> Baignait nerveusement ses ailes dans la poudre,
> Et disait, le coeur plein de son beau lac natal:
> "Eau, quand pleuras-tu? Quand tonneras-tu, foudre?"[20]

There is the same calling for the waters of life and inspiration as we see in Milton, and perhaps that is what "Lycidas" is to us now: a swan out of water.

For a long time "Lycidas" retained its importance in the English literary tradition, however, because it satisfied the old requirements of erudite authority while adapting itself to the new interrogative aesthetic that emerges with romanticism, unleashing a torrent of masks. The romantic *pathos* of art making as a struggle in which the artist does not have full control is enacted in the wild career of this poem, its spontaneous overflow of powerful feelings.[21] It is improvised with "eager thought" (line 189), coaxed out of unwilling muses ("Hence with denial vain and coy excuse!," line 18) and is often interrupted in its course by unexpected voices, if not by the singer himself, who seems to throw it down and take it up at will, as his mood changes. We feel the emotional drama of the making of the poem as it unfolds: "Begin!"; "Alas!"; "Now my oat proceeds"; "Return"; "Ay me!" (lines 15, 17, 56, 65, 88).

The poem's stance is one of continual, uncertain, and perilous questioning. Even its rhetorical questions have an air of mystery about them, as if a further, harder question waits behind each: "Who would not sing for Lycidas?"; "Where were ye, nymphs?"; "Alas, what boots it?"; "Were it not better done, as others use?"; "What hard mishap hath doomed this gentle swain?"; "Ah, who hath reft . . . my dearest pledge?"; "What recks it them? What need they?" (lines 10, 50, 64, 67, 92, 107, 122). We catch the interrogative contagion. *Should* "our frail thoughts dally with false surmise"? Where is Lycidas now, in the ocean or in Heaven? Exactly how will Lycidas be "good / To all that wander in that perilous flood"? And while we're asking, what are those "fresh woods and pastures new" (line 193) to which the mind of the singer is to be released on the morrow?

Primarily, "Lycidas" questions the experience of death, as we should expect, but also, more than has been supposed, it questions the experience of sexual desire, of *eros*, especially in the floral catalogue, though more directly, if less deeply, when we hear the young man regretting his squandered sexual opportunities (he is perhaps overconfident that that is what they were), of sporting with Amaryllis in the shade and in the tangles of Neaera's hair. The poem questions the natural and the supernatural, and on the latter it questions both divinity in nature and divinity beyond nature, since the two divinities cannot coincide, as death and desire cannot coincide.

Nor does this questioning proceed from a single interrogative voice. "Lycidas" is like a séance, in which different voices keep breaking in and other voices are implored; so it is not always clear who is speaking, or to whom. To this extent, Stanley Fish has a point, driven home by rhetorical exaggeration: the poem is intended at least in certain moments to be taken up by many voices at once, or by the pure spirit of song. W. G. Madsen went so far as to hallucinate a singing angel, Michael, who sings the consolation. One wonders if he inspired Fish's notion that everyone and no one is singing this poem.[22] Only at the end is everything unexpectedly attributed to an "uncouth swain" (line 186), whose voice is supposed to have contained and quoted theirs. Yet we feel haunted by the many voices we have heard, as we are by their questions.

As to the imagery, it is intensely strange and often menacing, though it is hard to say why. Dark sentinels are ranged along the path of this song: the "watery bier," the "destined urn," the "wizard stream," "the blind fury with th'abhorrèd shears," the god Apollo reaching out of the sky to touch the singer's trembling ear, the streams of Arcadia flowing into the earth and then through the currents of the sea, magically retaining their freshness, the "fatal and perfidious bark," "the sanguine flower inscribed with woe," the "blind mouths," the "two-handed engine," "the dread voice," the valleys of nymphs bearing flowers in their arms, the phantom hearse, the obscure bottom "of the monstrous world," and a mountain rising from the ocean waves: "the great vision of the guarded mount" (lines 12, 20, 55,75, 77, 85, 132, 100, 106, 119,130, 132, 136–40, 151,158, 161). On the summit of Saint Michael's Mount, we may suppose, the angel's wings are spread against the sky, like a *nike*. Finally, when we are not at the end of the text, though it feels as if we are at the end of the poem, we see expressed in the wish of the singer a dead body being borne on the waves by dolphins, homeward (line 164). Surely those dolphins are weeping.[23]

These images seem to have come down into the poem from outer space, not from the mind of its author. They stand before us as mysterious portents, like black monoliths reflecting light from off their surfaces but totally mysterious themselves: *outrenoir* as Soulages calls his paintings, "beyond black."[24] Everything in "Lycidas" seems to lead away from where we are, on the west coast of England, Cornwall, and Wales, to far distant places and times: to druidical groves and polar islands shrouded in mists; to the "high lawns" of Arcadia in archaic Greece and the mountain valleys of Sicily in the hellenistic age, where spring flowers are protected for a time from the blaze of the sun; to the throne of Jove on Parnassus above the Gulf of Corinth; to the death ships of northern memory and myth; to the bottom of the sea, with its monsters, of which we hear in *Beowulf*; and, finally, to a Heaven, where angels wipe the tears from our eyes—and the seawater from our hair. All these divergent places and times seem to have nothing to do with one another. "Lycidas" is a crowded street with traffic signs pointing away from it to far distant places—or "shores" (line 154). It seems pointless, therefore, to try to make these energetic portents converge on one meaning, for they insistently diverge. If we could pass through the event horizon of this darkness into the interior of one of these images, we would find ourselves in a different place and time—or, unexpectedly, in our own.

Even that final bodily image of Lycidas in the sea, after we have caught sight of his bones "hurled" (line 15) along the ocean floor or thrown against the rocky coastline, comes to us in the form of a request, the mood of which is subjunctive and interrogative: "And O ye dolphins, waft the hapless youth" (line 164). It is in truth hard to be exact about this mood. Peter Sacks draws attention to the "vocative mood" dominating the poem, which is "tautened by a sinew of address," but these moments of address often have a legal power, as when the "waves and felon winds" are put to question through their representative, Hippo-tades. Speaking of the sun simile at the outset of the peroration and comparing it to the more openly willed statement "Henceforth thou art the genius of the shore" (line 183), Sacks speaks of "a positing power manifested in the poet's *fiat*."[25] There seems to occur over the course of the poem a bidding up of the mood, from vocative address—"where were ye, nymphs"—to wishful subjunctive—"bid amaranthus all his beauty shed, / And daffadilies fill their cups with tears . . . Let our frail thoughts dally with false surmise"—and, finally, "O ye dolphins, waft the hapless youth" (lines 50, 149–50, 153, 164). It is important we un-derstand that the image of Lycidas's body wafted by dolphins is not something that is reported in the poem as actually taking place. It is not an assertion: that nature at last cares for us, as it seemed once upon a time to care for Arion, alive, and Palaemon, dead. It is a question: is there catharsis, if not salvation, in nature? Behind that lurks the ques-tion of the strength of this positing power, which is more tentative than that to which Sacks refers. What is its authority and its success, since it occurs in the final line before the Christian consolation and not in the final line of that consolation? Is the poetical image of wafting merely the pathos of an impotent hope, knowing as we do that dolphins do not bear poets to shore? Is it stronger than that? Is the wafting the psycho-logically efficacious expression of a moral charge imposed upon nature: that in an unfallen natural world dolphins would bear poets to shore? Or are we to understand it as a positing—"let nature be such that ceta-ceans carry drowned poets to shore"—to which we may respond in the negative or the positive? Let it not be such, since it isn't so; let it be so, since there is imaginative force in the thought, even though it isn't so, in the present state of the natural world. The image of the drowned shep-herd wafted by dolphins is like a question mark floating on the surface of the sea, a portent heading to land. We see a body in the sea carried by dolphins, and then the image dissolves and is gone. Was it ever there?

At just this charged moment we are exhorted to forget about the dol-phins and think of Heaven: "For Lycidas, your sorrow, is not dead" (line 166). The line is unpunctuated and could be misread, but *for* means "be-cause," and "your sorrow" is in apposition to "Lycidas," as in Latin, *vester dolor* "the object of your sorrow."[26] Regardless how one views Christi-anity, one could certainly argue (though I won't myself, in the end) that this poem would have been improved had Milton cut out the vision of Lycidas in Heaven and not asked us to dismiss that miraculous line, "And O ye dolphins waft the hapless youth" (line 164). We might have passed insensibly from the dolphins to the genius of the shore, which is what the drowned shepherd becomes: a protective god of the headland, warding passing ships from the rocks. He would also symbolize obscurely (obscurest is best) a higher salvation:

> Now, Lycidas, the shepherds weep no more.
> Henceforth thou art the genius of the shore
> In thy large recompense and shalt be good
> To all that wander in that perilous flood.
>
> *("Lycidas," lines 182–85)*

The strange imagery of "Lycidas" effects a transport to autumn, to adopt a phrase of Wallace Stevens's *Transport to Summer*. In that book the poem "Somnambulisma" seems to echo "Lycidas" in its opening verses: "On an old shore, the vulgar ocean rolls / Noiselessly, noiselessly, resembling a thin bird, / That thinks of settling, yet never settles, on a nest." We are transported in this poem not to summer but to late autumn, where the ocean is, or "would be," "a geography of the dead" (line 13).[27] The autumnal spirit of "Lycidas" is that of the prophet Jeremiah (8:20): "the harvest is past, the summer is ended, and we are not saved."

In the circumstances, however, which we cannot altogether dismiss, Milton would have been little inclined to remove his drowned shepherd "from the blest kingdoms meek, of joy and love" (line 177). The other poems in the collection of obsequies for Edward King do a remarkably poor job of giving Christian consolation, and in this last poem Milton succeeds where they fail. Much as some may prefer him to do so, Milton would not have abandoned Lycidas on the shore of the sea as a dead body, to which funeral rites are due, or even as a benevolent god of the headland. Yet we are not wrong to ask whether it would not have been better for Milton to have done so, giving a fading view of a headland in the sea, like the ending of *Beowulf*.

Doing so would also mean cutting the final stanza in *ottava rima*, that strange, one-handed engine by which we are lifted out the poem to look upon its singer from above, the "uncouth swain." It is a tactic of projection Milton seems to enjoy, as we have seen in "On the Morning of

Christ's Nativity" and in "The Passion," and as we will see in *"Mansus,"* too, at its conclusion. We have been given no hint before of the swain's existence, and the beauty of the lines, which have a filmic effect—giving another distancing shot, and a fade—is considerable:

> Thus sang the uncouth swain to th'oaks and rills
> While the still morn went out with sandals grey.
> He touched the tender stops of various quills
> With eager thought, warbling his Doric lay.
> And now the sun had stretched out all the hills
> And now was dropped into the western bay.
> At last he rose and twitched his mantle blue,
> Tomorrow to fresh woods and pastures new.
>
> *("Lycidas," lines 186–93)*

We are invited by these lines to watch the singer of "Lycidas" seated on a hillside, composing with "eager thought," that is, spontaneously, the elegy that we have just heard. We watch this archaic hellenized ancestor of A. E. Housman's west-country swains as the morning light passes him by in "sandals grey," in overcast weather. We watch the swain as the light lengthens on the hills in the late afternoon, still touching those "tender stops of various quills" as he sings. We watch the swain as the sun goes down into the western bay—the Irish sea, as seen from Wales, the land that, as we hear in *Comus*, "fronts the falling sun" (line 30). In Housman's "On Forelands High in Heaven," that sunset is "evening wrecked on Wales" (line 28). We watch the swain in the obscure evening light, still meditating on his song. We watch the swain as he rises abruptly, shrugging off the experience he has just had, and that he has just put us through: "At last he rose, and twitched his mantle blue, / Tomorrow to fresh woods and pastures new." The cameo is so good we can hardly wish the stanza away. But perhaps it is affected and unnecessary, and perhaps a modern poet would have cut it and let the poem end with dolphins and a headland, the fading sound of waves, and a lingering sea spray.

This is another point of aesthetic difference between Milton's time and ours. In an age of information saturation, we value economy of movement and purity of affect. We like our poetry stripped down and hard-hitting. Milton could write like that, especially in the sonnets, but the aesthetic of the Renaissance, and not just of its baroque epilogue, favored amplification and fullness, *copia:* the more the better, if what is more is also good. Economy of means and singularity of affect is for epigrams and short lyrics, like Ben Jonson's, not for the longer exercises of funerary organ music.

The purpose of the vision of Lycidas in Heaven and the unexpected sight of the Doric swain is to represent a turbulent boundary region between the pagan world and the Christian, when a new historical epoch is coming into view and an old one is fading away, but fading away slowly. These visions, or pictures, succeed one another like memories through which the older pictures can still be seen, each new one being "interposed," like the cascade of flowers interposed between us and the truth. It is a view of history that would inform *Paradise Lost, Paradise Regained,* and *Samson Agonistes.* We are radically historical, so Milton believes, because each of us lives in one time in history and not in another, and what period you live in historically to some extent determines and limits what you know, what you can believe, and even who you are—and above all, in the eyes of the revolutionary, whether you are saved. The Christian term for this terrible limitation of our freedom by our historical identity is *Providence*—our blind guide.

For example, if we live, as the swain who sings "Lycidas" does, before the coming of Christ, we are determinate and inalterable pagans. But the drama of the conclusion of the poem is in its fleeting, prophetic vision of other possibilities. A precedent for Milton would be Virgil's fourth, or "messianic" eclogue, which was viewed throughout the Middle Ages as a prophetic vision of Christian truth accorded to a pagan poet, and therefore as being only clear in part. This is a Pauline thought: now we know in part. The swain finally presented to us as having sung "Lycidas" is a development of those "shepherds on the lawn" in "On the Morning of Christ's Nativity" (line 85), of whom it is said "full little thought they then / That the mighty Pan / Was kindly come to live with them below" (lines 88–90). They speak more truly than they know, for this god is *kindly* because he is of the same kind as us, having become human. Those shepherds do not use the names *Jesus* or *Christ* because they are not, for Milton, what they are in the Bible: Jews in the area around Bethlehem, who would know Hebrew *Yeshua* and would have heard Greek χρίστος as the translation of Hebrew *messiah.* But these shepherds are not Jews; they are classical pagans, which is to say, indices of an historical epoch coming to a close, and intelligences to whom a new one is proclaimed. The only term they have to refer to what is now coming down into history is *mighty Pan*, whose service is perfect freedom. The irony is that mighty Pan himself, like the oracles later in the poem, will soon be purged by the very one to whom his name refers. The mighty Pan, too, will feel "from Judah's land / The dreaded infant's hand" (lines 221–22).

This inhabiting by Milton of an historically specific boundary region, signified by the classical imagery of pastoral, with Christian imagery emerging through it from below, may have more in common with the uses of primitivism than it does with the ahistorical and idealizing conventions of the pastoral elegy. The *primitive* is not an objective quality of any work of art, unless we mean art that is produced outside the context of teaching, something that certainly can't be said of "Lycidas." It took many years of humanist and Christian instruction, and many more years of self-instruction, to make the poet who could "build [this] lofty rhyme" (line 11). It also takes some years of instruction and self-instruction just to be able to read this poem and understand it superficially, and years, stretching to decades, of meditation (in the Latin sense Milton uses the word: repetitive practice, memorization) to feel confident writing about it.

Yet the essentially human is there, underneath all the masks. For Milton, this humanity is something ethical, and it is an essence he will try to extract, like distilled liquor, in the long, winding tube of sound that is *Paradise Lost*. What is this precious thing, the essence of the human? It is the righteousness truly existing in Adam and Eve before the fall into history. Another name for it is *liberty*. The fall into history obscures Milton's essential human thing and loses it in a chain of false substitutions, of tin wreaths, pastoral songs, and erotic liberties, those products of Virgilian *otium*, or leisure, which prove to be a vacancy within which there resonates an impotent classical song. Like the laureate hearse, which interposes temporary ease but proves to be an illusion, these images of our freedom are "frail thoughts" and "false surmise." "Since thy original lapse true liberty / Is lost," Michael says to Adam at the end of *Paradise Lost*, "which always with right reason dwells" (12.84). That is what Milton does not want to say in this poem because he wants us to feel the oceanic loss of the truth in the complexities of historical change.

In the end, we may venture to disagree with Milton on this matter of the question of the human, which is, as I said, like the body of Lycidas, washed far away and lost. Perhaps the essence of the human is not that noble thing, freedom, but caring, of which freedom may be only one part—caring plus courage. The Neanderthals who placed flowers on the bodies of those whom they loved—or perhaps only liked, and in some cases disliked—were not practicing sympathetic magic, as in *The Golden Bough*, to effect a resurrection in the spring or in another world. They knew they were doing something useless to their survival, or to the survival of the deceased, or to any of the practical purposes of life that they could identify. They were perhaps more like us than we think, knowing how to modify their feelings, as in Theocritus, where feelings are modified by flowers, wine, and song. No doubt these people were superstitious (as if we are not), but they were also in possession of the truth, the knowledge of the finality of death, that superstition only partly covers over. They strewed flowers because it felt good to do so, in defiance of the natural circumstances to which they were bound and to which, knowing of death, they knew they were bound. We recognize and greet them as humans like us because of this caring.

II

ENGAGEMENT

∽ 6

On the Interstitial Latin Poems and an English Fragment

Between "Lycidas" and the poems of the political period Milton returned to writing Latin verse because he was in Italy and was addressing persons for whom Latin was the universal language of learning and the elegant arts. Milton composed verses for the celebrated Roman singer Leonora Baroni; for the Roman poet Giovanni Salzilli (pronounced "salt-silly"); and for the Neapolitan nobleman, literary critic, and patron of letters Giovanni Manso (pronounced "Mantso").

But prior to these exercises there is an attractive two-verse fragment Milton wrote down before leaving for Europe. It is jotted on the back of the letter from Henry Lawes enclosing Milton's passport: "Fix here ye overdated spheres / That wing the restless foot of Time."[1] In a loose way these verses return to the mood and the imagery of "At a Solemn Music" and "On Time," and especially of the Nativity Ode (lines 117–40). We have noted how the music of the spheres, the *musica mundana*, measures out the time of the world until the Apocalypse, when this world and the heavens above are no more. Time's feet are of course winged, and they never rest but fly on indefinitely. The moving spheres are these wings, speeding time on. But the poet wants them to stop, to "Fix here," and that verb may remind us of another celestial pause, in the Nativity Ode: "Heaven's youngest teemèd star / Hath fixed her polished car" (lines 240–41). The pause of that one star over the stable where the Christ was born anticipates the stoppage of all celestial motions at the

Apocalypse, when the heavens disappear and Heaven opens her gates: "And Heaven as at some festival / Will open wide the gates of her high palace hall" (lines 146–47). The fragment sounds once again, almost for the last time, the theme we have followed through the early poetry: the expectation of transcendent ecstasy in Heaven, and a corresponding contempt for this world. The spheres are "overdated" because they have gone on moving past the date at which they should stop because the Apocalypse has come—or at least they have gone on too long so far as the poet's feelings are concerned. It is a purely subjective and emotional statement on the objective time of the world. Of course the spheres are not overdated, and the poet knows this; but to him it feels as if they are. He is asking them to annihilate themselves, so that he can transcend them.

The poems Milton wrote in Italy are three fine epigrams in elegiac meter, praising Leonora Baroni's singing at Rome (*"Ad Leonoram Romae canentem"*); a poem to comfort the ailing poet, Giovanni Salzilli, composed in "limping iambics," or *scazons* (*"Ad Salsillum poetam Romanum aegrotantem. Scazontes"*);[2] and a longer, ambitious poem in hexameters addressed to Giovanni Manso, entitled simply *"Mansus,"* thanking the older man for his gracious hospitality and fellowship in Naples; and, not incidentally, setting forth Milton's epic ambitions.

"Mansus" is the major poem in this group. But the epigrams to Baroni are, as I said, fine. The first says that the voice of God, or if not of God then of a "third mind" from Heaven, sounds through her as it winds and creeps (the verb is *serpere*, the root of *serpent*) through the secret passage of her throat: *"mens tertia . . . Per tuo secreto guttura serpit agens"* (lines 5–6). The phrase *"Serpit agens"* is immediately, and musically, repeated at the beginning of the following line, to say that this hidden, winding, and creeping sound easily and graciously teaches mortal hearts: *"Serpit agens, facilisque docet mortalia corda"* (line 7). Leonora's voice teaches our hearts the sounds of Heaven, accustoming us mortals to those sounds, in preparation for leaving this world for the better one. Although God pervades all things, on earth He is heard only in Leonora's voice, an earthly winding, hidden, interior sphere. This is a witty turn on the same transcendent theme we have heard in the earlier poems. Leonora Baroni seems a more grown-up version of the Lady of *A Masque Presented at Ludlow Castle, 1634*. Her purpose on earth is to turn our minds from the earth and fix them on Heaven.

The second epigram says, elegantly, that the great poet Tasso would have been cured of his madness at the sound of Leonora's voice, even if he had rolled his eyes more savagely than Dircean Pentheus (*"Quamvis Dircaeo torsisset lumina Pentheo / Saevior,"* lines 7–8); that *saevior* ("more savagely") makes a splendid enjambment. The third epigram appears to suggest that Leonora was originally from Naples but abandoned the raucous roar of the sea against the hill of Posillipo, on the northern shore of the Bay of Naples (*"Mutavit rauci murmura Pausilipi,"* line 6), for the agreeable waves of the Tiber (*"amoena Tibridis unda,"* line 5). There, in Rome, both men and gods are arrested and enraptured by Leonora's singing (*"Illic . . . homines cantu detinet atque deos,"* lines 7–8).

The poem to Salzilli, *"Ad Salsillum poetam Romanum aegrotantem. Scazontes,"* is interesting for the contrast Milton draws between the boisterous climate of England, where the winds blow violently, and the civilized beauty of Italy. This is a compliment nicely judged to reflect on Milton's own hardiness, while poor Salzilli suffers, for all his superior culture. Though Roman in speech, Salzilli builds lyric songs in Greek, in meters from Lesbos (lines 11–13 and 21–22). The fine mythological conclusion to the poem imitates the mythic digression in the Pindaric ode. Milton calls on Apollo, god of healing, to cure Salzilli, since, as a poet, Salzilli is Apollo's priest. Then, in a further and splendid pagan passage, the rustic oak groves and hills of ancient, pre-urban Rome are implored to bring whatever medicinal simples they have to cure the poet (lines 24–30). Once cured, Salzilli himself, through his song, will have a curative effect on the land. He will restore the land's ancient powers, bringing into view Numa himself, the legendary forest king, reclining with the wise water nymph Egeria in the dark woods (*"inter atros . . . lucos,"* line 33).

As I indicated, *"Mansus"* is the major poetic achievement of Milton's time in Italy, learned, charming, and socially suitable as these former exercises are. Milton in this poem introduces two major digressions on himself and his country—and he concludes the poem on himself, although, to be fair, he has lavished Manso with praise.

The first digression is a gesture similar to the briefer one in the poem to Salzilli: Milton is the youth sparely nurtured (culturally speaking) beneath Hyperborean skies and the icy constellation of the Bear, but who has dared, perhaps imprudently, to take his flight through the great cities of Italy: *"Imprudens Italas ausa est volitare per urbes"* (line 29). But we English are a not uncultivated nation, nor un-useful to Phoebus: *"neque nos genus incultum, nec inutile Phoebo"* (line 35). Chaucer himself (whom Milton, following Spenser, calls Tityrus) has visited Italy (line 34). The ancient Druids properly celebrated the gods, and they sang the praise of heroic deeds (lines 42–43). In splendidly Virgilian style, Milton says he believes he has heard in the depths of night swans singing on the Thames—he means, of course, English poets—the silver Thames that, from her pure urns, pours forth her streams and drenches her gray-green hair in the vortex of the Ocean:

> *Nos etiam in nostro modulantes flumine cygnos*
> *Credimus obscuras noctis sensisse per umbras,*
> *Qua Thamesis late puris argenteus urnis*
> *Oceani glaucos perfundit gurgite crines*
>
> ("Mansus," *lines 30–34*)

It is usual to celebrate the second passage in *"Mansus"* in which Milton again turns to himself, this time to meditate more narrowly on his own poetic plans (lines 78–84), which are to write an epic poem. He considers how he will, or may, bring back in poetry the ancient kings of Britain, beginning with Brute; how he will describe the famous Round Table with its knights, or "magnanimous heroes," as he calls them (line 83); and how he will tell of the deeds of their leader, King Arthur, which include making war even under the earth (*"Arturumque etiam sub terris bella moventem,"* line 81). Also, should the spirit be with him, he will—because he describes it—smash the enemy Saxon phalanxes beneath the martial valor of the Britons (*"Frangam Saxonicas Britonum sub Marte phalanges,"* line 84). In both the lines just quoted the hexameters are especially swaggering.

Milton is still meditating an English subject for the heroic poem he aspires to write, if he has the inspiration to do it: *"O modo si spiritus adsit"* (line 83). In Milton's view, Torquato Tasso, whom Manso had taken into his care in the poet's later years (as he did also Marino), is the great epic poet of the modern world. (The Portuguese poet Luis de Camões deserves the name, too, because he wrote a heroic poem on a modern subject—Vasco da Gama's voyage to India—but I do not know if Milton knew of Camões at this time.[3]) Manso took Milton to many places around the bay of Naples—no doubt to Cuma, famous to Pindar and

Virgil, and the Phlegraean fields, a premonition of the landscape of Hell—and Milton may well have thought of Manso as having conducted a sort of laying-on of hands, naming Milton the next great poet of the modern world, following Tasso's lead.

Perhaps Manso's accepting Milton as the future great poet of Europe was something Milton merely wished for. Or perhaps something like this happened between the older man and the young friend from England whom he so admired for his learning, genius, and ambition. The passage and its context suggests as much, as does the poem's remarkable conclusion, in which Milton imagines his own death, cared for by someone like Manso, who will bury him decently. Milton then imagines his tomb, at first with a simple urn but then with a marble bust of himself. He does not stop there but next imagines himself translated to Heaven, where he will not gaze upon God (as Dante does) but, as we should expect, on himself. That is, Milton will gaze from eternity on the days of his life in this temporal world, so that, considering his poetic achievements in that life, with a mind perfectly serene, and with his smiling face suffused with rosy light, he may applaud himself from ethereal Olympus: *"et tota mente serenum / Ridens purpureo suffundar lumine vultus / Et simul aethereo plaudam mihi laetus Olympo"* (lines 98–100).

We can see several things in this conclusion—Milton's self-controlling habit of viewing himself from above, for example—but it splendidly illustrates the change coming over Milton at this time. His desire for simple transcendence—to leave this world for another, better world, which is the prize of being good in this world (line 94)—is as yet unshaken. But no longer is he listening to Heavenly music and ignoring the lower world, which has been destroyed anyway. Instead, once Milton gets to Heaven, he immediately turns around and looks down upon this world he has left. He does so, for all his serenity, with something like longing. It is a longing to be involved, as the poet of his British race, so that his fame will live on in this world, a world that he has changed a little by means of his art. This is not yet engagement with the world and these are not a revolutionary's words. But the change of attitude and orientation is striking. It points toward what is to come.

In the autumn of 1639, after his return to England, Milton composed a long 219-line Latin pastoral elegy, *"Epitaphium Damonis"*—"Damon's

Epitaph"—to commemorate his close boyhood friend Charles Diodati, who died in Chester when Milton was in Italy. In the poem, the deceased shepherd is called Damon, and his mourner—a unique mourner, for no one else is qualified to mourn—is Damon's fellow shepherd, Thyrsis, Milton himself.

It can be fascinating to compare this poem in detail with "Lycidas," as has often been done. It can be fascinating also to compare their use of common sources. Many of the same pastoral allusions come up, and many allusions to Theocritus and Virgil in *Epitaphium Damonis* are from passages adjacent to those alluded to in "Lycidas." Milton has returned to this material—the body of traditional pastoral poetry—and is more assiduous in his study of it. Yet the result is much inferior to "Lycidas." Indeed—although on this point I differ from what appears to be the consensus of expert Latinists—much inferior to Milton's other Latin poetry. Perhaps Milton was now too old for the pastoral form. He does say, addressing his pastoral pipe in imitation of Virgil, that if his life is spared (*"O mihi tum si vita supersit,"* line 168), "you, pipe, will hang far off on the branch of an old pine tree, greatly forgotten by me": *"Tu procul annosa pendebis fistula pinu / Multum oblita mihi"* (lines 169–70). Virgil (*Eclogues,* 7.24)—*pendebit fistula pinu*—does not call the pine *old.* The added touch is a fine one, for the pastoral tradition is indeed like an ancient pine, continuous and old—and rough.

Perhaps, as is often suggested, Milton cared too much about the subject of this poem, Charles Diodati, to achieve the artistic distance necessary for free and original expression. The logic of such a proposition is questionable, for it comes down to the claim that the poem is bad because the poet was emotionally involved. In any event, I am less assured Milton cared so much about Diodati by this time, except as the companion, and therefore the symbol, of Milton's own ardent youth and his innocent delight in classical studies, now being displaced by political concerns.

It is striking that Milton spends much of the poem expatiating on his Italian experiences, but never once suggests it would have been pleasant to experience them with Diodati as his companion. How fine a fellow I was, Milton says (the allusion is to his participation in the Florentine academies), when lying at ease on the grass by the murmuring Arno, in a grove of elms, plucking violets and myrtles, I could listen to Lycidas and Menalcas contending in song. I myself even dared to contend! Nor did I altogether displease: *"Ipse etiam tentare ausus sum, nec puto multum / Displicui"* (lines 133–34). But surely, he says, such experiences are of no worth, in comparison with being present during his friend's dying hours. Was it so important, really, to see buried Rome (*"Equid erat tanti Romam vidisse sepultam?,"* line 115)? And to travel among those sublime peaks soaring in the upper air, in the snowbound Alps (*"Ire per aereas rupes, Alpemque nivosam,"* line 114)? Well, yes, it was important, and more important than staying at home in case someone got sick and died. These experiences were vital to Milton's aspiration to be a great poet, as he knew. It is insincere of him to say otherwise, lamenting the travels of which he is so obviously proud. A tinge of competitive satisfaction in his Italian experiences, unattractive but altogether human, is not far beneath the surface of this poem. Now Milton has seen what his friend Diodati never shall see more: Rome, Naples, Florence, Venice, the wild Apennines, and the soaring Alps. The friendship between them was always amiably competitive, even if Milton was the dominant one, the great studier, and Diodati the rapider student. The death of a friend should be the end of *lodevole invidia*, "noble and competitive envy." But the habits of friendship die hard, and Milton scores some points in this poem at Diodati's expense.[4] I was in Rome and you weren't. I fraternized on terms of equality with the intellectuals of Florence, and you didn't. I crossed the Alps; you never shall.

Perhaps politics, although they are rigorously excluded from this poem (except for one reference to concern for the flock, lines 14–15) is the reason for its slow-motion collapse. Politics were by no means excluded from "Lycidas." But they matter much more now to Milton, and personal, youthful friendship, with its shared idealism, now looks childish and self-indulgent. Greater issues are in hand: England is on the brink of civil war. Perhaps the poem is a farewell to youth because the poet, with his strong sense of a life divided into phases, feels obliged to bid his own youth farewell, at extravagant length. But his heart isn't in it. Perhaps—and I incline to this reason as much as any other—the ironical, playful detachment with which Milton conducted his Latin ululations in the past is no longer there. He lays it on with a trowel.

But more practical and specific reasons for the poem's failure to live up to, or nearly up to "Lycidas," are not far to seek. *"Epitaphium Damonis"* does not have the dramatic structure of "Lycidas," creating tension and surprise; it does not allow numerous other voices into the poem, as "Lycidas" does; it does not arouse moments of beauty, such as the floral catalogue, only to destroy them, or of horror, such as the vision of Lycidas's body in the depths of the sea, hurled by its violent waters. It does not arouse the complex array of feelings in us that "Lycidas" does, and, more surprisingly, it does not allow all living things in nature to lament the deceased, and resonate with sorrow, like the woods and desert caves of "Lycidas." This poem jealously guards the privilege of sorrow for its speaker alone, and in doing so it withers on the vine. Nor is there in *"Epitaphium Damonis,"* as in "Lycidas" (until the final eight lines of "Lycidas"), the pervading sense of mystery as to who the speaker is—and from which direction, so to speak, the song of lamentation is coming. In "Lycidas," the song seems to come from all directions at once, out of the earth and the sea and the sky. The lamentation can therefore be taken up readily by others. Unlike the monologic *"Epitaphium Damonis,"* the meaning of the loss of Lycidas is seen from many different points of view, all of them passionately felt and expressed. Milton's calling "Lycidas" a *monody* is of course technically correct, but the term ill suits the polyphonic character of that poem. The whole world mourns Lycidas—but not in unison. That dissonance in sorrow is profoundly expressive. This effect in "Lycidas" relies to a considerable extent on Milton's disclosing the singer, the "uncouth swain," only at the end of the poem and not at the beginning. If we were to see the uncouth swain at the beginning of "Lycidas," everything would be focalized through him and the polyphonic power correspondingly diminished.

From the beginning of *"Epitaphium Damonis"* the speaker obtrudes himself as its performer and conductor, calling on the Sicilian muses, as he did before in "Lycidas," but without the drama of "Lycidas" and with narrow officiousness. The muses show no reluctance in *"Epitaphium Damonis,"* as they do, dramatically, in "Lycidas," because now they are patently a literary fiction and compliant to any author's whim. There is no sense of the magic of invocation. These muses are easy and lack any numinous glow. They are brusquely summoned from Sicily to inspire the singer alongside the Thames, now that he is home and at leisure to be inspired, and at leisure to be sad. For when Damon died, he was detained by his love of culture—*amor musae* (line 13)—in a Tuscan city, Florence. Now he is less busy and so inclined to mourn.

The authority to mourn is jealously guarded by the speaker, as I said, although the muses are allowed to lament for *him,* for Milton, bewailing his wandering alone day and night, launching his wild cries of sorrow to the caves, the rivers and streams, the fountains and the woods. Only when Milton returned to England, which he did early, out of anxiety for the flocks, as he honestly says (to his credit), and not out of grief for Damon, does he visit familiar scenes and sit under the old elm (it recalls the beech tree in the opening lines of Virgil's *Eclogues*) where he and Damon sat. Then at last, feeling the absence of his friend, he began to unburden himself of his immense grief, saying, "Go home unfed, lambs, your shepherd has no time for you now":

> *Tum vero amissum tum denique sentit amicum,*
> *Coepit et immensum sic exonerare dolerem:*
> *Ite domum impasti, domino iam non vacat, agni.*
> ("Epitaphium Damonis," *lines 16–18*)

The last line, addressed to those unfortunate lambs, is sounded throughout the poem seventeen times, as a refrain, in the manner of the inset song in Theocritus's first idyll. But here Milton errs in not putting the refrain inside a song, for the poem itself is not sufficiently *cantabile* to carry it off. It grows more tedious and uncomfortable with every repetition, especially since we cannot help imagining those unfed lambs each time we hear it. The refrain is meant to compete with Virgil's address to his goats, in the beautiful final verse of the *Eclogues*. The speaker tells the goats to go home *well fed*: "*Ite domum saturae, venit Hesperus, ite, capellae*" (*Eclogues*, 10.77).

Such close imitation invites comparison, and Milton suffers by it. Virgil's speaker glances at the sky, where the evening star Hesperus is rising, indicating the hour grows late, and this gives the speaker his reason for telling the goats to go home now, since they have grazed to satiety. Because the evening star cannot be made to rise seventeen times in one poem, Milton substitutes his own, grieving indisposition as the reason for sending his lambs home unfed: he is too sad to attend to their feeding, so he is sending them home hungry from the meadow. Presumably the lambs do not move, for they are dismissed seventeen times, because they keep waiting to be fed. We may think of Saint Peter's remark in "Lycidas": "The hungry sheep look up and are not fed" (line 125). Much is lost by this substitution for Hesperus of the unfed lambs, and not only Virgil's fine effect of looking up into the evening sky, now in transition as the stars are coming out, before looking down at the goats and dismissing them from the scene: *ite*. Milton's speaker wants those lambs hungry because he is himself unsatisfied, hungering for his dead friend. If we take what he is saying seriously, then this is pathetic fallacy at its worst, because the suffering of the lambs is caused by the shepherd's emotional self-indulgence, not by a pervasive sadness in the natural world due to Damon's loss. It is the sadness of the speaker that matters, and the lambs have to pay.

Yet it would be wrong to dismiss *"Epitaphium Damonis"* altogether as catastrophically egotistical. There are in truth respectful and fond recollections of Charles Diodati, of his knowledge of medicinal plants (lines 150–54), for example, hellebore, crocus, and hyacinth, and the more secretive plants of the swampy fens, although these could do nothing to save him. Since they could not, may all medicinal plants perish, and all the arts of medicine, too, for they do could nothing for their master: *"Ah pereant herbae, pereant artesque medentum / Gramina, postquam ipsi nil profecere magistro!"* (lines 153–54). Earlier the speaker asks, "Who will bring back to me your suave sallies, who will bring back your smile, your Attic salt, and your humorously learned jokes?": *"Quis mihi blanditiasque tuas, quis tum mihi risus, / Cecropiosque sales referet, cultosque lepores?"* (lines 55–56). These sound like true recollections of Charles Diodati: brilliant, elegant, curious, learned, witty, and cheerful. An elegy that gets all that across cannot be called a failure.

At the level almost of individual lines, there are many things in this poem that please and even delight. I think the problems with this poem are more the result of bad artistic decisions, many of them enumerated above, by which Milton painted himself into a corner That is perhaps a surprising thing to say of such a great master of the art of poetry. But artistic decisions are the result of careful thought and planning, a detachment that Milton has not permitted himself hitherto, except when composing his earlier Latin verse, and then the detachment was in the direction of irony, not planning. *"Epitaphium Damonis"* is a spontaneous effusion, but so is "Lycidas" and so, too, is the beautifully articulated Nativity Ode, which *looks* planned. *A Masque Presented at Ludlow Castle, 1634*, had to be planned to some extent, in collaboration with Henry Lawes, because a dramatic presentation must be planned. But there is a lot of free and, from a later point of view, undisciplined writing in Milton's masque—inspired, to be sure, but undisciplined. I am not referring to anything Milton himself did not know. He knew genius and inspiration had borne him on their wings in the past and only occasionally failed him, as they did, we shall see, eleven days previous. He also knew that, to mature as a poet, and especially as an epic poet, he had to choose his subject with care, to plan in more detail and in advance, and to keep to the plan, alternately spurring and reining his Pegasus.

That is why we appreciate, and are not disgusted by, the passage in which he again turns to himself, although in doing so he apologetically fears he is now being a little turgid (*"dubito quoque ne sim / Turgidulus,"* lines 159–60). Indeed, he has been, but he is not in what follows. Intriguingly, he says that eleven days past he was sounding on his pipe some higher, grander strain, and when by chance he placed to his lips a new set of pipes, their fastening broke and they fell apart, being unable to bear any longer the weighty force of those sounds:

> *Ipse etiam, nam nescio quid mihi grande sonabat*
> *Fistula, ab undecima iam lux est altera nocte,*
> *Et tum forte novis admoram labra cicutis,*
> *Dissiluere tamen rupta compage, nec ultra*
> *Ferre graves potuere sonos.*
> > ("Epitaphium Damonis," *lines 155–59)*

We note how specific he is that what breaks is the pipes' *compages*, their jointure or framework, not the pipes themselves. Because Milton tends to be exact, I will venture to speculate he is describing an experience—one not unlike that of Keats in *Hyperion*—of trying to sing high epic strains without an adequate framework and plan. The epic subjects he considered are described in the following lines, which show that, as in *"Mansus,"* Milton was still meditating an epic theme from legendary British history, in the tradition descending from Geoffrey of Monmouth. He considers King Arthur, of course, although this time around the circumstances of Arthur's conception are what interests, a magical contrivance of Merlin, *Merlini dolus* (line 168), by which Uther Pendragon got access to Igrayne, disguised as her husband. Going back to the beginning, when Brute, the descendant of Aeneas, comes to Britain and is its first king, Milton promises to tell of Dardanian, which is to say, Trojan ships riding the swells off England's southeastern coast: *"Dardanias . . . per aequora puppes / Dicam"* (lines 162–63).

Those are his vague hopes for the future. But as to his recent effort to sing of such heroic deeds, his pipes' fastening broke, because he lacked a structural plan, so that it was impossible to go on making epic sounds to no purpose: *nec ultra / Ferre graves potuere sonos*. A younger Milton might have forged ahead anyway, hoping to pick up inspiration on the way, or to find a structure as he went. Now he has learned to stop and think about what he is doing. An addiction to planning has its dangers, as well, for planning—inspecting oneself, and what one is doing, from above, which as we have seen was a personal habit of Milton's—can become an end in itself. Milton would think for a long time, longer than he expected, before he would conceive, repeatedly alter, and draw out the plan for a drama that would become his epic poem. Its subject would turn out to be biblical, not English.

Now he bids Diodati a final farewell, consigning his virginal friend to the troops of the virgins in Heaven, as these are seen in the book of Revelation, bearing shady palms, wearing halos as saints, and eternally participating in the marriage rites of the Lamb. The rites are performed with surprisingly pagan enthusiasm. The saints dance like Dionysian bacchantes to the fury of the lyre in the orgies that take place beneath the thyrsus of Zion: *"Cantus ubi, choreisque furit lyra mista beatis, / Festa Sionaeo bacchantur et orgia thyrso"* (lines 218–19).

When Milton showed us Lycidas in heaven, the drowned shepherd's appearance there was a promise to us all, or to all of us who labor in virtue and faith in this world to deserve a place in Heaven, that is, to be *recompensed:* "Henceforth thou art the genius of the shore / In thy large recompense, and shalt be good / To all that wander in that perilous flood" (lines 183–85). What I find striking about the apotheosis of Charles Diodati among the rioting virgins in Heaven is the absence on the poet's part of any inclination to join him or to go there at last. To put it crudely but not inaccurately, Diodati is being got rid of so that Milton may attend to other things. But it is not quite Diodati who is being dismissed or set aside in another part of the poet's mind. It is Heaven itself that is being set aside. A civil war is imminent, and it will be fought over questions Milton thinks profoundly important in religion. He has decided it is time to be engaged with the world.

It was in the midst of civil war, in January 1647, that Milton composed his last Latin poem, *"Ad Joannem Rousium Oxoniensis Academiae Biblio-*

thecarium de libro Poematum amisso . . . Ode"—"To John Rouse, Librarian of Oxford University, on the Lost Book of Poems. An Ode." The poem is a learned performance, in elegant metrically and syntactically challenging Latin—"beautiful but pleonastic," as E. M. W. Tillyard says—in imitation of the style of the odes of Pindar. But the subject is lighter and more amusing than Pindar ever is.[5] It is a classic performance of mandarin social power. We are inclined nowadays to dismiss such poems as trivially occasional, with nothing important to transmit to later ages. But Milton never wrote anything—anything in verse—without an eye on the future, and without something to say about human experience in all times. In this instance, his true subject is the survival of the arts, and the importance of their preservation, a concern the more urgently felt in time of war.

John Rouse—*cuius inclyta / Sunt data virum monumenta curae* ("to whom are entrusted the glorious monuments of men," lines 50–51)—was the librarian of the Bodleian Library at Oxford. He had written to Milton to request a second copy of Milton's *Poems* of 1645, the first copy having gone astray in transit. Milton calls it a "twin-born book" because the *Poems* of 1645 (recall this book was published on January 2, 1646, by our reckoning) was actually two books, with separate signatures and separate title pages, one book containing the English poems up to that date, the other the Latin poems.[6] But the two books were bound together as one. Rouse already had in his possession the tractates on episcopacy and on divorce, which Milton had composed since 1641, but he was anxious to complete the full tale of Milton's works (see lines 47–51). Milton sent the second copy of his *Poems*, and with it this poem. Both are in the Bodleian today.

The title of the poem might suggest it is addressed to Rouse, but it is instead *dedicated* to Rouse, who is referred to in it only in the third person, in the most complimentary terms, which of course Rouse deserved. Milton refers to him as his "learned friend" (line 16), and his praise of Rouse's zealous, protective care for the treasures of learning has behind it Rouse's famous refusal in 1645 to allow Charles I, who was then occupying Oxford, to remove a book from the Bodleian. In defense of the cultural treasures of the ages, this man stood up to a king.

The addressee of the poem is not, however, Rouse but the book itself. The poet is sending it off on its journey to Oxford—"Go, litel bok," as Chaucer says—wishing it well and giving it confidence of a future life in the great library. There, Milton says to his book, you will be gathered with and read among (I take both actions to be implied in *legeris*) the authors of most exalted name, both Greek and Latin, the glorious lights of the ancients, and their true ornament: *"Illic legeris inter alta nomina / Authorum, Graiae simul et Latinae / Antiqua gentis lumina, et verum decus"* (lines 70–72). There is an amusing meditation on the probable fate of the lost copy, imprisoned in some cellar or roughly handled by some mercenary hawker, a thought that is keener in a time of war, when people were disappearing, as well, randomly imprisoned or executed, not least on the Oxford road. But you, Milton says to his book, are going to the sacred groves of the muses (I take "sacred" to be the strong sense of "pleasant")—*"lucos / Musarum ibis amoenos"* (lines 61–62)—and will enter again Apollo's divine habitation (the Bodleian Library) in the vale of Oxford, which the god prefers now to the island of Delos (his birthplace) and the twin peaks of Parnassus (his shrine at Delphi): *"Delo posthabita, / Bifidoque Parnassi iugo"* (lines 65–66).

Much had changed for Milton, and for his country, in the seven years between *"Epitaphium Damonis"* and the ode to Rouse. Milton was married. He had been deserted by his wife; he had been reconciled with her, not at his own initiative; and, to make the pill more bitter, her noisy royalist family, their fortunes now reversed, came back with her and lived in his house, to the confusion of his studies. And he was now a father. In his disillusionment, he might at this time have looked back with a sigh to the virginal orgies to which he had cheerfully consigned his friend Diodati, expecting something better for himself. As to his public life, Milton had been involved in exceptionally bitter and dangerous disputes, defying a parliamentary order and even being summoned before Parliament. He had worked ferociously on the prose tracts he composed in this period at white heat.

Of these by far the most important is *Areopagitica*, the only true classic among Milton's prose works, which he wrote to protest the Long Parliament's reinstitution of licensing books before they are printed, this being the former practice of the abolished and much-hated Star Chamber. This is not the place to speak in detail of *Areopagitica*, of its noble, soaring, yet sharply analytical and, for us, fundamental defense of freedom of thought and expression. That defense is far more important than the ways in which, undoubtedly, *Areopagitica* is limited by its the times, as all statements are by their times. But it should be mentioned here that in *Areopagitica* Milton does not content himself with expressing what we should now call a classic liberal view of the state and its authority: that reform should respond in detail—but not in general—to social problems as they arise, in the hope of achieving reasonable stability and justice. He has become instead a revolutionary in his thinking, in favor of reform and change, even tumultuous change—"strong and healthful commotions"[7]—as continuous and perpetual energies in our social and political lives.

In short, he was no longer the ingenuous, brilliant, but unknown poet from England who thought it daring of him, as he says in *"Mansus,"* to travel through the Italian cities for his own cultivation and meet their learned men. Nor was he any longer the naive idealist, author of *"Epitaphium Damonis,"* who returned to England in the summer of 1639 with a vague sense of giving his talents to the cause of liberty while setting up as a schoolmaster for elite boys. He was now a seasoned author and polemicist, accustomed to hard intellectual fighting. He was still a schoolmaster of sorts, but well seasoned by reality in that enterprise, too, writing texts on grammar and logic, composing a Latin dictionary, and implementing, as far as possible, the theories he had published in 1644 in *Of Education*.

With the abolition of the court of the Star Chamber in 1641, publication in London greatly increased, most of it political and religious in nature. Starting in that year, Milton published five hard-hitting anti-Episcopal tracts and four tracts on divorce (the first appeared again in a revised and expanded second edition). During this period, in 1642, King Charles I abandoned London, having failed to obtain civil peace by constitutional means. The civil war between the royalist forces of the king and the Long Parliament began with the indecisive Battle of Edgehill, outside London, in October 1642. The king then retired to Oxford (instead of pressing his advantage on London) and made it his headquarters, a matter not insignificant to Milton's poem to Rouse, in which he laments the civil war, which had become much bloodier after Edgehill, although Edgehill was bloody enough.

Civil tumults have caused the flight of the muses from England, Milton says, and especially from Oxford. If only some god or a son of a god would use his divine power to take away the abominable uproar

of civil tumults, to call back liberal studies, and restore the banished,
homeless muses to Oxford:

> *Modo quis deus, aut editus deo . . . :*
> *Tollat nefandos civium tumultus,*
> *Almaque revocet studia sanctus*
> *Et relegatas sine sede musas*
>
> ("Ad Joannem Rousium," *lines*
> *25–32)*

In the meantime, there is Rouse at Oxford, defending the fruits of
learning and liberal studies. Therefore, the muses are not altogether
absent from Oxford. Milton is sending his book to the same place he
sent the first copy, where it will be safely kept by Rouse in the *adytis
sacris* ("the inner sacred places") of the Bodleian (line 52). Which is just
what happened. You were taking, Milton says to his book, the illus-
trious way to the cradle of cerulean Father Thames (Oxford stands on
the Isis, the local name for this part of the Thames), where the limpid
springs of the Aonian muses and the sacred procession are known
throughout the world and through the immense revolutions of time as
the heavens turn round, famous in ages to come:

> *Illustre tendebas iter*
> *Thamesis ad incunabula*
> *Caeruli patris,*
> *Fontes ubi limpidi*
> *Aonidum, thyasusque sacer*
> *Orbi notus per immensos*
> *Temporum lapsus redeunte coelo,*
> *Celeberque futurus in aevum.*
>
> ("Ad Joannem Rousium," *lines*
> *17–24)*

Now it's there. Throughout the ode to Rouse there shines a noble confidence in the value and permanence of learning and art, a confidence
all the greater for the sad evidence of the forces ranged against culture
in human nature. These forces that are ruinous to culture are symbolized, in a remarkable simile, to harpies, the *Immundasque volucres* ("filthy

birds," because they defecate on food) who hover over us with their threatening claws (lines 33–34). That is, war both defiles and destroys art itself and slaughters its creators and protectors. May these harpies be transfixed by the arrows of Apollo and driven far from the river of the winged horse, Pegasus (*"procul amne Pegaseo,"* line 36)! By "the river of Pegasus" Milton does not mean the Hippocrene stream (Gr. "horse-spring") on Mount Helicon, in Boeotia in Greece, the spring tradition-ally sacred to the muses. It was opened by a strike from the hoof of Peg-asus. Milton means the river at Oxford. Culture occupies an intermediate region between the earthly world as we know it, chiefly in social and political terms, and the world that transcends our own, Heaven. For-merly for Milton, culture was a light leading us along the path of virtue and faith up to Heaven. In the ode to Rouse we see how culture has become something else: a means of preserving and fighting for what is good in this world. That of course implies that there *is* something good in this world, which is a change from Milton's youthful opinion, at least as he expressed it in his poetry. But there is more. Milton suggests in this ode to Rouse—in this, we recognize the author of *Areopagitica*—that culture is also means for creating a world better than the one we know now.

❧ 7

On the Sonnets and Shorter Poems of the Political Period

W̲ORDSWORTH WAS in France when the French Revolution broke out, and he never got over it, even when he was disillusioned with the result. When he sang, "Milton! thou should'st be living at this hour: / England hath need of thee," he was calling for the Milton of the rousing political sonnets, for example, Sonnet 18, "On the Late Massacre in Piedmont" (1655). Wordsworth was not perhaps interested in any clearly identifiable political cause. But he was interested as an artist in the voice of revolution, longing for its savage indignation and prophetic power, whether it be sounded by a reincarnated Milton or by some avatar of that "Soul aweful," such as Wordsworth himself. Blake had both of these things, savage indignation and prophetic power, but he never had them with the clarity and force of Milton's "On the Late Massacre in Piedmont," bearing down on a single event.

In this poem—it comes late in the period we are now to consider—Milton calls for vengeance on the Roman Catholic Duke of Savoy, and on the Roman Catholic Church in general, under the papal "triple tyrant." Their crime was the massacre by the Duke of Savoy's army—"the bloody Piedmontese"—under the command of the Marquis of Pianezza, of the proto-Protestant, Waldensian heretics, so called because they followed the twelfth-century ecclesiastical reformer Peter Valdes. The massacre took place on April 24, 1655, and Milton's sonnet dates from June of that year.

The Waldensians lived in remote villages in the Alps between France and Italy. They were marched on without warning and fled to higher villages, whither they were pursued and slaughtered, many being thrown from the cliffs and some, according to reports, bound together into balls and rolled down the mountainside—atrocities that are alluded to in the poem. Many others died of exposure trying to escape through the Saint Julien pass into France, when it was still blocked with snow, and others were taken prisoner and hanged.[1] Years before, Milton had crossed the Alps from Italy to Switzerland, farther to the east, and he knew the alpine terrain of which he was writing.

He prays for vengeance, but it is not at first clear what form he hopes this vengeance will take because in the sestet he says that the "martyred blood" of the victims will be like seeds (he is thinking of the parable of the sower in the synoptic gospels, especially Matthew 13:3–23), yielding "a hundredfold" of new Protestants in Italy itself, that is, on the main Italian peninsula south of the kingdom of Piedmont. In that case the vengeance for which Milton prays will be the confusion and overthrow of Roman Catholicism, "the Babylonian woe." In the Protestant imagination, Rome is Babylon, the city to which the Hebrews were carried into captivity after the fall of Jerusalem. (The conflation of Rome with Babylon is authorized by the book of Revelation, composed at the end of the first century A.D. It was an easy step for sixteenth- and seventeenth-century Protestants to add papal Rome to imperial Rome in the symbolic register.)

The vengeance Milton is praying for is not merely a sanguinary retaliation in kind for some seventeen hundred lives. It promises instead a revolution, a compensatory historical event proceeding from the evil of the massacre and, as it were, making use of it. The event Milton envisions is nothing less than the overthrow of the vast and ancient structure of the Roman Catholic Church. The plan of the sonnet, speaking a little approximately, is that the first eight lines, the octave, present to us the scene of the atrocity. The final six lines, the sestet, express the hope that the bones and ashes of the martyrs will multiply a hundredfold and start a revolution against the pope in Italy itself. But the scene of atrocity is carried over into the sestet as the moans of the dying are echoed by the mountains, from whence they reverberate to Heaven; Heaven, it is hoped, will hear those moans and answer Milton's prayer:

Avenge O Lord thy slaughtered saints whose bones
Lie scattered on the Alpine mountains cold,
E'en them who kept thy truth so pure of old
When all our fathers worshipped stocks and stones.
Forget not! In thy book record their groans
Who were thy sheep and in their ancient fold
Slain by the bloody Piedmontese that rolled
Mother with infant down the rocks. Their moans
The vales redoubled to the hills and they [the hills]
To Heaven. Their martyred blood and ashes sow
O'er all the Italian fields where still doth sway
The triple tyrant, that from these may grow
A hundredfold, who having learnt thy way
Early may fly the Babylonian woe.

("On the Late Massacre in Piedmont")

The sonnet is of some technical interest because it was written in the
period when Milton was meditating *Paradise Lost*, and it adumbrates
some of the stylistic characteristics of the epic poem. There is the indignant *hauteur* of the voice, which is above what it condemns, and there
is the assumption of the prophetic mantle. The poet scorns, like Jeremiah, and he prophesies, like Ezekiel. The verse is continuous and, so
to speak, "through composed," *durchkomponiert*, to use the musical term,
so that it rushes impetuously from the first line to the last, with hardly
a pause or repetition, despite the use of rhyme. To accomplish this,
Milton adopts the Petrarchan sonnet with octave and sestet, not the
Shakespearean sonnet, with its pointed final couplet. In the octave
Milton effects a subtler departure from English sonnets in general (English being far less rich in rhymes than Italian) by using only two rhymes
(**abbaabba**), in the Italian manner, instead of four (**abbacddc**). In doing
so, Milton avoids breaking down the octave into two distinct quatrains
and achieves an unbroken continuum of sound through those eight lines.
Nor is there any pause at the end of the octave, for the central "turn,"
or *volta*, between octave and sestet is nearly effaced by the strong enjambment: "their moans / The vales redoubled" (lines 8–9). That is immediately followed by another enjambment ("to the hills and they / to
Heaven," lines 9–10); and another ("Their martyred blood and ashes
sow / O'er all the Italian fields," lines 10–11); and still another ("where

still doth sway / The triple tyrant," lines 11–12); and yet another again ("that from these may grow / A hundredfold," lines 12–13). Only now do we have the sestet's single slight pause at a line end, before that striking final verse, the rhythm of which approximates heroic dactyls: "who having learnt thy way / Early may fly the Babylonian woe."

Uncertainty about the grammar of that *early*, as we shall see, creates the effect of an enjambment even here. The octave has only two noticeable terminal pauses, at lines 2 and 4, "cold" and "stones," making a total of three in a fourteen-line poem. Of the remaining eleven lines, two more (lines 3 and 5) are very lightly paused. Fully nine of the sonnet's fourteen lines are strongly enjambed into the next. The poem rushes forward, as if in a single breath, with no rupture in its fabric.

The effect of continuousness and of unidirectional development without repetition is further aided by the grammatical choice of non-substantives for rhyme words. In rhyming verse, nouns on the whole tend to create stronger mental pauses at the terminations than do pronouns or verbs. Milton therefore avoids nouns until the last two lines of the sestet. Five nouns are used in the octave, which is still a low proportion, but they are strong words, four of them sounding the long *Ohns* of the "a" rhyme, hammering home the brutality of the action described: "bones," "stones," "groans," "moans." The "b" rhyme—"cold," "old," "fold," "rolled"—uses the same long vowel sound—*O*—as the "a" rhyme, so that the two rhymes are nearly identical, like slant rhymes. This augments the effect of acoustical homogeneity and forward momentum, as if the poem were uttered in a single breath.

Although the penultimate line, ending on *way*—the true path of God's worship—is not enjambed, it is run into the next line by means of an effect of Latin poetry that will become familiar in *Paradise Lost:* the blending of two grammatical possibilities for the adverb *early*. Does *early* modify *learnt* or *fly?* Is the Lord's "way" *learned early*, instead of late; or is the "Babylonian woe" *flown* from *earlier* than it would otherwise have been? At first, *early* seems to modify *learnt*, thus making the termination on *way* run over into *early*, beginning the final line. The subject of the sentence is "hundredfold," which refers to the people inhabiting those "Italian fields" (line 11) who are indicated by the relative pronoun *who*. It is they who will learn the Lord's "way" and "fly the Babylonian woe" (line 14). At first we think they learn the Lord's way *early* because of the massacre. Without that example, the Italians would not *learn* the

Lord's way until later. But when we read the final line as a unit, we see that because of the Waldensians' martyrdom, the "hundredfold" inhabitants of the Italian fields will fly the Babylonian woe *early*, instead of at some later time, which later time is the Second Coming of Christ. That earliness is what the revolutionary Milton had been calling for since the 1640s: a new Chosen People to hurry on the advent of the kingdom of God on this earth.

As a revolutionary of the type whose mind is poetically disclosed in Walter Benjamin's *On The Concept of History* (*Über den Begriff der Geschichte*, 1940), Milton felt that the attainment of freedom was miraculously possible at any moment in history, like the coming of Christ. The Messiah, in the form of revolution, may step at any moment into time. For every "now-moment" (*Jeztzeit*) is a straight gate through which the Messiah might enter—as Benjamin says in the last sentence of this work. "On the Late Massacre in Piedmont" mentions, in a flashback, the moans of mothers and infants, and so appeals to our outrage. But it finally eschews pity because its purposes are sterner and higher. The poem opens when the victims of the massacre are already scattered bones, and it closes with their martyred blood and ashes turning to revolutionary seed.

Milton is instinctively disinclined to linger on the pathos or the outrage of the scene because it is, after all, over; it is no longer happening. Merely the bones, the blood, and the ashes are left to us—and to him, to use rhetorically. The victims will never be what they once were in the past, living people, and they should therefore not be thought of nostalgically as people anymore. These bones won't live—at least not as what they once were: living human bodies with souls. But the bodies might still become something of power in the future. The revolutionary way of thinking is not to be concerned retrospectively and pathetically with justice, that is, with retribution for what has been done, but rather to be concerned with how an event—truly or falsely reported—can be exploited in the future to advance a revolutionary cause, such as the struggle against Roman Catholicism. Only the physical remains of the victims enter into the now-moment of revolutionary possibility.

This will perhaps become clearer if we consider a biblical passage Milton is thinking of in the poem's sestet. Near the end of the book of Judges, chapter 19, in the Benjaminite city of Gibeah, a Levite's concubine is raped to death by the sons of Belial and is found dead in the morning, grasping the lintel of the door of the house from which she had been cast out to be raped. The scene is one of the most pitiable in the Bible. But the Levite, with no show of pity, swiftly and efficiently slices her corpse into twelve pieces and sends one to each of the tribes of Israel (Judges 19:30), inciting a civil war against the tribe of Benjamin. The dismembered body of the concubine is like the dragon's teeth sown by Cadmus, a multiple, independently targeted instrument of spontaneous violence. In Milton's poem, the Piedmontese have performed the dismembering already. It is a poet who scatters the incendiary ashes, bones, and blood of the victims of the massacre over all Italy, so that outrage will burst into flame.

In the famous ninth section of Benjamin's text, the one named after Paul Klee's *Angelus Novus*, an angel faces the accumulated horrors of the past, its wings forced open by a wind—Benjamin calls it a "storm" (*Sturm*)—blowing out of paradise across the growing pile of those horrors. In the final sentence, Benjamin says this wind is what we call "progress." For Milton, the wind blowing out of paradise, the first breath of which is Michael's narrative in *Paradise Lost*, is prophetic revolutionary hope. Such hope must never linger with the event in itself, which is soon to be cast onto the pile of horrors. Faced with such events, it is pointless to hope for justice, to demand answers of God, or even to shed tears of pity. It is better to be cold and efficient, like the Levite, and use the dismembered corpse to incite outrage and violent change. That is why every scattered bone of the Waldensians, every bloody parcel of flesh, and every cinder, becomes an incitement.

The technical achievements I have mentioned in respect of this sonnet, all of them so skillfully combined—the strict use of the Italian rhyme scheme; the avoidance of too many nouns for rhyme words; the very high proportion of enjambed lines; the accelerating modulation from octave to sestet by means of an especially strong enjambment; the use of grammatical blurring in the first word of the final line to blend that line, strong as it is, more seamlessly into the continuous whole—give the feeling of impulsive forward movement without repetition or noticeable pause, or even an awareness of structure. To see structure we have to look back. This is a one-way poem, hurtling into the time of the now.

The technical features I have described in "On the Late Massacre in Piedmont" are quite unlike those sought in the four political poems—three of them sonnets and one a tailed sonnet—written almost a decade before, around 1646 (just after the publication of the *Poems* of 1645). In these poems, Milton is engaged in polemics closer to home, having been attacked for his treatises on divorce, especially by his former allies, the Presbyterians, and having seen the rise in the Long Parliament of an oppressive Presbyterian ascendancy, supported by the infamous Westminster Assembly, which was charged with settling the terms of a national, established church, an abomination to Milton.

Two of these poems, Sonnet 11 (in the Trinity manuscript numbering), "I did but Prompt the Age," and the "tailed sonnet" *(sonnetto caudato)* of twenty lines, "On the New Forcers of Conscience under the Long Parliament" (this poem is not numbered among the sonnets) are technically very different from "On the Late Massacre in Piedmont." Instead of rushing forward in the manner of the verse of *Paradise Lost*, they advance by slow and deliberate steps, each line distinct from the last, so that it may be clearly heard and felt, like a blow. These are fighting poems, and they fight according to method (as Aristotle says), like a boxer, with balance and footwork. Each line is a stinging jab ("But this is got by casting pearl to hogs," line 8); or a careful setting up of the opponent for the main blow ("When straight a barbarous noise environs me," line 3); or the main blow itself: "License they mean when they cry liberty" (line 11).

These examples are from Sonnet 11, "On the Detraction which followed upon my Writing Certain Treatises." But the effect is even more apparent, and it is so from the start, in "On the New Forcers of Conscience under the Long Parliament." This poem opens with two lines of setup (you have thrown bishops out of the church and renounced the fancy Anglican liturgy); a stinging jab (but you have taken for yourselves the same corrupt, material rewards, "the widowed whore plurality"); and a sudden, right-hand blow (you are hypocrites who pretend to condemn sins you actually want to commit, "whose sin ye envied, not abhorred"):

> Because you have thrown off your prelate lord,
> And with stiff vows renounced his liturgy
> To seize the widowed whore Plurality [multiple livings
>   and appointments]

From them whose sin ye envied, not abhorred,
Dare ye . . .

("On the New Forcers of Conscience under the Long
Parliament," lines 1–4)

"Dare ye"—which means "how dare you?"—opens the next combination.

Because these are fighting poems, not poems calculated to mobilize indignation, they use enjambments much less frequently: two in Sonnet 11, "On the Detraction which followed upon my Writing Certain Treatises," and four in "On the New Forcers of Conscience under the Long Parliament." The end-stopped lines finish on strong substantives, adding to the independence of each line. Sonnet 11 turns from octave to sestet with a relative clause: "casting pearl to hogs / That bawl for freedom" (lines 8–9). The proverbial character of the biblical phrase—"neither cast ye your pearls before swine, lest they trample them under their feet, and turn again and rend you" (Matthew 7:6), with *swine* altered to the deeper-voiced *hogs*—creates a strong pause even here:

I did but prompt the age to quit their clogs
By the known rules of ancient liberty
When straight a barbarous noise environs me
Of owls and cuckoos, asses, apes and dogs.
As when those hinds that were transformed to frogs
Railed at Latona's twin-born progeny
Which after held the sun and moon in fee.
But this is got by casting pearl to hogs
That bawl for freedom in their senseless mood
And still revolt when truth would set them free.
License they mean when they cry "liberty";
For who loves that, must first be wise and good;
But from that mark how far they rove we see
For all this waste of wealth and loss of blood.

("On the Detraction which followed my Writing
Certain Treatises")

Milton's enemies are not accorded the respect of being distinguished from one another: they are a barbarous noise such as is made by chattering apes, barking dogs, braying asses, and vicious hogs squealing for their liberty. These abusive comparisons are stinging jabs preparing for the knockdown, which comes in the fourth line before the end: "License they mean when they cry liberty" (line 11). The line has an approximately dactyllic rhythm for heroic effect—"**LI**cense they **MEAN** when they **CRY LIB**erty—but its vehemence comes from the pronounced four beats of the old Anglo-Saxon line, with an emphatic caesural pause after **MEAN** and the last two beats—**CRY LIB**—hard up against each other.

The concluding three lines of the poem seem to be addressed to others, in an aside, explaining to us (not to them) the difference between license and liberty and reckoning up the damage these swinish fellows have done. In speaking to us, it is as if the poet is turning in contempt from a mortally stricken but as yet unextirpated foe.

In "On the New Forcers of Conscience" (from which I have already quoted the opening four lines), the turn strongly marks the separation of its three parts into phases of a counterattack. The octave is one long rhetorical question, a setup; the sestet is an insulting rebuke, raining blows down on the opponent; and the tail is a further setting up, with a menacing assertion of confidence in ultimate victory:

> Because you have thrown off your prelate lord
> And with stiff vows renounced his liturgy
> To seize the widowed whore Plurality
> From them whose sin ye envied, not abhorred,
> Dare ye for this adjure the civil sword
> To force our consciences that Christ set free
> And ride us with a classic hierarchy
> Taught ye by mere A.S. and Rutherford?
> Men whose life, learning, faith and pure intent
> Would have been held in high esteem with Paul
> Must now be named and printed heretics
> By shallow Edwards and Scotch What-d'ye-call.
> But we do hope to find out all your tricks,
> Your plots and packing worse than those of Trent,
>   That so the Parliament
> May with their wholesome and preventive shears
> Clip your phylacteries, though baulk your ears,

> And succour our just fears
> When they shall read this clearly in your charge:
> New *Presbyter* is but old *Priest*, writ large.
>
> *("On the New Forcers of Conscience under the*
> *Long Parliament")*

This a political poem, and it therefore speaks the language of the times, all of it crying out to modern students for annotation and historical understanding: *liturgy, plurality, civil sword, classic hierarchy, Trent, phylacteries,* perhaps even *Paul*—or what *Paul* means in this context. The ritual word *liturgy* may have suggested the "work" *(ergeia)* of praying *(lissomai).* But the word's contemporary association with Archbishop Laud—whose execution was engineered by these people only a year before—recall his deeply resented efforts to reform the Anglican liturgy in the direction of greater formality and beauty. Such associations overwhelm the original meaning of the word *liturgy,* or the generally positive meaning it has usually had and still has today. For Milton's audience *liturgy* meant a form of spiritual bondage to superstition that is analogous to the elaborately tied and, to Milton's audience, outlandish *phylacteries* of the Jews, signifying—for Jews as well as Christians, in fact—the elaborate bonds of the Law. *Pluralities* are lucrative parish "livings," an abuse of the now supplanted Anglican Church, roundly condemned by the Presbyterian divines, who have now changed their minds and greedily appropriated the livings to themselves ("whose sin ye envied, not abhorred"), and kept up tithing because the money is now flowing toward them, instead of away from them. *Presbyterian* means one who supports a church governed by the older and most respectable, godly men (Gr. *presbyteros,* "older man"), who are elected for the purpose by each congregation and have no one above them. Presbyterianism had overthrown the old-fashioned or *classic* government of bishops overseeing parish *priests,* beneath whom were deacons and curates doing the actual work in a parish, while the bishops were themselves overseen by an archbishop. That is the sense of *classic hierarchy* to which the Presbyterians—especially the grandees in the Westminster Assembly—now find themselves drawn, since they will be on top, riding the rest of us, as Archbishop Laud and his bishops did in the past. Hierarchy, with its material benefits, of course, is the sin the Presbyterians envied, when they said they abhorred it. Hence the hard-hitting final line, "New *Presbyter* is but old

Priest writ large." It means there is no difference (except the addition of two letters, hence "writ large") between the corrupt clergy of the Anglican Church, the priests, and the Presbyterians who overthrew them.

The *civil sword* refers to the power of the state and alludes to the Italian and Spanish states that the Roman Catholic Office of the Holy Inquisition infamously connived with to condemn to death and burn alive those it found guilty of heresy. *Trent* refers to the sessions of the Council of Trent (1545–1563), which was the basis of the Counter-Reformation. At the meetings of the Council of Trent over nearly two decades, the Roman Catholic Church worked out its doctrinal and disciplinary response to what it regarded as the heresies of Protestantism. The suggestion is that the Westminster Assembly of divines is no better than the ultra-Catholic Council of Trent. In taking up the civil sword to enforce its discipline and doctrine, the Westminster Assembly is no better than the hated English ecclesiastic court of the Star Chamber, and the still more hated Roman Catholic Holy Office of the Inquisition. Recondite as all this may seem to us now, these were fighting words because they were so intimate. They were aimed at well-known contemporary events and contemporary persons.

As for the great apostle Paul, not only is he the figure of deep integrity presented here, esteeming only men of great *learning*, pure *life*, and unshakable *faith*—he is also a byword for the Protestant movement as a whole from its origins, when Martin Luther—commenting on Paul's great Epistle to the Romans—raised the banner of justification by faith. We are justified before God by the inward act of *faith*, not by outward *works*, which the Roman Catholic Church defined as obedience to its *hierarchy* and submission to its *liturgy* and teaching—and its financial exactions. In "Lycidas," Peter had been the figure of ultimate authority, the symbol of the true church and the rock on which it is built. Now it is Paul, the symbol of faith, who is opposed to the corruptions of the church. In the Acts of the Apostles we see the kind of men who were held in esteem by Paul—and a considerable number who were not.

We're not done yet, for we still have those names to inform ourselves about. "On the New Forcers of Conscience under the Long Parliament" is a superb poem, but it is unintelligible without knowledge of the politics of the age, and perhaps the months, in which it was composed. It has elements of the political cartoon. The persons mentioned in the sonnet were forgotten within a few years, and after nearly four centuries are perfectly obscure. But the names were electric at the time: A.S., Dr. Adam *Stewart*, with an advanced degree for a fig leaf to hide his intellectual deficiencies; Samuel *Rutherford*, one of the pompous and venal Presbyterian divines of the Westminster Assembly; poor, shallow Thomas *Edwards*, who compared heretics like Milton to gangrene; and the supremely pathetic, because too contemptible even to be named, or remembered, Robert Baillie (if it is he), designated only by "Scotch What-d'ye'call." The reference to *ears*—"Clip your phylacteries, though baulk your ears" (line 17)—is an allusion to William Prynne, another of Milton's noisy antagonists, who had his ears cropped in 1634 for some offending passages in his attack on the theater, *Histriomastix* (1632). Some remarks by Prynne were taken to be insults directed at the queen, Henrietta Maria, who had recently performed in masques (too recently, however, to have been an object of attack in *Histriomastix*). The original of this line as it appears in the Trinity manuscript is more brutal, and better: "Crop ye as close as marginal P———'s ears." The second version, "Clip your phylacteries, though baulk your ears" (*baulk*, "to pass over, omit," is a term from plowing), is perhaps wittier because it suggests the phylacteries tied about the arm are cut off with the plow, while the ears are left, as ridges between the furrows. I say *perhaps* wittier, but without much conviction. Did Milton intend *baulk* to sound like *box?*

Two other sonnets were written in these years, one of them, the untitled Sonnet 14, is a suave, baroque elegy for Mrs. Catherine Thomason, observing the translation of her soul to Heaven, accompanied by her handmaids, who are the works of charity Catherine performed in her life. The superior figure of Faith clothes these handmaids with azure wings and purple beams and directs their course upward with her golden rod. When the handmaids tell the Judge, the Son, of Catherine's deeds, he bids her rest "And drink [her] fill of pure immortal streams" (line 14). The entire poem is sleek and well crafted, as we should expect. Beyond this it has Milton's compression, a rather faint but unmistakable trace of his genius, compensating for a banal final line. One prefers the more elegantly banal conclusion to the epitaph on the Marchioness of Winchester. The use of the Italian sonnet form with a sestet may not have served the poet well in this instance, although there is nothing in the poem strongly to blame. It may lack Milton's fire, but that is perhaps not always to be expected in an occasional and consolatory exercise. Any of the better poets of the age might have composed it. We should be happy Milton preserved it because it is so well mannered and suave; and because we are interested to watch him creating such a conventionally Christian scene.

Milton's boisterous genius reappears in the next sonnet, number 12 (following the Trinity manuscript numbering), which we might refer to as "On *Tetrachordon*." *Tetrachordon*, "Four Chords," that is, four biblical passages, and *Colasterion*, "The Instrument of Punishment," are the last two divorce tracts, published in March 1645, *Colasterion* being nothing more than a line-by-line jeering response to a critic of Milton's *Doctrine and Discipline of Divorce:* "I mean not to dispute philosophy with this pork, who never read any" (*YP*, 2:737). The four chords of *Tetrachordon* are four passages in the Bible referring to marriage, which Milton proposed to reconcile with one another in favor of divorce for incompatibility of mind. This is an impossible task, which makes the performance of it all the more virtuosic. Yet it is worth remembering, as Arthur Barker pointed out, that Milton's argument for divorce prompted a shift in his thinking from a "top-down" adherence to divine law to the "principle of human good" as a starting point for thought.[2] That is what we encounter in *Paradise Lost:* an anthropic theology.

It seems the title of the book, *Tetrachordon*, staggered many, as well it might, although Milton is not inclined to forgive them. The sonnet is a comic and, for Milton, good-natured response to critics who ridiculed him for the obscurity of his title:

> A book was writ of late called *Tetrachordon*,
> And woven close, both matter, form and style.
> The subject new, it walked the town awhile
> Numbering good intellects, now seldom pored on.
> Cries the stall-reader, Bless us! what a word on
> A title-page is this! And some in file
> Stand spelling false while one might walk to Mile-
> End Green. Why is it harder sirs than Gordon,
> Colkitto, or Macdonnel, or Galasp?
> Those rugged names to our like mouths grow sleek
> That would have made Quintilian stare and gasp.

> Thy age, like ours, O soul of Sir John Cheke,
> Hated not learning worse than toad or asp
> When thou taught'st Cambridge, and King Edward Greek.
>
> *(Sonnet 12, "On Tetrachordon")*

In the octave the book itself is described walking about town attracting the attention of the intelligent and the protests of the unintelligent "stall-reader," who grazes among the book stalls in Saint Paul's churchyard and is stumped by this erudite title. Others stand in line behind this vocal stall-reader, waiting their turn, filling the time trying to spell this hard word. You could walk out of London altogether, and back again, and they would still be at their orthographic contortions. At the turn in the eighth line of the octave the real target of Milton's scorn comes into view: as always at this time, the Presbyterians. The poet challenges them: is the Greek word *tetrachordon* really harder to pronounce than the names of all you Scots, *Gordon, Colkitto, Macdonnel,* and *Galasp?* Those are names that would have made Quintilian, the Roman rhetorician and arbiter of literary style, "stare and gasp" in dismay. *Gasp* is delightfully rhymed with the unfortunate *Galasp,* who hates learning worse than toad or *asp.* The poem concludes with an apostrophe to the soul of Sir John Cheke, the first professor of Greek at Cambridge and the tutor of Edward VI, the boy who succeeded to the throne after Henry VIII and who is remembered, despite his youth, as an exemplary Protestant king, and as learned.

The tone is burlesque from the start, when the difficult "a" rhyme of the octave is made more difficult still by rhyming on the last two syllables of last word of the opening line, *Tetrachordon: pored on, word on, Gordon.* John Carey observes that with the rhyme on *pored on,* Milton is mocking George Wither's all too serious rhyming of *pore on* with *Basilicon Doron.* The enjambments at lines 5, 6, and 7 are intentionally incompetent, sounding like prose that has been arbitrarily divided up into lines broken wherever breaks were needed for the syllable count: "what a word on / A title page"; "And some in file / Stand spelling false"; and, best of all, because it breaks up a word, "while one might walk to Mile- / End Green." We then have the cartoonlike picture of Quintilian in his toga (a picture worthy of James Gillray), appalled at the sound of names of those Scots—and perhaps at the sight of them, too. But the poet concludes on a note of disdain for the vulgarity of the Presbyterians, reading instead of buying at the bookstalls, thus acquiring superficial learning and hating real learning "worse than toad or asp" (line 13). The syntax of "like ours" is admittedly difficult. Carey reviews the interpretative debates on these lines. But the obvious sense was pointed out in the nineteenth century by David Masson, whom Carey cites: *like ours* means *as ours does:* "your age did not hate learning *as ours does.*"[3]

It is a technically difficult and largely satisfying performance. Notwithstanding its humor, the poem makes us feel great matters are in hand, recalling Milton's translation, in *Apology for Smectymnuus*, of a remark in Horace's satires in defense of satire: "Jesting decides great things / Stronglier, and better oft than earnest can" (*"ridiculum acri / fortius et melius magnas plerumque secat res"* (*YP*, 1:904).[4] But what exactly is decided in this poem? Englishmen who read books should learn their Greek? Scots should go back north of the Tweed? No: Presbyterians, for all their pretensions to learning, are vulgar.

We have thus far observed three principal voices in Milton's sonnets: the headlong, "through composed," prophetic voice of "On the Late Massacre in Piedmont" (1655); the punchy, vehement fighting voice of "On the Detraction" and "On the New Forcers of Conscience" (1646); and the genially ridiculing, humanist voice of the *Tetrachordon* sonnet (1646), which at the end brings out another, less public side of Milton's character: his learning.

But is any side of Milton's character not public? The fine early sonnet of this period, number 8, "When the Assault was Intended to the City" (1642), is a display of classical learning, and of the pleasure of classical learning, composed when London lay all but defenseless before the army of Charles I (it was not the only the military opportunity Charles would miss during the civil war). The city militia, or "trained bands," as they were called, were an inadequate force, and they were all that stood between a vengeful royalist army and the city. In the Trinity manuscript, Milton says he posted this sonnet on the door of his house, appealing to whatever "Captain or colonel or knight in arms" who should come there not to sack the house but to guard it against harm, because it is a place of learning: "Lift not the spear against the muses' bower" (line 9). The grateful poet can recompense the said captain or colonel with fame "o'er lands and seas" (line 7), as the conqueror Alexander the Great was famous for sparing the great lyric poet Pindar's house at the sack of Thebes, or as the timely singing of a chorus from Euripides's *Electra* prevented the destruction of Athens when it too lay at the mercy of an army:

> Captain or colonel or knight in arms
> Whose chance on these defenceless doors may seize,
> If deed of honour did thee ever please,
> Guard them, and him within protect from harms.
> He can requite thee, for he knows the charms
> That call fame on such gentle acts as these,
> And he can spread thy name o'er lands and seas
> Whatever clime the sun's bright circle warms.
> Lift not the spear against the muses' bower!
> The great Emathian conqueror bid spare
> The house of Pindarus when templ' and tow'r
> Went to the ground, and the repeated air
> Of sad Electra's poet had the power
> To save th' Athenian walls from ruin bare.
>
> ("*When the Assault was Intended to the City*")

"He knows the charms" (line 5). Milton means that he, the poet, knows the charms—the incantations, magical in effect—of deathless song, with power to immortalize a captain or colonel. But these charms are made possible by another, perhaps deeper charm, which is that of classical learning, arduously acquired. The charm with which the poet conjures whatever captain or colonel may come to his door is precisely that of classical allusion—to Pliny, Plutarch, and Horace. We see for a moment how in Milton's day, at the outset of the civil war, the classical tradition offered a ground for mutual protection and sympathy between men of a certain education and class. But the celebration of the power of learning's charm extends beyond the immediate purpose of saving Milton's home, or the selfish one of abandoning the unlettered to the tender mercies of war. It is about the power of learning itself against the violence of war. Alas, this power appears to be illusory.

For Milton, classical learning is not a private accomplishment. It is the *parole* of virtue and the bass note of the public voice. We hear it in Sonnet 10, "To the Lady Margaret Ley" (1642), calling for humanity, saneness and restraint. He praises Lady Margaret Ley, and her husband,

and her father, but in such a way as to promote public virtue. The closing lines read as follows:

> So well your words his noble virtues praise
> That all both judge you to relate them true
> And to possess them, honoured Margaret.
>
> *("To the Lady Margaret Ley," lines 12–14)*

There are of course more voices than the public one. An intimate voice has been briefly exemplified in the elegy for Mrs. Catherine Thomason (Sonnet 14), with its baroque decor. A stylistically audacious but very private sonnet—it is *about* a private life of devotion—is devoted to an unnamed lady (Sonnet 9, "Lady, that in the prime of earliest youth"). There is also the sonnet—number 13—to the senior partner and musical collaborator on *Comus*, "To Mr. Henry Lawes, on his Airs" (1646), which celebrates how music and verse, in Lawes's skillful hands, can complement each other—a favorite theme from Milton's earlier days, in "L'Allegro" and "Il Penseroso," in the poem to his musician father, *Ad Patrem*, and especially in "At a Solemn Music," with its "Sphere-born, harmonious sisters, Voice and Verse" (line 2).

There are three sonnets of sage counsel to leaders of the English Revolution: Sonnet 15, to the parliamentary general Thomas Fairfax (1648); Sonnet 16, to the brilliant and innovative general, Oliver Cromwell, now dominating the government (1652); and Sonnet 17, to Sir Henry Vane the Younger (1652), one of the most prominent figures of the revolution, executed in 1662. Joining together the private circumstances of the poet with his public persona are the two sonnets on his blindness and his public duty: the very famous Sonnet 19, "When I consider how my light is spent" (1655), and the impressive, more public Sonnet 22, "To Mr. Cyriack Skinner Upon his Blindness," "Cyriack, this three years' day these eyes" (1655).

But by far the most powerful, private, and personal of the intimate poems, Sonnet 23, "Methought I saw my late espousèd saint," is the last sonnet Milton composed, probably in the spring of 1658. It is a dream poem that describes how his deceased wife visited the poet in sleep. She had borne him a daughter, who also died. The poet imagines her, therefore, as having undergone ritual purification after childbirth, according to the "old Law," this ritual being described in Leviticus, chapter 12. The words *purification* and *pure*, as Edward LeCompte noted, play upon the Greek meaning of her name, Katherine, from *katharos* "pure." (I assume, with most students of Milton, that this is the poet's second wife, Katherine, not his first wife, Mary.) As readers of Mary Douglas's classic anthropological study, *Purity and Danger*, will recall, there is nothing disgraceful in the need for such purification after childbirth. One is more transcendently pure for having gone through it. The higher purity is dialectically produced.

In the dream, the poet sees her, though he never saw her in life, because he was already blind when they married. He does not see her entirely, however, because her face is veiled, although it seems to him as if her entire body—her "person"—expresses all the emotions the human face is capable of expressing. It is an exceedingly moving and tender account of a blind man's recollection of his wife's love, expressed through her entire body, her *person*: "Her face was veiled, yet to my fancied sight / Love, sweetness, goodness in her person shined / So clear as in no face with more delight" (lines 10–12). In *Paradise Lost*, in the famous passage on his blindness, Milton will call the human face *divine:*

> not to me returns
> Day or the sweet approach of ev'n or morn
> Or sight of vernal bloom or summer's rose
> Or flocks or herds or human face divine.
>
> (PL, *3.41–44*)

Perhaps this veiled face from his dream is the face he is thinking of here.

The dream occurred, and the sonnet was composed, in a time of deepening political troubles, when Oliver Cromwell, now Lord Protector, was dying and the English Revolution, not to mention the Excise office, where Milton's savings were lodged, was in danger of collapse (both would do so). None of these things is mentioned in the poem, but the privacy and the poignancy of the vision are a little augmented by our knowledge of the stress of the outer world, the world of day, which is physically dark for the poet when he wakes to it and morally dark for the nation. The poem ends after the illusion is dispelled (the poem's first word is *Methought*) by the returning darkness of the poet's waking hours: "But O as to embrace me she inclined / I waked, she fled, and day brought back my night" (lines 13–14).

Despite the Italian rhyme scheme, the octave breaks down into two symmetrical quatrains. The one quatrain bearing a classical allusion—to Alcestis, from Euripides's play of that name, who is brought back veiled to her husband by "Jove's great son" (line 3), Hercules. The other quatrain offers polysemous biblical allusions: first, to the old Hebrew law of Leviticus and then to the Christian promise of joyous reunion in Heaven. This stately manner of proceeding in the octave contrasts with the emotional release of the sestet. But that release is prepared for by the last line of the octave, in which the restraint of blindness falls away, as all human restraints on love fall away: "Full sight of her in Heaven without restraint" (line 8).[5] The sentence that begins with its grammatical subject *Mine*, at the beginning of line 5, produces its verb, *Came*, at the beginning of line 9, the first line of the sestet. This extension across the turn from octave to sestet of the sentence describing the main action of the sonnet ("my wife came") unifies the poem and allows the briefer action it recalls to frame the large biblical allusion of the second quatrain. There, the poet recurs to the deep past of the Israelites and looks forward to the promise of Heaven, in which he trusts. (We may note the decorous humility here, where the future is anticipated by faith rather than by prophecy.)

The action of the sestet is simple and direct, opening with that suspended main verb *came*. She comes to him with her face veiled but with her body expressing love, sweetness, and delight as intensely as any face could. She inclines to embrace him just as he is waking, and he loses her to the dream: "I waked, she fled, and day brought back my night." This final verse may disappoint because it seems to end the poem on nothing more than bitter complaint at an illusion. Yet although the visitation is presented as an illusory dream, and is concluded as a loss, we cannot help feeling that from a poetic point of view it was and is real. The poet wakes up to her great love for him, and to his love for her. If she is in Heaven, as the poet is assured she is, then she will be glad of how he has described their encounter:

> Methought I saw my late espoused saint
> Brought to me like Alcestis from the grave
> Whom Jove's great son to her glad husband gave,

> Rescued from death by force though pale and faint.
> Mine—as whom washed from spot of childbed taint,
> Purification in the old Law did save,
> And such as yet once more I trust to have
> Full sight of her in Heaven without restraint—
> Came vested all in white, pure as her mind.
> Her face was veiled, yet to my fancied sight
> Love, sweetness, goodness in her person shined
> So clear as in no face with more delight.
> But O as to embrace me she inclined,
> I waked, she fled, and day brought back my night.
>
> *(Sonnet 23, "Methought I saw my late espousèd saint")*

The three sonnets of sage advice to powerful men, Thomas Fairfax, Oliver Cromwell, and Sir Henry Vane, are Horation in tone, although the spirit of republicanism shines through them. They keep a steady pace between the headlong rush of the sonnet on the massacre of the Waldensians and the sharply separated, vehement lines of the fighting sonnets. In short, they are neither incendiary nor hostile, but firm. Their parts are carefully separated, generally into groups of four and three lines, and they march forward at a disciplined pace. Two of them— to Fairfax and Vane—return at their conclusions to the fighting style, with stinging contempt for corruption. All three poems are in the Trinity manuscript and two of them, to Fairfax and Cromwell, were unpublished and probably unpublishable in Milton's lifetime. The sonnet to Vane was published anonymously by Vane's biographer, George Sikes, in *The Life and Death of Sir Henry Vane, Kt* (1602), only months after Vane's execution.

Sonnet 15, "On the Lord General Fairfax at the Siege of Colchester" (1648), celebrates the numerous victories already won by the Long Parliament's head of the army and most successful general after Oliver Cromwell: "Thy firm unshaken virtue ever brings / Victory home, though new rebellions raise / Their hydra heads" (lines 5–7). But in the sestet the sonnet turns to say, "O yet a nobler task awaits thy hand" (line 9). The task is to sweep away corruption, or "public fraud" (line 13) in the state. The poem ends with a powerful apothegm: "In vain doth valor bleed / While avarice and rapine share the land" (13–14). But Fairfax would have no future in politics. Upon the execution of the king in 1649, he retired to his estate at Nun Appleton, in Yorkshire. It was there in all probability that his daughter's tutor, Andrew Marvell—a man who *did* have a political future, especially after the Restoration—wrote some of the finest poems of the age before *Paradise Lost*, on which he would write another of the finest poems of the age.

Sonnet 16, "To the Lord General Cromwell" (1655), also celebrates military victories, notably Cromwell's discomfiture of the Scots at the great battles of Preston (near "Darwen stream"), which was fought in 1648; Dunbar, fought in 1650; and Worcester, September 3, 1651, the concluding battle of the English Civil War, utterly routing and destroying Charles II's mostly Scottish army. Cromwell famously called the battle "a crowning mercy," which phrase is perhaps the source of Milton's "laureate wreath": "While Darwen stream with blood of Scots imbrued / And Dunbar field resounds thy praises loud / And Worcester's laureate wreath" (lines 7–9). Although the Battle of Worcester was widely and immediately recognized as the end of civil war, the turn into the sestet seems at first to say that more military victories will be needed: "yet much remains / To conquer still" (lines 9–10). It is then made clear that a different and nonmaterial order of victory is now in question, one having to do with peace, which is to say, politics: "peace hath her victories / No less renowned than war," when "new" but very different "foes arise" (lines 10–11): avarice, faction, and arrogant fanaticism.

We are struck by the contrast between, on the one hand, the blood choking Darwen stream and, on the other hand, the more abstract thinking required to master the political problem now to be introduced: whether to have an established church or no. The "new foes" are in London, subtle committee men all, and as dangerous as the bellicose Scots. They intend an established church in England, with a paid clergy and a doctrine of fifteen core tenets to be enforced by law against dissenters. Having the power of law, and the civil sword to enforce it, such a church threatens "to bind our souls with secular chains" (line 12).[6]

For Milton, the secular state should have no coercive power in spiritual things. The prospect of an established church rouses old hatreds in Milton, and enduring principles, too, principles he would enunciate in *A Treatise of Civil Power in Ecclesiastical Causes* (1659), which allows all religious opinions—the very word *heresy*, in a negative sense, is anathema—and therefore opposes all orthodoxy. He utterly rejects the possibility that civil power can be legitimately employed in matters concerning religion. The prospect of such an outrage also rouses old language, reaching back a decade to the antiprelatical tracts and still further back to "Lycidas," to the time in Milton's twenties when he declined to enter the church because it was corrupt and coercive. It was then that he was, as he said, "church-outed by the prelates" (*YP*, 1:823).

In the Cromwell poem we meet again with the language of "Lycidas": "the grim wolf with privy paw" (line 128) and the "blind mouths" (line 119) of the clergy. Milton is again denouncing ministers hired and paid by the state (through tithing) who instead of preaching the word of God to their flocks cram their own mouths and bellies with food, that is, with ill-gotten property and riches. "Help us," the poet implores Cromwell, "to save free conscience from the paw / Of hireling wolves whose gospel is their maw" (lines 13–14). The rhythm of this final couplet reminds us of the fighting sonnets. "**SAVE FREE CON**science" puts those three stressed syllables at the center of line 13, like the crown of an arch. The final line is stunning, not only for its pugnacious, Anglo-Saxon rhythm ("**HIRE**ling **WOLVES,** whose **GOS**pel is their **MAW**") but especially for the shock of that equation: the gospel these hirelings preach is nothing other than their own mouths. Where the gospel should he coming out of their mouths, in preaching, food is going in instead; the food is the very flock these wolfish preachers are supposed to protect and sustain by preaching the gospel. (Compare *A Masque Presented at Ludlow Castle, 1634*, line 777: "Crams and blasphemes his feeder.")

The third sonnet of sage advice, Sonnet 17, "To Sir Henry Vane the Younger" (1652), is more complicated than these other two, largely because it brings out a problem that is unacknowledged in them: how to overcome the contradiction of appealing to a man of war to safeguard matters of spiritual import, when force has no authority over spirit. The problem is more apparent when the sonnet is not addressed to a general but to a statesman. The political problem is to be solved by careful thinking and courageous adherence to principle.

Sir Henry Vane the Younger was a very different figure from Fairfax or Cromwell, although no less heroic. He was a statesman, not a general, and in the 1630s had been briefly governor of Massachusetts, where he saw the troubles that arise from using the power of the state, including the judiciary, to make judgments in spiritual matters, notably in the case of Anne Hutchinson, whom he admired, and whose meetings he attended. (He was also instrumental in the founding of Harvard College.) After returning to England, Vane showed his administrative skills as treasurer of the navy. As a member of the Long Parliament, he became an important figure in the English Revolution and notorious for the underhanded means by which he helped to secure the execution of the hated Earl of Strafford. Although he opposed the execution of the king, Vane remained a central figure in the Commonwealth and the Rump Parliament, until he split with Cromwell over the dissolution of Parliament in 1653, refusing thereafter to sit on the Council of State.

It was before this, in 1652, when Vane was thirty-nine, "young in years" for a person with his record, that Milton composed his sonnet and sent it to Vane, celebrating Vane's known opposition to an established church exercising civil power. Vane's retirement at forty was tactical—he continued to influence politics with his writing—but he would be back in the game in the chaotic final year of the Commonwealth. Despite his opposition to the regicide, he was executed on Tower Hill in 1662.

It is odd enough to see a military man such as Fairfax, more used to shedding blood in the field than conducting administration, being asked to root out fraud and corruption, mostly in financial affairs. It is very odd, if not absurd, to see another military man, Cromwell, first disqualified from having any authority in matters of "free conscience" and then asked to save free conscience from restrictions advocated by those who are exercising their free consciences arguing on the other side. In putting it this way, it would be quite wrong to plume oneself on having caught Milton out in his logic. Milton has identified a real political dilemma: do you accord freedoms to those who would deny them to others?

That Milton has meditated carefully on this problem is apparent in the way the Vane sonnet unfolds across its entire length, striving to break the problem down into parts. No longer is it a matter of simply turning, in the sestet, from bloody force to something altogether different from and incompatible with it. As Milton says in the Fairfax sonnet, "For what can war but endless war still breed / Till truth and right from violence be freed?" (lines 10–11). But truth and right cannot be separated from violence by violence alone, necessary as violence is to oppose evil. Violence in itself, separated from wisdom and right, only begets more of itself. If valor bleeds "in vain," it is not only because "avarice and rapine share the land" while valor is, as it were, occupied elsewhere. Valor is powerless to do anything about avarice and rapine, even if it should focus its attention on them at last.

Hence the need to distinguish between what violence can and cannot do, between the spheres of military action, diplomacy, and politics, and, again, between the spheres of secular authority and the spiritual realm of "free conscience." The very subject of the Vane sonnet is the difficult art of thinking clearly in the fog of political circumstances: on the one hand, of making distinctions where confusion exists and, on the other hand, of avoiding contradictions of principle.

In the Fairfax and Cromwell sonnets, Milton must say that these mens' works of peace—works consigned to an imaginary political future— will be different from and more important than their works of war. But Milton must also recognize Fairfax's and Cromwell's works of war as the basis of their imaginary works of peace. An uncertainty as to the importance of violence makes the literal sense of the sestet in the Fairfax sonnet blurry when you look at it hard. In the Cromwell sonnet this blurry spot is confined to the witty antithesis: "peace hath her victories" (line 10), a phrase that captures Cicero's poetic phrase "*cedant arma togae, concedat laurea linguae*" ("let arms cede to the magistrate's toga, and the military laurel crown to the tongue of civic eloquence").[7] This antithesis will be deployed again, more subtly, in the Vane sonnet: "gowns not arms repelled / The fierce Epirot and the African bold" (lines 3–4). The Roman senators were undismayed before the victorious Greek general and king of Epirus, Pyrrhus (from whom we derive the phrase "Pyrrhic victory"), as they were also before the Carthaginian (hence "African") general, Hannibal, even after his annihilation of a huge Roman army at Cannae, a disaster that left Rome all but defenseless. In *Areopagitica*, Milton saluted the firmness and confidence of Rome and the senate in this crisis, and compared it with that of London and the Long Parliament in 1642, when London was invested by royalist forces.

This idea of robes doing the office of arms is introduced at the beginning of the Vane sonnet, not at the end, so that it is no longer merely a turn of phrase for getting out of trouble. It is instead a means of stating the problem to be solved. How do togas, instead of arms, remove the state from danger?

They do so by mental firmness in the drawing of fine distinctions based on principle and by holding to those distinctions and those principles with military tenacity. Even the largest and hardest distinction to make in seventeenth-century politics, between secular and spiritual authority, is dealt with in this sonnet: "The bounds of either sword to thee we owe" (line 12). It opens with Vane, like the Roman senators, holding the helm of the secular state, and it ends with Religion leaning on his hand. The sonnet is about difficulty of making true judgments in the midst of continually changing complications of circumstance. The syntax is perhaps a little loose, so that reading the poem gives some experience of the difficulty that it describes. But it seems clear enough that the first eleven lines should be taken as a single sentence with the main verb at the end and the subject at the beginning (I have punctuated it accordingly): "Vane [line 1] . . . thou hast learned [line 11] . . . to settle [line 5] . . . unfold [line 5] . . . advise [line 7] . . . [and] know [line 9]."

The first four lines say who Vane is—"a better senator ne'er held / The helm of Rome" (lines 2–3)—before turning to what he has learned. The alternative introduced by "Whether" (line 5) is between making peace with Holland if her intentions are peaceful—Carey notes the pun on "hollow" (line 6)—or going to war with her, if her "drift" is hostile. Vane has learned how to "spell" (line 6; see *OED* 2a for *spell:* "to discover or find out, to guess or suspect, by close study or observation") the intentions of states. If war is decided on in consequence—as it was, in this instance—then Vane has also learned how to advise the conduct of the war, with regard to both weapons and finance, "iron and gold" (line 8). Besides, Vane has learned the difference between civil and spiritual power, "what each means, / What severs each" (lines 10–11), a thing "which few have done" (line 11). There the sentence ends, and the final three lines expand on this final point about civil power in spiritual matters:

> Vane, young in years but in sage counsel old,
> Than whom a better senator ne'er held
> The helm of Rome when gowns not arms repelled
> The fierce Epirot and the African bold,
> Whether to settle peace or to unfold
> The drift of hollow states, hard to be spelled,
> Then to advise how war may best, upheld,
> Move by her two main nerves, iron and gold

In all her equipage, besides, to know
Both spiritual power and civil, what each means,
What severs each, thou hast learned, which few have done.
The bounds of either sword to thee we owe.
Therefore on thy firm hand Religion leans
In peace, and reckons thee her eldest son.

("To Sir Henry Vane the Younger")

As I have said, "Settl[ing] peace" requires diplomatic negotiation, sage counsel and also resolution. Discovering the hidden intent or "drift" of states is hard to do. But Vane can do it. And when war is inevitable, Vane knows how to support a war effort with knowledge of munitions and finance. These abilities lead on to another deeper and more difficult one, which is how to "sever" spiritual and civil power. In the fog of politics and war, Vane sees where each has its just claims and will not encroach on the other. This is something, Milton says with understatement, "which few have done." "The bounds of either sword to thee we owe," he says, by which he means (1) the physical sword of the civil power, the power to execute and physically punish; and (2) the spiritual sword of the word of God in the Bible, the sword of faith. John Carey cites very appositely Milton's remark, in *Observations on the Articles of Peace*, that to extirpate spiritual sins, "heresy, schism, and profaneness," is "no work of the civil sword but of the spiritual, which is the Word of God."[8] A statesman who knows these principles and the fine distinctions they allow him to draw through every crowded issue, is someone on whose firm hand Religion may safely lean "in peace." The other hand remains free, as Cromwell's would be in Ireland, to take up the sword. But is the problem solved, even in this poem, notionally, with Religion leaning on the hand of a statesman?

The two sonnets of recreation, Sonnet 20, "Lawrence of virtuous father virtuous son," and Sonnet 21, "Cyriack, whose grandsire on the royal bench," both composed around 1655, are worth attention for themselves and because they remind us, as we do need reminding sometimes, that Milton was supremely urbane. They are elegant defenses, and celebrations, as well, of culture and sociability, in the tradition of Jonson's sociable poems, especially "Inviting a Friend to Supper." They inhabit a civilized atmosphere virtually created for literature by Horace. The first is indeed in friendly competition with one of Horace's most famous odes of recreational advice to a young man: the ninth ode of book one. The ode opens with a description of a winter landscape on Mount Soracte (modern Monte Soratte, north of Rome), the snow glistening on the heights and burdening the trees in the woods below, where the streams are frozen solid with the bitter cold. Do you see this, he asks:

> Vides ut alta stet nive candidum
> Soracte, nec iam sustineant onus
> silvae laborantes, geluque
> flumina constiterint acuto.

The speaker recommends staying indoors, heaping high the roaring fire, and liberally pouring the Sabine wine from its jar. Leave the rest to the gods (*permitte divis cetera* [line 9]), don't worry about what will come tomorrow (*quid sit futurum cras, fuge quaerere* [line 13]), treasure each day, and don't forget to dance and chase girls while you're young.

The last part is advice Milton perhaps finds supererogatory. Addressed to Henry Lawrence, his sonnet is about the wise measurement, the apportionment, of pleasures. It is also purely and uncomplicatedly delightful, despite the unpromising opening about virtuous fathers and sons. The final couplet introduces the problem that will be thought about at more length in the sonnet to Cyriack Skinner: how to *judge* wisely what true delights are and also to judge when to spare time for them, and even *interpose them oft*. Life is fundamentally serious, but without such intermissions one is not wise. Are rest and recreation departures from the serious life or are they contributions to it, actually helping one live a serious life? The delicate mental task of judging pleasure merits the light touch of humor of that final litotes: he who can so judge is *not unwise*. That cleverly posed intellectual puzzle is itself one of the pleasures to be reckoned up in this way, and it follows from an uncomplicated list of the others:

> Lawrence of virtuous father virtuous son,
> Now that the fields are dank and ways are mire
> Where shall we sometimes meet and by the fire
> Help waste a sullen day? What may be won

From the hard season gaining? Time will run
On smoother till Favonius reinspire
The frozen earth and clothe in fresh attire
The lily and rose, that neither sowed nor spun.
What neat repast shall feast us, light and choice,
Of Attic taste, with wine, whence we may rise
To hear the lute well touched or artful voice
Warble immortal notes and Tuscan air?
He who of those delights can judge, and spare
To interpose them oft, is not unwise.

("Lawrence of virtuous father virtuous son")

Winter is the time for staying indoors, for hard work and study, when the fields are wet and the roads clogged with mud. Spring and summer are for walking abroad, among lilies and roses, after Favonius, the west wind, breathes life on the frozen earth in spring. But winter should have its recreations. Following Horace, the poet proposes meeting sometimes for the entire rainy ("sullen") day, perhaps in an inn, where they can sit by the fire and talk, and where they can take an elegantly simple repast, "light and choice" (line 9): small portions but of the best quality. After which they will listen to music, perhaps some of it religious ("immortal notes," line 12), and some of it, in keeping with the elegance of the repast, in the most refined of the Italian dialects, Tuscan.

It is true the reader may stumble for an instant on the word *spare*, supposing it to mean "to refrain from these delights," and only after the enjambment see that the poet means "spare time for these delights." One may even quite legitimately enjoy making this correction, and find that in doing so the subtle point about judgment is reinforced. This is not what Aubrey meant when he called Milton "a spare man." The serious man's first impulse is sparely to refrain from these delights—or even to scorn them, as in "Lycidas," "and live laborious days" (line 72). But then he wisely spares a suitable quantity of time to "interpose" these delights between periods of work. I think it is wrong to suppose the word *spare* is deliberately ambiguous, as has been claimed, and of course the conclusion is turned into nonsense if the meaning is "can spare delights." Milton would hardly have committed the ambiguity intentionally, especially when one branch of it is absurd. Nor do I think Milton expected the reader to fall into an erroneous reading of *spare* as "to decline, to forbear" and then correct it. He expected the reader to suspend completing the sense until rounding the end of that strongly enjambed penultimate line and seeing that the meaning is this: "spare the time, often, to interpose those delights between periods of work." Because Milton was a Latin poet before he was an English one (as we have seen, before he was twenty-one he wrote far more lines of verse in Latin than in English), and because the very heart of his poetry is this syntactical suspense that accompanies the unfolding of the meaning, an ambiguity of this kind would not seem to Milton a deepening of the sense but a muddying of it, like those "ways of mire" (line 2). He expects from his English readers something of the vigilance of a reader of inflected, literary Latin, in which word order is artfully complex and the meaning is not clear until the verb has been grasped and put in relation with the other parts. Here, the main verb and its auxiliary are distributed across the end of the line, making an especially strong enjambment. The reader is expected to diet sparely on the meaning and refrain from gluttonous haste.

The point is illustrated in Sonnet 21, "Cyriack, whose grandsire on the royal bench," because the syntax is a little more difficult in this poem and the need for vigilance is correspondingly greater. The sonnet is addressed to the young man Cyriack Skinner, who was born in 1627, nineteen years after Milton. According to John Aubrey and Anthony à Wood, Skinner was formerly a student of the poet's. Milton addresses him with the affectionate care of a teacher as well as a friend, advising him not to work so hard at his studies that he declines to take time off at regular intervals to enjoy a "cheerful hour" (line 14). While you are still young, learn to apportion your time between hard work and cheerful recreation: "To measure life, learn thou betimes" (line 9). That is the lesson of the sonnet: live a life that is proportioned. The first half of the octave mentions Cyriack's grandfather, Sir Edward Coke, the eminent jurist and chief justice of the King's Bench:

> Cyriack, whose grandsire on the royal bench
> Of British Themis with no mean applause
> Pronounced, and in his volumes taught, our laws,
> Which others at their bar so often wrench.
>
> *("Cyriack, whose grandsire on the royal bench,"*
> *lines 1–4)*

An incautious reader might suppose that *pronounced*, at the beginning of the third line, is the verb for which we have been waiting (having *grandsire* in line 1 as its subject), and that this verb is meant intransitively, having no object: "Cyriack's grandsire sat on the bench and pronounced, and he did so to applause." But *pronounced* has a direct object, *laws*, and is paired with another verb, *taught*. The correct reading is, "Cyriack's grandsire pronounced our laws from the bench and he taught our laws in his books." We have to wait a little longer for the meaning. The next two lines of the octave will test the reader's patience and sense of proportion just a little more: "Today, deep thoughts resolve with me to drench / In mirth that after no repenting draws" (lines 5–6). *Deep thoughts* means "serious thoughts," and *drench* means "charm and put to sleep." To a reader used to English word order, *deep thoughts* looks at first like the subject of the sentence instead of its object, the correct reading being "resolve with me, Cyriack, to drench deep thoughts in mirth, the temperate kind of mirth that does not cause repenting"— repenting because of a hangover or embarrassment. It is true we can see a kind of found poetry in a misreading where deep thoughts resolve of their own accord to drench themselves in shallow ones, mirth. Such a misreading might suggest, not without a certain profundity, that there is no executive self apart from our immediate thoughts deciding, from above, as it were, when to be serious and when to be mirthful. This is the same executive self that appears at the openings and in the final couplets of "L'Allegro" and "Il Penseroso," respectively, banishing melancholy in the first and "vain, deluding Joys" in the second, and making bargains at the end of each: "These delights if thou canst give, / Mirth with thee I mean to live" (lines 150–51); "These pleasures, Melancholy, give, / And I with thee will choose to live" (lines 175–76). In these poems Milton exhibits some irony about that youthful executive self.

But far from criticizing in this sonnet the idea of an executive self, Milton is affirming its importance and authority. Proportion is never spontaneously produced: it requires decisive intervention. Deep thoughts have their own momentum and will never check themselves or grant an hour of repose. That requires a conscious decision, indeed a *resolution* and a habit of *resolve:* "Today, Cyriack, resolve with me to drench— that is, put to sleep—our deep thoughts in mirth." Milton intends the reader to suspend decisions about the grammar of the words until the phrase is complete, and especially until the imperative verb *resolve* is grasped. "Resolve with me, Cyriack!" "Resolve to do what?" "To drench something, put it to sleep." "What?" "Deep thoughts." "With what?" "Mirth." "When?" "Today!" The elegance and pleasure of the sentence is in the assiduity that must accompany our reading, the slight tension that comes from suspense, so that when we reach *mirth* all the parts fall into place, and the remaining clause, "that after no repenting draws" (line 6), affords an easy descent. It then comes over us that the Latinate syntax, which has compelled us to read in this way, suspending judgment, is an enactment of the lesson of the poem concerning due measure and proportion. The time of life, and of each day, should be carefully apportioned, just as we apportion the different parts of a sentence according to their respective grammatical functions. We should learn early to apportion our time: "To measure life, learn thou betimes" (line 9).

The final two lines of the octave are grammatically straightforward, but they too afford matter for thought: "Let Euclid rest and Archimedes pause / And what the Swede intend and what the French" (lines 7–8). It might be interesting to reflect what *resting* could mean to Euclidean geometry, since geometry is progressive, and what *pausing* could mean to Archimedes's mechanics. But the addressee is told not to do so. The point is only that geometry and mechanics are different forms of deep thought: one has to distinguish between them, as one does between the political and military intentions of the Swedish and French kings. It is not enough to study these things separately and diligently: one must reflect on the difference between them. That point has not yet emerged, but it is prepared for here. Because the sonnet is about due proportion and judicious apportionment, the octave concludes with a strong stop, reserving its lesson for after the turn, which here neatly coincides with the beginning of the sestet: "To measure life, learn thou betimes, and know / Toward solid good what leads the nearest way" (lines 9–10).

This is beautifully subtle. The second line seems to draw us back into the realm of deep thoughts and serious study. If we must think not only about Archimedes and Euclid but also about the difference between their respective disciplines, then the same work of distinction should be applied to learning as a whole, always asking what it is for and where it is leading. If the end or *telos* of learning is, as Milton said, "to repair the ruins of our first parents by regaining to know God aright" (*YP*, 2:366–67), the more secular version of this is "solid good," that is, the ethical. However hard you study your Euclid, you should not forget that virtue is the goal of your studies.

We may not always agree that every academic discipline is at bottom a discipline in ethics. But this sonnet is about education, the education or "guiding out" of the individual, not about the disciplines with which education is engaged. Education must put the student before the things studied, developing the "solid good" of the whole person. This, we will see, is the point of the discussion in *Paradise Lost* between Adam and the angel Raphael, who says that learning should be treated like diet, with temperance. It appears then that to "know / Toward solid good what leads the nearest way" (lines 9–10) is not just about apportioning attention within the disciplines of study—when to think about Archimedes, for example, and when to think about the Swede. It is about apportioning study itself within a larger and a higher view of life, which includes "other things" than arduous study, things that improve study rather than detracting from it. Too much care of study, though it seem very serious—"wise in show"—is as detrimental to intellectual proportion as overeating is detrimental to health:

> To measure life, learn thou betimes, and know
> Toward solid good what leads the nearest way.
> For other things mild Heav'n a time ordains
> And disapproves that care, though wise in show,
> That with superfluous burden loads the day,
> And when God sends a cheerful hour, refrains.
>
> *("Cyriack, whose grandsire on the royal bench,"*
> *lines 9–14)*

The recreative sonnets are about proportion, assigning all things in life to their proper spheres, including learning, and having the wisdom to spare time, as well—not too little and not too much—for cheerful and cultivated pursuits. These sonnets are ethical in what we may think of as the ordinary sense, in the management of the rhythm of the day, the word *ordinary* having the same Latin root as *order*. They are about the ecology of the ethos. The last two sonnets I shall discuss, Sonnet 19, "When I consider," and Sonnet 22, "To Mr. Cyriack Skinner Upon his Blindness," address the self outside the ordinary round of the day because their subject is the self in crisis after a major and, as it seems, catastrophic life event: the advent of total blindness, which happened to Milton early in the year 1652, perhaps on February 28. The poet is not now speaking about apportioning one's resources and powers to create a proper rhythm for the day. He is speaking about accommodating one's spirit to an irrevocable, crippling loss, and determining after it what one should do with one's life.

The first of the two is Milton's most famous sonnet, and perhaps his most famous short poem. I am inclined to agree with those who place it about two years after Milton went blind; however, those who think it earlier, following hard on the event, may be right. That Milton assigned this event to a single day is indicated in the opening of the second sonnet, to which I shall turn first:

> Cyriack, this three-years' day these eyes, though clear
> To outward view of blemish or of spot,
> Bereft of light their seeing have forgot,
> Nor to their idle orbs doth sight appear
> Of sun or moon or star throughout the year
> Or man or woman. Yet I argue not
> Against Heav'ns hand or will, nor bate a jot
> Of heart or hope but still bear up and steer
> Right onward. What supports me dost thou ask?
> The conscience, friend, to have lost them overplied
> In liberty's defence, my noble task,
> Of which all Europe talks from side to side.
> This thought might lead me through the world's vain mask
> Content though blind, had I no better guide.

> (Sonnet 22, *"To Mr. Cyriack Skinner Upon his Blindness"*)

Three years ago to the day, these eyes, he says, forgot how to see. He describes his eyes from the outside, as others see them, since he can see nothing. His eyes are clear, without blemish or spot, like a clear window, through which things on the outside should be seen from within: sun, moon, star, woman, or man. But they are not seen. And this is so, he adds carefully, throughout the year. He thus alerts us to a further dimension to the loss: the loss of the sight of seasonal change. It is not only the objects and persons themselves that are lost to sight but the relations between and among them. The phrase "throughout the year" (line 5) anticipates a little eerily what he will say in *Paradise Lost*, in the great apostrophe to Holy Light opening book 3:

> Thus with the year
> Seasons return but not to me returns
> Day or the sweet approach of ev'n or morn
> Or sight of vernal bloom or summer's rose
> Or flocks or herds or human face divine.
>
> (PL, *3.40–44*)

The turn in the sonnet comes early, in the sixth line, with the telltale *yet*, a word Milton likes for marking abrupt turns almost as much as he likes the word *but*. The remaining three lines of the octave modulate to the question Cyriack has asked—"What supports me dost thou ask?" (line 9)—which is then answered in the sestet. Indeed, the entire sestet is taken up by that answer. Approaching the question, he does not quite say he never regrets his misfortune. He says he does not argue with it, since it comes from God: "Yet I argue not / Against Heav'ns hand or will" (lines 6–7). Nor does he say he never complains of his misfortune, something the other sonnet gives evidence he does, if only inwardly. What he says is that he doesn't lose *heart*, even a little, or *hope*, even for a moment: the heart that gives him spirit to go on in life in pursuit of what he will call "liberty's defense" (line 11) and the hope that gives him the confidence to expect the cause of liberty to win out in the end. In a very fine phrase he then says, "but still bear up and steer / Right onward" (lines 8–9). He bears up bravely and bears his head erect—you can look him in the eye, as he has invited you to do in the opening lines of the sonnet—and like a ship in a naval engagement (is he thinking of the naval engagements with the Dutch?), he sails upright before the wind and steers directly on his foe.

That is what he does now. But he gets the confidence to do it from what he has already done in liberty's defense, although it was precisely from his literary labor on that defense (*Pro Populo Anglicano Defensio*, published in 1651) that cost him his eyesight, as his doctors had warned. But the book was famous—the most famous work Milton ever published in his lifetime—and he does not exaggerate when he says all

Europe speaks of it. The conclusion is splendid. The recollection of his achievement would be enough to *lead* him (as a blind man is led) contentedly through the vain pageant of the world. Unlike most people, the poet says he would be content, "though blind" (line 15), because of his achievement. But the final words come a surprise, one that is inevitable once it is heard: "had I no better guide."

It turns out that the *thought* he refers to—the thought of his achievement—is not the best thing to lead him through the world, and now we see why that it is so. The thought is a recollection; it is retrospective. If you are led by a guide who is looking back at where you have been, instead of at where you are going, you are poorly, indeed blindly, led, however *content* it may make you. Such blindness would be not only physical but spiritual, too. Are we readers expected here to change the meaning of *blind* in the final line of the poem from a physical to a spiritual sense—or to see at least that a spiritual sense is implied? This is the kind of semantic enrichment of meaning against which I have already urged caution, although in this case there is no inconsistency with the meaning of the poem or its direction. It may be a positive and beautiful effect produced accidentally by the interaction of different requirements and systems. It is conceivable it took Milton himself by surprise, as of course not infrequently happens with artists, when something not intended at the start is generated by the forces set loose in the work. Such an effect may not have been intended (fewer effects than we suppose are), but it is happily found. Milton would have been content, and complacent, and perhaps not unconceited, had he been led through the world by this retrospective guide: the thought of his "noble task," now complete, like a medal on his chest. But medals should not be worn every day. The poet has a better guide, which is his confidence that Heaven's hand, which took his sight away, will put another task before him. That is why he can nobly "bear up and steer / Right onward" (lines 8–9).

The central problem of Milton's poetic career, as of his life, is that of service, and it is the subject of Sonnet 19, "When I consider"—or, as it is often called, "On His Blindness." That is the first reason this sonnet is central in Milton's *oeuvre*. It is about the problem of service. It hasn't the scale and importance of "Lycidas," of course, which among other things is nearly fourteen times longer than the sonnet. But it comes out of the same central place. We are in this sonnet in the heartland of what motivates Milton's poetry: the intellectual, spiritual, and existential problem of service—and the mystery of service. How to serve God? And what does *service* mean? The word I have been using for it is *engagement*. We have just seen this matter in the sonnet the poet would address three years later to Cyriack Skinner, except that there service isn't a problem. What is at stake in that poem is doing one's duty when the problem of what that duty is has already been solved. The poet says, "I wrote my book, *Pro Populo Anglicano Defensio*, and it cost me my eyesight, but in doing so I was serving God (and my country)." It was clearly my duty, and I did it. Knowing that, and being proud of it, makes my affliction easy to bear as I go through the world. Besides, as the final clause tells us (we have noted the surprise), what truly leads me now is my readiness to serve again. In the Skinner poem, Milton is never for a moment off balance or uncertain. He steers right onward, under full sail. It is a brave sight.

But just because it is brave there is in this poem no emotional change, that is, no transition from one complex emotional state to another—something that is necessary to a poem if it is to be great. The change between emotional states in a poem is as important as the complexity of each—as we see demonstrated supremely in "Lycidas." Milton's poem to Cyriack Skinner on his blindness is just one proud emotion growing larger in sight as it bears down upon us. Nor is there any intellectual problem. We are never provoked by the poem to ask whether *Pro Populo Anglicano Defensio* really was the indispensable task in liberty's defense that Milton supposed it to be, and whether that is the task, and no other, God expected Milton to do (thank God it was not). So far as this poem is concerned, it just is. We have to take it for granted. The drama of the poem lies instead in the revelation, which comes in the last clause, that the thought of that duty performed is not, as we supposed, what now guides and sustains him. It is something that is not in the past but present now, which we may simply call "trusting in God," but which might also be new rousing motions for the composition of *Paradise Lost*.

In the great poem we are considering now, Sonnet 19, "When I consider how my light is spent," composed perhaps around the same time as the sonnet to Skinner, although, as I noted, some have placed it closer to when Milton became totally blind, we see where this confidence comes from, how it is earned, and what it has cost. The meaning and nature of *service* is not here taken for granted, as duty. Instead, the question, what is service, stands revealed as the central intellectual and spiritual problem of Milton's poetic career. That he grapples with it here would alone make this poem important, for the same reason "Lycidas" is important: they are both about searching for service. But, as in "Lycidas," this importance is compounded by emotional power released by the experience of trauma, "the wound." In "Lycidas" the wound around which the poem is bound, and out of which its energy flows, is the meaning of the death of Edward King, which by cutting off the possibility of service, calls everything else into question—including that service that is ritual mourning, and that higher form of ritual service, which is art.

The great emotional force of this poem is a response to the existential calamity that overtook Milton after he became totally blind: "Doth God exact day labor, light denied?" (line 7). The question is no longer, as it is in "Lycidas," that of annihilation: the Fury with the shears who "slits the thin-spun life" (lines 75–76). It is instead the annihilation of a poet's powers, leaving him an empty shell, unable to serve. He addresses the emotional problem with anguish and dignity—both of them together, but with the former dominating the early part of the sonnet, the octave, and the latter dominating the resolution, after the turn. The emotional resolution, however, which is dignified patience, does not provide an intellectual solution: "They also serve who only stand and wait" (line 14). Instead of an intellectual solution, we have a spectacular image of intellectual suspense, of serried ranks of angels at attention and perfectly still, waiting for a sign to tell them what to do, which, when they do it, might seem to be an answer to our question—except that they are doing it now.

That is what gives the conclusion to this poem its alluring and astonishing beauty. There is emotional resolution, but intellectual suspense in the form of a riddle. They are performing the answer in front of us, but we don't know what it is—though it feels good. The wound has healed, but it has left a fresh red scar, like an interrogative mark, in the shape of a question. Instead of being given brave but inadequate answers—service is writing *Pro Populo Anglicano Defensio* and whatever God tells me to do next—we are left with an open-ended question, which is more truthful to our own experience of life. It goes to the heart of the matter for Milton: What is our relation to God?

What is our relation to transcendence of this world, and what is the reflexive relation of that relation to this world? How does transcending the world—which is what faith is, and perhaps also what art is—make us more effective for good when we act in the world? What are we supposed to do?

Let us look back along the line of these questions to the point where they began. How does one serve God? Why does God need our service, if he does? Why does he want it, if he doesn't need it? If God doesn't need our service, what is service for? Service must therefore be for us, though we seem to be doing it for God: doing it for God is its *form*, whatever its substance. But the question remains, what is service for? That question is very close to asking, what are we for? How to serve God is a problem because it means, how is one to live? It means, what is one to do, and even, what is to be done? Service is a practical problem, and it is the problem of *praxis*, of what authentic action is. But service is also a mystery because God does not need it: "God doth not need / Either man's work or his own gifts" (lines 9–10). That is the mystery around which the poem is built:

> When I consider how my light is spent
> Ere half my days in this dark world and wide
> And that one talent which is death to hide
> Lodged with me useless, though my soul more bent
> To serve therewith my maker and present
> My true account, lest he returning chide.
> Doth God exact day-labour, light denied,
> I fondly ask. But Patience to prevent
> That murmur soon replies, God doth not need
> Either man's work or his own gifts, who best
> Bear his mild yoke, they serve him best. His state
> Is kingly: thousands at his bidding speed
> And post o'er land and ocean without rest.
> They also serve who only stand and wait.
>
> ("*When I consider how my light is spent*")

The opening metaphor is vaguely economic. All the light apportioned to him for life has already been spent, used up, before half his productive years are complete. Let us suppose this is the meaning of a phrase that has caused some consternation, "half my days." As the poem is about work, we may suppose working days are what is being counted, and at forty-four years of age, the poet has had some twenty-five years, with no reason not to think he will work for twenty-five more. However we calculate, "ere half my days" is the right expression, and "past half my days" is not.

"That one talent which is death to hide" is explained by the parable of the talents (Matthew 25:14–30), or at least the death and hiding are. In Jesus's parable the master of a house before going on a journey distributes his wealth to his three servants according to their merits: five talents to one (a "talent" is a measure of silver, a large one), two talents to the next, one talent to the last. When the master returns, the servant who received the five talents has invested them and doubled the amount entrusted to him; the servant who received two talents has done likewise. Both of them are welcomed into the kingdom of God: "enter thou into the joy of the Lord" (14:21 and 23). But the servant who was given one talent, fearing the harshness of his master, buried it in the earth and returned it without increase. He is rebuked, the talent is taken from him and given to the servant with ten (only now do we see the talents didn't have to be returned), and he is cast into outer darkness: "cast ye the unprofitable servant into outer darkness: there shall be weeping and gnashing of teeth" (14:30). As Milton says in the sonnet, it is "death to hide" that one talent. He identifies himself with the third servant, the one meriting the least trust and who is therefore given only one talent.

But what is the one talent? For a decade, Milton has been writing prose, although he never forgets, and never lets us forget, that he is a poet. Let us take the prudent path of the obvious and say the *talent* is his intellectual capacity, which is lodged useless in his mind because it can be active only when nourished by reading and expressed by writing, both of which require the eyes. His intellectual capacity is locked in, "Lodged with me useless" (line 4). It is as if he has buried it in the earth, except that it wasn't he who did the burying.

He then says something intriguing: because his talent has been rendered useless, his soul is *more* bent than it was before on serving God: "my soul more bent / To serve therewith my Maker" (lines 4–5). The reason given is that he feels fear, perhaps for the first time, that he will not be able to present his true account, as in the parable of talents, a cursory reading of which will explain his fear. What we recognize at this moment, however, is that, before he became blind, Milton didn't have the goad of fear to make his soul *more* bent to serve God. He was complacent (or so he imagines). He was secretary for foreign tongues to the Council of State, in charge of managing England's diplomatic correspondence. The press of work was immense, and so must have been the sense of importance. He had returned from Italy some fourteen years previous with every promise and advantage genius can have: a wealthy father, the best education money can buy, the advantages of European travel and contacts, all of which aided his social position and advantages at home. With all this cultural and social capital he dedicated himself to the cause of the English Revolution, to the Long Parliament and a free commonwealth, of which he had imagined himself to be the prophet, regarding the English as God's new Chosen People and comparing their struggle for liberty to the journey of the Israelites through the wilderness to the Promised Land. After the execution of the king, in 1649, three years previous, he had been ordered by the Council of State to vindicate the regicide against powerful attacks from at home and abroad. There was the anonymous *Eikon Basilike* published in England, in English (the title means "Sacred Image of a King"), which Milton demolished (though without much effect); there were attacks from abroad, in Latin, by the eminent scholar Salmasius, whom Milton also demolished, in *Pro Populo Anglicano Defensio*, with more effect. That was the fight that made him famous, as he tells us in the second sonnet to Cyriack Skinner (Sonnet 22): "My noble task / Of which all Europe talks from side to side" (lines 11–12). Years later, after the Restoration, when he was leading a private life, or as private a life as a famous man of letters can have, Milton would be regularly visited by travelers from the continent, not to see the author of *Paradise Lost* but the author of *Pro Populo Anglicano Defensio* and its mopping-up sequels, *Defensio Secunda* and *Pro Se Defensio*, which when this poem was written were yet to come. But at the time of writing the poem it was now clear these glorious accomplishments, the flood of publication throughout the 1640s, were now in his past and would not be repeated. (In fact, Milton's future accomplishments as a scholar, to say nothing of the accomplishments to come as a poet, would be impressive.)

How will he serve God now? Before, he could assume that serving God was what he was doing, and he couldn't work any harder than he *was* working; he couldn't try any harder than he *was* trying; and he couldn't care any more than he *did* care. When he was working, therefore, he had no reason to fear the remorseless accounting of the master in the parable of the talents. His soul was bent to serve his maker, but the bending was being done for him from the outside, by the press of work and by responsibilities placed on his shoulders. He didn't choose to demolish Salmasius: he was ordered to do it. All he had to do was do his duty, and hard as the work was, his duty was clear. But now he didn't know what to do. The flow of writing would come to a stop, or be greatly slowed; the habit from his childhood of massive and promiscuous reading, as he called it, could no longer continue; he couldn't work. (In fact, he would continue, although with assistants and, eventually, after three years with a much-reduced load.) The problem of service had been held at bay for a decade and more by externally imposed responsibilities. Now it was back, stirring and troubling his soul, which was *more* bent to serve his maker than it had been for years.

He says his soul is "more bent / To serve therewith my Maker, and present / My true account, lest He returning chide" (lines 4–6). The key word (after *more*) is the prepositional adverb *therewith*, modifying *serve*. He wants to serve in the same manner he has done in the past, with precisely that "one talent" (line 3), which is, he supposes, the only one he has. At this moment a small personification allegory starts up in the poet's mind. He imagines God as the master coming home from the journey and examining his servants, at last arriving at Milton, whose one talent, reading and writing, is buried, not in the ground but in his head. As the master chides in the parable—"thou wicked and slothful servant!" (14:26)—so Milton imagines God chiding him. In the scene he is now imagining, Milton answers with a question, "fondly," that is foolishly, although the question seems reasonable to me: "Doth God exact day labor, light denied?" (line 7). But a new personification of one of his faculties appears. Patience, "to prevent / That murmur" (lines 9–10), answers his question before it can even be asked. "Prevent" means to come before, as in "On the Morning of Christ's Nativity" (line 24). Therefore, in this little scene he is imagining, Milton never utters his question to God but only thinks of the question before another part of his mind suppresses it. Patience does so with a speech that occupies the entire sestet.

When Patience is introduced in the final line of the octave there is a strong enjambment (verb / noun) that throws the word *murmur* into relief, at the head of the line, and launches us into Patience's speech: "but Patience to prevent / That murmur soon replies" (lines 8–9). The rhymes chosen for the sestet (**cdecde**) are interesting because their vowels follow a sequence of three steps receding back into the mouth and descending in pitch: long *e*, short *e*, long *a: need, best, state; speed, rest, wait*. The effect is of an acoustic complement to two self-assured, singsongy assertions. Or the effect would be singsongy were it not for the muscular pull of the three enjambments in the sestet's first three lines "need / Either"; "best / Bear"; and "state / Is": "God doth not need / Either man's work or His [God's] own gifts. Who best / Bear his mild yoke, they serve him best. His state / Is kingly" (lines 9–12). Patience makes two assertions and this is the first. Like a good teacher, she points out the differences between God and the master in the parable of the talents. God's state is kingly, not like that of the clever and hard man of business shown in the parable. God doesn't need his own gifts, which are the talents. He gives them, it seems, to attract service, but he doesn't need them, and he also doesn't need the work a person can do to increase them.

Now Patience will cite scripture against scripture, opposing the mild yoke of Christ—"my yoke is easy" (Matthew 11:30)—against the harsh judgment of the master from the parable of the talents. Those who bear God's mild yoke *best*—which seems to mean serving God by not doing much of anything except knowing one is doing that service—also are serving him best. This is the second appearance in the poem of the word *service*, and Patience is using it pointedly to counter *serve therewith*, that is, "serve in the way that I choose to serve." But serving God's way is the best and indeed the only way to serve.

A further meaning drifts in from the scriptures, a few verses before that mild yoke, and in this case, it is unlikely to be a fortunate accident. It was Milton's habit to study scripture with attention in several languages at once. Matthew 11:28–30 is about rest and restoration, which we find in Christ: "Come unto me, all ye that labour and are heavy laden, and I will give you rest. Take my yoke upon you, and learn of me; for I am meek and lowly of heart; and ye shall find rest unto your souls. For my yoke is easy, and my burden is light." Jesus is speaking paradoxically: "if you are overburdened with labor [and Milton had certainly been overburdened], come to me and I will give you rest by urging you to put on an ox's yoke, which is of course for labor, but putting it on will not add to your exhaustion but bring rest to your soul." Not only is the discipline of following Christ easy and light; it makes everything else easier and lighter. That is the sense of this passage in scripture, which is perhaps more Christian in spirit than the harsh accounting shown in the parable of the talents. In the Latin, Vulgate Bible, that phrase from Matthew 11:28, "and I will give you rest," reads *et ego reficiam vos:* "I will restore you." This may not have been alluded to in order to propose the restoration of Milton's sight, but all the same it suggests a remaking, a rebuilding, a healing.[9] Formerly, as we saw, Milton didn't have to think about the problem of service, for events were doing that for him: he was racing merely to keep up with his tasks. He didn't have to exercise the spiritual resources necessary for sustaining devotion. Having faith is examining faith, and it wasn't necessary for him to do that, because he didn't have the time. Now he would have (as he supposed) a great deal of time for examining faith.

The assertion concerning God, "His state / Is kingly" (lines 11–12), is the pivot of the sestet. It looks back to God's kingly riches in the first half and forward to God's servants, who are angels, in the second half: "Thousands at his bidding speed / And post o'er land and ocean without rest: / They also serve who only stand and wait" (lines 12–14).

The image of God the Father as a great king on a throne surrounded by hosts of angels who are messengers *posting* "o'er land and ocean without rest" (line 13), known as a throne-vision, emerges in the Persian period of the development and recension of the Hebrew scriptures. This image of God was based on the Persian emperor Cyrus the Great, in the sixth century B.C., who was much admired by the Jews and is frequently mentioned in the scriptures. Cyrus freed the Jewish captives in Babylon (which city he conquered in 538 B.C.), urging the Jews to return to Jerusalem and rebuild Solomon's temple, which had been destroyed by the Babylonian king Nebuchadnezzar. Cyrus thus initiated what is called the Second Temple Period, which would last until the final destruction of the temple by the Romans in A.D. 70. But the temple building itself, and indeed the entire top of the mountain, Zion, on which it rests, would be transformed by Herod the Great in 19–20 B.C., who enlarged the platform on the summit in order to erect the largest complex of buildings in the Western world, not excluding Rome.[10] The great king Cyrus was famous for creating a system of rapid communications throughout his vast Asian empire, with messengers posting over land and ocean without rest. He is thought by some scholars to have been the model for an omnipotent and omniscient God whose acts are effected through his powerful word—the word from the lips of the king—which are immediately put into effect by his servants, or "messengers"—in Greek, *angeloi*, angels. Such a mighty and all-knowing king does not need men's work or their gifts (although he graciously accepts both) because the force of his word is sufficient to bring into effect all things needing to be done. The word of the king became sacred. The Greek idea of a pervading order connected with the word, or *logos*, the "reason principle," from which scientific law is derived, would interact with the Persian notion of the king's sacred word, to become the Word of the Gospel of John, the Word that creates the world and then comes into the world as its light, shining on its own truth.

What do all those messengers carry as they post over land and ocean without rest? They are of course carrying the Word, both the scripture and the Son of God, although it is perhaps best not to try to specify here. And what of those who "only stand and wait"? They are not so much waiting for commands as listening to the Word, hearing it all the time, with a vigilant, rapt attention that is suggested by *waiting*, which Milton would associate with Latin *attensio*, a "bending toward." They are perhaps listening to scripture itself, and in doing just that they seem to complete the meaning of the word that now appears in this poem for the third time: they *serve*.

I said the poem reaches an emotional resolution. It does so perfectly when we reach that quiet final line, which completes the suave, isotonal phrasing of the whole, deviating smoothly to either side of an acoustic midline. Beneath it we detect a very faint marching rhythm, as if heard in the distance—or in the future. The standing soldier waits for the command. But I said the intellectual and practical problem—what is service? and how shall I serve?—remains open. It remains open to a more authentic state of being than the frenetic, self-important activity in which Milton was formerly engaged, when he was writing books nobody much cares about today.

The imagery of that last line is emotionally satisfying, too. The vision of the waiting, listening, attentive angels in their beautiful ranks is not just an example to the poet, urging him to be like them and wait for whatever comes. It is almost as if Patience is urging him by this comparison to join the angels, to take a place in their ranks, and to listen.

What is listening? It is a discipline; it isn't easy, but it also isn't hard in the way busyness is hard. Listening isn't hard in the way that translating diplomatic correspondence is hard, or in the way that writing controversial prose in Latin and English amid hoarse disputes is hard. Listening is a light yoke and an easy burden, because listening isn't busy. Listening takes patience, which is why it seems so right that Patience should recommend it. To listen, you have to stop being busy. At first, when you listen to music, it feels as if you are not doing anything. Except in a concert hall, most people have difficulty listening to music without feeling restless, without getting up and doing something, even as they imagine they haven't stopped listening, which of course they have. Milton was a musician, a poet, a teacher, and a linguist, and he was fussy about the right pronunciation of Latin. He knew better than most do about listening. That is why it seems clear to me Milton in this sonnet is answering its rhetorical question in practical terms: he will serve God by listening, thus restoring in himself the quality of attention he had lost: *et ego reficiam vos.*

For him, the best thing to listen to is the Word of God in the Psalms, with their spiritual power issuing in a "diversity of lyric energies."[11] His next project, therefore, would be listening to the first eight of the psalms, in Hebrew, and translating them into English. Here are some of his lines from Psalm 1:

> Blessed is the man who hath not walked astray
> In counsel of the wicked, and i' the way
> Of sinners hath not stood, and in the seat
> Of scorners hath not sat. But in the great
> Jehovah's law is ever his delight,
> And in his law he studies day and night.
> He shall be as a tree which planted grows
> By wat'ry streams, and in his season knows
> To yield his fruit, and his leaf shall not fall.
>
> *(Psalm 1,1653, lines 1–9)*

Traditional interpretations of the psalms understand those watery streams by which the tree grows as the scriptures, the streams by which the tree is nourished and enriched, so that it bears fruit. Milton's reaction to blindness is to make himself into that tree. He stands and waits, but he is also rooted, and he will grow bearing fruit.

8

On the Romantics and the Principles of Milton

L IKE THE POETS and critics of the eighteenth century before them, the Romantics admired Milton almost to distraction for the
achievement of *Paradise Lost* and were inspired by him to strive for similar achievement and eminence.[1] They naturally wished to belong to
a great tradition of English poetry, the existence of which depended
in large measure on Chaucer, Spenser, Shakespeare, and Milton, but
especially Milton, whose *Paradise Lost* was widely considered in the
century that followed it to surpass any single work by any English author. The belief in English poetry as developing in time had begun in
Milton's day and was an established commonplace in the eighteenth
century, monumentalized in narrative form in Thomas Warton's *History of English Poetry, from the Close of the Eleventh to the Beginning of the
Eighteenth Century* (1774–1781).[2] This sense of a continuous historical
tradition largely replaced the earlier dominant view of English poetry in
the sixteenth century as striving to be worthy of the timeless standards
of the ancients. Milton strove to absorb and transcend the ancients,
largely by virtue of his being a Christian.

Yet with the partial exception of William Wordsworth, in the autobiographical poem *The Prelude*—which begins where *Paradise Lost* ends,
with the earth all before him (*Prelude*, 1.14; cf. *PL* 12. 646)—and with
the further, most unusual exception of William Blake, in his visionary
epic *Milton, Paradise Lost* was largely inimical to the sensibility of the

Romantics because of the religious, cultural, and, in a word, ideological gulf that separated them from Milton's epic. None of the major Romantics was concerned with Christian *theodicy*—that is, with the *justification* of an omnipotent and benevolent God—as Milton declares himself to be at the outset of *Paradise Lost:* "That to the heighth of this great argument / I may assert Eternal Providence / And justify the ways of God to men" (*PL*, 1.24–26). Nor were the Romantics concerned to accommodate in their own ideology the heterogeneous systems of Greek and Latin poetry and myth. Instead, they were the proponents, or they wished to be, of what Northrop Frye called "a new mythology"—perhaps it is better called "a new poetic philosophy"—in which a basis for communion across the gulf between the soul and nature might be formed.[3] Empathy succeeded to transcendence.

This was a profound change of circumstances for poetry across the entire European scene, one that is only obscured by talk of a tradition of prophetic continuity from Milton to the Romantics, "connected," as Wordsworth would express it in *The Prelude*, "in a mighty scheme of truth" (13.302). The most eloquent proponent of such a visionary, prophetic tradition has been Joseph Anthony Wittreich, the dean of studies in the relations between Milton and the Romantics and the founder of the field. He has recently expressed this prophetic continuity in the strongest terms: "what the Bible was for Milton, Milton came to be for the Romantics: the source for the visionary poetics that they (men and women alike) accommodated to their writings."[4] By affirming this continuity, the Romantics have become for the critics what they themselves so often wished to be: worthy sons of Milton, or instinctually rebellious but finally, having attained to their years of discretion, obedient sons. But is it ever a fine thing, in the arts, to be a worthy or a temporarily rebellious but finally obedient son? It may perhaps be fairer to the Romantics to consider how they differ from Milton, rather than how they follow in his wake, as lighter vessels.

There is a tendency among the Romantics to suppose the great Milton needed only to have several errors set right to be perfectly at one with them, spiritually and aesthetically, as well as politically, and that his prophetic revelations are furthered in theirs.[5] He would not have thought so. In the three centuries from Petrarch to Milton, the major preoccupation of European critical theory and poetic practice had been to make the pagan muse sing of Christ. Fairly suddenly, that long-standing preoccupation—beyond Petrarch, it went back to the origins of Christianity itself—disappeared like smoke. The Romantics certainly did not think one of the main purposes of poetry was to accommodate classical culture within the system of Christian belief, and to capture for Christianity the glamour and brilliance of that alien culture, like the spoils of the Egyptians. For the Romantics, poetry was the free creation of the human spirit in communion with the spirit of the world, continually, if not always, identified with liberty. Insofar as that spirit became incarnate, it was so for the Romantics in politics, the new realm of the sacred.

What classical poetry had been to the Renaissance—the allure of the profane—the Romantics tended to find in the East, following but also darkening the eighteenth century's delight in oriental tales employed for allegorical and satirical purposes. Romantic orientalism took the environment of such tales more seriously, as an exotic realm bathed in an aura of the beautiful, the cruel, the strange.

It is perhaps interesting that for Milton, living as he did before the height of European and especially British imperialism, the East held no especially exotic appeal and awakened no vague repulsion or horror, in the ambivalent sense for which Edward Said used the term *orientalism*.[6] Inaccessible remoteness seems to be the main theme of Milton's language for the East, as when mountains of ice in the Arctic Ocean bar the way to "the rich / Cathayan coast" (*PL*, 10.292–93). There are curiosities, such as "the barren plains / Of Sericana where Chineses drive / With sails and wind their cany wagons light" (*PL*, 3.437–39). And there is the panoramic sweep of Adam's view from the top of the mountain of Paradise to where the eight kingdoms of Asia will rise in the future:

> His eye might there command whatever stood
> City of old or modern fame, the seat
> Of mightiest empire from the walls
> Of Cambalu, seat of Cathaian Khan,
> And Samarkand by Oxus, Témir's throne,
> To Paquin of Sinaean kings and thence
> To Agra and Lahore of Great Mogúl
> Down to the golden Chersonese, or where
> The Persian in Ecbátan sat or since
> In Hispahan, or where the Russian Czar

> In Moscow or the Sultan in Bizance,
> Turkéstan-born.
>
> (*PL, 11.385–96*)

The scene is magnificent, as is the erudition, and the sense of historical depth complementing vast extension in space. But this view of the East is no more sinister or alluring than that of the kingdoms Adam sees prophetically to arise in Africa and America. For the Romantics, however, the orientalized East, with its barbarism and tyranny, its inertia, its horror, its bad infinity, and its oriental despotism, became the perfect scene on which to dramatize the struggle for freedom by individuals, noble youths awakened by love to the true nature of man, as in Shelley's *The Revolt of Islam* and Byron's Eastern tales.[7]

This is a view of the East that would be summed up, long after it was culturally established, in Hegel's *Lectures on the Philosophy of World History* (1821–1831), in which the East is despotic and fanatic because Orientals do not know that the individual is free. They therefore cannot struggle for individual freedom, having no conception of it. The consciousness of freedom was awakened in the Greeks, who therefore became free because they had some conception of it.[8] Because Greece is on the threshold of the East, and was the ancient scene—at the battles of Marathon, Salamis, and Plataea—of the struggle between oriental despotism and European liberty, the Greek War of Independence (1821–1832), to which Byron gave his life, served the purposes of the Romantics admirably, except of course Bryon's. The vision of the East would prove to be dialectically other—which is to say, opposite but necessary—to the Romantic vindication of the principles of liberty.

It is a trend that would come to its fullest realization across the Channel, in the paintings of Delacroix—*The Massacre at Chios* (1824); *Greece Expiring on the Ruins of Missolonghi* (1826); and the stupendous *Death of Sardanapalus* (1827)—and in Victor Hugo's great book of poems, *Les Orientales* (1829), which sets oriental tyranny and depravity against the Greek struggle for freedom. If revolution politicizes aesthetics, then the French Revolution found its artistic apotheosis in the East, and especially in Greece, which is both the gateway to the East and the bulwark against it.

England, however, had had its own revolution and its great poetic hero, Milton. The Romantics rightly attributed the principles of liberty to

Milton and naturally hoped to associate these with *Paradise Lost*. "The sacred Milton," as Shelley put it, was "a republican and a bold enquirer into morals and religion."[9] Shelley is blending together two distinct phases of Milton's career and two distinct movements of his mind, and in this he was typical of the Romantics. Milton was "sacred," *sacer*, in *Paradise Lost*, where he is *not* a particularly bold inquirer into morals and religion because he is no longer directly engaged with them as a means of altering his immediate world. There is no argument for divorce in *Paradise Lost*, but there is a vision of marriage as the companionship of body and mind, with the mind understood to be in first place. Nor is there in *Paradise Lost* any argument for abolishing established religion, that is, a religion legally entangled with the state. Adam and Eve are themselves a polity, with Adam the legitimate king, and a model of what the state should become. But their religion, which is to say, their prayers, is spontaneous and equal. That is not to say the old Milton of the years of engagement, which reach as far back as the tirade of Saint Peter in "Lycidas," never makes an appearance in *Paradise Lost*. He does so when he compares Satan's leaping the wall of the Garden of Eden to a bishop—or a Presbyterian—jumping into a fat living: "So clomb this first grand thief into God's fold. / So since into His Church lewd hirelings climb!" (*PL*, 4.192–93).

But such moments are infrequent and incidental. A good deal of wishful thinking is required—and it starts with the Romantics—to see the political Milton of the 1640s and 1650s in the Milton of *Paradise Lost*. It should always be remembered that *Paradise Lost* is a post-Restoration epic poem by a famous republican and regicide, which the royalist censor, the Reverend Thomas Tomkyns, domestic chaplain to the archbishop of Canterbury (and the author, in the same year as *Paradise Lost*, of *The Inconveniencies of Toleration*), nevertheless tolerated *Paradise Lost* with what were probably token objections, all of which were overcome (so far as we can know). Scholars have tended to accept the republican freethinker John Toland's report of this contretemps. He represents Tomkyns as maliciously or ignorantly trying to suppress all of *Paradise Lost* on the basis of frivolous objections, such as book 1, lines 594–99, ending "and with fear of change / Perplexes monarchs." Toland may be speaking the unvarnished truth, or not, but he is, of course, a strongly biased witness. In the twisted environment of censorship, as the recent history of Eastern Europe bears out, a censor may favor a book while protecting both himself and the author by raising trivial objections that can be overturned later or complied with while doing little harm. Whether or not this was the case with Tomkyns's supervision of the manuscript of *Paradise Lost*, he gave it his *imprimatur* and would not have done so had Milton been in this poem the bold inquirer Shelley describes.[10]

But Milton *is* a bold inquirer, in Shelley's sense, in the prose works, and in the poems we examined in the previous chapter. In the prose works, he explicitly separates himself from his other identity as a poet, soaring and singing (*YP*, 1:808 and 2:764). It was this political side of Milton that the Romantics valued and wished to associate with the universally praised sublimity of *Paradise Lost*. They therefore found themselves encumbered, in Walter Jackson Bate's famous phrase, with the burden of the past, wishing at once to be influenced by Milton and freed of his overshadowing sublimity. Their dilemma has given English literary criticism another famous phrase, Harold Bloom's "anxiety of influence," and a general theory of poetic tradition based on the distortive emulation of Milton.[11]

In transferring the aesthetic power and the cultural prestige of *Paradise Lost* to the principles of liberty enunciated by Milton in his prose works, the Romantics were responding to the application of those principles at the French Revolution, the great event of their time, as the English Revolution was the great event of Milton's. Milton did not, of course, change those principles and become an apostate to liberty, the charge of which Coleridge and Wordsworth would stand accused by the younger generation.[12] Writing in the *Examiner* on June 11, 1815—a week before the Battle of Waterloo—Hazlitt tore into Wordsworth, comparing his trimming with the political firmness of the poet whom Wordsworth most followed and revered: "We have no less respect for the memory of Milton as a patriot than as a poet. Whether he was a *true* patriot, we shall not enquire: he was at least a *consistent* one. He did not retract his defence of the people of England; he did not say that his sonnets to Vane or Cromwell were meant ironically; he was not appointed Poet-Laureate to a Court which he had reviled and insulted; he accepted neither place nor pension; nor did he write paltry sonnets upon the 'Royal fortitude' of the House of Stuart, by which, however, they really lost something."[13] Eight months later, on February 18, 1816, in the *Examiner*, Leigh Hunt, in "Heaven Made Party to Earthly Disputes:

Mr. Wordsworth's sonnets on Waterloo," less savagely but no less pointedly criticizes Wordsworth's encomia of restored princes and dynasties.
Milton's "tone of thinking," he says, "comes out very singularly sometimes among these panegyrics on modern princes and the restoration
of discarded dynasties. Mr. Wordsworth, we should think, must feel
some strange qualms on that point, especially as in one of his sonnets
["London, 1802"] he expressly said, that Milton ought to 'be living at
this hour,' and that the times 'had need of him.'" Hunt goes on to say,
"We hope to see many more of Mr. Wordsworth's sonnets, but shall be
glad to find them, like his best ones, less Miltonic in one respect, and
much more so in another."[14] Less pompously sublime, that is, and more
republican in spirit.

Milton never changed his principles. But in *Paradise Lost* he was exercising his liberty as an artist to do something else. What Milton was
doing in *Paradise Lost* was by no means inconsistent with his earlier political principles, which were now generalized in the most idealistic terms
by abstraction to the origin of humanity and the origin of the human
sins of cowardice and rapacity. That put him very far from the hoarse
noise of the political disputes of his day. Politics is the art of the possible, guided, one hopes, by principles. For Milton, *Paradise Lost* is the
art of what is.

What the Romantics looked for and longed after was a particular English sound, a magisterial *Stimmung*, which would express indignation
at tyranny, oppression, and greed; which would offer sage counsel to
liberty's friends, especially among leaders in the state; and which would
sound the high language of defiance to enemies and of encouragement
to friends. Above all they wanted political principles clearly expressed
in verse that future generations would not willingly let die. These are
the principles of Milton's prose works and of his poems of the political
period. But that sound, though far from absent in these works, is of
course preeminent in *Paradise Lost*, in which these principles do not appear, although nothing in the poem is inconsistent with them. It is hardly
surprising, therefore, that the Romantics would wish to associate those
principles with Milton's most celebrated work. Nor is it surprising critics
still wish to do so. But it is finally a misrepresentation of *Paradise Lost*.

The Paradise Lost (as the Romantics called it) was seen by them as one
of the twin summits of English poetry (an image Coleridge made use

of on several occasions), the other summit being the plays of Shake-speare. This high estimation of *Paradise Lost* was not new. It went back to the first appearance of the poem, which was hailed by Dryden, and it grew throughout the eighteenth century, when one hundred editions of *Paradise Lost* were published and "Time, the Avenger," as Byron said, acknowledging a fellow persecuted bard, made the word *Miltonic* mean *sublime*.[15] C. M. Bowra expressed as well as anyone can why Milton at-tained an insuperable limit: "Milton is the last great practitioner of literary epic. With him it found a finality which forbade any extension of its scope. No poem can include more than the whole of history or be set on a stage wider than the whole of space. It may even be doubted whether the grand style can be grander than Milton's or the heroic temper more sublime than his."[16]

A century and more may have helped this sublimity, this amalgam of grandeur and terror, to come fully into view. It was one of the cen-tral concerns of the Romantic critics who wrote on Milton. But from the beginning "the majesty that through thy work doth reign," as An-drew Marvell put it in the poem published with the 1674 edition, "On Mr. Milton's *Paradise Lost*," was there for all to see, and was recognized as something new in English poetry.[17] Dryden's epigrammatic lines on *Paradise Lost* subtly divide poetic sublimity into two qualities: loftiness of thought, which is seen in Homer, and majesty of manner, which is seen in Virgil:

> Three poets, in three distant ages born,
> Greece, Italy, and England did adorn.
> The first in loftiness of thought surpassed;
> The next, in majesty; in both, the last.
> The force of Nature could no farther go:
> To make a third, she joined the other two.[18]

What strikes one most about Dryden's epigram is his claim that Milton had no third thing to offer, in addition to loftiness of thought and majesty of manner, because nature has no higher stage of great-ness than these. Milton would have said, and he did say it, that he had the further and inestimable advantage of being a Christian. Dryden could anticipate that. But Dryden restricts the competition to the realm of aesthetics, of sense perception, and of the natural world. Milton

surpasses Homer and Virgil, says Dryden, not because he is in possession of a supernatural truth but because he joins Homer's natural kind
of greatness, loftiness of thought (what the thought is is not inquired
after), to Virgil's kind of greatness, majesty of manner. That is aesthetic perfection, in the full sense of the word *perfection* as completeness, a fulfillment beyond which one cannot go, a limit in nature itself.
For Dryden, there is no transcendental leap beyond the aesthetic. We
should therefore note that Dryden's compliment, handsome as it is, denies Milton his ambition, which he felt he had fulfilled, to go beyond
the classical poets and be a speaker of the truth.

By no means the least element of Milton's loftiness is geographical,
something that brings him closer to Homer, a great poet of the earth,
than to Virgil, a middling one in the *Aeneid* (but not in the *Georgics*). But
Milton surpasses even Homer on this point, for reasons that go beyond
knowledge of the earth to knowledge of space and of the cosmos. Not
until Milton is the grandeur of the physical world and of the forces of
nature elevated from a circumstantial effect (however sublime when it
happens in earlier poets) to a general atmosphere, a pervasive and defining mental state. We feel magnificent tremors of spaciousness and
distance, but we are continually astonished as well by the fine details
that arrive across these distances, something that was perhaps only possible to this degree in an age of maps and telescopes, telescopes that
can be turned on the heavens as well as on the earth. That telescopes
can render fine detail in what is seen at great distance seems to be the
reason for Milton's use of *microscope* instead of *telescope* in *Paradise Regained* (4.56–57), when Satan, having placed Jesus on a high mountain
in the Judean desert, shows him fine architectural details in the city of
Rome. Milton preferred *microscope* (Gr. *micros*, "small," +*skopein*, "to
look") because it is more purely objective than *telescope* (Gr. *telos*
"far," +*skopein*, "to look"), which includes the point of view of the observer. In *Paradise Lost* he perhaps avoids *telescope* when he uses "optic
glass" (1.298).

What are the poetic consequences of these scientific advances in which
Milton was so interested? Much has been written on this subject. I will
confine myself to a very subtle effect of the new spatial thinking, an
effect that is, however, totally original with *Paradise Lost* and not the
least of the reasons for its success. This effect lends a necessary gran-

deur to the intimate and unheroic main event of the poem, so that it feels heroic, though we can hardly tell why. My excuse for mentioning it here is that it is one lesson from Milton that the Romantics learned very well.

At any moment in *Paradise Lost*, whatever else is happening, we are aware of the immediate, even intimate, natural or infernal or heavenly or cosmic surroundings, and also of how these surroundings deepen insensibly into giant vistas, and deepen beyond these to the boundless. There is a powerful feeling of uniformity in space, so that any location is continuous with all others, however remote, enhancing the feeling of immediate presence by, so to speak, folding into it every other location. What is immediately present here is a part of what is present elsewhere and anywhere, even at vast distances. We may be standing in the Garden of Eden on the earth, or on Mount Niphates, but we feel that this location is continuous in space with the other side of the earth and with other worlds beyond the earth.

I would submit that this subtle effect of enhanced presence on the scenes of *Paradise Lost* is an unconscious result of the astronomical researches of Galileo and others, in which Milton was deeply interested and by which he was imaginatively excited. Milton utterly discards the old Ptolemaic systems of spheres, which divides space up into segments. He fully accepts not only the Copernican hypothesis—which describes the local event of the earth and the other planets orbiting the sun—but also the vaster Galilean idea of universal, continuous, and unlimited space, an idea soon to be propounded in Newton's *Principia*.[19] In *Paradise* Lost, more than in Homer and Virgil, we always feel we are there on the scene, looking at the surroundings as well as at the events that take place in them. The scene of action, however intimate, is also immense and unlimited because it is spatially homogeneous with every other scene and with any place in which a scene might occur, though it doesn't. We feel the reality of places where things never happen because they are continuous with places where they do, and as a result we feel the presence of this emptiness. This is a new effect in poetry, the spatial sublime, of which geographical sublime is only a surface effect. As I said, the Romantics learned this better than they learned anything else from Milton, as we shall see in Wordsworth's ascent of Mount Snowdon, and as we might have seen in many passages (I think of the scenes during the transit of Albania) of Byron's *Childe Harold's Pilgrimage:*

> There is a pleasure in the pathless woods,
> There is rapture on the lonely shore,
> There is society where none intrudes,
> By the deep sea, and music in its roar.
> I love not man the less, but Nature more
> From these our interviews, in which I steal
> From all I may be, or have been before,
> To mingle with the Universe and feel
> What I can ne'er express, yet cannot all conceal.
>
> (Childe Harold's Pilgrimage *canto 4, stanza 178*)

Breaking off a period of severe study, much of it devoted to Milton, Keats took his walking tour to the English lakes, Scotland, and Ireland to "gorge wonders" and "to load me with grander Mountains, and strengthen more my reach in Poetry."[20] Few poets before the Romantics believed that hard and prolonged travel in wild nature is necessary to extend one's reach in poetry, as Keats said. The Romantics were greater travelers and walkers than any English poets before or since: they found their landscapes in the world, not in books. What they inherited from Milton, however, was the sense of the earth as a defining artistic concern, which needed to be developed in an individual way through poetry. Blake was alone among the Romantic poets in his lack of travel, although he went to Felpham, for his "three years slumber on the banks of the Ocean," after which, he says, "I again display my Giant forms to the public."[21] Blake was a Londoner and a cockney. But he was also a visual artist, and the mental landscapes of his prophecies were sometimes more astounding than the realistic landscapes of the other major Romantics.

The Romantic poets also found grandeur in Milton's imaginary landscapes, in the violent abyss of chaos, the vast gothic landscape of Hell, and the still vaster landscapes of Heaven, over which, in the air, armies join battle with explosive force, like thunderheads at sea. Nor is Milton's featureless anti-landscape less imposing, that "boundless continent" formed by the outer convex surface of the universe on which Satan touches down after his voyage through chaos: "Dark, waste, and wild, under the frown of Night / Starless exposed, and ever threat'ning storms / Of chaos blust'ring round, inclement sky" (*PL*, 3.423–26). As Satan traverses this plain, searching for a way into the universe and at length to earth, with the intention of destroying the human race, he is characterized by means of a sublime geographical comparison:

> As when a vulture on Imaüs bred,
> Whose snowy ridge the roving Tartar bounds,
> Dislodging from a region scarce of prey
> To gorge the flesh of lambs or yeanling kids
> On hills where flocks are fed, flies toward the springs
> Of Ganges or Hydaspes, Indian streams.
>
> (PL, *3.431–36*)

These imaginary and supernatural landscapes are made the more real for us, as in this simile, by the precision and the sweep of Milton's terrestrial landscapes: the mountains and plateaus of central Asia; the torrid sands of Libya whipped up into storms; the volcanic regions of southern Italy; the Atlas Mountains across from Gibraltar, bounded by the sea and the floor of the desert; the snake-infested Balearic isles; the ice fields and violent winds of the arctic; and the dangerous sea-route around Africa and the "Cape of Hope" into the Indian Ocean, where the mariner is greeted—so Milton imagines—by the aroma of spices wafted from "Araby the blest" (4.163).

The effect is of what the ancient critics called "clearness," *enargeia*, a word that goes back to Homer and is perhaps the highest aesthetic character of Homeric verse, as Erich Auerbach famously pointed out in *Mimesis:* all objects and all scenes, human and natural, seem to shine with preternatural clarity.[22] Even the small area of the Promised Land is made sublime and exotic, as when we hear of the soaring heights above "the fount of Jordan's flood" to "Egypt and th'Arabian shore" (3.535–37). Geographical references such as these, with their evocative names—Imaüs, Sericana, Ganges and Hydaspes, Paneas and Beërseba—are more frequent in *Paradise Lost* than the biblical and classical allusions for which the epic was famous in the eighteenth century and for which it remains famous now. The geographical aspect of the poem is at least as important, investing every place mentioned in a mantle of stories, most of them remaining to be told. Milton traveled on the continent, but his passion for geographical knowledge, like Coleridge's, was built up by study and extended far beyond his personal experience. He was accurate about the geography of Greece, for example, which he never saw. One is not greatly surprised to learn that, years after he had gone totally blind, Milton inquired through a young friend, Peter Heimbach, after the price of an atlas recently produced on the continent, and joked ruefully about its cost. "I think it must be the Mauretanian mountain Atlas," Milton said, "and not the book which you say is to be bought at such a huge price."[23] I imagine that with a sighted person's aid, Milton could pose questions—no doubt, very specific ones—about places he was interested in, such as what a coastline now looked like, or what new and exotic names had appeared.

The romantic poets recognized Milton's geographical sublime as an achievement even more striking than his appropriation of the classical tradition. They gratefully took up his hair-raising vistas and mixed them with a world of fantasy and adventure drawn from Eastern and northern exotic tales, which, as we have noted, Milton encodes with a single phrase or place-name, such as "Araby the blest" (*PL*, 4.163). The Celtic and other Northern myths that lay behind the Ossianic epics, the Eastern tales gathered in *The Thousand and One Nights*, and exotic travel narratives from Herodotus to Marco Polo, Mandeville, Purchas, and Haklyut are most obviously the ingredients (heated and compressed under pressure) of Coleridge's "Kubla Khan" and "Rime of the Ancient Mariner."[24] Some of the same sources are present at the creation of Byron's *Childe Harold's Pilgrimage* and his Eastern tales, such as *Lara, The Giaour, The Bride of Abydos*, and *The Corsair*. Realistic landscape and fantastic tales contribute to the atmosphere of Shelley's *The Revolt of Islam* and *Prometheus Unbound*, of Keats's *Hyperion* and still more of *The Fall of Hyperion*. The same may be said, with modifications, of Wordsworth's rural scenes, haunted as these are by local memories, local legends and local presences, which in their very nearness ("almost as silent as the turf they trod") evoke a sense of distance equal to that of Arabian tales.[25]

Speaking, of course, very broadly, we feel we are in a Romantic poem when the substantial presence of the earth is evoked through the insubstantial presence of a tale or myth—in the case of *The Prelude*, an autobiographical tale. *Paradise Lost* likewise evokes for the reader the substantial presence of the earth—and of the cosmos, bounded by illimitable chaos—through the multiple and shifting lenses of myth. But these remain condensed within allusions sometimes no longer than a single word. The Romantic poets open up the tales.

In addition to the geographical sublime, the Romantics had the example of Milton's characters' speech before them. Above all, they absorbed what Shelley called the "high language" of the most stunningly original, eloquent, and contradictory character in epic literature since Homer's Achilles: Milton's Satan.[26]

An extensive prosopography of Romantic rebels—from Blake's Orc to Byron's Childe Harold, Cain, and Manfred, to Keats's Hyperion and Shelley's Prometheus and Demogorgon, to the monster of Mary Shelley's *Frankenstein*, a monster who learns of liberty and the nobility of the spirit from reading *Paradise Lost*—are all of the family tree of Milton's Satan and share the sullen exaltation of his speech.[27] But hardly less thrilling than Satan's speech is the haughty virtue of Milton's righteous angels; the soaring eloquence of Adam and Eve's hymns to their Creator (like the songs of the Romantic *improvvisatori*, these hymns are to be seen as more purely *creative* for their being spontaneously composed), and even the lower eloquence of Adam and Eve's common conversation, which is noble and yet familiar, ornate and yet direct, and which is closer than might at first be supposed (for they are both poets) to what Wordsworth called the language of a man speaking to men, although poetic discourse has been known to leap the abyss between men and women, as well.[28]

To achieve these effects Milton employed the superbly flexible instrument of blank verse, "English heroic verse without rhyme," as he called it in a note added to *Paradise Lost*, adapted from the later manner of Shakespeare and "our best English tragedies," and much refined technically.[29] It is a ten-syllable line using frequent enjambments, with heavier pauses at the midline break, or caesura, so that longer rhythms are built up above the level of the individual line. By "built up" I mean Milton uses carefully organized, parallel clauses, imitating the Latin periodic sentence, so that the reader has to hold the parts of the unfolding sentence in mind until its meaning is fully disclosed at the end. The sentences of *Paradise Lost* no doubt draw much of their power from Milton's long and voluminous experience writing prose in a looser periodic style. To its first readers, and even to Johnson, *Paradise Lost* seemed dangerously close to prose, and needed rhyme to give individual lines more articulation. Instead, the individual lines seem to burst at the seams under the strain of an inner, forward-driving power, as if the force of inspiration were breaking down, or breaking through the expected formalities of art. (The affinity of Milton with Michelangelo and Beethoven is apparent in this technical sense, too. In each of them, normative artistic conventions are swept away by the force of inspiration, to the consternation of contemporaries.) In Shakespeare's later career characters seem to be thinking up what they say even as they say it, and this effect is achieved by means that anticipate Milton: reducing rhyme, lengthening syntax, increasing enjambments, and relying less on the structure of the individual line to achieve poetic rhythm. The greater informality of Shakespeare's later verse is for dramatic effect: it creates a naturalistic sense of characters speaking their thoughts as they occur, often in a terrific rush of feeling. *Paradise Lost* has a single epic narrator, and for this reason Milton had to impose more syntactic regularity.

The lankier lines of Blake's prophecies, the looser blank verse of Coleridge's conversation poems, and, of course, the more obviously Miltonic cadences of Wordsworth's *The Prelude* are unimaginable without the blank verse of *Paradise Lost*. Even when the Romantics returned to what Milton called "the troublesome and modern bondage of rhyming" (for Milton, *modern* was not a flattering word), as Keats did in abandoning *Hyperion* and as Shelley admitted doing in *The Revolt of Islam*, the reason for doing so was defined by Milton. Shelley admits to avoiding "the blank verse of Shakespeare and Milton" because "there is no shelter for mediocrity: you must either succeed or fail."[30] Keats abandons his blank verse epic *Hyperion* because it is too obviously Miltonic. "There were too many Miltonic inversions in it," he said in a letter, observing more ominously of Milton, in another letter three days later, "Life to him would be death to me."[31] Note that this comment is not said about Milton generally but about Miltonic blank verse.

Byron shares with Wordsworth the thought—was it the only thought they ever shared?—that Milton's great innovation is to take the horns and tail from his devil and make him romantic. This aesthetic view of Satan is at a slight distance from Shelley's admiration of Satan's political defiance (though not his cause). It is a great distance from Blake's more radical identification of Milton's Satan with Orc, or the revolutionary principle, the engine of creativity. This view of Satan complements Blake's gnostic identification of God the father with evil, the Nobodaddy and Urizen against which Orc rebels.

Byron's views are less exotic and less radical, but they are interesting because they are his. He admires the first two books of *Paradise Lost* and finds the rest a heavy affair. But he admits not having read *Paradise Lost* since boyhood, unlike Wordsworth, who read Milton almost daily. Byron would have agreed with Baudelaire's statement that in Satan Milton represents ideal male beauty. He is perhaps the only Romantic poet who is not intimidated by Milton. For him—and in this he was simply more mature than the other Romantics—what mattered was verse. A man of the eighteenth century, he shared Johnson's preference for rhyme.

Byron issues a warning against the use of blank verse: "blank verse, which, unless in the drama, no one except Milton ever wrote who could rhyme, became the order of the day, or else such rhyme as looked still blander than the verse without it . . . I am not persuaded that the *Paradise Lost* would not have been more nobly conveyed to posterity, not perhaps in heroic couplets, although even they could sustain the subject if well balanced, but in the stanza of Spenser or of Tasso, or the terza rima of Dante, which the powers of Milton could easily have grafted on our language."[32] That is a splendid castle in the air. Perhaps Byron has in mind the *ottava rima*, the rapid measure of *Don Juan* (taken from Ariosto), in which he found a better medium even than the Spenserian stanza, which retards the pace with its lengthy closing line. We are not surprised to hear the author of *Childe Harold's Pilgrimage* finds the Spenserian stanza dear to his heart but too slow for narrative. *Childe Harold* is a great series of pageants and reflections on these pageants, but with no story, and for this reason the Spenserian stanza serves the author well. But in *Don Juan* there were stories to tell, and Byron makes the obvious adjustment to *ottava rima*, the measure of Ariosto and Tasso, whose "romantic" or romance tales were very popular. In this rushing style of verse the stanza effectively disappears but alternating rhyme is retained. It should be remembered that Byron composes splendid blank verse for his own dramatic poems, *Manfred*, *Marino Faliero*, and *Cain*. He is ready gently to chastise anyone else, such as James Hogg, who might venture to criticize Milton:

> You are mistaken . . . in thinking that I (or indeed that any living verse-writer . . .) can write as well as Milton. Milton's *Paradise Lost* is, as a whole, a heavy concern; but the first two books of it are the

very finest poetry that has ever been produced in this world—at least since the flood—for I make little doubt Abel was a fine pastoral poet and Cain a fine bloody poet, and so forth; but we . . . know no more of their poetry than the brutum vulgus—I beg pardon, the swinish multitude—do of Wordsworth and Pye. Poetry must always exist, like drink, where there is demand for it.[33]

We see how very highly Byron respected Milton, and how little he cared that he did.

With the exception of Blake and the partial exception of Wordsworth, both of whom composed epics without rhyme, the Romantic poets were committed to rhyme in their major works—unlike Milton. It was after some criticism of the absence of rhyme in *Paradise Lost* that Milton, at his publisher's request, added his note on the verse of *Paradise Lost*, with its polemical condemnation of rhyme as "tedious and modern," a mere "jingling sound of like endings." Keats's return to rhyme between April and September of 1819, his last and greatest year of composition, in "La Belle Dame Sans Merci" "Ode to Psyche," and the great odes—"On a Grecian Urn," "On Melancholy," "To a Nightingale," "On Indolence"—was one of the miracles of Romantic creativity. Milton, it would appear, had little influence on this achievement, except in the negative sense of being an example from which Keats at last fought free. Even so, the vivacity of the rhymes in "L'Allegro" and "Il Penseroso," and the absolute mastery of slant rhymes and assonance Milton shows in "Lycidas," may have been of some assistance to Keats. The exception is the greatest rhymester of the Romantics, Byron, who revered Dryden and especially Pope. But when it came to running up one's colors, even Byron couldn't leave Milton out: "Thou shalt believe in Milton, Dryden, Pope; / Thou shalt not set up Wordsworth, Coleridge, Southey."[34]

Wordsworth was the only Romantic poet who was able to rise to Milton's heights in blank verse, to sustain himself on those wings for longer than Milton did, and to transform them into an expressive instrument distinctly his own. Many passages of *The Prelude* recall Milton, some intentionally, some not, though they never seem unduly derivative. There is the famous tribute to Milton in the third book of *The Prelude*, the one devoted to studies at Cambridge, when, while visiting friends in Milton's rooms, Wordsworth poured intemperate libations to the "temperate bard."[35] He recalls the event with mock shame, but not before calling up the Milton of later life, who was for Wordsworth, as for all the Romantics, a symbol of political courage:

> Yea, our blind Poet, who, in his later day
> Stood almost single, uttering odious truth,
> Darkness before, and danger's voice behind;
> Soul awful! if the earth hath ever lodged
> An awful Soul, I seemed to see him here.[36]

Wordsworth's views on Milton, a poet to whom he resented owing a "debt immense of endless gratitude," are complex and inconsistent, as is to be expected of someone who wishes at once to acknowledge the debt—"still paying! still to owe!" (*PL*, 4.53)—and to discharge it at last, so as not to be thought inferior to his master forever. From the carping annotations to *Paradise Lost* and some injudiciously candid remarks to Hazlitt, we might conclude that Wordsworth's relation to Milton, whose bust he kept on his desk, was wholly emulous, if not envious. Hazlitt reports of Wordsworth, though with no friendly voice, that he thought "the only great merit of the Paradise Lost was in the conception or in getting rid of the horns and tail of the Devil, for as to the execution, he thought he could do as well or better himself."[37] But Wordsworth sometimes expressed warm appreciation of Milton's art, although he thought *Paradise Regained* the more polished work. He and his sister Dorothy often read Milton aloud to each other, and Charles Lamb records their weeping over the sorrows of *Paradise Lost*, book 11.[38]

But in the end Wordsworth much preferred to admire Milton as a figure of political courage and "republican austerity," singling out his "manly and dignified" political sonnets, which are "undisfigured by false or vicious ornaments." The latter phrase is perhaps a shaft directed at *Paradise Lost*, perhaps not. When he praises Milton, Wordsworth usually cannot withhold technical complaints, even when speaking of the political sonnets, which are dearest to his heart, but which he finds "in several places incorrect, and sometimes uncouth in language, and perhaps, in some, inharmonious."[39] These are criticisms for which it is hard to find corroborating evidence in Milton's political sonnets, which inspired Wordsworth to his best-known and finest tribute to the poet, "London, 1802":

> Milton! thou should'st be living at this hour:
> England hath need of thee: she is a fen
> Of stagnant waters: altar, sword and pen,
> Fireside, the heroic wealth of hall and bower,
> Have forfeited their ancient English dower
> Of inward happiness. We are selfish men;
> Oh! raise us up, return to us again;
> And give us manners, virtue, freedom, power.
> Thy soul was like a Star and dwelt apart;
> Thou hadst a voice whose sound was like the sea;
> Pure as the naked heavens, majestic, free,
> So didst thou travel on life's common way,
> In cheerful godliness; and yet thy heart
> The lowliest duties on itself did lay.[40]

This sonnet underlines an important point about Milton I have mentioned already: that he was for the Romantics, as he still is for most English readers, and increasingly for North American readers, more important as a political symbol than as a poet. Even so, Wordsworth could bring himself to sing, in *The Excursion*, of Milton's "mighty orb of song." He means Milton when he says "that from the blind hath flowed / The highest, holiest, raptures of the lyre; / And wisdom married to immortal verse."[41]

I said it is impossible to imagine the blank verse of *The Prelude* without the achievement of Milton behind it, and the debt is apparent in the passage shortly to follow below, which recalls some lines from the Creation in *Paradise Lost*—"Immediately the mountains huge appear / Emergent and their broad bare backs upheave / Into the clouds" (7.285–87)—from the episode of Eve's dream, and from the poet's famous invocation of the spirit that "Dove-like sat'st brooding on the vast abyss / And mad'st it pregnant" (1.21–22). The second of these is less obvious, perhaps, although it is a passage that resonates with much Romantic poetry, including the passage at hand:

> Why sleep'st thou, Eve? Now is the pleasant time,
> The cool, the silent, save where silence yields

> To the night-warbling bird that now awake
> Tunes sweetest his love-labored song. Now reigns
> Full orbed the moon and with more pleasing light
> Shadowy sets off the face of things—in vain
> If none regard! Heav'n wakes with all his eyes
> Whom to behold but thee, Nature's desire.
>
> (PL, 5.38–45)

For any frequent reader of Milton, Wordsworth's obvious and honorable borrowings upheave their backs above a more pervasive sea of resonances, the characteristic *lexis* and rhythms of Milton's verse. The wonder achieved in the following passage consists in its preservation of the presence of Milton—its transparency, so to speak—even as it emerges wholly independent of Milton. Saturated in *Paradise Lost*, it is unmistakably Wordsworth's and could not have been written by anyone else:

> I panted up
> With eager pace, and no less eager thoughts . . .
> When at my feet the ground appeared to brighten,
> And with a step or two seemed brighter still,
> Nor had I time to ask the cause of this,
> For instantly a Light upon the turf
> Fell like a flash. I looked about and lo!
> The Moon stood naked in the heavens, at height
> Immense above my head, and on the shore
> I found myself of a huge sea of mist,
> Which meek and silent rested at my feet.
> A hundred hills their dusky backs upheaved
> All over this still Ocean, and beyond,
> Far, far beyond the vapours shot themselves
> In headlands, tongues, and promontory shapes
> Into the Sea, the real Sea, that seemed
> To dwindle and give up its majesty,
> Usurped upon as far as sight could reach.
> Meanwhile the Moon looked down upon this show
> In single glory, and we stood, the mist
> Touching our very feet: and from the shore
> At distance not the third part of a mile

Was a blue chasm, a fracture in the vapour,
A deep and gloomy breathing-place through which
Mounted the roar of waters, torrents, streams
Innumerable, roaring with one voice. . . .
                            and it appeared to me
The perfect image of a mighty Mind,
Of one that feeds upon infinity,
That is exalted by an under-presence,
The sense of God, or whatsoe'er is dim
Or vast in its own being.[42]

A less successful appropriation of Milton by Wordsworth is the poem his sister Dorothy described as "the task of his life," *The Excursion*, published in 1814, itself but a portion of the vaster but inexistent cathedral of *The Recluse*.[43] The verse preface is Miltonic to an absurdly dependent degree. The story of the slow collapse of Wordsworth's grand ambition to create an epic poem on the human mind that would surpass Milton's *Paradise Lost*, and on the same grounds Milton claimed to surpass the ancients—because the new is *true* and the old is *false*—is long to tell. Suffice it to say Wordsworth made the same error Coleridge did, and of course Coleridge ceaselessly encouraged Wordsworth in the error: that a modern poem could be based on philosophy (or psychology) because philosophy (or psychology) is true and myth is false.[44] The truth is Wordsworth had stories to tell, but no story:

On Man, on Nature and on Human Life . . .
I would give utterance in numerous verse . . .
                        and the law supreme
Of that Intelligence which governs all,
I sing—"fit audience let me find though few!"
So prayed, more gaining than he asked, the Bard,
Holiest of men.—Urania, I shall need
Thy guidance or a greater Muse, if such
Descend to earth or dwell in highest heaven!
For I must tread on shadowy ground, must sink
Deep—and, aloft ascending, breathe in worlds
To which the heaven of heavens is but a veil.
All strength—all terror, single or in bands

> That ever was put forth in personal form;
> Jehova—with his thunder, and the choir
> Of shouting angels and the empyreal thrones,
> I pass them, unalarmed. Not Chaos, not
> The darkest pit of lowest Erebus,
> Nor aught of blinder vacancy—scooped out
> By help of dreams, can breed such fear and awe
> As fall upon us often when we look
> Into our Minds, into the Mind of Man,
> My haunt, and the main region of my Song.[45]

It is Miltonic travesty, further vitiated by the desire to surpass Milton, to enter directly into competition with him, rather than excelling on other terms. Hence Wordsworth misquotes Milton on "fit audience" and claims to be not only a poet who is *sacer* but one who is the "holiest of men." He asserts *droit du seigneur* over Milton's muse Urania, but then hopes to get a better one. He travels through a kind of chaos, like Milton on Satan's track in the invocation to book 3 of *Paradise Lost;* then he rises, like Milton, into "the heaven of heavens," emulously sequacious. But for him this heaven of heavens is no more satisfying than the tryst with Urania. The heaven of heavens is only a veil for higher, Wordsworthian truth. Whatever this truth is, it demands Wordsworth reject all "personal form[s]," that is, gods. He passes Jehovah and his "shouting" angels—*shouting* is Milton's word, but used in a different and newer sense—and remains "unalarmed" (a phrase that gave Byron meat for ridicule). Milton's chaos and Erebus breed no terror or awe in Wordsworth, for in comparison with *his* subject they are trivial. His subject is the "Mind of Man." The mind of man may be made the subject of stories, but not of one story, such as that of Achilles, or Odysseus, or Aeneas, or Adam and Eve.

Much more modest claims could be entered for the contribution of Milton's blank verse to the masterly yet informal eloquence of Coleridge's conversation poems, especially "Frost at Midnight," for some few passages in Keats's *Hyperion,* and for some in Shelley's *Prometheus Unbound.* But a rather different and difficult case must be made for Blake's independent achievement in verse. In the preface to *Jerusalem,* Blake condemns Milton's blank verse even as he echoes Milton's words in

defense of it. Blake says he first considered for his poem a "Monoto-
nous Cadence like that used by Milton and Shakespeare and all writers
of English Blank Verse, derived from the modern bondage of Rhyming."
What Milton saw as a breaking free, Blake saw as an extension of im-
prisonment: "as much a bondage as rhyme itself." "I therefore have produced," Blake went on to explain, "a variety in every line, both of cadences and number of syllables . . . the terrific numbers are reserved for
the terrific parts, the mild and gentle, for the mild and gentle parts, and
the prosaic, for inferior parts; all are necessary to each other, Poetry
Fetter'd, Fetters the Human Race."[46] Milton would have agreed with
that last statement, and he said as much when he spoke of his poem, in
the note on the verse he added to a later issue of *Paradise Lost*, as "an
example set, the first in English, of ancient liberty recovered to heroic
poem from the troublesome and modern bondage of rhyming." The
same association of metrical freedom with more important kinds of
freedom may be seen in Romantic verse across the Atlantic, in Whitman's *Leaves of Grass*, which is full of Miltonic cadences and echoes
and reads as if the energy barely contained by Milton's measure has at
last burst its confines. It is significant in this respect that the late
A. R. Ammons, a resolute antiformalist and a Romantic poet at heart,
was a continual reader of *Paradise Lost* and enjoyed hearing it read aloud.
Modern free verse, inheriting the spontaneous spirit of the Romantics,
owes more to Milton's verse than is generally acknowledged. Only
Byron, as we saw, stood out against the example of Milton's blank verse
for a long, quasi-epic poem, writing *Childe Harold's Pilgrimage* in Spenserian stanzas and *Don Juan* in *ottava rima*.

The influences we have so far observed flowing from Milton to the Romantics are the physical landscapes that both stretch and astound the
imagination of the reader; the entanglement of these landscapes with
Romantic tales sparked by exotic names; the cultivation of a "high language" more sublime than that afforded by the rhetorical tradition; and
the refinement of blank verse, which is a positive influence in some cases,
especially Wordsworth's, a negative one in others, notably Keats's, and
a mixed influence in at least one case—Blake's. Having also noted the
influence of the freer use of rhyme in Milton's early poems and in the
choruses of *Samson Agonistes*, we may turn now to another influence of
which the reader has perhaps been expecting to hear sooner, although
it was mentioned in connection with language: Satan.

We should perhaps not speak of the *influence* of Milton's Satan so much as of the *example* of his rebellious spirit. In the words of Satan's reputed but far from unqualified admirer, Shelley, Satan shows "courage, and majesty, and firm and patient opposition to omnipotent force." Satan is therefore an example of rebellious spirit. But Shelley's Prometheus shows these things without the "taints of ambition, envy, revenge . . . which in the hero of *Paradise Lost* interfere with the interest."[47] It is important to note that this is more than a matter of language, thrilling as Satan's soaring rhetoric is, especially in the early books of *Paradise Lost*. The virtues of courage and patient opposition to omnipotent force are what Byron saw in Milton's Satan, as well. He recast those virtues in his figures of Lucifer and Cain, although, as his letters in defense of *Cain* show, Byron's judgment of the devil is more nuanced than that of his youthful, fiery friend Shelley—if by "nuanced" we intend cunningly inconsistent and opportunistically worldly. Byron wrote to his publisher, John Murray, who had doubts about publishing *Cain*, "Are these people more impious than Milton's Satan?—or the Prometheus of AEschylus? . . . I was obliged to make Cain and Lucifer talk consistently—and surely this has been permitted to poesy."[48] In conversation Byron lamented there being no place in Westminster Abbey's Poets' Corner for the Roman Catholic Alexander Pope or the nonconformist and antiprelatical Milton, and asked, "Will men never learn that every great poet is necessarily a religious man?" But how serious he is is suggested by the sting in the tail of this remark, "so at least Coleridge says"—not Byron's highest authority on poetry or poets.[49] This may be true, but the point is which religion is in question. Byron may have been of the devil's party more than half the time in his private life, if drinking out of human skulls is any indication of his religion. But a fair reading of *Cain* shows only that the devil has a case to make, which he must if the drama is to be any good. As several of the Romantics justly observed, it was entirely Milton's innovation to represent Satan, the great enemy of the good throughout the Christian tradition, not as the repulsive monster of medieval art and literature, chewing and excreting the damned in Hell, but as what Baudelaire called "the most perfect type of virile beauty." "Nothing," said Shelley, "can exceed the grandeur and the energy of the character of the Devil as expressed in *Paradise Lost* . . . [the devil is] a moral being far superior to God, as one who perseveres in some purpose which he has conceived to be excellent, in spite of adversity and torture." He adds the point I have mentioned, which was made by Wordsworth and Byron as well: "Milton divested [the Devil] of a sting, hoofs, and horns [and] clothed him with the sublime grandeur of a graceful but tremendous spirit."[50] Shelley does not admire Satan, whose viciousness he sees, although he does admire his spirit and breathes it into his own, non-vicious hero. Shelley opposes in its entirety the theodicy of *Paradise Lost*, especially the implication that a God deserving any respect would torture for eternity a foe who has been entirely defeated.

Shelley's view of *Paradise Lost* is most clearly seen in the preface to *Prometheus Unbound*, in a passage worth considering more closely, for it anticipates the argument of William Empson's *Milton's God*. The problem for Shelley lies not in Milton's art but in the Christian religion to which Milton committed his art.[51] "The character of Satan," Shelley says, "engenders in the mind a pernicious casuistry which leads us to weigh his faults with his wrongs, and to excuse the former because the latter exceed all measure. In the minds of those who consider that magnificent fiction with a religious feeling it engenders something worse."[52] By those "wrongs" perpetrated on Satan that "exceed all measure" Shelley means what in *On the Devil and Devils* he calls God's "vindictive omnipotence," which "in the cold security of undoubted triumph inflicts the most horrible revenge upon his enemy—not from any mistaken notion of bringing him to repent of a perseverance in enmity, but with the open and alleged design of exasperating him [Satan] to deserve new torments."[53] The "something worse" engendered in the minds of Christian readers of *Paradise Lost* is the belief that inflicting unending torture on a defeated enemy is an act of sacred wisdom. But even for the nonbelieving reader of *Paradise Lost*, the tendency to excuse Satan's "faults" (though this is surely a light word for them) because they are outweighed by the monstrous punishment inflicted on him by God is a "pernicious casuistry."[54] However much we may be revolted by Milton's God, Shelley is saying, it would be pernicious casuistry to excuse Satan's crimes. To avoid that error, which is unavoidable within Christian ideology, Shelley chooses a classical hero, Prometheus, who is free of Satan's "faults." For Shelley, it is Prometheus, not Satan, who is "the type of the highest perfection of moral and intellectual nature, impelled by the purest and the truest motives to the best and noblest ends."[55] In short, Prometheus is friend to humanity and its greatest benefactor. Satan, as his name declares, is humanity's greatest enemy, intending its mass murder and enslavement.

But of course the Satan of Milton's *Paradise Lost* is not defying an illusion. He is defying the real God, who is a priori good, however many
difficulties this basic assumption draws the poet into, as Empson argued. For this reason, within its Christian context, the Satan of *Paradise
Lost* must be portrayed as evil, embodying, as Shelley says (again, somewhat mildly), "envy, revenge, and a desire for personal aggrandizement,"
to which we should add the intention to enslave and finally to annihilate
the human race. There is nothing noble about him that is not a performance for others. Milton makes sure that we see this in the squalid
declivity of Satan in *Paradise Lost*, and in his craven but dangerous obse-
quiousness in *Paradise Regained*. Shelley's admiration of Milton's Satan
begins only when the example of Satan's defiance is removed from the
Christian frame in which such defiance can only be evil. But once the
example is removed from its frame—surely it is a great mistake for criticism to do so, whatever poets do—Satan becomes innocent revolutionary power. To avoid confusion on this point, Shelley renames him,
Prometheus.

Blake's relation to Milton's Satan—and of course, his underlying relation to Milton—is a more complicated, not to say enormous subject, as
we should expect from a poet who titled one of his epic prophecies *Milton*.
But the outlines are reasonably clear, once we understand the depth of
Blake's revolutionary ideas and his sense of being on a mission to complete a revolution that Milton began. It is a revolution in the human
mind, throwing off the chains of mystery and sadism for which all the
religions of the world up to Blake's time, and not only or even especially traditional Christianity, are responsible. But traditional Christianity is certainly responsible, too, in its decadent form as deism, and
Christianity is nearest to hand, being in Blake's view the cause of all
European wars in his time. Yet Blake was a Christian. That is what made
him revolutionary. His intention was not to attack Christianity from
without but to overturn it from within, which is what the word *revolutionary* means. For Blake, the only place to stand outside Christianity
is in atheism or deism, which are for him indistinguishable, each being
the prisoner of a materialist science governed by the principle of reason,
which is set up as God.[56] Blake's figure for this god, this deified principle of reason, is *Urizen*, an old man in the sky with an immense white
beard. This is obviously God the Father, the God of Christianity, but

also the principle of reason separated from energy and given absolute authority to command and to create. (The name *Urizen* suggests both "reason" and "horizon," since for Blake reason is the horizon or outward circumference of energy. The most famous of Blake's engravings, the frontispiece to *Europe*, shows Urizen, "The Ancient of Days," drawing the circumference of the universe with compasses.[57]) Blake concludes that to try to find a secure place to stand outside Christianity is to fall back into the worst of the illusions for which traditional Christianity is responsible: the deification of reason as God, which Blake represents as Urizen. Reason as Urizen has the power to demonize energy and to condemn to Hell everyone who does not keep the moral law, a moral law devoted not to doing any good but only to suppressing desire and further promoting alienated reason. It is not possible, therefore, for Blake to regard traditional Christianity simply as error, erroneous as much of it is in his eyes: the living truth is still in it, though repressed by the Urizenic powers. That is why a revolution is necessary, to free the living truth from the prison that traditional Christianity calls "Hell."

From what has been said so far it should be clear that Blake is the only Romantic poet to engage Milton on the terms Milton himself thought most important: those of Christianity. Coleridge, Wordsworth, Shelley, Keats, and Byron all admire Milton's political morals and especially his principled firmness during the English Revolution and after, during the Restoration, when the poet was "in darkness and with dangers compassed round" (*PL*, 7.27). But Milton's Christianity is an embarrassment to them. What was most important to Milton, when he justified the ways of God to men, was the coming kingdom of God on earth, which would occur not by the vindication of principles and rights but by the Second Coming of Christ. It is Christ, and not a better version of the French Revolution, that will bring in final justice:

> respiration to the just
> And vengeance to the wicked at return
> Of Him so lately promised to thy aid,
> The woman's Seed, obscurely then foretold,
> Now amplier known thy Savior and thy Lord.

> (PL, *12.540–44*)

Vengeance to the wicked! The major Romantic poets treat Milton's Christianity as little more than a superstition, like the Olympian religion of Homer but without the aesthetic appeal of the latter. For them, Milton is essentially four things, none of which have anything to do with Christianity: (1) blank verse; (2) antimonarchical, republican politics, or rule by the most virtuous; (3) an organic vision of nature with the power of growth dwelling within; and (4) inspiration. Blake alone tackled what is most obvious and central to Milton: Christian ideology. More surprising still, he made Milton a savior who will return to the world.

Before turning to *Milton*, which was written and engraved between 1804 and 1808, we should note Blake's most famous remark about the poet, which was made in an earlier work, *The Marriage of Heaven and Hell*, dating from 1790–1793: "The reason Milton wrote in fetters when he wrote of Angels and God, and at liberty when of Devils and Hell, is because he was a true Poet and of the Devils party without knowing it."[58] The speaker of this remark, which is so often attributed to Blake's authorial voice, is a devil himself, eager to have the poet on his side. This of course does not mean, especially in Blake, that what a devil says isn't true, or that Blake doesn't think it true. But the fact does call for caution and some weighing of context.

In the preceding passage, beginning on plate 4 under the heading "The Voice of the Devil," the Devil is clearly Blake's mouthpiece, exposing errors that Blake also thinks are errors and affirming truths Blake also thinks true. The errors are that a person is a body and a soul; that energy is evil and reason good; and that eternal torment in Hell awaits those who follow energy, which they encounter through their desires. The truths—or, as Blake calls them, the *contraries*—are that a person is entirely soul, and the body is that part of the soul that the five senses discern; that energy is life, reason being merely the "outward circumference" of energy; and that energy, creative power, is "Eternal Delight," or what Christianity calls "Heaven."[59] But traditional Christianity condemns this creative energy to Hell. Recovering creative energy from the Hell to which it has been condemned, and revealing that this energy is Heaven, or "Eternal Delight," is what Blake means by the "Marriage of Heaven and Hell."

On the following plate, number 5, Blake surprisingly relates to *Paradise Lost* these claims of the Devil—that what is usually called "evil" is energy, which is in truth *good*, and that what is usually called "good" is reason, which, when separated from energy and set up on its own, is in truth *bad*. Blake regards *Paradise Lost* as a "history" of the development of these errors: the demonizing of energy and the deification of a principle of reason that has been removed from its life source in energy ("Reason is the bound or outward circumference of Energy"). It is important to understand that Blake's purpose in the passage is not to interpret *Paradise Lost* on its own terms, which terms Blake regards as erroneous: it is to interpret *Paradise Lost* on Blake's terms and above all to say something not just about one poet, Milton, but about *poets*. Blake is saying that poets give form to energy and are therefore always on the side of desire, the energy that gives poetry life. But conventional religions seek to restrain desire with common morality, not because desire leads to sensual indulgence—sensual indulgence is what conventional religion wants, in order to control energy within the economy of sin—but because in poets the freeing of desire leads to prophecy, which is the greatest threat to conventional religion. Conventional religion therefore enlists what it calls "reason" on its side, although this reason turns out to be preoccupied mostly with the repression of desire and the murder of prophets:

> Those who restrain desire, do so because theirs is weak enough to be restrained; and the restrainer or reason usurps its place and governs the unwilling.
> And being restrained it by degrees becomes passive till it is only the shadow of desire [i.e., reason].
> The history of this is written in *Paradise Lost*, and the Governor or Reason is call'd Messiah.
> And the original Archangel or possessor of the command of the Heavenly host, is calld the Devil or Satan and his children are call'd Sin and Death . . .
> But in Milton; the Father is Destiny, the Son, a Ratio of the five senses, and the Holy-ghost, Vacuum!
> Note. The reason Milton wrote in fetters when he wrote of Angels and God, and at liberty when of Devils and Hell, is because he was a true Poet and of the Devils party without knowing it.[60]

In this passage Blake is discussing what happens to traditional Christian ideas and images when they enter into Milton's epic where they are

exposed and stark: God the Father is destiny (the inescapable consequences of an implacable reason) and God the Son is "a Ratio of the
five senses," which is reason working up from mere sense impressions,
instead of following vision. For Blake, the Jehovah of the Hebrew scriptures, who becomes God the Father of Christianity, is the principle of
evil we call "Satan," seeking the death of the prophets and the repression of desire. And what we have learned to call "Satan" is the demon-
ized mask of energy, imagination, and poetic power. Milton's error, as
we are told in the "Note," is that he believed in the demonic mask without
seeing what is concealed behind it—his own poetic power. Milton therefore found himself writing about Satan in the first two books of *Paradise Lost* "with liberty" without knowing why he was writing so well.
He wrote "in fetters" when he wrote of "Angels and God" because these
figures are the masks of what is in truth repression. Blake's claim that
Milton is a "true Poet" and therefore "of the Devils party without
knowing it" means that what is best in Milton opposes the repressive-
ness of traditional Christianity, which is a wicked distortion of the teach-
ings of another true poet: Jesus.

However we interpret Blake's remarks on Milton in *The Marriage of
Heaven and Hell*, he clearly did not regard them as final, and returned
to what we may call "the problem of Milton" in the poem he named
after that poet. Blake was displeased with his earlier idea that Milton
was wholly ignorant of the true nature of the Christian ideology he ex-
pounded in *Paradise Lost*. For Blake, Milton is a prophet and deserves
more respect than he was accorded in *The Marriage of Heaven and Hell*,
in which the conscious Milton is wholly on the side of his rationalistic
God, parodied as Blake's Urizen. But Milton was also a "true poet," and
according him respect means reading him with broader awareness than
is shown in *The Marriage of Heaven and Hell*.

For Blake, this also means—to take us far beyond reading—that
Milton deserves to be appealed to in person. That is what happens in
Milton. But where is Milton, to receive this appeal? Part of him is in
Hell, for Satan is his "spectre," an alienated part of himself, his energy,
awaiting recuperation. But as a "true Poet" Milton is also in Heaven.
He is appealed to in person to make a terrible journey back into the
world as a prophet, risking eternal death to correct his mistakes and
vindicate the liberating truth buried in *Paradise Lost*. This he does,
descending through a bizarre Dantesque landscape and passing through
Albion's heart into the "tarsus" of Blake's left foot, a location signifying

the erroneous point from which Milton left the world, that is, a sinister religion of vengeance and Pauline repression (Saint Paul was from Tarsus):

> Then first I saw him in the Zenith as a falling star
> Descending perpendicular, swift as the swallow or swift:
> And on my left foot falling on the tarsus, enterd there:
> But from my left foot a black cloud redounding spread over
>   Europe.[61]

Milton rises from thence to become one with Blake. The old prophet is now taken up into the new, for the express purpose of correcting the old prophet's mistakes, with Blake's help. What are Milton's mistakes? The first ones have already been exposed in *The Marriage of Heaven and Hell*: the polarization of the universe into Heaven and Hell; the separation of reason from energy and the placing of reason above it; the alienation of this principle of reason to Heaven, calling it "God"; and the banishing of poetic energy, which is the source of this reason, to Hell. The other errors of *Paradise Lost* have been more apparent to readers: the subordination of women and the existence of hierarchy in the objective world as a permanent principle, justifying social distinctions as natural, rather than as according to merit. To this we may add Milton's materialism, to Blake the most inimical of all Milton's ideas.[62] Even so, Milton's materialism is monistic, which means he does not accept the division of creatures into bodies and souls, or of the universe into spirit and matter. Milton's materialism is therefore more nearly allied to Blake's monist belief that all is spirit than to the dualism both poets abhorred. "Materialism" is here the belief that there is an absolutely featureless, extended substance from which all things are made: "one first matter all," as it is called in *Paradise Lost* (5.472).

This matter comes ultimately from God, is alienated from God to become the "whelming" abyss of materials in chaos, and is worked on by God to create the Son, the angels, the world, and mankind (*PL*, 7.168–73). Because the matter of chaos is valueless as it is, being raised out of chaos by creation introduces the first step in a hierarchy, whereby all things on the ladder of being tend up to God "if not depraved from good" (*PL*, 5.471). Milton is fairly clear about Eve being lower on this hierarchy because she is closer to nature and to plants, so that her vision of God is not direct but through Adam, who is made in God's image. Milton's Eve is made not in the image of God but in the image of Adam's desire (*PL*, 4.288–31). Blake thought that Milton's cosmology inevitably leads to social distinctions of rank; to the disvaluing and impoverishment of artists; to the oppression of women; to commerce based on greed and enslaving a large part of humanity; to an abstract, deistical religion based on the senses (for everything, including God himself, is matter, not vision); to empirical science as the foundation and ultimately the substitute for such religion; and to ceaseless war, excellence at slaughter being regarded, as in the *Iliad*, as the human activity most deserving of praise. All these forces working together to enslave humankind make up the wheels of what Blake calls "dark Satanic mills."[63]

At the same time, Blake recognizes Milton as the greatest prophet of liberty in the modern world before Blake himself. Milton was against bishops and kings; Milton was for marriage as a union of minds; Milton was for poetry and prophecy as the voices of wisdom; Milton was for the visions of the individual spirit over the practices of organized religion (having attended no church in his adult years); and Milton spoke out against "wars" as the only proper subject for a poem, "hitherto the only argument / Heroic deemed" (*PL*, 9.28–29). For Blake, no prophet can be entirely in the right, for every prophet is as encumbered with almost as many errors as he or she is entrusted with truths. That is why there must be a *tradition* of prophets: one prophet is never enough. As each prophet carries the truth forward in time to the next, each is also a spiritual help for those who went before, as Blake is for Milton. That is why Milton can speak as he does in the following passage from *Milton* but could never speak this way in any poem he might have written in his own life:

> What do I do here [in Heaven] before the Judgment? Without my
>   Emanation?
> With the daughters of memory, and not with the daughters of
>   inspiration?
> I in my Selfhood am that Satan: I am that Evil One!
> He is my Spectre! In obedience to loose him from my Hells,
> To claim the Hells, my Furnaces, I go to Eternal Death.[64]

Some poets are better than others, and some are much better than others—Mount Parnassus is not a democratic place—but poetry never gets better or worse over time because genius is a continual, not a continuous, occurrence. Poetry therefore cannot be counted on to advance with civilization, to improve when opinions improve, or to inscribe itself within the continuity of a tradition. Poetry reaches the heights unpredictably, under barbarous or civilized conditions. Education appears to be the only social force that is unambiguously in poetry's favor because education is the nursery of genius. Their own education and thought, and their own experience, did more for the Romantics than Milton did.

I began this chapter observing that literary criticism, following the example of the Romantics themselves, has adhered to an illusory logic of continuity extending from Milton to the Romantics. A visionary, political, and prophetic *tradition* has been affirmed in preference to the artistic differences between Milton, on the one hand, and the Romantics, on the other, the differences that make them distinctive. What happens when we attend to the differences?

If we do the thought experiment of setting Milton's influence on the Romantics at a minimum, confining it to certain technical features of blank verse, to certain arresting locutions, and to that new sense of continuous and illimitable space, then the Romantics immediately benefit and look more original. They are not required to be Christian, or to explain why they are not and what they are instead. They do not have to substitute for Christianity something putatively as coherent, such as Kant, with his giant's hand, in which Coleridge was taken up. Nor do the Romantics, in their eyes or in ours, have to make up for, or blush at, their comparative ignorance of Greek and Latin poets (comparative with Milton); for the Greeks and the Romans had little importance to them and did not need to have any. The world had changed in their time and a new epoch emerged.

Without having to affirm their continuity with Milton, the Romantics also do not have to worry about *his* limitations, as they see them, if a poet so great can meaningfully be said to have limitations, instead of circumstantial eccentricities. Freed from invidious comparisons, the Romantics can be seen doing what they finally did, which is to affirm their authenticity: their right to be what they are, clearly and splendidly. We have to look across the Channel once again, to Byron and the Shelleys in Italy, to Goethe in Weimer, and to Hugo in France, to see that Romanticism had much less to do with Milton than it did to its being a European, epochal event. In short, the Romantic poets were more original than they knew, at least at those times when they were crouching in Milton's shadow, though Byron never crouched. Had Milton spotted them there he'd have told them to stand in the light, as they deserved.

III

TRANSCENDENTAL ENGAGEMENT

❧ 9

On History in Paradise Lost

My title speaks of history *in Paradise Lost* because I suggest that all history is transcendentally implied—"folded in"—in Milton's greatest poem. In *Paradise Lost*, Milton uses a "true myth" to pierce through the veil of confusing, superficial events so as to explain history in its moral interior. But there is some irony in the fact of Milton's turning away from contemporary events, at the midpoint of the composition of *Paradise Lost*, at the moment when these events were historically decisive, and most dangerously apparent to him. When Charles II returned to London at the Restoration, in 1660, Milton's name was published as one of those who were excluded from the general pardon. During the following summer he was in hiding from the authorities, in danger of being legally executed by the disagreeable method of partial hanging, castration, evisceration, and disarticulation. After August, when it was supposed he was quit of all charges and could come out of hiding, Milton was imprisoned for several months on what may have been a misunderstanding, or may not have been, and some formal act of submission was probably required of him. In any event, what appear to have been larcenous prison fees absorbed much of the money he had been able to rescue, after losing his savings in the collapse of the Excise Bank. (The case of the fees was brought up in Parliament by Andrew Marvell, with what result we do not know.)[1]

Although a decade previous Milton had loyally defended the execution of Charles I, he no doubt escaped punishment in 1660 because he had taken no part in promoting the execution before it occurred. Indeed, it seems doubtful he would have approved of it, had anyone thought it worth asking him, for the simple reason that executing the king would tie the legitimacy of England's revolutionary project to the legality of a single shocking act, rather than to the revolution's broader intellectual, political, and moral justification. (Charles I was not the only victim of judicial homicide in the 1640s.) Killing Charles Stuart was worse than a crime: it was a mistake. But once the execution was done Milton defended it with his usual vigor, emphasizing that the executed king delegitimated himself by being lawless and a tyrant.[2] It is hardly surprising that immediately after the Restoration Milton was a hunted man. It is more surprising he survived and received clemency. It is even possible, as was later affirmed, Milton received an offer to employ his pen in the service of the new regime. If he did, he declined without contumely and no doubt politely.

The death blow of the English Revolution was struck by the army, under General Monck, which after much agonizing delay—and after frenzied speculation on all sides—came down from the north and allowed free elections. Now the old, purged members of the Long Parliament were recalled—those who were still alive—and this Parliament sat long enough to dissolve itself and call new elections. At the invitation of the newly elected and overwhelmingly royalist Convention Parliament, Charles Stuart returned from the continent to be crowned King Charles II. The Restoration had begun. Milton believed that when the mass of the people want slavery instead of liberty, the few have the right to preserve their own freedom by forcing the rest to be free.[3] This means a dictatorship of the free. Although it is nobly and no doubt sincerely expressed by Milton, the sophistry of this argument is apparent. Nobody wants to be a slave, but few could want liberty or, rather, the promise of liberty, on Milton's revolutionary terms. Exhausted by twenty years of war and political turmoil, the mass of the people of England wanted stability and peace, in which most find whatever liberty is to be found in this world. They also wanted a representative government, however limited. Yet in the end, both the revolutionary fervor and equally fervent royalist-parliamentary reaction to it were necessary elements of the bloodless "Glorious Revolution" of 1688, by which England would become a constitutional monarchy. In stages, real power would pass over to Parliament and stay there, without the further inconvenience of beheading any kings.

It seems, then, not wide of the mark to conclude that the years during which Milton composed *Paradise Lost* were for the poet years of intense emotional strain, heroic effort, personal danger, public scorn, financial difficulty, and physical pain (the poet was probably already suffering from gout, racking all his joints), tinged no doubt with guilt at the executions of men (most of them in October 1660) who suffered the death he escaped. These included his personal friend Sir Henry Vane, beheaded in 1662. There is no reason to withhold our assent to the poet's claim that excellence at slaughter, though it has long been deemed heroic and virtuous, as well as being the proper subject of an epic poem, is inferior to "the better fortitude / Of patience and heroic martyrdom" (*PL*, 9.31–32). Putting his own body at risk, and suffering for his integrity while never ceasing to create, Milton earned that brave and unusual claim.

Paradise Lost was first published in August 1667, in a handsome quarto volume, to immediate fame and slow but steady sales. Milton's epic may have been substantially complete as early as 1663, according to John Aubrey's dubious hint, or by 1665, when Thomas Ellwood was given the manuscript—or, shall we say, *a* manuscript?—and asked to comment on it.[4] In any event, publication was delayed by a number of factors: by the licensor, by the Great Plague of London, from which Milton and his family escaped to Chalfont St. Giles (their London home at the time was near one of the mass burial pits), and by the Great Fire of London in September 1666, which destroyed eighty-nine of the city's ninety-seven parish churches. Samuel Pepys describes the smoke, the intense heat, the panic, and the astonishing noise, which included the destruction of houses deliberately blown up to prevent the fire's spread. He also describes pigeons catching fire on the wing.

In the aftermath, finding a printer may well have been difficult. The fire destroyed the shops and equipment of many printers and booksellers, which were concentrated around Saint Paul's churchyard, the cathedral having been destroyed in the fire along with presses and printing stock. Much of this valuable paper was stored beneath the cathedral in underground chambers, which were thought to be fireproof. The huge falling stones of the arches opened those chambers and the flaming timbers of the roof followed the stones.[5] As *Paradise Lost* was being printed, the center of the city was still a charred ruin. To add to the calamities of that annus horribilis, England, already a great power at sea, suffered a humiliating naval defeat at the hands of the Dutch in June 1667, ending the Second Anglo-Dutch War. The Dutch fleet sailed into the Medway, where the English fleet was harbored, destroyed many ships and towed two away, one of them the Royal Charles, the English flagship, named after the restored king and the symbol of the new order. Pepys's account of the event is valuable for its record of the general horror that was felt when these events were known, and the dread of the social chaos and violence that could ensue as a result. Milton's feelings were no doubt somewhat different.

Amid plague, fire, and war, it was perhaps not unreasonable for poets closer to the court to transform these disasters into providential expressions of hope, enunciated with polished coolness. That is what John Dryden did, in his *Annus Mirabilis* ("the year of wonders"), composed in neat, alternately rhyming quatrains, the stanza used by the royalist poet, Sir John Davenant, for his attempted epic, *Gondibert*. *Annus Mirabilis* was published in the same year as *Paradise Lost*, 1667, although before the Dutch raid on the English fleet. Dryden's comments on the war, comparing Holland with Carthage and England with Rome, reflect confidence in England's ultimately prevailing, as indeed she did:

> What peace can be, where both to one pretend?
> (But they more diligent, and we more strong)
> Or if a peace, it soon must have an end;
> For they would grow too powerful, were it long.[6]

Such icy and shrewd *Realpolitik* is entirely foreign to the spirit of *Paradise Lost*, but very much in the spirit of the times. Dryden's poem was brought out by the most fashionable publisher of the day. Milton was not so fortunate.

Paradise Lost was unfashionable in every respect: it didn't rhyme; it didn't address current events; it was biblical; it was classical; it was moral; it was densely allusive and astonishingly learned; it was hard to follow; its plot was complex; it was serious (its subject being the origin of history in original sin, the will of God for humanity, and the possibility of liberty for all mankind); and it was huge. I say "huge" and not merely "long." Among the skipping satires and lighter elegancies of profitable compliment, *Paradise Lost* paced with a mastodon tread, a book dedicated to no one, moving inexorably on its own power. The order of the day—after the convulsions of the civil war, after the Bible-spewing fanatics and hypocritical Presbyterians, after Cromwell's dictatorship and the despotism of his major generals—was for lightness, ease, and relaxed moral standards, including tolerance of cynicism and the adulation of wealth and power for their own sakes. The age demanded a poetry that was disinclined to remember the withering idealism of the immediate past, the years of the Interregnum, except with advantageous distortion. (The very word, *interregnum* "between the reigns," suggests a kind of empty space, a time already forgotten, a zero or a bubble in history.) It would be a poetry that was formally as well as morally indifferent to history, devoted to present fashions and current events. These circumstances all but ruined Andrew Marvell as a poet, despite the flashy brilliance and savage indignation of the satires he now composed against the corruption of the times. Whatever is given over to the fashions or concerns of the present, forgetting the past, will not please or interest long. Milton lasted, and continues to please, because he embarked on the farthest journey it was possible to take into the past, so as to roll up history from the beginning.

Paradise Lost appeared like some antediluvian monster hauled up from the deep, covered with barnacles and ooze, but still fighting and still dangerous, as Marvell himself acknowledged in the great poem he wrote to appear with the second edition. (It is surely the best poem in English on another English poem.) *Paradise Lost* was antediluvian in the full sense of the word because it went back "before the Flood," to the origin of humanity, and traced out human history forward from thence. Yet despite its unfashionable style, and the general obloquy in which its author was held, the greatness of *Paradise Lost* was never in doubt. One of the smartest poets of the age, Sir John Denham, is said to have brought a sheet of the poem then printing into the newly opened Parliament (or its antechamber), describing the wet sheet he was holding as "part of the noblest poem that ever was wrote in any language or any age."[7]

This new epic in an old style—a style as old as that of Homer—did not employ rhyme, which was now de rigueur, thanks to Edmund Waller, Sir John Denham, and of course Dryden. Samples of each of these poets will show how far *Paradise Lost* was removed from the taste of the time. But they will also help to show, by contrast, how the style of *Paradise Lost* was well suited for the task of imagining history. Waller was the pioneer of the serried couplet, that is, of couplets that are each contained in themselves but lined up crisply in ranks, like soldiers:

> The soul's dark cottage, battered and decayed,
> Lets in new light through chinks that Time has made:
> Stronger by weakness, wiser men become
> As they draw near to their eternal home.
> Leaving the old, both worlds at once they view
> That stand upon the threshold of the new.[8]

The most famous lines in this new manner were composed at the beginning of the civil war by Denham, in "Cooper's Hill" (1642), describing the flow of the Thames:

> O could I flow like thee, and make thy stream
> My great example, as it is my theme.
> Though deep, yet clear, though gentle, yet not dull,
> Strong without rage, without o'erflowing, full.[9]

Finally, to quote the master of the serried couplet, here are lines from Dryden's *Astraea Redux* (1660), celebrating the Restoration of Charles II, each couplet delivering its packet of compliment just in time, as on a conveyor belt. Read the first line of each couplet with a rising intonation and the second with a declining:

> Inured to suffer ere he came to reign,
> No rash procedure will his actions stain:
> To business, ripen'd by digestive thought,
> His future rule is into method brought:
> As they who first proportion understand,
> With easy practice reach a master's hand.[10]

In the sixteen lines of verse I have just quoted from these three poets, there is one enjambment, Denham's "O could I flow like thee, and make thy stream / My great example, as it is my theme." (Enjambment occurs when the enunciation runs over the end of one line into the next without pause, so that the syntax appears to strain against the metrical order by which it is contained.) The couplet remains, however, tightly closed in on itself, and the enjambment, by flowing easily into the second line without flowing any further, wittily imitates what is said of the easy-flowing Thames. Denham's couplet is full "without o'erflowing."

Paradise Lost is composed in blank verse, which is always overflowing. Such verse allows Milton to develop rhythms above the individual line and to extend them over long sentences in the periodic style, in which the final sense of a grammatical unit is suspended over many lines. The opening phrase of *Paradise Lost*—"Of Man's first disobedience . . ." does not find its main verb—"Sing"—until the sixth line. No sooner is this grammatical unit concluded in the middle of the sixth line than a dependent clause is opened with a relative pronoun—*that:* "Sing Heav'nly Muse, that on the secret top" (*PL*, 1.6). We now learn that the muse who has been commanded to sing once inspired Moses—*didst inspire* being the main verb of this new clause—who taught the Hebrews "in the beginning, how the heav'ns and earth / Rose out of chaos" (*PL*, 1.8–9). A new unit is now opened, but one beginning with the conjunction *or*, thus compelling the reader to treat what has gone before as part of this new unit and to keep the first of the alternatives in mind, even as a new one is opened: "Or if Sion hill / Delight thee more and Siloa's brook that flowed / Fast by the oracle of God, I thence." Now we must wait, across an enjambment, for the main verb of this new subject, *I:* "Invoke thy aid to my adven'trous song" (*PL*, 1.9–13). Not unreasonably, the reader expects a pause for rest at this moment, but the rest is denied as new clauses are opened successively, all of them modifying *song* and answering the questions (they are the perennial questions of historical investigation) *what? where?* and *when?:* "That with no middle flight intends to soar / Above th'Aonian mount while it pursues" (*PL*, 1.14–15). We are again hanging at the end of a line, in suspense, and only now is the full sense of what was begun in the opening words of the poem brought to a rhythmical and grammatical termination: "Things unattempted yet in prose or rhyme" (*PL*, 1.16). The continuous, kinetic, overflowing experience of reading *Paradise Lost* is remarkably like our experience of reading and thinking about history.

The style of *Paradise Lost* is a periodic style, like Latin prose, punctuated, as such prose is, by rhythmical closures that fall into units like this one: "Things unattempted yet in prose or rhyme." But the rest that even this closure gives us is brief. Nor are we allowed altogether to dismiss from memory what has just been closed off. The next line opens with a parataxis hanging from the conjunction *and*—"And chiefly thou, O Spirit, that dost prefer" (*PL*, 1.17)—with the result that the reader must now run through another ten lines of suspended, forward-falling sense until a new rhythmical unit concludes the development: "And justify the ways of God to men" (*PL*, 1.26). The question what constitutes a *sentence* in our modern understanding of the term is inadequate to the grammatical style of *Paradise Lost*, which is highly syntagmatic—what I characterized as "forward-falling," like running—so that grammatical units that we might subdivide into sentences are really dependent on larger structures that keep the mind in suspense. The first twenty-six lines of *Paradise Lost* work like a single, developing, and complicating sentence with a brief resting point in the middle—"Things unattempted yet in prose or rhyme"—and a strong rest at the end, for emphasis: "And justify the ways of God to men." The next line, at last, opens a new thought: "Say first, for Heav'n hides nothing from thy view, / Nor the deep tract of Hell, say first what cause" (*PL*, 1.27–28). At the outset of *Paradise Lost*, two contrasting themes, or musical subjects, are introduced, like first and second subjects in sonata form, and are then elaborately combined and developed: (1) the historical depth of human sinfulness, which goes back to the first humans; and (2) divinely inspired prophetic song, which happens in the midst of history, fighting to reverse the effects of the Fall.

Milton's contemporary readers, accustomed to rhyme, found this exhausting. As we have seen, rhyming couplets use enjambment more sparely, and when they do, the run-on seldom extends beyond more than one line. Couplets give a dry sort of pleasure, brisk and urbane. They also give the reader continual breaks, moments in which attention to the forward movement of the verse (the syntagmatic "axis of combination") is relaxed, allowing the cleverness of what has been said to be savored by happy comparison to circumstances outside the poem (the paradigmatic "axis of selection"). The couplet is the most unhistorical of poetic forms because it is continually capturing the truth, the truth as understood in this moment, in what Hegel would describe as the impoverished "now."

I mentioned Milton did not manage to place his epic poem with the fashionable printer of the day. Instead, he published with the more obscure Samuel Simmons, who drove a hard bargain.[11] After two years and six reissues—reprintings with minor alterations—the first edition sold out. The definitive edition of the poem, the last in Milton's life, appeared in a smaller, unprepossessing octavo volume in the late summer of 1674. The poet died on the following November 9, a month short of his sixty-sixth birthday.

What appeared in 1667 was in several ways different from this definitive edition of 1674. The first, 1667 edition was called *Paradise Lost: A Poem Written in Ten Books by John Milton.* It had no front matter of any kind: no dedicatory poems, epistles, or commendatory verses, and no prefatory note on the verse, proclaiming that the poem's "measure" is "English heroic verse without rhyme, as that of Homer in Greek, and of Virgil in Latin." In the edition of 1667, as soon as one turns the title page, one is in the presence of the opening lines of the poem, which is attractively set with lined borders, making each page look like a framed picture, as Masson observed. This directness, this eschewing of all flourish, must have appeared surly—or challenging—in that age of exaggerated compliment. There were no prose summaries at the head of each book (the "arguments"). The poem was ten books long, not the twelve it would have in 1674. The eventual change to twelve books would be accomplished—notwithstanding the publisher's description of the new edition as "revised" and "augmented"—by a redistribution of the existing poem and the addition of only a handful of lines. Book 7 of the first edition of *Paradise Lost* was divided in 1674 to become books 7 and 8 and, as a result, the material of former book 8 was moved forward to become book 9, the book of the Fall. The domino effect continued as the former 9 moved up to become 10, the longest book of 1674 poem, describing the immediate consequences of the Fall for Eve and Adam. The former book 10 was next divided in half, yielding the two new books, 11 and 12, most of which are given to describing the remoter consequences of the Fall in history. Books 11 and 12 are very suitably divided at the Flood, "Betwixt the world destroyed and world restored" (*PL*, 12.3). Although the Flood comes early in the first book of the Bible, it was traditionally thought of as marking a break at the middle of history, before which little is known about the civilizations that rose and fell after Cain founded the first city. To facilitate these transpositions, very brief passages—of only three and a half and five lines, respectively—were added to the incipits of books 8 and 12. There were some additions to the list diseases tormenting humanity after the Fall, of which more later.

It has been suggested that the initial choice of ten instead of twelve books is attributable to a republican preference for the unfinished ten-book epic, Lucan's *Pharsalia*, on the Roman civil wars—with its iconic martyr to liberty, Cato—over the imperial twelve books of Virgil's *Aeneid*, which celebrates the victor in those wars, Octavian, the first emperor and the man who effectively ended the Roman Republic.[12] The suggestion is intriguing and persistent but improbable. To convince, it would have to be shown Milton was less republican in spirit in 1674 than he was in 1667, though he was not; that *Paradise Lost* resembles the *Pharsalia* in some other broadly significant way, though it does not; and that the twelve-book arrangement was not otherwise an improvement, though it is.

Paradise Lost is better proportioned in twelve books than it is in ten. For one thing, the new arrangement throws into the foreground the great circuit of the action in the epic's first half. The action begins with the opening scene, where the fallen angels are seen prostrate on the fiery lake of Hell. The action comes full circle at the end of book 6, when those angels are cast out of Heaven and pursued by the Son's lightning bolts of wrath through chaos to Hell. When at the end of book 6 we watch Hell open upon the rebel angels and swallow them whole, we have returned to the scene on which the poem began, witnessing the action now from above instead of from below. Moreover, the war in Heaven, which has occupied book 6 and ended with the casting out of the rebel angels, is now balanced, in book 7, across the midpoint of the epic, by the book of Creation. That Milton would elicit these symmetries of design at a stage later than that of actual composition is unsurprising.

Of greater significance, however, is the earlier change in the tenor of Milton's thinking as he began *Paradise Lost*. The change had been stirring for some time, at least since Oliver Cromwell's death in 1658 and probably earlier, during the Protectorate, when Milton was no longer engaged so intensely in public affairs. His renewed work on *History of Britain* was a factor in this change, as was his elaborate cutting up and pasting of biblical texts into a theological system, *De Doctrina Christiana*. Immediate political concerns began to fade into the background, giving way to large expanses of historical time. The enduring or, shall we say, persistent principles of human nature and conduct now moved to the fore. The change of perspective is consistent with the designing of a long epic poem, which must by its nature lay claim to universal truth, abstracting itself from immediate crises.

A contrasting example is given by the royalist poet Abraham Cowley. In the 1640s he tried to write an epic poem on the English Civil War as events were unfolding, based on newspaper accounts and royalist propaganda. It is an interesting, uninspired work by a gifted poet. Satan is seen in Hell, in the center of the earth, trivially stirring up his devils to incite the London puritans to rebellion. When he found himself on the losing side, Cowley left the poem incomplete. Milton was in a similar case when, as an excited and hopeful idealist, he wrote *Of Reformation* (1641), expecting to record in panegyrical and epic song the glorious deeds of the Long Parliament. But the Long Parliament proved to be a great disappointment to Milton, as parliaments always are to those who want collective action instead of principled dissent or unprincipled self-seeking.

In winter and early spring of 1660 Milton made one last convulsive effort at direct political intervention, in the two editions—the second even more rashly brave than the first—of *The Ready and Easy Way to Establish a Free Commonwealth*. This, however, was an uncharacteristic act for Milton at this stage of his life, a resumption of the prophetic voice of the 1640s in a new state of emergency. The work was undertaken more out of a sense of duty than out of any practical hope. I say "practical hope" because it is obvious in this work, as in its very title, that Milton does think a political miracle is just possible, even if it is, in the nature of miracles, improbable. Perhaps the English would at the last moment come to their senses and, after the shedding of so much blood in the cause of liberty, not surrender abjectly to a king.

Yet the main direction of Milton's thoughts at this time is a tactical retreat from the kind of presentist thinking we see in his poetry in the middle phase of his career, from the outburst of Saint Peter in "Lycidas" (1637) to "On the Late Massacre in Piedmont" (1655). Milton's thinking moves now toward a determinate negation of political presence, effected by a turn to biblical myth. Determinate negation (as opposed to negation in formal logic) does not affirm that what it negates is wholly and always not so, untrue. Logical negation exists out of time. What determinate negation negates has been mostly true in its historical moment, and is now not so much untrue as increasingly incomplete. This mode of thinking may sound later than Milton's period and it is, or the language for it is, but such thinking is also implicit in the Christian reading of the Bible, regarding the Hebrew scriptures as contingently true, as true in their time. By this way of thinking, it was altogether right in Milton's eyes for him to have risked his life and fortune for a permanent English Commonwealth, and to promote war in the cause of liberty, despite the outcome. But it isn't right now. The opportunity was there, and it would have been wrong not to urge seizing the moment. But that moment of *kairos* has passed. What *is* right now, as the later 1650s become the early 1660s, is a turning away from political presence, thus clearing the stage on which universal principles will emerge. The question is, what are these principles and where are they to be found?

They cannot be plucked out of the sky, like the principles of Plato's *Republic*. But neither can they be fished out of history, because every period of history reveals the consequences of the same human problem, which for Milton could be summarized by the term "the Fall," or by "Mans first *disobedience*" (*PL*, 1.1), a disobedience not only to God but to human nature founded on liberty. Idealized figures in history turn out to be morally compromised, and to have feet of clay—or, like King Arthur, the hero of Spenser's *Faerie Queene*, to be of dubious veracity. It therefore becomes necessary to step out of history into myth, although not any myth. Such a myth must fulfill two conditions: first, it must be a *true myth* and, second, it must be a myth that stands in a causal or *aetiological relation* to history (from Greek *aitios*, "cause" but also "crime, charge, accusation"). Only one myth fulfills these conditions. It is the story of Adam and Eve, from the opening chapters of the Bible, on which, accordingly, Milton based the story of *Paradise Lost*. The biblical myth is not necessarily true as fact but rather because it is a story inspired by God, by the Holy Ghost, and is accommodated to the human mind as light to the eye. The real circumstances of the origins and character of human nature may have been different, and much more complex (as we now know), but this myth is the one God inspired Moses to record, as a comprehensible and memorable image of the truth. The myth of Creation and the Fall stands in an aetiological relation to history because history acquires its enduring character from Adam and Eve's "disobedience" (*PL*, 1.1); Milton is probably thinking of the word *aitios*, rather than the biblical *hamartia*, in connection with *disobedience*. This new movement of thought in Milton's work demands that he turn his attention away from immediate political concerns to what appears to be their opposite: biblical fiction.

Nor does Milton follow the usual distancing stratagem of the Renaissance epic poet, which was authorized by Italian critical theory based
on Aristotle's *Poetics:* to select an exemplary historical event from the
past as the basis for "a true epic poem" (*YP*, 2:404–5). That had been
Milton's intent in the past, following the examples of Boiardo and Ariosto
(on Charlemagne defeating the Saracens), of Tasso (on Godfrey of
Bouillon, leader of the first crusade), and of Trissino (on the late
Roman general Belisarius, who defeated the Goths). Milton describes
this strategy as finding the "pattern of a Christian hero" in history, and
preferably, as he puts it, in "our own [i.e., British] ancient stories" (*YP*,
1:813–14). Indeed, a little earlier than this, around his thirtieth year, in
the Latin poems *"Mansus"* and *"Epitaphium Damonis,"* Milton expresses
a desire to base an epic poem on Brutus and Arthur and the Trojan narrative of England's origins, the subject of Spenser's *Faerie Queene*.[13] But
this way of proceeding would have been an ineffectual half measure,
only a partial turning away from the contingencies of history. Past events
may be safer to treat than present ones are—he who follows history too
close at the heels, said Walter Raleigh, is liable to be kicked in the
teeth—but they are not fundamentally different.

The right thing to do, therefore, was for Milton not only to negate
his earlier engagement with present political concerns but also to negate
historical contingency itself and to step outside history altogether—
but not far outside it.[14] This is what I mean by *transcendental engagement*, a diagnostic investigation of history from a mythical platform
outside history. Transcendental engagement is altogether different from
simple transcendence, going to Heaven, which we saw was the aim of
Milton's early poetry: to condemn this world from the point of view of
the next world. Transcendental engagement entails negating a positivist and presentist engagement with the unmediated events of the
historical world and turning to a mythic truth that does not belong to
history but that does not belong to Heaven either. Such a truth will be,
so to speak, pointed toward this world instead of away from this
world. The true myth will take up such causes as human nature, human
dignity, the principles of liberty, and also the forces—which may be collected under the general term *sin*—that vitiate human nature. I mentioned at the outset of this book that these forces may be divided between
acts of cowardice and acts of rapacity, the roots of human sin and the
drivers of history. Transcendental engagement involves the diagnosis of

the problem of history from its inception. Transcendental engagement
is therefore *radical* thinking (from Latin *radix*, "root").

An example of the value of such a turn in Milton's thoughts—if such
a turn requires any defense—may be seen if we adopt a more skeptical
reading than is usual of the poem that is perhaps the strongest statement of Milton's previous way of thinking, "On the Late Massacre in
Piedmont." What did Milton hope for in this poem? Its first word is
avenge, and it is a reasonable enough hope, expressing desire for justice. That word, and the description that follows, properly registers
outrage at a pitiless act of indiscriminate slaughter, as does Picasso's
Guernica. But Milton hopes the martyred blood and ashes of the slain
will be like a seed sown "O'er all th'Italian fields" (line 11), causing a
general rebellion of Roman Catholics against the church and against
the pope. Unlikely as that eventuality is, its occurrence would not redeem the tragic fate of the slaughtered, or make the slaughter worth-
while. Moreover, had such a revolution occurred it would no doubt have
been a disappointment too, instituting new forms of oppression in place
of the old ones: "For what can war but endless war still breed / Till Truth
and Right from Violence be freed" ("On the Lord General Fairfax at
the Siege of Colchester," lines 10–11). The principles underlying our
experience of history, such as truth, right, and violence, cannot be
plucked out of historical examples. They must be *freed*.

It would, of course, have been unwise of Milton, even if it were not
suicidal, to protest the decisive results of the election of the new Convention Parliament, or the overwhelming joy at the return of Charles II.
He had to accept what had occurred and think about that. Direct political engagement was no longer possible, not only in action but also, as
I have suggested, in thought. His new thinking would not be defeatist
and it would not be despairing. But it would have to take a different approach to the problem of liberty—how to win it and keep it—beginning
with the labor of diagnostic understanding. He would have to seek engagement with humanity in universal human terms emerging from history rather than in the contingent ones given by circumstances. Where
did Milton learn this? He learned it, of course, from the Bible.

No doubt Milton thought the English had shown themselves unworthy of liberty at the present time, and for a long time to come. Liberty was not to be attained, as he once erroneously hoped, by this generation. In one of the terrible phrases of *The Ready and Easy Way*, the

English had run their necks under the yoke of servitude again, "basely and besottedly." In *The Ready and Easy Way*, Milton is saying that this shameful cowardice is what the English *would* be doing if they were to allow Charles II to return. But now they have done precisely that. What is he to do, and what is to be done? For Milton, the answer begins with reading the Bible for its fund of hard political truth. The analogy of the English Revolution with the Israelites leaving Egypt and passing through the wilderness to the Promised Land continues to hold, although at greater length than he had hoped. The story of the Israelites does not end with the conquest of the Promised Land, in the book of Joshua. The story goes on in the book of Judges, where we see a people continually alternating between the states of freedom and bondage. They are able to win liberty, often with God's help, or the help of some exemplary person, such as Deborah or Jael, but they are unable to keep it. The pattern continues until the Israelites, at their own request, are given a king by God, to be anointed by his prophet Samuel, although God is most displeased with the Israelites for wanting a king. This next period in their history has turned out to be the fate of the English, as well.

For in surrendering their liberty, the English continued to follow the pattern of the ancient Hebrews. First, they win liberty but cannot keep it; next, they cannot even win liberty in the first place, because they lack the courage to do so, even when the opportunity appears. That is the situation near the end of the book of Judges, on Milton's reading of it, the scene of *Samson Agonistes*. Although the biblical Samson cares nothing for such abstractions, the failure to seize offered liberty is mentioned on more than one occasion by Milton's hero. But instead of seizing liberty, the Hebrew tribes fall into a bloody civil war, as England had done, and as England threatened to do again in 1659.

In the next historical book, the first book of Samuel (after the pastoral interlude that is the book of Ruth), the Israelites are subjected to a crushing military defeat at the hands of the Philistines. They therefore implore God, through their prophet Samuel, to give them a king, "that we also may be like all the nations, and that our king may judge us, and go out before us, and fight our battles" (1 Samuel 8:20 and 8:5). God tells Samuel that in asking for a king the people are not rejecting Samuel as their leader and judge. They are rejecting God, who says they have done so in their usual way: "according to all the works which they have done since the day that I brought them up out of Egypt even unto this day, wherein they have forsaken me, and served other gods" (1 Samuel 8:8). It was by serving God alone that Israel had in the past, when she came out of Egypt, continually recaptured her liberty. But in wishing now to serve a king who will fight their battles for them the Israelites are giving way to cowardice and serving another god, that of their own fear. God therefore lets them enslave themselves and gives them a king, Saul, because they have shown themselves unfit for liberty—just as Saul will prove unfit to be a king. That is Milton's reading of the book of Samuel and his view of the English in the 1660s. They have chosen their captain back for Egypt—the more famous of the condemnatory phrases from *The Ready and Easy Way*—and this too is God's hard but irresistible will, his "unsearchable dispose" (*Samson Agonistes*, line 1746).

There remain, of course, the friends of liberty, few in number, as Milton supposed his readers would be: "fit audience, though few" (*PL*, 7.31). But what are they to do, and what is Milton to do? The course of history for the time being, and for the indefinite future, has been decided—against liberty—and direct engagement with the present is futile. What the friends of liberty can do is hold firm to its principles and keep them alive for more propitious times. What are these principles, and how can they be known, preserved, and inculcated? Milton's answer, in the first instance, is *Paradise Lost*, which returns to the origin of human beings in the world and examines from the beginning the foundations of liberty in human nature itself. The second instance is *Paradise Regained*, in which Milton demonstrates those principles as they are borne witness to in the midst of history by one exemplary man. The third instance, *Samson Agonistes*, is a more realistic and grim demonstration of what historical existence is like under oppression, when the principles of action are hard to discern.

I mentioned that the second and definitive edition of *Paradise Lost* in 1674 is substantially the same as the one published in 1667 and that a small number of verses were added to facilitate the divisions of books necessary to bring the number up to twelve. A little puzzlingly, in the middle of book 11, three lines were added to the impressive list of diseases to be endured by us after the Fall. They would be much criticized by later critics but are a good example of how Milton's verse at times,

in the last phase of his career, seems close to the threshold of pure poetry, delighting in the sound of technical words: "Demoniac frenzy,
moping melancholy, / And moon-struck madness, pining atrophy, /
Marasmus and wide-wasting pestilence" (11.485–87). Is it significant
that most of these are psychological? In *Samson Agonistes* Milton would
have his hero state that the afflictions of the mind are worse than his
considerable afflictions of body.

In the fourth of the six issues of the 1667 edition, that of 1668, the
publisher added to the book's preliminary pages two documents, both
by John Milton, in response to criticisms that the poem was hard to
follow and that, as the publisher says, it "rhymes not." "Arguments," or
prose summaries of each of the books, were introduced for the first time,
but all together in one batch, not distributed throughout as they would
be later.[15] There appeared also a somewhat defensive and haughty note
entitled "The Verse," which for all its brevity (considering the importance of the subject) is not on every point clear. When the new edition
came, in that summer of 1674, the "arguments" were distributed to their
present places, each over its corresponding book, and the note on the
verse stayed at the front. Dedicatory poems appeared: by Samuel Barrow,
in Latin, and by Andrew Marvell, in English. Barrow rightly says that
Milton's epic tells the story of all things, not just the events in this poem,
and for this reason Barrow may be taken as the first to say what I am
arguing here: that all history is implied in *Paradise Lost*. Marvell gives
a sense of how the first readers of *Paradise Lost* were affected:

> At once delight and horror on us seize,
> Thou sing'st with so much gravity and ease;
> And above human flight dost soar aloft,
> With plume so strong, so equal, and so soft.
> The bird named from that paradise you sing
> So never flags, but always keeps on wing.
>
> *("On Mr. Milton's* Paradise Lost," *lines 35–40)*

We hear often of the sublimity of *Paradise Lost*—its manner is high and
even haughty, "above human flight," with much storm and stress—but
we should not forget the sustained confidence underlying these effects
to which Marvell here draws our attention. Milton sings with "gravity
and ease." Like the mythical bird of paradise that never lands, Milton

never sinks down to earth or is common. His "plume"—by which Marvell means Milton's wing, but also his pen and his style—is "so strong, so equal, and so soft." Beneath the wild grandeur and the astonishing sights and sounds of *Paradise Lost*, there is a sustained and almost placidly confident equanimity of tone.

Despite early readers' complaints, *Paradise Lost* was an immediate success. It was mentioned in Parliament—or, as we saw, in the antechamber to Parliament—and was accorded the highest praise by the reigning poet of the day, John Dryden. It sold well, and it sold out. Even readers implacably hostile to Milton on political grounds acknowledged the poem's greatness, as Samuel Johnson would do, a century later. In his life of Milton, Johnson was irritated by the poet's revolutionary personality, his impatience of all authority but his own. Yet Johnson ranked Milton beneath only Homer, and then only because Homer was first: "By the general consent of critics the first praise of genius is due to the writer of an epic poem, as it requires an assemblage of all the powers which are singly sufficient for other compositions." Johnson's final words on Milton are as follows: "he was born for whatever is arduous; and his work is not the greatest of heroic poems, only because it is not the first."[16] For some reason, Johnson's life of Milton was thought to be mean-spirited, its judgments distorted by party and prejudice. That is nonsense. Johnson was morally honest and direct, as always, and if he found Milton (as Eliot would) personally antipathetic, he nevertheless accorded him a breathtaking compliment: that he was second to Homer only because he came after Homer. The greatest admirer of Milton might reasonably decline to say *Paradise Lost* is as great an epic poem as the *Iliad*, or greater, falling into second place only by the accident of its coming later in time.

Midway between the two editions of *Paradise Lost*, a single volume appeared—it was licensed in 1670 and came out in 1671—containing the two other long poems of Milton's mature years: *Paradise Regained*, "to which is added," as the title page says, *Samson Agonistes*.[17] These two works are neither of them as long as *Paradise Lost*, but they are very substantial works. *Paradise Regained* is a brief epic (the genre was a recognized one in the Renaissance, not without ancient precedent).[18] *Samson Agonistes* is a Greek tragedy, that is, a drama modeled on the Greek tragic poets, Aeschylus, Sophocles, and Euripides, rather than on Shakespeare, but using a biblical tale for its subject rather than one from Greek legend.

As Milton says in his preface on tragedy, *Samson Agonistes* is intended for reading—perhaps reading aloud—rather than for the stage. The ritual, religious, civic, and ceremonial setting of ancient Greek tragedy means that these plays do not travel well in performance, although Sir Richard Jebb argues in his editions that Sophocles, at least, still has exceptional power on the stage. Greek tragedies were never purely or even in large part intended to "entertain," in our sense of the word. New plays were performed annually as entries in a competition at the festival of the god Dionysus, and they were anticipated through the year, as other annual religious festivals are in other cultures. This makes Greek tragedy different from the English stage in the reigns of Elizabeth and James, which because of its focus on commercial entertainment does indeed travel well: it is always current and always entertaining.

If a sequel such as *Paradise Regained* is to be a success, it must not try to extend the success of the original work; it must find what was lacking in the original work, or left incomplete, and supply or repair it. *Paradise Regained* does so. It is a brilliant and still underappreciated account of Jesus's mental fight in the desert with Satan. (The setting reminds me of Blake's weird poem, "The Mental Traveler.") It is a fight in which history itself is at stake, and the future of humanity, perhaps even the future of the dead. Milton will always be known for *Paradise Lost*, not *Paradise Regained*, as Melville will be for *Moby Dick* and not for *Billy Budd*, and certainly not for *Pierre* or his interesting long poem, *Clarel*, even if these later works tell us more about the mind that made *Moby Dick*. *Paradise Regained* gets to the intellectual heart of the vision that is opened in *Paradise Lost*. It does not leave the world for Heaven but stays grounded on the earth, even when its hero is balanced in midair. Yet the hero accepts none of the values of the world, as the world understands them, and this is what makes him effective in the world. He is detached from the world but concerned with the world absolutely. Like Milton himself, he is transcendentally engaged.

The late date of *Samson Agonistes* has been questioned in the past because in the 1640s, as the Trinity manuscript shows, Milton was much preoccupied with tragic subjects drawn from the Bible. There is no external, documentary evidence for the dating of *Samson Agonistes*. Internal evidence for its being a post-Restoration work is, however, decisive. It is impossible to imagine this work being written before the poet was blind and in physical pain, and it is still more impossible to imagine it being written before the collapse of the English Commonwealth and the savage executions meted out on the regicides after 1660. Some scholars, including the historian Christopher Hill, and John Carey in his second edition of the *Shorter Poems*—weighty voices, indeed—have maintained *Samson Agonistes* was composed immediately after the Restoration, perhaps before the completion of *Paradise Lost*, and certainly before the composition of *Paradise Regained*.[19] But there was little time to be composing both works and completing them by 1663, or even 1665. It seems to me, moreover, that the traumatic memory of the events of the Restoration would have taken time to be digested and transmuted into art. Poetry brings forth powerful emotions recollected, if not in tranquility, then at a certain distance in time. As I observe in Appendix II, for long works date of publication is more important than date of composition, the latter being fuzzy and extended. Efforts to dislodge *Samson Agonistes* from its traditional place as Milton's last work have been persistent but remain unconvincing. In the simplest and most important sense applied to long works, *Samson Agonistes* comes last, because it does.

The two works published together complement each other and make a fascinating study in contrasts. Whereas *Paradise Regained* is subdued in tone and intensely cerebral, after the *Sturm und Drang* of *Paradise Lost*, *Samson Agonistes* exceeds even *Paradise Lost* as an explosively passionate work. It is the poet's cri de coeur over the political disappointments and personal afflictions of his life. Yet it ends cathartically, in what are probably the last words in verse Milton wrote, with "calm of mind, all passion spent."

The story how Milton composed *Paradise Lost* is hard to tell because so little is certain, for example, when he began, and what counts as a beginning, and when he finished, and what counts as finished. We have seen that with long projects the date of publication, in this instance 1667, is the safest and most reasonable terminus, whatever Milton showed Thomas Ellwood in 1665. A long poem is finished when it goes out in the world.

But when did Milton begin *Paradise Lost* and how did he begin? How did he proceed? *When* is of course less important than *how*. Just enough has been reported from the early lives of John Aubrey and the poet's nephews, John and Edward Phillips, among others, including the poet himself, to form a picture of how Milton composed his poem, mostly in the winter months, between the autumn and spring equinoxes, sometimes in the evening, with one leg thrown over the arm of a chair, sometimes at night and in the early morning, with verses coming to him spontaneously. We do not know when Milton planned out *Paradise Lost*—or when he converted into an epic four different plans for a tragedy on the loss of Paradise—and exactly how long the process of composition went forward after the plan was complete. We can know little of his manner of working, although seriatim composition—starting from the beginning and going on to the end—is most likely. The poet suggests as much at several stages of the epic. In particular, the invocations to books 3 and 7 and the introduction to book 9 transmit the excitement and drama of getting on with the project of what he calls his "advent'rous song" (*PL*, 1.13). Yet to repeat, just enough facts, or tantalizing quasi-facts have been dangled before us—such as Milton's holding quantities of verses in his head in the morning, waiting for an amanuensis to arrive (he is reported to have joked he was like a cow that wanted to be milked); of his spending the later morning, with the amanuensis's help, compressing those lines into more concentrated units; and of his being unable to compose between the spring and autumn equinoxes—to make total abstention from conjecture impossible. To imagine the blind poet building his poem—shaping it under the force of his breath with the different parts of his mouth and throat, occasionally counting it out on his fingers (at least for some lines), and stopping to think, or to listen—is part of the pleasure of reading it. What is more, Milton intended this to be so. It is an important critical fact about *Paradise Lost*—I shall be repeating it—that the poem is to a considerable degree about the excitement of its own creation. Romanticism, with its celebration of the poet as creative hero and its reverence for the shaping spirit of imagination, has its origin here. I have observed that in their poetic identities the major Romantic poets were unlike Milton in being neither Christian nor classical (with the exception of Blake, who was explicitly if very strangely Christian in his work). They owed less to Milton than some of them supposed—and this is true even of Wordsworth—because they were more original than they knew. If we set aside the verse of *The Prelude*, which is indeed Miltonic, Wordsworth's great poem is entirely different from *Paradise Lost*. Yet in being about the growth of the poet's mind, it takes the author of *Paradise Lost* as the type of such a mind.

Milton intended us to see the composition of his poem as a prophetic act, an adventure of the spirit in quest of the truth; and he invites us to join him. In doing so he departed from what was widely supposed, at least in neoclassical critical theory, to be the impersonal decorum of epic, which requires readers to admire and adore from afar. Milton was too familiar with the *Iliad* to think it impersonal, and he was too well acquainted with the ancient treatise on the sublime, *Peri Hypsous*, to think the reader is not supposed to feel excited when the action is exciting because the poet is excited by creation. From the outset, the singer of *Paradise Lost* tells us of the thrill of inspiration and the dramatic risk of soaring far above Mount Helicon—the source of classical poetry—to tell of things never told of before:

> I thence
> Invoke thy aid to my adven'trous song
> That with no middle flight intends to soar
> Above th'Aonian mount while it pursues
> Things unattempted yet in prose or rhyme.
>
> (PL, *1.12–16*)

Elsewhere, the poet prays for visionary power as compensation for his physical blindness, so he might "see and tell / Of things invisible to mortal sight" (*PL*, 3.54–55). He prays likewise for safety to complete his grand task. For a period during the composition of *Paradise Lost*, as we saw, Milton was in real danger, in hiding and later in prison (*PL*, 7.32–39). As a blind man, a public figure against whom strong resentments lingered, he risked assassination in the London streets. But these dangers are presented to us, mutated by art, as the danger of poetic flight, of actual soaring outside the universe, through Hell and chaos: "Thee [Holy Light] I revisit now with bolder wing / Escaped the Stygian pool . . . Thee I revisit safe" (*PL*, 3.13–21). Having traversed chaos and returned to the world, "Though hard and rare" (*PL*, 3.21), he has also soared up into Heaven and breathed its fiery *(empyreal)* air, which has been tempered for him by Urania, his muse. The Greek hero Bellerophon, showing a similarly dangerous *hybris*, rode the winged horse Pegasus up Mount Olympus (Pegasus is associated with epic poetry), intending to join the gods on its heights. But Zeus sent a gadfly to sting the horse and Bellerophon fell to earth. Milton alludes to this tale, with

his typical ambition, to affirm he has soared far higher than Bellerophon ever did soar or attempted to soar—and he succeeded where Bellerophon failed. He has done so with the help not of the winged horse
of classical poetry but with the help of his celestial muse, Urania (her
name means "sky-lady"), the medieval muse of astronomy (to Milton,
she is much more than that). With her he has soared into the true
Heaven, and heard the counsels of God the Father and the Son, on the
fate and the future of humanity. (In a youthful poem, "Vacation Exercise," he imagines himself soaring through the clouds into Heaven, to
eavesdrop on the classical gods.) The poet now asks to be guided down
safely, after the extreme danger of such a flight:

> Up led by thee
> Into the Heav'n of Heav'ns I have presumed
> An earthly guest and drawn empyreal air,
> Thy temp'ring. With like safety guided down
> Return me to my native element
> Lest from this flying steed unreined (as once
> Bellerophon, though from a lower clime)
> Dismounted on th'Aleian field I fall
> Erroneous there to wander and forlorn.
> Half yet remains unsung.
>
> (PL, 7.12–21)

With the words "Half yet remains unsung," he speaks with measured
satisfaction of how far he has come and of how far he has yet to go:
"Standing on earth, not rapt above the pole, / More safe I sing with
mortal voice unchanged / To hoarse or mute" (*PL*, 7.23–25). By the *pole*
he does not refer to our north and south terrestrial poles; he means one
pole of the cosmos, above the pole star. When he is seized or "rapt" by
the spirit into Heaven, or into chaos, he can look down on the entire
globe of the universe, seen from outside. The poet says he is now to
sing standing on earth because the main course of the narrative will be
concerned with events on earth, the temptation and the Fall, the immediate consequences of the Fall in the Garden of Eden, and the more
distant consequences of the Fall on the whole earth, in history.

In the proem to book 9, just before relating the Fall, the singer
loftily defends his many departures from the stock conventions of

epic, especially as these are narrowly understood by the fashionable Italian—and latterly, French—critical theorists. But it is not only the theorists of epic whom Milton spurns: he spurns Homer and Virgil as well, because he will accept no line of separation between their aesthetics and their politics, the latter broadly understood to include morals and even religion. The ancient epic poets cannot help their pagan religion—it was the best to be had in their time—but even their positive morals are hopelessly entangled with sin. This sin is what Milton in the first line of *Paradise Lost*, employing a word that does not ring so well to our ears, calls *disobedience*. By this he does not mean departure from any constituted or conventional authority, for Milton had a strong record of that kind of disobedience, including defying the law to publish illegally, abusing the bishops and wishing them in Hell, to be trampled on by all the other damned, and defending the regicide. He was not an obedient man. By *disobedience* Milton means disobedience of God alone, as God is known in our conscience, and according to our reason. *Disobedience* thus turns out to mean failing to do what the best part of you wants to do, according to the lights of your conscience and reason. *Disobedience* is departure from the good and also from the free. This means what Milton admires above all else and promotes in his epic is the free exercise of one's conscience and reason. This exercise is something anyone may do, and everyone must do. It is not restricted to heroes, as the highest values of the ancient epic are. Homer and Virgil admire, respectively, the glory *(kleos)* to be won by giving free rein to deceit, greed, hate, slaughter, and pillage, and the majesty *(maiestas)* to be won by terrorizing and oppressing all the known peoples on earth. The aesthetic form of the epic, which was brought to perfection by Homer and Virgil, and never equaled since, cannot be separated from its values. This may seem an unremarkable point now, after Marx, Benjamin, Adorno, and others, but in Milton's day it was a radical thought, hardly to be understood in the two centuries that followed. Yet Homer and Virgil are poets Milton admired enough to have large passages of them by heart.[20]

Milton also defends his neglect of the courtly routines of what he regards as the late derivative of epic, medieval and Renaissance romances, with their pointlessly elaborate accounts of jousting, of riddlingly complicated escutcheons and shields ("impreses quaint"), of magic swords, disappearing castles, fleeting maidens, wondrous transformations, and the endless array of knightly tackle and equestrian gear, superbly mocked by Thomas Nashe, and later by Cervantes. An air of immorality hung about the genre of romance for English humanists. Queen Elizabeth's old schoolmaster, Roger Ascham, condemned Sir Thomas Malory's *Morte d'Arthur* as a book the whole pleasure of which "standeth in two special points, in open manslaughter and bold bawdry." The noblest knights are those "that do kill most men without any quarrel [i.e., "cause"] and commit foulest adulteries by subtlest shifts." Milton would have agreed, notwithstanding his admiration of Spenser—a "sage and serious" teacher, as he called him—who strove to make romance morally serious.[21] But Milton seems especially annoyed by the tedium of romance, and in this he is as modern as Cervantes. In short, Milton regards the technical and mechanical requirements of the epic and romance genres as beneath him because he has far more important matters to address in the spiritual adventure of poetic truth. These more important matters are gathered under the phrase "higher argument," where *argument* means what we would call the *content* of a work, as opposed to its form. (The Greek word translated by Latin *argumentum* is *hypothesis*, which is perhaps closer to what we should understand Milton to mean by *argument*: it is the subject matter but also the meaning.) The higher content or "argument" of *Paradise Lost* is moral and spiritual truth. It is how to be good and how to be free, instead of the usual subject of epic, which is war:

> Not sedulous by nature to indite
> Wars, hitherto the only argument
> Heroic deemed, chief mastery to dissect
> With long and tedious havoc fabled knights
> In battles feigned, the better fortitude
> Of patience and heroic martyrdom
> Unsung. Or to describe races and games
> Or tilting furniture, emblazoned shields,
> Impreses quaint, caparisons and steeds,
> Bases and tinsel trappings . . .
> The skill of artifice or office mean,
> Not that which justly gives heroic name
> To person or to poem. Me of these
> Nor skilled nor studious, higher argument

Remains sufficient of itself to raise
That name [i.e., "heroic"].

(PL, *9.27–44*)

Milton defends his decision—an astoundingly original one—to write an epic poem on the un-martial subject, or "argument," of the Fall of Adam and Eve and their expulsion from the Garden of Eden, together with the creation of the world, the defeat of the rebel angels in Heaven, and their escape from the Hell, far off in chaos, into which they have been thrown, under the leadership of Satan, to mount an assault on humanity. The successful temptation of Adam and Eve by Satan is the cause of "all our woe," and more generally, of history. Such is the argument Milton describes as "long choosing and beginning late" (*PL*, 9.26). Quite apart from Milton's public duties during his forties, it is small wonder the choice of his subject took him so long, considering its originality. We know that twenty years before Milton was meditating a national epic poem on King Arthur, imitating the *Iliad* and extending the project of Spenser's *Faerie Queene*. No doubt such a poem, had it ever been composed (or one of the others Milton was considering, such as an epic on King Alfred in imitation of the *Odyssey*), would have been a serious affair, "doctrinal and exemplary to a nation," as he said such a poem should be. It would have been more narrowly English and nationalistic, instead of universal, and it would also have been just the sort of poem described in the passage above, full of elaborate ornaments for the horses as well as the knights. In the end, his main characters are majestically naked, like Greek sculptures.

Thinking especially of Homer's *Iliad* and Virgil's *Aeneid*, Milton serenely declares himself "Not sedulous by nature to indite / Wars." He thus takes the fight into the enemy's camp, expressing his disdain for the notion, which most of us share, that war, if it is not the essence of epic, is an indispensable part of epic poetry because it is essentially noble. Milton's subject, however, is more original, in the etymological sense of the word as "going to the origin," because it is diagnostic. It is "Man's *first* disobedience" (*PL*, 1.1; cf. 9.8), which is not itself a war but the cause of all wars, war being only a special case of the broader problem of evil, including, for example, that of environmental degradation.[22] From this broader perspective—and here Milton makes another astonishing, intuitive leap—the primal *disobedience*, the originative departure from the good and the free, is something we all compulsively repeat. The first disobedience, the first departure from conscience, from what Adam and Eve knew to be the good and the true, is therefore the cause of history. We keep history going by repeating this disobedience of our own consciences and of our own reason. History is therefore understood as a *series calamitatis* (the phrase is Saint Augustine's), a long sequence of human calamity, including the one closest to Milton, the collapse of the English Revolution.[23] Yet it is for him a special case, one "lamentable to think on":

> That a nation should be so valorous and courageous to win their victory in the field, and when they have won it, should be so unwise in their counsels as not to know how to value it, what to do with it, or with themselves, but, after ten or twelve years prosperous war and contestation with tyranny, basely and besottedly to run their necks again into the yoke which they have broken . . . will be an ignominy, if it befall us, that never yet befell any nation possessed of their liberty.[24]

Even this singular and exceptional moment of abjection (Milton here leaves aside the example he almost always thinks of, Israel) is according to his analysis of history a repetitious amplification of the sin of the Fall.

For this reason, the diagnosis of human calamity that begins with the opening words of *Paradise Lost*, "Of Man's *first* disobedience," is judged by Milton to be "Not less but more heroic than the wrath / Of stern Achilles" (9.14–15). Milton is deliberately pointing to the first line and indeed the first word of the *Iliad*, "wrath," or *menis:* "Sing of the wrath, goddess, of the son of Peleus, Achilles, / the terrible wrath." Homer isolates this *wrath* and gives it prominence as the diagnosis of a single cause, and it is from Homer that Milton will learn to do the same with *disobedience.* Homer says the wrath of Achilles, which breaks out in the midst of a war, "thrust many noble souls of heroes down to Hades and made their bodies a meal for buzzards and dogs, thus fulfilling the intentions of Zeus." The wrath is a cause, an *archê*, or originative beginning. But in Milton's estimation even the wrath of Achilles is but one small, almost insignificant result of the event that Milton describes in *Paradise Lost.* The city of Troy can no longer be found, except as one thin layer on a mound of ruined cities, and the consequences of the wrath of Achilles have all been run out. But the consequences of the Fall still continue, destroying, for example, the English Revolution. In Milton's account, what Homer describes with such overwhelming power in the *Iliad* can be understood only when *Paradise Lost* has been written and read, some twenty-three centuries after Homer. That is because Milton's description of the first human beings, Adam and Eve, tells of what is prior to what happens in Homer, and to what happens and is happening in history. Yet Milton has learned from Homer himself how to do this with the Fall, that is, from Homer's diagnostic analysis of the consequences of *wrath*. In Harold Bloom's terms, Milton renders even the *Iliad*, the oldest epic poem in the Western tradition, belated with respect to *Paradise Lost* because the later poem explains what the earlier cannot explain about itself.[25] Milton's poem is better than all others because it understands them when they cannot understand themselves. It possesses the truth they lack. For Milton, all previous poems, whether epic or romance—including, alas, even *The Faerie Queene*—wander in the mists of uncertainty about ultimate questions. Where did the world come from? Where do we come from? Why is life so cruel? And why are we cruel to one another? Milton pursues answers to these fundamental questions and will accept nothing less as his task.

To summarize, all previous poems fail, in comparison with *Paradise Lost*, either because they are not morally diagnostic or because their diagnoses are wrong. As we see time and again in his prose works, Milton is seldom content to defeat an opponent with a single blow. In polemical controversy he seems always to be saying, "Your diagnosis is wrong; I defeat you because my diagnosis is deeper; because I understand more; and because I understand you better than you understand yourself; *but I also defeat you at your own game.*" *Paradise Lost* beats all previous epic poems at their own game. That game is heroism and manly excellence (Homer's *aretê*), and Virgil's more complicated version of heroism and excellence, *pietas*, the epithet of Virgil's hero, Aeneas, which means the firm observation of duties to the gods, to one's relations and ancestors, and to covenants with others. Achilles and Aeneas are heroes, and their respective poems, which celebrate their heroic deeds, are therefore heroic, but the poems about them are heroic as artistic achievements, and their poets are artistic heroes, because epic is the highest and hardest form of poetry—"of highest hope and hardest attempting," as Milton said.[26] This is so, in the first instance, simply because the consequences of choosing the wrong subject are so high. If you choose the wrong subject for a short poem and it doesn't work out, you can try again tomorrow. If you choose the wrong subject for an epic poem, you have chosen wrong for life.

Paradise Lost is not less but more heroic than the *Iliad* and the *Aeneid* because its subject is more important but also because it beats them at their own game, that of martial heroism. Milton makes this astonishing boast three-quarters of his way through *Paradise Lost*, when it is less astonishing to us because we have already witnessed some of the most convincing and original set battle pieces ever composed. We have also experienced eight books of Milton's majestic style, notably in his use of the epic simile, which surpasses Virgil and is nearly equal to Homer. Milton goes so far in the direction of Homeric *aretê* and Virgilian *pietas* as to include an *aristeia*, or solo demonstration of excellence in battle, when the Son, after much modest observation of his subordination to the Father's will, drives onward with dark fury against the armies of Satan, hurling thunderbolts and confounding them utterly: "So spake the Son and into terror changed / His count'nance too severe to be beheld / And full of wrath bent on his enemies" (*PL*, 6.824–26). Books 1, 2, 4, much of 5, and all of 6 explicitly and honorably rival Homer. As for book 6, the war in Heaven, it contains the finest battle scenes in poetry since Homer, scenes not equaled in poetry again until Byron's *Don Juan:*

> Nor stood at gaze
> The adverse legions nor less hideous joined
> The horrid shock. Now storming fury rose
> And clamor such as heard in Heav'n until now
> Was never: arms on armour clashing brayed
> Horrible discord and the madding wheels
> Of brazen chariots raged.
>
>   (PL, *6.205–11*)

We have observed that from Milton's point of view even Homer is inferior to him because his diagnosis is poorer. Homer does not know (or much care about) the underlying causes of war, or the meaning of a just war—that latter being an idea utterly foreign to him. But because even Homer, according to Milton's view of human nature after the Fall, retains a spark of our original innocence, he has occasional flashes of insight, as when Hector, responding to a bird-diviner's warning against a counterattack, famously says, "One bird-sign is best, to fight for your fatherland."[27] But Milton's poem accounts for these flashes of insight, too, and tells us why Homer can have them. Homer's character, Hector, the defender of civilization—or at least of a city—is a responsible, good man with a family, and he is a great warrior in his own right. But Hector is beaten by Achilles, the seeker after glory, or fame *(kleos)*, a man with greater *aretê*—and Ilium is destroyed. From Milton's point of view, however, there have been many Iliums and Hectors and there will be many more. Good men and women, and great cities, are destroyed because Adam, the best man, and the father of the human race, departed from goodness and surrendered his freedom. Adam was beaten by Satan, a Miltonic Achilles, and Eden, the original pattern of civilization—and, for Milton, of the state—was lost. Such is Milton's idea of the relation of his epic to Homer's: he gets behind Homer and explains him.

Lastly, Milton is most modern and even avant-garde (despite his use of the word *modern* with contempt) when he anticipates that he will be read only by the few, and even that few, he fears, will not understand him: "Still govern thou my song / Urania, and fit audience find, though few" *(PL*, 7.30–31). These are the "vulgar readers" we have seen Milton speaking of in his note on the verse of *Paradise Lost*, and by *vulgar* he means conversant only in the common tongue, English, not in Latin and Greek. The irony is that Milton's lofty disdain of the common opinions and ideas of his day, and of uneducated but boundlessly pretentious vulgarians, made him a poet not for the learned but for the many, for all of us. In a real sense—and one can say this of only a few very great works of art, such as Michelangelo's Sistine Ceiling, or Melville's *Moby Dick*, or Beethoven's *Eroica* symphony—the meaning of *Paradise Lost* resides in large measure in the drama and the terror (the grand *terribilità*) of its creation. Any person, however unsophisticated in such matters, immediately feels and knows these are great works of art.

What did Milton achieve when, in his fifties, he completed *Paradise Lost*, the hope of a lifetime? There are several ways to answer this question, which in its simplest form is this: What is *Paradise Lost?* A literary-historical answer, restricted to English literature, is that *Paradise Lost* is the greatest monument of English poetry between Spenser's *Faerie Queene* (1596) and Wordsworth's *The Prelude* (1805). A broader literary historical answer would be that *Paradise Lost* is the last epic poem of any stature to be written in Europe, and one of only two great and fully epic poems to be written in the modern world, the other being Tasso's *Gerusalemme Liberata*, on the subject (not so popular now as it was in the eighteenth and nineteenth centuries) of the first crusade. Some might wish to include Camões's *Lusiads*, published in 1572, in Portuguese, a splendid poem with some epic decoration on a nearly contemporary event: Vasco da Gama's sailing around Africa to India. Milton may have known the poem in the Portuguese (the Latinate diction made it easier for him to work out). He may also have known the superb English translation of Sir Richard Fanshawe, although too late for it to influence *Paradise Lost*.[28] There are, of course, epic aspects to the greatest of the continental long poems of the Renaissance, Ariosto's *Orlando Furioso*, and also to Spenser's *Faerie Queene*—both of which are, in part, "dynastic epics" in the Virgilian manner.[29] But these are blended works and not fully epic poems in the manner of Virgil and Homer.

A more complex, social, and literary-historical answer to the question, what is *Paradise Lost?*, one that I have had occasion to propose before, is that *Paradise Lost* is the last major work of European literature in which the act of creation is centered in God and the first major work of European literature in which the act of creation begins to find its center in the human. Let me take a little more time to explain this. The displacement of theological and ethical focus taking place in the poem, a displacement of divine Creation by human creativity, is important to understanding how the subject of *Paradise Lost* is in large measure the excitement of an epic being made.[30]

A Janus-faced work standing at a threshold in history, *Paradise Lost* looks back to an age of faith in which the world is created by God and all other creative acts are imitations of this better Creation, or perversions of it, as with mythical beasts and grotesques, so disturbing to Saint Bernard of Clairvaux. Saint Bernard saw very clearly that such inventions are in an unspoken rivalry with God, encroaching on God's status as the Creator, and are therefore impious.[31] Even in the Renaissance, art continues to fall under this shadow of inferiority and subversion with respect to divine Creation. Milton pays tribute to the ancient and venerable thought—the thought that everything that truly *is* is created by God—in the sixth book of *Paradise Lost*, in which the account of Creation that opens the Bible is vastly and sublimely improved on, great as the original is. Joshua Sylvester's long and not unimpressive poem on Creation—a very free translation from the French of Du Bartas—was the favored English reading of Milton's boyhood, and phrases from Sylvester find their way into Milton's early poems. The idea of universal Creation by God is the joy of Milton's youth, and in *Paradise Lost* it remains a fundamental ethical standpoint, underlined at the end of book 8.

There, Satan's evil is first seen clearly (first, that is, in the chronology of events the epic relates, but not of course in the epic itself) when, having withdrawn with his rebellious followers far into the north of Heaven, he questions this doctrine that all things are created by God, proposing, on the contrary, that they emerge by and out of their own "quickening power" (*PL*, 5.861):

> who saw
> When this Creation was? Remember'st thou
> Thy making while the Maker gave thee being?
> We know no time when we were not as now,
> Know none before us, self-begot, self-raised
> By our own quick'ning power.
>
> (PL, 5.856–61)

This is Satan's skeptical response to the angel Abdiel's rebuke of him for feeling his liberty has been impugned by the Father's proclamation of the Son as ruler over all the angels, the "pow'rs of Heav'n." It is for this purpose—to challenge that proclamation—Satan has withdrawn those angels who owe allegiance to him to his palace in the north parts of Heaven. Once Satan makes his purposes clear, only one of these angels, Abdiel, stands up to oppose him:

> shalt thou dispute
> With Him the points of liberty who made
> Thee what thou art and formed the pow'rs of Heav'n
> Such as he pleased and circumscribed their being?
>
> (PL, 5.822–25)

Satan's skeptical response soon turns to violence: he threatens to besiege the throne of God itself and, while the rebel angels support his threats with "Hoarse murmur" (*PL*, 5.873), he invites Abdiel to make himself scarce: "fly, ere evil intercept thy flight!" (*PL*, 5.871). Abdiel's response is a magnificent reply to such insolence. He is happy to fly—not for fear of Satan, however, but for fear that God's wrath upon Satan and his rebel angels will accidentally strike him, too:

> Well thou didst advise,
> Yet not for thy advice or threats I fly
> These wicked tents devoted, lest the wrath
> Impendent raging into sudden flame
> Distinguish not. For soon expect to feel
> His thunder on thy head, devouring fire.
>
> (PL, *5.888–93*)

Abdiel's final words are, as it seems, definitive in their affirmation of who creates and who is created: "Then who created thee lamenting learn / When who can uncreate thee thou shalt know!" (*PL*, 5.895–96).

The entire exchange between Satan and Abdiel is a parley before a *monomachia*, an epic "single combat," one that does not issue in a fight, however, although they will meet later in battle. For a more famous parley before a *monomachia* that does not result right away in a fight, we might consider the exchange of words between Gabriel and Satan at the end of book 4 (lines 874–1015). The parley occurs when the guardian angels Zephon and Ithuriel find Satan in Eden at night, crouching like a toad at Eve's ear. At the touch of a spear that undoes all deception (a fine detail borrowed from the literature of romance), Satan resumes his proper shape and accompanies the angels to meet their chief, Gabriel. The fight between them is avoided—for its violence might have torn the universe apart—by God's hanging his scales above the contestants to show Gabriel will win, at which Satan, without further contest, retreats: "The Fiend looked up and knew / His mounted scale aloft. Nor more, but fled / Murmuring, and with him fled the shades of night" (*PL*, 4.1013–15). This is the ominous conclusion to the book.

In the parley between Satan and Abdiel, however, it is the moral victor who retreats. For Milton, such a mild, Christian reversal of heroic values, accompanied though it is with searing words, is not satisfying, even when it is accompanied by Abdiel's departure, so much more dignified than Satan's before Gabriel. Abdiel does not "swerve from truth or change his constant mind" (*PL*, 5.902)—we recall this is what Milton means by *obedience*—but passes fearlessly through the ranks of hostile angels, indifferent to their angry threats, and turns his back on them, knowing that for all their pride they are doomed:

> From amidst them forth he passed
> Long way through hostile scorn which he sustained
> Superior, nor or violence feared aught
> And with retorted scorn his back he turned
> On those proud tow'rs to swift destruction doomed.
>
> (PL, 5.903–7)

This is another ominous conclusion to a book.

If Milton is singing the better fortitude of patience and heroic martyrdom this scene of passive moral courage—we may venture to call Abdiel a self-portrait—should be enough for him. The rebel angels, so vast and terrifying, are like so many towers of Babel, strong in appearance but foolish, like the Maginot line, and now doomed to destruction. Vengeance is God's, not Abdiel's. In the following book, however, Milton gives himself further satisfaction by staging a true *monomachia* between Abdiel and Satan (*PL*, 6.111–98).[32] It ends when Abdiel delivers a "noble stroke" (*PL*, 6.189) on Satan's crest, causing the leader of the rebel angels to stagger back, in good Homeric fashion, "ten paces huge" (*PL*, 6.193):

> as if on Earth
> Winds under ground or waters forcing way
> Sidelong had pushed a mountain from his seat
> Half sunk with all his pines.
>
> (PL, 6.195–98)

That is Milton's martial spirit, challenging Homer at his own game.

While Milton never, of course, denies, as Satan does, the divine Creation described in book 6, nor God's creation of him, he continually celebrates the human act of creation as he creates *Paradise Lost*. He does so, as we have seen, with humility, attributing his inspiration to the celestial muse, and implicitly (through her) to God. But one cannot help feeling he does so as much out of fear of his own humanistic *hybris* as out of religious devotion. Milton has the strength of humility, which is a kind of confidence, but he is no devotional poet. He feels in his bones the grandeur of the human power to create, and not only a great poem but a great political order and a great world, modified according to virtuous desire, like the cities of the future we can imagine, the traces of which are visible in some cities now. These teach us how nature (in our engagements with the world) is contained by human creativity, rather than the other way round. Parks are enclosed by cities, and even the largest areas of wilderness on earth are encompassed by communications networks, pierced by roads and telephone lines—in the wilds of the Amazon, Claude Lévi-Strauss followed the telegraph line—and surveyed by satellites from space. The entire world is either cities or extensions of cities. We live inside a human world of our own construction, and nature, God's Creation, which once circumscribed the human world, is now circumscribed by it—or so it seems to us now, as we come to terms with our waste, and find there is no "outside" to put it into. We are, of course, contained by nature and subject to it in the long run, as long as we survive as a species. But it does not seem so to us now. Milton stood on the threshold of this emerging vision of a human world, the product of heroic creativity, including science and engineering, which one suspects would have interested him more than subsequent literary art. He sensed the turbulent majesty of the coming centuries of human invention that would transform the world. I have spoken so far of Milton's engagement with history as a question of going back to an origin just before history and outside it. But for him, as a biblical Christian, history has a future as well, its vague outlines limned in the Book of Revelation, which concludes with the appearance of Heaven as a great city enclosing nature in itself, as the Tree of Life, or the Trees of Life, growing on either side of the river out from God's throne. Its name is Jerusalem, and Blake would write an entire epic poem on it, or rather, an epic prophecy. Blake saw the Milton of *Paradise Lost* as concerned with the daughters of Memory, that is, with the historical past rolling forward out of Eden up to the present day, Milton's present day. Reading Milton and the Bible at once, Blake turned this originative procedure on its head and prophesied the history of the future.

At some level of his consciousness, Milton knew that while God has created him, Milton, in his, God's, own image, he has in turn created the God of *Paradise Lost* in his, Milton's image: that of a magisterial Creator.

This irresolvable contradiction, lodged deep in Milton's consciousness, because it was not dialectical, generated a rapid oscillation between incompatible points of view that I referred to in the past as *delirium*, the driving power of Milton's daemonic creativity in the making of *Paradise Lost*. He is at once sublimely deferential to the Creator—like that other sublime poet of Creation, Michelangelo—and energetically committed to human creativity as a driving force in the history of the future. This may make *Paradise Lost* the first romantic poem. But it also makes the poem a prophecy of the built environment of the modern world as the *telos* of history. That is perhaps the largest answer to our question: what is *Paradise Lost?* With respect to its content, *Paradise Lost* is an epic, transcendental engagement with history at a point just before the origin, in the true myth of history's *archê*, the Garden of Eden. With respect to its form, by which I mean its energetic awareness of its own making, *Paradise Lost* is a transcendental prophecy of the future, in the true myth of history's *telos*, the Heavenly Jerusalem.

What then, to conclude, did Milton achieve in the making of *Paradise Lost?* He achieved a morally and metaphysically coherent vision of history, something that had never been accomplished before, certainly not in the Book of Revelation, which is incoherent in both respects, and not even in Dante's *Commedia*, which for all its historical concerns, is not finally an historical poem. *Paradise Lost* is the only successful classical epic composed in the modern world, in a modern language, on a Hebraic theme altogether foreign to the values and outlook of the classical world. It is a grand, moving, morally serious, spiritually sublime, spectacularly cosmic and visionary poem, in which the forces of evil contend against good for command of prophetic-historical time. Grandiose as such statements about it may seem, they are not out of proportion to what Milton achieved. But *Paradise Lost* is also a poem about the fate of the world in which everything comes down to one man and one woman, because everything begins with them. Few of us are heroes or princes like the important characters in classical epic and tragedy. But we are all of us women or men. *Paradise Lost* is that seemingly impossible thing: an epic poem about everyone, everyone as seen through the figures of Adam and Eve. Their tragedy is the beginning of history. They are the true origin of all actions described in subsequent epic poems. But they are also the origin of our own moral actions, insignificant as these may appear when considered from an historical point of view.

Milton elevates our actions onto that historical stage. From its first book, in Hell, we see that *Paradise Lost* is continually and yet transcendentally engaged with all human history to come, and that the poem gives a moral explanation, from the outset, for the accumulating horrors through which history is usually imagined by us. That moral explanation might be summarized as follows. At the root of every horror, though it may be hidden from sight, is our preference for easy and inferior solutions to challenges that demand toughness, honesty, and courage, so that we will take the decisions we know to be right. Whether or not history, in all its complexity, can be commanded by such a moral diagnosis—so simple and clear in its outlines, once it is uncovered—is another matter. But simple solutions to complex problems are always the most intellectually and practically satisfying. And since we are speaking of art, it should be said that simple solutions to complex problems are also beautiful and have aesthetic power. Milton's undertaking, which is to make moral sense of everyone's experience in the most sublime and august of the literary genres, is an inspiring and courageous act of hope. It almost persuades us we might begin to save ourselves with its help. I do not think any other great English poet—nor, in saying this, have I forgot Blake and Shelley—placed so much confidence in the potential of literature.

10

On the Origin in Paradise Lost

THE CIRCUMSTANCES in which this chapter originated have some bearing on its subject. The fall of 2008 saw the stock market take a giant slip almost indistinguishable from a crash, causing financial chaos around the world, and of course in universities, even at plush and, as we imagined, flush Harvard. Everywhere, universities were canceling building projects, programs, appointments, and even events, such as conferences and visiting lectures. But wherever some budgetary leeway survived, and even where there was none, festivities were taking place in celebration of the four hundredth anniversary of John Milton's birth, which occurred before sunrise, on December 9, 1608. At Harvard, thanks to the generalship of Chris Barrett, then a graduate student in our English program, symposia, readings, visiting lectures, and other celebratory events took place regularly, the high point of which was a holiday production by the students of *Comus*, with original music and instruments, directed by Lawrence Switzky, also a graduate student at the time. At the conclusion of the masque, before the epilogue, my colleague Barbara Lewalski, playing Sir Thomas Egerton, gravely removed the monsters' masks to disenchant them and make them humans again. It was a gracious touch.

In the general mood of retrenchment, I found myself heading off to Mexico City—the National University had not, they assured me, canceled my lecture—to speak to a conference in celebration of Milton. To my further surprise, the audience was large and enthusiastic, and the hall was so full people sat up the steps of the aisles. The mood was festive, and all seemed filled with enthusiasm for Milton, as the question period showed. Faculty asked, among other things, about Milton's "mortalism"—the heterodox belief that body and soul die together and are resurrected together at the Apocalypse. Graduate students asked theoretical questions, citing Benjamin, de Man, Adorno, and Deleuze, among others, even one of my teachers, Northrop Frye. Undergraduates asked about Satan, Sin, and Death, but especially about Death. For the festive atmosphere, and the interest in mortalism, was due to its being October 31, the night before the two-day celebration of the Day of the Dead (*El Día de los Muertos*), a combination of the Christian celebration of All Hallows Evening, All Saints Day, and All-Souls Day, and an Aztec festival dating back as far as three thousand years, devoted to the skeletal goddess of the underworld and Lady of the Dead, Mictecacihuatl, popularly known as La Calavera Catrina, Kate the Skull. The skulls one sees everywhere at this festival are fashioned from sugar, the skeletons from wire, papier-mâché, and other materials. Catrina is always elegantly attired, and is less cosmically menacing that Mictecacihuatl, whose gaping jaw swallows the stars.

The Day of the Dead is the largest celebration in Mexico, when votive displays of skeletons—*ofrendas*—are to be seen in all locations imaginable, gaily arrayed, accompanied by nuts, candied pumpkin, and tequila for the dead—and also, touchingly, toys for dead children, *los angelitos* "the little angels" and *los innocentes.* The *ofrendas* are festooned with beautiful, golden bouquets of marigolds, the Aztec flower of the dead, which has the power to attract the departed spirits to the offerings. People dance in the streets in skeleton suits, and even children, closely watched by their parents, sit on the ground in public places, including the vast, enclosed courtyard of the public library, watching puppet shows—complete with elaborate stages and curtains—performed by skeleton puppets. As in Kleist's *Über das Marrionetten theater,* the puppets seemed electric, more alive than alive, having no flesh to obstruct them in their motions.

On the grounds adjacent to the main university building (its outer walls decorated with revolutionary art), each faculty raised its own altar, an enormous display of skeletons representing great figures in its field. I shall never forget the physics department's display, which was a towering structure of wire and cheesecloth representing the mushroom cloud explosion from a detonated atom bomb. Out of the cloud, extending from its column and also from its bulbous summit, the skeletons of famous physicists, Einstein, Bohr, Heisenberg, and Oppenheimer prominent among them, were projecting from the blast. To one side was a small apple tree made out of wire and there, reclining nonchalantly under its boughs, was the skeleton of Isaac Newton, indifferent to the violence nearby.

The Day of the Dead is a celebration of ends, of things brought to their conclusion. You celebrate a skeleton, or you celebrate if you are a skeleton, because the processes of rotting are ended and your bones are hard and clean. The skeletons dance joyously because they have reached stability at last, having passed through the extended transformations of death and reached the finality of an end, not the anxious moment of a beginning, or the still more anxious moments we know in the middle of the way in our lives. The skeletons have done what they have done, lived as they have lived, and now they have nothing further to suffer, to regret, or to grieve. They have no potential; they are *bare* bare life.[1] They cannot grow into anything else; they have no freedom, but they also have nothing to lose. These bones are dry, and happy to be so. Therefore, they dance.

They are, it would seem, in every respect different from Milton's Adam and Eve, whose skeletons are well clothed with comely and magnificent flesh, although one of them, for a moment, has been an exposed bone, with blood streaming from it, until God fleshed her out with a body. There they are, at the origin of everything, dwelling in the place of the origin, the first and determining moments of human being in the world. All humanity waits inside them, as pure potentiality, *dynamis*, ready to begin coming out of Eve and her daughters. They are not yet in history but rather before it, just before it, for entering into history will be the result of the Fall. History, therefore, has as yet nothing to do with the original state, the transcendental *archê*. The children of Adam and Eve, as the Angel Raphael relates, are certain to go on into the future (but not necessarily into history), filling the world, filling even Heaven, doing heaven knows what, and changing unimaginably, perhaps growing wings like the angels', for to be human is to change without knowing it and without knowing the future. These humans have no institutions and no clothes, and they are, biologically speaking, a community yet to come. They are not anxious about the future because they are innocent. They have something of the lightness of those skeletons at the Day of the Dead, but without the frenetic festivity. Adam and Eve do not dance. They are the beginning, not the end. Their motions are graceful and slow, like the figures on the Parthenon frieze.

There is one future possibility, however, one source of anxiety that does lie in Adam and Eve's power to transcend: whether or not to eat the fruit of the tree of the knowledge of good and evil. Before their Fall, as Milton remarked in an aside long before, in *Areopagitica*, the tree is to them the visible sign of their freedom and in an odd sense it is responsible for their freedom, for on nothing else are they free to exercise this freedom But the tree is also an image of the future, as if it stood on a point at which a river divides in two courses that will never meet again, that of the fallen and that of the unfallen future. They can take either course. As God says with his usual efficiency, "they themselves ordained their Fall" (*PL*, 3.128). Eating of the tree of the knowledge of good and evil is, however, an original act, in our sense of *original*, which is later than Milton's. It is something novel and bold never done before, and barely thought of before it is done. More importantly, eating of the fruit of the tree of the knowledge of good and evil is also an *originative* act, one that is cause of history and also, ever since, the determining factor in history. Subsequent historical events will be largely repetitions of this act. That is one reason the episode Milton invented in book 10 is so brilliant, when the devils, having been changed into serpents, are driven by thirst into a seemingly limitless orchard of trees, each tree a reproduction of its model, the Tree of Interdiction, in the Garden of Eden. The serpents are compelled to devour the ashen fruit, which only worsens their thirst and drives them to bite it again, thus deepening their agony. This self-inflicted torment is a prophetic image of what is happening in the interior of history, hidden from us by the visible events, but driving them on from within. Milton's visionary scene is at least in one respect more accurate an image of history than is Benjamin's highly cinematic image of the Angel of History, its wings spread, being blown backward into the future by a wind blowing out of Paradise, staring in horror at the ever-growing heap of disaster by which it is pursued. Milton's scene reveals where the agency lies, and demonstrates that we are the perpetrators as well as the victims of this ongoing disaster.

It is noteworthy that, by eating the fruit, Adam and Eve move away from the origin of history with a plan, the result of anxious meditation on the future: we are of course aware with what success—mixed, at best—statesmen at war, or pretending to be at war, implement plans for the future. They do so anxiously, with internal dialogue, such as we see for the first time in Eve and Adam, when each contemplates the decision to eat. Eve plans aloud before us, elaborately, intending to be a goddess by eating the fruit, in order to satisfy what Augustine rightly identified as the driving power of history, the unquenchable lust of dominion, *libido dominandi*—or fear of that libido in others, as the Spartans feared Athenian power. Adam plans to keep Eve for himself, by eating the fruit, and thus falls—however we may be inclined to debate the point—into the party of those who make history possible for the strong, because of the lust of possession, *libido habendi*. Eve and Adam become power and wealth.

Had Adam and Eve chosen not to fall, nothing they could do would have moved them away from the original state in which they dwell. Future time would be for them like a spatial enlargement, an expansion of the present moment, one corresponding to their promised, or nearly promised expansion beyond the confines of the earth, to other worlds, and to Heaven. It is impossible for us to dwell at the origin and remain there—the language is Heideggerean, and to be used advisedly, as we shall see—because we busily plan things and because busyness is what it means for us to be alive, cast into circumstances not of our making. The Garden of Eden is not itself the beginning of history but is rather the scene where the beginning takes place. The tranquility of Eden, on which Eve is especially eloquent, is one of the less celebrated but original glories of *Paradise Lost*. Happy states are usually the most briefly described. But in *Paradise Lost*, the transcendental scene that for a brief time precedes history is expandable in time, so as to be shown to be potentially eternal. The Garden of Eden is not eternal as an objective place, and to emphasize that point Milton violently destroys it. But it is, so to speak, subjectively eternal, at once particular and ideal, as a vision of the truth about history.[2]

The title of my lecture in Mexico was originally "The Problem of Originality in Milton." I intended to speak about Milton's counterintuitive and yet somehow old-fashioned decision to write an epic poem on Adam and Eve, that is, on the Bible and on the most naive story in it, the most obviously primitive. What later scholarship has divided into the "P" and "J" accounts of Creation need not concern us here. The point is that to

Milton, and not only to Milton but to believers in his time and before, there is a qualitative difference between the opening chapters of the Bible and the historical narratives to follow—not a difference in truth but in necessary style. The naive style, which was God's choice when inspiring Moses, is not "mythic" in our common sense of the word as "untrue" or "made up." It is mythic (not, I must emphasize, allegorical) because that is the style in which to relate wonders that exceed human experience.

But epic poems are poems of harsh, realistic experience, their mythic episodes being hardly more than entertaining diversions even when they bear on the action, as so often they do. The *Iliad* is founded on war, the *Odyssey* on return and recovery, the *Aeneid* on conquest and founding. Heightened as they are, these themes have a mimetic and probable basis in experience we know. The opening chapters of the Bible have none. In my lecture I intended, therefore, to point to the originality of Milton's choice of subject and the extremity of its departure from all epic subjects before. I intended likewise to point out how our concept of artistic originality developed after Milton's day, and to argue that Milton's telling the story of mankind from the origin has conditioned our sense of what is "original," rather than the other way round. Milton's dwelling at the origin, his insistence on remaining centered in Eden for the duration of an entire epic poem (though he flies to Heaven and Hell), generated the poetic and artistic concept of originality that was to be celebrated after his day. So I intended to argue, and it still seems to me true.

But lecture titles must be given in advance, before the lectures are written or planned out in detail. As I reflected on the problem of originality in Milton, I became preoccupied with the somewhat different and more traditional problem of the *origin* as Milton's theme: the origin of matter and of the world, the origin of humanity, the origin of marriage, the origin of politics, and the origin of history. Milton would write about all these things but only at their very beginnings, that is, not encyclopedically, to show how much he has learned, but radically, to show how deep he can think. The subjective and aesthetic idea of poetic originality—Romantic originality—is thus displaced by an objective phenomenon, the mystified place or site (in Heidegger's German, *der Ort*) in which Milton decided to dwell. To go there and hold on to that place, to remain there poetically, is a higher achievement than being "original" in our usual sense.

Dwell suggests the Heideggerian word *Wohnen*, with its emotionally positive sense of authentic living, as opposed to mere residing at one convenient address or another. As I warned, in what follows some Heideggerian notes will be sounded, in particular those of patience, remaining, and listening as these bear upon Milton's Garden of Eden, that place of an opening, or *Lichtung*, in the complex pathways of the earth, where what we are is seen by the blind poet through patience, obstinate remaining, and heightened acoustic attentiveness. Patience, obstinacy, and listening with attention are three things at which Adam and Eve fail.

New disclosures about Heidegger's fascist politics, his anti-Semitic prejudices, and his despicable acts continue to be made, with more to come by report, as the pages of his notebooks are published. Even so, we have not fully confronted the truth that until 1945 Heidegger was our enemy, and would have acquiesced—no doubt with suitable expressions of regret—not only to the destruction of the Jews, but to the destruction of Britain and America to the west, as he would have, with less regret, to the destruction of Bolshevik and Slavic *Untermenschen* to the east. Nor did his views change after 1945. Heidegger was as unrepentant as the Nazi jurist Karl Schmidt, though more cowardly. Yet because Heidegger's thought is on the border, and under the border, between philosophy and poetry, as Milton's was, it remains provocative for thinking about Milton's conception of prelapsarian dwelling and place.[3] I am very far from proposing a Heideggerean reading of Milton, which would be false because of one glaring difference: like his hero, Hölderlin, Heidegger is nostalgic and turned to the past. An idealized time in the past, like an idealized place, has value for Heidegger, as it never does for Milton.

Milton, in contrast, is a revolutionary fired with prophetic zeal, as we see him, for example, in *Areopagitica*. He turns to the future, not to the past. There is no possibility of returning to the Garden of Eden, or of recreating the conditions in the Garden of Eden at some time in the future. That original clearing in the forest of Being—Dante wonderfully describes Eden's ancient trees—is gone forever, and what may be recovered of it at the Apocalypse is utterly changed. Milton's urbanity has nothing in common with Heidegger's rustic idiocy or his conservative nostalgia for folkways, field paths, and forests. It is Heidegger's imaginary world that Milton is erasing when he describes the burning of the Garden of Eden, then its being torn loose by the Flood and washed down the Euphrates to the Persian Gulf:

> To teach thee that God áttributes to place
> No sanctity if none be thither brought
> By men who there frequent or therein dwell.
>
> (PL, *11:836–38*)

This means that *sanctity* is *attributed* to some places by God, merely as a courtesy, if such a place has become *sacer* to humans, that is, set apart as treasured.[4] Places become treasured to humans because their ancestors have lived there, perhaps over generations, and their own repeated actions are worn into habitual time, as was the case for Milton with London. This is a not a sacredness that comes from mystical communion with Being or with God. It is not holiness. Even Jerusalem—a holy site to the three Abrahamic religions—would not be holy to Milton. To visit the holy city is to be repelled, as Milton would certainly have been, by the violence, absurdity, and exceptional folly that attaches to religious belief when it sanctifies place. In *Paradise Lost* Milton places the pilgrims who go to Jerusalem to find God—the poet allows himself this one moment of Dantean grimness—in the chaotic Paradise of Fools: "Here pilgrims roam that strayed so far to seek / In Golgotha Him dead who lives in Heav'n" (*PL*, 3.476–77). The Garden of Eden is transcendent and yet intimately close to history; it is near and yet quite apart. Its purpose, so far as Milton is concerned in *Paradise Lost*, is to be turned upon history, like a lens.

The etymological trail of *dwell* stretches back through Old Norse and Germanic antecendents to connote remaining in a place instead of moving on. It is an obstinacy that commands a certain respect, even awe, easily mistaken for authenticity, as when people are forcibly evacuated while still sitting in their chairs, from land that is about to be flooded, or overwhelmed with fire. We all have that inclination in little, but we also have the opposite one, which is to journey on to somewhere else, however ill conceived and groundless the journey. This is a strong temptation for the writer, and I suppose especially so for the writer of an epic, to get on with it, to move forward in time and forward in action, to write many pages by recording many things. (Gian Giorgio Trissino's epic poem, *L'Italia Liberata dai Goti* [1547–1548], is very long and often tedious, but it is also classically impressive, and full of events. Milton knew the poem, and although Trissino's unrhymed hendecasyllabic lines were a precedent for the blank verse of *Paradise Lost*, the poem was a warning to him. It is better to be obstinate and patient.) The mystery to be opened in the first place lies at or behind the origin, not at some point further downstream. Hölderlin famously said, "Ein Rätsel is Reinentsprungenes. Auch / Der Gesang kaum darf es enthüllen" ("The purely-sprung-forth is an enigma. Even / Song scarcely is able to reveal it").[5] These lines seem to me the truest words possible to speak about *Paradise Lost* because they address the riddle of human nature in history and trace the riddle back to the pure springing forth of what history will afterward complicate and overwhelm. Song may be able scarcely to reveal the riddle of the transcendental origin in Eden, but it has a better chance than anything else because song presents the mystery as a mystery, a thing essentially veiled.[6] The first poet, Adam, said it more simply, if anthropocentrically: "For man to tell how human life began / Is hard" (*PL*, 8.250–51). Resisting both extremes—that of leisurely curiosity and that of purposeful direction—Milton forced himself to become accustomed to the original place, the first place, and to become familiar with its ways. He remained there and dwelt, listening to the sounds of the place, feeling its deeper resonances and slowly, without effort or planning—for effort and planning, if they come at all, should only come after this patient remaining—to discover its secrets. We may call this obstinate refusal to be moved or to move—as Milton's Samson refuses to be moved, unless dragged—the foundation of genius, or at least of genius of a certain kind. We may also call it courting the muse. For the muse demands nothing less than this self-denying rejection of alluring but shallow goals. The muse demands stillness while waiting for sunrise, as in the Nativity Ode.

The word *origin* has much to do with rising light. The word comes from Latin deponent *orior*, "to rise up," and the participle *oriens*. The *orient* was understood to be both the place of the rising sun and also, more precisely, the point at which the sun crosses the *horizon*, the *oriens zonos*, a false etymology of *horizon*, as it happens, but a poetically irresistible one.[7] In Milton's day, the Greek word *horizein*, "to draw a boundary," was supposed to be related to *orior*. Milton would have known the correct etymology. John Donne did too, as may be seen in the inscription above his statue in Saint Paul's in London. But the similar sounds of the words, and the association of sunrise with a visible line in the east, would have invited Milton to associate origins, the rising into appearance of beings, with the rising of dawn as it crosses the line of the horizon. Milton is fascinated by such crossings, as when Adam crosses the boundary between sleeping and waking: "Now morn her rosy steps in th'eastern clime / Advancing sowed the earth with orient pearl" (*PL*, 5.1–2); "sacred light began to dawn / In Eden on the humid flow'rs that breathed." Like all other creatures, which seem to come into being again under the first light, the flowers breath forth "morning incense" that rises up as "silent praise" to God, "and His nostrils fill / With grateful smell" (*PL*, 9.196–97). The elaborate description of the cave in Heaven, which is "within the Mount of God fast by his throne" (*PL*, 6.5), is derived from the Cave of the Nymphs episode in the *Odyssey*, and Porphyry's allegorical commentary on it. There, Milton has night and day entering and leaving at opposite ends. Morning goes forth from the cave in fiery gold, shooting "orient beams" at night:

> And now went forth the Morn
> Such as in highest Heav'n, arrayed in gold
> Empyreal. From before her vanished Night,
> Shot through with orient beams.
>
> (PL, *6.12–15*)

When Milton uses *orient* he means something like "rosy-yellow," the light of the dawn; but he also means "rising" and "auspicious." This sense of origin is the crossing of a line, a moment of glorious transition. But it is this sense of the origin that Milton opens in *Paradise Lost* by treating the line of the horizon, the moment of rising, as a place to remain.

Like the word *history* for Hegel, the word *origin* appears to carry objective and subjective meanings. We have seen how the problem of the objective origin in Milton—and of Milton's dwelling at this origin, this sunrise, this coming into appearance of things—needs to be thought about in more depth before Milton's *originality* as an artist can be assessed. As a term of aesthetic evaluation, *originality*, like *creative genius*, comes into use after Milton's day, notably in Edward Young's *Conjectures on Original Composition* (1759), in no small part because of Milton's example. Young, the author of the poem "Night Thoughts," was one of the creators of German and English romanticism. It is in the light of the beams of the rising sun of genius, Young says, that the original composition also rises: "nothing *Original* can rise, nothing immortal can ripen, in any other sun."[8]

For Milton, however, poetic originality does not flow from any power that resides in himself, such as incomparable intelligence, which in his late forties, when he began *Paradise Lost*, he could take for granted. For Milton, what makes him great is what he knows and what he has to say, after a lifetime of hard study and harder thought. But he needed the patience to wait, and the strength to wait, to gain access to what he deeply knows and what he deeply has to say. His originality consists, therefore, in his choice of subject, his "higher argument" (*PL*, 9.42), as he calls it, rather than in the technical skill with which he treats that argument. If there is an ethical and subjective side to the originality of the poet of *Paradise Lost*, it consists in the courage it took to compose a heroic poem on the primitive tale of Adam and Eve in the Garden of Eden, to stick with it and to stick with its uneventful scene. Among the objections Milton raises to other epic poems, especially at the opening of book 9, the underlying objection is their trivial busyness. The main event of *Paradise Lost* is for Milton almost the only one that matters in the world, because it underlies history. The other event in history that will matter, and matter more, is the event that will overturn the consequences of this one, the subject of *Paradise Regained*. Milton, as I said, shows the artistic courage to remain near the origin of things, at the origin of the world and the origin of the human, without succumbing to the urge to plunge into the middle of history, with its "tedious havoc" (*PL*, 9.30). For if he were to take the plunge, he would be as ignorant as all the epic poets before him were of what the world, the human, and the historical are.

It was held by the most authoritative literary theorists of the Renaissance and notably by one of Milton's models, Torquato Tasso, that an epic poem must be founded on some action in history, real or partly imagined, such as Charlemagne's war with the pagans, or Justinian's liberation of Italy from the Goths, or the conquest of Jerusalem in the first crusade, which was Tasso's subject in *Jerusalem Delivered*. Even the poet Milton called his "original," Edmund Spenser, composed a Romantic epic intended to prepare the way for a fully epic poem on Arthur and

the Fairy Queen's defense of English Christendom against Saracen in-
vaders. "Faire Goddesse," the poet says to his muse,

> lay that furious fit aside,
> Till I of warres and bloudy *Mars* do sing,
> And Briton fields with Saracen bloud bedyde,
> Twixt that great faery Queene and Paynim king,
> That with their horrour Heaven and earth did ring,
> A worke of labour long and endlesse prayse.
>
> (The Faerie Queene, *2.11.7*)

The classic idea of what an epic poem should do is to recall, in brilliant detail, some dimly remembered but glorious event in the past. But
history is a shifting foundation and anything grounded thereon will be
undermined and forgotten, or regarded with opprobrium instead of with
praise—as is the case now with the first crusade. Milton realized this
during the period of study after he left Cambridge, when researching
the early Christian Church, so idealized by his fellow Protestants. He
discovered it again when researching his *History of Britain.*[9]

Milton thought an epic about history, history considered as a whole,
should be grounded on something more secure than historical events,
something such as the origin of history. But the origins of human things
generally do not belong to scientific knowledge and documentary evidence; they belong to poetic myth, to the aetiological tale. The scientific paleontologist will not speak of the origin of the human, especially
when *origin* is in the singular, any more than the scientific historian
is likely to speak of the *origin* of history. With regard to the first, we
know that certain emergent "human" features and developing skills—
bipedalism, stereoscopic vision, opposable thumb, alterations in the
structure and shape of the throat—accelerated the development of others
which in turn accelerated them, in feedback loops over evolutionary
time, which moves in sudden pulses as a result of such feedback. The
human brain, like human language, is as much a product of developing
human culture (including the culture and physiology of tools) as the
brain and language are the producers of culture.[10]

But in mythic terms, the origin of history is when Adam and Eve are
driven forth from the Garden of Eden, after which one of their children, the murderer Cain, founds the first city, the city being an engine

of history. When, therefore, he composes *Paradise Lost*, Milton is not drawn downstream by the current of events, far from the truth out of which history springs. Nor is he drawn downstream in the great biblical narrative, stretching from Eden to the Apocalypse, which occupies half of the eleventh and most of the twelfth books of *Paradise Lost*. For every moment in that history, which includes sickness and death—the Tower of Babel, the Flood, the calamities of Israel, the life of Jesus, the beginnings of the Church and its corruption—is an opening out of the origin in which it is implied. As the story of human history unfolds in *Paradise Lost*, we are always in the Garden of Eden, and never allowed to forget where we are. The poet returns to this origin, moreover, when the narrative is closed, in the final moments of the poem, so that we may feel the momentum of history building up in front of Adam and Eve, waiting to be loosed into time. In defiance of every successful example of epic before him, Milton dwells at the origin of history, so that the essence of history is disclosed.

The subject matter Milton treats in *Paradise Lost* centers on the Fall of Man, but it encompasses, in Andrew Marvell's astonished description, "Heaven, hell, earth, chaos, all."[11] In the technical skills usually thought necessary to the composition of heroic poems Milton disdainfully says he is "nor skilled, nor studious," although he shows himself to have mastered all the technical requirements of the epic—"what the laws are of a true epic poem"—and had done so when he was still a young man.[12] I mentioned that Milton did not begin *Paradise Lost* until he was almost fifty. Spenser died in his forty-seventh year, having composed a work three times as long as *Paradise Lost*, and by fifty Shakespeare had completed his astonishing career of some thirty-six plays, dying at age fifty-two. Milton, as he himself put it, was "long choosing and beginning late" (*PL*, 9.26), and unsurprisingly, *Paradise Lost* has some of the irascible qualities Adorno associated with the late work of Beethoven in the *Missa Solemnis*. Among these is an insistence on returning to archaic forms—in Beethoven's case, the traditional form of the mass, in Milton's, the traditional form of the epic—and inhabiting them with cold detachment, aggravating the dissonance of content and form.[13]

It is well known that Milton first planned *Paradise Lost*, or *Adam Unparadized*, as a drama, not unlike the Italian *dramma per musica*, or the German *Trauerspiel*.[14] The *dramma per musica* was a fashionable new genre in Milton's day, eminently modern, the forerunner of the oratorios and operas of the eighteenth century. This form would have drawn on skills Milton had demonstrated in his greatest English poems to date: "On the Morning of Christ's Nativity"; in *A Masque Presented at Ludlow Castle, 1634*; and in "Lycidas," with its masterly interplay of contrasting voices. Indeed, one of the most stunning soliloquies in *Paradise Lost*, Satan's hostile address to the sun, delivered from the summit of Mount Niphates, was originally part of this earlier drama. In *Paradise Lost* Satan's passionate discourse on the top of Mount Niphates remains a great baroque aria in the style Monteverdi invented, with its skillful variation of intense passions and contrasting tonalities. There is no reason to suppose Milton wouldn't have succeeded, had he wished to, in creating an eminently performable dramatic work on the loss of Paradise. Still less is there any reason to suppose Milton himself wasn't confident of success. Perhaps he abandoned the dramatic composition because it was too easy, too in harmony with long-cultivated, natural skills, and too likely merely to please, not astonish. Instead, Milton chose a literary form that, it is true, he had long aspired to write, but that for all its prestige was now, in the modern age, improbable and unfashionable. It was the irritable disharmony of form and content, each throwing the other into relief by the force of repulsion between them, which made the change to the epic form attractive to Milton.

To compare him with the greatest of his predecessors is to see the point more clearly still. Dante's great poem begins *nel mezzo del cammin di nostra vita*, in the *middle* of the journey of our lives—our lives as well as his. Virgil's *Aeneid* is preoccupied with the foundations of those soaring walls and battlements of Rome. The *Aeneid* is about power, the *regnum Caesaris*, which holds the sufficiency of human will to dominate history from within. The *Odyssey*, as its first word suggests, is about manhood, mostly in the middle of life, but also, with the education of Telemachus, how to become man and remain one; how to be an exemplary man; and how to exercise the manly resources of courage, endurance, and cunning. That there are so many interesting women in this poem, themselves not without courage, endurance, and cunning, only underlines the point. The *Iliad* is a poem about the origins of a human catastrophe, the *menis*, or wrath of Achilles, that sent so many noble souls of heroes to Hades, preparing their bodies—or "fashioning their bodies into" (there's a grim suggestion in the verb of technical construction)—a meal for dogs and birds.[15] Milton's great predecessors all begin in the middle of things, in the middle of a life or in the middle of a war. Any reference to origins as such is brief and obscure, an embarrassment to be moved away from as swiftly as possible.

For Milton, knowing the origin of something will tell you what it is. We've come back to that way of thinking in the modern world, to breaking things down into their radically constituent parts, the "first principles of things," as Lucretius called them, the *primordia rerum*. Milton's great epic poem, *Paradise Lost*, is an investigation of the origin of history, and Milton dwells there, at the origin, in the Garden of Eden, among the *primordia rerum*, in order to find out what the essence of history is. His purpose could hardly be a more important one, for history, whatever else it is, is the temporal environment within which human life unfolds. It is as impossible for us to step out of history as it is to step out of the world. We see such an effort to step out of history dramatized in Milton's youthful hymn, "On the Morning of Christ's Nativity," when the music of the angels provokes the speaker to imagine the heavenly Jerusalem descending from above, almost to the ground on which we stand, and opening her gates in invitation: "And Heaven as at some festival / Will open wide the gates of her high palace hall" (lines 47–48). It seems as if by taking one step through those opening gates we can leave behind us the catastrophe of history. That fantasy, however, is immediately broken: "But wisest fate says no, / This must not yet be so" (lines 149–50). It *will* be so at the end of time, at the Apocalypse. Milton has proven one thing, however, in this typical episode of arousing and then canceling a fantasy: that it is possible to step out of history, however briefly, in order to see history, as it were, from above. In *Paradise Lost* Milton will step out of history again, but this time he will not be so brief, and he will step out of history not into the heavenly Jerusalem at the end of time but into the garden, the Paradise, at the beginning of time.

To find out what history is, therefore, Milton inhabits the Garden of Eden, long after its inhabitants have gone, and long after the garden itself has been destroyed in the Flood, torn loose from its foundations and washed down the Euphrates to the Persian Gulf, where it is now: "an island salt and bare, / The haunt of seals and orcs and sea-mews' clang" (*PL*, 11.834–35). This description of the Garden of Eden in latter times, after the Flood, is an erasure, a wiping clean of the slate, so that vital information is lost. Travel will not take us back to the origin: it will take us to an island, salt and bare. Only poetic inspiration will take us back in time to an origin that has since been removed.

Paradise Lost is about "liberty lost," and the loss of liberty is the origin, and therefore the essence, of history. As often happens in Milton, something immense—the whole course of human history—is seen through the aperture of something small, a single couple in the evening, seeking out a place of rest. As they do so, we view them for the last time from what feels like a great and rapidly increasing physical distance, as if our earlier intimacy with Adam and Eve were dissolving as our temporal distance from them is restored. In these closing lines, every reader begins a journey back to the future, to his or her own situation in time:

> The world was all before them, where to choose
> Their place of rest, and Providence their guide.
> They hand in hand with wand'ring steps and slow
> Through Eden took their solitary way.
>
> (PL, *12.646–49*[16])

As we journey back to our places in the future, we are aware of traversing all human history between the time to which we are bound in our own lives and the time of Adam and Eve, who originate history. Much has happened in between, not much of it good, although a considerable amount of it hopeful. The "Providence" that guides Adam and Eve here in this passage, as they leave the garden, is the "Eternal Providence" (*PL*, 1.25) mentioned at the outset of *Paradise Lost:* God's plan for history. As the word *providence* suggests, together with the word *guide*, this is an assurance that history has a direction, that beneath the repetitive cycle of catastrophe and partial recovery, history is progressive.

To uncover the origin of history by dwelling at this origin, in the Garden of Eden, is also to uncover what history essentially is in the fallen, historical world. Milton will show in *Paradise Lost* that at the origin of history is a single, though compound event: the loss of liberty, which occurs with the Fall of Adam and Eve. "Since thy original lapse," the angel Michael tells Adam, "true liberty / Is lost" (*PL*, 12.83–84). But Adam

and Eve's loss of liberty is not total, as it is for the rebel angels, who
have become devils, and whose experience of time is not historical
but purely catastrophic: "And in the lowest deep a lower deep / Still
threat'ning to devour me opens wide, / To which the Hell I suffer seems
a Heav'n" (*PL*, 4.76–78). This is Satan on the top of Mount Niphates,
in that soliloquy some lines of which were composed when Milton was
planning a drama. The loss of liberty, which is the beginning of history, is a very grave but still a partial loss, which humanity must struggle
to restore, although with divine help. That is the meaning of *covenant*,
a coming together of the human with the divine. But history remains
in large measure humanity's struggle with itself, and the process of history, its advance through this struggle, is the dialectic of liberation and
enslavement. Milton means political enslavement, that is, subjection to
tyrants, but he also means enslavement to our passions, an inner subjection leading to the outer, political subjection:

> Immediately inordinate desires
> And upstart passions catch the government
> From reason and to servitude reduce
> Man till then free. Therefore since he permits
> Within himself unworthy pow'rs to reign
> Over free reason God in judgment just
> Subjects him from without to violent lords
> Who oft as undeservedly enthrall
> His outward freedom. Tyranny must be,
> Though to the tyrant thereby no excuse.
>
> (PL, *12.90–96*)

At the heart of history, therefore, as history moves forward in time
and further from its origin in the Garden of Eden, two contrary forces
in our nature are continually at war. The first is what Hegel revealed as
the master-slave dialectic, the inclination to dominance and submission, to tyrannize out of fear of the mob and to submit to tyranny out
of fear of the tyrant. In both cases, whether of domination or submission, we surrender our liberty to fear. Milton's term for this is *sin*, the
Fall of Man being the loss of our original, perfect liberty, which we had
in the Garden of Eden before the origin of history. The second and contrary force, aided by God, is our struggle to recover that original lib-

erty, which remains central to our humanity, defaced though this original liberty is by sin. Milton's term for this second force is *right reason, recta ratio*, which is the rediscovery of what we already know deep in our conscience, conscience being the Law of God written in the heart: "Since thy original lapse true liberty / Is lost which always with right reason dwells / Twinned and from her hath no dividual being" (*PL*, 12.83–85). History, therefore, is the struggle between cowardice and reason; between, on the one hand, the perverse dialectic of domination and submission wherein each position, dominant or submissive, depends on the other, nurtured by mutual fear, and, on the other hand, the true logic of reason, which is the fearless recollection of who we are in the presence of ourselves. Through this reason we recover enough freedom to affirm our independent and erect human nature. Sin makes us cower; reason lets us stand upright. The difference between them is learned by eating the fruit of the tree of the knowledge of good and evil.

To see these struggling forces at the beginning of history, or just before the beginning of history, is to see them as they truly are, allowing us to understand subsequent historical events. Milton's most powerful image of the struggle is not from *Paradise Lost* but from *Areopagitica*: "it was from out the rind of one apple tasted, that the knowledge of good and evil, as two twins cleaving together, leaped forth into the world. And perhaps this is that doom which Adam fell into of knowing good and evil, that is to say of knowing good by evil."[17] By dwelling at the origin in *Paradise Lost* Milton shows us the birth of these struggling twins in the discord between Adam and Eve, so that, as I have said, we may understand later historical events, beneath which the struggle between good and evil goes on.

One such event Milton sought to understand was the failure of the English Revolution, to which Milton had dedicated his life, and for which he nearly lost his life. He thought the English Revolution a God-ordained mission comparable to the delivery of the Israelites from Egypt and their forty-year wilderness journey to the Promised Land. The English were the Israelites of the modern age and would show the rest of humanity the way through the wilderness of illegitimate tyrannies—modern kings—to the Promised Land of a free commonwealth. Milton had been the chosen prophet of this great enterprise. Its utter collapse, the experience of defeat, as Christopher Hill called it, was a major driving force behind the composition of *Paradise Lost*, a poem that dwells at the origin in order to understand historical events remote from it in time, but especially *this* historical event, which would end in 1660, at the Restoration, when the English would find what Milton called their "captain back for Egypt" and would "basely and besottedly . . . run their necks under the yoke of tyranny again."[18] There were those who not unreasonably felt that by siding with the Long Parliament in the 1640s they ran their necks under what would become the tyranny of a Lord Protector and his major generals. They were right, of course, from their point of view, but Milton had the longer historical perspective.

What does it mean to look for the origin of something that happens in history? In historical explanation, whenever we try to fix the origin of an event, we understand that there is something provisional about this origin, which depends on our own choice and is partly subjective. Is there a historical event that assured the failure of the English revolution? Was it the death of Oliver Cromwell? Was it Cromwell's assumption of total power at the Protectorate? Was it earlier, at the purging of the Long Parliament? Was it the habit of submission acquired during the long years of Charles I's personal rule and during the tyranny of the Church of England under Archbishop Laud? Milton gave it an immediate and nonhistorical cause, a moral cause: the failure of the English to be courageous in the face of adversity, preferring ignoble ease to hard liberty. But all these causes and others, even when taken together, seem inadequate to explain the event, for which the original and determinative cause lies in human nature. For the failure of courage in the English, and their preference for ease over liberty, as Milton knew very well, was hardly a local event. He found their weakness in the Bible, written out time and again in the history of the Israelites, from the moment of their arrival in the Promised Land (and indeed from before) up through the period of the judges and the two kingdoms, until the Babylonian conquest. He found it written also in the history of the Christian Church, from the time of the apostles to the sects and schisms of his own day. The real cause of historical experiences such as the failure of the English Revolution is *sin*, making it necessary to go back not to any moment within history but to the origin of history and the origin of sin, in the Garden of Eden.

For the historian, presumptive starting moments within the stream of history have antecedent causes making these causes look like effects:

the origin is always receding before us. It will be better for the historian, therefore, not to dwell too much upon the chimera of an origin but instead to plunge as soon as possible into the stream of events, and to move forward in time, not back toward the origin of time. For the historian, the origin is a way of getting started.

Epic narrative engages history, as well, although at a higher level of artificial order than the chronological one of the historian. But like the historian, the epic poet has to plunge in, too. Horace's advice to the epic poet is to plunge *in medias res*, into the midst of events, as Homer does by beginning in the ninth year of the Trojan War, instead of launching forth from the absolute beginning, *ab ovo*, from the egg.[19] Instead of starting there, the poet is supposed to plunge into the middle, as into a stream, moving with the current of the action some distance before stopping to have previous action recounted in a retrospective tale. After that, the main action may be resumed and pursued to the end, and future events may be hinted at through prophecies. The point for Horace and the rest is *not* to start from the origin.

Nor does Milton do so, at least in the narrower, technical sense, in which he carefully follows Horace's prescription. Among its many other virtues, *Paradise Lost* is a masterpiece of epic architecture. Milton assures us of the fact, lest we miss it, in the argument to book 1, in which he goes so far as to translate the key phrase from Horace. After introducing the "whole subject" of *Paradise Lost*, which is "Man's disobedience and the loss thereupon of Paradise," caused by the serpent, "the poem," Milton says, keeping to the Latin use of a verb of motion *into* something, "hastes into the midst of things," beginning with the sight of Satan and the other fallen angels lying on the burning lake of Hell, thunderstruck and astonished. How they got there will not be shown until the midpoint of *Paradise Lost*, at the end of book 6, when the rebel angels are driven through an opening in the wall of Heaven. With the thunder driving them downward, they begin their nine-day fall through chaos into Hell, which has been formed by a portion of the thunder that pursues them, overshooting its mark. Our last sight of them is horrible: a great mouth swallows them up, as if they were disappearing down the gullet of a shark: "Hell at last / Yawning received them whole and on them closed" (*PL*, 6.874–75). But what is shut away from our sight here, as Hell's mouth closes, is what we have already seen when the narrative of the epic opens: Satan and the other rebel angels lying unconscious on the lake of Hell, rolling like dismasted hulks in its fiery waves: "he with his horrid crew / Lay vanquished rolling in the fiery gulf / Confounded though immortal" (*PL*, 1.51–53). We recognize at this moment, at the midpoint of *Paradise Lost*, that we have completed a vast circuit in the epic's design and have returned to the place from which we set forth.

The war in Heaven, which has brought us to this point, has been the subject of the angel Raphael's narrative, the purpose of which is to explain to Adam why an enemy is coming to the Garden of Eden with the intention of destroying him—and, of course, Eve. In book 7, a new and deeper phase of Raphael's narrative opens, introducing Creation to make a contrast with the destruction of the war we have seen in book 6. We are shown the origin of time and the Creation of the world. In book 8, after some astronomical speculation, Adam will relate his own tale, which is of everything he remembers of his brief but astonishing existence: of how he woke to find himself created, outside the Garden of Eden, of how he was transported to the garden, of how he met his Creator, of how Eve was taken out of his side, of how he met her as she came toward him from the pool, led by their Creator, and of how they live together in the Garden of Eden, which we are startled to find to be the origin of sexual desire: "Here passion first I felt, / Commotion strange!" (*PL*, 8.530–31).

Only in book 9 is the course of the main action resumed from where it was left at the end of book 4, when Satan was found disguised as a toad, whispering in Eve's ear as she slept, and is brought before the angel Gabriel. In that stern confrontation, as we saw, Gabriel and Satan prepare to fight, but to prevent it, lest the created universe be destroyed by their encounter, God's scales are suspended in the heavens above them, showing Satan to be certain to lose. At this, Satan "fled / Murmuring, and with him fled the shades of night" (*PL*, 4.1014–15).

The next four books will be taken up almost entirely with retrospective narrative as the principal action is held in suspense. Only in book 9 does Satan, having fled before Gabriel and flown around the earth, cloaked within "the space of seven continued nights" (*PL*, 9.63), return to earth again, at night, "improved / In meditated fraud and malice bent / On Man's destruction" (*PL*, 9.54–56). After searching the earth over for the perfect beast in which to hide himself—he earlier disguised himself as a cormorant and as a toad—Satan finds the serpent and conceals himself in it as it sleeps, "waiting close th'approach of morn" (*PL*, 9.191). From this moment, the action rushes forward to the catastrophe: the Fall of Adam and Eve, with its immediate consequences, their judgment by the Son, their prayers of repentance, the merciful instruction that follows upon these prayers of repentance, and their expulsion from the Garden. A further marvel of the poet's achievement is that, for all the brilliance of its management of action, pacing, and structure, the poem dwells at the origin, with all of history before it.

The instruction Adam and Eve receive—or that Adam receives, to be communicated later to Eve—is the occasion of the large prophetic narrative of history, which stretches through half of book 11 and most of book 12. It extends forward from Adam and Eve's present moment in Eden until the end of time: "the race of time / Till time stand fixed" (*PL*, 12.554–55). That narrative is what Milton has been dwelling at the origin for: to explain the conditions in which we live, as historical beings.

Prominent among those conditions is death, the penalty for original sin. But dying is not in itself historical. Only when we begin to inflict death on one another, only when we kill and, more important, when we can threaten very plausibly to kill, thus originating power, does history become possible.

If we are to understand the origin of history in the threat of killing, it will useful to turn to the tenth book of *Paradise Lost*, specifically to the judgment pronounced on Adam and Eve by the Son before he clothes them. They must both die, but not before they have had time to suffer and to be humiliated. Eve will bring forth children in sorrow and will be subjected to her husband's will, enslaved by her own sexual desire to the production of those children and to obedience to a man who is no longer reasonable or particularly kind. Adam is condemned to labor, too, not, as Eve is, within his own body, but in the ground or, to use Aristotelian language, in his material cause, the dust from which he was taken. He will sweat to wring from a cursed soil the bread that he and Eve and their children will eat, as a reminder that they come from dust and will return to it when they die. It is an absurd cycle, not a historical development: they come out of dust, they eat the bread that grows from this dust, and when they die they will return to this dust. Every day's labor will be a reminder of the life cycle from dust to dust as they bend over the earth, looking into their origin, and also into their graves.

How are they to break out of that cycle, into something progressive, into history? Among those children is the first murderer, Cain, who will spill his brother's blood in that dust, mingling "dust and gore" (*PL*, 11.460), from which the blood will cry out: "the voice of thy brother's blood," as the Lord says to Cain in the Bible, "crieth unto me from the ground" (Genesis 4:10). Killing one another gives us a hand in the death to which we have been condemned, hurrying it along, so to speak. Cain's spilling of his brother's blood appears to be another origin of history, and of civilization, for Milton would not forget that Cain is an agriculturalist and the founder of the first city. Nor was Milton ignorant that the ancient city was itself a weapon, an instrument for the coordination of agricultural production and capital accumulation for the purpose of making of war on other cities and spilling their inhabitants' blood in the streets. That is history, or a part of it, and it is a mystery.

Here then, once again, is that final scene of *Paradise Lost*, at the origin of history, and on the threshold of history. The troop of fiery cherubim descending the neighboring hill, led onward by that blazing sword above, advances toward Adam and Eve. As the sword torches the Garden of Eden, it poses a real, physical danger to them:

> High in front advanced,
> The brandished sword of God before them blazed
> Fierce as a comet which the torrid heat
> And vapor as the Libyan air adust
> Began to parch that temperate clime.
>
> (PL, *12.632–36*)

There is a sense of real urgency when the angel Michael catches Adam and Eve in either hand. In expelling them, he is also leading them to safety from this fiery apparition of the wrath of God:

> Whereat
> In either hand the hast'ning angel caught
> Our ling'ring parents and to the eastern gate

> Led them direct and down the cliff as fast
> To the subjected plain, then disappeared.
>   (PL, *12.636–40*)

Even at this moment of danger, the movement of the troop of cherubim, which should be terrifying, is compared to what at first appears to be a more tranquil, almost pastoral scene of mist rising from the river and the marshes at evening while the laborers return from the fields. It is an astonishing poetic conjuncture of extreme heat and, as the careful reader will perceive, of insidious cold:

>   All in bright array
> The cherubim descended, on the ground
> Gliding meteorous as evening mist
> Ris'n from a river o'er the marish glides
> And gathers ground fast at the laborer's heel
> Homeward returning.
>   (PL, *12.627–32*)

The laborers are sweaty from the day's work and eager not to be caught in the chilling damp of that startlingly fast-moving mist, for almost as certainly as that troop of flaming cherubim to which it is compared, the mist carries death. All future human labor is captured at this moment, but it is a moment of intermission between labor and rest, as the word *homeward* implies. Where else, except at this origin, could such a complex but compelling picture of our ordinary lives be achieved?

As for Adam and Eve, it must not be forgotten that they are at the origin not only of our ordinary lives but of history, as well, as they turn from the dreadful faces and menacing arms at Eden's gate, wipe their tears, and set forth in search of a place to rest for that evening, "with wand'ring steps and slow" (*PL*, 12.648). Milton says, "The world was all before them" (*PL*, 12.646), which it is. And so we are.

One of the most decisive of the principles at the origin to which Milton returns is matter, the substance out of which everything is made, including angels and Heaven, and even humankind, for humans have no souls apart from matter. This principle is commonly referred to as Milton's *materialism* or *monist materialism*, although for reasons that will become apparent I think *physicalism*—from the Greek *physis*, "growth"—is the better term for what Milton generally means. He is interested in nature as a unified, growing, ecological, and hierarchical system, all the parts of which nourish and complement one another, although generally the lower created beings feed higher ones, and the total system moves upward, like a growing plant. The growing plant is the figure, the simile (beginning with "So") that the angel Raphael employs when he is explaining to Adam how nature works. Note that the simile is never formally closed. When it ends on the words "last the bright consummate flower / Spirits odorous breathes" (*PL*, 5.481–82), the figural structure is not left behind as a figure standing apart from what it refers to. It is instead reassimilated to the whole. It is small wonder Coleridge placed the entire passage at the head of the thirteenth chapter of *Biographia Literaria*, to affirm that the symbol differs from the allegorical sign by participating in what it refers to. At some level, Milton's imagination is stirred by the similarity between *simile* and *assimilation*:

> Till body up to spirit work in bounds
> Proportioned to each kind. So from the root
> Springs lighter the green stalk, from thence the leaves
> More airy, last the bright consummate flower
> Spirits odorous breathes: flow'rs and their fruit,
> Man's nourishment, by gradual scale sublimed
> To vital spirits aspire.
>
> (PL, 5.478–84)

Everything in the system is moving upward to higher states of refinement of matter, angels being spiritual, or "spiritous," only in the sense that they are almost the highest of these material refinements. Humans—Adam and Eve and their offspring—are destined for a like ascent, so that at length they will leave earth and ascend to Heaven, and yet still return to earth when they wish, to visit their original home. Earth itself will ascend on the "scale" or ladder of being. For Milton, the natural home of humanity is Heaven and earth together, and humans, like angels, will be able to travel wherever they like on the hierarchy of being, unlike other creatures who are fixed in place on the hierarchy. Adam and Eve's freedom of movement recalls the freedom emphasized in the most distinctive ideological statement of

Renaissance humanism, Pico della Mirandola's *Oration on the Dignity of Man.*

In the Garden, Adam and Eve eat and digest food, and inoffensively exhale waste through their pores (excretion isn't necessary yet). They also enjoy sexual love, or rather, they celebrate it together, and from their union the entire human race is destined to spring. Angels also mix in love, sexually, but "Easier than air with air" (*PL*, 8.626). They mix their bodies entirely, "and obstacle find none / Of membrane, joint or limb . . . nor restrained conveyance need / As flesh to mix with flesh" (*PL*, 8.624–29). Angels do not produce offspring, however, which underlines Milton's stated belief, in the divorce tracts, that marriage is not for procreation but for love. Nor are the angels, apparently, monogamous, as the ancient Hebrew patriarchs were not monogamous, a thing Milton also approved of. The angels' genders are not fixed, either. They are polymorphously erotic. Because physical sex is pure, there is no reason for angels not to indulge in it, too, and because the physical expression of love is necessary to the happiness of conscious beings, and angels are happy, they enjoy sex "in eminence" (*PL*, 8.624). They enjoy sex more than we do—but not more than we shall. In nothing is Milton's revolutionary consciousness more apparent than in this. In the future, when real and substantial liberty is attained, even sexual intercourse will be better, not imposed on by social conventions, monogamy, and laws of marriage and divorce; not channeled in one direction or another by difference of gender; and not confined by the limitations of the body, either by its barriers to total penetration or by specialized sexual organs.

Milton emphasizes the homogeneity of his materialist system by having angels eat, too:

> nor seemingly
> The angel, nor in mist (the common gloss
> Of theologians) but with keen dispatch
> Of real hunger and concoctive heat
> To transubstantiate.
>
> *(PL, 5.434–38)*

Like us, the angels need to eat to be sustained, and they "cook" what they eat inside their bodies, transubstantiating it to their own substance. In the Bible, before the Fall, only humans eat. In Milton, everything

eats: "whatever was created needs to be sustained and fed" (*PL*, 5.414–
15). Even the spots on the moon can be explained as lingering vapors
risen up from the earth that have not yet been drawn in and digested
by the moon's body:

> Of elements
> The grosser feeds the purer: Earth the Sea,
> Earth and Sea feed Air, the Air those Fires
> Ethereal and as lowest first the Moon,
> Whence in her visage round those spots unpurged,
> Vapors not yet into her substance turned.
>
> (PL, *5.415–20*)

The passage continues on to "higher orbs" (*PL*, 5.422) such as the sun,
to indicate the fully systematic, benevolent, and courteous, but also hierarchical, upward-moving character of this cosmic nourishment system:

> Nor doth the Moon no nourishment exhale
> From her moist continent to higher orbs.
> The sun that light imparts to all receives
> From all his alimental recompense
> In humid exhalations and at ev'n
> Sups with the Ocean.
>
> (PL, *5.421–26*)

Humans will inhabit the entire earth, all of which, though different from
the Garden of Eden, is no less ideally delightful. Milton's Garden of
Eden is not a shelter from a harsh external world. It is a special place of
honor, like a royal palace, where the benevolent king and queen, the
father and mother of humanity reside. In the future, they will be frequently visited and honored by their offspring. This condition is the
original state of what in the prophet Isaiah would be the idea of Jerusalem as the holy city at the center of the earth, from which the Messiah will reign over the earth, and all the kings of the earth will come
to do him homage (Isaiah 9.7, 11:9).

   With the Fall of Adam and Eve, all these possibilities are swept away.
Eden will not be Jerusalem and Whitehall Palace at once; sex will not

get better but worse; restrictive laws of all kinds, over the mind as well as over the body, will increase; superstition, paganism, and irreligion will arise; sickness will rage, and so will wars; and humans will not rise to Heaven but sink down into the earth, and die. Efforts to restore liberty will rise from time to time, only to be crushed and rise again. When humanity falls, all of nature falls, too. The earth's axis is tilted and the seasons begin; animals prey on one another; just as men war with one another; earth becomes a wilderness; and Paradise, the Garden, is destroyed by unleashed natural forces, the waters of the Flood, which loosen the mountain from its place and wash it down the Euphrates or the Tigris (or both rivers together, now joined by the rising waters of the Flood) to the Persian Gulf, where it stands a barren, inhospitable rock (*PL*, 11.829–35).

We have seen that instead of being a dualist—accepting, with Descartes, and indeed with the entire Christian tradition, that there are two primary substances, soul and matter—Milton is a monist and accepts only one substance: matter. It is the burden of monists to have to variegate their primary substance on the basis of an originative difference, like the "swerve" in Lucretius, or the simple difference made by the spaces between atoms. For Milton, this originative difference is the will of God and God's effectual Word. The difference is transmitted to matter, which exists in many states, hierarchically arranged: "one first matter all / Endued with various forms, various degrees / Of substance" (*PL*, 5.472–74). The highest, the most refined degrees on the continuum may be referred to as "spirit" or, rather, by the adjective *spiritous:* "But more refined, more spiritous and pure / As nearer to him Him placed or nearer tending" (*PL*, 5.475–76). This one first matter becomes more "spiritous" as it gets nearer to God, but it also has its origin in God, who says, "Boundless the deep because I am who fill / Infinitude, nor vacuous the space" (*PL*, 7.168–69).[20] For Milton, matter does not, as in traditional Christianity, come out of nothing, *ex nihilo*, but rather out of God, *ex deo*. This does not mean God is for Milton altogether reducible to primary matter, even if it is his substance, his body. God transcends matter, as he does everything else, but God is not any substance—for example, pure spirit—apart from or other than matter. He is not a spirit, and he is not Spirit. Milton does employ the word *spirit*, but in a sense different from that of traditional Christianity and Christian metaphysics. When he has decided to send the Son to create the world, God calls him *my Word*: "And Thou, my Word, begotten Son, by Thee / This I perform: speak thou and be it done!" (*PL*, 7.163). God then adds, "My overshadowing *Spirit* and might with Thee / I send along: ride forth and bid the deep / Within appointed bounds be Heav'n and Earth!" (*PL*, 7.165–67; emphasis added). In orthodox Christianity the Spirit is the Holy Ghost, the third person of the Trinity, equal with God; the second person, the Son, also is equal with God. I would not say Milton is altogether an anti-Trinitarian, or an Arian, believing Jesus to be nothing more than a specially elevated man.[21] But in a departure from orthodox Christian doctrine, Milton's monism requires he be a subordinationist within the Trinity: the Son is inferior to God and the Spirit is inferior to the Son. Milton remains a Trinitarian, however unorthodox a one, because the Son and the Spirit are persons in the godhead. In the passage above, as in others, Milton is at pains not to reduce the Spirit and especially the Son to *faculties* of God, and he is at pains for the good reason that the possessives, "*my* Word" and "*My* . . . Spirit" bring him almost vanishingly close to that position. By *Spirit* Milton means God's creative power, which the poet invokes at the beginning of *Paradise Lost* (1.17), and which is the *ruach*, or "breath," of the Creation in Genesis 1:2: "And the Spirit of God moved upon the face of the waters." If we speak metaphysically, instead of in the personal terms required by theology, we may conclude that those originative differentiae in Milton's monism are the Son— *will*, or *decision*, or *command*—and the Spirit, which is *power* or *force*. If we insist on asking what God is substantially, behind the prime matter from which everything comes, it is best to call him light: "God is light" (*PL*, 3.3). He is essential, or "unapproachèd" light, rather than radiant light. (It is unclear whether light is to be understood as material, like everything else.) Even so, in a moment of sublime slippage—that is, of contradiction suggesting a higher, impenetrable mystery—God transcends this light with which he has been identified because he *dwells* in it, too:

> Since God is light
> And never but in unapproachèd light
> Dwelt from eternity, dwelt then in thee,
> Bright effluence of bright essence increate.
>
> (PL, *3.3–6*)

Lucretius's system is mechanistic; Milton's is vitalist. We see this when that Spirit, whom God has sent along with the Son, gets down to work on the whelming abyss of chaotic matter, which has just been calmed by the Son's command, "'Silence, ye troubled waves and thou, deep, peace!' / Said then th'Omnific Word, 'Your discord end!'" (*PL*, 7.216–17). The Son rides far out into chaos, and then with golden compasses (the scene is famously represented by Blake, as the act of Urizen) measures out the "horizon" or circumference of the world: "One foot He centered and the other turned / Round through the vast profundity obscure" (*PL*, 7.228–29). The scope of the universe has been delineated and the primal matter is calm, though "unformed and void" (*PL*, 7.233). Everything now depends on what kind of system will be realized, a mechanical or a vitalist one. This decision does not lie in the command of the Son but rather, we must presume, in the will of the Father, because without any prompting the Spirit starts to work:

> Darkness profound
> Covered th'abyss but on the wat'ry calm
> His brooding wings the Spirit of God outspread
> And vital virtue infused and vital warmth
> Throughout the fluid mass.
>
> (*PL, 7.233–37*)

The aesthetic unity of Milton's physio-theological system—his ontology and his cosmology, his anthropology, ethics, and historiography, his physics and his metaphysics, and of course his theology—depends for its unity on everything being made at the origin out of one substance, which comes out of God, the origin of all.

❧ *11*

On the Verse of Paradise Lost

A POET *IS* SOMEONE, *makes* something, and *says* something. These are the *ethical*, the *technical*, and the *prophetic* aspects of being a poet. Clearly, making verses belongs to the second and is the basis of our word for the poet. To be a "maker"—Greek *poiêtês*, Old English *scop*, Middle Scots *makar*—does not define the essence of what it is to be a poet. A poet is a special kind of "sayer" as well as a special kind of maker; and a poet is a special kind of person, quite apart from what the poet makes or says. Perhaps being a poet is a spiritual state, like that of the Hebrew prophets, or a certain way of being in the world, as Robert Graves said, and as Keats said, and as Blake showed, regardless what the poet does, so far as making verses is concerned. Perhaps to be a poet is to be a primal sayer, as Heidegger said, a speaker of the truth of what we are in relation to the gods and the earth, to time, and to others in the past as well as in the future. The Greek muses are the daughters of Memory, and in oral cultures from Homer's time to ours (in western Crete and Sicily, for example, in the Balkans and the Caucasus), the poet's role is like the herald's in medieval war: to note, to remember, to report. Perhaps to be a poet is to be a prophet of the future, as Mao thought, and as Majakovskij thought, without as much regard for the past, and for roots we have sunk into the past; perhaps poets are uprooters, not rooters: "the homeland of creative poetry is the future."[1] Perhaps poets speak to our hearts, as they have always done in the past, back to Sappho and further back still; perhaps poets speak for their own hearts, regardless of ours, as Sappho does, and her follower, Catullus, but are all the same cordial to us. Perhaps poets are the modern version of what shamans were—and still are, in some places—in more primitive societies, mysterious channels for dark forces moving through the world, benevolent and evil. Such poets are unintelligible criers of the unimaginable truth. These examples may suffice to show it is widely supposed that being a poet does not essentially have to do with the making of verse, even if nearly every poet makes verses. It seems to me one reason poets occasionally write prose poems—from Baudelaire's *Petits poèms en prose* to Paul Celan's "Meridian" address to Louise Glück's "A Foreshortened Journey"—is to establish that the concept of the poet, and the glory of the poet, the poet's *aura*, are not confined to the technical art of versification. Sir Philip Sidney made this point as wittily as anyone has. Verse is merely the outside, the muddy vesture of true poetry, which is inward and spiritual: "it is not rhyming and versing that maketh a poet (no more than a long gown maketh an advocate, who though he pleaded in armor should be an advocate and no soldier), but it is that faining notable images of virtues, vices, or what else, with that delightful teaching, which must be the right describing note to know a poet by."[2] "Faining notable images"—*mimesis*—is of course just as technical a concern as making verses. But for Sidney, it is the prophetic aspect of poetry—"delightful teaching," as he calls it—that counts for most.

It counts the most for Milton as well, and in the last two chapters I have been speaking of what Milton is saying in *Paradise Lost* about history. The underlying question for Milton is what kind of engagement with historical events in the present—with politics—is legitimate and possible for the poet. I have argued that the reason for his choosing the subject he did for *Paradise Lost*—the Creation of the world, and the first human beings—is to engage history in a new way, radically, at its root and origin, and from the transcendental platform of myth, where *myth* does not mean something untrue but rather what philosophy would call *a priori*. Milton accepts that the biblical myth contained in those opening chapters of Genesis is divinely inspired and is therefore fundamentally true. It would seem then—and Milton's comments on verse might be taken to support this—that the poem's style is altogether secondary to what it represents and says. Yet that is surely not the case: there is nothing secondary about the thundering rhythms of *Paradise Lost*. The reason is that the verse of *Paradise Lost* unites who the poet is and what he says. Verse then is a serious matter, and while it is a technical concern, to be sure, its physical force is the unifying medium between the ethical and prophetic aspects of poetry. The image I like to think of for verse is that of the chemical bond.

The English word *verse*, French *vers*, is from Latin *versus* and implies "a turning," an indirection or a change of direction. Verse changes direction and turns back on itself; but verse is also a going forward, a setting out for somewhere else and a settling in to travel. You set out on a journey, and you settle in to the rhythm of walking. As William Hazlitt reports, "Wordsworth always wrote (if he could) walking up and down a straight gravel walk, or in some spot where the continuity of his verse met with no collateral interruption."[3] You set out on a narrative, and you settle in to the rhythm of the verse. Verse turns, however, because it is not just a pace; it is also a measure. Keeping measure, a single verse can only go so far, and then it has to turn. Where does it turn? It turns into another verse. There is something metamorphic in this turn, a "turning into something else," as we say in English, and the transformation comes as a surprise. If there is rhyme, the element of surprise is only greater. In Philip Larkin, "frail" becomes "exhale," and "lace" becomes "pace": "Lost lanes of Queen Anne's lace, / And that high-buildèd cloud, / Moving at summer's pace."[4]

There is something laborious to this continual turning, however, this going down a row to the end and then turning, or turning back, to go down another just beside it. In making verses, we keep continuity from one row to the next, and the next, but we also keep the rows apart. Each stands out; each moves into the next. Keeping the verses straight in the mind, forcing oneself to turn back at the end of each row, feeling one is starting all over again after each turn, and yet having to make the new act of attention fit in with the last, so that they lie neatly together in the mind, is laborious, or can seem so. I think this impression of laboriousness is why some readers say they find poetry intimidating, in contrast to prose. Indeed, the comparison of putting down rows of verse to plowing a field is obvious and ancient. A form of ancient writing that went in both directions, like plowing, was called *boustrophedon*, "turning of the ox."[5] Verse is like plowing a field. It is a turning, therefore; however, as in plowing, it is also a straightness. It is direct. Plowing a strait furrow, especially the first one, is very hard to do (harder than turning the team around at the end of the furrow).

There is something direct about a straight line of verse. That is why we call it a line. The Greeks called a single line of verse a *stichos*, an arrow, something straight and swift and fast. Straight lines are unnatural. To draw one you need a ruler, as you need a compass to draw a regular curve. An arrow therefore has something magical about it: it flies straight on its own, without continuing aid. A line of verse imitates this wonder. The term from Greek drama, *stichomythia* ("arrow speech"), of which there is an example in *A Masque Presented at Ludlow Castle, 1634*, when Comus first addresses the Lady and she responds to his questions, does not mean rapid-fire exchange. It means only that each speaker gets one entire verse at a time, one straight shot. Other words for what we call "verse" are a *thread*—Latin *filus*—and a *path* or *way through*, Greek *oimê*. These terms imply directness over a distance longer than a single line, or a handful of lines. They refer to a discipline in the making of verses that is above and beyond the level of the line, and that goes on for some time. A feat of memory is involved, as with Homer's catalogue of the ships, Virgil's catalogue of the Italic tribes, or Milton's catalogue of devils, long after known in Palestine.

These feats of memory are in turn emblematic of a greater: the poet's holding the thread of an entire epic poem. We speak of keeping to the thread of the discourse, or of losing the thread of discourse. It is hard to keep the thread disentangled from others. There are many turns to a pathway, as there are many turns in verse, although these are more regular. A pathway, like verse, is always going somewhere, but it is easy to lose one's way on this path, to turn onto false paths, of which there are many. Although this is less apparent today, in the era of highways and street signs and global positioning, it is hard to keep to the path, to the find true and best way to get through. (Hunter-gatherer societies have penetrative terms for a route that gets you through difficult terrain, such as the Algonkian-Anishinaabe word, *nastawgan*, "the way through."[6])

Anyone may turn a verse, or compose a straight line. But it is hard to compose many verses, many lines that go well together, and harder still to find and keep to the way when the way is long. It is good to have directions, or a guide. Animals can show the way through (human paths follow older animal ones), and so too can a spirit, a goddess. That is what we mean by inspiration.

It is for this reason—that the way is hard to keep to, that it is difficult, and long—that Milton calls again upon the muse, after the beginning of *Paradise Lost*, when he approaches his narrative subject more closely. The subject is the Fall of Adam and Eve, "Man's first disobedience" (*PL*, 1.1), and more largely it is the beginning of history itself, which has been caused and conditioned by this first disobedience. For history is a falling from bad to worse, perpetuating the original Fall. The subject is also our being rescued from this falling, and from ourselves as its continuing cause, by the sacrificial act of "one greater Man," Jesus Christ (*PL*, 1.4). The "Heav'nly Muse" is invoked and identified as the same muse that inspired Moses, on Mount Sinai, and David, on Mount Zion. She will lead the poet higher than Mount Helicon, which with the stream Hippocrene, is the source of the classical muses, so that he, the poet, may report "Things unattempted yet in prose or rhyme" (*PL*, 1.16). After this seeming conclusion, the majesty of the invocation is augmented further, as the poet goes on. "Chiefly," he says, he calls on the "Spirit," which works inwardly, in the heart, instead of in temples or churches, the same spirit or breath, the *ruach*, that at the opening of the Bible moved upon the face of the waters, making the waters pregnant with being and preparing them for the appearance of light, which will make them appear (*PL*, 1.17–22). The poet prays for this spirit to perform the same action of enlivening and illumining on him so that he may rise to the height of his "argument"—this theme. For his intention is nothing less than to be the champion (L. *assertor*, "a liberator, a champion") of providence, defending God's will before the rest of humanity and asserting the right of that will over our minds: "I may assert Eternal Providence / And justify the ways of God to men" (*PL*, 1.22–26). He has stated his great argument in grandly abstract terms: it is divine Providence and the "ways" or *mêtis* ("counsel") of God. But the story is more specific, though perhaps no easier to tell. It is about Adam and Eve's Fall. What or who caused them to fall from the high estate of being masters of the earth into the low estate of being subjects of history? The question imitates Homer, and so does the answer, placed at the beginning of a line. It is Satan, or as he is called here, the serpent, for that is the form in which he appears to Adam and Eve in the Garden of Eden. We have the answer, but where is the thread to be grasped? When did the serpent do this and what was the reason, the occasion? The reason was his being cast out of heaven with all his rebel angels, and he tempted Adam and Eve after that. The poet has now found the place to grasp the thread of his discourse at the start, which is not the Fall of Adam and Eve but of Satan:

> Say first, for Heav'n hides nothing from thy view,
> Nor the deep tract of Hell, say first what cause
> Moved our grand parents in that happy state,
> Favored of Heav'n so highly, to fall off
> From their Creator and transgress His will
> For one restraint, lords of the world besides:
> Who first seduced them to that foul revolt?
> *Th'infernal Serpent.* He it was whose guile
> Stirred up with envy and revenge deceived
> The mother of mankind, what time his pride
> Had cast him out from Heav'n with all his host
> Of rebel angels.
>
> (PL, *1.27–38; italics added*)

This chapter is about verse, but it is also about narrative, which is the environment of verse, and we shall see that it is about drama, too. The difference between a versifier and a great poet, so far as epic is concerned, is the management of narrative, keeping to the *oimê*, the pathway of song, taking hold of the thread at the right place, and keeping it disentangled from others. Narrative is the long-range challenge of verse, verse as it is stretched out by *durée*. It may come as more of a surprise that, in being about verse, this chapter is also about Satan, especially as we see him in the opening verses of *Paradise Lost*. That the problem of Satan is relevant to the problem of verse may be supported by the observation that Satan is the first to *turn* against God, to trope upon obedience and compel Providence in a new and surprising direction—as poetry does. There can be no epic of *Paradise Lost* without Satan's first turn. But perhaps we may first observe an obvious literary-historical fact. It is that with the peculiar kind of verse opening *Paradise Lost* (which, yes, owes something to the verse of the Elizabethan and Jacobean stage, "our best English tragedies," as Milton acknowledged), a new sound in poetry came into the world. This sound, for which the adjective I have already employed, *thunderous*, is not out of place, is inextricably associated with the character, as Milton creates it, of Satan. The first two books of *Paradise Lost* are vocalized by, about, and around the figure of Satan. They give us the blast and roar and blare of Hell, the noise of chaos beyond Hell, and also of the devious (turning) and slashing words of the master of Hell. In his note on the verse of *Paradise Lost*, Milton mentions that his poem is "without rhyme," and it is only when we reflect upon Satan, on what he sounds like and how we see him in these two books, that we know it could not be otherwise. Milton says his rhymeless verse is like that of Homer and of Virgil, but Milton was well aware of the difference. The difference is that in Homer and Virgil, because of the quantitative line, it is never unclear when one line or row ends and another begins, even when enjambment is used. But in Milton's blank verse this clear articulation of the line is lost, as we shall see, in multiple enjambments, and the "poetical" sound of the verse is correspondingly diminished. The verse therefore sounds like vehement and continuous speech—a "surging maze," as Milton will say of Satan's coils (*PL*, 9.499).

We can hear this—the vehemence, the flexibility, the headlong rush and excitement, the thunder—by continuing with the passage from which I have been quoting:

> Of rebel angels, by whose aid aspiring
> To set himself in glory above his peers
> He trusted to have equaled the Most High
> If he opposed, and with ambitious aim
> Against the throne and monarchy of God
> Raised impious war in Heav'n and battle proud
> With vain attempt. Him th'Almighty Pow'r
> Hurled headlong flaming from th'ethereal sky
> With hideous ruin and combustion down
> To bottomless perdition, there to dwell
> In adamantine chains and penal fire
> Who durst defy th'Omnipotent to arms.

> (PL, *1.38–49*)

Of these twelve lines five are strongly enjambed, which is to say that even the slightest pause at the end of the line is disruptive to sense. But in fact, none of these lines, not even those that are end-stopped (e.g., "To set himself in glory above his peers," line 39, and "In adamantine chains and penal fire," line 48), invites us to pause at the end of the line but urges us forward into the next. The first six lines seem to climb upward with Satan's own "aspiring," each line turning like a switchback in the mountains, until reaching a line that feels like a complete rhythmical unit promising a rest at its end: "Raised impious war in Heav'n and battle proud." But to our surprise, this line, which sounds so complete in itself, flows into the next with a second strong enjambment, "With vain attempt," compelling us to stretch our attention beyond the resting point we thought we'd reached to absorb the new hemistich into the total phrase: "Raised impious war in Heav'n and battle proud / With vain attempt" (line 44). A new sentence begins immediately, after the caesura— "Him the Almighty Pow'r . . ."—and carries on through the next five lines with impetuous force augmented by our own sense of imbalance in reading them. The effect is developed from Homer, who for speed often begins with an accusative pronoun, which Milton imitates with the pronoun *him*, for example, *ton d'apameibomenos prosephê podas ôkus Achilleus* ("[to] him replying spoke swift-footed Achilles"), and the identical phrase with a change at the end, *kreiôn Agamemenôn* ("[to] him replying spoke lordly Agamemnon"), and so on; or when Achilles addresses Athena, *ten d'apameibomenos* (*Iliad*, 1.85, 130, 215) "[to] her replying."[7]

There are at least two other moments like the unexpected enjambment at line 43: at line 46, "combustion down / To bottomless perdition"; and the "little closure," or *clausula*, of line 48, "In adamantine chains and penal fire," which leaves us unprepared for the following relative clause: "Who durst defy th'Omnipotent to arms."

The passage goes up one steep side and descends on the other. We climb upward to line 43—"Raised impious war in Heav'n and battle proud"—which is rhythmically extended into line 44, "With vain attempt," although this rhythmical extension is also the beginning of the descent, as its meaning implies. Satan's attempt, "Against the throne and monarchy of God," so impressive just a moment ago, is a vain, empty act. Its punishment follows, contemptuously reducing Satan to an accusative pronoun, "Him," and naming the punisher in a manner suitable to the action to follow, "the Almighty Pow'r."

We note also how the six ascending lines tend to abstraction. They are sonorous, not visual or sensuous. But in the second half of the passage the only faintly abstract word is *perdition*, although when modified by *bottomless* we feel it in the pit of our stomachs. Otherwise the second part of the passage is astonishingly visual, as if the lights have just been turned on for us. We see something hurled forth and shooting down in flames out of the blue, making a long arc toward the horizon as it descends through the sky, collapsing and exploding as it falls (in *ruin* Milton recalls, L. *ruor*, "to collapse"). It falls into a place without any bottom, and yet is chained there with unbreakable bonds. *Adamant* is the hardest substance, and in Homer *adamantinos* is an epithet of Hades, the king of the underworld. The falling thing is also roasted with more punishing fire, for there is indeed something thing-like about Satan in his fall. Or is he a thing, after all, when he lands? The last line begins with a relative personal pronoun, "Who durst defy th'Omnipotent to arms," only now reminding us that this explosive, collapsing descent, ending in bottomless perdition and chains, is endured by a conscious, willing agent, one who has challenged "the throne and monarchy of God." The reconversion of thingly thing, a giant meteor, back into a conscious agent prepares us for the lines to follow, in which Satan "with his horrid crew" lies for nine days unconscious, "rolling in the fiery gulf." He is still the mere thing that he was, now a damp squib, senselessly rolled over and over again in the flood. But he will revive:

> Nine times the space that measures day and night
> To mortal men he with his horrid crew
> Lay vanquished rolling in the fiery gulf
> Confounded though immortal. But his doom
> Reserved him to more wrath, for now the thought
> Both of lost happiness and lasting pain
> Torments him. Round he throws his baleful eyes
> That witnessed huge affliction and dismay
> Mixed with obdúrate pride and steadfast hate.
>
> (PL, *1.50–58*)

The frequency of enjambments has risen (only line 52 stands independent). The narrative opens the scene on Satan and his army of fallen angels rolling, as I said, like dismasted hulks on a sea of fire. Because they are immortal, destined to awaken, and to do something, the verse hurtles on as our attention is directed to the interiority of the conscious agent that suffers: "his doom / Reserved him to more wrath." This new and worse suffering is not of the body but of the mind. We are to imagine Satan reflecting on what he has lost in the past, and of what he must endure in the future—forever. Forever isn't even the future. It is a *now* from which there is no escape. We are then transported outside Satan's mind to see that his psychical torment shines forth in his "baleful eyes." We wake when he wakes; we see him when we see his eyes, as if they are looking at us. The sympathy we cannot avoid having in response to the description of Satan's mental torture (it is stronger than any sympathy we have for his being physically burned), is now stopped by the eyes of a predator, the red eyes we see at night in the dark. We now know he is not only the enemy of God but more especially of us, and he is coming our way.

The passage divides in two parts in the way the previous passage did, at line 53: "Confounded though immortal. But his doom." This time, however, the division is not between an ascent and a descent but between, on the one hand, a scanning view of Satan and his army on the fiery lake and, on the other hand, a brief, inner experience of his mind. We recognize here that if "bottomless perdition" is not literally true of Hell, when Hell is considered spatially, bottomlessness *is* true, and more terribly true, of the rebel angels' punishment in Hell. Milton's word alludes to the etymology of *abyss*. It is bottomless duration, a present that cannot become anything else. That is why any thought of escape from the merely spatial structure of Hell is as vain as Satan's earlier attempt "Against the throne and monarchy of God."

Only now, when this point is established, do we begin to look around at the physical structure of Hell. But we look at it—and it is a wonderful touch, learned from Virgil—through Satan's eyes. Later, we have our first panoramic sight of the Garden of Eden through Satan's eyes, when he is perched like a cormorant on the Tree of Life, and gazes around him. In an early plan of *Paradise Lost* as a drama, Milton has Moses "prologuizing" (προλογίζει) to the audience, saying that they cannot see Adam in the state of innocence "by reason of thire sin" (*Columbia*, 18:229). That intuition is beautifully recaptured in *Paradise Lost* when our first sight of Eden, and of Adam and Eve, is through Satan's eyes, by reason of our sin. Here, in Hell, Satan gazes around his prison, his baleful eyes turning like a periscope:

> At once as far as angels' ken he views
> The dismal situation waste and wild:
> A dungeon horrible on all sides round
> As one great furnace flamed, yet from those flames
> No light but rather darkness visible
> Served only to discover sights of woe,
> Regions of sorrow, doleful shades, where peace
> And rest can never dwell, hope never comes
> That comes to all, but torture without end
> Still urges, and a fiery deluge fed
> With ever-burning sulfur unconsumed.
>
> (PL, *1.59–69*)

Though all but two lines (60 and 64) are enjambed, this passage is not (like the former one) impetuous and unbalanced in its forward rush. Instead, the verse proceeds with measured pace, increasing and varying the torture with every new phrase. Being an angel himself, Satan sees as far as angels can see, which is very far, farther than the length of the cosmos, yet he cannot see beyond the wilderness of his torment, "waste and wild." That very limitlessness, however, is now refigured as what it is: a dungeon, flaming on all sides, because endlessness itself is a limit to hope and an absolute limit to escape. As with the bottomless bottom of the fiery lake, what seems a contradiction stands revealed as a dreadful bifurcation into two ways of suffering one thing: claustrophobic panic and agoraphobic despair.

From falling through the bottomless bottom to suffocating in the limitless enclosure we pass on to another contradiction, which is, again, sublimely overcome: "yet from those flames / No light but rather darkness visible." How can there be vision in the dark? No light issues from the flames because light is a good thing, the effluence of God: "Bright effluence of bright essence increate" (PL, 3.6). There is something primordially comforting about light, when night is past and with it the terrors of the night. Light gives us hope. Death tends to come in the early morning hours, before hope for another day appears with the dawn. Even the smoky light of a torch is preferable to the dark. The flames in hell do not afford even the slight comfort of torchlight but only such visibility as terrors require in order to terrify more, to reveal "sights of woe." Those sights are described as a vaguely psychologized landscape— "regions of sorrow, doleful shades, where peace / And rest can never dwell"—and in this moment we recognize how darkness can be visible: by translating space into time. Time has its usual emotional rhythms, which are here made unusual by being deprived of all relief. In even the most reduced life (one thinks of the works of Samuel Beckett) rest comes inevitably, however poor it is, if one survives. Sorrow inexplicably lifts; cheerfulness unjustifiably arises; and peace settles upon us, if only because exhaustion drives wild sorrow off for the time being. If you have nothing else to hope for, you can at least hope for that, the reprieve of exhaustion. Such hope "comes to all." But not here, not for Satan. Wild sorrow is his inner condition, carefully concealed from the rebel angels he will master and command. The "darkness visible" that serves "only to discover sights of woe" is the state of perfect mental clarity in which one understands there isn't any hope, nor will there be rest or relief. Speaking subjectively, the flames of Hell *are* Satan's mental clarity, showing him the agony of torture without end.

Once this inner mental meaning of the flames is established, our perspective on them is changed to the outer world again, where they are a raging storm of falling and enveloping chemical torment: "a fiery deluge fed / With ever-burning sulfur unconsumed." The fire is unconsumed because inexhaustible, but we realize as soon as we think this that the fuel—the physical bodies of the devils, and the clarity of their minds—is unconsumed, too. The surviving clarity of a fallen angel's mind is the flame of Hell. That is a thought as majestic as any in Dante. We note how this splendid line, "With ever-burning sulfur unconsumed"—marks the most definitive break in the verse we have encountered since line 26, "And justify the ways of God to men" ("*JUStiFY* the *WAYS* of *GOD* to *MEN*"). It has the identical trochaic rhythm of the earlier line, the five strong accents falling on the first syllables: "*EVer, BURning, SULfur UNconsUM'D.*" The trochees fall like hammer blows.

Now the poet resumes his more detached, narrative voice, the voice that is not only describing what it wants us to see but speaking to us about it, telling us that the prison was made in advance (how far in advance is explained later: just in time, while the rebel angels were actually falling) and giving more precise information about its placement, as far from Heaven as three times the distance from the center of the earth to the uppermost pole of the cosmos:

> Such place Eternal Justice had prepared
> For those rebellious, here their pris'n ordained
> In utter darkness and their portion set
> As far removed from God and light of Heav'n
> As from the center thrice to th'utmost pole.
> O how unlike the place from whence they fell!
>
> (PL, *1.70–75*)

Four of the six lines are enjambed, but they fall between the firm stops of line 69, "With ever-burning sulfur unconsumed," and line 74, "As from the center thrice to th'utmost pole," which is then followed by another self-sufficient and freestanding line: "O how unlike the place from whence they fell!" That emotional exclamation gives us a strong break and a pause within which we can step back and consider the entire scene before us, from Heaven down to Hell, a scene that will later be filled out in wonderful detail and with magnificent power. For the present, the line reminds us of another place, Heaven, which we will see. That place will be entirely in contrast to this one, as ecstatically pleasing as Hell is relentlessly cruel. The contrast allows the poet briefly to return to the description of Hell, "With floods and whirlwinds of tempestuous fire," while introducing Satan again, so that at last he may speak.

To do so, the passage must also introduce the addressee of Satan's first words in the poem: his nearest associate among the devils. At present this mate is "weltering" (that is, "rolling") beside Satan in the flood. It is of course Beëlzebub, or Baal-Zebub, the "Lord of the Flies," a Philistine god who in Matthew 12:24 is called "the prince of the devils" *(archonti tôn daimoniôn):*

> There the companions of his fall o'erwhelmed
> With floods and whirlwinds of tempestuous fire
> He soon discerns. And welt'ring by his side
> One next himself in pow'r and next in crime,
> Long after known in Palestine and named

Beëlzebub. To whom th'Arch-Enemy,
And thence in Heav'n called *Satan*, with bold words
Breaking the horrid silence thus began:

> (PL, *1.76–83*)

Enemy is a translation of Hebrew *ha satan*, "the adversary." Satan is the *arch*enemy in the Greek sense of the word as originative as well as original: he is the first enemy as well as the cause and source of all enemies since. Of the three enjambments, the first two (lines 76, 77) take us back for a moment to the spectacular violence of Satan's fall and the relentlessness of his torment in Hell. After that, the passage begins to climb toward the opening of the first speech in *Paradise Lost*, that of Satan himself. The only remaining enjambment in the passage is at line 80, before the name "Beëlzebub," and the reason is the same as that for the placement of "Th'infernal serpent" at the beginning of the line, after the epic question. Here the effect is especially powerful because of the menacingly obscene exoticism of the name, "Long after known in Palestine."

With that phrase, Milton introduces one of the most brilliant ideas of *Paradise Lost*, which is to bring in here the false gods in the Bible that tempted the nation of Israel to abandon their God, causing the Israelites to commit idolatry in vicious, cruel, and obscene forms of worship, including the sacrifice of children. He will name the chief devils by the names they would later assume as they sought to draw human worship away from God. In "On the Morning of Christ's Nativity," the twenty-one-year-old Milton imagined the pagan gods—the gods of Palestine as well as of Greece and of Egypt—being driven back to Hell at the birth of Christ:

And sullen Moloch fled,
Hath left in shadows dread,
His burning idol all of blackest hue.
In vain with cymbals' ring
They call the grisly king,
In dismal dance about the furnace blue.
The brutish gods of Nile as fast,
Isis and Orus, and the dog Anubis haste.

> (*"On the Morning of Christ's Nativity," lines 205–12*)

The Greek gods are included in this cleansing of the world:

> The oracles are dumb,
> No voice nor hideous hum
> Runs through the archèd roof in words deceiving.

Milton is more explicit about Moloch in the first of the Hell books of *Paradise Lost*, giving us, first, an indication of how children were sacrificed to him—they were thrown into the mouth of a brass idol representing the god and incinerated—second, how music was played by attendants so the parents could not hear the screams; third, how he was worshipped in Israel's neighboring lands, on the other side of the Jordan River and across the Dead Sea; and, fourth, how Solomon built a temple for him on the Mount of Olives—just opposite the Temple Mount—and in the valley between these hills, called Hinnom, Tophet, and Gehenna, where, according to Jeremiah (7:21), the Israelites "burn[ed] their sons and daughters in the fire":

> First Moloch, horrid king, besmeared with blood
> Of human sacrifice and parents' tears,
> Though for the noise of drums and timbrels loud
> Their children's cries unheard that passed through fire
> To his grim idol. Him the Ammonite
> Worshipped in Rabba and her wat'ry plain,
> In Argon and in Basan to the stream
> Of utmost Arnon. Not content with such
> Audacious neighborhood the wisest heart
> Of Solomon he led by fraud to build
> His temple right against the templ' of God
> On that opprobrious hill and made his grove
> The pleasant valley of Hinnom, Tophet thence
> And black Gehenna called, the type of Hell.
>
> (PL, *1.392–405*)

As in "On the Morning of Christ's Nativity," Milton mentions the nonbiblical gods of the pagans, as well, including the Greek gods, but his store of information is much greater now: "Then were they known to men by various names / And various idols through the heathen world" (*PL*, 1.374–75). This idea leads to a spectacular epic catalogue, which is the virtuosic showpiece of book 1 of *Paradise Lost*. With its elaborate invocation of the muse, it corresponds delightfully with Homer's more elaborate invocation of the muses before the great catalogue of ships in the *Iliad*, listing the commanders of the Achaean forces and of the Trojans and their allies. The feat of memory represented by the catalogue, preceded by a special invocation of the muse or the muses for aid in achieving such a feat, was an established feature of the epic tradition, famously imitated—but with much more literary elaborateness, in contrast with Homer's "divine simplicity"—in Virgil's catalogue of the leaders of the Italian federation opposing Aeneas and the Trojans.[8] Milton's catalogue of the devils likewise cultivates complex literary effects, visual cameos, allusions to rites and future history, and so on. Beginning with the invocation, "Say Muse, their names then known, who first, who last / Roused from their slumber on that fiery couch" (*PL*, 1.376–77) and ending with "All these and more came flocking" (*PL*, 1.522), Milton's catalogue is 146 lines in length, as compared with Virgil's 203 and Homer's massive 383. With wonderful biblical detail, supplemented by Plutarch on the gods of Egypt and John Selden on the gods of Syria and Palestine, Milton gives an account of leaders of the devils who are marshaled in Hell, on the "bare strand" (*PL*, 1.379) beside its burning lake, raising "A forest of huge spears and thronging helms" above "serried shields in thick array / Of depth immeasurable" (*PL*, 1.547–49).[9] They are marshaled to the sound of trumpets and clarions as Satan's "mighty standard" is raised (*PL*, 1.533). But once marshaled they move forward, "Breathing united force" (*PL*, 1.560) like Homer's Achaeans, and like the noblest heroes of old, Milton says, showing cool, "Deliberate valor" (*PL*, 1.554). One might have expected Milton to show the devils as Homer shows the Trojans, in contrast with the Achaeans, advancing noisily, like a flock of birds, crying out excitedly in many languages. It would be a subtle way to undercut the devils' presumed nobility, making them a cruel but unvalorous horde. Milton has done so in an earlier place, just before the catalogue, when newly awakened devils, flying off the burning lake, are compared first to the "pitchy cloud" of swarming locusts in Egypt, called up by the "potent rod" of Moses (*PL*, 1.338). They are here directed by Satan, as an oriental sultan, indicating their landing-places with his "uplifted spear":

> Till as a signal giv'n th'uplifted spear
> Of their great sultan waving to direct

> Their course in even balance down they light
> On the firm brimstone and fill all the plain.
>
> (PL, *1.347–50*)

This is followed immediately by another simile suggesting barbarism, although the barbarians in question are not oriental but northern. They are the hordes that descended from the frozen regions under the pole to cross the northern boundaries or *limes* of the Roman Empire, the Rhine and Danube Rivers (Milton's *Rhene* and *Danaw*) into the Roman provinces and eventually into Italy itself, destroying the empire. Some of them, the Vandals, conquered through Spain, another Roman province, crossing from Gibraltar to establish barbarian kingdoms in four provinces of North Africa, the last being Cyrenaica, next to Egypt— Milton's *Libyan sands*. In five verses, which is rather less space than Gibbon will afford the subject, Milton evokes the gathering momentum of the disaster that ended ancient civilization:

> A multitude like which the populous north
> Poured never from her frozen loins to pass
> Rhene or the Danaw when her barbarous sons
> Came like a deluge on the south and spread
> Beneath Gibraltar to the Libyan sands.
>
> (PL, *1.351–55*)

Only after the poet's catalogue do the devils acquire the order and discipline with which they are represented advancing silently, breathing deliberate valor, to the tune of flutes, like the fearsome Spartan infantry. Milton's purpose is to magnify the threat—for no army can or will oppose them—and to magnify Satan, thus making him more fearsome. But we cannot be wholly insensible to the admiration Milton is expressing, and perhaps also wishes us to feel.

The catalogue itself does something more striking, which is to name the leaders of the devils after idolatrous gods worshipped by humans much later, in history, after the fall of Adam and Eve, when obscene idolatries will flourish. They will do so because the devils wish to seduce human worship away from the worship of the true God, and so to compound human sinfulness, thus winning more souls for Hell. The devils' names in Heaven are lost, "blotted out and razed" (*PL*, 1.362) and they can be known and named now only according to what they will become.[10] To give himself aid for accomplishing this superhuman task of historical reconstruction, nothing less than what Kierkegaard would call recollecting forward, the poet reinvokes the muse:[11]

> Say, Muse, their names then known, who first, who last,
> Roused from the slumber on that fiery couch
> At their great emperor's call, as next in worth,
> Came singly where he stood on the bare strand
> While the promiscuous crowd stood yet aloof.
>
> > (PL, *1.376–80)*

Promiscuous means "mixed," undistinguished one from another, unlike the leading devils, who will speak individually at the "great consúlt" (*PL*, 1.798). These gods are seen here as gigantic devils, that is, as they truly are and as they were long before they assumed their divine roles in the human world around the Mediterranean, whether of Apollo or Hephaestus among the Greeks or Beëlzebub and Moloch among the Philistines and Moabites:

> By falsities and lies the greatest part
> Of mankind they corrupted to forsake
> God their Creator . . .
> And devils to adore for deities.
>
> > (PL, *1.367–73)*

That development is still far off in the future, which is why Beëlzebub is known "long after" in Palestine. His present name is never given, nor is that of any other rebel angel: "Though of their names in Heav'nly records now / Be no memorial, blotted out and razed / By their rebellion from the books of life" (*PL*, 1.361–63).

In his famous preface to *Cromwell* (1827), the manifesto of the Romantic movement, Victor Hugo identified drama as the quintessential modern form of expression. Milton adopted the verse, or measure, of *Paradise Lost* from the stage, from "our best English tragedies," as he said, and indeed *Paradise Lost* began life as a baroque tragedy, modeled on the Italian *dramma per musica* and early opera. The early plan has elements that resemble the pageantry masque, except, of course, that it is tragic. It is perhaps futile to attempt to determine the genre of a proposed drama that never existed in more than four very brief drafts in the Trinity manuscript, before it was transformed into a classical epic. Of that astounding transformation we have no evidence at all, except for one passage in the epic, part of a speech of Satan's, of which more in a moment, which was reported to belong to yet another draft, a longer one, which has not survived.

The third and fourth drafts both have a chorus of angels singing at the end of each act, and they carry over from the first two drafts (which are merely untitled lists of *dramatis personae*) a small cast of biblical characters—Michael, Moses, Adam and Eve, Satan, called "Lucifer"— plus numerous personified abstractions, some speaking and debating, such as Justice, Mercy, Wisdom, Heavenly Love, the Evening Star, and Conscience. Others mutely process before Adam and Eve after the Fall: Labor, Grief, Hatred, Envy, War, Famine, Pestilence, and so on, to Death, fifteen named personifications, plus a trailing "& etc." These represent to Adam and Eve the consequences of their Fall, and as the figures pass they are named by an informative angel who is not himself named, although this function will eventually be discharged by Michael in *Paradise Lost*, when Adam sees the pageant of history. By that time the personifications will be translated into actual scenes from human history, most of them extrapolated from the Bible and recollected forward. Not biblical, however, is the hospital scene in which Michael shows Adam actual sicknesses, instead of mere abstractions: "Convulsions, epilepsies, fierce catarrhs, / Intestine stone and ulcer, colic pangs . . . pining atrophy, / Marasmus and wide-wasting pestilence" (*PL*, 11.483–87). It should be noted, however, that abstract personifications continue to stalk this scene in *Paradise Lost*: "Despair / Tended the sick busiest from couch to couch / And over them triumphant Death his dart / Shook, but delayed to strike though oft invoked" (*PL*, 11.489–92). In *Adam Unparadized*, after witnessing this depressing allegorical spectacle, our hero is comforted and instructed by Faith, Hope, and Charity (Eve is present, but the focus is on Adam). The chorus then briefly concludes. The drama would doubtless have been much better than this description makes it sound, and the differences between the third and fourth drafts show Milton already thinking out a more dramatic presentation and connection of scenes, which thinking would lead ultimately to his changing his plan from a drama to an epic poem. We see this especially with the figure of Lucifer, who, as it says in the fourth draft, "appears after his overthrow, bemoans himself, [and] seeks revenge on man." These words designate a speech of Satan's that Milton would compose later, when he was still thinking of the work as a tragedy. According to the testimony of Milton's nephew Edward Phillips, the speech survives in ten lines of the completed *Paradise Lost:* "This subject was first designed for a tragedy, and in the fourth book of the poem there are ten verses which several years before the poem was begun were shown to me, and some others, as designed for the very beginning of the said tragedy. The verses are these."[12] Phillips then quotes the lines:

> O thou that with surpassing glory crowned
> Look'st from thy sole dominion like the god
> Of this new world, at whose sight all the stars
> Hide their diminished heads, to thee I call
> But with no friendly voice and add thy name,
> O Sun, to tell thee how I hate thy beams
> That bring to my remembrance from what state
> I fell, how glorious once above thy sphere,
> Till pride and worse ambition threw me down,
> Warring in Heav'n against Heav'n's matchless King.
>
> *(PL, 4.32–41)*

This moment in the draft is of interest for several reasons, not least because one of the greatest characters in English literature makes his trace-like appearance for the first time. We have come a long way from "The old dragon under ground" who in rage "Swinges the scaly horror of his folded tail" ("On the Morning of Christ's Nativity," lines 168, 172). Lucifer is merely named in drafts one and two, and is described in only four words in draft three: "Lucifer contriving Adam's ruin." Milton first chose this odd name, which means "Light Bearer" and refers to the Morning Star (employed in the Latin translation of Isaiah 14:12), because in the early Christian tradition "Lucifer" refers to Satan at the time of his rebellion and defeat, before he became "the enemy" Satan, the name by which he is introduced and consistently referred to in *Paradise Lost:* "th'Arch-Enemy, / And thence in Heav'n called *Satan*" (*PL,* 1.81–82). In *Paradise Lost* Milton keeps to himself whatever Satan's name was in Heaven before he fell, after which he was 'thence' referred to in Heaven as *Satan.* A curious passage in Book Five shows Milton by this time had scholarly doubts that *Lucifer* was Satan's original, Heavenly name. The passage occurs when Satan withdraws to his palace or "royal seat" (*PL*, 5.756) in the north parts of Heaven to begin his rebellion: "The palace of great Lucifer (so call / That structure in the dialect of men / Interpreted)" (*PL*, 5.760–62). *Lucifer* is now a human translation in the dialect of men ("interpreted" means "translated") of an original Heavenly word that is no longer known, one standing behind the Hebrew word *helel*, "shining one." In Luke 10:18 Jesus says he saw Satan, or "the Satan" *(ton Satanan)*, fall like lightning from Heaven. This passage was associated with the one in the prophet Isaiah comparing the king of Babylon to the morning star, the "shining one, son of the dawn" *(helel ben shachar):* "How you have fallen from Heaven, O star of the morning, son of the dawn!" In line 74 of "On the Morning of Christ's Nativity"—"Or Lucifer that often warned them thence"— Milton uses this name simply to refer to the morning star (our planet Venus), who commands the lingering night stars to depart from the sky. No association of *Lucifer* with *Satan* is intended there.

Perhaps Milton's shunning the name *Lucifer* in *Paradise Lost* had something to do with the morning star's being insufficiently bright, as compared with the brilliance of Satan before he fell, when he was far brighter even than the sun. That at least is implied in those ten verses Edward Phillips saw, when the great work was still undergoing its metamorphosis from a baroque tragedy displaying the Fall of Man to an epic on the consequences and meaning of the Fall. Satan's address to the sun now stands near the outset of book 4 of *Paradise Lost*, once Satan has descended to earth and landed on the top of Mount Niphates. The verses open a long and passionate soliloquy, Satan's first (which in the previous chapter I suggested has proto-operatic effects), in which he reflects on the disaster of his rebellion against God and draws a picture for us of the psychological torment he suffers ("Which way I fly is Hell, myself am Hell," [*PL*, 4.75]). Once again, we see his mental torment is worse than the physical pains of Hell. In this long soliloquy, Satan reviews why he rebelled against God; why God did not deserve such perfidy; how God's love is now to him a curse; how he, Satan, deceived the angels he led into rebellion; how he continues to deceive them with his empty vaunting; how intense but concealed his suffering is; how hopeless is any thought of submission, because he would only rebel again; how pointless, therefore, is any thought of pity or remorse; how resolute he is to promote evil as something good for him ("Evil, be thou my good" [*PL*, 4.110]); and how fixed his purpose is on the destruction of humankind.

The opening ten lines of the speech, the ones Milton originally placed as the opening of a tragedy, are in a different vein from all this, but their effect is marvelously complementary to these inward thoughts. As we have seen, instead of talking to himself in a soliloquy, Satan addresses hostile words to the sun, modulating—at the exclamation, "Ah wherefore!"—into inner debate with himself. He does so only after that outward address is complete, as if turning from the sun in contempt:

> O thou that with surpassing glory crowned
> Look'st from thy sole dominion like the god
> Of this new world, at whose sight all the stars
> Hide their diminished heads, to thee I call
> But with no friendly voice, and add thy name,
> O Sun, to tell thee how I hate thy beams
> That bring to my remembrance from what state
> I fell, how glorious once above thy sphere
> Till pride and worse ambition threw me down,
> Warring against Heav'n against Heav'ns matchless King.
> Ah wherefore!
>
> (*PL, 4.32–41*)

That "Ah wherefore!" may have been written as many as fifteen years after the line preceding it, when Satan recalls, "Warring in Heav'n against Heav'ns matchless King." I called the change a modulation, because the earlier passage is so neatly mortised into the later one. When the proud assertion of having warred in Heaven against its matchless king is joined to the passionate question, "ah! wherefore?" we have the beginning of the to-and-fro struggle between defiance and abjection, fight and fright, that now unfolds in Satan's mind. But we should not miss the abruptness, as well. He tells the sun why he hates the sun's beams—because they make him remember he too was once bright, brighter than the sun, which now shines down on him with superior brightness. (Unbeknownst to him, the regent of the sun, Uriel, is at this moment observing his wild gesticulations and threats.) After Satan tells the sun he was "glorious above *thy* sphere"—we note the Ptolemaic language of crystalline *spheres*, which is more in keeping with Milton's ideas in the 1640s—the process of introspection begins, as the mind by "wily subtleties and refluxes" (*YP*, 1:817), to use Milton's phrase in another context, is turned back on itself: "Till pride and worse ambition threw me down." (The sense of pride is very bad indeed, but ambition is even worse, because ambition is pride put into action.) The line is especially striking because it is the first time since Satan woke in Hell—and we have seen much of him since then, addressing the devils in Hell, confronting Sin and Death at the gate of Hell, flying across chaos and speaking to Chaos himself, landing on the outer shell of the cosmos, flying down through an aperture in that shell to the sun, disguising himself and speaking to the regent of the sun, Uriel, and then flying down to the top of Mount Niphates—that he tells us what it is like inside his mind. In book 1 it is the narrator who tells us what it is like inside Satan's mind; we do not hear him confess it: "But his doom / Reserved him to more wrath, for now the thought / Both of lost happiness and lasting pain / Torments him" (*PL*, 1.54–56). It is the narrator in book 1 who insists on the difference between what Satan says and what he feels: "So spake th'Apostate Angel, though in pain, / Vaunting aloud but racked with deep despair" (*PL*, 1125–26). Moments such as this one have been taken to reveal a flaw in the poet's handling of Satan because Satan is "very dangerous for Milton's scheme," to quote from the classic statement of this position, by A. J. A. Waldock, decrying the "long line of automatic snubs [and] perfunctory jabs" To see the claim that Satan's being "racked with deep despair" as equal in authority to his "vaunting aloud" "is surely very naive critical procedure."[13] The implication is that Milton is naive or incompetent, at least in his handling of Satan.

Waldock's influential book created a dilemma that lasted twenty years, until Stanley Fish finessed it, in a book that bears its argument in its title: *Surprised by Sin: The Reader in "Paradise Lost."* The reader finds herself or himself lured into agreement with Satan—later, into agreement with the sinning Eve and the sinning Adam—and then corrected again by Milton (by the text) in the course of reading on. After our psychological participation in the sin we read of in the poem, a participation the poet himself draws us into, we are suddenly drawn up short and implicitly chastised. The reader is the focus of the poet's art, which is experienced as a corrective or cybernetic process. What might have been, and was, a difference of opinion *among* readers—Satanists versus traditionalists—turns out to be a difference Milton has cunningly started up in the mind of the *individual* reader.[14] Milton, at least, is exonerated, while it is the reader who is subject to those perfunctory but efficacious jabs.

Once they become lodged in the tradition, critical dilemmas are resilient things. But the starting point in Waldock seems to me a wild misjudgment. In fact, the moment in which we see Satan's inward despair in contrast with his outward vaunting has nothing like the effect on us Waldock describes: of perceiving "anxiousness" in the poet because the vaunting is a "demonstration" we have just read in Satan's speech, whereas the despair is an irresponsible "allegation" having "no comparable authority." This distinction can have no authority whatever in a narrative poem. What is called the "demonstration," Satan's vaunting speech, is just as much "alleged" by the poet as is the despair; it is merely "alleged" at more length. Milton's Satan is entirely imagined. Satan's despair will be described at length—or "alleged" at length—later in the poem. The single verse—"Vaunting aloud but racked with deep despair"—far from being the collapsing balloon Waldock presents it as being, is terrific and sublime. It projects the terrible majesty of Satan's character in two directions. We have seen it extended far outward, in a forty-line speech that climbs upward from abjection ("into what pit thou see'st / From what heighth fall'n" [*PL*, 1.91–92]) to soaring defiance:

> We may with more successful hope resolve
> To wage by force or guile eternal war
> Irreconcilable to our grand Foe
> Who now triúmphs and in th'excess of joy
> Sole reigning holds the tyranny of Heav'n.
> So spake th'Apostate Angel though in pain,
> Vaunting aloud but racked with deep despair.
>
> > (PL, *1.120–26*)

That addition, "but racked with deep despair," discloses to us, at a stroke, that the soaring defiance has at least an equal and perhaps a greater opposite motion, one leading inward, into to a psychological abyss. This is what we hear later from Satan himself, and we are now allowed to look into that abyss:

> Which way I fly is Hell, myself am Hell,
> And in the lowest deep a lower deep
> Still threat'ning to devour me opens wide,
> To which the Hell I suffer seems a Heaven.
>
> (PL, *4.75–78*)

In book 1, this inner abyss comes upon us like a flash of lighting in the dark, illuminating the landscape for only an instant, but assuring us of its existence.

The last moment of a pathos we are shown in book 1 comes when Satan is about to address the fallen angels he has called up from the lake of Hell and marshaled to war:

> Attention held them mute.
> Thrice he assayed and thrice, in spite of scorn,
> Tears such as angels weep burst forth. At last
> Words interwove with sighs found out their way
>
> (PL, *1.619–21*)

He is still an angel, although he is rapidly decaying from his original state. We are touched for a moment by his being moved to tears by what he sees before him (the three times is a Virgilian formula): "O myriads of immortal spirits, O Pow'rs / Matchless but with th'Almighty" (*PL*, 1.622–23). Even this great moment does not match in power the confession Satan makes in book 4, when he is alone: "Till pride and worse ambition threw me down" (*PL*, 4.40). The phrase is coldly factual. Satan's refusal either to extenuate or to exaggerate what he has done is now seen as coldly by us as Satan sees it himself. This settles our view of him, so that we are prepared for what is to come, an experience of what it is like in Satan's mind: "Me miserable! Which way shall I fly / Infinite wrath and infinite despair?" (*PL*, 4.73–74). The wrath of God being infinite, the despair of Satan must be, too. But the wrath of God is the cold contemplation of evil punishing itself. After a moment's reflection we begin to see that this fiery and intense wrath, which Satan calls infinite, is generated within him. He is entirely alone in the dungeon of himself, where his own wrath pursues his own despair.

It is worth recalling that "Till pride and worse ambition threw me down" was written long before the rest of *Paradise Lost* was composed, when Milton was thinking of a tragedy instead. The tragedy would of course have been the tragedy of Adam and Eve, but the majesty of Satan's evil comes in large measure from tragic potential. Satan talks like a tragic hero, and like a tragic hero he is ground between the contrary engines of fate, the difference being that these engines are not, as they are for a tragic hero, outside him, in the world. Disastrously free, and being an environment to himself ("Myself am Hell"), Satan has borne inside him his own fate and the necessity that follows from his terrible choice. This confers on Satan's torment a greater majesty still:

> The more I see
> Pleasures about me so much more I feel
> Torment within me as from the hateful siege
> Of contraries: all good to me becomes
> Bane.
>
> (PL, *9.119–23*)

He is not so much a cosmos to himself as he is an anti-cosmos, a chaosmos, enclosed on itself, always flying apart, as in an explosion, but unable to achieve release from the pressure within, not even that of collapse and dissipation. Satan is a strangled explosion.

How are these effects produced by the verse? Could they ever have been achieved in rhyme, as Byron supposed? In the background of this verse is a fascinating effect not unlike the resonance produced by a guitar played in an open tuning: a seemingly articulate but unintelligible drone still to be heard in major long poetry today, for example, in the longer poems of John Ashbery and James Merrill. It is like the rumble and noise of the world, a resonance that is pushed into the background, where it continues, a dark *sostenuto*. This is the effect Matthew Arnold was referring to when he said, "Milton has always the sure, strong touch of the master. His power both of diction and of rhythm is unsurpassable, and it is characterized by being always present—not depending on an access of emotion, not intermittent."[15]

It was not for nothing that unrhymed, decasyllabic poetry with varying end-stops and enjambments was called "blank verse," for when it appeared around the middle of the sixteenth century, in Richard Stanyhurst's partial translation of the *Aeneid*, and then on the English stage, in the tragedies of Marlowe and Kyd, and again in Shakespeare's mature tragedies in the early years of the seventeenth century, it did not sound like poetry: it sounded like passionate speech. Surely poetry should sound poetical. Or surely it should not.

Milton's blank verse, inherited from the stage, was the beginning of the great modern bifurcation of poetry from the poetical, such that for one side, true poetry, deep poetry, just barely escapes sounding like poetry and sounds instead like passionate or complicated or in some other way interesting speech.

Milton's comparison of his verse to that of Homer and Virgil is accurate enough, and it is justified by the high seriousness and rapid movement of *Paradise Lost.* I mentioned that the hexameter line in these ancient poets stands out more distinctly than does the shorter, usually ten-syllable blank verse line of *Paradise Lost.* The quantitative, ancient hexameter line generally runs to fourteen or more syllables. You can see and hear the difference when you compare the measure of *Paradise Lost* with the "fourteeners" of Arthur Golding's translation of Ovid's *Metamorphoses* or George Chapman's translation of Homer's *Iliad*, on which Keats wrote a famous sonnet, "On First Looking into Chapman's Homer." Keats must have been more disconcerted than he lets on. English fourteeners do not have the rapidity of the quantitative verses of Homer, Virgil, or Ovid—indeed, to our ears they are tedious, unless they break down into ballad measure, which is also tedious—but they do show how each line remains distinct, as compared with blank verse. The ancient hexameter line is never submerged in larger syntactical structures, even when there are strong enjambments, because these do not reach as far as the caesura, or medial pause, in the following line. The caesura therefore does not become what it does become in *Paradise Lost:* a frequent and pronounced stopping place equal to the end of a line, such that the ear often loses the difference between the middle and the end of the line. If you listen to *Paradise Lost* being read for any length of time, there will be moments where you cannot tell whether the slight pause in the verse is coming from the end or the middle of a line.

The reading eye, following in the text, does not lose this difference. Milton was blind when he composed *Paradise Lost*, and the poem is primarily an artifact in sound, which the poet himself never *wrote*, that is, inscribed with a writing instrument. He shaped it with his mouth, his palate, his tongue, teeth, and lips, sculpting the breath that rose from his lungs to pass across his vocal cords. When I say *Paradise Lost* is an artifact in sound I do not mean to say the poem can be appreciated only by being read aloud. I mean that even when reading it silently, *Paradise Lost* is a poem you hear, because it excites the acoustic imagination.[16] I have heard that when we read silently nerve signals are still sent to the muscles of the throat and the tongue, which are imperceptibly activated, as if we were ourselves speaking the sounds we imagine—as a sleeping dog's feet twitch when it dreams it is running. This account seems plausible to me because of the exceptional strength of the aural hallucination we experience when we read, and especially when we read poetry. The hallucination happens more powerfully still when we hear or read music. One thinks of Glenn Gould's involuntary low singing while playing Bach. Unawares, we do something similar, activating the organs of speech, when we read Milton silently. Over the years as we read verse or prose rapidly, and perhaps when we are still very young, we take the strength of the aural experience of reading for granted; we may even learn to suppress it, as anyone who has read large amounts of poetry before an examination will know. It is hard to see afresh the miracle that as one's eyes travel over the lines on the page one's organs of speech—not just one's imagination—are helping one to hear the poet's voice by subtly, imitatively manufacturing the sound. The voice one experiences as Milton's is not his at all but one's own—an imaginary modification of one's voice to mimic Milton's that occurs unawares by our making subtle use of the organs of speech. We read a poem with the body, not with the isolated brain.

Whereas Homer and, perhaps, though to a lesser extent, Virgil composed their poems for oral recitation and acoustic reception, *Paradise Lost*, *Paradise Regained*, and *Samson Agonistes* (Milton said of *Samson* that it was never intended to be performed) are poems that are meant to be seen on the page. The eye has some part in discerning the structure of the individual line, but in doing so it leaves the poet free to build up larger syntactic structures extending through a great many lines—like the mile-long but only inches high ripple of a tsunami, far out at sea. The eye is therefore of some assistance in making the acoustical effect of the poem still more subtle and complex, combining the rhythms of the individual line with the longer rhythm of the sentence, something that is nearly impossible to develop with any consistency when using rhyme, especially couplets. Consider two great English translations: Dryden's translation of the *Aeneid* and Pope's translation of the *Iliad*. In both these translations the unit of attention demanded of the reader seldom reaches more than half a line beyond any couplet. In *Paradise Lost* it can stretch to ten or more lines.

Let us be clear we have understood this point, that the visual cueing supplied by the textual characteristics of *Paradise Lost* does not diminish its acoustical force but rather augments it, in the same way that following a musical score allows one to hear more of the music, that is, to hear things one would not have heard with the unaided ear. One does not at first hear the quiet *ostinato* in the bass line, or when one first began to hear it. It comes upon us, as we say. But one does hear the quiet *ostinato* in the bass line, and one does know exactly when one begins to do so, when one sees it first on the page, cueing the ear. To hear the music fully, you have to see it. So it is with Milton's artifact in sound.

Of particular interest in Milton's note on the verse is the not unprecedented but in his day unusual deployment of the word *expression* to mean what it generally means now: to bring out in words a meaning that is latent but already complete in the mind. Milton's use of it implies something we should expect to be affirmed more naturally of prose, not of poetry: that content—that which is expressed—is more important than form. This privileging of content over the medium of verse suits Milton's hot revolutionary temperament. When the sonorities and rhythmical effects of the verse are in the foreground, creating the sense as it goes, as in *The Faerie Queene*, the effect is of cool involvement in the poetic experience for its own sake.[17] The improvisatory character of the thinking in *The Faerie Queene* allows the story as well as the thought to develop by contingency and unforeseen association, partly as a consequence of rhyme. In *Paradise Lost* the relation of verse to sense is opposite to what it is in *The Faerie Queene*. In *Paradise Lost* the thinking is rigidly structured, and the verse is comparatively free.

Yet structure is certainly there in the verse; it is the recipe for that articulate, underlying drone: "apt numbers, fit quantity of syllables, and the sense variously drawn out from one verse into another." "Apt numbers" means the number of syllables to the line (ten or eleven in the case of an unaccented syllable at the end of the line) in decasyllabic verse. "Fit quantity of syllables" is meant to suggest the varying length of time a syllable is sounded in unrhymed, Greek and Latin "quantitative" verse. The verse of *Paradise Lost* is not quantitative in this sense, however. Earlier Renaissance efforts to domesticate quantitative measure in English—for example, in the eclogues of Sidney's *Arcadia*, and in the letters exchanged between Spenser and Gabriel Harvey—were failures, except for occasional local effects, as in the final line of Spenser's *Shepheardes Calender*. In the stanza with which this line concludes, every line but the last has ten syllables ending in an iamb, a classic iambic pentameter. The last line sounds awkwardly out of step at first because it has eleven syllables and still ends with an iamb, "a**DIEU**." Ending in an unaccented syllable is the only circumstance in which the decasyllabic line may be allowed an extra syllable, as in "The care that budden faire, is burned and blasted" (*The Shepheardes Calender*, "December," line 99):

> Adieu delightes, that lullèd me asleepe,
> Adieu my deare, whose love I bought so deare;
> Adieu my little Lambes and lovèd sheepe,
> Adieu ye Woodes that oft my witnesse were:
> Adieu good *Hobbinol*, that was so true,
> Tell *Rosalind*, her *Colin* bids her adieu.
>
> (The Shepheardes Calender, *"December,"*
> *lines 151–56)*

That last line is far from unsuccessful in English because the extra syllable seems to come in the name *Rosalind*, a dactyl, which breaks up the iambic march-tune of the overregular meter up to that point, giving splendid emphasis to that hallowed name, which can also be shortened to *Ros'lind*. The line is also a success because of the transposition of the word *adieu* from the beginning of each of the previous five lines to the end of the sixth. The effect is deliciously pathetic. Moreover, although the word *adieu* is rhythmically an iamb, its French origin (though in French it has the same rhythm) and elongated final syllable, like the fading note on a flute, has a trailing effect that overcomes, after a moment, its accentual force. "Tell **ROS**alind, her **COL**in, **BIDS** her a**DIEU**ewwww. . . ."

But for the cognoscenti among Spenser's original readers, notably Hobbinol, Gabriel Harvey, what is splendid about that final line is that it can be sounded quantitatively, as well, like the second verse in an elegiac distich: a trochee followed by two spondees, a trochee and a final spondee with the second syllable cut off (/,, // // /,, /). The result is a splendid arch of sound in the middle of the line, when the syllables— *lind her col in bids*—are all drawn out: "**TELL** Rosa**LIND HER COLIN BIDS** her a**DIEU**." It is a good line spoken in the English manner, and a little daring, too, as befits its position, making one pause to think and also pause to feel. But it is an even better line when pronounced in its secret quantitative form. It is best of all when you hear both, which is to say, when you hear either version with the other in the background.

Because *Paradise Lost* is not quantitative in this sense, we may reasonably conclude that the phrase "fit quantity of syllables," is employed to legitimate Milton's choice of "English heroic verse without rhyme, as that of Homer in Greek and of Virgil in Latin." For rhyme, as he goes on to say, "is no necessary adjunct or true ornament of poem or good verse, in longer works especially." It is true that rhyming English verse also has a fixed number of syllables to a line ("apt numbers") and that by enjambment rhyming verse can draw out the sense variously from one verse into another, although certainly not to the degree that blank verse does. Spenser enjambs at least once in every stanza of *The Faerie Queene*, but the enjambment is followed immediately by a strong pause either at the end of the next line or, sooner yet, in the caesura. This may be seen in the following example from the proem to book 3, with enjambments of the first line, ending with *farre*, and of the penultimate line, ending with *constraine*:

> Ne Poets wit, that passeth Painter farre
> In picturing the parts of beautie daint,
> So hard a workmanship adventure darre,
> For fear through want of words her excellence to marre.
>
> How then shall I, Apprentice of the skill,
> That whylome in divinest wits did raine,
> Presume so high to stretch mine humble quill?
> Yet now my luckelesse lot doth me constraine
> Hereto perforce. But O dred Soveraine
>
>   (The Faerie Queene, *3, proem 2–3*)

The slight acceleration that enjambment creates, an increase in forward momentum, is arrested in the following line for the sake of stability, and to keep the harmony of those rhyming terminations in the foreground.

It is this forward momentum that Milton sets free by throwing off the chains of rhyme. The immediate aesthetic result is a shift in the balance of attention from the axis of selection to the axis of combination (to employ Roman Jakobson's powerful formula for analyzing verse); from diction to grammar; from the paradigmatic to the syntagmatic; from particular words and their sounds—which are, as it were, orthogonal to the direction of the narrative—to the vast, organ-like harmony in the accumulating rhythm of the sentences, which are aligned with the direction of narrative and so add to its momentum.

The result, however, for the original audience, is something that no longer sounds the way poetry is supposed to sound, but something that sounds much closer to prose, if not indistinguishable from prose, although cunningly divided into ten-syllable units that at least look like verses on the page. What is the difference between the verse of *Paradise Lost* and vehement, rhythmical prose? It isn't easy to hear, even for us, on the other side of Wordsworth, and more accustomed as we are to the blank verse of the Elizabethan and Jacobean stage than was Milton's original audience. We can answer our question. The difference between good prose and the verse of *Paradise Lost* is the ten-syllable line or "tone row," with its unmistakable rhythm, and the cunning variation of pauses between line ends and caesuras, so that the syntax—what Milton means by *sense*—is "variously drawn out." Something Milton doesn't mention in his note on the verse, unless he means it by "the sense variously drawn out," is his use of the grammatical architecture of the periodic sentence (such as we encounter it in Cicero, or, in English, in Hooker's *Laws of Ecclesiastical Polity*, and, indeed, in Milton's own prose), to build up much longer and more flexible rhythms creating that pulsatile effect. The effect is augmented by these longer rhythms being laid on top of the regular metronomic beat of the ten-syllable line. It is these two systems—the long syntax and the shorter ten-syllable line—working in harmony (and at other times fighting against each other) that creates the effect of a continuous drone beneath the train of images that flows across the surface of the mind as one reads. T. S. Eliot was right: *Paradise Lost* changed how we hear poetry.

It is a change in the disposition of attention, in which what is being said is moved into the foreground and poetical effects are pushed back. If you look at the passages of Spenser above, you see how the sense is a little more in the background, harmoniously blended with the sound to create a general unified feeling in which the emotional tone of the speaker—of pathos in the passage of *The Shepheardes Calender*, of humility in the passage from *The Faerie Queene*—is more important than exact sense. The exact sense is there, but it is laid back into its sonorous and emotional effects, as one mixes a recording so that the voice is behind the instruments, instead of in front of them. (The phrase *laid-back* appears to have been invented by J. J. Cale for this purpose.) By removing rhyme from narrative verse on the page, Milton did more than turn the axis of attention from what the verse sounds like to where the verse is going. He also shifted the disposition of attention by moving poetical effects into the background and bringing the sense forward. This is a poet who has something to say. He assumes a prophetic authority.

Milton's influence would be gradual. Except for Wordsworth, rhyme is still predominant in the verse of the Romantics, a century and a half after Milton, and indeed even Wordsworth, except for "Lines Written a Few Miles above Tintern Abbey," *The Prelude*, and *The Excursion*, wrote mostly in rhyme or in unrhyming stanzas, even in his narrative poems, such as "Michael," "Resolution and Independence," and the Salisbury Plain poems, these last in Spenserian stanzas. But modern poetry with rhyme, regular syllabic line lengths, and stanzas, from Yeats to Richard Wilbur, is the exception today. The norm has become poetry with irregular but rhythmical lines, poetry in which expression, to recall Milton's use of the word, has been pressed into the foreground.

To summarize, the verse of *Paradise Lost* is labile, pulsative, elastic, and strong. It camouflages the individual line to blend in with the syntax, and it camouflages the syntax to blend in with the dramatic voice, with the movement of the thought, and with the astonishing visual effects. There is a resulting shift in the balance of attention around from the ear to the eye. The ear is lulled not quite to sleep, but to a lower level of vigilant attention to detail, and the eye is correspondingly excited. The verse builds up longer rhythms above the level of the line, and because these longer rhythms are of varying lengths, unconfined by stanzaic divisions and uninterrupted by rhyme, they give the verse this pulsing *sostenuto*. In 1667 it must have sounded radically new and disconcerting. As late as the Romantics, despite the towering figure of Wordsworth, blank verse was not evidently the way forward in poetry.

When I first heard the music of Philip Glass, in *Satyagraha* and *Einstein on the Beach*, with its breathlessly sustained, incantatory monotony, it seemed to me the startling effect of this new kind of music afforded insight into how *Paradise Lost* was heard by readers accustomed to the more poetical sounds afforded by stanzas and rhyme. From Stravinsky's *Rite of Spring*, the audience for modern orchestral music—Bartok and Hindemith, Boulez and Ligeti—had become inured to hyperactive arrhythmia and dissonance. When people heard Glass, they were startled to be lulled. Many loved it, but many also wondered if it had the right to be called orchestral music, there seemed so little to it. I imagine the verse of *Paradise Lost* had much the same effect at the start. What right did it have to be called poetry? Rhymed verse, especially as it appears in shorter lyric poems—English poems from Sidney and Herbert to Dickinson, Yeats, and Larkin—has an ornamental surface, agitating the reader's attention. The effect is cool, in McLuhan's sense, because the message is in the background and the medium holds our attention. Nor is this contrast true only for short lyric poems. In *The Faerie Queene*, the elaborate stanza, especially with its longer, terminal line, has the granular effect of separating each stanza as an independent unit standing partly apart from the whole. The effect is of a *ritardando*, a slowing of the forward impulse of the narrative to invite meditative delay. This effect is certainly augmented by Spenser's allegory, which slows reading down to involve our attention in surface features that suggest a deeper meaning within. That "within" tends to spatialize the experience of reading, as is typical of allegory, and to slow reading down.

In contrast with the effect of Spenser's *Faerie Queene*, the verse of *Paradise Lost* impels us forward with little invitation to delay, even in the ring-composition structure of Eve's poem on the sweetness of life in Eden with Adam (*PL*, 4.639–56). Such local effects are wonderful, and are worth pausing over, but there is nothing in the character of the verse—not even the texture of exotic names, which we glide over insensibly—that encourages meditative delay. The reader may want to look back, to reread and appreciate, to pause and reflect, but it is hard to find a safe place to stop, where one is not in danger of losing one's place in the continually developing thought. When you read Milton you feel as if a giant hand is on your back, gently but firmly pushing you ahead.

You can hear in Milton's note on the verse of *Paradise Lost* the tone of every avant-garde manifesto to come in the turbulent arts of the modern world, from the "Preface to the Lyrical Ballads" to Charles Olson's "Projective Verse," in which an analogy is suggested between artistic and political progress, so that not to approve of a technical change in the arts is to be regressive in another realm, too: that of politics. That is certainly how Milton regarded his Restoration audience, or that part of it that expected a narrative poem to rhyme, after the fashion of the royalist Sir William Davenant and the wise timeserver Dryden. It may amuse us to see how the appeal to "ancient liberty" from Sonnet 11 ("I did but prompt the age to quit their clogs / By the known rules of ancient liberty," lines 1–2), which recalls the more incendiary, revolutionary appeal to the "reviving liberty" of *The Ready and Easy Way* ("God may raise of these stones to become children of reviving liberty; and may reclaim, though they seem now choosing them a captain back for *Egypt*, to bethink themselves a little and consider whither they are rushing" [*YP*, 7:463]), is deployed here on what might not unreasonably be considered a trivial question of versification. But for Milton the analogy is real. Meter is political. In the "jingling sound of like endings," he hears servile royalist poetasters rattling their chains. When the rhymes are struck off, as a prisoner's chains are struck off, a free poet can say what he will, and concentrate on *expressing* it well, that is, on moving content into the foreground, increasing the temperature. The verse throws eloquence into relief, to give an underlying acoustical ground against which that eloquence soars. In such verse, it becomes possible to speak seriously about freedom.

The verse of *Paradise Lost* is in any event free enough to afford a precedent for later, freer verse in English, from William Blake to Walt Whitman and even to the less than grateful T. S. Eliot—and onward, to the present. *The Waste Land*, "The Hollow Men" (with its ostentatious enjambments), and *Four Quartets* are strongly indebted to Milton. This fact may confirm, rather better than Eliot might have wished, his historical point about Milton changing the direction of poetry in English. Much of Ezra Pound's *Cantos* will remind the ear of Milton, as will its glaring erudition. In another groundbreaking long modern poem, Wallace Stevens's *The Comedian as the Letter C*, which appeared in Stevens's first book, *Harmonium*, published in 1923, a year after *The Waste Land*, the poet composes actual blank verse, but in a voice that is entirely different from Milton's. The same measure underlies Stevens's still more ambitious poems, from "The Idea of Order at Key West"—an ode with the high solemnity of Milton's odes and monodies—to *The Auroras of Autumn*. Even William Carlos Williams's mysterious "triple foot" could be considered a physician's anatomizing of the Miltonic line. Robert Lowell, in a deliberate reappropriation of the authority of public eloquence in verse, is perhaps the most self-consciously vatic and political of Milton's American poetic descendants.

Among the late twentieth-century poets, A. R. Ammons acknowledged a debt to Milton for the ability to create an unbroken, rhythmical flow of thought, which Ammons supremely achieves in his poems from *Tape for the Turn of the Year* (composed between December 6, 1963, and January 10, 1964) to *Garbage* and *Glare*.[18] Jorie Graham's sonorous long lines and syntactical complexities, mirroring the linear progress of feeling and thought, are in the tradition of *Paradise Lost*. At the time she was working on *Overlord*, Graham paced the mile of sand on Omaha Beach, looking at the sea and sky and listening to *Paradise Lost*. She was also contemplating what would be her next book, concerning the currents offshore, *Sea Change:*

> . . . North Atlantic Deep Water
>   which also contains
> contributions from the Labrador Sea and entrainment of
>   other water masses, try to hold a
>   complete collapse, in the North Atlantic Drift, in the
>   thermohyaline circulation, this
>   will happen,
>   fish are starving to death in the Great Barrier Reef, the new
>   Age of Extinctions is
>   now
>   says the silence-that-precedes—you know not what
>   you
>   are entering, a time
>   beyond belief.[19]

To other poets, Milton's Christianity is alienating, his morals forbidding, and his classicism unimmediate and emotionally false. These criticisms go back to Johnson. Milton transgresses the prime rule of modernity set down by Paul Verlaine, which is to take eloquence and wring its neck (*"Prends l'eloquence et tords-lui son cou"*).[20] But eloquence of a kind, sometimes in disguise, as in John Ashbery, has proven to be more resilient than the imagists and their descendants have hoped—because in fact poetry *is* eloquence submitted to measure.

Part of eloquence is flow, the sense of discourse moving onward in a stream, altering course frequently, undermining formerly resilient shorelines, opening new channels for thought, tumbling over rocks and abrupt ledges, rushing past the walls of a canyon, or rolling gently between overgrown banks, with flowers and succulents bending over dark eddying pools. Not without reason was poetry anciently compared to the Hippocrene stream flowing down from the side of Mount Helicon through such a various terrain—or that that particular stream (as its name implies) should have had its source opened by a strike from the hoof of the winged horse, Pegasus, the symbol of epic poetry. It is true that Chaucer and Spenser have this eloquent flow, and they also soar. That is what every poet is striving to achieve, or self-consciously turning away from, though in a manner that is still lofty and fluent. Spenser is the great master in English of poetic streams, and like Chaucer (at the end of *Troilus and Criseyde*) he soars above the earth, in the *Mutabilitie Cantos*, mounted on an Irish Pegasus. But Milton's innovations in English verse, giving measure to eloquence without stanzas or rhyme, have had a greater influence on much of modern poetry since, especially of the avant-garde kind.

Only Milton's Christian religion may be thought in some quarters, decidedly not all, to put him dangerously out of step with the modern world, or to be deserving of censure. William Empson blamed Milton, or rather, Milton's God, that is, the God of the Christian tradition Milton inherited, for adhering to a religion glorifying human sacrifice—though it must be said Milton did everything he could to minimize the Eucharistic side of Christianity in favor of individual liberty and revolution modeled on Christ's sterner and more subversive side. Whether such a reformation of Christianity along these lines is possible, cleansing it of mystery and nonrational belief is another matter. In any event, the turbulent religious tradition of patriarchal monotheism from which later Judaism, Christianity, and Islam derive is hardly extinct in the modern world and well worth understanding better, not least in the prophetic form given to it by Milton.

At least since the time of Milton's younger contemporary, John Dryden, Chaucer, Spenser, and Milton have been seen as the highest examples of the tradition of the heroic poem in English, passing the baton from one age to the next. Somewhat surprisingly for us, Chaucer's huge tale of love and betrayal, *Troilus and Criseyde*, with the Trojan War in its background, can be traced back through many intermediaries to Homer, supposedly: Joseph of Exeter, the quality of whose hexameters prompted Milton to call him "the only smooth poet of those times," Benoît de Sainte-Maure, Guido delle Colonne, and of course the legendary combatants on either side of the war, pseudo Dictys Cretensis and pseudo Dares Phrygius.[21]

The seven-line stanza of *Troilus and Criseyde*, lengthened by two lines in Spenser's *Faerie Queene*, was long understood to be the proper measure for heroic poetry in English. Spenser saw himself as a son of Chaucer, and Milton called Spenser his "original": "Milton was the poetical son of Spenser . . . for we have our lineal descents and clans as well as other families. Spenser more than once insinuates that the soul of Chaucer was transfused into his body, and that he was begotten by him two hundred years after his decease. Milton has acknowledged to me that Spenser was his Original."[22] Why then does Milton speak to us today with more force than the other two? Might the appeal Milton has for us reflect some limitations in the outlook of his poetry, as well as the more obvious strengths? It is not inconceivable we would be better off favoring Chaucer's more relaxed and tolerant view of human nature. As for Spenser's ethical idealism, committed as it is to a more open and complex reflection on Aristotelian ethics as an intellectual problem, it might be argued that treating ethical truths as real has advantages over Milton's powerful and very modern reduction of ethics to decision, in a line that leads straight on, though with many turns—it is the straight way of verse—to Nietzsche and the existentialists. You are what you choose to be. That you *should* choose obedience to God's will as the manifestation of reason easily falls away from such decisionism. Milton's higher idealism, the superstructure of reason and conscience, "the law of God written in the heart," rests on the unstable basis of the will. Self-creation by decision is the lesson of the great works of Milton's later career, *Paradise Lost*, *Paradise Regained*, and *Samson Agonistes*.

In any event, it appears that the sound, the characteristic tone, of this extreme subjectivity was first heard by Milton in those dramatic lines in blank verse that he wrote for Satan at the origin of what became *Paradise Lost*, the tone we hear in Satan's unforgettable and magnificent opening speech. In this sort of verse, Satan can express fully, without interference or constraint, the passions he felt welling up from within him. It was in this verse that Milton would give the power of expression to others as well, to the Father and the Son, to the angels, and above all to Eve and to Adam. He would of course also give it to himself, preserving in new measure the vehement authority he had won in the prose.

~ 12

On the Sublime in Paradise Lost

Sublimity has been attributed to Milton more than to any other English poet—sublimity, or what Dr. Johnson called "gigantic loftiness":

> He had considered creation in its whole extent, and his conceptions are therefore learned. He had accustomed his imagination to unrestrained indulgence, and his conceptions therefore were extensive. The characteristic quality of his poem is sublimity. He sometimes descends to the elegant, but his element is the great. He can occasionally invest himself with grace; but his natural port is gigantic loftiness. He can please when pleasure is required; but it is his peculiar power to astonish.[1]

Johnson's composite formulation, taking in the objective and subjective sides of Milton's art—his "natural port" and his "power to astonish"—may be clearer than that somewhat abstract and much-theorized term Johnson also employs, *the sublime*. We know that Milton is gigantic and lofty, and we feel that some connection exists between the hugeness of the scenes Milton describes and the high moral seriousness with which he undertakes to disclose the origin of history and the cause of all evil.

But when we use the word *sublime* we tend to mean it more in the first sense than in the second, as an *aesthetic* term describing sensational hugeness, rather than as a *moral* term bearing on the consciousness of evil in history—or of good. The word *aesthetic* comes from the Greek word for sense perception, *aisthêsis*, and the treatise on aesthetics by Alexander Baumgarten, in the middle of the eighteenth century (*Aesthetica*, 1750), first proposed to add judgments of taste in the arts to the philosophy of sense perception. In the *Critique of Judgment* (1790), Immanuel Kant would take this idea further and employ aesthetics not for *perceptions* but exclusively for *judgments*, judgments of the beautiful and the sublime. As for Johnson, he was attracted to the term by its use in a famous treatise of some two decades previous by his friend Edmund Burke, *A Philosophical Inquiry into the Origin of our Ideas of the Beautiful and the Sublime* (1757). It was Kant who developed a connection between the sensational or "gigantic" sense of the sublime, the thrill of grandeur, and the moral loftiness that the term also implies—at least when we read *Paradise Lost*.

The ancient Greek work of literary criticism called 'On the Sublime,' or 'The High Effect in Literature' (*Peri Hypsous*), is of uncertain authorship and date, although the first century CE seems likely and the authorship has traditionally gone under the name of 'Longinus' or 'Pseudo Longinus.' *On the Sublime* is a work of criticism and theory that is unlike anything else that has come down to us from the ancient world. It has nothing of the technical pedantry of the hellenistic rhetorical treatises before it, nor does it succumb to the continuing delusions of the allegorical interpreters of Homer. It makes no excuses for literary pleasure because it sees literary genius as itself heroic. As we read the treatise, we see we are in a late, highly sophisticated literary culture, in which artistic achievement for its own sake is as ennobling as prowess in war.

On the Sublime is therefore very different from, as well as much later than, Aristotle's *Poetics*. But in the Renaissance, after its publication by the same publisher who brought out the *Poetics*, Francesco Robortello, *De Sublimitate*, as it would be titled in Latin, enjoyed an authority almost equal with Aristotle. *On the Sublime* was widely disseminated in the later sixteenth and seventeenth centuries, and its appeal was that it filled an emotional need Aristotle's *Poetics* could not. Aristotle is highly analytical, and dry as a stick. One reads him and worries about whether one is keeping to rules, as so many did worry, including Milton. But Longinus is filled with enthusiasm for strong and noble effects in literature and he seeks to rouse us with the same feelings for them. Aristotle cites few examples outside Sophocles' *Oedipus Tyrannus* and the epics of Homer. Longinus, more catholic and florid in his tastes, cites and describes a great number of works, including the opening of Genesis, largely for the purpose of sharing his enthusiasm for them.[2] Aristotle's *Poetics* presents itself as an instruction manual on how to make a tragic poem. Longinus' *On the Sublime* teaches us to read, or rather, how to feel as we read. If the *Poetics* dominated critical theory of the sixteenth century and the high Renaissance, *On the Sublime* came into its own in the seventeenth century with the heroic exuberance of the baroque. Milton of course knew this work and recommended it in *Of Education* for the literary instruction of youths.[3] From his comments on criticism in this period, it is reasonable to assume he thought *On the Sublime* was for boys and *The Poetics* for men. By the time he composed *Paradise Lost*, that assessment would be turned upside down. Milton would outgrow Aristotle's *Poetics*, regarding it as elementary, an early stage in preparing for greatness. But he would grow into *The Sublime*. The reason is simple. For Aristotle, the thing of first importance in poetics is technique. The rest is natural talent, which cannot be taught, and is therefore out of account. For Longinus, the thing of first importance for attaining the sublime does not lie in the realm of technique or even in art. It is to have great, or vigorous conceptions. Milton's term for these is "higher argument" (*PL* 9. 42).

Largely because of Nicolas Boileau's translation of it as *Traité du Sublime, ou du merveilleux dans le discours, traduit du grec du Longin*, published in 1674, the year of Milton's death, the influence of Longinus was still greater in the eighteenth century, and was canonized in the famous treatise I have already mentioned, by Johnson's friend, Edmund Burke, *A Philosophical Inquiry into the Origin of our Ideas of the Beautiful and the Sublime*. Burke's essay occasioned one of those not infrequent events, when a fresh new idea, brilliantly expressed, is seized on by a great thinker and transformed for his own purposes, as when Einstein seized on Riemannian geometry for the General Theory of Relativity. Burke's analysis was taken up by Immanuel Kant, in the *Critique of Judgment* (1790), in which the aesthetical concept of the sublime is, so to speak, sublimed into an ethical one, providing the means to unify reason with moral consciousness in the Kantian system.[4]

In the analysis of the sublime, especially of what Kant calls "the mathematical sublime," the experience of greatness, of what is vast or high (*das Erhabene*) is also the experience of a failure adequately to perceive, or to imagine this greatness. This check provokes a dialectical reaction in which the mind now grasps, by reason, what it could not perceive, which compensatory movement awakens moral consciousness as reason. The "dynamical sublime" works a little differently but comes out the same, with moral consciousness emerging at the end. Remote as this way of thinking about the sublime may appear—its haste to get beyond the aesthetic to morals has much to do, as I have suggested, with holding the Kantian system together—we shall find considerable resonance between it and *Paradise Lost*. That is largely because the sublime in Kant is not a static structure but a process, a series of steps.[5] The sublime effects of Milton's poem are not there for themselves, to thrill us with a sense of our inadequacy before them: they are meant to awaken moral consciousness in us.

The Greek *hypsos* means simply "height, top, summit, crown" and by extension such things as "grand," "magnificent," "lofty," "haughty." Homer's Zeus is *hypsibremetês* ("high thundering"), and Milton is, too. Simple highness, loftiness, is what Longinus means by the term. Although he advances subtle analyses of its effects, the sublime to him never refers to more than a direct elevation of subject and tone, accompanied by emotional grandeur.

Latin *sublimitas* (n.) or *sublimis* (adj.) is a little more difficult. For one thing it is also a verb, *sublimo,* and something can be "sublimed" or "raised up." (In Greek a separate verb is required, for example, "to seize or take hold of highness," *hypsos lambanein*). The elements of Latin *sublimis* suggest something that is beneath a limit or boundary, the *limes,* but which transgresses this limit—hence the verbal meaning of the word *to sublime:* "Sublimed with mineral fury" (*PL,* 1.235). In speaking of the sublime as concerned with the unbounded, *Unbegrenztheit,* Kant was clearly thinking of the Latin word, and of a process of transgression proceeding from one step to another, and then another. Milton would have known the word from alchemy, among other sources, of course, including Ovid and Virgil. In alchemy the verb *to sublime* meant the refinement of a base metal from a lower state into a higher, or from a less volatile condition to a more volatile one. *De Sublimitate* means "on things in literature that have been raised up from a lower condition into high-ness." These things that have been sublimed, as with mineral fury, are more volatile, more explosive. The Latin title of the work disposes us to think Longinus' treatise is all about greatness of size. Yet this is not true in him, or in Milton.

What is most striking about Milton's poetry, especially in *Paradise Lost*, is not just that it is sublime, that it is elevated and "high." What is striking is that at every moment we feel its uplifting power in a moral sense, too, as a development subsequent to the experience of this height, without leaving the highness behind. Milton's poetry has the baroque quality of being continuously in motion, and of continuously rising. In-deed in all Milton's poetry there is an active, verbal meaning to the ef-fects of the sublime. Even Satan, who descends morally throughout the epic, explodes upward, "like a pyramid of fire" (*PL*, 2.1013). Nothing is fixed; everything is in motion—flowing, growing, ascending, descending, transforming. Good things tend to rise up with stately magnificence by their natural power, their loftiness, as if extending the moment of their creation. The entirety of the Creation scene in book 7 is an as-cension of not-Being into Being, and of Being into beings. It is this quality, at once metaphysical and aesthetical, that gives Milton's poetry its astonishing energy, flexibility, and power.

That is indeed the attitude we find in the famous introduction to book 9 of *Paradise Lost*, when Milton appears at first to be saying that his subject—the Fall of humankind—is more heroic than the "long and tedious havoc" (*PL*, 9.30) of war. But then Milton says that the heroic belongs as much to the poet as an artist as it does to the subject of the poem. As a genius and an artist, the poet must be worthy of his high subject and rise up to it, if not above it:

> Not that which justly gives heroic name
> To person or to poem. Me of these
> Nor skilled nor studious, higher argument
> Remains sufficient of itself to raise
> That name unless an age too late or cold
> Climate or years damp my intended wing
> Depressed, and much they may if all be mine,
> Not hers who brings it nightly to my ear.
>
> (PL, *9.40–47*)

"That name" (line 44) refers back to *heroic* (line 40), but it now includes Milton himself in its meaning. At this moment we are struck, however, by the poet's humility, because instead of affirming his strength, he affirms his weakness in three respects: his living in a late age of the world; his living in a northern climate, away from the Mediterranean, where all other major epics had been composed; and his being old. In each of these things he is assessing the power of his genius and finding it possibly too weak to complete his task, weighing him down with dampness and cold, depressing—that is, pressing downward—his soaring poetical flight. These things may weigh him down ("much they may") if he relies on his genius alone. But at this moment of admitted weakness, he finds an unexpected strength in recalling that he depends upon a higher power: "and much they may if all be mine, / Not hers who brings it nightly to my ear." The Romantic sublimity of this passage— for it is indeed sublime—comes from a failure imagined, which is fol- lowed by a new and unexpected source of power, a power not within but above. Milton does not here even mention his blindness as another disability menacing his success, the blockage of a "universal blank" (*PL*, 3.48). We never find this movement of *compensatory hyperbole* in Longinus. But we do find much more that is relevant to *Paradise Lost*.

On the Sublime is concerned mostly with the effects of the high and the grand, of cosmic magnitude, of unimaginable height and unimagi- nable depth, of vast, violent power, like that of Poseidon the earth shaker, of fearsomeness in war, or at sea, of flashing wonder and of divine, bounding speed. But these things are predicated not only on what the poet describes when telling of the power of the gods, or of the terror of battle. They are predicated also on the poet in his creation, which is also unimaginably grand, stirring, fearsome, dazzling, and fast. The au- thor's examples are drawn from very wide reading, and not only in po- etry, for he considers oratory, too, especially Demosthenes, and even Latin authors, such as Cicero. But he means poetry chiefly, and Homer is his supreme example of all these effects: a poet who is sublime and even godlike because of his genius. Because it takes great genius to pro- duce these effects, the poet's genius is to be marveled at for its sublimity as much as for what the poet describes. As readers we capture some of this greatness by repeatedly exposing ourselves to it and being caught up in the poet's divine enthusiasm. The purpose of reading is "to turn the soul upward" (*anatrephein*) toward what is grand. What is not in

Longinus but will be in Burke and Kant—and is also there in Milton's poem—is any sense of progressing through stages, beginning with an inadequacy that, by being overcome, suddenly transports us over the obstacle we were formerly trying to clear.

For example, Longinus quotes a passage from Homer on the horses of the gods, which at a single leap cover a distance farther than a lookout can gaze over the ocean—"so far spring the high-neighing [*hypsêchées*] horses of the gods."[6] On this the author remarks that it is with supreme grandeur that Homer "makes the divine large" by making the horses' stride as long as the world, or *cosmos*, so that if they took two such strides no place for them would be found in the cosmos. That effect is created time and again in *Paradise Lost*, where we are required to imagine the unimaginably large, and where the poet travels outside the cosmos altogether, to Hell and to Heaven. One of the great sublime passages is when Satan, having crossed chaos, spots the entire created universe—not only the earth but the whole cosmos—appearing to him in the distance as a tiny star, faint because close to the moon: "This pendant world in bigness as a star / Of smallest magnitude close by the moon" (*PL*, 2.1052–53). Yet in the following book this faintest of objects becomes an unimaginably vast, convex plain, the outer surface of the cosmos:

> A globe far off
> It seemed, now seems a boundless continent
> Dark, waste, and wild, under the frown of Night
> Starless exposed and ever threat'ning storms
> Of chaos blust'ring round.
>
> (PL, *3.422–26*)

The rapid transition from one way of perceiving something to another, by a violent stretching, is one of the effects named as "high" by the author of the treatise on the sublime.

In section 8 of the treatise Longinus says there are five causes of the sublime. The first two—robust ideas and the representation of high passions—belong to the natural productions of genius beyond the reach of art, of a "great nature." Longinus says the remaining three causes—the management of figures, the splendid phrasing of noble sentiments, and the harmonizing of all these effects into one—belong to technique, although conscious effort is perhaps the better term. The distinction between those elements of sublimity that are attained by natural talent and those that are attained by technique is still less convincing when the author says that we can acquire robust ideas and strong passions "by frequently turning our souls upwards towards great things." One does this by reading, in particular by frequent reading in great authors, from mighty Homer to rugged Aeschylus and terrifying Demosthenes, whose language descends on us like a thunderbolt out of the blue. The synthetic effect, that which unifies the whole (Longinus's number 5), is attained by Milton's blank verse, the homogenizing efficacy of which we have already had occasion to consider. The splendid phrasing of noble sentiments we see from the outset of the poem in the high language of Satan, as when he says, "Better to reign in Hell than serve in Heaven" (*PL*, 1.263), shows a splendor of expression that has always made Satan the interpretative problem that he is. Longinus divides figures or *schemata* into those involving thoughts and those involving merely words (an example of the latter would be the carefully sewn internal rhymes in Milton's blank verse). For figures or ornaments of thought the most prominent are the great epic similes of *Paradise Lost*.

The sublime is concerned with the tropes of impossibility and contradiction, of perceptual blockage and blank darkness in the face of the unimaginably huge: of the mind's returning upon itself after failure with a new and unexpected knowledge of its powers:

> a huge Cliff,
> As if with voluntary power instinct,
> Upreared its head: I struck, and struck again,
> And growing still in stature, the huge Cliff
> Rose up between me and the stars, and still,
> With measured motion, like a living thing,
> Strode after me.[7]

For many days after, Wordsworth says (for this is he, the most Miltonic of the English poets), "my brain / Worked with a dim and undermined sense / Of unknown modes of being: in my thoughts / There was a darkness."[8] This is from the episode of *The Prelude* (1805) where the poet recalls as a schoolboy coming by chance, at night, upon a moored boat beside a mountain lake. It is irresistible: "The moon was up, the lake was shining clear / Among the hoary mountains" (1.383–84). As he rows outward on the water, by a trick of perspective a black and ominous cliff seems to rise between him and the starry sky overhead:

> When from behind that craggy Steep, till then
> The bound of the horizon, a huge Cliff
> As if with voluntary power instinct,
> Upreared its head: I struck and struck again,
> And, growing still in stature, the huge Cliff
> Rose up between me and the stars, and still,
> With measured motion, like a living thing,
> Strode after me. With trembling hands I turned,
> And through the silent water stole my way . . .
>   for many days my brain
> Worked with a dim and undetermined sense
> Of unknown modes of being: in my thoughts
> There was a darkness, call it solitude,
> Or blank desertion, no familiar shapes
> Of hourly objects, images of trees,
> Of sea, or sky, no colours of green fields;
> But huge and mighty Forms that do not live
> Like living men moved slowly through my mind
> By day and were the trouble of my dreams.[9]

The reader may hear in the verb *upreared* Milton's description of Satan on the fiery lake of Hell, "with head uplift above the wave," and in Wordworth's "huge and mighty Forms" Satan's rising from that lake: "Forthwith uplift he rears from off the pool / His mighty stature" (*PL*, 1.193 and 221–22). The "measured motion" of the pursuing cliff—an objective impression unwittingly created by the measured beat of the oars—recalls the stride of Death when approaching and challenging Satan: "The monster moving onward came as fast / With horrid strides" (*PL* 2. 675–76). Wordsworth's "darkness" or "blank desertion" will recall the famous passage on Milton's blindness, in which a "universal blank" and "ever-during dark" cuts him off from the sight of ordinary things, "sight of vernal bloom or summer's rose / Or flocks or herds or human face divine" (*PL*, 3.43–44). In Wordsworth these common sights—"familiar shapes / Of hourly objects, images of trees, / Or sea, or sky, . . . colors of green fields" are obliterated by a darkness in his thoughts, not the physical darkness imposed by blindness. Even the sudden and alarming rising of the cliff in Wordsworth's description, and the mighty forms that haunt the poet after, recall Milton's violent description of a sheer hill torn from the side of Mount Etna, in Sicily on the Strait of Messina, at Cape Pelorus, which extends into the strait from under the brow of the volcano:

> As when the force
> Of subterranean wind transports a hill
> Torn from Pelorus or the shattered side
> Of thund'ring Etna whose combustible
> And fueled entrails thence conceiving fire
> Sublimed with mineral fury aid the winds
> And leave a singèd bottom all involved
> With stench and smoke.
>
> (PL, *1.230–37*)

The difference between the two passages is that in Wordsworth the mind is in the foreground of our attention, mediating the sublime sights of the world, or blacking them out. In Milton, following a similar passage in Virgil, the sensorium is temporarily reduced to insignificance by the force of the real. But the "universal blank" (*PL* 3. 48) proceeding from the loss of the sense of sight becomes a step towards seeing and telling what is "invisible to mortal sight" (*PL* 3. 55).

Not the least of the achievements that make Milton modern is that he was the first poet to imagine all the lands on the globe more or less as we know them today. (Australia, of course, would not be known to Europeans until the voyages of Captain Cook in the following century.) If Homer speaks of divine horses taking a single leap out of the world, Milton has a more gigantic sense of how far such a leap would be. Milton seems to have a preternatural, physical intuition of the huge size of the earth, such as no poet ever had before him. From his early education, he gained knowledge of and passionate interest in geography; in the treatise *Of Education*, he recommends teaching the subject to young boys, including the use of globes and maps, and memorizing old and new place names (*YP*, 2:389). Even in old age, when he was blind, Milton inquired into purchasing the most recent and advanced modern atlas.

But Milton earned his physical intuition of the earth between the ages of twenty-nine and thirty-one, when he traveled in Europe, from Paris to as far south as Naples. What libraries and societies Milton visited, and who he met in the great centers of Italian Renaissance civilization, has proven easier to record than the effects on him, arduous but stimulating, of traveling such distances through France and Italy, and over such astonishing terrain.

In Florence, Rome, and Naples, and doubtless in Venice (we have few particulars of his stay in this last), Milton proved to distinguished Italian men of letters, including Galileo, that he was learned, civilized, and clever, that he could speak Latin and Italian well, and that he could write Latin and Italian poetry very well indeed. The last is impressive, of course, and was important to Milton, who proudly mentioned it later in life. Nevertheless the artistic value of these achievements was largely expended in Milton's career by the time he returned to England. It was the actual traveling, which in those days was laborious and slow—and dangerous—that was important for Milton's future literary production, especially *Paradise Lost.* The landscape of Italy is far more varied and dramatic than that of southeast England. Passing through France would have taken Milton along the Loire through comparatively featureless landscape until reaching the *Massif Central* and Provence. Although Milton would have seen nothing like this landscape before, the varied geography of France changes over long distances and in stately stages. In Italy, as one travels, the tempo is faster, as Milton would have seen making his way from Livorno on the coast (the usual English name is Leghorn) into Tuscany to Florence, following the route Montaigne had taken some sixty years before.[10] Even more striking and rapidly changing is the geography of the high road that descends from Florence to Rome through Siena, Arezzo, and the Umbrian hill towns, with the Apennine mountains on the left of the route (Dante had written of their wildness and soaring heights) and the Tyrrhenian Sea on the right, though far off. Milton had referred to this landscape in his early poetry, in *"In Quintum Novembris"* (lines 49–51), in which Satan flies down the Italian peninsula from the Alps to Rome, and in *A Masque Presented at Ludlow Castle, 1634,* where Bacchus meets Circe while "Coasting the Tyrrhene shore, as the winds listed" (line 49). Milton must have paid keen attention when he at last saw these places (although what he "coasted" was not the "Tyrrhene shore" but the Ligurian to the north). Traveling south from Rome to Naples, in the Campania, Milton saw Mount Vesuvius and the volcanic region around Naples, which Pindar and Aeschylus refer to as having chained beneath it—all the way down to Mount Etna, in Sicily—the great monster Typhon, vomiting lava and fire. The Phlegraean fields to the north of the Bay of Napes gave Milton the objective correlative for his landscape of Hell, with its "burning marl" underfoot. On his return north through Florence Milton crossed the Apennines—his first serious mountain traverse—from Florence to Bologna, on his way to Venice, across the broad plain of the Po River, doing much of it by boat on canals. Milton would next travel westward across that plain from Venice through Verona to Milan, with the snow-capped Alps visible to the north through much of his journey. He would cross the Alps into Switzerland—which was no light undertaking in those days—and then travel to Geneva along the shore of the beautiful (in fact, it seems to unify the beautiful and the sublime), mountain-ringed Lac Léman. Milton must have been astounded at the sight of the wild and chaotic massif of the Alps, its passes in June only recently opened after the winter, its valleys descending into the abyss, its snow-clad peaks hanging above him, like frozen waves of gleaming rock—all of it belonging to a world he believed to be created by God. This was Milton's firsthand experience of the earth. It imparted to him, through his legs and his lungs as well as his eyes, a sense of the insignificance of one's perception in comparison to what is there to perceive.

Giants are limited by having their feet on the ground. They have, of course, no sense of the sublime. The high style in poetry must therefore be more than large or, to use Johnson's word, gigantic; it must also be lofty; it must soar. From his youth, Milton liked to imagine the act of flying, which is almost the only means of transport in *Paradise Lost*. The angel Uriel, the guardian of the sun, glides down to earth on a sunbeam, "swift as a shooting star" (*PL*, 4.556), and returns thither by the same means of conveyance. We feel this to be perfectly normal. The flight of the angel Raphael, sent to earth from Heaven to warn Adam and Eve of Satan's approach, is spectacularly imagined, showing remarkable powers of hypothesis about the principles of flight, which Milton conceives of partly by analogy to propulsion through water. Raphael flies *down* to the level of eagles soaring at their greatest height (the technical term from hawking is *tower*) and then as low as the other birds, who gaze on him in wonder:

> Down thither prone in flight
> He speeds and through the vast ethereal sky
> Sails between worlds and worlds with steady wing
> Now on the polar winds, then with quick fan
> Winnows the buxom air till, within soar
> Of tow'ring eagles, to all fowls he seems
> A phoenix . . .
> At once on th'eastern cliff of Paradise
> He lights and to his proper shape returns.
>
> (PL, *5.266–76*)

Milton imagines flying through space not so much to explore other worlds as to see our own from above, and from all around, as when Satan makes his complicated, serpentine, evasive flight around the earth:

> Thence full of anguish driv'n
> The space of seven continued nights he rode
> With darkness, thrice the equinoctial line
> He circled, four times crossed the car of Night
> From pole to pole traversing each colure,
> On th'eighth returned and on the coast averse
> From entrance or cherubic watch by stealth
> Found unsuspected way.
>
> (PL, *9.62–69*)

Keeping out of sight of Uriel, the angel who is in charge of in the sun and who spotted him on a previous occasion—and keeping out of sight of the other angels to whom Uriel had reported him, including Zephon and Ithuriel, who arrested him the night before—Satan flies along the equator (which before the Fall coincides with the "equinoctial line"), staying just inside the revolving cone-shaped shadow of the earth. Perhaps because this tactic of concealment is fairly obvious, and bound to be discovered, Satan then turns ninety degrees and flies around the poles, "traversing each colure," always veering on a sinuous course away from the light. The flight itself, and Milton's ability to imagine it, is of course sublime: it is amazing. But it is also devious and hidden. Of Satan's flights, especially his flight across chaos in book 2 and his return across chaos in book 10, there is more to say. But what is most interesting about them is Milton's and our own ghostly presence. To see them, we have to fly along, too. Milton's making this psychological fact explicit, by saying he has flown to Hell and back, is audacious.

No epic poet before Milton—although shamanistic poets did so—represents himself gathering his knowledge of the events in the poem by flying to the scenes he describes, in Hell, in Heaven, and through chaos. It comes as a surprise, during the hymn to Holy Light, "offspring of Heav'n first born," at the beginning of book 3 of *Paradise Lost*. He says he is "revisit[ing]" the light after having escaped from Hell, the "Stygian pool," and flown "through utter and through middle darkness," tracking Satan's flight across chaos. This sublimely naive account of the making of the poem is very different from what we see at the opening of *Paradise Lost*. There, Milton calls on the "Spirit" to inform him of the events he is to describe, including the Creation, without his having to change place. Considering the position of this passage at the poem's outset, it is appropriately austere, without the enthusiasm of flight. But what he describes is sublime, having primordial and abyssal magnitude:

> And chiefly thou, O Spirit, that doest prefer
> Before all temples th'upright heart and pure
> Instruct me, for thou know'st, thou from the first
> Wast present and with mighty wings outspread
> Dove-like sat'st brooding on the vast abyss
> And mad'st it pregnant.
>
> (PL, *1.17–22*)

By a daring and original analogy, Milton implores the Spirit to make him *creative*, to illuminate the dark potential within him and to elevate anything in his character that is as yet unequal to this task, so that the task may be done:

> what in me is dark
> Illumine, what is low raise and support,

> That to the heighth of this great argument
> I may assert eternal providence
> And justify the ways of God to men.
>
> (PL, 1.22–26)

In Kant, reason compensates conceptually for the failure of the senses adequately to perceive what surpasses human sense. This compensatory moment is an effect of the sublime because without warning it makes us aware of the greatness of the mind's power to grasp the (literally) ungraspable. The new respect for reason that is acquired thereby provides a foundation for morals. In Milton, this unexpected compensatory power to rise and soar comes from without, from inspiration. That is of course a more sublime assertion than Kant's reflection of the mind upon its moral power, and Kant knows this. Kant's point at this moment is to turn back toward the world, with a new, transcendental consciousness of it: that the moral is real. But that is the turning movement Milton will effect in *Paradise Lost* as a whole, descending from the transcendental mythos to engagement with history.

There is no suggestion at the opening of *Paradise Lost* that the poet will be a personal witness to anything described in his epic. Instead, the suggestion is that he will become a fit instrument for imagining what he will describe. In the process of cosmic creation the Spirit foments and warms the materials of chaos, preparing them for the Creation proper, which is performed by the Son, all of which we see in book 7. When the Spirit makes the abyss *pregnant*, Milton does mean the word in our sense. Thinking of *dynamis* in Aristotle, he means "potent" or "capable," ready for the definitive imposition of form, according to the Creator's "Idea." Likewise, as I have suggested, the Spirit makes the poet worthy by exalting him: "what is low raise and support." Unlike Homer, who asks the muse to tell him what to sing, and to sing through him— "*Sing* [*aede*] of the wrath, goddess"—Milton is asking the Spirit to develop the potential in him, to make him the singer and creator of this song. In the hymn opening book 3, he gives a more literal and naive account of himself following the action on the wing, until Satan reaches the shores of light.

Satan reaches those shores at the end of book 2. He is likened to a ship battered by a long and tempestuous ocean voyage, wafting gently off the coast of Creation. The universe hangs in the distance, looking like a star; so far does Satan still have to journey when his journey is done: "in a cursèd hour he hies" (*PL*, 2.1055). For Satan, unsurprisingly, there is a sense of relief when he attains the shores of light, the terror and uncertainty as well as the huge effort of his voyage being now over. We feel the relief, too, for a moment, by the strange sympathy any literary representation of a character creates, no matter how bad the character is. We feel almost as if we have made the journey across chaos ourselves, accompanying Satan. The impression takes only a moment. It is one of the uncontrollable feelings we have when we are reading, feelings that are no small part of literary pleasure. But these impressions are soon forgot if not selected for further attention—or reinforced in some way by the author. This Milton will do, when speaking of his own flight. We thus have a second sublime movement in the opposite direction from the last, that is, from visionary understanding to actual, sensual presence.

That is why we are startled by the moment in the hymn opening the following book by the poet's claim he has flown across chaos and eternal night. That brief, nearly forgotten impression we had at the end of Satan's voyage, a relief that is like a fading coal in our minds, is suddenly rekindled by the author. He too feels relief:

> Thee I revisit safe with bolder wing
> while in my flight
> Through utter and through middle darkness borne
> With other notes than to th'Orphéan lyre
> I sung of Chaos and Eternal Night,
> Taught by the Heav'nly Muse to venture down
> The dark descent and up to reascend
> Though hard and rare.
>
> (PL, 3.13–21)

This is one instance where a literary effect is illumined and raised up on a level with the poet, soaring through space. If he really flew, so did we. A fleeting and inchoate feeling is suddenly made literal. The effect is sublime, but it is also naive. We are excited by the thought while at the same time finding it, just because of this naivety, daring. It is daring not because Milton has risked grandiosity but because he has risked naivety. We are thrilled both by the thought of this flying and by the aesthetical trap the poet has contrived for himself. How will he escape this over-zealous and unsustainable enthusiasm (he has nine books to go) and make the flying figurative again?

He will do so, in the most famous and moving personal lines in *Paradise Lost*, by speaking of his physical blindness. Milton cannot witness anything while flying, so there is nothing to be gained by such flight, understood in the most literal sense. Therefore he has flown in the spirit, like Ezekiel, which here means in a poetic and figurative sense. Blindness gets him out of the trap. The blindness is a moment of what Neil Hertz calls "blockage," a necessary stage in the experience of the sublime that provokes a recoil. In Hertz's account, the denial of access, the feeling of having reached the "end of the line" without breaking through, causes a buildup of psychic energy that is released in a moment of "sublime turning," opening upon vistas unsuspected before and inaccessible by direct approach.[11] When Wordsworth is confronted with the "upright face" of a blind beggar propped against a wall, with a paper pinned to the shirt, he says, "My mind did at this spectacle turn round / As with the might of waters."[12] The sight of God's eternal and "unapproachèd light" (*PL*, 3.4) cannot be approached by us, and is felt as darkness: "dark with excessive bright thy skirts appear," Those words are the angels', who praise God in Heaven, and their minds too "turn round":

> Thee, Father, first they sung omnipotent,
> Immutable, immortal, infinite,
> Eternal King, Thee Author of all being,
> Fountain of light, Thyself invisible
> Amidst the glorious brightness where Thou sit'st
> Thron'd inaccessible. But when thou shad'st
> The full blaze of thy beams and through a cloud
> Drawn round about Thee like a radiant shrine,
> Dark with excessive bright thy skirts appear
> Yet dazzle Heav'n that brightest seraphim
> Approach not but with both wings veil their eyes.
>
> (PL, *3.372–82*)

The angels are blinded in Heaven as Milton is blind on earth, and they must mentally turn away, as he does:

So much the rather thou, celestial Light,
Shine inward, and the mind through all her powers
Irradiate. *There* plant eyes. All mist from thence
Purge and disperse, that I may see and tell
Of things invisible to mortal sight.

(PL, 3.51–55)

At the midpoint of *Paradise Lost*, when he invokes the Heavenly muse Urania to descend to his aid, Milton again imagines himself soaring, only to cancel the idea—and again, the effect is sublime. He renounces soaring beyond the bounds of the earth and indeed of the cosmos, up into Heaven, where he has drawn "empyreal air," which is to say, the element of fire. But in renouncing such powers he does so in language that evokes the thrill of flight:

Descend from Heav'n, Urania . . .
                              whose voice divine
Following above th'Olympian hill I soar,
Above the flight of Pegaséan wing . . .
                              Up led by thee
Into the Heav'n of Heav'ns I have presumed
An earthly guest and drawn empyreal air,
Thy temp'ring. With like safety guided down
Return me to my native element
Lest from this flying steed unreined (as once
Bellerophon, though from a lower clime)
Dismounted on th'Aleian field I fall
Erroneous there to wander and forlorn.
Half yet remains unsung but narrower bound
Within the visible diurnal sphere:
Standing on earth, not rapt above the pole,
More safe I sing with mortal voice unchanged
To hoarse or mute.

(PL, 7.1–25)

Milton may formally renounce flight at the beginning of book 7 to tell the rest of his tale "standing on earth," for that is where the remainder of the poem's action takes place. But when Adam sees half the earth from the top of the highest mountain, the effect of the passage for the reader, as for the poet, is of flying. It is gigantic and lofty. Toward the end of *Paradise Lost*, in book 11, after the Fall, the angel Michael takes Adam to the top of the mountain to show him the rest of the world. It is the world into which Adam and Eve will shortly be expelled, thus initiating what we call *history*. Because of the curvature of the earth, however, there is a limit to how much Adam can see from any fixed point, no matter how high, even if it were from outer space, this limit being the distance at which the horizon of sight and precisely half the earth—its *hemisphere*—coincide:

> It was a hill
> Of Paradise the highest from whose top
> The hemisphere of earth in clearest ken
> Stretched out to th'amplest reach of human prospect lay.
>
> (PL, *11.377–80*)

There follows a description of the kingdoms of the earth as these will rise up in the future, though the earth is, of course, devoid of human presence at the time of Adam's vision, with all of history still to come. The effect of temporal anticipation reminds us to what extent our perception of the space of the earth depends on temporality itself, anticipating the struggle for power through time. The passage allows Milton to indulge his learned delight—which we share—in exotic place names and distant cultures, gathered in a sweeping vision that is at once historical, anthropological, and cross-cultural. We feel as if we are not merely seeing with Adam, or through Adam's eyes, but are flying over the territory described, and over history, as well. History in this vision is mythically transcended and recollected forward. Yet the vision of history, though abstracted from time, is concrete and particular with respect to the earth. Milton never loses sight of Adam's eye, of where it is and what it can see:

> Nor could his eye not ken
> Th'empire of Negus to his utmost port
> Ercoco and the less maritime kings
> Mombaza, and Quiloa and Melind
> And Sofala thought Ophir, to the realm

> Of Congo and Angola farthest south.
> Or thence from Niger flood to Atlas mount
> The kingdoms of Almansor, Fez and Sus,
> Morocco and Algiers and Tremisen.
> On Europe thence, and where Rome was to sway
> The world. In spirit perhaps he also saw . . .
>
> (PL, *11.396–406*)

Adam's vision has swept in a great circle round Asia and down into Africa, where I have picked up the passage, making another great circle there and returning north again across the Sahara, from the river Niger to the south of the Sahara to the Arab kingdoms in the desert itself and on to the Mediterranean coast. His eye travels along the coast to the west, to Mount Atlas, which faces Gibraltar from across the narrow strait dividing Africa from Europe. As Thomas Newton noted, in the middle of the eighteenth century, it would have been impossible for Adam to see anything that follows in this catalogue, which now turns to America, over the horizon on the Atlantic. Since vision travels in a straight line, Adam would have had to see through the earth—and the sea—to view the continent on the opposite side. Milton therefore says Adam saw the opposite hemisphere "in spirit." The qualification may strike us as weak, especially from Milton, a literalist if ever there was one. But the point is that although the story requires Adam to see what he sees from a fixed position on earth, the poet who shows us what Adam sees is flying around the earth in his imagination, and carrying us, as it were, on his wings. "In spirit" means, or it almost means, in the air, in flight:

> in spirit perhaps he also saw
> Rich Mexico, the seat of Montezume,
> And Cusco in Peru, the richer seat
> Of Atabálipa and yet unspoiled
> Guiana whose great city Geryon's sons
> Call El Dorado.
>
> (PL, *11.406–11*)

Other passages that would illustrate Milton's gigantic scale are much better known. These include the astounding visions of the devastated landscape of Hell, likened, as we have seen, to the shearing off of land from Cape Pelorus in Sicily (from Greek *pelôr*, "gigantic"); "the shattered side / Of thund'ring Etna" (*PL*, 1.232–33); the warring angels in Heaven, hurling entire mountains through the air, as artillery ("terror seized the rebel host / When coming tówards them so dread they saw / The bottom of the mountains upward turned" [*PL*, 6.648–49]); and the oceanic terror of chaos, with its churning elements, its vast vacuities and tumultuous blasts, and its mountainous waves of rocky liquid out of which the universe was made:

> the vast, immeasurable abyss
> Outrageous as a sea, dark, wasteful, wild,
> Up from the bottom turned by furious winds
> And surging waves as mountains.
>
>   (PL, *7.211–14*)

Perhaps the most sustained episode of gigantic imagining is the building in chaos of the immense mole, or sea wall, far greater than the entire earth, that is bulldozed against the gate of Hell by Sin and Death to support one end of a high, arching bridge, a bridge they then throw across chaos—"a ridge of pendent rock / Over the vexed abyss" (*PL*, 10.313–14). Like "pendent rock," "Vexed abyss" is a wonderful, sublime phrase: *vexed* means churning, tormented; and *abyss* means without any sea bottom (Gr. *byssos*). Sin and Death, infernal engineers, then secure the other end of this bridge to the distant created universe "with pins of adamant" (*PL*, 10.318). Milton compares this labor in its different stages to several things on earth that, huge as they are, are microscopic by comparison: mountainous icebergs clashing on the polar sea of the undiscovered, but in Milton's day eagerly sought, Northwest Passage; the island of Delos, which was once floating and then fixed firm in its place by Zeus; and, lastly, to conclude with a historical event, the bridge made of ships lined up side to side, which the Persian king Xerxes built across the Hellespont (his purpose being to enslave the Greeks), after madly scourging the waves for foiling him at his first attempt:

> So if great things to small may be compared,
> Xerxes the liberty of Greece to yoke
> From Susa his Memnonian palace high
> Came to the sea and over Hellespont

Bridging his way Europe with Asia joined
And scourged with many a stroke th'indignant waves.

(PL, *10.306–11*)

"Europe with Asia joined": one of earth's vast continents is here joined
to another: that is the *small* thing to which a far greater is compared.
In all these passages we see how what is gigantic in Milton's imagination proceeds by way of this mind-stretching comparison of the smaller
with the greater. Johnson's phrase "gigantic loftiness" captures, on the
one hand, how Milton's imagination tends to the gigantic in scale and,
on the other hand, how Milton's personal tone, his moral intensity, is
always lofty without condescension.

The gigantism of Milton's imagination is inseparable from the loftiness of his manner, the conviction he shows at every moment that
nothing can be of greater importance, morally and spiritually, than what
he is speaking of now—just as nothing could be on a greater *scale*. What is
cosmic in scale, and nearly unimaginable—until Milton imagined it
for us—is also of ultimate importance to humans. In medieval biblical
exegesis, the term for the highest level of meaning is *anagogy*, which
means "an ascending" or "going up." *Anagogy* looks like another way of
saying *the sublime*. Milton did not approve of medieval biblical exegesis
because it is too mystical and inward and too fanciful: it is not literal
enough for him, and therefore not *true* enough or *high* enough. The
problem with abstracted sublimities is that they are *abstract*. Milton col-
lapses the literal and the eschatological levels of biblical meaning in his
poem, so that the poem is always beckoning its readers to ascend to its
level of grandeur and moral seriousness.

If there is one moment of the poem we might venture to say is not sublime, because it is elegiac and pastoral, it is in book 11, just before the
arrival of the angel Michael and his troop of cherubim, with their order
to expel Adam and Eve from the garden: "If patiently thy bidding they
obey," God says in his commission to Michael, "Dismiss them not dis-
consolate" (*PL*, 11.112–13). They do bear it patiently, just. The shock is
prepared for, and its force augmented, by the irony of the speech Eve
delivers just before, in which she imagines an Eden in which pastoral
contentment is possible, though in the midst of sadness. Erwin Panofsky finely describes this effect in the pastoral tradition as a "vesper-

tinal mixture of sadness and tranquility which is perhaps Virgil's most personal contribution to poetry."[13] Milton raises this mood of tranquil acceptance of sadness in order to crush it, as false consciousness, although it will survive in the human heart and be expressed in future ages as literature:

> But the field
> To labor calls us now with sweat imposed
> Though after sleepless night. For see! the Morn,
> All unconcerned with our unrest begins
> Her rosy progress smiling. Let us forth,
> I never from thy side henceforth to stray,
> Where'er our day's work lies, though now enjoined
> Laborious till day droop. While here we dwell
> What can be toilsome in these pleasant walks?
> Here let us live, though in fall'n state, content.
>
> (PL, *11.171–80)*

Those first five lines are splendidly true, especially the image of the morning being unconcerned with Eve and Adam's exhaustion (they have been up all night), and beginning her rosy progress through the hours, "smiling." The second five lines are weak, or rather, they are a deliberate and, on the poet's part, ironical cliché, the originative moment of the pastoral tradition. They faintly echo the rhetorical question with which the delusional speaker of Andrew Marvell's "The Garden" concludes: "How could such sweet and wholesome hours / Be reckoned but with herbs and flow'rs?" "What can be toilsome in these pleasant walks?"

Milton's diagnosis of Eve's moral problem is harsh but acute: it is narcissism, the aesthetic contemplation of the self from outside the self, as a picturesque and, in this case, a pastoral other. Eve can *see* the two of them there, in the garden, growing old, but together. If how Eve is thinking at this moment is culpable, it is the crime of literature. Narcissism and literariness are closely allied, and Milton (like Brecht) guards against the danger of their becoming one and the same. Art, Milton thinks, must be for something else and something higher than imagining oneself as an Achilles, or even an Antony. Poetic art must therefore break the circuit of mutual reflection, when the faces we see in the texts seem to look back at us as our friends displaying our own passions and allowing us, in them, to pity or admire ourselves without shame.

Milton now breaks this picture of contentment, incidentally turning Virgil against himself: "but Fate / Subscribed not" (*PL*, 11.181–82; cf. *Aeneid*, 2.428). Adam observes predatory behavior among the animals and birds—an eagle stooping on "birds of gayest plume" (*PL*, 11.186) and an unnamed "beast that reigns in woods" (*PL*, 11.187) pursuing deer toward the eastern gate of Paradise—the same gate through which Adam and Eve will be exiled. These portents show that Eve and Adam's lives will be worse than any life they can imagine for themselves, let alone for their offspring. The final portent Adam sees is the rosy glow in the western sky, which turns out to be a troop of angels under Michael's command making halt on a nearby hill, "a glorious apparition" (*PL*, 11.211). Michael comes forward, a "princely hierarch" (*PL*, 11.220), severe and military in his bearing and armor, like a conqueror, demonstrating in his approach how matters have changed since the sociable Raphael visited Adam and Eve. Michael is now to "seize / Possession of the Garden" (*PL*, 11.221–22), and he looks it. Eve retires and conceals herself, but in a place where she can listen, and Adam goes forward to meet Michael. With no flourish of compliment—for Adam no longer has title to this place or any other—Michael pronounces the eviction, "to remove thee I am come" (*PL*, 11.260). At this, Adam stands, "Heartstrook with chilling gripe of sorrow / That all his senses bound" (*PL*, 11.264–65). The shock is worse for Eve, who by crying out in pain now reveals "the place of her retire":

> O unexpected stroke, worse than death!
> Must I thus leave thee Paradise? thus leave
> Thee native soil, these happy walks and shades,
> Fit haunt of gods, where I had hope to spend,
> Quiet though sad, the respite of that day
> That must be mortal to us both?
>
> (PL, *11.268–73*)

Thus far, Eve's speech has the purpose of recapitulating the sentiment of her earlier, pastoral one, which ended "Here let us live though in fall'n state content" (*PL*, 11.179–80). In her apostrophe to the Garden she addresses it as if it were a person: "thee Paradise . . . thee native soil." The literary habit is growing on her. But she is mostly concerned about herself, in particular, about the loss of her fond hope to spend the rest of her days in this place, her home. We sympathize with her pain, and we feel it, but we do also notice she laments for herself, not for any other, such as Adam, whose loss is as great. She continues in this state of mind, and her lament resonates down the valley of echoes which is the future, pastoral tradition.

But for seven lines before this something different occurs. It is one of the more inconspicuous but fine touches of genius in this poem. Our hearts are won when Eve laments the fate of her flowers, dismayed she will no longer be able to care for them. As soon as Eve cares about others, the flowers who depend on her, we start to care more about her:

> O flowers,
> That never will in other climate grow,
> My early visitation and my last
> At ev'n, which I bred up with tender hand
> From the first op'ning bud and gave ye names,
> Who now shall rear ye to the sun or rank
> Your tribes and water from th'ambrosial fount?
>
> (PL, *11.273–79*)

The angel must interrupt her—we note the need to *interrupt*—and remind her to be patient: "Lament not, Eve, but patiently resign / What justly thou hast lost . . . with thee goes / Thy husband" (*PL*, 11.287–91). This is a reminder: her husband is standing there. The angel tells her that her home now is with him, wherever they wander: "Where he abides, think there thy native soil" (*PL*, 11.292).

Yet the passage on the flowers is heart-rending to us not only for Eve's pain, but also for the pain and loneliness to be suffered by the flowers. We feel the pain Eve feels for them, the long days and nights with no sound from Adam and Eve, and no touch from Eve, no caring—and no water. We do not know the worst, which is that that very evening the flaming sword of God, waving over the Garden as fiercely as a comet, will reduce those flowers to ash (*PL*, 12.633–36). Because we do not know this, we fall in with Eve's sentiment instead of recognizing its ironical inadequacy to the fate of these flowers shortly to be incinerated. But few readers are likely to miss what Eve herself misses at this moment, which is that she is as yet childless, and the care that will be denied to these flowers by her exile from the Garden of Eden will be given to her children, and by the mothers among these to their children. By this thought about children, which cancels its predecessor and yet raises its tenderness up to complete it in time, the episode touches the sublime.

With the exception of this last, which is sublime in the way Virgil's tenth eclogue is sublime, the examples I have given of the sublime in *Paradise Lost* have been unimaginably powerful and vast, taking us within sight of the abysses of space and of time. Johnson said very well of Milton, in the passage with which we began, that "his peculiar power is to astonish." Indeed, we may detect a note of critical irony a little earlier in this passage when Johnson accounts for this power by Milton's "having accustomed his imagination to unrestrained indulgence"—meaning, of course, in political and theological matters, in which, by Johnson's lights, proper restraint should have been shown. Milton accustomed himself to transgression (another word associated with the sublime) "and his conceptions therefore were extensive." There are sublime passages in Johnson's *Rasselas*, but they are spoken by persons in moral danger. Yet there are hints in Longinus—one of them, for example, is a discussion of some exquisitely delicate lines in Sappho—that the elevating transport we are to associate with the literary sublime does not always need to come from the vast. Any moment where the trance of literariness is especially intense, and then broken, or opened, as in the last episode I have considered, achieves the effect Longinus and his followers describe.

Milton's motto was adopted from Saint Paul, 2 Corinthians 12:9, changing the person and tense of the verb: "In weakness I am made perfect."[14] Milton *assumes* loftiness in *Paradise Lost*—he takes it and puts it on, as his singing robe—not to make himself great but to speak with a voice equal to the gigantic subject he treats. He does so by aesthetic means but not to an aesthetic end. His end is to call us upward, out of the world as we find it into the regions of moral engagement. So that we may witness Johnson's sturdy fairness—and, more, his generosity to a man as great as himself but as different as it is possible to be from himself—let us hear him last: "such is the power of [Milton's] poetry, that his call is obeyed without resistance, the reader feels himself in captivity to a higher and nobler mind, and criticism sinks in admiration."[15]

13

On Temptation in Paradise Lost

THE MAIN DRAMATIC ACTION of *Paradise Lost* is taken from the third chapter of Genesis as interpreted by the Christian tradition.[1] This action is the temptation of Eve by Satan—he who "deceived / The mother of mankind" (*PL*, 1.35–36)—which leads to Eve's and later Adam's "disobedience" (*PL*, 1.1) of God's command not to eat the fruit of the tree of the knowledge of good and evil. This action continues through its chain of necessary causes to the judgment of Eve and Adam by God—in the person of the Son, who will redeem them—and their exile from Paradise, which occurs in the final lines of the epic. The poet names *disobedience* as the subject of his poem, which it is. But the event of temptation is the cause of this disobedience and is the key to the poem's main action. From a literary point of view, there could hardly be a more important subject for criticism of *Paradise Lost* than this of temptation.

The ancillary action of *Paradise Lost*—the rebellion of Satan, the war in Heaven, and the Creation of the world and of Adam and Eve (they and their children are intended as replacements for the fallen angels)—is on a larger scale, indeed, the largest scale imaginable. This action takes up most of five books of the epic, books 1 and 2, and books 5 to 7. But these gigantic events are structurally and causally subordinate to the intimate events of the poem's main action, the temptation, transgression, judgment, and exile. As the poet announces in the invocation to the poem, and reminds us in the introduction to book 9, the rest is mere background to what happens quietly in the Garden of Eden between a serpent, a woman, and a man.

Three more books of *Paradise Lost*—books 10 to 12—are devoted to the consequences of the temptation and Fall in the cosmos and in history—all of history, biblically considered, from the first murderer, Cain, who founds the first city (in general, the Bible does not regard cities with favor), to the last city, Babylon, the symbol of Rome, a whore drunk with the blood of the saints. All of which is Adam and Eve's fault, or is supposed to be. That leaves four books out of twelve—books 3 to 4, and 8 to 9—through which the main action of the poem is threaded and briefly tied up at the end.

Everything is at stake in this action. Its critical event is the temptation, which occurs in book 9 in two phases or scenes, one leading directly and swiftly to the other: first, the temptation of Eve by Satan, and second, the temptation of Adam by Eve, or of Adam by Satan through Eve, or of Adam by himself, through Satan, to Eve. It is hard to know for sure, and perhaps this question—who, if anyone, tempts Adam—depends on how far we stretch the meaning of *temptation*, and how and where Milton uses the word and its cognates (*intent* and *attempt*) in book 9.

The root meaning of *temptation* is from Latin *tendere*, "to stretch," and implies a trial of something to know how far it can be stretched before breaking. Milton would also have associated the word with the Greek *peirasmos*, which is used in the New Testament for the temptation of Christ by Satan and, more prominently still, in the Lord's Prayer: "lead us not into temptation," echoed by the poet when Adam says, "Seek not temptation" (*PL*, 9.364). In the Greek, the word also denotes a testing, as when one tests the silver content of a coin. Milton therefore associates *temptation* with *trial*—"trial will come unsought" (*PL*, 9.366; cf. 380)—and with *proof*, "*proof* / Against temptation" (*PL*, 9 298–99). Following Shakespeare, *proof* is a word Milton often uses for "invulnerable," as with armor, but which has the primary sense of "a testing" (L. *probare*). The semantic field of *temptation* stretches as far as proof by scientific experiment, which Bacon compared to torturing a prisoner on the rack, stretching out the victim. Temptation is nearly allied with torment in a legal trial. Lead us not into it.

Temptation and its cognates, *attempt* and *intent*, appear twenty times in book 9, five of them substantives with the definite article, *The Tempter*, the epithet for Satan during his temptation of Eve (*PL*, 9.549, 567, 655, 666, 678). Of the remaining appearances, one is of less semantic importance, being close to our looser sense of the word, which does not imply deception and attack. This is when the narrator tells us the mere sight of the fruit might tempt one to eat it (*PL*, 9.736). Six concentrated appearances of *tempt* occur in the discussion between Adam and Eve, during what is called "the separation scene" (*PL*, 9.281 *tempt*, 296 *tempts*, 297 *tempted*, 299 *temptation*, 328 *tempting*, 364 *temptation*). Also, Satan speaks of his "dark *intent*" (line 162) and Adam of the "attempt . . . *intended* by our foe" (line 295). The word *attempt* in this line is used again when Adam entertains the possibility of Eve being *attempted* (line 369); and it is used twice more retrospectively, near the close of book 9, when Eve says the *attempt* might just as well have succeeded on Adam (line 1149), and when Adam says he thought "no evil durst *attempt* thee" (line 1180).

When she has just returned from the tree of the knowledge of good and evil and is presenting Adam with a *fait accompli*, Eve refers to her eating the fruit as "this my *attempt*" (*PL*, 9.978). It must be emphasized that that is the only use of *temptation*, or of a cognate of *temptation*, when Eve offers Adam the fruit. For the present it is enough to observe that Milton appears studiously to have avoided the word *temptation* on the second occasion the fruit of the tree of knowledge of good and evil is eaten.

The crucial appearance of *temptation*, from a dramatic point of view, is when Satan first speaks to Eve:

> He, glad
> Of her attention gained, with serpent tongue
> Organic or impulse of vocal air
> His fraudulent *temptation* thus began.
>
> (PL, *9.528–31*)

Milton understands *temptation* to denote a hostile act of testing with the *intent* to destroy. Satan prepares to enter the "mazy folds" of the serpent, "To hide me and the dark *intent* I bring" (*PL*, 9.162). The like meaning for *intent* appears later when Adam uses both cognates of *temptation* in a single line: "*Th'attempt* itself *intended* by our foe" (line 295). In *Paradise Lost* an *attempt* is hostile, as when Satan says that God, by concealing his power, "*tempted* our *attempt* and wrought our fall" (*PL*, 1.642). God hostilely lured us kindly angels into revolt.

In book 9, *attempt* appears on five occasions, on four of which the word clearly means "attack" (*PL*, 9.295, 369, 1149, 1180). On the other occasion, to which I have alluded, the apparently innocuous meaning is "an effort." But the dramatic situation causes the word to draw in darker senses. Eve is offering the fruit she has eaten to Adam, so that he will eat of it also. She says if she thought death would ensue from disobedience, as was promised, she would never ask Adam to eat: "This my *attempt* I would sustain alone" (line 978). The dramatic irony, especially after she has herself said she will make Adam eat precisely because death remains a possibility for her (*PL*, 9.826–31), urges a meaning remote from what Eve intends: her *attempt* on the fruit *tempts*—it tests, and it torments— Adam. He says to himself, "How art thou lost, how on a sudden lost, / Defaced, deflow'rd, and now to death devote!" (*PL*, 9.900–1).

Does the irony in Eve's use of *attempt* reach so far as to suggest she is tempting Adam, submitting him to a trial, with hostile intent? Do her words, "Confirmed then I resolve / Adam shall share with me in bliss or woe" (*PL*, 9.830–31), make it certain she is *tempting* him, which in Milton's sense is a hostile testing, a *trial* (e.g., *PL*, 9.370)? If we may judge from where the poet uses *temptation* in book 9, we must conclude Eve does not *tempt* Adam as Satan has tempted her, nor does she tempt in some diminished sense that permits us to consider her in analogy to Satan, although Adam, at his lowest moral point, will propose just such an analogy: "Out of my sight, thou serpent!" (*PL*, 10.867). Eve appears to be doing something else, not something praiseworthy, to be sure, but something human, not diabolical. I shall return to this point when I examine the scene in which, having eaten the fruit already, Eve tries to persuade Adam to eat of it, too. I say "tries" because Adam doesn't need persuasion further than the fact of Eve's having already eaten the fruit. Adam sees she is ruined and instantly knows he is ruined with her. Eve therefore does not tempt, in Milton's sense of the word. But Adam is tried all the same. Within the ideological terms of the poem, he fails.

I have mentioned the concentration of uses of temptation in the exchange, or rather the much-debated debate, between Adam and Eve, before they separate, when they speculate on the assault intended by their enemy. This is the famous "separation scene." Eve wishes to work separately, for the sake of efficiency, she says. Adam prefers they stay together because, he says, their "malicious foe" is "nigh at hand," intending, among other possibilities, "to withdraw / Our fealty from God" (*PL*, 9.253, 256, 261–62). Speaking of her own fealty, Eve says it should not be called in doubt merely because "we have a foe / May *tempt* it" (*PL*, 9.280–81). Later, she says "only our foe / *Tempting* affronts us with his foul esteem / Of our integrity" (*PL*, 9.327–29). That is, he affronts us with his foul esteem of us, but not with any worse result, and as for the affront, which Adam thinks serious enough in itself to avoid, she says, rather finely, "His foul esteem / Sticks no dishonor on our front but turns / Foul on himself" (*PL*, 9.329–31).

That is her reply to Adam's thought that the mere insult of an attempt—setting aside the danger—is offensive enough to avoid, by staying together. It is surely a trivial argument to venture in a serious cause:

> To avoid
> Th'*attempt* itself *intended* by our foe.
> For he who *tempts*, though in vain, at least asperses
> The *tempted* with dishonor foul, supposed
> Not incorruptible of faith, not proof
> Against *temptation*. Thou thyself with scorn
> And anger would resent the offered wrong
> Though ineffectual found.
>
> (PL, *9.294–301*)

In all these instances of the word's use, *temptation* is understood to be hostile, a "sly assault" (line 256) by an enemy intending to destroy by fraudulent seduction, capturing the will of another and winning that other, as Satan says, "to what may work his utter loss" (*PL*, 9.131). This is the "dark intent" that Satan brings (*PL*, 9.162). When Adam says, "Seek not temptation" and "Trial will come unsought" (*PL*, 9.364, 366), he clearly believes something much more grave than that an insult is impending. But as the passage quoted above shows, he has let himself be maneuvered into a position—or he has let himself be cowed into it—where a successful assault by Satan on Eve cannot be entertained as a possible danger, lest he impugn Eve's faith: "Thoughts which, how found they harbor in thy breast, / Adam, misthought of her to thee so dear" (lines 288–89). Since she is so dear to him, he'd better get rid of those thoughts. Adam thus accepts Eve's position that to think Satan dangerous is an insult to Eve. As I said, it is a trivial argument in such a cause as this, and it does not leave Adam much room to dissuade Eve from working apart. He is forced by his own logic to assume what he does not believe—that Satan is no danger—and then to affirm weakly that Satan will *try* to be dangerous, which would be rude.

Adam shows more spirit later. He replies "fervently" (*PL*, 9.842) to Eve's irresponsible claim they are not happy if they have to stay together out of "fear of harm" (*PL*, 9.326). To Eve's "Frail is our happiness if this be so / And Eden were no Eden thus exposed" (*PL*, 9.340–41), Adam retorts that God did not make Eden deficient (Satan did, if anyone), and that whatever danger there is in the enemy's assault lies in human nature, particularly in the will, which should always be governed by reason. But the will is free and follows reason freely. The *reason* he is referring to is "right reason" *(recta ratio)*, which is another term for "conscience," the law of God written in the heart. Right reason is always innately right. But reason must "beware" of deception and falsehood and remain "still erect"—that is, always upright—so as not to be taken by surprise by some "fair appearing good." If reason is deceived by an apparent good it will dictate to the will to choose this apparent good over a higher good (e.g., a moral duty), or, worse, the deceived reason will dictate to the will to transgress God's law outright. That is what happens to Eve, and its cause is temptation:

> Within himself
> The danger lies, yet lies within his power:
> Against his will he can receive no harm.
> But God left free the will, for what obeys
> Reason is free, and reason he made right
> But bid her well beware and still erect
> Lest by some fair appearing good surprised
> She dictate false and misinform the will
> To do what God expressly hath forbid.
>
> (PL, *9.348–56)*

The speech is a formulation in brief of Milton's ethical psychology, with its hierarchy of reason, will, and appetite, although the last, appetite, is left out of account here—a significant omission for this speaker. Except in cases of devilish perversity, sin, in Milton's liberal judgment, is the preferring of a lesser good to a higher, in effect, a misunderstanding. Sin is indulging "some fair appearing good" (*PL*, 9.354) that we talk ourselves into acceding to, against our better judgment. A harsher view, Saint Augustine's, is that sin is no misunderstanding but is always perverse, a rebellion against God, however trivial the crime, because one sins not for love of the inferior good obtained, as Milton supposes, but for love of the crime in itself. Of course, the truth for the most part is somewhere in between, in the swelling of a bell curve, as no doubt Milton knew, when not theorizing.

After the Fall, when Adam and Eve wake from their slumber, Milton applies this psychological model again when describing their "inward state of mind," formerly "calm . . . And full of peace, now tossed and turbulent":

> For Understanding ruled not and the Will
> Heard not her lore, both in subjection now
> To sensual Appetite who from beneath
> Usurping over sov'reign Reason claimed
> Superior sway.
>
> (PL, 9.1125–31)

What follows, however, is no longer sensual appetite but mutual recrimination.

Milton does not think, as has been affirmed, and as he himself affirms in *De Doctrina Christiana*, that all possible sins are included in the crime that Eve and Adam commit.[2] That is to give too metaphysical and magical an account of original sin for Milton's inclination in this poem, which is always physicalist and ethical. Without diminishing the ethical gravity of the original sin, its importance for the fate of the world, which will fall with Adam and Eve, Milton's view of their sin is surprisingly tolerant and mild, so far as their personal responsibility is concerned. Eve was deceived (the point is mentioned several times, even by God), and, like Romeo, she thought all for the best. Adam was not deceived, and so has less excuse than Eve does, but he too thought he was making the best of a bad situation.

For Milton (his psychology is traditional, and can be found, for example, in Richard Hooker's *Laws of Ecclesiastical Polity*), the demands of

appetite and will are good things in their places, the former being necessary to life and the latter to action. Reason is necessary to direct the
will into correct judgments and upright actions. The demands of appetite and will are good when appetite is subordinate to will and will is
subordinate to reason. For example, eating—and not daintily but "with
keen dispatch / Of real hunger" (*PL*, 5 436–37)—is good when kept in
check by the will. The same is true for the sex drive (*PL*, 4.764–65).
The will should indulge both according to the dictates of reason: at
proper mealtimes, and after proper marriage. Sin, as I said, is letting
something appetitive overpower and misdirect the will, or letting something merely willed overpower reason. What Adam is saying is that we
are vulnerable because our will is free: an enemy might try to deceive
either him or Eve (if they are separated from each other) by interposing
some fair appearing good between the reason and the memory of what
God has forbid. He gives an excellent account of what Milton means
by *temptation*.

Adam will conclude his argument against Eve's working separately with the stiffer assertion—he has come a long way from his first
argument—that if she wants to prove her *constancy* against real danger,
she should first prove her *obedience* to him. She should do so, he argues,
because the former, constancy, cannot be known or evidenced (*probare*)
except by trial, which is dangerous and should not be sought, whereas
the latter *can* be known—by her staying: "Wouldst thou approve thy
constancy? Approve / First thy obedience, Th'other who can know /
Not seeing thee *attempted*, who attest?" (*PL*, 9.367–69). No ordeal, no
proof. But why actively seek an ordeal, which will come anyhow? Adam
judges it is better to listen more carefully to him. When Milton uses a
word, such as *obedience* (L. *ob* "to," "against," +*audire* "to listen"), he uses
and whole word, pulling it up by the roots. *Obedience* means the readiness to execute a command, and indeed Eve will later ask Adam why he
failed to command her to stay (*PL*, 9.1155–56). Adam refuses to issue a
command—"thy stay, not free, absents thee more" (*PL*, 9.372)—yet he
does demand to be heard all the same, to be *obeyed* in this less stringent
sense, listened to, as to an authority. Eve is not bound to obey, but she
can *approve*—that is, test, give witness of—her capacity to listen. Milton
has not arrived there yet, but he is moving toward a conception of
Adam and Eve as equals capable of listening to each other, even when
the other does not speak.

Adam has established that an attempt against Eve will seek to pervert her reason to misinform her will, such that she will be made to think she is doing the right thing. But he has also made it clear—not least from the sense that he and Eve have established for the words *temptation* and *attempt*—that this attempt will be an attack, not an insult. In his final words to Eve, Adam returns to Eve's claim that the external world of Eden is imperfect if they are exposed to temptation in it, and to his counterclaim that Eden is not imperfect, but that they are vulnerable within themselves. He summarizes this with the injunction, "God towards thee hath done his part: do thine" (*PL*, 9.375).

Before he says this, Adam has given Eve permission to go: "But if thou think trial unsought may find / Us both securer than thus warned thou seem'st, / Go, for thy stay, not free, absents thee more" (*PL*, 9.370–72). (She acknowledges that her departure is a permitted one: "With thy permission then" [*PL*, 9.378].) Adam's statement, "thy stay, not free, absents thee more," is to my mind the truest in the poem. Doing anything against your own will and good judgment, to please someone else, is slavery and morally destructive to both parties. Eve should go, if she thinks they are secure; she shouldn't go if, after hearing Adam out, she no longer thinks they are.

Every time I read it, I am surprised at Eve's departure because it means she still thinks they are secure. Of course, for the functioning of the narrative, she must go. But the narrative is not her concern. She is her concern. To say otherwise about her departure is like saying Hamlet must delay killing the king because otherwise there wouldn't be a play. That is true enough, but it is changing the subject: the problem of Hamlet's character is not so easily circumvented. It is right to call to mind that Hamlet is a character in a play, and to reject florid psychological speculation, at least for the purposes of literary criticism and knowledge. But it is wrong to forget why plays are written in the first place. Plays are written so we may watch characters as they are thrust into action, or as they hold themselves back from it. Plays are also written so we may speculate, from hints given in the text, or from soliloquies that disclose motivation, what inner drives *move* characters to act or not to act.

So it is also with the character of Eve at this moment. She must go. The third chapter of Genesis begins with the serpent speaking to her alone, tempting her to eat the fruit, which she gives to Adam. Milton will exploit this biblical fact, the unexplained but also, in the Bible, narratologically necessary separation of Adam and Eve. From it, Milton will build the astonishing scene of Satan's approach to Eve and his temptation of her. That separation will also allow Milton to build the powerful operatic scene of Eve and Adam's reunion, with the trial and fall of Adam, thus completing "the mortal sin / Original" (*PL*, 9.1003–4).

Necessary as it is, Eve's working separately is debated between her and Adam, and Milton never quite succeeds in finding a plausible psychological reason for Eve's separating herself. Nor is this a fault on Milton's part. It is not unreasonable to think Milton composed the scene to find a plausible psychological reason for the separation of Adam and Eve in the Bible and deliver it. He has Adam deliver his own best reasons against such a separation: "the wife where danger or dishonor lurks / Safest and seemliest by her husband stays" (*PL*, 9.267–68).

Adam could plausibly speak these lines, but they sound rather more like Milton reflecting on his own deserting wife, the one who would return to bear him three children, and die bearing the fourth. It would have been more seemly for Mary Milton, long ago in the spring of 1642, to have stayed with her new husband, rather than going home, though with her husband's permission (however hardly obtained), for a period of four entire months, from Whitsuntide to Michaelmas, May 29 to September 29. Not going would have safeguarded her honor, which was impugned when she failed to return at the agreed time. And it would have kept her safe from the impending war, as well as from the malicious persuasions of her family and friends. These memories bear on Milton's mind as he composes this passage. Soon, war closed traffic on the roads between Oxford and London, and Mary was lost to John, as he then supposed. The fortunes of war would prove otherwise.

I mentioned my continual surprise that Eve does not prefer to stay after what Adam has said, and especially after agreeing with him that, as she says, "our trial when least sought / May find us both perhaps far less prepared" (*PL*, 9.380–82). Adam's argument has had the opposite of its intended effect. It has sent her off, as she puts it, "The willinger" (*PL*, 9.382), but it is hard to see why she is now more willing, if she is, than she was before. This is what leaves the reader speculating after causes. Perhaps the dream Satan whispered into Eve's ear has had an effect, and she is longing after independence because of it (*PL*, 5.32–93).

Perhaps it is merely natural and right for a human being to want to be alone from time to time, as Adam guesses: "For solitude sometimes is best society / And short retirement urges sweet return" (*PL*, 9.249–50). Adam and Eve are still finding out what it is to be what they are, human. Unlike any humans since, they have never been children, and never watched and learned from adults. The thought that a period of solitude, if desired, may cause no breach but actually reinforce a human bond is here a purely theoretical discovery by Adam, who has never been separated from Eve before. We approve his words. But we are apt to forget that, although he was solitary after his creation, and felt the imperfection of his state, Adam is not speaking from experience.

The truth is, we do not know any reason Eve wants to work separately from Adam, except the reason she gives herself, that they will work more efficiently that way (*PL*, 9.320–25). This may be the best reason she has, and strictly speaking, morally speaking, she does not have to give any other, although it may be opposed because of the present emergency. Adam points out that the garden is for them, rather than they for the garden, but this comment is not followed up: "For not to irksome toil but to delight / He made us and delight to reason joined" (*PL*, 9.242–43). Politeness perhaps requires some reason for wishing to be solitary, such as the one Eve gives. We are often in life pressed to give reasons why we wish or intend to do something when in fact we do not know, and out of politeness we half invent our excuses. We do not particularly care, at least not as much as others seem to, why we choose what we do and decide as we do. Within the limits of morals and prudence, life is an affair of living and taking decisions, often by "fine slicing"—adjusting decisions from within the flow of action ever more finely as the moment approaches—rather than by detached reflection. Discovering the deepest cause of every decision, however trivial, and only then acting, would paralyze action.

The morality of a proposed action must certainly be discussed, if the morality of it is in question, and so too must the prudence of an action, if its prudence is in question. In a couple, the efficacy of an action may also be discussed, as in a family or an association. But not every decision can or should be accounted for all the way down, so to speak, even to partners, or to parents, or to children. (The tension in relationships comes from differences over where this line is or should be drawn.) Eve wants to go and is free to do so. That is enough for her; it should be enough (and it is) for Adam, after an attempt at a reasonable assessment of the danger. It should also be enough for us, without indulging in one thought too many.[3] I think Milton would have accepted the account I have just given of why we are not required to know Eve's motive beyond the one she gives. But if he did, it might be a little impatiently. So far as he is concerned, the Bible says Adam and Eve were separated, and therefore God wanted Eve to be tested first, alone.

So Eve is alone, and the temptation goes forward, not as a theoretical matter for prudential discussion, but as a real event, an assault, and a trial. The temptation is prepared for with exceptional literary skill, even, if I may venture to say so, for Milton. Milton gives a close-up of Eve drawing her hand out of Adam's, and he lingers painfully (and a little pointedly) on the word *husband:* "Thus saying, from her husband's hand her hand / Soft she withdrew and like a wood-nymph light" (*PL*, 9.385–86). Their hands will not be joined again until after both have fallen, and we are of course meant to notice the difference of circumstances in the difference of verbs, *withdrew* and *seized:* "Her hand he seized and to a shady bank / Thick overhead with verdant roof embow'red / He led her nothing loath" (*PL*, 9.1037–38). Eve departs from Adam looking like a goddess, half-wild, half-domestic: she is like Delia, the wild huntress, but she promises to return at noon and have the meal ready, like Pomona, goddess of fruit. The sad irony of her assurance calls forth an apostrophe imitating Homer's aside concerning Patroclus, in book 16 of the *Iliad*, when Patroclus asks Achilles to permit him to don Achilles's armor and fight alone, since Achilles will not: "a great fool, not knowing he was asking for his own death, his evil and his fate."[4] The word "fool," *nêpios*, is taken up at the end of this, the sixteenth book, by Hector, when he kills Patroclus: *nêpie*.[5] Milton improves on it, if anything in Homer can be improved on: "O much deceived, much failing, hapless Eve, / Of thy presumed return! Event perverse!" (*PL*, 9.404–5). In contrast with Homer's judgment on Patroclus, Milton says the *event* is perverse "upside-down, backwards, turned-around." The *event* is contrary to Eve's fortune, and the cause of her death; however, she is not the cause herself; the weight of guilt is being subtly and of course partly shifted to the event in itself. Eve is therefore not a fool like Patroclus, even when she asks for what will prove her destruction. When Milton says she is "much failing," it is important to take into account how he finishes the sentence. She is "failing . . . of [her] presumed return" (*PL*, 9.405). She is not failing ethically. She is failing to return as planned:

> she to him as oft engaged
> To be returned by noon amid the bow'r
> And all things in best order to invite
> Noontide repast of afternoon's repose.
> O much deceived, much failing, hapless Eve,
> Of thy presumed return! Event perverse!
> Thou never from that hour in Paradise
> Found'st either sweet repast or sound repose,
> Such ambush hid among sweet flow'rs and shades,
> Waited with hellish rancor imminent
> To intercept thy way.
>
> (PL, *9.400–10*)

As she trips lightly through the groves and by the ranks of flowers, an ambush has been set to intercept her and send her back despoiled (*PL*, 9.408–11). Not her only her but Adam, too, and in them both "The whole included race" (*PL*, 9.416). But as for Eve, the telling word is *hapless*, unlucky—*hap* is related to *happen* and denotes what occurs, what takes place and emerges (cf. Ger. *geschehen*), what comes about by chance, by circumstances out of our control. After showing Eve a little strong-headed—not a bad thing in anyone, from time to time—Milton goes out of his way to free her of any blame for leaving Adam's side. She has a right to, she chooses what she has a right to, and she is unlucky to be waited for by Satan, through no fault of her own. She is a tragic figure, and her leaving Adam is a *harmartia*, a mistake, but not a flaw. I myself would blame her more than Milton does. She is courting disaster, and she knows it. But Milton takes as much blame off Eve as he can.

The camera (let us use anachronism for the better understanding of the poet's art) has turned to Satan: "For now, since first break of dawn the Fiend, / Mere serpent in appearance, forth was come" (*PL*, 9.412–13). Eve is now seen as Satan sees her, through his borrowed serpent eyes, red as carbuncles (*PL*, 9.500). Two great similes will follow. Satan's sight of Eve rouses feelings like that of the person, no doubt a man, who walks out of London into the country, having been "long in populous city pent" among "houses thick" and "sewers." Wordsworth would make much out of these lines. The solitary walker is delighted by all he meets, dairy farms and cattle, the smell of grain and grass. But his wandering delight is concentrated—"sums" is Milton's word—in the sight of a "fair virgin," who passes "with nymph-like step" (*PL*, 9.445–56). Is her name Lucy? So Eve appears to a briefly Wordsworthian Satan, leaving him for a moment "abstracted . . . From his own evil" and "Stupidly good" (*PL*, 9.463–65). (Milton means Satan is in a *stupor*, immobilized, not that he is *stupid*, in our sense of the word: far from it.) With his usual swift insight, Adam suspects their enemy envies their conjugal love, "than which perhaps no bliss / Enjoyed by us excites his envy more" (*PL*, 9.263–64).

Satan now is given another soliloquy, condemning his own sexual attraction to Eve, which is, as he rightly judges, a lingering trace of goodness in him. (Are we supposed to picture a *serpent* saying this?) He must therefore renounce it, and "all pleasure . . . Save what is in destroying" (*PL*, 9.477–78). Satan shrewdly remarks that under normal circumstances beauty is intimidating, and the feeling of love—by which he means arousal—makes beauty more intimidating still, arousing "terror" as well as desire (*PL*, 9.490). But the terror can be overcome by hate, "Hate stronger under show of love well-feigned" (*PL*, 9.492). Where did Milton learn such a thing, we may wonder—the efficacy of hate to seduction? From a chance remark of one of the "young sparks" with whom he would "venture his body so far as to spend a gaudy day" in London, when he was studying at Horton?[6] Classical authors, Euripides, for example, or Catullus—*odi et amo*, "I hate and I love"—might have led him to the thought. Or did he learn it from Shakespeare, in *The Rape of Lucrece, Measure for Measure, Othello,* and *Cymbeline*? Perhaps he put the thought together unconsciously out of hints from all these sources. Such is the mystery of the knowledge poets have.

In the run-up to the second simile the camera changes again: the picture shifts from Satan's view of Eve to our view of Satan in the serpent, "inmate bad" (*PL*, 9.495). He does not undulate on the ground with "indented wave" (*PL*, 9.496)—*indented* is from *As You Like It*—but floats aloft on his coils, his head and neck rising from the middle of them, burnished with "verdant gold" (*PL*, 9.501). His coils are piled on top of one another and continually in motion, waving and curling delightfully, like a "surging maze" (*PL*, 9.499). This wonderful expression, *surging maze*, at once beautiful and sinister, but simply beautiful to Eve, suggests the style of temptation Satan will undertake. Eve will be overwhelmed by a maze of arguments—specious non sequiturs and unapparent contradictions—that surge over her head.

We learn a little later, after the simile, that Satan's "sleek enameled neck" supports a head that has a "turret crest," or "mural crown," as it is called, suggesting city walls, worn by Cybele, the earth goddess of Phrygia, adopted by ancient Rome, and associated by the church fathers with obscene rites to Attis (*PL*, 9.525). Perversion, tyranny, and arrogance are suggested all at once. Even so, the serpent fawns on Eve and lowers his turrets so far as to lick the ground on which she treads (*PL*, 9.526), hoping she will catch sight of him and "mark his play" (*PL*, 9.528), which of course she does.

The description of Satan in the serpent as a maze of gorgeous coils floating and curling in all directions is followed by a virtuosic passage of classical allusion—virtuosic and, perhaps to our eyes, being accustomed to the novel—a form that emerges after Milton—pedantic. Classical allusion is a vital aspect of the texture of Milton's aesthetic appeal. It is not necessary to follow everything, to track every reference down and read it, with its entire text, in the original language, unless one has a professional interest. It is enough to luxuriate in the resonant sounds of burnished antiquity. The passage describes serpents in ancient myth that were not what they seemed: a king and a queen, Hermione and Cadmus; the god of healing, Aesculapius, who traveling from Epidaurus in the form of a great serpent was once lodged for a night in the poet Sophocles's house; and Jove himself, who in the form of a serpent begot, on separate occasions, Greek and Roman conquerors, Alexander the Great and Scipio, "the heighth of Rome" (*PL*, 9.510). The simile reminds us serpents are powerful and dangerous, especially mythical ones who aren't serpents except in appearance, as with Satan here. But the chief aesthetic effect of the passage is to give repose to our attention, delighting in remote associations, which are of interest in themselves, so that we will be returned to the main action refreshed. As with simile, the point is not to develop a comparison but to break the attention—and then restore it—awakening the reader from a trance.

Instead of breaking the trance yet, a second simile opens on an English coasting vessel—that, or more probably the vessel on which Milton was carried along the coast of Liguria to Livorno, past mountainous headlands and the mouth of the Arno, descending from Milton's inland destination, Florence. Like a ship at the mouth of a river, or rounding a headland, where the wind keeps changing direction, the serpent moves, as serpents do, "with tract oblique" and "sidelong" (*PL*, 9.510 and 512). The shifting winds cause the ship's pilot to tack, to reset the sails rapidly and often, continually changing direction so as to make way obliquely toward his goal. To an inexperienced eye, the pilot will even appear to be heading in the direction opposite to what he intends, or nearly so: "So varied [Satan] and of his tortuous train / Curled many a wanton wreath in sight of Eve / To lure her eye" (*PL*, 9.516–18). We are already put on alert—as Eve is not—to the deceitfulness of the temptation to follow.

Eve notices the serpent's "play," and the mere notice invites him to speak. In typical fashion—for Milton does believe in giving an account wherever physical things are concerned—the poet speculates on how this speaking would have been accomplished, whether by using the serpent's tongue or by emitting pulses of air that vibrate in the elongated tube of the serpent's body, as in a flute. By the one or the other means, Satan begins his "fraudulent temptation" (*PL*, 9.531).

With the word *temptation* we have reached the intensest moment of the epic's action: the first words of Satan to Eve. The defining word added to *temptation* is *fraudulent*, a nonrestrictive adjective: all temptation is fraudulent, not this one in particular (*PL*, 9.532–732). The restrictive sense would imply there are some temptations that are fraudulent and some that are not (may I tempt you to a glass of wine?). But that is not Milton's meaning. *Fraudulent* is for him almost the definition of temptation, plus destructive intent directed at another's will.

Satan's speech of temptation extends for more than two hundred lines (*PL*, 9.532–732), the ending clearly marked by the words, "He ended" (*PL*, 9.733). Another fifty lines are needed for the work of the temptation to take effect on Eve's thoughts and prompt her to "reach and feed" till "all was lost" (*PL*, 9.733–84).

I mention this first to show how well proportioned the entirety of book 9 is, without sterile exactness. Its six scenes (excluding the forty-seven-line introduction) may be divided between three dramatic tableaux, each exceeding two hundred lines, of which the longest is this, Satan's temptation of Eve, and three shorter, narrative scenes, which are transitional, falling under two hundred lines each. The narrative scenes are (a) Satan's preparation, with his entering the serpent; (b) Satan's approach to Eve, beginning when the serpent wakes at dawn; and (c) the closing scenes of book 9, when the effects of eating the fruit begin to be seen. The first (a) is a transition from book 4 (the last time we saw Satan on earth). The second (b) is a transition from Satan's waking and moving the serpent to his addressing Eve for the first time. The third (c) effects a transition to book 10, in which the consequences of the Fall are further expatiated on—or, to use Milton's word in the argument to book 9, extenuated. These transitional scenes, to repeat, are narrative in character and frame the three dramatic tableaux.

The three dramatic tableaux are the separation scene between Adam and Eve; the temptation of Eve by Satan and, after her fall, her soliloquy; and Eve's return to Adam and her giving him the fruit. The alternating narrative and dramatic scenes of book 9 of *Paradise Lost* may be laid out as follows:

Introduction: 47 lines
1. **Satan's Preparation** (narrative): 144 lines
2. **Adam and Eve's Separation** (dramatic): 219 lines
3. **Satan's Approach** (narrative): 119 lines
4. **Eve eats the Fruit** (dramatic): 254 lines
5. **Adam eats the Fruit** (dramatic) 227 lines
6. **Consequences of the Fall** (narrative) 178 lines

Throughout Satan's temptation of Eve the poet is careful to give us Eve's point of view: she sees and hears only a serpent, who talks. In this scene, he is never called "Satan." He is referred to chiefly by a name that denotes the action he performs, "the Tempter" (*PL*, 9.549, 567, 655, 666, and 678). Of course, Satan appears only much later in the Old Testament, and until his dramatic role in Job, only for brief mention in 2 Chronicles and 2 Kings, and in this last he is not named. Satan has no part whatever in the story in Genesis—that is a later, mostly Christian invention. In Genesis, Eve is tempted only by a serpent, who has no identity other than being one of the beasts of the field invented by God: "Now the serpent was more subtle than any beast of the field which God had made" (Genesis 3:1). The phrase is closely followed when Eve addresses the serpent: "Thee, Serpent, subtlest beast of all the field /

I knew, but not with human voice endued" (*PL*, 9.560–61). He is addressed by her again as "Serpent" (*PL*, 9.647) and referred to as such in her thoughts: "How dies the serpent?" (*PL*, 9.764). The narrator refers to "the spirited sly snake" (*PL*, 9.613)—a quiet reminder the serpent has an evil spirit inside—"the wily adder" (*PL*, 9.625), the "dire snake" (*PL*, 9.643), and finally, as this creature slinks back into the thicket while Eve, eating the fruit, is preoccupied, "the guilty serpent" (*PL*, 9.785).

In this crucial tableau Milton wants to keep as close as he can to the text of Genesis. He narrates the action on a double plan: Eve sees only the serpent, in keeping with Genesis, but we know this is Satan tempting Eve, and his brilliance continually reminds us of his presence. Describing the serpent lying asleep on the grass, "in labyrinth of many a round self-rolled" (*PL*, 9.183), Milton appears to have enjoyed inserting Satan into the serpent as surely and slyly as author of all evil has been inserted into the Book of Genesis:

> In at his mouth
> The Devil entered and his brutal sense
> In heart or head possessing soon inspired
> With act intelligential, but his sleep
> Disturbed not, waiting close th'approach of morn.
>
> (PL, *9.187–91*)

For narrative and especially moral reasons Milton also wants to emphasize how much Eve knows, but especially how much she does not know. Milton repeatedly says in the poem that she is deceived, starting at the start: the "infernal serpent . . . deceived / The mother of mankind" (*PL*, 1.34–36). Eve's simple and dignified statement before her judge—unlike Adam's, it is not "Bold or loquacious" (*PL*, 10.161)—is not challenged because it is true: "the serpent me beguiled and I did eat" (*PL*, 10.162; Genesis 3:13). She does not, like Adam, transgress the prohibition open-eyed and undeceived.

The serpent begins by telling Eve that she, not Adam, is the fairest resemblance of her Maker, that all creatures gaze on her with ravishment, but that because they are "shallow to discern / Half what in thee is fair" (*PL*, 9.544–45), no one really sees her for what she is—except one, "and what is one?" (*PL*, 9.546), a thought captured from Marlowe's *Hero and Leander* ("one is no number"), when Leander addresses Hero "like a bold sharp sophister."[7] The concept of number is grounded in difference, the difference of one unit from another: one, therefore, if it is alone, is no number. One man seeing Eve's beauty is equal to no one seeing her beauty, "who should'st be seen / A goddess among gods adored and served / By angels numberless" (*PL*, 9.546–48). This immoral multiplication is caught by Adam, after his fall, when he says "it might be wished / For this one tree had been forbidden ten" (*PL*, 9.1025–26), and it catches the devils when they are punished in Hell for seducing humanity. They are forced to eat the bitter fruit of a huge grove of trees, each one an image of the tree of the knowledge of good and evil (*PL*, 10.547–76).

By multiplying Eve's adorers, Satan has planted the seed of vanity, but also of discontent. His entire temptation will build on this point wisely drawn by Milton from the twisted logic of desire. Eve is made to feel she deserves something that at once belongs to her and yet is also somehow denied her. Like a credit card, the fruit will set this contradiction right. As she will observe just before she puts her hand to the fruit: "Here grows the cure of all" (*PL*, 9.776).

When Eve expresses her astonishment that the serpent can speak, he tells her he learned to do so by eating the fruit of a certain tree, which he then offers to show her. The description of his leading her to the tree is well known for its imitation of how he will lead her on in his tempting speeches, making intricate seem straight, when in truth he is involving her in further tangles of logic: "He leading swiftly rolled / In tangles and made intricate seem straight / To mischief swift" (*PL*, 9.631–33). We may note also his description of how he became articulate, or "speakable of mute" (*PL*, 9.563), as Eve tersely puts it. He did so by eating the fruit, having got up into the boughs of the tree, while the other beasts stood below watching, "Longing and envying" (*PL*, 9.593). He appeals to the pleasure of exclusiveness, unknown to Adam and Eve before. To be exclusive, like a universal goddess, is to exclude. But it is also to be vulnerable to the sense of being excluded from what one should have by right. To be exclusive is always to be excluded at the same time. The wedge is slipped a little further in.

Brought to the tree of prohibition, Eve says they might have spared their coming thither because they are forbidden to eat from this one tree, and it is God's only command, "Sole daughter of his voice" (*PL*, 9.653). Of course, she hasn't said before she would eat of it, too, only that she was curious to see it; so her remark they might have spared coming to the tree is not consistent with their reason for coming.

It is clear Milton is interested in the legal status of the tree. The prohibition against eating of it is a law, the only one, and therefore questioning the reasonableness of the prohibition (or how far it extends: to snakes?) is beside the point: "The rest we live / Law to ourselves: our reason is our law" (*PL*, 9.653–54). The serpent acts surprised at this, and asks a question that cleverly turns on the ambiguity of the word *all*—"Hath God then said that of the fruit / Of *all* these garden trees ye shall not eat?" (*PL*, 9.656–57). Eve catches the ambiguity and carefully corrects it—"Of each tree in the garden we may eat / But of the fruit of this fair tree" (*PL*, 9.660–61); then, for the first time, she mentions the penalty for eating of this tree: "Thereof ye shall not touch it, lest ye die" (*PL*, 9.664).

On this point, capital punishment, the real temptation begins, as the serpent "Fluctuates disturbed" (*PL*, 9.668) on behalf of poor humanity, and especially on Eve's behalf, nobly orating in her defense against a punishment she hasn't yet deserved for a crime she hasn't yet committed, although the punishment is threatened by "the Threatener," a splendidly insinuating and shocking epithet for God, which Eve will imitate ("Our great Forbidder, safe with all his spies" [*PL*, 9.815]):

> Queen of this universe, do not believe
> Those rigid threats of death! Ye shall not die.
> How should ye? By the fruit? It gives you life
> To knowledge. By the Threatener? Look on me!
> Me who have touched and tasted yet both live
> And life more perfect have attained.
>
> (PL, *9.685–89*)

The serpent tells her if she eats the fruit she will not die and will be a goddess, or at least rise to be like one, since he, the serpent, acquired human speech and reason, but not human form, after eating the fruit. Far from punishing you for such a petty theft, he says, God will praise you for your audacity in defying his prohibition of the fruit. It is a test, not a law: God is tempting you. The serpent's circling coils are now, as it were, recapitulated in his circular arguments. A just God would not allow anything fearful, such as death, to exist; so because you fear death, this fear proves the inexistence of death: "Your fear of death itself removes the fear" (*PL*, 9.702). It is a subtle elenchus (in the slightly looser sense Milton uses the word), and Eve is taken in, encircled.[8]

It follows, or it seems to, that the prohibition has some other purpose: "to keep ye low and ignorant," for otherwise you will rise to God's level, "and ye shall be as gods" (*PL*, 9.704, 708). For as he, a serpent, by eating the fruit, acquired human mental powers, so she, by eating likewise, shall acquire divinity; the analogy is "but proportion meet" (*PL*, 9.711). (Milton has a low opinion of such Neoplatonic, analogical reasoning.) Moreover, as Satan's masterly speech advances, a singular God is metamorphosed into a plural, beginning with an inconspicuous pronoun, *they* (*PL*, 9.709). Before long, the *they* is explicitly the gods: "The gods are first and that advantage use / On our belief that all from them proceeds" (*PL*, 9.718–19).

Satan has of course advanced the same argument in Heaven, against Abdiel. Creation does not descend from on high, "by task transferred / From Father to his Son" (*PL*, 5.854–55). The angels are instead "self-begot, self-raised / By our own quick'ning power . . . the birth mature / Of this our native Heav'n, ethereal sons" (*PL*, 5.800–3). Satan says to Eve that production rises up from below, with the earth "producing every kind [species], / Them [the gods] nothing" (*PL*, 9.721–22). (A new way of thinking about production appears.)

So why then is the tree forbidden? The serpent has just suggested the reason is envy and fear, lest humans become gods like God. But now he says the opposite: that because God is incapable of envy, there must be no reason for the prohibition, which therefore is not real and not in effect. The tissue of non sequiturs and contradictions ends with a perfect non sequitur. Yet this one resumes what was established, that is, insinuated, at the beginning: that Eve lacks something she has. She is queen of the universe, admired by all, and yet she is not quite a queen, and she is admired by none, or by only one, which by Marlovian mathematics is equal to none. That is why she *needs* the fruit, to set these odds even again. And to this of course the serpent adds that there are many more reasons to eat the fruit just as good as this one, but there is unfortunately not enough time to list them: "These, these and many more / Causes import your need of this fair fruit. / Goddess humane, reach then and freely taste!" (*PL*, 9.730–33). People who read student essays professionally (or catch themselves using this ploy) will recognize the statement. For many reasons I have no time to go into, what I say is true.

The serpent ends with this last conjuration and Eve stands before the fruit, his arguments ringing in her ears, "impregned / With reason (to her seeming) and with truth" (*PL*, 9.737–38). Speaking to herself—this is the first time a human being speaks privately—she repeats his arguments, taking them for her own: "his words replete with guile / Into her heart too easy entrance won" (*PL*, 9.733–34). Milton troubles to mention, as well—for he never forgets his theory of the faculties of appetite, will, and reason—that the hour of noon had come and the smell of the fruit awakened an "eager appetite" (*PL*, 9.740) and "Solicited her longing eye" (*PL*, 9.743).

Knowledge grows here, she says, and nowhere else of any interest to her now, and knowledge, all knowledge, must be wise. Why does God forbid us to be wise? "Such prohibitions bind not!" (*PL*, 9.760). Death is a possible consequence, since it is threatened, but unlikely, given the experiment already performed by the serpent, a reliable witness to his own experience: "author unsuspect, / Friendly to man, far from deceit or guile" (*PL*, 9.771–72). The irony is a little heavy, though not unsuitably. Why then should she fear? The last non sequitur follows as she says the fruit will cure all, for she has not said exactly what this *all* is that she lacks, or what it is she suffers from, which the fruit will cure. The famous lines in which she reaches for the fruit to eat remind us of what we may have forgotten in the drama of this moment: that the world, being created for humanity, will be wounded by the crime Eve now commits:

> Her rash hand in evil hour
> Forth reaching to the fruit, she plucked, she eat:
> Earth felt the wound and Nature from her seat
> Sighing through all her works gave signs of woe
> That all was lost.
>
> (PL, *9.780–84*)

Immediately, she gorges on the fruit without restraint and then praises the tree, promising to worship it each morning and tend it, "Till dieted by thee I grow mature / In knowledge as the gods who all things know" (*PL*, 9.803–4). To repeat: she does not think knowledge or wisdom are to be found anywhere else. She then considers whether she has been observed, and her language becomes reminiscent of the English stage: "And I perhaps am secret: Heav'n is high" (*PL*, 9.811); "But to Adam in what sort / Shall I appear?" (*PL*, 9.816–17).

Eve is considering whether to keep to herself the advantage of superior knowledge gained by eating the fruit, or share the fruit with Adam, and let him also have the knowledge and wisdom therein. She inclines toward keeping the fruit to herself, "for inferior, who is free?" (*PL*, 9.825). But if God *has* seen her—and she appears now to believe the punishment is real—then she will die and Adam will be wedded, as she supposes, "to another Eve" (*PL*, 9.828). The mere thought of this, she says, not knowing at all whereof she speaks, is "A death to think!" (*PL*, 9.830). Of course, it is unpleasant to think of your love with another, and yourself "extinct" (*PL*, 9.829). But it isn't as unpleasant as death. In any event, the thought of Adam enjoying himself with someone else, while she is extinct in his memory, is enough to decide Eve on sharing the fruit. With splendid hypocrisy, a hypocrisy of which she is still unaware, being deceived, she concludes:

> Confirmed then I resolve
> Adam shall share with me in bliss or woe.
> So dear I love him that with him all deaths
> I could endure, without him live no life.
>
> (PL, *9.830–33*)

With a low bow, she departs from her new god, the tree.

The next tableau shows Eve's reunion with Adam, when she gives him the fruit to eat. Note I do not say she *persuades* him to eat the fruit, only that she gives it to him. Eve certainly tries to persuade, but Adam is far from persuaded by what she says: he sees that what Eve says is false, and that she has been deceived. He eats the fruit for his own reasons, not disclosed to her. He cannot bear to be separated from her and would rather die at approximately the same time she does than be compelled to live without her.

Eve's tone has already changed noticeably. Instead of the stately addresses we are used to between Adam and Eve, she greets him happily, but rudely, with a question, "Hast thou not wondered, Adam, at my stay?" (*PL*, 9.856). She speaks of the agony of love she has felt in his absence, and hopes he has suffered such agony, too, only more so. With "countenance blithe" (*PL*, 9.886) she tells him she has eaten the fruit, prompted thereto by the "serpent wise" (*PL*, 9.867). She did it so that Adam and she might be gods, "which for thee / Chiefly I sought, without thee can despise" (*PL*, 9.877–78). We have, of course, just seen the untruth of this. She adds a threat: that if Adam does not soon eat the fruit, she may rise so far above him in divinity it will be impossible to come down to his level again: "Thou therefore also taste . . . Lest not tasting, different degree / Disjoin us and I then too late renounce / Deity for thee when fate will not permit" (*PL*, 9.881–85).

None of this nonsense has the least effect on Adam, except perhaps the threat, although he understands it in a different way. If he does not join her soon in eating the fruit, she will indeed pass into another state where he can no longer reach her, or reach for her. But it is a lower state, death, not a higher, godhead. In his shock, the roses Adam has woven into a crown for Eve fall from his hand, fading and dying as they fall (*PL*, 9.892–93). This bold image is from Ovid, and Dante saw its beauty long before Milton: *"tu mi fai rimembrar dovè e qual era / Proserpina nel' tempo che perdette / la madre lei, ed ella primavera."*[9] These are the Dante's words upon seeing Matelda, in the Garden of Eden, and she reminds him of Ovid's Proserpina, or Persephone, when she lost her flowers and her mother, Demeter, lost her. Matelda represents the spirit of innocent human nature, which has remained behind in this place of innocence when humans were thrust out of the garden, into history. The flowers to which allusion is made in Dante are those Ovid describes being gathered in the field of Enna, in Sicily, and they fall from Persephone's hand, dying, when she is seized by Hades, god of the underworld. So it is with Adam: he feels the hand of death seize him.

Still more important to Milton, however, is the moral sense implied when Adam's joints all relax and his hand goes slack, dropping those flowers (*PL*, 9.891–92). This loss of physical rigor foreshadows the collapse of his will, or displays the collapse as it occurs: "How art thou lost," he says, speaking to himself but apostrophizing Eve, "how on a sudden lost, / Defaced, deflowered, and now to death devote" (*PL*, 9.900–1). He rightly assumes she has been deceived by "cursèd fraud / Of enemy" (*PL*, 9.904–5), although by what enemy he doesn't yet know. This is followed by startling words, startling for their suddenness, because we expect

him to take time to reflect. But it is too late: he has already decided to join
Eve in death: "And me with thee hath ruined, for with thee / Certain my
resolution is to die!" (*PL*, 9.902–3). Even if he were to give another rib
and get another Eve (how many ribs can he spare for such emergen-
cies?), the first Eve would never be forgotten and would never leave his
heart. The "link of nature" draws him, "flesh of flesh . . . and from thy
state / Mine never shall be parted, bliss or woe" (*PL*, 9.911–16).

He then speaks aloud to Eve, and in very different terms, suggesting
the outcome might be favorable, as she says, approving her bold deed,
and agreeing to eat the fruit. His specious arguments need not be re-
hearsed; they mirror what Eve has said. The point is that Adam thinks
one thing and says another: marriage as we know it starts here. The
author of the first serious tracts advocating divorce for incompatibility
of mind knows whereof he speaks.

Adam's resolution is moving. Eve responds movingly, too, weeping
for joy—and her joy is sincere, as is her love—that Adam is willing to
risk "Divine displeasure for her sake, or death" (*PL*, 9.993). Responding
to her emotions, Adam complies all the more readily. Indeed, the scene
is so moving, and so familiar in happier contexts ("yes, I will go with
you to France, since you insist on going"), that Milton is obliged to break
in a little severely: "for such compliance bad / Such recompense best
merits" (*PL*, 9.994–95).

Adam therefore eats the fruit "not deceived / But fondly overcome
with female charm," at which the natural world is again struck: "Earth
trembled from her entrails as again / In pangs and Nature gave a second
groan" (*PL*, 9.1000–1). Adam and Eve do not, however, notice the earth's
agony, for now they are both intoxicated with their crime and feel "Divinity within them breeding wings / Wherewith to scorn the earth" (*PL*,
9.1010). The earth may be trembling in agony, but they scorn it.

Why do they eat? Each is convinced she or he lacks something that
only eating the fruit can restore. Eve lacks adoration; Adam lacks Eve.
Unlike *seduction*, which occurs between two agents when one of them
captures the will of another, *temptation* requires this third, phantasmal
object, which multiplies as sin propagates. As Adam says, in a statement
I have already had occasion to quote, "it might be wished / For this one
tree had been forbidden ten" (*PL*, 9.1026).

The final, dramatic tableau of the book ends here, and the conclusion to book 9 begins in the second half of the line beginning, "Where-

with to scorn the earth": "But that false fruit / Far other operation first displayed" (*PL*, 9.1011–12). A new kind of sexual intercourse is only the first of these operations of the fruit. Others will be the sense of lost innocence, of shame and remorse, of mutual recrimination from which they cannot extricate themselves, although both want to, and the consciousness of what they have done to the earth—that is, to the general system of nature—and to their children for all the generations to come.

I return to the question, who has tempted Adam? Eve hasn't, even if it can be argued that she tried. She isn't deceitful—she is deceived—and *pace* C. S. Lewis, who calls her a murderer, she isn't hostile, although she contemplates Adam's death with immoral equanimity. (A lower charge of manslaughter might stick.) We saw that the word *temptation*, so frequent earlier in the book, appears to have been studiously avoided when Eve returns to Adam after she has eaten the fruit. She has certainly been foolishly bad, but not so bad as to be her husband's tempter. No analogy with Satan may be allowed, although, as we have noted, Adam will suggest it at his lowest moral point. The poet means us to disapprove when Adam calls Eve a serpent. (But he will not expect us to disapprove when the chorus in *Samson Agonistes* calls Dalila a "manifest serpent by her sting" [*SA*, line 997].) Does Adam tempt himself even in a looser sense than Milton's, dandling and toying with the prospect of a sin, resisting it, but only to make surrender more delightful? Not at all. His action is impulsive, leaping to rescue. Does Satan tempt Adam, that is, test him with the intent to destroy, using Eve as bait? In an obvious, narratological sense, he does. Satan may hope Eve will draw Adam with her into sin, as they both draw the earth into sin. But Satan does not deceive Adam. It seems Adam is not tempted to fall, but he does.

The truth is, there are worse things than succumbing to temptation, to being deceived and then misled by your will, whether to greed or to power. A worse thing is willful disobedience of a just law, however poorly understood. That is what Adam has done. He has done so for what we think is the best of reasons, although Milton apparently does not: loyalty to the person who is nearest to you in the world, loyalty to a spouse, and unconditional love of a spouse. But Adam has broken a law, the only law, without hesitation and without remorse, although remorse will come later. Later, he is not so noble as he seems to us to be at this moment.

The psychological schema of a hierarchy of reason, will, and appetite, where sin entails the usurpation of executive authority by a lower level over a higher, can aid us in seeing something most important about the Fall in *Paradise Lost:* Eve falls first, but Adam falls farthest. Eve's will to power gets the better of her reason, and she falls, violating the transgression and eating the fruit. Her appetite is indeed awakened by the fruit, but it is the promise of power based on knowledge that draws her. Eve's will to power through knowledge gets the better of her reason. Adam's physical and appetitive connection to Eve (Milton appears to subsume what we call "emotions" in appetite) makes Adam afraid he will lose Eve. He therefore lacks the will to resist doing what he knows to be wrong. His limbs lose their strength, and his hand goes slack. In his panic, he also lacks the will to think of alternatives to compounding Eve's crime, for he knows it is a crime. I myself, who have more time than Adam did, can think of none, except prayer, C. S. Lewis's suggestion.[10] Adam should trust God to find a better solution than his own. He forgot to trust, and might have remembered to if he had taken more time. One of Milton's phrases for the crime of Adam and Eve, pointedly so called at the beginning of book 9, is "foul distrust" (*PL*, 9.6).

If this analysis is approximately faithful to Milton's intentions, then we may discern how Milton is evening out responsibility for the Fall, correcting a long and well-established tradition that the Fall is woman's fault: *mulier in pricipio hominis confusio est*, says Chaucer's rooster, Chauntecleer ("in the beginning woman was the destruction of man"), which he blandly mistranslates for the benefit of his wife, the hen Pertelote: "Dame, the sentence of thys Lateyn is, woman is mannes love, and all his blis."[11] The hope of a condescending peace in the henhouse did not appear to influence Milton. He wanted men and women to be equals, notwithstanding the official ideology of *Paradise Lost*, in which nothing is equal to anything else and no one is equal to anyone else. But as the divorce tracts show, Milton adhered to the rising bourgeois expectation of companionate marriage, because it makes better economic sense for the middle classes, and because companionship is more pleasing than hierarchy as a way of living with a fellow human being—even if universal hierarchy, including complementary subordination and superiority in marriage, has its aesthetic appeal. Marital hierarchy belongs to the total system of creation, in which all persons and things (and, before the Fall, many "things" are vestigial "persons") complement one another and nothing and no one is equal to anything or anyone else. It is beautiful to contemplate from an aesthetic distance, for example, in a poem.

As I suggested before, a great poem is under no obligation to be always morally reassuring to us, and a great poem is better if it isn't, partly because it provokes us to thought about our own morals, and mostly because it permits us the tolerant and humane experience of traveling to different moral worlds. Hierarchy may be aesthetically attractive from a distance, and it is useful to contemplate. But in our own world it is no way to live with the person you love.

Poets tell the truth, in spite of themselves. They do so even when they are trying to "feign"—the most true poetry is the most true feigning—a universal system of great aesthetic beauty, such as that of *Paradise Lost*, into which everything in life must be forced. Allegory is the most extreme example of this, where making a world fit into a system must be done by force (Gr. *bia*) or "violence' (L. *vis*). Dante's *Commedia* is a powerful, violent system as John Freccero's readings of it have shown, and as Dante inadvertently shows us, as well, in the episode of Paulo and Francesca. So too is *Piers Plowman*, where persons from the field full of fair folk are captured one by one and compelled to perform self-tormenting roles. So too is Spenser's *Faerie Queene*, in which persons are forced into similarly self-tormenting allegorical roles (Phedon, Cymocles, The Squire of Dames, Mirabella), tortured in perpetuity by the concepts they are made to represent. The stress of forcing persons—*personification* is already, as we see in *The Faerie Queene*, a kind of violent capture—into a rigorous and abstract system causes eruptions of violence and pain.[12] Kafka's fable of the harrow is the emblem of allegory. *Paradise Lost* is no allegory. But the worldview, the cosmology, that Milton develops—a physicalist, hierarchical, organic whole, growing up to God, with each part feeding on another, and being fed on in turn—has a powerful, systematic force that is finally, because it is a system, untrue, even to the poet who made it.

Despite himself, therefore, or in spite of his system, Milton evens out responsibility for the Fall because he wants Adam and Eve to be equals after the Fall, and perhaps even before it. What I meant when I said Eve falls first, but Adam falls farther is as follows. Eve is deceived, but she is direct, and aspiring, falling because of her will, not her appetite. Adam is undeceived, indirect when speaking to Eve after the Fall, evasive when confronted with his crime, and morally abject. He falls much farther than Eve does. By thus inverting their positions in the ideological hierarchy of *Paradise Lost*, Milton does more, perhaps, than he intends. The inversion calls the entire system into question, shaking it—soliciting it—to its foundations.[13] Creation itself has been touched, and called into question, as Satan has called it into question. Creation must give way at last to its rebellious offspring, creativity.

Adam's decision to remain with Eve is moving, and surely right, even if, within the frame of the poem's ideology, eating the fruit isn't the best way to do this or to care for her. We are moved by it. This is one of those interesting moments in *Paradise Lost* over which critics are divided because the expansive force of the poetry breaks out of the field of the poem's ideology. The place of criticism is not to take sides at such moments. It is not good criticism to feel liberated from Milton's intentions if they happen to be disagreeable to us (assuming we understand his intentions). But criticism also falls short if it is too zealous to do the poem's ideological work for it (assuming we understand what that work is). Both cases—the latter less obviously, but even more so—imply incompetence on Milton's part. It is better to trust a great artist, up to a point, and after that to trust the tensions at work in great art. That means criticism should inhabit and observe and aesthetically embrace the rupture, the discontinuity, which opens at this moment in *Paradise Lost*.

After they take "their fill of love and love's disport" (*PL*, 9.1042), Adam and Eve fall into a heavy sleep and wake ashamed of their nakedness: "Innocence that as a veil / Had shadowed them from knowing ill was gone" (*PL*, 9.1054–55). They seek broad fig leaves to cover themselves, "what best may for the present serve to hide / The parts of each from other that seem most / To shame obnoxious" (*PL*, 9.1092–94). Before they do so, Adam laments their condition, brought on because Eve "in evil hour . . . didst give ear / To that false worm of whomsover taught / To counterfeit man's voice" (*PL*, 9.1067–69). He does not yet appear to know this is Satan, and will only work it out in book 10. He blames Eve for separating from him, to which charge she retorts he should not have let her go, since she is the inferior: "Being as I am, why didst not thou, the head, / Command me absolutely not to go?" (*PL*, 9.1155–56). Yet in the two previous lines she says the opposite: "Was I t' have never parted from thy side? / As good as grown there still a lifeless rib!" (*PL*, 9.1153–54).

Adam is incensed—"To whom then first incensed Adam replied" (*PL*, 9.1162). He predicts that this will be the lot of men, to "overtrust"

(*PL*, 9.1183) women and let them rule themselves. But when these women bring evil on themselves, they will blame men for giving them the freedom that they themselves sought: "Restraint she will not brook / And left t' herself if evil thence ensue / She first his weak indulgence will accuse" (*PL*, 9.1184–86). How these women will shift back and forth at convenience, from insisting on their independence and equality to profiting from the excuse of their weakness! All this to the confusion (in both senses) of men! If Milton is recalling his first marriage, or at least drawing on something of that experience to compose this scene, then he is not representing himself through Adam in any positive light, although it may be admitted he does get to *say* these things at last, even if he has to put them in the mouth of a speaker whose words neither he nor we can approve. Poets have the last word and can afford to be generous, or at least fair, if they choose. But they do get the last word—as Eve did when she left Adam. The conclusion of book 9 is a judgment on them both: "Thus they in mutual accusation spent / The fruitless hours, but neither self-condemning, / And of their vain contést appeared no end" (*PL*, 9.1187–89).

We observe that the source of this vain contest is hierarchy. He says she should have been subordinate, when she was acting superior. She says he should have been superior, when he was acting subordinate. Neither is self-condemning because in a hierarchy, where one is always above and below at the same time, responsibility shifts—as with linguistic "shifters"—from one position to another, according to use. Against his own system, Milton has them share responsibility, so that it becomes bearable at last, if only just. To bear the responsibility at all, they must bear it equally, as equals. That is what the great final scene of this poem will show us. Adam and Eve have failed one test, one *temptation*. They have perhaps not failed another.

∾ 14

On the End in Paradise Lost

IN ARISTOTLE'S ACCOUNT of tragedy, a well-made play imitates a complete action with a beginning, a middle, and an end. A play thus shows how an action is articulated, with separate moving parts forming a unity, like an animal. Allowing for its greater size and looser organization, an epic poem has roughly this unified and articulated structure, as well. But there is room for subjective judgment, and hence for disagreement, concerning exactly where we place these divisions, or rather, these jointures, and even concerning whether, in particular cases, such jointures are there. After all, joints—*arthroi*—take up a certain amount of space for themselves and are transitional regions. Dr. Johnson affirmed Milton's *Samson Agonistes* is faulty because it has no middle. It is not perhaps evident what Johnson means—the three visitations, or at least the second and third, Dalila and Harapha, certainly look like a middle—unless he means the action has no complication, although Aristotle allowed for simple as well as complex plots.[1] In any event, Johnson thought *Samson Agonistes* has no middle, no thorax, so to speak, like a monster with its legs coming out of its head, and the great critic never thought anything without having good reason for it. But to see what he means we have to look to his mind, not to the page. Do we have a necessary or accidental chain of events?

As this example may show, the word *structure*, when it is not used for architecture, which is where it originated, is a tendentiously objective word. It places what it names entirely outside the mind as a thing merely perceived. But structure is always to some extent an action (L. *struo*) of the structuring, the schematizing mind.[2] In short, structure is responsive to the questions we ask of the world and of literature in particular, according to what we ask and how.

This subjective element in determining structure must increase when we are considering an epic poem, with its many episodes, its preparatory actions, and its parallel, subordinate, and principal actions. The matter will be complicated further by an impulse to draw more lines of division within these divisions—including divisions within whatever we choose to call "the end." Does the end start immediately after the crisis, after the moment of decision: the killing of Hector in the *Iliad*, when two books remain; the slaughter of the suitors in the *Odyssey*, when, likewise, two books remain; or the eating of the fruit in *Paradise Lost*, when three books (formerly, two) remain?[3] Or does the end start nearer to the *end*, in the terminal sense of the word? Is the end something built up into parts? May we speak of an *architectonics* of the end, independent of the division of the epic poem into books? For example, may we speak of the end of book 9 of *Paradise Lost*, starting with the words, "But that false fruit / Far other operation first displayed" (*PL*, 9.1011–12), as the "turnaround" or *peripeteia* out of which the poem's final movement develops?

Certainly, this moment is when we see how Eve and Adam's circumstances are reversed, contrary to what they expect. Adam has been eating the fruit given to him by Eve, and there is just a suggestion his eating is a preoccupied devouring, not the social act eating is supposed to be among humans. German, like other languages, distinguishes between animal *fressen*, "to devour, to feed," and human *essen*, "to eat"; Adam's eating is more like the former than the latter, a greedy engorging: "Adam took no thought, / Eating his fill" (*PL*, 9.1004–5). For a Puritan, and especially for Milton, whose portions were famously exiguous, not taking thought while you eat—and so "eating [your] fill"—is far from a good thing. Eve eats more of the fruit too, not for nourishment but to keep Adam company, "the more to soothe / Him with her loved society" (*PL*, 9.1006–7)—also, not good. The effect on both is exhilarating, and is more like alcohol than food:

> As with new wine intoxicated both
> They swim in mirth and fancy that they feel

> Divinity within them breeding wings
> Wherewith to scorn the earth. But that false fruit . . .
>
> *(PL, 9.1008–11)*

Eve tasted the fruit first because she thought it would bring on divinity in her. Adam was not so deceived: he ate in order to stay with Eve. But his mental clarity is lost as soon as he eats, and he too feels divinity within him, "breeding wings." Like her, he now believes, or feels he believes, he will scorn the earth and fly up to heaven. The *peripeteia* comes when the narrator breaks in with the single adjective, *false*, and with the ironic words, "Far other operation." Far other than what? He means far other than flying, because Adam and Eve want to lie down, being carnally inclined. Adam says, fatuously, "If such pleasure be / In things to us forbidd'n it might be wished / For this one tree had been forbidden ten!" *(PL*, 9.1124–26). He is speaking of the anabolic effects of erotic stimulation, which always wants more stimulation. Never before, he says to Eve, have his senses been so inflamed "with ardor to enjoy thee" *(PL*, 9.1032). The language of selfish objectification is meant to be noted by us, ironically, although it is not noted, or not given any importance, by Eve, who feels the same as Adam does, her eyes igniting "contagious fire" *(PL*, 9.1036). Adam leads her to a couch of flowers—not, and this is important, their bower—to which conduct Eve is "nothing loath" *(PL*, 9.1039). The episode to follow is closely based on the scandalous one in the *Iliad*, the *dios apate*, "deception of Zeus," much criticized in antiquity, including by Plato, in which Hera, to deceive Zeus, seduces him into making love *en plein air*, and the earth pushes up flowers beneath them, to soften their exertions:[4]

> Flowers were the couch,
> Pansies and violets and asphodel
> And hyacinth, Earth's freshest softest lap.
> There they their fill of love and love's disport
> Took largely, of their mutual guilt the seal,
> The solace of their sin, till dewy sleep
> Oppressed them, wearied with their am'rous play.
>
> *(PL, 9.1039–45)*

We expect what is to follow. The exhilarating effects of the "fallacious" fruit, which made their inmost powers "err," wear off *(PL*, 9.1046–49), and they fall into "grosser sleep / Bred of unkindly [unnatural] fumes" (*PL*, 9.1049–50), haunted with accusing dreams. They wake, "As from unrest," and look upon each other with dismay, seeing "their eyes how opened and their minds / How darkened" (*PL*, 9.1052–54).

We should note two things about this watershed passage. The first is that the level of irony has not so much increased as separated itself from horror and suspense. When Eve is contemplating the fruit before eating it, and even when she is meditating after, we read her words with irony, but irony tinged with horror and suspense. The same is true when she separates from Adam, confident of her return. But once Adam and Eve have both eaten and are inflamed to seal their guilt with lovemaking, we read with an irony that is much more distanced, tinged with repugnance. (If we are ourselves a little stimulated by this sexy passage, perhaps more so than by the description of "good" lovemaking formerly, so much the worse for us. We take guilty note of that, too.) This is a new kind of reading in the poem, cooler and more detached, but also more hermeneutically active. For the first time, we are comparing one passage with another.

The other thing we should note about the passage, however, is nearly opposite to this. The *peripeteia* is transitional—it is a joint, or *arthros*—and therefore it continues to elicit a mimetic response, that is, one involving emotional identification and sympathy. That mimetic effect will continue for the remaining 135 lines of the book, up to its conclusion, as we shall see, when Adam and Eve are hopelessly entangled in "mutual accusation" for their crime, "but neither self-condemning" (*PL*, 9.1087–88). For a moment, repugnance gives way—or gives *some* way—to sympathy, as we recognize ourselves in them. On the whole, in the following books, we will read with more detached irony and interpretative textual engagement, but with correspondingly less mimetic sympathy, except for the moment when Adam and Eve are told they are to be expelled from the garden, and the moment when they are.

Milton wants to keep our mimetic sympathy alive and in the mix of our responses, but he wants this sympathy laid much farther back than formerly, allowing other responses to come to the fore. This reversal of the predominating detachment in favor of mimetic sympathy, which we see at the end of book 9, and which returns in book 11 when the exile is announced (*PL*, 11.263–85), returns again at what I will venture to call the end of the poem, when Adam runs to wake Eve but finds her awake; they are rushed out of the garden; and they make their first steps in the world, "with wand'ring steps and slow" (*PL*, 12.648–49). Our detachment gives way, as in a great tragic *exodus*, to the overwhelming pathos of the scene, which I shall return to twice more in this chapter.

But first, I resume the question of the end in *Paradise Lost*. When is the beginning of the end? Is the terminal end part of a larger ending, a final movement? Questions of structure may appear arid, but they will not appear so if we keep in view their rapport with *action*. The quest for structure, that is, for clear divisions between one part and another, belongs to life itself and is produced by the questions we ask of our lives as we live them, and of course also by the questions, or the simple affirmations, imposed on us by the societies in which we live. We ask ourselves when something begins, when something is over, and when a critical point of decision has come. Social rituals help us to make clearer these articulations within the flow of life and more structured, more unanimous, than they actually are. They mark out and articulate the difference between one state of mind and the next. We are forever trying to discern more order in the events of our lives—articulate, jointed order, with separate moving parts—than the events actually warrant.

The mild but pervasive anxiety produced by this noncoincidence of our descriptions of ourselves and the truth is surely among the most important reasons for our attraction to and fascination with literature. Literature gives us life with a higher degree of articulate order, indeed, an order that life itself seems altogether to lack, but that we want it to have, and that we try to create. Similarly, literary characters, however tragic the situations they find themselves in—Creon and Antigone—have less uncertainty about who they are and what they must do in response to events that are simple in comparison with life. Not less terrible, perhaps, but simpler. The point is the clarity and the simplification. If characters *are* uncertain, then, as in *Oedipus*, this uncertainty is magnified—it becomes blindness—and is moved from the periphery to the center of attention, as the subject of the tragedy. But then the pleasure—it is called *irony*—lies in our ability to contemplate the sight (*théama*) of this blindness in another, finding it repugnant but pitiable.[5]

Consider how we reflect on disaster. When did this disaster begin, we ask, when the disaster in question had no beginning in the linear sense that the question intends. What was this disaster's cause, we ask,

when any cause we can identify is a retrospective and unreliable interpretation, a possible but not probable cause. (Satan? Acid reflux? The
first cigarette? The first touch?) At what critical moment, we ask, was
a decision taken that made the onset of disaster inevitable? How long,
we ask, must we endure the consequences of this disaster, when there
will be no end to them. When we are under the stress of disaster, we
cannot help asking such questions, as if true answers would give us some
comfort and some confidence we will survive and even master such
things in the future—and never even die. But whatever we do, however convincing our answers may be, at least to others, we are haunted
by the feeling that we are making a *fiction*—a mimesis, with a beginning,
a middle, and an end. We feel that the fiction we are making has only
a tenuous, imaginary relation to the truth, to what has really occurred,
which remains largely mysterious.

In literature, however, which is deliberate fiction by experts, this *écart*,
this distance or space between answers and truth does not exist. Literature is written with conviction. That is most satisfying. Every question
about disaster I mentioned above is asked in the opening lines of *Paradise Lost*, and every question is answered in the poem, with total conviction of truth. That is why *Paradise Lost* continues to matter to us, quite
apart from any theological or factual claim it offers, and quite apart
from its ideological specificity: it matters because of its *conviction*. With
masterly art, and with magical song, *carmen*, *Paradise Lost* removes the
space of doubt between the answers and truth. It does so on its own
terms, of course, but to its own complete satisfaction, which is the point.
The conviction of *Paradise Lost*—unhesitating, decisive, and passionate—
is a revelation of the human spirit.

That is why we care about literature, and it is also why structure in
literature makes us care about it the more, for structure is the enabling
frame within which conviction convinces. Without its rigorously formal,
dancelike structure, Greek tragedy would not be convincing. Without
the intricately continuous structure of its rhyming *terzine*, sustained
from the beginning to the end, Dante's *Commedia* would not be convincing. It takes a powerful, determined, and convinced character to
do what Dante did. Milton shares with Dante the same obstinate character and the same powerful conviction. I do not mean religious, ideological, or political convictions, although Milton certainly has those,
as Dante does. I mean artistic conviction. Both poets may have acquired

such conviction from their political and religious convictions. But it is an independent thing. Milton's artistic conviction, pursued with great obstinacy, is that nothing less will do for his magnum opus than a full-scale epic poem in the ancient manner for the making of a biblical poem. Milton's holding to that structure so firmly is what makes us feel that the answers he gives to the great questions of life are without any doubt true, in the frame of this work. We want such conviction in a great poet, and structure gives us much of what we want.

It does so especially when it gives a frame for disaster. We want to contemplate disaster clearly, with no distance between answer and truth. Zeus sent a phantasmal idol of Helen—an *eidôlon Helênes*—to Troy, "that hatred might flourish and the slaughter of men."[6] We may not like Zeus, but this is a *satisfyingly true* answer to the question what caused the greatest war of all time and, implicitly to the question, what causes war. Zeus causes war, to lighten the earth of our encumbering presence. What causes bad history, foul sin, incessant and frustrating labor, sickness and death, failed marriages and failed revolutions? God judged Adam and Eve.

To accept such an answer as this as satisfyingly true within the frame of its world means we are concerned with that frame and with the manner in which it affirms a distinction between inside and outside, and also the manner in which it effects a transition from one to the other.[7] What then is the end in *Paradise Lost*, and where is the beginning of this end? What is the poem's endgame, its *fin de partie?* How does it play out, as we say, and how do we play it out, that is, how do we read it from the end of book 9 to the end of book 12? The crisis of the epic, its moment of decision, is the temptation. When that decision is complete, it remains for the consequences of this decision to follow, independently of Adam and Eve—for they no longer decide. But Adam and Eve are still at the center, as the immediate objects of this playing out. If we count from the middle of line 1011 in book 9—"But that false fruit / Far other operation first displayed" (*PL*, 9.1011–12)—there remain almost three thousand lines in the epic (2,917), during which we adjust to and reflect on what has recently occurred, at the temptation. For the temptation, as we have seen, is the moment of decision, the crisis when Adam and Eve judge, after which they are themselves judged, and, as I said, no longer decide. (They no longer decide their fate, but they do decide not to commit suicide and, crucially, they decide to pray.)

In these three books we are not only watching the consequences of the Fall: we are being prepared, and are preparing ourselves, for not being inside the poem at all, for no longer being, for the time being, under the spell of its charm. We cannot see the finish as yet, but we know it is coming, and we feel it coming for the first time. We therefore begin to expect signs that we are not centrally inside the work, in its wooded interior, so to speak, where the temptation occurs, although we are not yet outside. We are approaching the margins of the forest, where the trees and plants begin to change as we go: hemlocks and mosses, and light-fleeing, serpentine Indian Pipe, give way to birches and alders, grasses and ferns. A different kind of imagery surrounds us, less classical, and more biblical. Fewer intimate circumstances are described, especially in contrast with book 9, where what happens, as I said, happens quietly, between a woman, a serpent, and a man. The scene begins to open out upon enormous vistas.

A different kind of reading is now required. The irony, instead of erupting violently, as when Eve departs from Adam, confident of her return, is more pervasive and broadly displayed. The irony also depends more on our vigilance, beginning with the exhilaration of Adam and Eve after the Fall. We also begin to read less dramatically and more interpretatively, connecting what we find on the page with later, heterogeneous phenomena. Biblical typology makes its appearance, and we are now expected to read typologically. We seem almost to be in a new poem, a "region of unlikeness" in which the difference between appearance and truth is continually before us.[8] We are aware we are looking at the page.

We know that, with three books remaining, this is to be a slow denouement, a gradual loosening of dramatic tension, during which new and different tensions arise. *As dramatic tension declines, interpretative tension increases.* This process of transitional exchange may not in its entirety be what we would like to call "the end." We have to find the end in it, or rather the beginning of this end, since the very end of it we know, or think we do: the moment of expulsion. But even the approach to this end is implicated in that end and is nearly indistinguishable from it.

Although the event of the Fall has brought on this new phase of *Paradise Lost*, strangely enough, the event of the Fall swiftly recedes into the distance, as soon as it is past. Already at the opening of book 10, we read of it as if we are reading tabloid headlines, which are shrill but unreal. This just in: a "heinous and despiteful act" (*PL*, 10.1) of Satan "perverted Eve, / Her husband she, to taste the fatal fruit" (*PL*, 10.3–4). In book 9, this facile and mechanical analogy between Satan's act and Eve's is denied. But as the event recedes in the distance, moral distinctions, however important, become hard to discern. The rumor mill has started: Eve is in league with the devil! All women shortly to follow! The Fall itself—not the headlines about it—falls off behind and is nearly lost to sight. It has become the horizon of human beings in the world (or rather it is placed at a point on the wider horizon of time), and, like any horizon, it is far off from where we stand. These last three books of the poem therefore belong more to the very end, almost three thousand lines on, than they do to the crisis that has recently passed, two hundred lines earlier. It is not quite a paradox to say that in books 10 to 12 of *Paradise Lost* the end is anticipated and prepared for in a region of transition that does the work of making the end end. The transitional region is auxiliary to the ending of the poem, but like any auxiliary, any supplement, it is implicated in the identity from which it is more or less formally excluded. In this respect, the transitional region that flows into the ending is part of this ending. It builds up pressure for the debouching of Adam and Eve. How does *Paradise Lost* end itself, inside itself? And what are the signs of the approaching end?

Wherever and whatever the signs are, they will have to do with time. The transitional region of the poem must give us time to consider, to reflect on history—at length, as it happens—but also on what it now means to be human. We must also have time to begin gauging what the poem's consequences will be for us, and what its relevance is to us, while we are still in its presence, still reading, and still under the poet's spell. We do so because we are aware for the first time that the spell will indeed come to an end. We never thought so before.

Milton is telling us that everything human will now be thrust forth in time, defined and determined by change. What does that mean? What will we be, in that case, with change underneath us, like shifting sand? As a consequence of this temporality, everything human will emerge under the limiting conditions of blindness to what is coming in the future, and of myopia with respect to the past. What does *that* mean? What will we know, in that case? Before they fall, whenever they speak, Adam and Eve make poetry spontaneously, but they never invoke the Muses, the daughters of memory. They are never inspired, that is, breathed through by an assisting and benevolent other. They do not have to invoke the daughters of memory because, unlike us, they know. As Homer says, invoking the Muses, "For we have heard only the rumor (or fame, *kleos*), nor do we truly know."[9] The transitional region introduces temporality as the ground of our being and epistemic blindness as the impossible condition of the possibility of knowledge. After Eden, we never quite *exist* and we never quite *know*. Metaphysics and epistemology begin after the Fall, a rather long time after, to repair the ruins of our first parents, or at least to afford a clearer view of the wreckage.

With this latter portion of the epic we pass into a different aesthetic register from the heart of book 9, when the long-awaited, long-prepared-for crisis comes upon us and we are breathless with expectancy and terror, as in a tragedy. There is no time then for detachment. But we feel it immediately upon Adam and Eve's eating the fruit and regard their exhilaration with irony, knowing it is false, and being shocked at how fatuous Adam's language suddenly is. There is less detachment at the sight of Adam and Eve at the close of book 9, their loins inadequately covered with leaves, overcome with anger and shame and unable to stop blaming each other, although they already know they should stop. We pity them, but we have already joined the poet in converting them into objects for contemplation; we are watching the experiment play out. Even so, the hard edge of our irony is dulled by compassion, which overcomes what repugnance we may feel, as at the end of Sophocles's *Oedipus Tyrannus*, with its hardier repugnance and its more savage test of compassion.[10] As book 9 concludes we seem to see Adam and Eve from an increasing distance as the darkness comes on and their voices are fading to unintelligibility: "And of their vain contést appeared no end" (*PL*, 9.1189).

In sum, we discover after the close of book 9 that there is a surprising amount of work to do before we are done, and much of this work—in addition to the simple amount of poetry remaining to be read—is interpretative. The catastrophe, "Man's first disobedience" (*PL*, 1.1), has at last taken place, after long preparation. We let out our breath: we seem to have arrived. But we have not yet arrived at and "captured the end" (*finem capere*), as soldiers returning to Rome on the march at last "capture the gate" (*portam capere*). Moreover, the process of reading is now more laborious and less swiftly moving. Our concentration is no longer concentrated, as through a burning lens, on what is before us. Instead, our attention must be dispersed. The result is less brilliant, of course, but more far-reaching, throwing a blue light on distant and shadowy regions. These include biblical typology, social order, and a narrative spanning the entire scope of the Bible, including the history of Israel and then of the Church, and the Apocalypse. And, of course, the experience of each of us, each reader, is dimly illuminated, too.

A ready but, as might at first appear, unfruitful answer to the question, what is the end of *Paradise Lost*, is that this poem ends with its final line or, for grammatical completeness, with its final two lines: "They hand in hand with wand'ring steps and slow / Through Eden took their solitary way" (*PL*, 12.648–49). This is the first sight we have of Adam and Eve to correspond with and contrast the fading sights and sounds at the end of book 9, when, to their mutual accusations, there "appeared no end" (*PL*, 9.1189). Now they are hand in hand. They are together, not apart. Nor are they any longer divided by mutual and addictive accusation. But there is no end in sight for them, or for our looking at them. This moment of the very end, the final two lines, trails off and fades out, so that exactly when the poem *does* end eludes us, or seems to. Eve and Adam have not as yet reached the place of rest for which they are searching (*PL*, 12.646–47); we linger with them as they search.

And what, we must ask ourselves, is the meaning of *through*, so prominently set at the head of the line, the last line? The literal answer will have much to do with water. Literally, Adam and Eve have left the Garden of Eden, the "Paradise" (Gr. *paradeisos*, "garden"), as it is called in the Septuagint Bible, and now they travel in a southwesterly direction through the much larger country of Eden, *terra Edenensis*, which is bounded by the upper reaches of the Tigris and Euphrates Rivers, to the east and west, respectively: "And the Lord God planted a Garden eastward in Eden; and there he put the man he had formed."[11]

In the Bible, an unnamed river comes "out of Eden," a larger country, to enter and, irriguously, by many channels, as in Babylonia, waters the garden, which is *in* Eden. This river, after passing through the entire garden—a detail Milton will alter—then emerges from the other side of the garden ("from thence"), after which it divides into "four heads," two of which are the Tigris ("Hiddekel") and the Euphrates (Genesis 2:10–14).

Milton follows this arrangement, but he elaborates on it. A "river large" flows "Southward through Eden" (*PL*, 4.223), that is, the country of Eden, but not Paradise, and then passes underneath the treed mount, or "shaggy hill" (*PL*, 4.224) of Paradise itself: "for God had thrown / That mountain as His garden mold high raised / Upon the rapid current" (*PL*, 4.225–27). The water rises up through the porous stone to create fountains and rills in the garden, a more attractive hydraulic arrangement than the original, like an Italian garden. (Did Milton see the gardens of the Villa d'Este, outside Rome?) The fountains and rills then flow gradually downhill, joining at last to form a waterfall on the south slope of the mountain, outside the garden. The outlet of the pool at the foot of the waterfall (and at the foot of the mountain) now rejoins the main current, which, having under-flowed the entire mountain, emerges from the ground: "Which from his darksome passage now appears" (line 232). After that, south of the garden but still in the country of Eden, the river divides into its four heads: "And now divided into four main streams / Runs diverse wand'ring many a famous realm / And country. Whereof here needs no account" (lines 233–35).

Milton returns to this disposition of the waters and says that the original river flowing southward under the mountain of Paradise is the Tigris itself, a portion of which wells up into the garden as a fountain by the Tree of Life, thus providing Satan with his second means of ingress:

> There was a place,
> Now not (though sin, not time, first wrought the change)
> Where Tigris at the foot of Paradise
> Into a gulf shot underground till part
> Rose up a fountain by the Tree of Life.
> In with the river sunk and with it rose
> Satan involved with rising mist, then sought
> Where to lie hid.
>
> (PL, *9.69–76*)

At the end of the poem, therefore, Adam and Eve have been expelled from the garden by its eastern gate, and are now traveling *through* the country of Eden as it opens out to the south and west. The waterfall is not mentioned, nor the main current emerging from the earth, nor the confluence of these two currents, nor, farther downstream, the division of this recently united current into the four great rivers of the world—"whereof here needs no account" (*PL*, 4.235). But Adam and Eve are moving southward into Mesopotamia, traveling downhill with the rivers as these flow and spread out.

As for that original stream flowing southward in Eden and plunging beneath the mountain of Paradise, many years later it will swell with the rising waters of the Flood and tear the mountain out of its place, pushing it southward, down "the great river" to the Persian Gulf, where, like the island of Delos, it will "take root" as a barren rock, "an island salt and bare" (*PL*, 11.834).

With these geographical considerations we may explain the meaning of "through" at the head of the poem's final line—"Through Eden took their solitary way"—or explain it away. Even in Milton's day, however, *Eden* and *the Garden of Eden* were taken by metonymy to be one and the same, except by close students of the Bible and of biblical atlases. It is, of course, right for the annotator of *Paradise Lost* to point out that by *Eden* Milton means the much larger country in which the garden is situated, and that after their exile from the garden and their descent from its mountain, Adam and Eve must pass through the *country* of Eden, already making their way in the fallen world.

But it seems to me likely that Milton intended us, for a brief moment, to see Adam and Eve *in* "Eden" and *out of it* at the same time, still in a state of transition, notwithstanding the gate we see behind them, "With dreadful faces thronged and fiery arms" (*PL*, 12.644). Not being in history, not having seen death at firsthand, not having borne children in sorrow, not having eaten bread by the sweat of their brows, they are not yet out of Eden, as we are not quite out of the poem. They *are* wearing animal skins, possibly killed and dressed for them by their judge, "pitying how they stood / Before him naked to the air that now / Must suffer change" (*PL*, 10.211–13). The "coats of skins" (Genesis 3:21) is an uncomfortable biblical detail Milton is at pains to transmute, or at least to offer an alternative to. The beasts were either slain or shed their skins, as snakes do, "with youthful coat repaid" (*PL*, 10.217–18). As always with Milton, everything physical, especially if it is mentioned in the Bible, must be explained.

Note that the effects of the Fall—predation, blustery weather, seasonal change, cold nights, and, in humans, diminishing faculties—are registered *in* the garden, not *out*. The garden has been turned inside out when its inhabitants are exiled. They too have been turned inside out: formerly, the garden was outside them; now, they bear a "paradise within" (*PL*, 12.587). The final verse, "Through Eden took their solitary way," is not so much a falling cadence as it is a *diminuendo sostenuto*, as in Mahler, a sustained diminishing that seems to reach out longingly even as it recedes and disappears. Adam and Eve disappear from the image-holding screen of our minds, exactly when it is difficult to say, but some moments after we have read the last line. The end itself seems not quite an ending.

During the crisis in book 9, we watch the action from close up, seeing nothing to the left or the right. We have little or no peripheral vision. But the distanced and critical attitude demanded by the text after the Fall means that new, alien, and unexpected things begin to crowd into our peripheral vision. Above all, the historical events from the Bible that are recounted over so much of books 11 and 12 are familiar, especially for a readership long familiar with the Bible, or at least with the stories of some of its principal figures. But the feeling of historical familiarity, of a growing proximity to us in comparison with the archaic figures of Adam and Eve, is present whether we know the Bible or not.

More familiar still are changes in the natural world that the poet describes in some detail, including their efficient causes: the angels who are sent to push the axis of the earth a little off center (*PL*, 10.668–714). Adam takes note of the results anxiously, for Eve and he are cold, as the winds "Blow moist and keen, shattering the graceful locks / Of these fair spreading trees" (*PL*, 10.1066–67). From the need to create warmth for themselves beyond those animal skins with which God clothed them, Adam brilliantly hypothesizes the possibility of fire, and how to capture it, whether by a lens that will "gather" the beams of "this diurnal star"—the sun—or "by collision of two bodies [that will] grind / The air attrite to fire" (*PL*, 10.1069–73). Milton's anthropological perspective on hard primitivism enters.[12] Later, as Eve proposes a life of soft primitivism—"Here let us live, though in fall'n state, content" (*PL*, 11.180), Adam notices signs portending otherwise:

> But Fate
> Subscribed not. Nature first gave signs impressed
> On bird, beast, air, air suddenly eclipsed
> After short blush of morn. Nigh in her sight
> The bird of Jove, stooped from his airy tow'r,
> Two birds of gayest plume before him drove.
> Down from hill the beast that reigns in woods,
> First hunter then, pursued a gentle brace,
> Goodliest of all the forest, hart and hind:
> Direct to th'eastern gate was bent their flight.
>
> (PL, *11.181–90*)

Passages such as this one demand a distanced and complex perspective on what we read, as we relate what is happening here—note that the prey is still "Goodliest of all the forest"—to what we will know in our world, when, as hunters, we will account ourselves lucky to find prey such as this and not to be preyed on ourselves. As human hunters, we think of it not as *prey* but as *game*. Even so, something more is implied, a satirical view of our social existence as a predatory and exploitative game, not excluding our relation to food, however cruelly processed, arduously farmed, or recklessly hunted to extinction. As we follow Adam's gaze, we are meant to feel the excitement and pleasure of the hunt, and the prospect of venison, while at the same time we are meant to read what Adam sees as the sign of our fallen state, and as a social sign, too, not just of recreational venery. "Man is a wolf to man," *homo homini lupus.* The hunt Adam sees is one degree toward the allelophagic social hierarchy to follow, satirized in the nursery rhyme (the first stanza derived from a poem of Jonathan Swift, the second from the Victorian mathematician, Augustus de Morgan), "Siphonaptera":

> Big fleas have little fleas
> Upon their backs to bite 'em,
> And little fleas littler fleas,
> And so, *ad infinitum.*
>
> And the great fleas themselves, in turn
> Have greater fleas to go on;
> While these again have greater still,
> And greater still, and so on.[13]

This could stand as a travesty of the cosmic hierarchy described before the Fall: "The grosser feeds the purer: Earth the Sea, / Earth and Sea feed Air, the Air those Fires / Ethereal" (*PL*, 5.416–18).

Complex social reflection is thus encouraged in the final books of *Paradise Lost*, as it is not earlier, except on the rare occasions when Milton does it for us: "So clomb this first grand thief into God's fold. / So since into his Church lewd hirelings climb!" (*PL*, 4.192–93). (*Political* reflection is unobtrusively encouraged before the Fall: Adam and Eve are for Milton the first and only just polity, with Adam as the head of state, and Eve as all the citizens.) Note the difference between the sideways jibe at the hirelings—benefice hunting priests and, when these are ejected, the very Presbyterians who ejected them—and the portent of the beast pursuing prey. When the hirelings are mentioned, we are not implicated ourselves: we look askance with Milton at those scoundrels. In contrast, when we read of the first hunt, we reflect differently on what we read because it reflects back on us. Each reader may even see herself or himself coursing the spoor—or the benefice. Together with all the other things we must attend to, we slide, so to speak, into our own peripheral vision. Milton does not have to point the way, as he did formerly. We react less and reflect more.

The Christian biblical and typological perspective is opened earlier still in book 10, exactly where we should expect it: at the judgment of Adam and Eve—and of the absent serpent. We may pass over the judgment on Adam and Eve, which remains as close as possible to the text of the just-so story in the Bible: why it hurts and sometimes kills to have babies, why men boss women, and why you sweat when you farm. Milton can tackle the larger and, to him, more important implications of the Fall in the later historical vision the angel Michael will give Adam, in books 11 and 12. But the judgment on the serpent is the more interesting one at this moment, and by far the most important for Milton's total vision of Christian history.

Following the text of the Bible, the Son judges the serpent mysteriously, "Her [Eve's] seed shall bruise thy head, thou bruise his [the Seed's] heel" (*PL*, 10.181). Here too is a folktale etiology: why do serpents crawl on the ground and kill us with poisonous bites? Milton is committed to more complicated questions and answers, which take us from the beginning of Genesis to Satan in the Gospels and the dragon in Revelation. Following the Christian interpretation of Genesis, Milton has put

Satan in the serpent and given us the magnificent scene of his temptation of Eve. The punishment of crawling on the ground, mentioned in
Genesis, will be brilliantly interpreted by Milton in the scene in Pan-
demonium, now a "Pandraconium," when the devils are changed into
serpents and forced to wriggle on the ground, with more indignities to
follow (*PL*, 10.504–84). Satan will not hear of this prophecy by the Son
until he returns furtively that night and overhears it repeated by Adam
and Eve (*PL*, 10.341–45), nor does he understand it. He knows only that
it refers to a distant "future time" (*PL*, 10.345; cf. 495–99). Adam and
Eve do not know its meaning, either (*PL*, 10.169–70). The riddle will
be at the center of Milton's *Paradise Regained*, when Satan meets Jesus
in the desert, not knowing Jesus is the Son, and tries to find out what
this head-bruising means, having been tormented by the thought of it
down through the ages.

The traditional Christian meaning connects the riddle to the Atonement and Judgment in New Testament. The Seed is not mankind in
general but Jesus Christ in particular, the only son of God. The bruised
heel of the Seed is Jesus's crucifixion. The bruised head of the serpent
comes at the Apocalypse, with the locking up of Satan in Hell. The connection to Satan of the prophecy on the serpent goes back to the earliest Christian writings, and is alluded to by Saint Paul: "And the God
of peace shall bruise Satan under your feet shortly" (Romans 16:20).

Note that it is *your* feet Paul mentions, not *his*, the God of peace's
feet—a riddle Milton preserves with "*our* feet" (line 190). We are reading
in a very different way from how we read in book 9. We are being asked
to step back from immediate events and consider them in terms of later
ones, and in biblical perspective, with suitable biblical texts ready to
hand. Immediately after the Son delivers the serpent prophecy, the
poet adds,

> So spake this oracle, then verified
> When Jesus son of Mary, second Eve,
> Saw Satan fall like lightning down from Heav'n,
> Prince of the Air; then rising from His grave
> Spoiled principalities and pow'rs, triúmphed
> In open show, and with ascension bright
> Captivity led captive through the air,
> The realm itself of Satan long usurped,

Whom he shall tread at last under our feet,
Ev'n he who now foretold his fatal bruise.

(PL, *10.182–91*)

This is a difficult passage of telegraphic typologizing. It alludes to the Psalms, "Thou hast ascended on high, thou hast led captivity captive" (68:18); to the Gospel according to Luke, "I beheld Satan fall as lightning from heaven" (10:18); to Paul's Epistle to the Romans, which I have quoted above; and, in detail, to the twentieth chapter of Revelation. The passage ties up the length of the Bible in a single textual node. We await the denouement, in the world, in history, but also in this poem.

The "oracle" who speaks these words is of course the Son, who has been sent by the Father to judge Adam and Eve, and the serpent. But as we are reminded, the Son is also Jesus, or he will be when he is incarnate (*PL*, 10.191). The Son foretells Satan's "fatal bruise," a bruise the Son himself will deliver, first as Jesus on the cross, thus overcoming sin and death, and then as the risen and enthroned Christ of Revelation: "And the devil . . . was cast into the lake of fire and brimstone . . . and shall be tormented day and night for ever and ever" (20:10). From the clause opening with the preposition *when*, Jesus, "son of Mary, second Eve" (already, we are to see Eve, standing shivering at her judgment, not as Eve alone but also as Mary) performs every action to follow. He *sees* Satan fall; he *rises* from his grave; he *spoils* the kings of the earth; he *triumphs* openly, unfurling his banner; he *ascends* into the heavens; he *leads* captivity (Satan, our captor) captive through the air—the air being the region long held by Satan; and he *treads* Satan under not his, but our feet, as Paul says in Romans. The Son tramples Satan under *our* feet because we are who Jesus is, ideally. That is because Jesus became human to assimilate us to him. The Son has imputed to humans—that is, given them credit for—everything he accomplishes thereafter, starting with the Crucifixion, which pays for human sin and undoes what Adam and Eve have just done. We have in fact already been informed of all this by the Son himself, and rather more clearly than here, in book 3 of *Paradise Lost* (lines 236–65).

The effect of the judgment on Adam and Eve is seen first with the reappearance in the poem of Sin and Death. This comes as a surprise.

We had not expected to see them again. Nor have we expected, after the poet has told us he will sing the remainder of the epic "standing on earth" (*PL*, 7.23), to see again the vastness of the cosmos. But in book 10 it is opened once more to our astounded sight, as Sin and Death "shoal" their bridge across chaos and Chaos himself lashes out in fury: "Disparted Chaos overbuilt exclaimed / And with resounding surge the bars assailed / That scorned his indignation" (*PL*, 10.416–18).

When Sin and Death arrive on earth all living flesh is "seasoned" by Sin to be ready for Death, "sagacious of his quarry from so far." He smells the carnage to come:

> As when a flock
> Of rav'nous fowl through many a league remote
> Against the day of battle to a field
> Where armies lie encamped come flying, lured
> With the scent of living carcasses designed
> For death the following day in bloody fight,
> So scented the grim feature and upturned
> His nostril wide into the murky air,
> Sagacious of his quarry from so far.
>
>   (PL, *10.273–81*)

Johnson criticized what he took to be the "allegory" of Sin and Death because, among other faults, that bridge is "a work too bulky for ideal architects."[14] Ideal figures have done bulkier things. But we have seen that these are not so abstract personifications, mere signs for a reality beyond them. They are Homeric and Hesiodic daemons and the real revealed force of what they do in the world. She *is* Sin and he *is* Death.

Milton is not an allegorical poet like Spenser. Yet we see in this passage how the daemonic figure of Death has been reduced to a "grim feature" and has started disappearing into the simile of the vultures, which simile was intended to make him more clear. *Feature* recalls Latin *facture*, "a made thing," something put together but chiefly the forming of a face—associated with French *figure* and Latin *figura*—out of the grim and yet nebulous fact of death. The giving of a face to nebulosity is the forming of a *persona* or "mask" (*persona* was popularly derived from *per+sonare*, "to sound through," as an actor sounds his voice through a mask). This occurs by what is called *personification*, "mask making," or, to use the Greek rhetorical term, *prosopopoeia*, the "making," or *poiesis*, of a *prosopon*, "a mask."

I have argued elsewhere that Milton's Sin and Death are not allegorical figures, in the traditional sense of rhetorical constructions consciously invented and deployed as signs. Milton reaches back to something prior to and more archaic than allegory: the *daemons* of Homer and Hesiod, such as Hate, *Eris*, and Madness, *Ate*, who are not conventional figures derived from the phenomena but actual beings from which the phenomena derive.[15]

But in any quasi-allegorical system there are principles that seem to mediate between the abstract ideal and the material real, transmitting the influence of the former onto the latter. In the allegorical frescoes lining the walls of the Salle des Fêtes in the former Museum of the Colonies, in Paris, the main tableau represents "France Colonizing"—*la France colonisatrice*. The allegorical figure of France is sending doves of peace out into the world. As the doves fly farther away from her, into the frescoes on adjacent walls, their white wings turn into the sails of the great French sailing ships, the *caravelles*, bearing goods to the colonies and bringing back raw materials in return. Having left Lady France's hands as doves, these doves then become ships, and we see the ships landing in actual ports.[16]

Something similar is happening with Milton's Death, except that he seems to be disappearing before our eyes into the figures to which he is compared in a simile: the vultures following armies about to fight. The vultures become more insistently present in the mind's eye than he was. Death is the fading personification of devouring death and is likened to vultures scenting their prey. But the vultures are also the representation, or the *avifaction* of him, carrying his being into actual war, where they will feed on the slain, perhaps returning to him, like those French ships, with regurgitated flesh. What is left of Milton's Death, snuffing the air for his victims? Only the huge dark hole of his nostril thrust upward in the murky air, with vultures flying out of it.

Except for the Son, the angel Michael is the first (and last) messenger from Heaven after the Fall, and his purpose is to execute the sentence of exile. Michael briefly announces that Adam and Eve's prayers have been heard, that the sentence of death is suspended to give Adam and Eve more days to repent their crime, and that God may in the end be "appeased" and "Redeem thee quite from Death's rapacious claim" (*PL*, 11.258). Michael then adds the startling announcement, "But longer in this Paradise to dwell / Permits not. To remove thee I am come" (*PL*, 11.259–60). Hearing this from the place to which she has retired upon Michael's appearance, Eve cries aloud in pain at this loss and touchingly, as I have mentioned before, speaks an apostrophe to the flowers, which must now subsist without her care (*PL*, 11.273–79). Adam indulges in nostalgic fantasy of how he might have shown his sons the places God appeared, and raise altars of turf and stone on those hallowed spots (*PL*, 11.317–27). We are hearing an alternative history, directing our attention at once to this fantasy and to the reality that took its place. No place is hallowed anymore, not Jerusalem and not the site of Eden, if it can be found. Those who think otherwise are blown about in Milton's Paradise of Fools. The Paradise of Eden is the last and only sacred place, and it is not sacred anymore. That is why, as I have mentioned, Milton destroys it.

We are now given an alternative history. Michael tells Adam that the garden might have been Adam's "capital seat," to which generations of Adam and Eve's children, from all the ends of the earth, had come to do them reverence (*PL*, 11.342–46). A new and final action has begun, the one for which the poem has been named: the loss of Paradise. We read with a certain critical distance, reflecting with the characters themselves on what might have been as well as what is.

After Michael has announced the exile from the garden, he and Adam ascend the high hill nearby for the vision of history that is to follow in the rest of this book (a little over half its length, 58 percent) up to Noah's Flood. The prophetic account of history to come continues—no longer as a vision, however, but as a narrative—for most of the last book (85 percent). About 70 percent of the remaining verse of the poem will be given to this vision of history.

Milton has displayed his huge cosmos before, but our sight is now directed to the vast extent of the terrestrial globe, outside the garden. We have seen the earth darkly before, when Satan flew around it, keeping to the shadow of night, "for seven continued nights" (*PL*, 9.63). Satan then traveled on the surface, over sea and land, starting in Eden, in search of a beast in which to hide. He traveled north to the Caucasus and south to Antarctica, and from the Orontes river in Asia Minor to the Pacific Ocean beyond the Isthmus of Panama—"the ocean barred / At Darien" (*PL*, 9.79–80). The ocean is barred, but not Satan. He passed from thence over the Pacific Ocean to India—"the land where flows / Ganges and Indus" (*PL*, 9.81–82). He then overflew the Himalayas and Persia to return to Eden (*PL*, 9.76–82).

That account of Satan's travels is meant to focus our attention on Satan, on his determination, resourcefulness, and power, not on the world to come beyond the poem, and beyond the boundaries of the garden. Now, however, we are given a sweeping panorama of what will be the scene of human history, shortly to be foretold:

> It was a hill
> Of Paradise the highest from whose top
> The hemisphere of Earth in clearest ken
> Stretched out to th' amplest reach of prospect lay.
>
> (PL, *11.377–80*)

There follows a virtuosic catalogue of the kingdoms of Asia, from China in the Far East to the regions bordering Europe, around the Hellespont and the Bosphorus. From there, as I mentioned in the chapter on the sublime, Adam's eye is directed south to the kingdoms of Africa—of course, none of these are kingdoms yet—from the Congo in the south to the Maghreb in the north, up to the Atlas mountains (across from Gibraltar), the closest point to Europe. I shall quote the passage again, at slightly greater length:

> Or where
> The Persian in Ecbátan sat or since
> In Hispahan, or where the Russian Czar
> In Moscow or the Sultan in Bizance,
> Turkestan-born. Nor could his eye not ken
> Th'empire of Negus to his utmost port,
> Ercoco, and the less maritime kings,
> Mombaza and Quiloa and Melind,
> And Sofala, thought Ophir, to the realm
> Of Congo and Angola farthest south.
> Or thence from Niger flood to Atlas mount

> The kingdoms of Almansor, Fez and Sus,
> Morocco and Algiers and Tremisen.
>
> (PL, *11.392–404*)

Europe is then described, or at least Roman Europe, "where Rome was to sway / The world" (*PL*, 11.405–6). Then, over the horizon of the terrestrial hemisphere—that is, beyond what would be visible to perfected sight, because the curvature of the earth is in the way—Adam sees, "in spirit perhaps" (*PL*, 11 406), the great kingdoms of North and South America, destroyed by the Spanish, "Geryon's sons" (*PL*, 11.410). We are much more aware than we have been before, that is, up to the end of book Nine, of what is outside the garden, in the space of the world. We take these as signs of the beginning of the end of the poem, because now we see places outside the garden, and in the future time beyond the time of the action of *Paradise Lost*. The world is empty, now. But Adam's vision is of a world filled with kingdoms that rise up one upon another and violently fall, like those serpents in Hell, wriggling in heaps.

I said earlier that the two modes of reading in *Paradise Lost* are dramatic and interpretative, or, to express it in technical terms, *mimetic* and the *hermeneutic*. This is perhaps to put the matter too starkly, if no qualification is made. Of course, we read and interpret, and are aware we are reading, when we read of the Fall. For the meditative reader, the terrible phrase, "all was lost" (*PL*, 9.784), can start a chain of reflections on original sin. And when we read of the consequences of the Fall as described in the last three books of *Paradise Lost*, we are some of the time affectively engaged in what is described, as when Adam is shown a hospital of people in agony from a shocking list of diseases— "Convulsions, epilepsies, fierce catarrhs . . . Marasmus and wide-wasting pestilence." The sick call upon Death, "as their chief good and final hope," who shakes his dart over them, sadistically withholding the blow. The only figure caring for the sick, moving "busiest from couch to couch," is, appallingly, Despair (*PL*, 11.477–93). The scene is at least moving to Adam—he weeps at the sight—but of course the allegorical machinery added to it (one is reminded of the allegorical fresco in the *Camposanto* of Pisa, and another by Orcagna, painted for Santa Croce, in which the sick plead with Death and reach out to him, hoping to be taken out of life) is meant to generalize our response and make us reflect on innumerable other instances of lingering, tormenting sickness. The scene has an imaginatively centrifugal power.[17]

The same tendency to a double hermeneutic reading is apparent in the first, terrible scene Adam is shown: the murder of his son Abel, who groans out his soul, "with gushing blood effused" (*PL*, 12.447). Abel, the shepherd, is killed by Adam's other son, the first murderer and first agriculturalist, Cain. "These two are brethren, Adam, and to come out of thy loins," Michael, who is "also moved," informs him (*PL*, 11.53–55). Although we see Abel "rolling in dust and gore," we do so only through the screen of biblical allusions and portents, which we are supposed to interpret:

> th' unjust the just hath slain
> For envy that his brother's off'ring found
> From Heav'n acceptance. But the bloody fact
> Will be avenged and th'other's faith approved,
> Lose no reward though here thou see him die,
> Rolling in dust and gore.
>
> (PL, *11.455–60*)

Cain goes on to found the first city, the prototype of Babel and Babylon. With all agricultural oppressors of semi-itinerant, pastoral peoples—that would be the Hebrews—Cain will go to Hell at last, and stay there, chief among them his avatars, Pharaoh and Nebuchadnezzar. But the faithful shepherd Abel, whose sacrifice was accepted, will have his faith "approved" when his distant descendant, Abraham, will be the "father of faith" and be promised Canaan for his descendants forever. In time, the seed of Abraham will bring forth King David and at last Jesus Christ, who is the Seed that will bruise the serpent's head (*PL*, 10.181). Jesus Christ will do so by dying on the cross, paying for the sins of humanity. But he will rise again and return at the end of the world to judge those living at the time and also those many more who have already died—the quick and the dead. The damned will go with Cain into Hell, and the faithful, Abel among them, will at last be rewarded with Heaven. Thus, Abel will "Lose no reward though here thou see him die" (*PL*, 11.459). All this the reader is expected to call to mind, looking behind and beyond what is presently seen, which is now to be understood as a literal or surface meaning: "*though* here thou see him die" (*PL*,11.459). What the vision is to Adam—a point of departure for further thoughts and further understanding—the text is to us. We are at the other extreme from the kind of reading we do in book 9, responding immediately to the drama before us.

It seems clear enough that when we read the event of the Fall in book 9 the balance is tilted toward passionate engagement, toward mimesis. After book 9, especially, as we have seen, in the visions Adam is given by Michael, the balance starts to shift toward a predominantly detached, hermeneutic response—until the moment, after these visions, when Adam runs to the bower and wakes Eve (*PL*, 12.607), whereupon the balance swings back suddenly to the other extreme, the dramatic. The final, moving scene of *Paradise Lost* is about to occur.

We have moved from a point of view in which Adam and Eve are outside us, as objects of our just condemnation to a point of view in which we want to fight on their behalf against the injustice of the system as a whole, with its improbable supposition they are free. Nether position can be sustained in the absence of the other because neither coincides with a full experience of the poem. Indeed, neither can be sustained exclusively without abandoning the poem, either for theology or for an attack on theology, on the very idea of a Creator God and blood sacrifice, and so on. From both points of view we see Adam and Eve outside ourselves, as our sinful first parents, although their sin explains our own, or as victims we can succor or pity, although their suffering merely explains our own, insofar as we are under the boot of God. As we read book 9 of *Paradise Lost*, quieter versions of both these points of view, the transcendental and the engaged, supplant each other in turn. The two begin to merge, as transcendental engagement, when what we see of ourselves in Adam and Eve, from both points of view, moves from the background into the foreground. We see that the system that condemns them from the start is like the world we live in. It should be changed by action we must perform against the world and its systems. At the same time, we see truly that we are not innocent, transcendental subjects, that our tendency to do evil is rooted in the system we would change, and that an analysis of the system, through art, is necessary (and frustratingly slower) to bring about change that lasts. At the beginning of *Paradise Lost* we see Adam and Eve as the cause of "all our woe" (*PL*, 1.3). It's all their fault. If we are bad, it is because they were—and because Satan is worse. By the third book of *Paradise Lost*, if not sooner, we have begun to blame the poem itself, and the ideological system on which it runs.

But everything cannot be Milton's fault, either. He is drawing on a broad nexus of discursive formations, contributing to an archive in which *Paradise Lost* is only one item. Do we turn to this vastly larger archive instead and concentrate our indignation on it? To do so is inevitably to abandon this poem for something else. But what if we stay with the poem, and persist? A great poet does not have to be right, and cannot be "right" in any sense we can mean that is wholly outside the discourse of which the poem partakes. But a great poem may be wiser than the rest of its archive together, because it gives us the means of taking apart from within the assumptions by which this archive is organized. This is what happens in *Paradise Lost*, if we persist. Our indignation on Adam and Eve's behalf melds with our desire to play out the game, so that indignation is recycled as something like compassion, a "suffering together." At the beginning we see Adam and Eve as the cause of all our woe. At the end, we see them as ourselves.

Who are these people whom we see for the last time, at the end of *Paradise Lost*, ourselves, or some others? Let us start with where they are, physically. They are apart. Eve is sleeping in the bower and Adam is on the hilltop with the angel Michael, having been shown the future of humankind. Adam has been told of the Redeemer, and he has learned that of all the virtues, love—"by name to come called *charity*"—is "the soul / Of all the rest" (*PL*, 12.583–84). This is not erotic love, the love Adam and Eve have for each other as man and wife, which is only one part of the total love they have for each other. It is the other, less focused because more general love of one's "neighbor"—in effect, anyone you may meet. It is called *caritas* in Latin and *agapê* in Greek, the word always employed by Jesus in the gospels.

Agapê is not a personal or private ideal but a social one. It is mere sentimentality, and poor reading, to suppose that by the "paradise within thee, happier far" (*PL*, 12.587), Michael is referring to the private paradise Eve and Adam will have with each other, "Imparadised in one another's arms" (*PL*, 4.506)—the phrase with which Satan enviously describes them. It does not take virtue for Adam and Eve to love each other. But *charity*, to use Michael's language (and Jesus's) is the soul of all the rest of the virtues. What does this mean? I think the phrase will mean more to us if we think of charity not as the soul but as the ground, or foundation. Without it, the other virtues have nothing to stand on. Like a foundation, it must be always there. Charity therefore marks the most fundamental decision in life, a decision we are inclined to think is merely temperamental, but which Christian ethics insists on regarding as a choice. We have a choice in life, which is how to be disposed toward others in general all of the time, whether we are normally in a state of suspicion, or of (wary) trust, a state of general dislike, or of affection to all; whether we wish to harm others or to help them. As usual with Christianity, which was extremely radical when compared with the Roman ideology through which it erupted in later antiquity, there is no middle way, the classical ideal. You must and you will love or hate others, with feeling; no stoical apathy is possible. You will either suspect others unreasonably, all of the time, or you will trust them, unreasoningly; so that, to the untrusting, you will look foolish, a fool for Christ. You cannot go through life being fair and just to others, with an equal mind, *aequo animo*, the Roman ideal. If Adam and Eve have each other and their descendants in charity, a charity that is strongly committed, righteous and passionate, instead of calculating, this will help to re-create Paradise. The Paradise so created may not be—indeed, it cannot be—a utopia, a possibility Milton rejected even at his most sanguine moment of social hope, when he wrote *Areopagitica*. But by having others in charity in this righteous and passionate way, even when they do not have you in charity, you will be carrying paradise inside you: "A paradise within thee, happier far" (*PL*, 12.587). I think this is a reasonable claim, even when we include the word *happier*. But *far* may be going too far. In any event, the hierarchical and benevolent cosmos, which the angel Raphael described, has disappeared. Nature is now the savage scene we know it to be. What was once in nature, a system of mutual exchange and mutual concern, is now inside us, in our society, or it is not. Reason may be the highest of our faculties, but social charity is the most fundamental.

But this idealized, physical universe which has been seen from Eden does not merely fade from sight. It has to be destroyed, as it is, and in so doing the idea of it must be exposed as a eudemonic aesthetic fantasy from which one is excluded when one closes the book, as we are shortly to close *Paradise Lost*. "See!," says the angel Michael,

> the guards
> By me encamped on yonder hill expect
> Their motion, at whose front a flaming sword
> In signal of remove waves fiercely round:
> We may no longer stay.
>
> *(PL, 12.590–94)*

Note the kindness of that *we*.

Eve has been instructed in her dreams and "her spirits composed / To meek submission" (*PL*, 12.596–97), or so the angel says, who belongs to this departing world. Adam and Eve will live for many years yet, and they will be redeemed from death at last by the "woman's Seed" (*PL*, 12.600–1). They will be sad for their "evils past," but "much more cheered / With meditation on the happy end" (*PL*, 12.603–5). Most important, they will be "unanimous" in one faith (*PL*, 12.603).

Michael and Adam descend the hill and Adam runs to the bower to find Eve awake, receiving him without the majesty of former days, but with the dignity and beauty of this patterned line: "Whence thou return'st and whither went'st I know" (*PL*, 12.610). After falling asleep in sorrow, she has been instructed and comforted by propitious dreams. She speaks to Adam in the beautiful words of Ruth to Naomi (Ruth 1:16), but the passage is richly textured with other phrases captured from the writers of the past, chiefly Homer and Virgil:[18]

> But now lead on.
> In me is no delay. With thee to go
> Is to stay here; without thee here to stay
> Is to go hence unwilling. Thou to me
> Art all things under Heav'n, all places thou,
> Who for my willful crime art banished hence.
> This further consolation yet secure
> I carry hence: though all by me is lost,
> Such favor I unworthy am vouchsafed,
> By me the promised Seed shall all restore.
>
> *(PL, 12.614–23)*

Let us call the messianic seed "hope for the future," that without which we humans cannot live, however dark the prospects at the moment. Eve is perhaps the better poet of the two, or the more classically refined: her lines are delicately balanced, and stately in their poise. There is majesty even in her gesture of submission. We note the grace—astonishing, after the end of book 9, but less so after their reconciliation in book 10—of Eve's saying Adam will be to her "all things under Heav'n" because (the connection is not quite so strong as "because," but almost) he has been banished from Eden for her crime. Since the passage in which she touchingly laments for her flowers, we have been waiting for her to care about Adam.

There is no time for Adam to answer her generous, and perhaps overly generous, statement, which is the more gracious and loving for going so far. The archangel Michael is standing too close, requiring their attention. The troop of burning cherubim is descending the other hill to enforce the expulsion, and Michael must lead Eve and Adam away, for their safety. The expulsion from Paradise is still an expulsion, but it is also, in Milton's telling of the scene, a rescue:

> So spake our mother Eve and Adam heard
> Well pleased but answered not. For now too nigh
> Th'archangel stood and from the other hill
> To their fixed station all in bright array
> The cherubim descended.
>
> (PL, *12.624–28*)

The silence of Adam is circumstantial and sufficiently explained by this motion. Yet it is eloquent, too. He doesn't need to answer—for example, by taking some responsibility himself, or by expressing the pleasure he feels at Eve's loving and generous words. He does not need to answer—although he would have, had circumstances permitted—because the two of them are of one mind, in the way well married couples can be, with complicity. I would venture to say this is the first moment of the poem in which marriage is represented in both a realistic and a positive light. We have already seen marriage as we know it, realistically and negatively, when Adam and Eve have private thoughts for the first time, thinking one thing and saying another. Now we see Adam having a thought—we are not told what it is, except that Eve's words give him pleasure—which is not private because Eve can sense it. Yet it is private because Michael, although he stands "too nigh," cannot overhear it. Nor can we. Nothing is said, and there is nothing to hear. But Eve and Adam have communed.

Milton thought more about marriage, and more deeply about marriage, than anyone in the seventeenth century, even if this thinking was hampered by absurd attempts to be grounded in the Bible. For Milton, the law seized basely on the carnal side of marriage, the bed and board, especially the former, while failing to address marriage—and the reasons for dissolving a marriage—at the highest level, that of the mind. The married mind enjoys cheerful conversation, where conversation is understood in the widest sense as a continual exchange, a going back and forth together by turns (L. *con*, "with, together"+*versare*, "to turn"). This means that at any point in a married conversation where something is said the response, the turnaround, is already implied, and does not always need to be enunciated. The response "goes," as we say—it travels, it returns—"without saying." Intuitive communication is not uncommon among the higher mammals, notably wolves and lions, which are highly social. Such behavior is especially efficient for cooperative hunting, which may be the reason for its evolution. If so, it soon spread into other areas of social exchange. Our awareness of such communication in ourselves—in body language and visual saccades—is suppressed because of the power of our unique communicative system: language. We become aware of our intuitive powers of communication (developed in training and practice) in those circumstances where language is of less use, for example, in team sports and in battle. In normal circumstances, marriage may be the principal arena in which intuitive communication persists—the sense of being of one mind, the sense of complicity, of being folded together, of not needing to speak.

Many things in Milton's portrait of Adam and Eve are touching, and many more are interesting to think about, for example, their beautiful, formal, articulate manners, which Milton manages to avoid making stiff and peculiar: "Sole partner and sole part of all these joys, / Dearer thyself than all" (*PL*, 4.411–12); "O thou for whom / And from whom I was formed flesh of thy flesh / And without whom am to no end, my guide and head" (*PL*, 4.440–4). Each address is as intimate as a caress.

Yet this inconspicuous moment between Adam and Eve, when speech is cut off but something is said, expresses something that Eve's first address to Adam in the poem does not. It expresses equality. Not equality based on independence, and self-reliance. It expresses equality based on interdependence and communion. Milton is suggesting our first parents, the parents we started out with, those original sinners, are not so bad as we might have supposed. This moment of silence, the most touching between them, supports and is worthy of the great, elegiac passage to follow, the passage with which the epic ends.

The sun has set. It is early evening, when there is still glimmering light, and mist is rising from the ground. Adam and Eve are lingering, understandably, as the archangel stands by. Throughout the brief scene to follow, in which the long-promised "loss of Eden" (*PL*, 1.4) will at last occur, we must imagine the light falling and the night coming on. Adam and Eve will be led out the gate and down the cliff, during the descent of which, although the angel is holding each by the hand, the path will become harder to see as they go. By the time they reach the bottom, the "subjected plain" (*PL*, 12.640), it will be dark on the ground, and the last light of the last day of human life in Paradise will stand in the sky. The angel will disappear and Adam and Eve will stand there together, looking back to the gate of Paradise—which is behind and above them, "so late their happy seat" (*PL*, 12.642). As darkness falls, we see the blazing sword waving over the eastern gate of the Garden of Eden, and the fiery arms of the cherubim guarding that gate, *thronging* it (*PL*, 12.644).

   The expulsion from Paradise begins when the troop of cherubim, at the precise time commanded, descend the other hill and advance across the intervening ground,

> Gliding meteorous, as evening mist
> Ris'n from a river o'er the marish glides
> And gathers ground fast at the laborer's heel
> Homeward returning.
>
>   (PL, *12.629–32*)

The angels float and glide in mid air: that is what Milton means by *meteorous* (Gr. *meta*, "across," "through," suggesting motion within + *aêr*, "air"). That image of evening mist at the heel of the laborer returning from the field evokes the daily round of labor to come. It is also, as we have seen, sinister. For workers sweating from the heat of the day, those fast-moving evening mists rising from the river and crossing the swamps can be fatal. The troop of cherubim *is* fatal, if encountered, and Michael's charge is to see they are not. Before the troop the sword of God blazes, "Fierce as a comet" (*PL*, 9.634), burning the ground. It is destroying Eve's flowers. It would also destroy flesh:

> High in front advanced,
> The brandished sword of God before them blazed
> Fierce as a comet which with torrid heat
> And vapor as the Libyan air adust
> Began to parch that temperate clime.
>
> (PL, *12. 632–36*)

Michael seizes Adam and Eve each by the hand, hurries them through the eastern gate of Paradise, and without slowing leads them down the high cliff to the plain below. Then, without a word, he disappears:

> Whereat
> In either hand the hast'ning angel caught
> Our ling'ring parents and to the eastern gate
> Led them direct and down the cliff as fast
> To the subjected plain, then disappeared.
>
> (PL, *12. 636–40*)

As I mentioned, the first parents of the human race now look back up the cliff they have descended to see the flaming sword waving over the garden, destroying it. They weep; they compose themselves; and they turn to face the world, which is now "all before them" (*PL*, 9.646). We are part of what is before them, although they cannot see us.

For simplicity and greatness, Milton's art in these lines is unexampled, even by him. As Adam and Eve turn to face the world, there is a shift of register from space into time, from the terrestrial *distances* before Adam and Eve to the *ages* between them and us, ages filled with the turbulence of history. The effect is increased when Adam and Eve begin to move, tentatively, "with wand'ring steps and slow" (*PL*, 12.648), to find their place of rest for the night. The slight motion suggests, and seems even to impel, the great human movements to come, the rise and fall of civilizations, the ceaseless wars, the moments of hope—for Providence, Milton says, is their "guide" (*PL*, 12.647)—and the times of despair. At a stroke, the poet has joined the main dramatic action of his epic poem with the action of history. Mythic time flows into historical time, which flows into contemporary, political time. I said Adam and Eve face us at last but cannot see us. They are instead looking for something between them and us, and much closer to them, a place of rest. As in a mirror, we see ourselves in them. Yet we hope to become more than what they are, or than what they were. Blindly, they have hoped this for us, too.

∽ 15

On Late Style in Paradise Regained *and* Samson Agonistes

In 1671, THREE YEARS before his death, Milton published in a single volume two very sizable poetic works, of 2,070 and 1,758 lines, respectively, four years after the gigantic accomplishment of *Paradise Lost*. The title page of the volume reads, *Paradise Regained, a Poem, in Four Books, to which is Added Samson Agonistes. The Author John Milton.* Once more the aged eagle stretched his wings.

We might say that the first work is about Milton's hope for the future, including the future of liberty in England, the second about his judgment of the past, including the failure of the English Revolution. That is their emphasis. But each is concerned with both the future and the past, within the framework of the Bible, the first with the deep past, in the garden of Eden, the second with the heroic spirit of a nation to be revived at some very uncertain time in the future.

Paradise Regained is a brief epic on Jesus's meeting Satan in the wilderness (read, "wilderness of history") where Satan tempts him, as Adam once was tempted. The action is based on a brief and unusual episode in the three, synoptic gospels, one immediately following the baptism of Jesus by the charismatic figure of John the Baptist, when a voice from Heaven proclaims Jesus the Son of God and a dove, symbolizing the Holy Ghost, settles on him when he rises from the water. Then the Holy Ghost drives Jesus into the wilderness—in the compulsive phrase of

Mark—where Satan awaits him. The temptation in the wilderness appears to belong to the earliest oral traditions about Jesus. It therefore could not be dropped, despite the generally ethical and pedagogical emphasis of the gospels. The episode could not be dropped until, of course, John, the author of the very different, more philosophical fourth gospel, did drop it. Instead, John expanded the event of the baptism, and Milton drew liberally on John's account, while spectacularly expanding the temptation itself.

For the authors of the synoptic gospels, as for Milton, the temptation in the wilderness gives proof of Jesus's worthiness ("proof" is one of the meanings of the Greek word for temptation), and is therefore a boundary dividing the first two phases of Jesus's life: the private life of his youth (including his birth) and the public life of his ministry. The latter will begin when he returns from the desert. The third phase of Jesus's life is its final week, the Passion, with Jesus's crucifixion on Friday and his resurrection on Sunday. Milton's title might lead one to suppose, mistakenly, that *Paradise Regained* is about the Passion, which in orthodox Christianity is the sacrifice that redeems humanity from Satan and makes it possible for those who believe in this sacrifice to go to Heaven at last, resurrected from death, as Jesus was. This Heaven to which believers will go is the "paradise" of the title, the typological fulfillment of the first paradise, which was the garden in Eden. The crucial line of the introduction depends on this typological thinking: "And Eden raised in the waste wilderness" (*PR*, 1.5).

Of course, the actual garden, destroyed at the flood, will not be recovered or "raised." That word "raised" suggests something built, which is the city of God, the heavenly Jerusalem of Revelation, for which Christ is the cornerstone and in which Christ is the mystical Lamb. All this is traditional and orthodox Christian thinking. The surprise is that Milton's poem is not about Jesus's crucifixion but rather about his temptation by Satan in the wilderness, a brief episode that in all three synoptic gospels, as mentioned, immediately follows John the Baptist's baptism of Jesus in the Jordan River.

Jesus does three things in *Paradise Regained*, and typologically raising Eden in the wilderness is the third of these. The other two are his successful resistance to Satan's temptations, which he refutes with scorn, and his defeating Satan at the end, a victory that is nowhere present in the gospels, where the devil simply leaves Jesus (Matthew 4:11, Luke

4:13). We do not see Satan again in the gospels, except when Jesus, quoting a prophecy, says "I beheld Satan as lightening fall from Heaven (Luke 10:18).[1] That detail is used for the climax of *Paradise Regained:* "Satan smitten with amazement fell" (*PR*, 4.562). As is typical of this poem, the full significance of the event lives in an allusion two steps removed and then three steps removed, in a prophecy against Babylon: "How art thou fallen from Heaven, O Lucifer, son of the morning" (Isaiah 14:12). In Isaiah, Lucifer, the morning star, is Babylon; but for Christian readers of the Book of Revelation, Babylon means all the kingdoms and powers of this world. The victory on the pinnacle explicitly recalls—as it does for the astonished and horrified Satan—the Son's victory over Satan's armies on the battlefield of Heaven, at the end of book 6 of *Paradise Lost*, which of course also recalls Isaiah and Revelation. Indeed, Satan, Jesus, and the reader all find out at the same climactic moment of *Paradise Regained* (*PR*, 5.538–39; 560–62) what the meaning of the emphatically repeated word *Son* is. The word is important because, at the baptism, it was spoken by the Father's voice from Heaven, pronouncing Jesus his son (*PR*, 5.1.32; 85; 285; 329–30). We find out, as I said, that *Son* means the militarily victorious Son of *Paradise Lost*, but *Son* also means a second, better Adam. The two are brought together in Jesus. Satan's horror comes from recognizing in a flash this fusion of horizons of meaning. The typological thinking is underlined from the opening lines by the repetition of the phrase *one man*, which means "Adam" the first time it is used and "Jesus" the second:

> I who erewhile the happy garden sung
> By one man's disobedience lost, now sing
> Recovered Paradise to all mankind
> By one man's firm obedience fully tried
> Through all temptation, and the tempter foiled
> In all his wiles, defeated and repulsed,
> And Eden raised in the waste wilderness.
>
>   (PR, *1.1–5–7*)

Paradise Regained is linked to *Paradise Lost* by this tight biblical and typological connection, which is captured in the double referent of *man*. But here too is the departure from orthodoxy: instead of dying to *pay* for Adam's sin, Jesus *undoes* Adam's sin.

Jesus then defeats Satan with mere words, while balancing on the pinnacle of the temple, whither Satan had taken him to see him fall, a stunningly original and dramatic transformation of the episode as we find it in the gospels. With this victory—to continue with the typological thinking Milton intends us to do mostly ourselves—the direction of history is reversed, from fall to restoration, although history is far from complete. The work of restoration has only begun, as we hear near the end, in the angels' chorus: "Queller of Satan. . . . Now enter, and begin to save mankind" (*PR*, 5.634–35). Jesus's ministry is about to begin. From this moment humanity is assured of salvation and the world itself, the world with which Milton was politically engaged, is now gradually improving—so gradually, however, it will often look like the series of continuing and worsening disasters prophesied in Daniel and the Book of Revelation. The English Revolution is one of the disasters. But Milton is now looking to the future.

Eve, who was so important to the action and psychology of *Paradise Lost* and who is so tragically noble at the end of that poem, is in *Paradise Regained* left out of this settling of accounts with her tempter. To make up the deficit, Jesus's mother Mary comes in unexpectedly, in her son's recollection of what she told him of his birth (*PR* 1.229–58), and in the second of three artful digressions opening book 2, anxiously meditating on his youth (*PR*, 2.60–108). She is not outright called a virgin mother, as she is in *Paradise Lost* (12.368; cf. *PR* 1.239), but that she is present at all is a surprise, the cult of Mary being so abhorred by radical Protestants. Milton makes her fully human, and with a poet's insight imagines her "Motherly cares and fears" (*PR*, 2.64). We readers of the poem may have forgotten Mary by book 4, but Milton has not. The poem's final line is powerfully evocative: "Home to his mother's house private returned." (Mary's recollections in book 2 also allow Milton to include—perhaps it is better to say, "to not entirely omit"—the nativity narrative from the gospels of Matthew and Luke.)

Samson Agonistes is a tragedy in the Greek manner on the Hebrew hero, Samson, famous for slaughtering Philistines, first at Ramathlehi, "the hill of the jaw bone," and last in Gaza, when he pulls down the Philistines' temple on them—and also, unavoidably, on himself. It is a drama meant for reading instead of for the stage, which is sensible because its formal models are all from the Athenian stage of two thousand years previous, plays created for a religious context that was entirely lost. Making a drama, even one meant for solitary reading, allowed Milton to complete the process already begun in *Paradise Regained*, which is the withdrawal of himself from the scene of creation. Now he moves his pieces like a chess player. I have said no small part of the meaning of *Paradise Lost* is the excitement of an epic being made. It is possible that with some displeasure Milton recognized this truth about *Paradise Lost* and in these severer works renounced the bardic pose.

Samson Agonistes opens with Samson accorded a day of rest outside his prison, in the fresh air, "pure and sweet" (*SA*, line 10). The opening lines are addressed to a guide leading him to a bank on which he can sit. With the beauty of simplicity, these lines anticipate the action of the whole, and also the feeling of this action, which advances uncertainly but is always going somewhere: "A little onward lend thy guiding hand / To these dark steps, a little further on." The respite from toil is occasioned by a Philistine holy day to celebrate the god Dagon. Attended by a chorus of Hebrew youths, Samson laments his condition, his fall from greatness, and the folly that led him to it. He will very slowly get round to the most important thing: his betrayal of God's trust. He is visited by his father, Manoa; by his "wife," Dalila (for so she is in Milton's account); by the Philistine giant Harapha, who is related to Goliath; and lastly by an officer who brings him the command of the Philistine lords that he perform feats of strength for the crowd at the festival of Dagon. After refusing categorically to participate in idolatrous rites, Samson complies, impelled from within by "rousing motions" (*SA*, line 1382), and goes off with this officer. Manoa returns with hopeful news of Samson's release, which he discusses with the chorus until they hear a "hideous noise" (*SA*, line 1509), which the chorus describes: "Blood, death, and deathful deeds are in that noise" (*SA*, line 1513). They huddle together in fear, like the chorus in Aeschylus's *Agamemnon*, uncertain whether to run or find out what has happened. A messenger arrives and relates the catastrophe. The chorus sings a paean to Samson's violent achievement, contrasting his "inward eyes illuminated" (*SA*, line 1689) with the Philistines' blindness to the doom that unfolds before their very eyes, coming "speedy upon them" (*SA*, line 1681). Manoa is swiftly reconciled to the death of his son, his old heart cheered by the manner of this death. He imagines a splendid tomb for Samson that will inspire "matchless valour" (*SA*, line 1740) in more young men ready to die for their country. And the tomb will be decked with flowers by virgins singing anthems, "only bewailing / His lot unfortunate in nuptial choice, / From whence captivity and loss of eyes" (*SA*, lines 1742–44).

From whence this "from whence"? The great strength of Milton's mind tends to compression, so necessary to the writer of blank verse. These lines are farcically compressed, perhaps because they are too nearly inspired by the poet's resentments. His wife Mary imprisoned him, as he thought, by returning when at last he felt free. But she did not make Milton blind. He did, if anyone did. Yet how satisfying it would be for him if it could be proved Mary Powell *was* after all responsible for his blindness and subsequent miseries, including his daughters, perhaps even the collapse of the English Revolution, long after her death. It's all her fault! The splendid final lines, spoken by the chorus, fall into rhyming couplets, although with lines of unequal length, as in "Lycidas." But even better, more moving, because more true, true especially in their refusal to lie about those who die in battle, are the elegiac lines in Milton's familiar style, unrhymed decasyllabic verse:

> Nothing is here for tears, nothing to wail
> Or knock the breast, no weakness, no contempt,
> Dispraise or blame. Nothing but well and fair,
> And what may quiet us in a death so noble.
>
> (SA, 1721–24)

There was a flurry of publication by Milton in the late 1660s and early 1670s, which saw the appearance in print of a textbook on grammar, another on logic, a substantial history of Britain, Latin epistles and prolusions, and so on, partly because of the fame of *Paradise Lost* and partly, no doubt, because Milton's life was coming to a close and he knew it, as did those around him, not excluding his publishers. He was clearing his desk, or it was being cleared for him. Other works appeared after his death. That Milton was no quietist in his final years is indicated by his publishing in 1673 *Of True Religion, Heresy, Schism, Toleration: and what best means may be used against the growth of Popery*. This work pleads for toleration for all sorts of religious nonconformist sects, however crazed, but not for Roman Catholics, because they are agents of a foreign power. Under the circumstances, this was not so inconsistent a position to take as it might now appear. The early poems published in 1645 were republished in 1673, in the year before the poet's death, together with unpublished poems subsequent to 1645, the poems of the political pe-riod, although there were prudential omissions. These were the son-nets to Thomas Fairfax, the parliamentary general, to Oliver Cromwell, "our chief of men," to Sir Henry Vane the Younger, beheaded in 1662, and the second sonnet to Cyriack Skinner, in which the poet says he is sustained in his blindness by having lost his sight "In liberty's defence" (line 11).[2] No one was defending that kind of liberty now.

The definitive, twelve-book *Paradise Lost* was published late in the summer of 1674. Milton died the following November, a month short of his sixty-sixth birthday. Even in Milton's day his death came early for someone who escaped the plague and avoided syphilis, who came from the upper-middle classes, and who led a temperate life with reg-ular exercise. Milton's sudden aging must therefore have surprised him. He refers to *"crude* [that is, early, or 'unripe'] old age" in *Samson Ago-nistes* (*SA*, line 700) and he uses the expression "old age" on three other occasions in this work.[3] In both *Paradise Regained* and *Samson Agonistes* the poet knows he has little time left in which to say what he has still to say. He also has little time left in which to explore the further re-gions of his art. These are late works that know they are late.

Milton's nephew Edward Phillips says *Paradise Regained* was "begun and finished . . . in a wonderful short space, considering the sublimeness of it."[4] We know from the witness of Thomas Ellwood, Milton's Quaker friend and pupil, that *Paradise Regained* was composed not long after *Par-adise Lost* and completed around the time the latter made its first appear-ance in the world, in 1667. Ellwood says that Milton entrusted him with the manuscript of *Paradise Lost* and asked him what he thought of it:

> After some further discourse about it, I pleasantly said to him, Thou hast said much here of Paradise lost; but what hast thou to say on *Paradise found?* He made me no answer, but sate sometime in a muse: then brake of that discourse, and fell upon another subject.
>
> After the sickness was over, and the city well cleansed and be-come safely habitable again, he returned thither. And when after-wards I went to wait on him there (which I seldom failed of doing, whenever my occasions drew me to London) he showed me his second poem, called Paradise Regained; and in a pleasant tone said to me, *This is owing to you: for you put it into my head, by the question you put to me at Chalfont; which before I had not thought of.*[5]

We have no external evidence of this kind for the date of composition of *Samson Agonistes*. As I argue in Appendix II, the longer the work, the more important is the date of *publication* and the less important or clear is the date of *composition*. (With short poems, the opposite is generally true.) The structural outline of *Samson Agonistes* may have been meditated for some time. Milton considered several versions of a tragedy on Samson in the early 1640s, more than twenty years previous, including the one in which the hero sets alight foxes' tails and releases the unfortunate beasts into the wheat fields of the Philistines: *Samson Pyrsophoros* "fire bearer." Why was this done? The riddle Samson proposed at his first marriage, which his Philistine wife disloyally revealed to her countrymen, provoked this incendiary revenge, which was harder on foxes than Philistines. The episode is referred to only by the most remote and dignified allusion in *Samson Agonistes*. When the chorus sees the giant Harapha approaching and is too frightened to say so directly, the blind Samson replies, "Be less abstruse: my riddling days are past" (*SA*, line 1064). His clowning and whoring days are, as well. He supposes the same to be true of his military feats, one of them performed with the "trivial weapon" of the jaw of an ass, his "sword of bone" (*SA*, lines 142–43). But in this assumption Samson is wrong. One trivial weapon remains to him: a Philistine temple.

The restricted focus and rugged style of this work, its nearly transparent recollection of distressing events from the 1660s—"their carcasses / To dogs and fowls a prey, or else captíved; / Or to the unjust tribunals under change of times, / And condemnation of the ungrateful multitude" (*SA*, lines 693–96)—and the powerful expression of the hero's sufferings in body and mind, so like those of John Milton in his later years, make it certain *Samson Agonistes* is a late work, and indeed Milton's latest work. Any date after the Restoration earlier than 1667 can be ruled out by Milton's preoccupation in these years with *Paradise Lost* and after with *Paradise Regained*. That *Samson Agonistes* was completed not long before the date of publication, 1671, may be supposed. One may also suppose it took some time for the trauma of the Restoration and its attendant disasters—and evidently the trauma of Milton's first marriage—to heal sufficiently for the poet to be able to displace his anger and despair onto his Old Testament hero and convert them into art.

It has been fashionable of late to follow Edward W. Said in speaking of *late style (Spätsil)* as a general aesthetic category applicable to great masters at the end of their careers but coherent in its own right, apart from biography. The term is used in this way by the Germanist Peter Szondi with respect to the late hymns of Hölderlin (though these were written in Hölderlin's thirties, before his descent into madness), and by Theodore W. Adorno in his reflections on some of Beethoven's late compositions. In its perhaps unnecessarily idealized form, late style is held to be invariably difficult and exceptionally demanding of its audience, refusing to fulfill expectations, rebelling against harmony, logic, and perspicuous structure, and obstinately reviving outmoded forms.[6] Much of this description is applicable to Hölderlin's hymns, with their metrical intricacies, imitating Pindar, and also to Beethoven's late quartets, especially the obsessive "Great Fugue," which was separated from quartet number 13 in B-flat major because of its incomprehensibility, and the wild and wonderful Diabelli Variations, perhaps Beethoven's most adventurous work, according to Arnold Schoenberg.[7] Some of Szondi and Adorno's accounts of late style are applicable to Milton, whose *Paradise Regained* and *Samson Agonistes* are both more cerebral than *Paradise Lost*, more uncompromising, more adventurous, and more difficult to grasp. But there is a classical simplicity to both works that differs from usual description of late style, although such simplicity is not unheard of in artists at the end of their careers.

Two factors are likely to influence almost all great masters in the last stage of their careers, simply as a consequence of their being recognized and old. The first is the assurance that comes of having already proved oneself artistically, so that there is less urge to impress or to please, thus allowing new priorities to emerge, such as the conviction that art is *for* something else that is higher than art, even if art affords the only avenue to it. The second is the feeling that one has much to say not *in* but *through* art, and little time in which to say it, so that one had better be clear and compressed. The compression can indeed produce difficulty, and is no guarantee against length. But clarity of design and difficulty in the medium are not incompatible. Both Milton's late works force us to think more and think harder than we ever have to do in *Paradise Lost*. They are in this sense slower and more difficult to read, to get through. But they are also both more simply and clearly designed. At the end of both, we feel we know pretty clearly what they mean, which is to say, we know what we have been told.

Paradise Regained is a fine poem in its own right, with, as we have seen, a clear, single action drawn from the biblical New Testament instead of the Old. But *Paradise Regained* is also a retrospective commentary on the great epic from which it takes its name and its theme. It demands more of the reader because it completes the intellectual design of *Paradise Lost* as a transcendental engagement with the problem of history. It also brings this design into prominence and makes it intelligible for the first time, especially to the reader who is willing to think typologically throughout: Adam's story tells us what is wrong, Jesus's what is to be done. Everything Jesus says in *Paradise Regained* is a lesson to us and is possible for any ordinary person to follow. Readers who expect to revisit the thunderous cosmic scenes of *Paradise Lost* will of course not find them here. The action is almost entirely a debate, an intense one between exceptionally gifted contestants, with the fate of the world at stake. This is not a Heaven-storming poem because it is already in the Kingdom of God, where thinking and truth coincide. (The antagonist does not recognize this until the end.) It is nobly unified and simple. No formal or metrical innovations are ventured because Milton wants the reader to see through the art of poem, as through a windowpane, to the thinking that is on the other side. But this thinking is an insurgency against the whole world, an overturning of its corrupt and violent norms.

Although both *Paradise Regained* and *Samson Agonistes* have much in common with Greek drama, *Samson Agonistes* is of course a drama, ostentatiously Greek, with no narrative voice, not even the dry and detached one of *Paradise Regained*. If the style of both works is leaner, less superficially agreeable, less lyrical, more focused and intense, that of *Samson Agonistes* is also explosively violent, and not only at the end. It is emotionally wrenching throughout. But no longer does Milton appear to be creating his work from within, as in *Paradise Lost*. We feel the difference immediately when we read the businesslike opening lines of the dry narrator of *Paradise Regained*. No grand cosmic panoramas appear, no roiling chaos, no furnace of Hell, no battles between armies in the sky, no hurling of mountains, no ten thousand thunders resounding on the wide plains of Heaven, no calling up of new worlds out of the deep. The actions of these two works unfold in the desolate Judean desert and in sun-baked Gaza. Milton is bearing down with all the force of his mind on the hard matter before him, striving for deeper penetration of insight.

It is true that the extravagant manner of *Paradise Lost* is occasionally revived, as when the chorus recalls how Samson crushed under his heel tough old warriors, who "groveling soiled their crested helmets in the dust," and how Samson carried off Gaza's gates from the sea to the mountain fastness of Hebron, "seat of giants old" (*SA*, lines 141 and 148). The storm scene in the wilderness, in *Paradise Regained* (4.409–25), is in the style of the description of chaos in *Paradise Lost*, from which some locutions reappear:

> Nor slept the winds
> Within their stony caves but rushed abroad
> From the four hinges of the world and fell
> On the vexed wilderness whose tallest pines,
> Though rooted deep as high, and sturdiest oaks,
> Bowed their stiff necks, loaden with stormy blasts
> Or torn up sheer.
>
> (PR, *4.413–19*)

But such effects are now deployed with a purpose, which is to register the shock of the chorus at their hero Samson's changed and calamitous state, and to show Jesus's physical and mental toughness, in preparation for the climactic moment of truth.

Although they were published together and are of comparable length, it is not surprising *Paradise Regained* and *Samson Agonistes* are regarded as altogether separate entities, because of their different genres.[8] One is a brief epic related by its title and subject matter to *Paradise Lost*, and differences in style between it and *Paradise Lost* can be accounted for in some part by the difference of scale. The other is a tragedy that for its passionate and irregular style harks back to "Lycidas," not least for the strong personal feelings expressed in it. But there is a deeper connection between *Paradise Regained* and *Samson Agonistes* that is related to their both coming after *Paradise Lost*. After the quietism of the final two books of *Paradise Lost*, *Paradise Regained and Samson Agonistes* make a powerful artistic statement about the necessity of fighting. The fighting in question, especially in the first work, is for the most part what Blake called "mental fight," but for Milton that is no less intense or important than actual combat, as the second work shows.

Why did Milton compose *Paradise Regained?* After *Paradise Lost*, Milton had nothing to prove to the world, but he had something to say, and of course he had the energy to say it. *Paradise Lost* addresses the Old Testament from the beginning of its action, the creation of the world. *Paradise Regained* addresses the New Testament from what Milton sees as the beginning of *its* action: the temptation of Jesus in the desert by Satan.[9] The earlier events in Jesus's life recounted in Matthew and Luke are not actions *by* Jesus. Only after Jesus's baptism by John the Baptist, after he goes into the desert and is tempted, does he "begin," as Milton puts it in the final line of *Paradise Regained*, "to save mankind."

In *Paradise Regained* the old adversaries from the battle in Heaven, recorded in book 6 of *Paradise Lost*, meet again. But in Heaven they were hardly adversaries: the Son's victory over the armies of Satan is sudden, overwhelming, and total. This time Satan, who is prince of this world (John 12:31), has supernatural powers, and Jesus, the incarnate Son of God, has no powers above human, although he is a perfect human being in every way. But surely even a perfect human being would not be equal to the powers Satan now has. Or might he be?

Nor does Jesus have any memory of the war in Heaven, of who he is or what it means to be God's "Son." As we have seen, the word *Son*, obsessively repeated, is the riddle of this poem. Satan wants to find out the meaning of the phrase, "This is my son beloved, in him am pleased" (*PR*, 1.85), and whether it applies to the prophetic judgment on the serpent uttered by the Son when Adam and Eve were judged: "Her Seed shall bruise thy head, thou bruise his heel" (*PL*, 10.180). Is the meaning of "Seed" the same as the meaning of "Son"? For the climactic episode of *Paradise Regained*, when Satan tries something harsher and more direct than temptation, he reveals his uncertainty on this question: "Therefore, to know what more thou art than man / Worth naming Son of God, by voice from Heav'n, / Another method I must now begin" (*PR*, 4.538–40). Satan recalls the Son's judgment shortly after the action of the poem begins and refers to this wound as "fatal" and "long-threatened" (*PR*, 1.53 and 59). What does this wound consist of? Satan conjectures the prophecy means he and the other devils will no longer be left free to range in "this fair empire won of earth and air" (*PR*, 1.63). They will be driven back to Hell, as they are in the Nativity Ode. Is Jesus this "Seed" who will inflict the bruise? That is what Satan wants to find out above all. But whether Jesus is the "Seed" or some other sense of "Son of God," Satan intends to corrupt him if he can and destroy him if he must—and if he can.

If Jesus can defeat Satan's efforts to tempt and destroy him, he will have undone Adam's crime, which persists in the entire human race as original sin, and which Milton understands as the lust of dominion and the lust of possession, but also, especially now, after the collapse of the English Revolution, as cowardice. If Jesus wins, he will have become a perfect instrument for his ministry, which will start after the close of this poem.

Paradise Lost expands upon the biblical Creation and Fall in the most literal and physical sense. The essential thought of *Paradise Lost*, about the Bible as well as about human ethics, is direct and uncomplicated. It affirms human freedom, and the exaltedness of human reason, within the horizon of our createdness. We are created beings and owe God thanks and praise for our existence. We also owe God obedience to what was originally a single command: not to eat the fruit of the tree of knowledge of good and evil. But after the Fall this original command branched out into many prohibitions, not all of them reasonable and free. The many laws are an effort to plug the leaky holes in the hull of our corrupted nature, while the ship slowly sinks. We are still reasonable and free beings, but overwhelmed by the sins we commit and even more by the sins we inherit from all who have been sinning before us, which inherited sins cumulatively may be termed "history." History is our great excuse, but it is also our greatest burden. The Son of God comes into the world to remove this weight of sin and restore us to our original state of innocence—although this, as it happens, will take time, and will require, in conventional Christianity, a sacrifice. To remove the weight of sin means for Milton to reverse the direction of history, to turn Paradise lost into Paradise regained—or, rather, to turn the desert of history into a new Paradise that exists only in the barest of outlines. The new Paradise, for which the secular version is Utopia, is for Milton in the process of being slowly built. That is the meaning of the phrase in the introduction to *Paradise Regained*: "And Eden raised in the waste wilderness" (*PR*, 1.7).

Paradise Regained is biblically allusive, conceptually challenging, and stylistically spare. It also makes an unexpected advance, intellectually speaking, upon *Paradise Lost*, which becomes strikingly quietist, with nothing more to recommend than obedience, suffering, and meekness, ideas not well coordinated with Milton's ethically paramount, humanist concepts of freedom and reason. In books 11 and 12 of *Paradise Lost*, the synthesis of classical values and Christian faith comes apart and Christian faith overwhelms humanist values. Transcendental engagement—that is, engagement with the world, because human beings are inherently noble and deserve better—begins to regress into transcendence pure and simple, because human beings deserve what they get from one another. In these final two books of *Paradise Lost* Milton almost seems to recommend giving up on the world and hoping for Heaven.

Paradise Regained shows renewed intellectual vigor, and the thinking, the *dianoia*, which is to say, the thought expressed by the characters, is more immediate, disclosing a reawakened engagement with the world. The engagement is dialectical and transcendent because it will have nothing to do with improvement. It begins by rejecting all that the world has to offer and all that the world thinks it needs, in order to begin making a new world out of the old. In a further dialectical subtlety, the thinking in *Paradise Regained* does not struggle, as we might have expected, to fight its way free from an unalloyed Christian tradition that comes to dominate the final books of *Paradise Lost*, nor does it welcome back the classical, humanist values that make up the anthropology of *Paradise Lost*. Instead, *Paradise Regained* goes straight into the heart of the Christian tradition, in the New Testament gospels, and includes for good measure a stern condemnation of the classical tradition. In *Paradise Lost*, Milton expresses thinking he had already done before beginning the poem, mostly in the prose works written over nearly two decades. In *Paradise Regained*, we feel the pressure of thinking as it is happening now.

The Jesus of *Paradise Regained* is like the supremely authoritative Jesus of John's gospel, but in a state of becoming. It is almost as if Milton set out to discover where Jesus got his strength of mind from and sought an answer by expanding imaginatively on an episode that is not in John's Gospel, but that is in the other three. The temptation by Satan is understood by Milton, and so presented by him, as the final and decisive stage in the formation of Jesus's mind, preparing Jesus for his ministry and also testing him to see if he is worthy. The portrait we are given of his mind is fascinating, in his private thoughts as well as in his statements to Satan. It is an entirely human mind, without divine knowledge, but it is the mind of a genius and an idealist, one who has read intelligently enough in the Hebrew scriptures to know he is the coming *Messiah* to which the prophets refer. But what exactly does this mean, and what is to be done? Jesus has come into the desert to think this over, and Satan will have some solutions to offer him.

In the choice of the temptation episode, Milton discovers a thought we see clearly expressed nowhere else in his work: that the Crucifixion, the climactic episode of all four gospels, is less important than the temptation in the desert, a minor episode at the outset of the synoptic gospels. As Milton sees it, Jesus's Crucifixion is a victory over the *consequences* of the original sin of Adam and Eve, the chief consequence being death. But Jesus's victory in the desert is a victory over the *cause* of original sin, the temptation of Adam and Eve. This is a more radical solution.

It is hard to emphasize enough how unorthodox and extreme this idea is, got from thoughtful and repeated reading of the Greek text of the gospels, with attention and with total disregard for tradition—or for other parts of the Bible, notably the epistles of Paul. As we have come to expect with Milton's thought, his solution to the problem of what Jesus actually does to save us goes down to the root.

In the Book of Judges, Samson is a brutal, inarticulate strong man, who nevertheless ends as a hero, although his intention is only to revenge the loss of his eyes. Milton's considerable achievement is to make Samson intelligent, eloquent, public-spirited, and even something less of an egotist. He makes Samson's revealing to Dalila the secret of his strength a credible and likely thing, in Aristotle's sense of the "probable," and above all he makes the intensity of Samson's moral agony almost unbearable to us. If such speeches are Sophoclean in their power, the speech of the Messenger describing Samson's last act has an explosiveness worthy of Euripides. For the poet who wrote so unforgettably of Paradise and of the Creation of world, this scene of slaughter is a remarkable farewell.

The contrasts between the two works, not only with respect to genre but also mood and philosophy, appear to be very great, so much so a celebrated collection of critical essays on them is entitled *The Prison and the Pinnacle*.[10] *Paradise Regained* and *Samson Agonistes* are in contrasting genres, on contrasting subjects, drawn from the contrasting testaments of the Christian Bible, in what appear to be contrasting styles, the majestic and the passionate. In *Paradise Regained* Jesus praises the "majestic, unaffected style" (*PR*, 4.359) of the Hebrew prophets, and Milton has evidently taken the phrase to heart in this new work, having, as I said, nothing to prove to the world after *Paradise Lost*. Yet we hear of, and see, what Jesus is shown: strong-armed, superbly mounted Parthians, who fill the plain with glinting steel; stately but luxurious and lascivious Romans, pillaging the world for their insatiable greed; and clever, plausible, but morally abject Greeks, who sing, as Jesus puts it, "The vices of their deities, and their own, / In fable, hymn, or song, so personating / Their gods ridiculous, and themselves past shame" (*PR*, 4.340–46). The style of *Samson Agonistes* is passionate, as befits a tragedy and as befits the characters in the state of crisis they find themselves in, especially Samson. But of course that puts the author in a still more majestic stance, as never having to speak in his own voice. As for Samson, his tone changes over the course of the drama from the wrenching pathos of his lamentations to cold fury when faced with Dalila, a "cleaving mischief" (*SA*, line 1039) as he calls her, and to colder, lethal scorn when confronted by Harapha, whom he defeats with the first words he utters, "The way to know were not to see, but taste" (*SA*, line 1091). Finally, as he leaves with the officer, and as we hear by report, Samson maintains a stern but amused self-control before the mocking Philistines. There is grim irony in his taunting invitation to them to watch what marvelous thing he is going to do next: "such other trial / I mean to show you of my strength, yet greater / As with amaze shall *strike* all who behold" (*SA*, lines 1643–45). In the end, as the title foretells, Samson is an agonist in the stadium, confident of victory. This athletic sense of the word is confirmed by the Messenger, who says—in what otherwise makes little sense—that when Samson did his feats of strength at the temple, no one dared to compete with him: "None daring to appear *antagonist*" (line 1628). The other meaning of *agonistes* refers to one who is in a struggle to the death. The Philistines learn that meaning the hard way.

Both works are also biblical and, although their biblical subjects could hardly be more different, both contribute to the comprehensive vision of history that is opened in *Paradise Lost*. Unlike *Paradise Lost*, however, which is diagnostic and hortatory, *Paradise Regained* and *Samson Agonistes* are militant works, and *Paradise Regained* is no less *agonistic* than *Samson Agonistes*. In the severer mental fight of *Paradise Regained*, the fate of the world hangs in the balance—a balance in midair. The hero of *Samson Agonistes* fights against his sworn and proven enemies. But he also fights against the more banal and amorphous manifestation of evil in every age, in which the hand of Satan is harder to discern: social, political, religious, and moral corruption. The Philistines are tyrants, but tyrants can be agreeable and even humane, as Manoa discovers when seeking Samson's freedom—for a bribe, of course. The Philistines do not think of themselves as tyrants, and would repel such a thought with indignation: they are patriotic. The Philistines represent *bien-pensant*, ruling-class opinion in a state that was at the time one of the great powers of the region: self-satisfied, triumphalist, sensationalist, and, always, for one plausible excuse or another, at war. But the truth is, they like war for its own sake, although they like military defeat rather less. The Philistine ruling class is therefore not absolutely evil, like Satan, the metaphysical origin of evil. It is well meaning, banal, and corrupt, and therefore harder to spurn and less easy to condemn—or to crush. In *Paradise Regained*, we watch the fight against the evil of evil. In *Samson Agonistes*, we watch the fight against elusive but omnipresent everyday-ness of evil.

What was Milton's intention in *Samson Agonistes?* It does not appear in his substantial theoretical preface, "Of That Sort of Dramatic Poem Which Is Called Tragedy," in which the poet is at pains to describe the work to follow as a proper Greek tragedy, correct in all details because it follows the principles set forth by Aristotle, which are familiar to those who are "not unacquainted" with Aeschylus, Sophocles, and Euripides. (Such acquaintance may make one more aware of the differences between them and Aristotle's theory.) Shakespeare is not deemed worthy more particular mention than by the puritanical statement that tragedy is today held "in small esteem, or rather infamy," for such faults as bringing "trivial and vulgar persons" on stage in the midst of grave matters, to please the vulgar in the audience, which is wrong. Against these aberrant poetasters, Gregory Nazianzen, "a father of the church," is held up in favorable contrast, because he put together an ingenious patchwork—the technical term is a cento—of verses and half-verses from ancient tragedies to make the play, *Christ Suffering* (χρίστος πάσχων).[11] At such moments Milton sounds like Theodore W. Adorno writing on music. There is a philosophically correct way to compose music, which

Adorno has discovered and Schoenberg practiced, and Stravinsky must be scorned as a degenerate. If people approve of Stravinsky's music, which they do—as they do of Shakespeare's plays, to Milton's seeming annoyance—so much the worse for them.

After some more of this swaggering, Milton confesses that *Samson Agonistes* was never intended for the stage. His reasons for saying this are somewhat circumstantial. As a Puritan, Milton was suspicious of popular commercial theater (the Puritans closed the London theaters in 1642). The fashionable Restoration stage—with, for the first time, women actors—seemed to him even more immoral than Caroline masques. It should be added that Greek tragedy existed then—as for the most part, despite some performances, it still does today—on the printed page. Milton naturally wants *Samson Agonistes* to be thought of as meeting the high *poetic* standards of Greek tragedy, and he therefore emphasizes its literary qualities by deprecating its suitability to performance. And indeed, performance of such a work is almost unthinkable at the time. English theater was moving in a different direction. Shakespeare and his colleagues introduced commercial theater to the world, or reintroduced commercial theater for the first time since antiquity, drawing from the popular ancient models, Terence, Plautus, and Seneca. From Shakespeare's time forward, despite the hiatus of 1642–1660, theater has been about entertainment, the growing culture industry, to use Adorno and Max Horkheimer's term, now global in its reach. The truest words in Shakespeare concerning the purpose of his work are in the last line of *Twelfth Night*, "We'll strive to please you every day." That is not the aim of *Samson Agonistes*, which is not about distraction but *purification*, or *catharsis*, which Milton tries to explain in his preface.

Happily, Milton's absurd theorizing has no harmful effect on his actual tragedy. With wonderful deftnesss, the complex and highly episodic story of Samson in the book of Judges is given unity by focusing on the last hours of Samson's life and having earlier episodes referred to retrospectively by the chorus, by Samson's father, by Manoa, and by Samson himself. The circumstances of Dalila's corruption by the Philistines and her betrayal of Samson are fascinatingly expatiated on—from her own mouth. Milton says the action takes place "*within* the space of twenty-four hours," but that figure is for the benefit of readers of Italian critical theory, who will want to be reassured on this point. In fact, the action extends from dawn to early afternoon, a perfect length of time for a play with this action.

To a considerable degree Milton's having Greek tragedy in mind as he composed appears also to be true of *Paradise Regained*. Most of the work is dialogue, and the exchanges between Satan and Jesus—leading up to a dramatic recognition, or *anagnorisis*, to use the technical term from Aristotle—have the character of Greek drama, as well. Milton's Satan bears at least a structural resemblance to the insolent usurper, Aegisthus, a figure in the well-known revenge plays by the three tragedians whom Milton mentions in his preface to *Samson Agonistes:* the *Choephorae* of Aeschylus, and the *Electra* plays by Sophocles and Euripides. Aegisthus fears one thing, the return of Orestes, the son of great Agamemnon, whose murder Aegisthus contrived with Agamemnon's wife, Clytemnestra. The recognition of Orestes is a terrifying moment for these two, who understand that the time of reckoning they have dreaded for so long has at last come. Milton contrives just such a moment of recognition at the climax of *Paradise Regained*, when another son is revealed. Milton cannot get away with having Satan struck down like a slaughtered ox, as Aegisthus is struck down—while sacrificing—in Euripides's *Electra*. But Milton is so attracted to the idea of a physical fall and collapse he repeats the word *fall* seven times (*PR*, 4.567, 568, 571, twice, 576, 581, 620).

Famously, and startlingly, Milton chooses this moment of Satan's "fall" to insert two elaborate similes from Greek myth. The first is Antaeus (*PR*, 5.563–68), who is thrown down repeatedly and keeps rising, stronger from each fall, until Heracles throttles him in mid-air: "Throttled at length in air expired and fell" (*PR*, 4 568). The other is the Theban sphinx (*PR*, 4.572), who when Oedipus answers her riddle throws herself over the cliff on which she is perched, "th'Ismenian steep" (*PR*, 4.575).

To these brilliant, physically impressive similes Milton adds three New Testament allusions to falling: the Gadarene swine falling into the sea (*PR*, 4.629–30); Satan falling like lighting from heaven (*PR*, 4.619–20); and the defeat of Satan at the Apocalypse (*PR*, 4.622). Milton further adds an allusion to his own account in *Paradise Lost* of Satan's being cast down after his first rebellion (*PR*, 4.604–7). The discomfiture of Satan occurs by means of a *peripeteia*, or "turnaround," combined with an *anagnorisis*, or "recognition"—the key elements of what Aristotle says is the best sort of tragic plot, a "complex" or "folded together" one *(symplokê)*.[12] A *peripeteia* occurs when the action seems to be tending in one direction and is suddenly reversed, as when Satan puts Jesus on the pinnacle in order to see him fall, and falls himself: "Fell whence he stood to see his victor fall" *(PR*, 4.571). The turnaround is combined with the *anagnorisis* when Satan, in the instant before falling, recognizes Jesus as the "Son of God," in what is, for him, the worst possible sense of that phrase. This is the Son who is the visible expression of the wrath of God.[13] Deviating from the biblical accounts, Milton has Satan put Jesus on the pinnacle fully expecting him to fall. Milton makes sure we understand this intention when he says that Satan's words to Jesus, once Jesus is in position, are *added in scorn*. All the action of *Paradise Regained* has been tending to the point where Satan will have no resources left with which to destroy Jesus except violence:

> There, on the highest pinnacle, he set
> The Son of God and added thus in scorn:
> "There stand, if thou wilt stand; to stand upright
> Will ask thee skill. I to thy Father's house
> Have brought thee and highest placed: highest is best.
> Now show thy progeny; if not to stand,
> Cast thyself down. Safely, if Son of God;
> For it is written, 'He will give command
> Concerning thee to his Angels; in their hands
> They shall uplift thee, lest at any time
> Thou chance to dash thy foot against a stone.'"
> To whom thus Jesus: "Also it is written,
> 'Tempt not the Lord thy God.'" He said, and stood;
> But Satan, smitten with amazement, fell.
>
> *(PR, 4.549–62)*

For these reasons it seems likely that after completing *Paradise Lost*, or while he was doing so, Milton returned to his long-standing interest in Greek tragedy and the theory of *catharsis*—"cleansing" or "purification"—which he describes in the preface to *Samson Agonistes*, alluding to the medical origin of the theory: "for so, in physic [medicine], things of melancholic hue and quality are used against melancholy, sour against sour, salt to remove salt humors."[14] The theory is all but explicitly referred to in the closing lines of *Samson Agonistes*. After the catastrophe, God's servants are dismissed with "peace and consolation," and "calm of mind, all passion spent" (*SA*, lines 1747–48). It is true that the agonizing passions were the poet's, too, which he was spending in this play, in order to be rid of them. The result is Milton's most personal work since "Lycidas," in the most impersonal of literary forms. In terms of the actual tragedy, however, Israel is purified of its slackness and cowardice. Her youths will in the future visit Samson's tomb and be inspired with courage, as will the maidens of Israel, who will sing anthems in Samson's praise. We notice that the site of the tomb Manoa will build for his son is swept and *clean*, because the hero honored there has been purified, and has purified Israel.

That at least is the idea. Milton makes no allusion to the events to follow after the story of Samson in the book of Judges. They are anything but pure.

The title of *Paradise Regained* indicates it follows from and completes the thought of *Paradise Lost*, which it does. But in *Paradise Lost* there is a real Paradise that is really lost by Adam and Eve, and later destroyed at the Flood. In contrast, neither word in the title of *Paradise Regained* is what it is or means what it says. There is no *Paradise* and nothing is *regained* or even *gained*. In the anthems they sing at the conclusion, the angels do refer to the earthly, paradisal Garden, which has "failed": "For, though that seat of earthly bliss be failed, / A fairer Paradise is founded now / For Adam and his chosen sons" (*PR*, 4.612–14). What is *founded*, but not *planted*—we take note of the architectural metaphor—is the heavenly Jerusalem of Revelation, which may be figuratively referred to as *Paradise* because it has the fountain and tree of life, from which the Son is refreshed by the angels at the end of Milton's poem: "fruits fetched from the tree of life, / And from the fount of life ambrosial drink" (*PR*, 4.589–90). At the end of the poem the angels exhort Jesus to begin his great work of reversing the direction of history, from downfall to gradual ascent: "Now enter, and begin to save Mankind" (*PR*, 4.635).

In *Paradise Lost*, everything is what it is and not another thing. It is a poem of astonishing presence. In *Paradise Regained*, nothing quite is what it is. Satan has been thrown down by Jesus, and although we do not see this overthrow actually occur, the proof that it did occur will come when Satan shall fall like the autumnal star prophesied in Isaiah and the lightning prophesied by Jesus. But before that happens, "ere this" (*PR*, 4.621), the proof that it *will* happen is that Satan now feels his wound, which is not a real wound but a darkly prophesied one. As bad as this wound is, though Satan has not yet received it, it is not as bad as the last and deadliest wound, which is to come in the future, at the Apocalypse, and is not further described, except by the original prophecy. The final wound is already this present wound, which is not a wound but the renewed prophecy of one:

> Like an autumnal star,
> Or lightning, thou shalt fall from Heaven, trod down
> Under his feet. For proof, ere this thou feel'st
> Thy wound (yet not thy last and deadliest wound)
> By this repulse received.
>
> (PR, *4.619–23*)

Paradise Regained asks us to read differently from how we read *Paradise Lost:* we are asked to be always vigilant, always aware of reading a text, instead of forgetting we are reading and enjoying the show. *Paradise Regained* opens up the allusive and ever-shifting textual system of the Bible, wherein the true meaning of anything is distributed around a vast circuit extending from Genesis to Revelation and returning again, in a *ricorso* of images that are only partially inhabited by the more fluid currents of meaning. We are always looking forward to the Apocalypse, back from thence into the prophets, and forward again from all the points we have looked back to, a maze of mirrors. We find ourselves in such a maze when we try to state flatly the meaning of the title of *Paradise Regained*.

The verse of *Paradise Regained* and *Samson Agonistes* is changed from that of *Paradise Lost*. It is more vehement, suiting the speech of the heroes of these works. The difference is more obvious in *Samson Agonistes*, where the ten-syllable tone row is no longer invariant, although it remains the foundation. But there is considerable deviation, in keeping with the decorum of Greek tragedy, which uses a variety of meters of some complexity, especially in choruses. The matter is wittily summarized by John Creaser when he says *Samson Agonistes* is not written in *vers libre* but in *vers libéré*.[15]

I turn first to the more challenging case of *Samson Agonistes*, and to its first speech, a soliloquy by Samson of fully 114 lines, starting at the opening line. It is an astonishing journey, dramatically as well as poetically. But up to line 82 and the phrase "Without all hope of day," the speech is entirely in blank verse, sinewy and powerful as ever, indeed more than ever. Three following lines in blank verse may lead the reader to suppose the hypometrical line 82 is a sport, but then we have three six-syllable lines (*SA*, lines 86–88) and realize Milton is taking us into metrical territory unexplored since his Latin and English poems of more than twenty years previous.

In his opening speech Samson performs the role of a prologue in supplying background information concerning the feast of Dagon on that day, allowing him rest. Such rest, however, affords "Ease to the body some, none to the mind" (line 18) because his thoughts attack him (I emphasize where the stresses fall) like a "**dead**ly **swarm** / Of **hor**nets **armed**" (*SA*, lines 19–20). He is stung with the thought of what he was—a hero, chosen by God and announced at birth by an angel, and Israel's proposed deliverer—and of what he is now: "**Ask** for this **great de-liv**erer **now,** and **find** him / **Eye**less in **Ga**za at the **mill** with **slaves,** / Him**self** in bonds **un**der Phil**is**tian **yoke**" (*SA*, lines 40–42).

Already, the meter of these lines is more adventuring than that of *Paradise Lost*, homogenized as the latter is by the narrative voice. These lines are passionate and springing, but also unexpected in their rhythms. They imitate the dactylic rhythm of heroic poetry, especially in the rolling rhythm of the last. But the middle verse intrudes another aggressively vehement rhythm (following the terminal trochee of the preceding line: "**find** him"): a choriambic, "**Eye**less in **Ga**za"; followed by a cretic, "**mill** with **slaves.**" This is followed by a contrary train of thought in a speculative mood, showing the energetic side of Samson's mind: "Yet **stay,** let me **not rash**ly **call in doubt** / Di**vine** pre**dic**tion. What if **all** fore**told** / Had **been** ful**filled** but **through** mine **own** de**fault?**" (*SA*, lines 43–44). As blank verse, this is more regular meter, especially the second line. But the two, anapestic rhythms—"let me **not**" and "what if **all**"—suggest a mind eagerly searching for truth. He has himself to blame, he says, for telling the secret of his strength to a woman (as if a man might keep a secret better), but this conclusion of his guilt is soon troubled by the thought that his God-given strength should have been accompanied by wisdom, a beautiful echo of Horace's *vis consilii* *inexpers mole ruit sua* ("strength without the good counsel of intelligence causes the collapse of its own defensive wall"):[16] "But what is strength without a double share / Of wisdom? Vast, unweildy, burdensome, / Proudly secure, yet liable to fall / By weakest subtleties" (*SA*, lines 53–56). Such a person is unfit to command. He should serve those who are wiser, if less strong.

This thought leads to the bitterest statement in the speech, **"God, when he gave me strength, to show** with**all** / How **slight** the **gift** was, **hung** it **in** my **hair"** (*SA*, lines 58–59). The three emphatic words **"Gave me strength,"** are followed by iambs that modulate at the end into hammer-like trochees, forming that emphatic cretic at the termination of the line: "**gift** was, **hung** it **in** my **hair**." The same movement as earlier follows this ("But peace!"): from bitter reproach of God to a deep uncertainty that is covered over by self-reproach for questioning God. God's purpose no doubt is being fulfilled, but if so, where does that leave Samson? His miseries are "So many and so huge that each apart / Would ask a **life** to **wail**" (*SA*, lines 65–66).

Of these the greatest, the most insupportable, is blindness: "Blind among enemies, O worse than chains, / Dungeon, or beggary, or decrepit old age!" (*SA*, lines 68–69). At these passionate words—and the lines following, which recall the invocation to light beginning *Paradise Lost*, book 3—we recognize Milton is speaking for himself, through Samson, of his own affliction, of his being blind among enemies, in hiding and then in jail. Milton can bring Samson to life before our eyes all the more convincingly, and cathartically, because his own life circumstances have come to resemble those of Samson, if not Job. (Job seems to be the other biblical model for Milton's character of Samson.[17])

First, blindness came to Milton and was total by early 1652. Then came the deaths of two wives and two infants. Then came political disaster, and the return of tyranny, as Milton saw it, immediately followed by internal exile and prison. As Frank Kermode points out, it is likely Milton had to make a personal submission and sue for grace.[18] There was no shame in that. Refusing to do so would have been useless, and suicidal, and Milton had children to care and provide for. Tradition has it Milton was also offered service with the new government, which he declined. There is no evidence for this, nor, in the nature of the thing, would there be. Such an offer would have been informally and discreetly made, but surely it would have been made to a man of such talent, ability, and fame—and a defeated enemy, too—if only for the publicity such a service would afford. What could have been more welcome to the new regime than that the only truly famous intellectual of the Commonwealth, who "fulmined" (*PR*, 4.270) over Europe in defense of the cause of the English Revolution (and the execution of the king), should have been shorn like a "tame wether" (*SA*, lines 538) and brought into service, grinding at the mill of low-level diplomatic correspondence—or better, made to compose encomia of the new king?[19] The point would not have been the work itself, translating barbarous Latin into good English and barbarous English into good Latin. The point would have been the humbling of an enemy, and a great man. Samson refuses, too, and his first refusal is one of Milton's additions to the tale. But after that, when Samson is moved by God to obey the command to go to the temple of Dagon, his and Milton's stories diverge. Milton watched him in his mind, with admiration and envy, as the close of the work shows.

As emerges later in this speech, blindness and political failure made Milton feel dead and buried, a moving grave. The absence of a single beam of light separates him from all creation, and puts him in his grave before his time, his open eyes staring at black earth pressed to his face:

> O dark, dark, dark amid the blaze of noon
> Irrecoverably dark, total eclipse,
> Without all hope of day!
> O first-created beam, and thou, great Word,
> "Let there be light, and light was over all"
> Why am I thus bereaved thy prime decree?
> The sun to me is dark
> And silent as the moon
> When she deserts the night,
> Hid in her vacant interlunar cave . . .
> To live a life half dead, a living death,
> And buried, but O yet more miserable,
> Myself my sepulchre, a moving grave,
> Buried, yet not exempt,
> By privilege of death and burial
> From worst of other evils, pains and wrongs

> But made hereby obnoxious more
> To all the miseries of life,
> Life in captivity,
> Among inhuman foes.
>
> (SA, *lines 80–109*)

Not even Adam's theologically intriguing despair, in *Paradise Lost*, or the lyrical—and so, secretly alluring—despair of "Lycidas" ("Alas! What boots it with uncessant care," line 64) can approach the deadly vacuity of this speech, out of which nothing but agony rises. It is not so much nihilism—which is still a philosophical position—as it is an articulate scream. A new phonic instrument is needed to make this savage sound into art. I will venture a few more technical points, consideration of which will help to attune the ear to the subtler energies of *Samson Agonistes*.

The extraordinary qualities of this new kind of verse—Milton's calling it *apolelymenon*, which means only "freed up," is a schoolmaster's joke—are hard to summarize. As I mentioned, there truly is a freeing up after the lockstep tone row of ten syllables (eleven for occasional un-accented terminations) in *Paradise Lost* and *Paradise Regained*. We see the return from "Lycidas," three decades before, of the expressive six-syllable line, for syncopation, but now in the rhythmical equivalent of tone clusters: "The **sun** to **me** is **dark**, / And **silent as** the **moon**, / When **she** de**serts** the **night**" (*SA*, lines 86–88). The simplicity—only two words exceed a single syllable—and the startling force of these lines is followed in the next line by a well-positioned polysyllable with two tro-chees ("interlunar"), the latter, admittedly, a technique familiar from *Paradise Lost*, but especially effective after the series of short lines, the like of which is not in *Paradise Lost*.

Eight-syllable lines are employed, providing openings for expressive dactyls—"<u>**mis**eries</u> of **life**"—and even anapests, although not here, and dactyls are more frequent in the longer lines, too, in the words "<u>**privi**lege</u>" and "<u>**bur**ial</u>." When eight- and six-syllable lines are placed together, they recollect the old-fashioned, English fourteener, used, for ex-ample, by Chapman in his translation of the *Iliad*, and conferring on this primitive scene a burnished effect. Of still more interest for the verse of *Samson Agonistes*—and this applies, as well, though more subtly, to *Paradise Regained*—are the expressive line endings, choriambics ("**to**tal ec**lipse**"), and combinations of punchy cretics (**long**-short-**long**), created by a slight detachment of the second syllable of a penultimate iambic foot that then attaches to the finishing iamb: "**blaze** of **noon**"; "**hope** of **day**"; "over **all**"; "**living death**"; "**moving grave**"; "**not** ex**empt**"; "**pains** and **wrongs**"; "ob**nox**ious **more**"; "in**hu**man **foes**." These terminations are like blows.

The effect is ubiquitous in *Samson Agonistes*, when aggression or triumph is registered: "**Ga**za **mourns**" (*SA*, line 1753); "**see,** but **taste**" (*SA*, line 1091); "**thine** or **mine**" (*SA*, line 1155); "**small** en**force**" (*SA*, line 1223).[20] One imagines Milton spoke this way, arming his phrases with barbs, so they will stick in. Many of these terminations may be scanned doggedly as two iambs, but to the attentive ear Milton has developed a new rhythm closer to the way he spoke, especially when ironical, or satirical: "extreme pleasant . . . but satirical. He pronounced the letter *R* very hard."[21]

Milton's composing a drama, thus disengaging himself as a narrator, has something to do with this rugged style. The instinct of a narrator is to achieve homogeneity, like equal temperament in music, toning down the sharper, more dissonant edges. Now Milton was hearing differently, and in *Paradise Lost*, even in the Hell books, there is nothing remotely like the vehemence of these lines:

> If **Da**gon **be** thy **god,**
> **Go** to his **tem**ple, in**voke** his **aid**
> With **sol**emnest de**vo**tion, **spread** be**fore** him
> How **high**ly it con**cerns** his **glory now**
> To **frus**trate and dis**solve** these **magic spells,**
> Which **I** to be the **pow'r** of **Is**rael's **God**
> A**vow,** and **chall**enge **Da**gon **to** the **test,**
> **Then** thou shalt **see,** or **ra**ther **to** thy **sor**row
> Soon feel, whose God is strongest, **thine** or **mine.**
>
> (SA, *lines 1145–55*)

Note how the strong accents of the line terminations, which fall thick and fast at the outset, become still more concentrated at the end of the passage, especially in the final line. Samson says that with only an oaken staff he will raise an outcry on Harapha's clattered armor, and one seems already to hear the clanging.

One could conduct a similar analysis, with similar results, throughout *Samson Agonistes*, notably in the terrific scene of snarling and snapping, interspersed with lyrical pathos, and ending with a roar, which occurs when Samson and Dalila square off. One would find a wider range of metrical effects calibrated nicely to the passions, especially in the choruses, and most especially the central one, beginning "Many are the sayings of the wise" (*SA*, line 652), which is sung before the entrance of Dalila.

The *antistrophe*, as I am tempted to call it, the second paragraph of this chorus, begins with the question, "God of our fathers, what is Man?," a clear challenge to what is perhaps the most famous chorus of the Attic stage, from Sophocles's *Antigone* (lines 332–75). Throughout Sophocles's chorus the same question is implicitly asked, but without any transcendental answer: "Many things that endure are marvelous [*deinos*, which includes in its semantic field 'terrible, portentous'], but none is more marvelous than man" (lines 332–33). Unlike all other creatures, man has intelligence and language, and is armed against every assault except death, sailing the seas even in winter, tormenting the earth with the plough, catching birds, and subduing powerful beasts to his will. He devises ingenious solutions with technical knowledge, but for all this cleverness he can still take the road of evil or good, and so, because of evil, he is the greatest danger and mystery to himself, and to the city.

Milton seems to have these verses in his sights when his chorus speaks of "ancient books" extolling patience as the truest fortitude against "all chances incident to man's frail life" (*SA*, line 656). For what do such books, including Sophocles's chorus extolling patient cleverness and endurance, ignore? They ignore the *afflicted*, those who are cast down and irreparably abject, and can take no comfort in how marvelous human achievements are. For them, humanism is beside the point, and rubs salt in the wound. Extolling human greatness is "harsh and dissonant" (*SA*, line 662) in the ears of the afflicted unless—and this, Milton judges, Sophocles completely ignores—there is for the afflicted a transcendental source of consolation and of hope:

> Unless he feel within
> Some source of consolation from above,
> Secret refreshings that repair his strength

> And fainting spirits uphold.
> God of our fathers, what is man?
>
> (SA, *lines 663–67*)

The first two lines, of six and ten syllables, could be from "Lycidas," and march on confidently in iambs. The third line, "**Se**cret re**fresh**ings that // re**pair** his **strength**," varies the rhythm with two dactyls in the first half, giving a sense of the miraculous, and two iambs in the second, although I would be inclined to pronounce **his** with an accent, as well, so that the line ends with three strong beats. The next, concluding line is six syllables (*spirits* is pronounced as one syllable, *spearts*) and has the definitiveness of a trochaic tetrameter, with its emphatic, one-beat conclusion: "and **faint**ing **spearts** up**hold**."

The final line in the passage quoted begins the *antistrophe*, although Milton in his preface says he eschews such terms because his play was never intended for the stage. (At the end, however, he divides the chorus beginning at line 1659 into two semi-choruses, at line 1667 and at line 1689, a division that is supererogatory apart from performance, more so than the division of *strophe* from *antistrophe*, which exists in lyric poetry as well, without specific reference to performance.) An *antistrophe* is a contrasting stanza, or group of stanzas, that "turns back, or against" what was previously said. With the Greek love of symmetry and dialectic, even—especially—in states of high excitement, the *antistrophe* is the perfect instrument for raising the emotional temperature, as if by friction, when what is said forces itself back against what has already been said.

Hence the question, which bursts upon us: "**God** of our **fath**ers, **what is Man?**" (*SA*, line 667). The *is* can be accented or not, although, again, the three beats lends force to the end of this powerful line, the beginning of which joins an initial dactyl to a trochee, giving vehement force to the question.

The remainder of this chorus is a true masterpiece of complex rhythms for passionate effect, including obsessively obstinate rhymes (*various/contrarious*, *SA*, lines 668–69). The last words of the following six lines all rhyme (the first with a slight slant), ending with the sound, *oot*:

> Not evenly, as thou rul'st
> Th'angelic orders and inferior creatures mute,

> Irrational and brute.
> Nor do I name of men the common rout,
> That wand'ring loose about
> Grow up and perish as the summer fly.
>
> (SA, *lines 671–76*)

The irritable disregard for the normal propriety of verse, and for what Milton once called "the jingling sound of like endings," is a manifestation of pure artistic will.

We also encounter what we have not seen before, hypermetrical lines that stretch the phrase out, as if the emotional pressure of the thought were too intense to be contained within the normative frame of ten or eleven syllables. (And there is an unusually high concentration of feminine lines to contribute to this effect.) We see such a line above, beginning "Th'angelic orders," having twelve syllables ending on an accent, and framed by short six-syllable lines. In the following lines the same triadic structure appears—6–12–6—(reducing *countenance* to two syllables), which is followed, as before, by a return to the standard ten- or eleven-syllable row (in this case eleven, because of the unaccented final syllable). The closing effect is reassuring, like returning to the tonic key:

> Amidst their height of noon,
> Changest thy countenance and thy hand with no regard
> Of highest favors past
> From thee on them or them to thee of service.
>
> (SA, *lines 683–86*)

The elegance of that final verse—every word a single syllable, except the last word, providing the unaccented terminal syllable of a feminine line—makes a perfect conclusion.

Except that the chorus now presses on even deeper into doubt and despair. "Not only," they begin, does God appear to turn his face utterly from those on whom in the past he has conferred honor, including the honor of serving him. He abases and humiliates our heroes. Indeed, everyone who has placed their hope in these heroes and has taken them for an example is likewise cast down. This is expressed with another stretched-out line: "But throw'st them lower than thou didst exalt them high; / Unseemly falls in human eye" (*SA*, lines 689–90). They are jailed and reviled by the mob; they are left to the hostile sword of the heathen and the profane; their carcasses (I have quoted these lines already) are fed to dogs and birds; and even if they escape these things, they are afflicted with old age and disease (as Milton was), even if they have led (as Milton did) temperate lives, lives "not disordinate" (*SA*, line 701), though now they suffer "The punishment of dissolute days" (*SA*, line 702). It would not be a fair criticism to say none of these latter complaints have any bearing on Samson but considerable bearing on Milton. The chorus is addressing the general system of divine injustice, of which Samson's fate is only one example—and Milton's another.

The conclusion of the chorus, the epode, is if anything still more remarkable. Its first two verses derive their force from Milton's powerful syntax, and are not unlike the verse of *Paradise Lost* for their sinewy and flexible strength, made more eloquent by their bi-syllabic unaccented terminations (all three syllables of *glorious* are pronounced), which sound like dactyls: "So deal not with this once thy glorious **cham**pion, / The image of thy strength, and mighty **min**ister" (*SA*, lines 705–6). After the dignity of this, we are startled by the outburst of the following line, which seems to take up again the tone of reproach: "What do I beg? How hast thou dealt already?" (line 707). We have two vehement choriambs—"**What** do I **beg?** // **How** hast thou **dealt?**"—followed by an equally vehement termination, whether the *al* in *already* is accented or not. If the *al* is accented, the line concludes, before its unaccented termination, with three strong beats: ***dealt al- read*-*y!*** This striking protest is followed by a two-line exhortation and prayer that is so strongly expressed it sounds like a command addressed to God: "Look at Samson, God! Turn his fate around! We know you can do it! So do it!"

The first of these two lines is hypermetrical, with twelve syllables, as we have seen before, and its final two syllables—"and turn!"—are especially strong, even heartrending, as they stretch the thought and feeling out through a strong enjambment into the following line: "and turn / His labors." Even now, as we anticipate the closure of the thought after the enjambment, the thought is unfinished. Turn his labors—for we know you can!—to a peaceful end. The second line is a regular ten-syllable row, and the meter settles back into standard rhythm, although we note the emphasis, so common in Milton's late verse, at the end of the line (**peace**ful **end**): "Behold him in this state calamitous, and turn / His labors, for thou canst, to peaceful end" (*SA*, lines 708–9). How splendid it is that the following episode—the arrival of Dalila—should be introduced by the chorus as an interruption of its thoughts, but one that provokes a slant rhyme (end / land) with what has just be said: "His labors, for thou canst, to peaceful end. / But who is this, what thing of sea or land?" (*SA*, line 710).

The chorus—as we are to imagine the scene—now turns to look off-stage. A visitor is arriving, unrecognized at first, except as a grand lady, "Some rich Philistian matron" (*SA*, line 722) by appearances, perfumed and attended by servants, a "damsel train" (*SA*, line 721). She is compared to magnificent ship in the distance, sailing this way from afar. The description recalls Shakespeare's *Antony and Cleopatra*, in particular Enobarbus's description of another seductive vessel, a real one and an instrument of seduction: Cleopatra's barge. This description is briefer and more restrained, but alluring: "sails filled and streamers waving, / Courted by all the winds that hold them play" (*SA*, line 718–19).

One great difference is the sinister effect created by indistinction, which in the culture of the Hebrew law is unclean and sinister. First, the chorus cannot tell *who* or *what* this is; next, whether the thing discerned moves on the *sea* or on the *land*, whether it is fish or flesh. Is it a *thing* or a *person*, and if a person, of what *sex* is it, male or, as is more likely (but not certain: it or she merely *seems* so) female. She is like a ship—and ships, at least, are female—but if the nautical likeness holds, then it is uncertain as well what port she issues from and where she is bound. Everything in the description, after we have noted how alluring it is, recalls Satan's sideways and indirect approach to Eve, like a ship sailing in the mouth of a river, veering oft and shifting sail (*PL*, 9.499 and 513–17):

> **Chorus.** But who is this, what thing of sea or land?
> Female of sex it seems
> That so bedecked, ornate and gay
> Comes this way sailing,
> Like a stately ship
> Of Tarsus bound for the isles,
> Of Javan or Gadire,
> With all her bravery on and tackle trim,
> Sails filled and streamers waving,
> Courted by all the winds that hold them play,
> An amber scent of odorous perfume
> Her harbinger, a damsel train behind.

> Some rich Philistian matron she may seem
> And now, at nearer view, no other certain
> Than Dalila, thy wife.
> **Samson.** My wife, my traitress! Let her not come near me.
>
> (SA, *lines 710–25*)

With these words of Samson's in response to the chorus's description, the central and most dramatic scene in this play is about to begin. But the poet is not finished with this lyrical moment and now extends it, drawing the note out and combining it with another in a minor key, for pathos. She is beautiful and sad, like a flower bent down with the weight of morning dew on it, glistening. Her tears wet the border of her veil. Samson, of course, cannot see her, and so the chorus sees for him and directs him how to feel:

> Yet on she moves; now stands, and eyes thee fixed
> About t' have spoke, but now with head declined,
> Like a fair flower surcharged with dew, she weeps,
> And words addressed seem into tears dissolved,
> Wetting the border of her silken veil.
> But now again she makes address to speak.
> **Dalila.** With doubtful feet and wavering resolution
> I came, still dreading thy displeasure, Samson.
>
> (SA, *lines 726–33*)

After her long speech of repentance, Samson's response is in another key: "Out, out hyaena!" (line 748). But we are expected to ask if she is indeed a voracious hyaena—and whether her repentance is sincere, as it appears. For the following scene to be interesting, Dalila must be allowed to make an alluring case for reconciliation with Samson and a reasonable excuse for her betrayal of him to the Philistines. If truth were told, and as he must surely be willing to admit (at least if she can touch him), Samson is in some small part also responsible: "Ere I to thee thou to thyself was cruel" (line 784).

Milton is "not unacquainted" with Euripides—the *Medea*, for example—and knows that now is the time for agonist and antagonist to square off in brilliant forensic debate. Nothing is quite so powerful in ancient Greek theater than when a known and manifest criminal of legend—an Aegisthus, or a Clytemnestra, or, indeed, a Medea—stands before us without shame and justifies his or her crimes. Everyone knows the story of Samson and the wicked Dalila. What can she say in her defense?

The result is dramatically successful because Milton exerts all his powers to give Dalila's arguments specious plausibility and attractive grace—so that he can have his hero rip these arguments down and spurn them under foot: "I thought where all thy circling wiles would end: / In feigned religion, smooth hypocrisy" (*SA*, lines 871–72). In betraying Samson to the Philistines, Dalila has violated the law of nature and of nations—this point is made with inescapable logic, although one suspects Dalila is not interested. But she does hear Samson when he says he is a freer man chained in the prison and laboring at the mill as a slave than he would be under her care: "This jail I count the house of liberty / To thine, whose doors my feet shall never enter" (*SA*, lines 950–51).

Without further resources of debate, Dalila asks—it is another touch from Greek tragedy—if she may at least approach and touch Samson's hand. "Not for thy life," he replies, "lest fierce remembrance wake / My sudden rage to tear thee joint from joint" (*SA*, lines 952–53). The physical rejection seals the moral one. Samson dismisses Dalila with ironical forgiveness and invites her to cherish well her ill-gotten wealth, obtained at the cost of his life: "Cherish thy hastened widowhood with the gold / Of matrimonial treason: so, farewell" (*SA*, lines 958–59).

She does not leave without a shameless speech—another Euripidean touch. In northern Dan—Samson's tribal homeland—and in Judah, where the kingdom of Israel will rise, she, Dalila, may be traduced "for falsehood most unconjugal" (*SA*, line 979). But in her own country of Philistia, in the cities of Ecron, Gaza, Ashdod, and Gath—she might also have mentioned Ascalon—she will be "the famousest / Of women" (*SA*, lines 982–83), outstripping the inhospitable Jael (she, Dalila, is at least being hospitable) who knocked a nail through Sisera's head. It is an unfortunate comparison. The ineuphonious mouthful of *s*'s in *famousest* is one of Milton's ways of indicating mental aberrancy, as when Adam says Eve seems "wisest, virtuousest, discreetest, best" (*PL*, 8.550). Dalila is wrong, of course, and the irony is strongly felt: the Hebrews, not the Philistines, will write her story and give it to the world.

It may seem a strange thing to say, but close inspection of this exchange shows Milton thinking as intensely as he ever did since the divorce tracts about the nature of love and the bond between a woman and a man. This particular bond has not gone so well, but much is said by the way about the connection (not easily understood) between loyalty and love. Milton has lost his illusions but not his idealism.

Dalila ends on defiance: "At this whoever envies or repines / I leave him to his lot, and like my own" (*SA*, lines 995–96). Samson has become a *whoever* and a *him*. She disdains to name or notice him further. "She's gone," the chorus says, "a manifest serpent by her sting / Discovered in the end, till now concealed" (*SA*, lines 997–98). To which Samson replies—it is perhaps the most devastating thing he says about her, and one would have liked to have seen her hear it—"God sent her to debase me" (*SA*, line 999).

The exchange between Samson and Harapha, although not equal to that between Samson and Dalila, which nothing could equal, is important for its showing Samson's returned confidence in his strength, his courage to do a heroic deed and fight anyone, though blind, unarmed, and chained: "My heels are fettered, but my fist is free" (*SA*, line 1235). Put on your plated armor, Samson says to Harapha, your vaunt-brace, greaves, and helmet, enumerating all the giant's "gorgeous arms" (*SA*, line 1119):

> I only with an oaken staff will meet thee
> And raise such outcries on thy clattered iron
> Which long shall not withhold me from thy head,
> That in a little time, while breath remains thee,
> Thou oft shalt wish thyself at Gath, to boast
> Again in safety what thou wouldst have done
> To Samson, but shalt never see Gath more.
>
> (SA, *lines 1123–29*)

This is exciting but, as I suggested before, not so efficiently intimidating as the first words Samson addresses to Harapha. Harapha says he has come to gaze on Samson and see if his appearance "answer[s] loud report" (line 1090). Samson growls, "The way to know were not to see but taste" (line 1091). From that moment, Harapha keeps his distance, and his bafflement is certain: "His giantship is gone somewhat crest-fallen," says the chorus (line 1244).

A chorus follows Harapha's departure, in which they observe that on this day of rest Samson's mental labors have been greater than his phys-ical ones (*SA*, lines 1297–99). But physical labor is now to be required of him. A Philistine officer arrives, asking for Samson, and demanding him, though with some respect, to appear at the temple of Dagon—unchained, cleaned, and dressed—to perform feats of strength before the lords. Samson refuses the demand because it is against the law of Moses for a Hebrew to appear at a pagan rite. The officer leaves with this refusal for answer, after warning Samson, not without some show of kindness, that such an answer will not please the lords. The prudent thing to do is to comply.

Samson is now alone with the chorus, which fearfully urges Samson to comply, arguing he is not guilty if forced. But of course he is not forced until dragged to the temple, which would not be easy for them to do. He then notes—and we are to feel Samson is surprised at his own thought—that God may choose to *use* him, or anyone else, at idolatrous rites. In that case a direct impulse or message from God would super-sede the injunction of the law: "Yet that He may dispense with me or thee / Present in temples at idolatrous rites / For some important cause, thou need'st not doubt" (*SA*, lines 1377–39). The chorus expresses per-plexity at this moment of high tension, as choruses must do. "Be of good courage," Samson tells the Hebrew youths, for he feels "rousing mo-tions" that incline his thoughts to an "extraordinary" act (*SA*, lines 1381–83). He will go along with the officer when he returns, as return he will, with commands expressed in harsher terms ("Art thou our slave . . . And dar'st thou at our sending and command / Dispute thy coming?" [*SA*, lines 1392–95]). Samson tells the chorus, "This day will be remarkable in my life / By some great act or of my days the last" (*SA*, lines 1388–89). We know it will not be one or the other: it will be both.

With some irony, Samson responds to the officer with compliance: "Masters' commands come with a power resistless / To such as owe them absolute subjection" (*SA*, lines 1404–5). Of course, the master he is obeying now is God, whose "rousing motions" have sent him to the temple of Dagon. His last words to the chorus of Hebrew youths are that they should expect to hear of him nothing that is dishonorable or unworthy "Our God, our Law, my nation, or myself" (*SA*, line 1426).

A closer examination of the play than has been possible here will show how this series—God, law, nation, self—expresses an order of priority in importance: God's direct command or intimate impulse comes first; then comes obedience to the law of Moses; then comes loyalty to the nation of Israel as a political entity; and lastly comes loyalty to oneself, to who one is and what one should do because of who one is. These are all important, but the order of importance among them is important, too. From the beginning of the play, Samson had this order of importance backwards. His crime, as he supposed, was to have betrayed himself as a Nazarite, and as a hero. Next, Samson understands his crime as the betrayal of the nation of Israel, which because of his error still serves the Philistines. (Provoked by the chorus, he exonerates himself of that fault: the Hebrews did not seize their chance when he gave it them.) Next, Samson focuses on the importance of the law, not because his fault violates the law but because going to the Philistine temple would violate the law against idolatry. At the crucial moment when he says, "Yet," he understands that God is above the law and can do what he likes, including sending his hero to the Philistine temple with its idolatrous rites. In this way, Samson reestablishes a personal relationship with God, and his mind is purified when his original order of priorities is reversed and so corrected.

After Manoa's interlude of hope, a messenger arrives in a state of shock and, with the usual delay and suspense, relates how Samson pulled down the temple on the heads of the Philistine ruling class, and on himself, "tangled in the fold of dire necessity" (*SA*, lines 1655–56). In Aeschylus's *Agamemnon*, Clytemnestra describes how she killed Agamemnon as he was coming out of his bath. The robe she "threw around" him—"so he might not flee nor beat away his fate"—is "an inescapable purse-net, as for fish, a golden robe of evil."[22] She then strikes him twice, presumably with an ax, bringing him down. Delivering a third blow, after he is dead, she makes a sacrifice of his blood to Zeus of the underworld. "Dire necessity," *dira necessitas*, is a phrase from Horace, but Milton knew it to be a translation of Greek tragic *anagkê*.[23] What is the "fold" that tangles? A net entangles and a robe can catch one in its folds. However consciously or unconsciously, it may be concluded from his treatment of the chorus as it hears the two shouts, and from the slightly strange image of an entangling fold, that Milton has the *Agamemnon* in mind as he composes the conclusion of *Samson Agonistes*.

The later plays of Aeschylus's *Oresteia*, and indeed the plays by Sophocles and Euripides on the revenge of the children of Agamemnon, present
Agamemnon as a hero, although one for whom our approbation is qualified, because of the injuries and crimes of which Clytemnestra speaks.
Agamemnon is a *polluted* man, the bearer of a *miasma*, and Samson is,
too. But Samson is the more perfect hero because his achievement comes
at the same time, and by the same means, as his death. Agamemnon,
the conqueror of Troy, dies afterward, squalidly, tricked and struck down
in his bath, like an ox. Samson likewise destroys a city—he decapitates
its ruling class—but at the same time and by the same action he expi-
ates his crime, which is of course what he has always wanted to do. To
Milton's mind, this is a more efficient and tightly organized tragic action. Samson is still polluted, because he is "soaked in his enemies'
blood," as his kindly but bloodthirsty father cheerfully says (line 1726).
But that stain can be washed away, unlike the other, which could be
washed away only with Samson's own blood. His own blood cleanses
him; his enemies' blood defiles him, requiring a second and more literal purification:

> Let us go find the body where it lies
> Soaked in his enemies' blood, and from the stream
> With lavers pure and cleansing herbs wash off
> The clotted gore.
>
> (SA, *1725–28*)

Only then, for the readers as well as for the Hebrew youths of the chorus,
whom Manoa addresses, is there a catharsis. By washing the body, and
raising a tomb to put it in, "calm of mind" is restored, and "passion" is
"spent":

> Oft He seems to hide His face
> But unexpectedly returns
> And to his faithful champion hath in place
> Bore witness gloriously, whence Gaza mourns,
> And all that band them [unite themselves] to resist
> His uncontrollable intent.
> His servants he with new acquist
> Of true experience from this great event

> With peace and consolation hath dismissed
> And calm of mind, all passion spent.
>
> *(SA, 1749–58)*

The conclusion of *Samson Agonistes*, its blind hero dead, the Philistine ruling class destroyed, and Israel, as the next episode of the book of Judges will show, on the point of anarchy—all this as a prelude to kingship—is a dark conclusion to Milton's poetic career. The state of Israel at the close of the Book of Judges is an analogy, as Milton saw it, to his own historical moment, when King Charles had come in at the people's request and General Monck, their captain, led them back to Egypt: "yet Israel still serves" (*SA*, line 240).

The sharp aesthetic contrast between *Paradise Regained* and *Samson Agonistes* reflects their following the two biblical testaments, especially with regard to blindness and insight. Even so, caution must be exercised on this point. In medieval typological exegesis the two testaments are deeply identical: the New Testament is concealed in the Old and the Old is revealed in the New. Everything in the Old Testament is a polyvalent symbol of what is to come in the New Testament. Nothing in the Old Testament can resist the disintegrating power of this chemical conversion, with the result that everything solid, the sense of history especially, melts into air.

Milton held too strongly to the density of history, and to the weight of the text literally read, to accept such an extreme way of reading scripture, and such an easy one. He would believe in and allow only those typological symbols from the Old Testament that the New Testament authenticates explicitly. Moses is a type of Christ, as is "Joshua," which is Jesus's name in Hebrew; so is David, the branch of Jesse. But to anyone who actually reads the Old Testament, these figures are so different from Jesus that what strikes us most is their substantiality as historical actors in a past that is real and other. Yet God was at work in this historical past, and *Samson Agonistes* is about this other kind of work God was doing. Samson is a witness or *martyr* to that faith in that time—so he is called in the Epistle to the Hebrews (11:32)—and not to the faith still to come.

The irony of being a blind witness is perfectly suited to a tragedy, especially one in the style of classical Greek tragedy. The blind prophet

Tiresias is a common figure in Greek tragedy, and is never listened to, though he is always right. Samson is something of a prophetic figure in this kind, but a prophet of deeds. None of his heroic deeds are followed up by others: the Hebrews have no king, yet. Sophocles's *Oedipus at Colonus* is an important source of *Samson Agonistes*, as is widely recognized, but so too is *Oedipus Tyrannus*, the tragedy of a morally blind man fiercely seeking the truth, to his own destruction. Oedipus becomes at the end of the play what Samson is throughout *Samson Agonistes*, a *théama:* a frightful sight, a thing gazed on, the unseeing object of horrified yet pitying speculation.[24] Samson's final act is a way of covering himself so he will no longer be exposed to others' gaze.

Demonstrating the splendors of Milton's rhythms can become tedious, even when there is much more to say. The point is to demonstrate enough to show the fineness and force of his expression, thanks to his deep experience of reading and writing in Greek and Latin meters. At the time he was composing *Samson Agonistes*, Milton had perhaps not heard much Greek and Latin poetry in years and he had done no extended Latin verse composition since the 1640s. But these complex systems of overlaid rhythms were imprinted in his brain, and as is the way with such things, they became more, not less available with the passage of time, having seasoned and settled in him.

Superficially, the verse of *Paradise Regained* is the same as that of *Paradise Lost*—unrhymed, decasyllabic lines making frequent use of enjambment but less frequent use of the strong medial pause—differing from the former only in sounding a little routine, as if the poet were more interested in what he has to tell us than in the artistry with which it is told. But that too is a calculated effect. There is an extraordinary tightness and efficiency in the verse, such as only a master can achieve. The metrical effects already noted in *Samson Agonistes* begin to appear in this poem, especially in Jesus's words to Satan: "Thy pompous delicacies **I** con**demn** / And count thy specious gifts no **gifts** but **guiles**" (*PR*, 2.390–91); "I seek not **mine,** but **His,** / Who **sent** me, and **there**by **wit**ness **whence I am**" (*PR*, 3.106–7); "No. **Let** them **serve** / Their enemies, who serve idols with **God**" (*PR*, 3.431–32, a choriambic); "plain thou **now** ap**pear'st**" (*PR*, 4.193); "that Evil one, **Sat**an, for ever **damned**" (*PR*, 4.194); "which ex**pect** to **rue**" (*PR*, 4.181); "**worth** a **spunge**" (*PR*,

4.329); "Desist, thou **art** dis**cerned** / And toil'st in vain, nor me in **vain** mo**lest**" (*PR*, 4.497–98).[25]

The great theme of Milton's entire poetic career is temptation. Temptation is for him always personal, and it always hides a game of power. Milton seems to have discovered this in *A Masque at Ludlow Castle, 1634*: there is no indication of it before. But there, Milton seems to grow up in a single line of verse, when the Lady makes an ethical statement that sounds very like the Milton of ten years later and nothing like the Milton of two years before: "none / But such as are good men can give good things" (701–2). Temptation is of course the central ethical problem of *Paradise Lost*, and it is of great importance in the drama of *Samson Agonistes*, in which Dalila represents the greatest danger. In *Paradise Regained*, the focus on temptation is intense.

There are three temptations in Matthew's and Luke's Gospels, and Milton follows Luke's order: Jesus is tempted to turn stones to bread; to accept the kingdoms of the world at Satan's hand (in return for worshipping Satan as Lord); and to throw himself down from the pinnacle of the temple, to prove he is the Messiah by fulfilling a prophecy. Milton divides the first temptation into two parts, the second part being a table set in the wilderness. He divides the second temptation into four parts and draws it out from the middle of the second book to the middle of the fourth: accept wealth to become king of Israel; accept the kingdom of Parthia, in order to free Israel and repatriate the lost ten tribes; accept the Roman Empire, so as to rule the world, free Israel, and bring in universal justice; and accept mastery of Greek learning (chiefly philosophy and political thought) so as to develop a mind fit to rule the world. Nothing works. Satan says he has found Jesus "Proof against all temptation as a rock / Of adamant, and as a center, firm," and must therefore use "another method" (*PR*, 4.533–34 and 540). He puts Jesus on the pinnacle of the Jerusalem temple, expecting Jesus to fall, but adding, "in scorn," the prophecy that angels will bear up the messiah if he should chance to strike his foot against a stone (*PR*, 5.530; cf. Psalm 91:11–12). Jesus responds, "Also it is written, 'Tempt not the Lord thy God,'" and stands, whereupon Satan falls (*PR*, 4.560–62; cf. Deuteronomy 6:6 and Luke 4:12).

Returning to the opening of the poem, and the first meeting of Jesus with Satan, Jesus wanders in the wilderness for forty days without eating before he feels any hunger. He thinks, and we watch and hear him do it.

Out of the distance in this bleak landscape, gathering sticks for his fire, a poor, old, and, as it seems, illiterate desert dweller stops to address Jesus, being concerned for Jesus's safety in this wild place, and in particular with what Jesus will eat, since he has not eaten for so long, and is unprovisioned for a wilderness journey. The desert dwellers live sparely, and are nearly starving themselves, scraping the ground for tough roots. But Jesus is town bred, with soft hands used more to reading the scriptures than digging. How will he subsist? The desert dweller has an idea. When he was wandering closer to civilization, bordering the east bank of the Jordan, he heard that voice from Heaven, proclaiming Jesus a "Son." Would Jesus care to try out his powers, right now, and turn stones into bread, thus relieving the general hunger? Milton makes it more interesting by having Satan propose the relief of the hungry in general, not just the relief of Jesus's own hunger.

In the second part of the first temptation Jesus is presented with an elaborate table with every sort of food, with attending spirits at his command. We are modulating into the next temptation, which is the temptation to power, and this episode, when read closely, shows Milton's remarkable anthropological insight into eating and relations of power: what do you eat (animals, and if so which ones)? who serves you as you eat? and who gives you what you eat?

Formerly, Jesus was tempted *on his own power* to turn stones to bread; now he is tempted to accept food as the gift of another. Unlike Eve, but very much like the Lady in *A Masque Presented at Ludlow Castle, 1634*, Jesus understands that the gift—and the more dazzling the gift, the more this is true—always masks a bond of power with the giver. Moreover, he swiftly discerns that Satan is offering him what is in fact his own, so Satan has in effect stolen from Jesus what he then offers to him: "I can at will, doubt not, as soon as thou, / Command a table in this wilderness / And call swift flights of angels ministrant" (*PR*, 2.383–85). Jesus refuses the gift as Satan's superior, because the gift presumes Jesus should be grateful for it and so for an instant relinquish his authority over Satan: "Why should'st thou then obtrude this diligence / In vain, where no acceptance it can find?" (*PR*, 2.387–88). In a scene from the *Aeneid*, much imitated in the literature of romance up to Shakespeare's *The Tempest*, the refused meal is swept away, "with sound of harpies wings and talons heard" (*PR*, 2.403). This is presented as Satan's angry decision, after the meal is refused. But we recognize it as the danger that was there all along: if accepted, the meal would have been fouled and the talons thrust in.

The second temptation, which takes place on a high mountain, to which Satan carries Jesus, is that Jesus accept from Satan rule of all the kingdoms of the world, only prostrating himself before Satan, and calling him "Lord," in order to attain this gift. Milton places this mountain from which Satan shows Jesus the kingdoms in the highlands of ancient Armenia, at the headwaters of the Tigris and Euphrates Rivers, thus suggesting an analogy with the mount of Paradise, which was destroyed at the Flood. The kingdoms of the world become in Milton the two greatest world powers in Jesus's day: the Parthians to the east and the Romans to the west.

The Parthian Empire—in Persia—is seen first, viewed from the east side of the mountain. When Jesus refuses it he is conducted to the west side of the mountain, to look upon Rome, far off in the Mediterranean, on the long Italian peninsula. Italy is seen as a near paradise shielded from the cold north by the great wall of the Alps.

As a Jew, and as a king in David's line, destined to rule, Jesus is offered wealth (we are still in the early stages of the second temptation) as the means of leading a rebellion against the Romans, as Judas Maccabaeus did against Greek overlords. Judas also retired to the desert, as Satan points out, "but with arms" (*PR*, 3.166).

The offer of the Parthian Empire includes the opportunity to recover the lost ten tribes of the northern kingdom of Israel, which were conquered and dispersed by the Assyrians two centuries before Nebuchadnezzar destroyed Jerusalem and carried the Jews of the remaining two tribes, Judah and Benjamin, into captivity in Babylon. Freed by Babylon's conqueror, Cyrus the Great, these two tribes would return to Jerusalem and rebuild the Temple. But the dispersed and assimilated ten tribes were forever lost, as was supposed. Their remnant became the hated Samaritans, who on Jesus's standard account "serve idols with God" (*PR*, 3.431), in particular the calf statues at Bethel and Dan, set up long ago by the rebel king Jeroboam, when, after Solomon's death, the kingdom of Israel divided. The point of this episode, which may appear arcane, is an encoded account of Milton's judgment of England

and the English after the failure of their revolution. The revolution failed because the English, like the ten lost tribes of Israel, are inwardly slaves, abjectly serving idols, especially that of monarchy, but also of bishops and of the archbishop, of powerful lords, and secretly, but soon openly if the powerful have their way, of popery, returning Roman Catholicism to England, by force. Jesus declines the opportunity to free people who are enslaved to themselves, leaving it to God to move their hearts to repentance in God's own time.

If the Jews and the English have failed, what about the rest of humanity? The temptation from the other side of the mountain, which is to take control of Rome, would make Jesus an emperor and put him at the head of the world, capable of instituting, in real terms, not "allegoric" ones, as Satan puts it, an age of peace and justice on the earth for all humanity. The illusion is that the evils of human life—poverty and war—can be overcome by political means, if we can get the right man or woman at the top. The illusion is that politics do not corrupt their own ends. We might object, and we would be right to do so, that when politics are the only means to improvement of the human condition—and in general, that is the case—then political means must be used. But Jesus's kingdom is to be a spiritual and eternal one, outside history and, as it happens, outside the world altogether. Were Jesus to become a Roman emperor, he would be accepting a lower definition of what it means for him to be the "king" or *Messiah*, and Satan would be safe. That is true. But we should not ignore Milton's turning a little from the delicate balance of transcendental engagement, in which he is apart from the world, in the realm of myth, but turned toward the world instead of away from it. Here, we may sense Milton again turning his back on the world, as he seems to be doing at some moments in the last two books of *Paradise Lost*, returning to the simple transcendence of his youth.

In the midst of these offers Jesus interrupts Satan with a pointed question:

> But what concerns it thee when I begin
> My everlasting Kingdom? Why art thou
> Solicitous? What moves thy inquisition?
> Know'st thou not that my rising is thy fall,
> And my promotion will be thy destruction?
>
> (PR, *3.198–202*)

At this, Satan is "inly rackt" (*PR*, 3.203) and expresses himself in language that Byron would value and use: "My error was my error, and my crime / My crime" (*PR*, 3.212–13). "Though to that gentle brow," he says, "Willingly I could fly" (*PR*, 3.215–16), as shelter from the wrath of God, "Whose ire I dread more than the fire of Hell" (*PR*, 3.220).

Milton introduces another subtler version of the temptation to rule the kingdoms of the world. When Jesus refuses Rome, Satan offers Greece, which is to say, mastery of Greek culture, of Greek poetry and philosophy, which Jesus is invited to study *in situ*, at Athens, or "here at home," by correspondence, thus wasting no time. In looking at Rome from the west side of the mountain, with Rome far off across the sea in the west, they have literally been overlooking Greece, the peninsula jutting down into the Mediterranean from the north, with Athens on its nearer branch. What is now offered is mastery over the kingdom of the mind, which even today, and far more in Jesus's day, as in Milton's, is associated with the culture and the very language of the Greeks. After the scriptures Greek literature was Milton's dearest possession. It is almost as if, in seeking to differentiate his hero from himself, Milton was moved to put in one temptation that he would have found hard to resist—although resist it he did.

Seeing Greece, and especially Athens, was an opportunity Milton had surrendered long ago because of the imminent English Revolution. He returned home from Naples, instead of going south, as planned, to Sicily, rich in Greek antiquities, and from thence to Greece itself. Perhaps funds were short, or not forthcoming, and Milton's father's patience was running out. But Milton gave as his principled reason for returning to England at this point his concern that his countrymen were fighting for liberty without him, while he was traveling abroad for his private improvement. A higher duty kept Milton from seeing, in Sicily, Segesta, Seliunte, Acragas, and Syracuse, Greek buildings such as he could never see in Italy (Paestum, south of Naples, was as yet undiscovered). It kept him from seeing the harbor of Syracuse, where the Athenian fleet was destroyed, a catastrophe recounted in the greatest passages of Thucydides and Plutarch (in the life of Nicias). It kept him from sailing from Sicily to Greece and entering by the Gulf of Corinth, with Parnassus and Helicon on the north shore, and high on the side of Parnassus, Delphi, with Corinth at the end of the gulf and the road to Athens. I could go on for a long time. Milton knew Strabo and Pausanius, and no doubt had studied them closely, especially Pausanius, in preparation for this journey. At this time, he likely could have reeled off sixty names of places in Greece. It must have been a wrenching decision not to go. Satan's temptation of Jesus to go to Athens to study is therefore a temptation Milton refused, and found it harder to refuse.

Jesus rejects this temptation in the severest terms. For anyone interested in Milton personally, it is the most fascinating passage of the poem. If some of the language is surprising—Greek poetry is "varnish on a harlot's cheek" (*PR*, 4.344)—the outcome surely is not. The Greeks worship idols and numerous gods, including a catch-all "unknown god," according to Saint Paul (Acts 17:23). They tell ridiculous and morally reprehensible stories about their highest gods. They are themselves immoral, "past shame": Milton is referring to aristocratic pederasty, or naked athletic competition, or both. They talked and thought cleverly about politics, and they created the first democracy. But the Greeks never solved their own political problems—we have seen Sophocles's comment on politics—and were conquered from without, first by Alexander of Macedon and then by the Romans.

Milton had a character that was born to command, and he believed learning was created to serve us, not the other way around. Jesus is more entitled to this attitude than anyone: he is the king at the head of humanity, and for Milton he is the last legitimate king. Even so, in the course of his rejection of Greek learning Jesus shows he has an impressive mastery of it.

At the beginning of book 4, Milton unexpectedly introduces a compound epic simile. What is striking about this simile, however, is that its initial portion, comparing Satan to a man who, out of frustrated spite, continues to deceive when discerned, is really a direct novelistic description of Satan's mind. It feels strangely modern. That novelistic moment is then followed, as if to recover the antique decorum, by two comparisons drawn from Homer, swarming flies and beating waves:

> But—as a man who had been matchless held
> In cunning, over-reached where least he thought,
> To salve his credit, and for very spite,
> Still will be tempting him who foils him still,
> And never cease, though to his shame the more;
> Or as a swarm of flies in vintage-time

> About the wine-press where sweet must is poured,
> Beat off, returns as oft with humming sound;
> Or surging waves against a solid rock,
> Though all to shivers dashed, the assault renew,
> (Vain battery!) and in froth or bubbles end—
> So Satan, whom repulse upon repulse
> Met ever, and to shameful silence brought,
> Yet gives not o'er, though desperate of success,
> And his vain importunity pursues.
>
> (PR, *4.10–24*)

Jesus will at last order Satan to desist from the insolence of tempting him to no purpose.

That command finally breaks Satan's mask of amiability. With a thrill, we hear for how long Satan has been tracking Jesus, and with what anxiety Satan has done so, as well as rage and hate. The entire biblical significance of Jesus is summed up in the passage that prepares us for the poem's climax:

> Desist. Thou art discerned
> And toil'st in vain, nor me in vain molest.
> To whom the fiend, now swoln with rage, replied,
> 'Then hear, O son of David, virgin born,
> For Son of God to me is yet in doubt,
> Of the Messiah I have heard foretold
> By all the prophets, of thy birth, at length
> Announced by Gabriel, with the rest I knew,
> And of th'angelic song in Bethl'em field
> On thy birth night, that sung thee Saviour, born.
> From that time seldom have I ceased to eye
> Thy infancy, thy childhood, and thy youth,
> Thy manhood last, till at the ford of Jordan . . .
> Heard thee pronounced the Son of God beloved.
>
> (PR, *4.497–513*)

After Jesus has defeated Satan the angels bring him down from the pinnacle and celebrate his feat, calling him "Queller of Satan" (Milton knew the Anglo-Saxon source of *quell* in *cwellan*, "to kill," but doubtless not

the Indo-European root, **gwel-*, "to let fall, make fall"). The angels conclude their anthems not on what the hero has done, which is immediate
and simple, but on what he will now begin to do, which is neither immediate nor simple:

> Hail, Son of the Most High, heir of both Worlds,
> Queller of Satan! On thy glorious work
> Now enter, and begin to save Mankind.
>
> (PR, *4.633–35*)

Much is said in these three lines, which conclude the angels' hymn.
The earthly man, Jesus, is the Son of God the Father, the "Most High,"
and he is not only the heir of this world, as a royal king in David's line,
an "anointed one" (Hebrew *messiah*; Greek *christos*), but also the heir of
Heaven, the Kingdom of God, which will last for eternity. As the Son of
the Most High he will at last kill Satan, or lock him up in the pit forever,
which is as good as killing him. In the meantime, by way of preparation
for these apocalyptic events, Jesus will enter time and history again—
"Now enter"—by reentering human society. He will "begin to save
mankind" by destroying, not Satan, but Satan's works in humanity.

That outcome is a thought carried forward from *Paradise Lost*: Adam
is told his Savior will win, "Not by destroying Satan but his works / In
thee and in thy seed" (*PL*, 12.394–95). This suits the more quietist
mood of the final books of *Paradise Lost*. But now the quelling of Satan
looks to Milton like unfinished business. The final four lines of the
poem, which are given to the narrator, resume the mild temper of Jesus
himself—now he is "meek"—as if seeking to cover over the flash of violence in *quell*, extinguishing it as soon as it appears, lest Jesus seem too
much like Satan:

> Thus they the Son of God, our Saviour meek,
> Sung victor and, from Heavenly feast refreshed,
> Brought on his way with joy. He, unobserved,
> Home to his mother's house private returned.
>
> (PR, *4.636–39*)

If Milton's only interest were to vindicate his understanding of the Bible
and of Christianity, and to round off his vision of history, justifying the

ways of God to men, this would be the place for him to end his entire poetic career. It is a magnificent conclusion to that career, or it would be if it were a conclusion, providing, as the word *conclusion* implies, a satisfying closure. But it is not so much a closure as it is a signpost, the indication of a path we are to follow. The reader may take it from here, which means taking up the Bible and reading on from this point, understanding far better, thanks to John Milton, what everything to follow in the Gospels will mean. Jesus has already won. Milton's vision of history is therefore objectively complete, and nothing decisive is omitted, because nothing stands in the way of our completing it ourselves, simply by reading the Bible. Milton has peaceably disappeared. We no longer require his guidance.

But perhaps we would like his guidance and are loath to part with him. If we look very closely, we may indeed find Milton, or traces of him, in three words: in the word *queller*, in the word *vanquishing*, and in the word *avenged*. These are violent and emotional words, especially *avenged*, and they belong, accordingly, not to the realm of objective totality but to that of subjective infinity, to emotion, not reason. The poet remains before us as a remainder, a residue, emotionally unsatisfied with the beautiful things he has made, and with the way in which his creations meekly lead us back to the Bible, to the Gospel of redemption, of love and forgiveness.

Satan has been quelled, or he will be at length, if we are very, very patient. But what about those others, who are here now, all around us, the filth of this world, whom we hate? For we do have this hate and do not know what to do with it. Why isn't Jesus—or someone else capable of chastising, such as Samson or Milton himself—quelling them all? Milton's revolutionary spirit is awakened, and although his objective vision can end here, with Jesus going home to his mother, a private man, Milton is unable to desist, because by the end of *Paradise Regained* he is larger than what he has created. As the alienated subject of that vision, as its poet, he counts.

Is this perhaps the remoter significance of the strange architectural metaphors used in *Paradise Regained* for the "fairer paradise" that is regained? I mentioned them before, as incipiently Utopian. The Paradise is "raised" in the wilderness, and is not planted, but "founded" (*PR*, 1.7 and 4.613). As I suggested before, I suppose that in the first instance we are intended to understand these architectural metaphors as referring mysteriously to what this "fairer paradise" is: a heavenly city with the twelve apostles for its foundation stones and the twelve tribes of Israel for its gates. That vision comes at the end of the Bible, and in the Bible, everything must unfold in its proper order, and in its proper time, book by book, event by event, and covenant by covenant: Genesis before Exodus, Matthew before Mark, Abraham before Moses, Jesus before Paul, the Old Testament before the New. To reverse anything in this order, for example, to put circumcision *after* the law, or the Flood after the Exodus, or Samson after Jesus, is to overturn the Bible, to shake it and cause it to fall, as Samson shakes the temple of Dagon:

> those two massy pillars
> With horrible convulsion to and fro
> He tugged, he shook, till down they came and drew
> The whole roof after them with burst of thunder
> Upon the heads of all who sat beneath,
> Lords, ladies, captains, counselors, or priests,
> Their choice nobility and flower.
>
> (SA, *lines 1648–54*)

The overturning is done by reversing the expected order of things in his vision, which likewise rests on two columns, the Old and New Testaments. Under the covering shade of the Bible, where their hypocrisy is sheltered from the sun of righteousness, sit lords, ladies, captains, counselors, and priests, the "choice nobility and flower." *Paradise Regained* and *Samson Agonistes* together with *Paradise Lost* are a single poetic statement, independent as each work also is. Think of the words, "to which is added *Samson Agonistes*." In them, the order of the Testaments is shaken: the Old Testament story of Samson is placed not before its fulfillment in the better covenant of the New Testament, the subject of *Paradise Regained*; it is "added." There are Philistines to take care of.

Jesus will choose—he has already chosen—not to be politically engaged with the world, although he will indeed be engaged through performance art and the spiritual politics of the Kingdom of Heaven. Unlike the Neoplatonists of his own day, disgusted with the body and with the material universe, Jesus does not propose a simple transcendence of the world. We saw that that was Milton's Christian position in the early stage of his career, when we will at last leave the filth of the world and be "attired with stars." Unlike the stoics of his day, Jesus does not choose indifference, refusing the world the attention and importance it wants. Jesus's Kingdom is not of this world, he says, answering a political question, and yet he does not reject this world as beneath him or despise it with contempt. That would be to reject the poor, the sick, and the comfortless, all those who live on the edge of despair.

Jesus does not even despise the dead, who stink—as he is warned when he raises Lazarus—for even the dead are included in his love, his *agapê*. Heaven will be filled with what were once dead bodies. This Heaven turns out not to be a transcending of the world but the largest embrace of the world possible, one that includes the dead, which, normally, politics cannot include. There are no politics among the dead or for the dead. Filling Heaven with the dead is engaging the world, all of it, even what the most worldly of us are eager to rid ourselves of.

I am not quite sure Milton sees this far into the phenomenon of Jesus, or this way into it. But he does see that while Jesus remains engaged with the world as his ministry begins, it is not to be a political engagement but one of a very different sort. Milton recognizes that this is the right decision for Jesus to make. That Satan offers Jesus political and military success is not the reason these are wrong.[26] Satan's offering them is the proof they are wrong in this case. If we want more general reasons, Jesus gives them. That Satan offers political and military power, fraud and force, as the final solution to the problems of the world (if, of course, these powers, fraud and force, are in capable hands) is clearly wrong, whether it is Satan who makes the offer or not. Politics are the management of the world (management is, of course, needed), but politics are not the final answer to the problems of the world, which are more deeply rooted in our nature. Jesus will address them at this deeper level, and renounce politics to do so. Milton saw he was right, but renunciation of power—the negation of the world on its own terms—is not the decision Milton would have made, had he had it to make.

In another, typically quiet ending, the final verse reads (I mention it yet once more), "Home to his mother's house private returned." The word *private* is emphasized—it falls into position, emphatically, after the caesura—because Jesus's private life is now ending. These are its final moments, so far as we are concerned, although the journey will take about three days (Milton's geography is always exact). Jesus will henceforth be pressed in on all sides by large crowds, and he will die a very public death, nakedly exposed, tormented, and reviled. As the hero of

Paradise Regained leaves the Judean desert and begins the journey home to his mother's house, Milton's eye follows him on the northbound road through Samaria that leads up to the Galilean hills, to Nazareth and the high country around the Galilean lake, until he disappears from sight.[27] But Milton has taken a different road, toward his next work. At least we may allow ourselves to imagine him doing so, for he is a poet who always saw himself *in situ*, in the place about which he was writing, whether it be in Hell, in chaos, in Heaven, or anywhere on or above the terrestrial globe. Milton is headed southwest to the low-lying plain running down to the sea, to Gaza, where Samson is imprisoned. He therefore parts ways with Jesus here, at a desert crossroads, and does not look on him again.

Appendixes

Notes

Index

APPENDIX I

References and Texts

We LIVE IN A TIME of enterprise in Milton studies, and the scholarly editing of Milton's texts is no exception. A new, complete, multivolume edition of Milton's works is under way at Oxford University Press; another major series is appearing from Blackwell. Both are "diplomatic" editions, preserving (by collation) the spelling and punctuation of the published seventeenth-century texts. So, too, does the standard edition of the prose, Don M. Wolfe, gen. ed., *Complete Prose Works of John Milton*, 8 vols. (New Haven, Conn.: Yale University Press, 1953–1982), which prints the Latin prose works only in English translation. The Yale prose is in need of revision in the light of scholarship over the past decades, and new annotated texts of the prose works are currently in progress at Oxford, with the Latin texts in the original and translation. What is known with due reverence as the Columbia edition, Frank Allen Patterson, gen. ed., *The Works of John Milton*, 18 vols. (New York: Columbia University Press, 1931–1938)—with a two-volume index—remains the only comprehensive, coherent, and indexed edition of all Milton's works. But it is not annotated and will soon be seventy years old. In the meantime, Milton scholars and critics cite from an array of texts differing widely in matters of spelling, punctuation, order of presentation, and annotation. The somewhat various state of affairs in the contemporary editing of Milton's texts is to be expected at times of transition in the study of any great and complex author. It will be desirable to explain how I have quoted Milton's poems.

I have followed my own edition of *Paradise Lost* (New York: W. W. Norton, 2005), which ignores the "accidentals" of the seventeenth-century printed texts (spelling, punctuation, italicization, and capitals) in favor of modernized spelling and very light punctuation. This is done to preserve the resonance of several meanings at once and especially to preserve the Homeric speed of Milton's narrative verse, which is unnaturally impeded by the heavy, often misleading, seventeenth-century punctuation, very little of it original with Milton. The evidence we have—the Trinity manuscript text of *A Masque*; the letter to Peter Heimbach, August 15, 1966 (in which Milton mentions as exceptional his having to specify punctuation); the accounts by Edward Phillips and Cyriack Skinner of the composition and copying of *Paradise Lost*; the poet's blindness; and his experience of composing Latin verse; his musical culture; even his insistence on the Italian pronunciation of Latin—may not prove but strongly suggests that Milton let others attend to punctuation. I have therefore reduced punctuation to a minimum and introduced it only where the reader would stumble without it.

Comparison to the recording of music may help to clarify the issue of punctuation. An audio recording of a string quartet can be too "bright"—with the notes too defined, eliminating resonant undertones, or too noisy, blurring the melodic line and even capturing the turning of pages, the breathing of the musicians, and the shifting of their feet. Modernized punctuation runs the risk of the first; original punctuation (because of the "noise" of the print shop) runs the risk of the second. I have sought a solution between these extremes. But I have also sought to shift the current sense among readers of what the authentic experience of Milton's verse is—visible marks on the page—into the acoustic register, treating Milton's poems as artifacts in sound. I have for the same reason indicated elisions and unusual accents where they occur, when these affect meter. In doing all this, some interpretation on my part—that is, judgment by the ear—has been inevitable. But every text, no matter how "diplomatic," involves interpretation. I have followed the same principles in quoting from the shorter poems as well, altering the punctuation and sometimes the spelling (in the case of elisions) as these appear in the printed texts.

The reader is warned that this acoustical and, as it were, anti-typographical approach to Milton's text has proven to be controversial, after nearly half a century of strong commitment to the seventeenth-century punctuation as substantive and authorial. My reason for opposing this orthodoxy, which may be termed *typographical essentialism*, is that it distracts from Milton's art while presuming to represent it better. For the orthodox view on punctuation, see the introduction to John Carey and Alastair Fowler, eds., *The Poems of John Milton* (Harlow: Longmans, 1968); Mindele Anne Treip, *Milton's Punctuation and Changing English Usage* (London: Methuen, 1970); and Stephen B. Dobranski, "Editing Milton: The Case Against Modernization," in *The Oxford Handbook of Milton*, ed. Nicholas McDowell and Nigel Smith (Oxford: Oxford University Press, 2009), 480–95.

Carey and Fowler gave reasons, following Adams and especially Shaw-cross (see below), for not accepting the *spelling* of the original texts as substantive. But the recent authoritative editions from Blackwell and Oxford have returned to the older, more conservative model of the Columbia edition, producing "diplomatic" texts, presumably to be faithful to the visual experience of sighted readers in Milton's day. Readers interested in these matters may wish to consult John Creaser's two-part study, "Editorial Problems in Milton," *Review of English Studies* 34 (1983): 297–303 and *Review of English Studies* 35 (1984): 45–60; and R. G. Moyles, *The Text of "Paradise Lost": A Study in Editorial Procedure* (Toronto: University of Toronto Press, 1985), 16–17, 29. For classic discussions of spelling cited by Carey and Fowler, see J. T. Shawcross, "One Aspect of Milton's Spelling: Idle Final 'E,'" *PMLA* 78 (1963): 501–10; and Robert Martin Adams, *Ikon: John Milton and the Modern Critics* (Ithaca, N.Y.: Cornell University Press, 1955), 73–75. For a broader perspective on the circumstances of book production, see Stephen B. Dobranski, *Milton, Authorship, and the Book Trade* (Cambridge: Cambridge University Press, 1999).

For the shorter poems, I have in the first instance followed the edition of John Carey, *Complete Shorter Poems*, rev. 2nd ed. (Harlow: Pearson, 2007), but without accepting his punctuation or his argument that the *Poems* of 1673 should be accepted as copytext. For the latter, see Dobranski, *Milton*, 155–72. As John Creaser has demonstrated, in "Textual Cruces in Milton's Shorter Poems," *Notes and Queries* 29 (1982), "1645 provides consistently the better text" (27). But Carey's text is otherwise a joy to work with: the commentary is magisterial, especially on classical sources, and, crucially, Carey prints the poems in chronological order. Although I do not always agree with his decisions regarding chronology—notably, in the case of *Samson Agonistes*—this seems to me the right way to present Milton's shorter poems, instead of reproducing the order of the 1645 *Poems* and adding on the rest. I have benefited from the editions of Stella Revard, *Complete Shorter Poems* (Malden, Mass.: Wiley-Blackwell, 2009); of Barbara Lewalski and Estelle Haan, *The Shorter Poems*, vol. 3, *The Complete Works of John Milton* (Oxford: Clarendon, 2012); of John Leonard, *Complete Poems* (London: Penguin, 1998); and of Jason Rosenblatt, *Milton's Selected Poetry and Prose* (New York: Norton, 2010). I have also consulted the original, 1645 *Poems of Mr. John Milton*, and, for poems written subsequently or not included in that edition, the *Poems* of 1673.

I have checked the Carey text of *Paradise Regained* and *Samson Agonistes* with the commentary and texts of Laura Lunger Knoppers's edition, *Paradise Regain'd and Samson Agonistes* (Oxford: Clarendon Press, 2012). For the three earlier versions of Milton's *A Masque Presented at Ludlow Castle, 1634*, I have used S. E. Sprott's comparative edition, *A Maske: The Earlier Versions* (Toronto: University of Toronto Press, 1973), which sets alongside one another the texts of the Trinity manuscript, the Bridgewater manuscript, and the first published text of 1637. Because Carey's text of the masque follows 1673, in which the lineation is different, I have followed John Leonard's edition of the *Complete Poems* for the 1645 text of the masque.

In referring to Milton's prose, I have followed Don. M. Wolfe, gen. ed., *Complete Prose Works*, 7 vols. [vols. 4 and 5 are each in two parts] (New Haven, Conn.: Yale University Press, 1953–1982). This edition is referred to in the text as *YP*. I have also used Patterson, gen. ed., *The Works of John Milton* (vols. 1, 2, and 3 are each in two parts), referred to in the text as *Columbia*, especially for the Latin texts. Associated with the Columbia edition is Frank Allen Patterson and French R. Fogle's *An Index to the Columbia Edition of the Works of John Milton* (New York: Columbia University Press, 1940). *De Doctrina Christiana* is referred to in the edition of John K. Hale and J. Donald Cullington, with Gordon Campbell and Thomas N. Corns, *The Complete Works of John Milton* (Oxford: Clarendon Press, 2012), vol. 8 (in 2 vols.). I have repunctuated the prose wherever doing so makes the sense clearer, and I have modernized spelling.

Shorter poems quoted in this book are referred to by name, in quotation marks, followed by line numbers. References to *Paradise Lost*, *Paradise Regained*, and *Samson Agonistes* are shortened to *PL*, *PR*, and *SA*, respectively. *PL* and *PR* are followed by book and line numbers, for example, *PR*, 1.3, and *SA* is followed by line numbers, for example, *SA*, lines 1–9. For reasons set forth in Chapter 3, I refer to *Comus* as *A Masque Presented at Ludlow Castle, 1634*, occasionally shortened.

Classical texts such as the *Aeneid* and the *Iliad* are referred to in the same manner as *Paradise Lost*, by book and line number, for example, *Aeneid*, 2.1. References to Shakespeare's plays are to act, scene, and line, for example, *Macbeth*, 1.2.3. References to Spenser's *Faerie Queene* are to book, canto, and stanza, for example, *The Faerie Queene*, 3.4.40. References to classical texts are to scholarly editions from Oxford's Clarendon Press or to the volumes in the Loeb Classical Library.

Standard translations of foreign and classical texts, which are meant for continuous reading at length, are often unsuitable for closer analysis. I have therefore provided my own translations, or indicated the meaning in paraphrase. I have striven for specificity to the matter in hand, rather than for elegance. For elegance I recommend the translation by David Slavitt, *Milton's Latin Poems* (Baltimore, Md.: Johns Hopkins University Press, 2011); and William Cowper, trans., *Latin and Italian Poems* (London, 1808). Estelle Haan's translations in the Lewalski-Haan *Shorter Poems* are valuable, as are Lawrence Revard's, in Stella Revard's edition. I hope that by the time this book appears William Shullenberger's translation of Milton's Latin poems—some of them published in Jason Rosenblatt's *Milton's Selected Poetry and Prose* (New York: Norton, 2011)—will have appeared in print.

References to the Bible are to the Authorized (King James) Version of 1611 and are given in standard form by book, chapter, and verse, for example, 1 Corinthians 1:12. I refer to the Old Testament when the context indicates the Christian view of the Hebrew scriptures. However, Milton had a strong textual understanding of the Hebrew Scriptures themselves and was interested in the historical element in them. When he is referring to this element I refer to them as the Hebrew Scriptures, or, in the Greek version, the Septuagint.

Some words in quotations will appear in *italics*. In all cases, the italics are mine, added for emphasis. The same is true of words or parts of words quoted in **bold** type, to indicate a strong metrical beat.

APPENDIX II

Chronology of the Poems

FOR ANY POEM, the relative importance of date of publication and date of composition will vary with circumstances, one of the most important of these being length. In general, the longer the poem, the more important the date of publication and the more extended and fuzzy the period of composition. The opposite is the case for short poems, which are usually saved up over a period of time and then published all together, as with Milton's 1645 *Poems*. In that case, date of composition is often more important and also, alas, harder to determine. Many of Milton's shorter poems are of uncertain date, and sometimes he has himself apparently misremembered his age at time of composition. For a discussion of problems, see Gordon Campbell, *A Milton Chronology* (New York: St. Martin's, 1997), 1–7. For the purposes of this study, it is usually enough to know Milton's approximate age at composition, for example, whether he was a teenager, in his early, mid-, or late twenties, or in his early thirties. With one exception mentioned below, we do know that much.

When Milton began *Paradise Lost* is uncertain (1658 is the usual, but I think late, guess). It is a question Milton perhaps could not have answered himself. The same obscurity hangs about the question of when *Paradise Lost* was completed. (We may learn about Milton by comparing our modest efforts with his great ones. I would be hard-pressed to say when I began this book, and I have "finished" it more than once in the past.) John Aubrey says Milton completed *Paradise Lost* "about" 1663.[1]

In the summer of 1665 Milton lent a manuscript to Thomas Ellwood, who later wrote, "When I had come home, and had set myself to read it, I found it was that excellent poem which he entitled *Paradise Lost*."[2] It would seem reasonable, on the face of it, to suppose the poem was complete at this time, when Milton was fifty-six, and that publication was delayed by one or more of the following: the plague, the Great Fire of London, the need to find a publisher, and the legal requirement that the poem be licensed, which it was only after delays. But Aubrey's phrasing is approximate, no doubt on purpose, because he didn't know. Nor can we be certain what exactly the prison-prone Quaker Thomas Ellood was lent. It is improbable he was lent a unique copy. Perhaps he was lent one soon to be superseded, and so expendable. Nor can we be sure, as I suggested above, that over the next two years Milton didn't work on the poem further. For a poem the length of *Paradise Lost*, a stupendous and complicated labor, fixing termini post and ante quem is uncertain. But the dates of publication, 1667 and, for the definitive text, 1674, are clear and secure. Those publishing events are like the signature on a painting, which as long as it is unsigned must be considered incomplete. It is reasonable to conclude *Paradise Lost* has no clear date for its beginning—for Milton was meditating a heroic poem from his youth, and false starts were part of the work—and that it was completed not once but twice: in 1667, when it was first published in ten books, and again in 1674, when it was published in twelve books, only months before the poet died. The later signature lies on top of the earlier one, which shows through, like a palimpsest.

With the exception of "On Shakespeare," *A Masque Presented at Ludlow Castle, 1634*, "Lycidas," and some juvenilia published later, Milton's early poems—those composed between the ages of fifteen and thirty-seven—did not see the light of day until they were published all together on January 2, 1646. The arrangement of the poems in that publication has been a subject for much interesting and valuable comment. An unfortunate consequence, however, is that it has become customary in modern authoritative editions, except for John Carey's, to publish Milton's shorter poems as they were arranged in 1645–1646 and again in 1673, instead of chronologically. Of course, a chronological edition is more difficult to do, but despite rare exceptions, such as George Herbert's *The Temple*, an editor's task is not to reproduce books already in print in a collated and dubiously idealized form. It is to give the best texts possible of poems in the order they were composed, so far as this can be determined. Especially in Milton's case, chronology is a key to understanding.

Dates of composition for Milton's shorter poems are of course harder to determine than dates of publication, and yet, as I said, date of composition is for these poems more important. In at least one case the date of composition is impossible to determine and nearly impossible to guess: Milton's very close translation of the fifth ode from the first book of Horace. There has been considerable discussion of the date of composition of *Samson Agonistes*, which was most probably after *Paradise Regained*, and hence the last work Milton composed. A tragedy on Samson was conceived early, in the 1640s, and it is now impossible to say how much work, and what sort of work, if any, was done on this sketch before the Restoration in 1660. I imagine very little. References to the pains of age, to the sorrow of blindness, and to public and barbarous executions of men who have served their country and their God date *Samson Agonistes* as a late work, after 1660. The executions took place between 1660 and 1662, the first of them around the time Milton was imprisoned, having narrowly escaped execution himself. There is no reason to think these events would be forgotten, and every reason to think that a few years of distance rendered them more assimilable to art. I remain convinced by the exhaustive arguments of Mary Ann Radzinowicz supporting the later date, in *Toward "Samson Agonistes": The Growth of Milton's Mind* (Princeton, N.J.: Princeton University Press, 1978), 387–407. The later date is confirmed by Laura Lunger Knoppers, ed., *The 1671 Poems "Paradise Regain'd" and "Samson Agonistes,"* vol. 2, *The Complete Works of John Milton* (Oxford: Oxford University Press, 2008), lxxxviii–xcviii. But to apply again the general rule I have set forth, because *Samson Agonistes* is a long work, its date of publication, 1671, and its placement after *Paradise Regained* in the same volume, is more important than its date, or dates, of composition. I have spoken of both works as composed in a late style, and despite superficial differences in manner I hear rhythms that are common to both and less frequent in *Paradise Lost*.

For summary discussion up to 1970 of scholarship on Miltonic chronology, see *A Variorum Commentary on the Poems of John Milton*, vol. 1, *The Latin and Greek Poems*, ed. Douglas Bush; *The Italian Poems*, ed. J. Shaw and A. Bartlett Giametti; vol. 2 (New York: Columbia University

Press, 1970); and *The Minor English Poems,* ed. Douglas Bush and A. S. P. Woodhouse (New York: Columbia University Press, 1972). For a chronological edition of the shorter poems with discussion of scholarship up to the twenty-first century, see John Carey, ed., *Complete Shorter Poems,* 2nd ed. (Harlow: Pearson, 2007). An indispensable resource is Gordon Campbell's *A Milton Chronology* (London: Macmillan, 1997). I have followed Campbell's numbering of the sonnets.

For the sake of clarity, the following chronology is restricted to the poems, eschewing parallel events in Milton's life, including the prose works. I relate the poems continually to Milton's age at the time of composition, which is more relevant than the calendar year, supplied in square brackets (*our* calendar year, not Milton's, which still ended in March). Question marks are supplied where there has been reasonable scholarly doubt whether Milton composed the poem in the year shown. The first line of each poem is given in full.

Chronological List of Milton's Poems with His Age at Composition

AGE YEAR

15 [1624]   Psalm 114, "When the blest seed of Terah's faithful son . . ."
                      Psalm 136, "Let us with a gladsome mind . . ."

?   *Apologus de Rustico et Hero* Fable of the Farmer and the Lord *("Rusticus ex malo sapidissima poma quotannis . . .").*

?   *Carmina Elegiaca* For Early Rising *("Surge, age surge, leves, iam convenit, excute somnos . . .").*

?   *Ignavus Satrapam* "Unworthy of a Ruler" *("Ignavus satrapam dedecet inclytum . . .").*

?   *Philosophus ad regem* "A Philosopher to a King" *("Ω ἄνα εἰ ὀλέσῃς με τὸν ἔννομον, οὐδέ τιν' ἀνδρῶν . . .").*

17 [1626]   Elegy 1, *"Ad Carolum Diodatum,"* "To Charles Diodati" *("Tandem, care, tuae mihi pervenere tabellae . . .").*
                      Elegy 2, *"In Obitum Praeconis Academici Cantabrigiensis,"* "On the Death of the University of Cambridge Beadle" *("Te, qui conspicuus baculo fulgente solebas . . .").*
                      Elegy 3, *"In Obitum Praesulis Wintonienis,"* "On the Death of the Bishop of Winchester"

("*Moestus eram, et tacitus nullo comitante sedebam . . .*").

"*In Obitum Praesulis Eliensis,*" "On the Death of the Bishop of Ely" ("*Adhuc madentes rore squalebant genae . . .*").

"*In Obitum Procancellarii Medici,*" "On the Death of the Vice Chancellor, a Doctor" ("*Parere fati discite legibus . . .*").

? | "*In Proditionem Bombardicam,*" "On the Gunpowder Treason" ("*Cum simul in regem nuper satrapasque Britannos . . .*").

? | "*In Eandem,*" "On the Same" ("*Siccine tentasti caelo donasse Iacobum . . .*").

? | "*In Eandem,*" "On the Same" ("*Purgatorem animae derisit Iacobus ignem . . .*").

? | "*In Eandem,*" "On the Same" ("*Quem modo Roma suis devoverat impia diris . . .*").

? | "*In Inventorem Bombardae,*" "On the Inventor of Gunpowder" ("*Iapetionidem laudavit caeca vetustas . . .*").

? | "*In Quintum Novembris,*" "On the Fourth of November" ("*Iam pius extrema veniens Iacobus ab arcto . . .*").

18 [1627] | Elegy 4, "*Ad Thomam Junium praeceptorem suum*" "To Thomas Young, his Teacher" ("*Curre per immensum subito mea littera pontum . . .*").

Elegy 7, "To Alluring Amathusia" ("*Nondum blanda tuas leges Amathusia noram . . .*").

19? [1628] | "*Naturam non pati senium*" "Nature doesn't Decay" ("*Heu quam perpetuis erroribus acta fatiscit . . .*").

"*De Idea Platonica*" "On the Platonic Idea" ("*Dicite sacrorum praesides nemorum deae . . .*").

"At a Vacation Exercise in the College" ("Hail native language, that by sinews weak").

20 [1629] | Elegy 5, "*In Adventum Veris*" "On the Coming of Spring" ("*In se perpetuo Tempus revolubile gyro*")

? | Sonnet 1, ("O Nightingale, that on yon bloomy spray . . .").

? | "Song: On May Morning" ("Now the bright morning star, Day's harbinger . . .").

? | Sonnet 2, "*Donna leggiadra il cui bel nome onora . . .*"

?		Sonnet 3, *"Qual in colle aspro, al imbrunir di sera . . ."*
?		*Canzone* "song" *("Ridonsi donne e giovani amorosi . . .")*.
?		Sonnet 4, *"Diodati, e te 'l dirò con maraviglia . . ."*
?		Sonnet 5, *"Per certo i bei vostr'occhi, Donna mia . . ."*
?		Sonnet 6, *"Giovane piano, e semplicetto amante . . ."*
?		"The Fifth Ode of Horace, Lib. 1, rendered almost word for word" ("What slender youth bedewed with liquid odours . . ."). The date of this translation is especially uncertain.
21	[1629] [December 25, 1629]	"On the Morning of Christ's Nativity" ("This is the month, and this the happy morn . . .").
	[Dec.–Jan. 1629–1630]	Elegy 6, "Ad Carolum Diodatum ruri commorantem" "To Charles Diodati, in the Country" *("Mitto tibi sanam non pleno ventre salutem . . .")*.
	Easter 1630	"The Passion" ("Erewhile of music and ethereal mirth . . .").
22	[1630–1631]	"On Shakespeare" ("What needs my Shakespeare for his honored bones . . .").
	[1631]	"On the University Carrier, who sickened in the time of his vacancy" ("Here lies old Hobson, Death hath broke his girt . . .").
		"Another on the Same" ("Here lieth one who did most truly prove . . .").
		"An Epitaph on the Marchioness of Winchester" ("This rich marble doth inter . . .").
?		"L'Allegro" ("Hence loathèd Melancholy . . .").
?		"Il Penseroso" ("Hence vain deluding Joys . . .").
23?	[1632]	One surviving line—there were originally two—written in Milton's copy of Ariosto: *"Tu mihi iure tuo Iustiniane vale."* "You, Justinian, with your law, farewell."
?		"Arcades" ("Look nymphs, and Shepherds look . . .").
24?	[December 9, 1632]	Sonnet 7, "How Soon Hath Time" ("How soon hath Time, the subtle thief of youth . . .").
?	[1633]	"At a Solemn Music" ("Blest pair of sirens, pledges of heaven's joy . . .").

?		"On Time" ("Fly envious Time, till thou run out thy race . . .").
?	[Jan. 1]	"Upon the Circumcision" ("Ye flaming powers and wingèd warriors bright . . .").
25	[1634]	*A Masque Presented at Ludlow Castle, 1634* ("Before the starry threshold of Jove's court . . ."). Psalm 114 ("Ἰσραὴλ ὅτε παῖδες, ὅτ᾽ ἀγλαὰ φῦλ᾽ Ἰακώβου . . .").
28	[1637] November	"Lycidas" ("Yet once more, O ye laurels, and once more . . .").
29?	[1638]	*"Ad Patrem"* "To His Father" *("Nunc mea Pierios cupiam per pectora fontes . . .").*
?		"Fix here" ("Fix here ye overdated spheres / That wing the restless foot of time"). Two lines written on the back of a letter sent by Henry Lawes with Milton's passport for his upcoming journey abroad.
?		*"Ad Salsillum poetam Romanum aegrotantem" ("O musa gressum quae volens trahis claudum . . .").*
30	[1639]	*"Ad Leonoram" ("Angelus unicuique suus [sic credite gentes] . . ."). "Ad Eandem" ("Altera Torquatum cepit Leonora poetam . . ."). "Ad Eandem" ("Credula quid liquidam sirena Neapoli iactas . . ."). "Mansus" ("Haec quoque Manse tuae meditantur carmina laudi / Pierides . . .").* Published in a private edition, 1640.
	[1640]	*"Epitaphium Damonis" ("Himerides nymphae, nam vos et Daphnin et Hylan . . .").*
32	[1641]	Translations from *Of Reformation*, Dante, Petrarch, Ariosto ("Ah Constantine, of how much ill was cause . . ."). Translation from *Reason of Church Government*, proverbial, probably from Euripides ("When I die, let the earth be rolled in flames . . .").
33	[1642]	Translations from *Apology for Smectymnuus*, Horace and Sophocles ("Laughing to teach the truth . . ."). Sonnet 8, "When the Assault was Intended to the City" ("Captain or colonel, or knight in arms . . .").

34?	[1643]	Sonnet 9, "Lady, that in the prime" ("Lady, that in the prime of earliest youth . . .").
?		Sonnet 10, "To the Lady Margaret Ley" ("Daughter to that good Earl, once President . . .").
35	[1644]	Translation from Euripides, on title page of *Areopagitica* ("This is true liberty, when freeborn men . . .").
36	[1645]	Translation of Horace Epistles 1.16.40–45, from *Tetrachordon* ("Whom do we count a good man, whom but he . . .").
?		Appended to Elegy 7 for publication with *Poems* 1645 (January 2, 1646): "*Haec ego mente olim laeva studioque supino . . .*"
		For publication with the engraving of the poet published with *Poems* 1645 (January 2, 1646): "*In Effigiei eius Sculptorem*" ("Ἀμαθεῖ γεγράφθαι χειρὶ τήνδε μὲν εἰκόνα . . .").
37	[1646]	Sonnet 11, "On the Detraction which Followed upon my Writing Certain Treatises" ("I did but prompt the age to quit their clogs . . ."). The order of Sonnets 11 and 12 is the order in the Trinity manuscript. In the 1673 *Poems* their order is reversed.
?		"On the New Forcers of Conscience under the Long Parliament" ("Because you have thrown off your prelate lord . . .").
?		Sonnet 12, "On *Tetrachordon*" ("A book was writ of late called *Tetrachordon* . . ."). This sonnet is numbered 11 in the 1673 *Poems*.
		Sonnet 13, "To Mr. Henry Lawes, on his Airs" ("Harry whose tuneful and well-measured song . . .").
38	[Late December 1646]	Sonnet 14, "On the Religious Memory of Mrs. Katharine Thomason" ("When faith and love which parted from thee never . . .").
	[January 1647]	"*Ad Joannem Rousium Oxoniensis Academiae Bibliothecarium*" ("*Gemelle cultu simplici gaudens liber . . .*").
39	[1648]	Psalms 80–88 (April) ("Thou shepherd that dost Israel keep . . ."); ("To God our strength sing loud and clear"); ("God in the great assembly

stands . . ."); ("Be not thou silent now at
length . . ."); ("How lovely are thy dwellings
fair! . . ."); ("Thy land to favor graciously . . .");
("Thy gracious ear, O Lord, incline . . .");
("Among the holy mountains high . . ."); ("Lord
God that dost me save and keep . . .").
Sonnet 15, "On the Lord General Fairfax at the
Siege of Colchester" ("Fairfax, whose name in
arms through Europe rings . . .").

40 [1649]
Translation from *Tenure of Kings and Magistrates*,
from Seneca ("There can be slain . . .").
Translations from *The History of Britain*, from
Geoffrey of Monmouth and from the *Flores
Historiarum*.

42 [Perhaps late
December 1649]
Epigram from *Defensio Pro Populo Anglicano*
("*Quis expedivit Salmasio suam 'Hundredam'* . . .").

43 [1652]
Sonnet 16, "To the Lord General Cromwell"
("Cromwell, our chief of men who through a
cloud . . .").
Sonnet 17, "To Sir Henry Vane the Younger"
("Vane, young in years, but in sage counsel
old . . .").

44 [1653]
Psalms 1–8 (August 8–14) ("Blessed is the
man who hath not walked astray . . ."); ("Why
do the gentiles tumult, and the nations . . .");
("Lord how many are my foes . . ."); ("Answer
me when I call . . ."); ("Jehovah to my words
give ear . . ."); ("Lord in thine anger do not
reprehend me . . ."); ("Lord my God to thee
I fly . . ."); ("O Jehovah our Lord how wondrous
great . . .").
Verses from *Defensio Secunda*, adapting lines
from Juvenal ("*Gaudete scombri, et quicquid est
piscium salo* . . .").

46 [1655]
Sonnet 18, "On the Late Massacre in
Piedmont" ("Avenge O Lord thy slaughtered
saints, whose bones . . .").
Sonnet 19, "When I consider how my light is
spent."
Sonnet 20, "Lawrence of virtuous father virtuous
son."

		Sonnet 21, "Cyriack, whose grandsire on the royal bench."
?		Sonnet 22, "To Mr. Cyriack Skinner Upon his Blindness" ("Cyriack, this three years' day these eyes, though clear . . .").
49	[1658]	Sonnet 23, "Methought I saw my late espousèd saint" ("Methought I saw my late espousèd saint . . .").
51	[1660]	From the title page of the second edition of *The Ready and Easy Way*, adapting Juvenal *("et nos / Consilium dedimus Syllae, demus populo nunc")*.
56?	[1665]	*Paradise Lost* completed? ("Of man's first disobedience and the fruit . . .").
57–	[1666–1667?]	*Paradise Regained* completed?
58?		("I who erewhile the happy garden sung . . .").
58	[1667]	*Paradise Lost* licensed and under contract in the spring, published in the fall.
62	[1671]	*Paradise Regained* published in May. *Samson Agonistes* published with *Paradise Regained*, in May ("A little onward lend thy guiding hand . . .").
65	[1674]	*Paradise Lost*, definitive edition, published in late spring or summer.

Notes

Introduction

1. Austin Woolrych, *Britain in Revolution, 1625–1660* (Oxford: Oxford University Press, 2002), 6. Were events in England between the Petition of Right in 1628 and the Restoration in 1660 a *rebellion* or a *revolution?* Edward Hyde, the Earl of Clarendon, a courtier to Charles I and a minister to Charles II, began his great *History of the Rebellion* in the midst of events, in March 1646. A rebellion, or armed insurrection, is a failed revolution. *Rebellion* would therefore seem to be the proper term, as Blair Worden sensibly argues, for a process ending in 1660 with the Restoration of Charles II. But any full understanding of the period must take 1688–1689—the flight of King James II, the last king of the Stuart line, the accession of William and Mary, and the passage of the Bill of Rights—as the terminus of events that were set in motion sixty years before by the Petition of Right. It seems to me, therefore, that the English seventeenth century was indeed a period of revolution, an overturning of the political order, such that by the end, Parliament and not the throne was the chief power in the land. Of course, it is perfectly consistent with a revolution for people in its early stages to conceive of their aims as a recovery of natural and legal rights enjoyed in an earlier time, in this instance, the time of Queen Elizabeth, frequently alluded to in Parliament by supporters of the Petition of Right, notably Sir John Eliot. Parliament also saw itself striving to protect the ancient rights of all Englishmen enshrined in *Magna Carta*, according to Sir Edward Coke's controversial interpretation of that document. Were the bellicose events taking place between 1642 and 1651 a civil war? Yes, in an obvious sense, but unlike, say, the Wars of the Roses in the fifteenth century or the American Civil War in the nineteenth century, the English Civil War was part of a larger revolution. Was the period between the death of Charles I in 1649 and the Restoration of Charles II in 1660 an *interregnum,* "a period between the reigns"? Yes. There seems to me nothing partisan in that accurate phrase, so often branded as royalist. Was the government of England during the interregnum a *republic* or a

commonwealth? The government called itself a *commonwealth*, but educated persons of the time, including Milton, saw its form as that of a *republic*, so terming it in Latin, on the model of the Roman Republic and the more recent example of the Venetian Republic. The term *commonwealth* has the advantage of historical literalness. The term *republic* may be used, however, to denote the actual commonwealth plus the aspirations held out for it by men such as John Milton, a hope for which the soldiers coined the phrase "good old cause." Does the *republic* or *commonwealth* period include the *Protectorate* (1653–1659), when Oliver Cromwell dismissed an already greatly reduced Parliament and assumed all power? Or does the commonwealth end with the Protectorate? Much depends on point of view. But Milton's view, that of a committed revolutionary, was that the Protectorate is an unfortunate but necessary stage on the way to a free commonwealth. G. M. Trevelyan describes the period between the execution of Charles I and the Restoration of Charles II as that of the "revolutionary governments." See *England under the Stuarts*, 3rd ed. (1946; repr., London: Folio, 1999), 261. For a valuable analysis of the relations between politics, economics, and ideas, see Christopher Hill, *The Century of Revolution, 1603–1714*, The Norton Library History of England (New York: W. W. Norton, 1982). See also Christopher Hill, *The Experience of Defeat: Milton and Some Contemporaries* (New York: Viking Penguin, 1984). For a detailed, chronological account of events, see Godfrey Davies, *The Early Stuarts, 1603–1660*, vol. 9, *The Oxford History of England* (1937; repr., Oxford: Clarendon Press, 1945). The radicalized parliamentary army roused stronger feelings for basic social as well as political change, expressing the feeling "that after so much blood there should be no better an issue for the Commons" than to have to have everything again at the disposal of the King and the Lords. See A. S. P. Woodhouse, ed., "The Putney Debates," in *Puritanism and Liberty: Being the Army Debates (1647–1649) from the Clarke Manuscripts*, 2nd ed. (Chicago: University of Chicago Press, 1965), 123. For a more skeptical view of the period as being one of revolution, see Hugh Trevor-Roper, "The General Crisis of the Seventeenth Century," in his *The Crisis of the Seventeenth Century: Religion, the Reformation, and Social Change* (Indianapolis: Liberty Fund, 1967), esp. 79–81. My sense of the period is formed to a considerable degree by Crane Brinton's classic work of theoretical history, *The Anatomy of Revolution*, 2nd ed. (New York: Vintage, 1957). While preparing this book for press I happened to read Fredric Jameson's, "Religion and Ideology: A Political Reading of *Paradise Lost*," in *Literature, Politics and Theory*, ed. Francis Barker et al. (London: Methuen, 1986), 35–56. It drives home the point that religion in the preindustrial world is not merely false consciousness. Religion *is* ideology, and theological debate is the form "in which groups become aware of their political differences and fight them out" (39). I recommend the essay for other valuable points, in addition to this one.

2. See Appendix II and Mary Ann Radzinowicz, *Toward "Samson Agonistes": The Growth of Milton's Mind* (Princeton, N.J.: Princeton University Press, 1978), 387–407; Gordon Campbell, *A Milton Chronology* (London: Macmillan, 1997), 4–5.

3. That attachment to an imaginary original liberty, and indignation at one's equally imaginary "enslavement," can be a serviceable instrument of violence, and enslavement, is the argument of Mary Nyquist's *Arbitrary Rule: Slavery, Tyranny, and the Power of Life and Death* (Chicago: University of Chicago Press, 2013), 1

and 229. For the other side, see Joan S. Bennett, *Reviving Liberty: Radical Christian Humanism in Milton's Great Poems* (Cambridge, Mass.: Harvard University Press, 1989). It seems to me brave and right for Nyquist to look closely at that the admired concept of liberty as an instrument of enslavement.

4. I develop this point at more length in the chapter "Revolution in *Paradise Regained*," *Delirious Milton: The Fate of the Poet in Modernity* (Cambridge, Mass.: Harvard University Press, 2006), 166 and 179. It is interesting to note that the *epiphany* or "revelation" of Jesus's divine nature is celebrated in Western church as the visit of the Magi (Matthew 2:1–11), but in the Eastern church as the baptism of Jesus in the Jordan River, when the heavens open, a dove descends, and a voice from above declares Jesus "my beloved Son" (Matthew 3:17; Mark 1:11; Luke 3:22).

5. Hugh of Saint Victor, *De Sacramentis Christianae Fidei*, vol. 176 in *Patrologiae Cursus Completus, Series Latina*, ed. Jacques-Paul Migne (Paris, 1854), 184. Hugh's technical definition of *opus restaurationis* is *incarnatio Verbi cum omnibus sacramentis suis*, "the incarnation of the Word with all its sacraments," which means both the scriptures and the sacraments administered by the church. On the one hand are the scriptural prophecies of Christ's sacrifice, *ab initio saecli*, "from the beginning of time"; on the other hand, the positive consequence of the Crucifixion, the restoration of humanity, which goes forward through time *ad finem mundi*, "to the end of the world." Humanity is what is being restored, and what it is being restored from is sin.

6. "Christ died for our sins, according to the scriptures" (1 Corinthians 15:3), where "according to the scriptures" means in fulfillment of the Hebrew Scriptures, especially the prophets. Milton could not have explicitly denied this central Christian belief. But he could displace it in his poetry, most startlingly in the subject for *Paradise Regained*, which shows Jesus as a victor and a moral example, rather than as a victim. When Milton wrote *De Doctrina Christiana* in the 1640s and 1650s, he acknowledged that Christ redeemed all believers at the cost of his own blood *(sanguinis sui pretio)*, citing thirteen biblical texts in support (although not 1 Corinthians 15:3). But the entire chapter "On Man's Restoration, and Christ as Redeemer" says nothing further on the blood sacrifice and hastens to Christ's nature and office. It seems to me that, even here, Milton is avoiding the issue of blood sacrifice. *De Doctrina Christiana*, ed. and trans. John K. Hale and J. Donald Cullington, with Gordon Campbell and Thomas N. Corns, vol. 8 (in 2 vols.), *The Complete Works of John Milton* (Oxford: Clarendon Press, 2012), 1:468–72. I am grateful to an anonymous reader who pointed out that the doctrine of penal substitutionary atonement has not always and everywhere been held by Christians. That is a fair point. I have no doubt Milton kept what Sir Thomas Browne called "the honorable stile of a Christian" because there was nowhere else for him to go and, more important, because of a fundamental loyalty to the person of Jesus. But as far as doctrinal Christianity is concerned, Milton seems to have begun moving in his poems into something like eighteenth-century deism. For three theories of the atonement, see Gustav Aulén, *Christus Victor: An Historical Study of the Three Main Types of the Idea of Atonement*, trans. A. G. Hebert (New York: Macmillan, 1951).

7. This story is told in the classic study of Charles Norris Cochrane, *Christianity and Classical Culture: A Study of Thought and Action from Augustus to Augustine* (Oxford: Clarendon, 1940).

8. Charles I ruled without Parliament from 1629 to 1640, in the period of "personal rule," as it was called, and what those of Milton's party would call the Eleven Years' Tyranny. "Lycidas" was composed in 1637 and published in 1638.

9. Don M. Wolfe, gen. ed., *Complete Prose Works of John Milton*, 8 vols. (New Haven, Conn.: Yale University Press, 1953–1982), hereafter referred to as *YP* with book and page number cited. See Appendix I for texts and references.

10. In *Über den Begriff der Geschichte* (online source: www.mxks.de) "On the Concept of History," the famous angel of Walter Benjamin's commentary on Paul Klee's painting "Angelus Novus" has its wings spread and cannot close them, because it is being driven backward by a storm-force wind blowing out of Paradise. As the angel flies backward the rubble—dead bodies—piles up at its feet, a huge and always increasing pile, a *Trümmerhaufen* rising up to heaven. Benjamin says the storm is progress, whatever he means by the word; Milton would say it is sin.

11. References to *Paradise Lost, Paradise Regained,* and *Samson Agonistes* are shortened to *PL, PR,* and *SA,* respectively. *PL* and *PR* are followed by book and line numbers, for example, *PR,* 1.3, and *SA* is followed by line numbers, for example, *SA,* lines 1–9. For citations and quotations from *Paradise Lost,* I have used my own edition: *Paradise Lost* (New York: W. W. Norton, 2005).

12. Powerfully argued by Irene Samuel, "The Regaining of Paradise," in *The Prison and the Pinnacle,* ed. Balachandra Rajan (Toronto: University of Toronto Press, 1973), 111–34.

13. G. C. Moore Smith, ed., *Gabriel Harvey's Marginalia* (Stratford-Upon-Avon: Shakespeare Head Press, 1913), 161.

14. *YP,* 7:462–63. Oddly, the reference to Jeremiah 22:29 is not noted. The passage from *The Reason of Church Government* is a shortened quotation from Jeremiah 15:10. For the antiquity of the supernatural role of the poet, see M. L. West, *Indo-European Poetry and Myth* (Oxford: Oxford University Press, 2007), 26–33. For the romantic association of poetry with Hebrew prophecy, and of the Bible with poetry, starting with Robert Lowth—much of which is applicable to the Hebrew-reading Milton—see Ian Balfour, *The Rhetoric of Romantic Prophecy* (Stanford, Calif.: Stanford University Press, 2002), 55–56. Balfour's insightful discussion of Friedrich Hölderlin as a prophet is applicable to Milton, as well; see Chapter 7 of the same volume, "Hölderlin's Moment of Truth: 'Germanien' and the Oracle to the Nation," 173–249.

15. Pindar, *Pythian* 4. 177–78: *aoidan patêr . . . euainêtos Orpheus* ("father of song . . . much-renowned Orpheus"). See Stella Purce Revard, *Pindar and the Renaissance Hymn-Ode* (Tempe, Ariz.: ACMRS, 2001). For the dismemberment of Orpheus as a central figure in Milton's work, see Michael Lieb, *Milton and the Culture of Violence* (Ithaca: Cornell University Press, 1994).

16. Wordsworth, *The Prelude* (1805), 1.233. See Simon Jarvis, *Wordsworth's Philosophic Song* (Cambridge: Cambridge University Press, 2007), 9 passim.

17. Matthew Arnold, *On Poetry and Poets* (London: Faber, 1957), quoted in *PL,* ed. Teskey, 398.

18. On the continuing ideals of Greek thought and art, see Jacqueline de Romilly, *Ce que je crois* (Paris: Fallois, 2012), 151. See also Jacqueline de Romilly and Monique Trédé, "A propos du verbe (voix, modes et temps)," in *Petites leçons sur le grec ancien* (Paris: Stock, 2008), 83–96; B. F. C. Atkinson, *The Greek Lan-*

guage (1931; repr., London: Faber, 1952), 136–39; and J. D. Denniston, *The Greek Particles*, 2nd ed. (1954; repr., Oxford: Clarendon Press, 1959), xxxvi: "a loss of definiteness has been accompanied by increased subtlety of nuance." Caveats are from time to time issued against regarding the syntax of *Paradise Lost* as Latinate. See Thomas N. Corns, *Reading "Paradise Lost"* (London: Longman, 1994), 117–19. Yes, *Paradise Lost* is in English and its long sentences with dependent clauses resemble the prose Milton wrote in English. Yes, English isn't Latin, and long sentences in English will be more obscure than long sentences in Latin, at least by the great masters who have come down to us. The style of *Paradise Lost* has nevertheless a Ciceronian rhythm in its bones, of which the most important English model was Richard Hooker, in his *Of the Laws of Ecclesiastical Polity* (1593–1597). Of course, Milton's grand style has much else. See Christopher Ricks, *Milton's Grand Style* (Oxford: Clarendon Press, 1963).

19. Nigel Smith, *Is Milton Better Than Shakespeare?* (Cambridge, Mass.: Harvard University Press, 2008).

20. H. D. F. Kitto, *The Greeks*, 2nd ed. (1957; repr., London: Penguin, 1991), 25.

21. In well over one thousand lines, I count only fifty-five periods in the Trinity manuscript text of *A Masque 1634* (with the crossed-out passages), excluding periods after speech tags and abbreviations, but not excluding stage directions. Milton tends to use periods as dividers for speech ends or in places where a long pause is expected from the speakers: they are not syntactical markers. Even these numbers do not give an adequate picture of the lengthy passages in which exceptionally few periods or "full stops" are used. In the opening lines there is no punctuation of any kind after *sainted seats* (line 11), *eternity* (14), and *mould* (17), the first period being after *task* (18). The 1637 text has periods after *seats* and *mould* and a colon after *eternity*. From *to my task* (18) to the end of the Daemon's first speech, at *viewless now* (92), just before Comus enters, a stretch of 74 lines, there are only nineteen commas and two periods, including the final one after *now*. The other is after *scepter* (36). Comus's opening speech, 93–144, contains only one period, at line 118, after *elves*, and only three commas. Within that speech there is no punctuation of any kind at the strongest break, marked by an end-stopped line, "To roll with pleasure in a sensual sty" (77). John Milton, *A Maske: The Earlier Versions*, ed. S. E. Sprott (Toronto: University of Toronto Press, 1973).

22. Samuel Johnson, "Life of Milton," ed. Stephen Fix, vol. 1, *Lives of the Poets*, gen. ed. John H. Middendorf, in *The Collected Works of Samuel Johnson XXI* (New Haven, Conn.: Yale University Press, 2010), 200: "Such are the faults of that wonderful performance *Paradise Lost;* which he who can put in balance with its beauties must be considered not as nice but as dull, as less to be censured for want of candour than pitied for want of sensibility."

23. William Empson, *Milton's God*, 2nd ed. (London: Chatto and Windus, 1962); and C. S. Lewis, *A Preface to "Paradise Lost"* (London: Oxford University Press, 1942). Both texts cited in *PL*, ed. Teskey, 437–39.

24. Richard Dawkins, *The God Delusion* (Boston: Houghton Mifflin, 2006), 98. Sir Thomas Browne, *Religio Medici*, in *The Works of Thomas Browne*, ed. Geoffrey Keynes (London: Faber and Faber, 1964), 1:9.

25. MacCallum is here paraphrasing Milton's statements on scripture in his theological treatise, *De Doctrina Christiana*, especially 3.33, in which treatise every point is rigorously tagged to a passage of the Bible, since the Bible is revealed

truth and must anchor every Christian belief; see Hugh MacCallum, "Milton and Figurative Interpretation of the Bible," *University of Toronto Quarterly* 31 (1962): 397–415, reprinted in Feisal G. Mohamed and Mary Nyquist, *Milton and Questions of History: Essays by Canadians Past and Present* (Toronto: University of Toronto Press, 2012), 77.

On the Early Poems

1. Gordon Campbell and Thomas N. Corns, *John Milton: Life, Work, and Thought* (Oxford: Clarendon Press, 2008), 8. Barbara K. Lewalski, *The Life of John Milton: A Critical Biography* (Oxford: Blackwell, 2000), 2.

2. *The Complete Poetical Works of John Milton*, ed. Douglas Bush (Boston: Houghton Mifflin, 1965), 25; and A. S. P. Woodhouse and Douglas Bush, *A Variorum Commentary on the Poems of John Milton*, vol. 2, part 2, *The Minor English Poems* (New York: Columbia University Press, 1972), 503–5. See Barbara Lewalski, *The Life of John Milton*, 26–27.

3. G. M. Kirkwood, *Early Greek Monody: The History of a Poetic Type* (Ithaca, N.Y.: Cornell University Press, 1974), 21.

4. This is the continual argument of Northrop Frye's *The Return of Eden: Five Essays on Milton's Epics* (Toronto: University of Toronto Press, 1965); see, for example, 112–13. I have been unable to find in his writings a remark Frye made in a lecture, to the effect that freedom is what humanity is desperately trying to avoid and is the one thing God is determined humanity shall have.

5. John Leonard, *Faithful Labourers: A Reception History of "Paradise Lost" 1667–1970*, 2 vols. (Oxford: Clarendon Press, 2013), 705–820.

6. *Lumina*, literally "lights," is a common term for eyes. I am inclined to approve Charles Knapp's conjecture that the word here means "bright rays," a metonymy for Phoebus's "radiant head." *Elegia Quinta*, line 88; *Columbia*, 1 part 1, 202–3.

7. The point applies to *Paradise Lost*, as well, and the notion that contemporary context is the only grounds for reading the poem. See Helen Gardner, *A Reading of "Paradise Lost*," The Alexander Lectures in the University of Toronto (Oxford: Clarendon Press, 1965), ix: "I have never felt happy at the attempt to confine the meaning of *Paradise Lost* to the meaning that it had for its own century, even if this were discoverable with certainty, which I doubt."

8. Philip Larkin, *Collected Poems*, ed. Anthony Twaite (New York: FSG, 1989), 183.

9. See Martin Heidegger, "The Origin of the Work of Art," in *Poetry, Language, Thought*, trans. Albert Hofstadter (New York: Harper and Row, 1971), 42–43; "Der Ursprung des Kunstwerkes," in *Holzwege* (Frankfurt: Klostermann, 1950), 27–29.

10. *Furor* (in Greek, *enthousiasmos*, "being filled with a god") and *mystery* were closely associated in Renaissance poetic and esoteric thought. It took divine fury to see into the mysteries behind mythical signs. This is the common theme of Natalis Comes's *Mythologiae* (Venice, 1581). See John Mulryan and Steven Brown, ed. and trans., *Natale Conti's Mythologiae*, 2 vols. (Tempe, Ariz.: ACMRS, 2006). See also D. P. Walker, "Esoteric Symbolism," in *Poetry and Poetics from Ancient Greece to the Renaissance*, ed. G. M. Kirkwood (Ithaca, N.Y.: Cornell University

Press, 1975), 218–32; Edgar Wind, *Pagan Mysteries in the Renaissance* (New Haven, Conn.: Yale University Press, 1958), 24–30; E. N. *Tigerstedt*, "Furor Poeticus: Poetic Inspiration in Greek Literature before Democritus and Plato," *Journal of the History of Ideas* 31, no. 2 (1970): 163–78; *Plato's Idea of Poetical Inspiration* (Helsinki: 1969); William Chase Greene, "Plato's View of Poetry," in *Harvard Studies in Classical Philology 29* (Cambridge, Mass.: Harvard University Press, 1918), 15–17; Marcel Detienne, "The Memory of the Poet," in *The Masters of Truth in Archaic Greece*, trans. Janet Lloyd (Cambridge, Mass.: MIT Press, 1996), 39–52.

11. T. W. Allen, W. R. Halliday, and E. E. Sikes, eds., *The Homeric Hymns* (Amsterdam: Hakkert, 1980), lxiv–xcv; Aimé Puech, ed., *Pindare*, vol. 1, *Olympiques* (1930; repr., Paris: Belles Lettres, 2003), xxii. See also Stella Purce Regard, *Pindar and the Renaissance Hymn-Ode, 1450–1700* (Tempe, Ariz.: Arizona Center for Medieval and Renaissance Studies, 2001), 110, for the Greek muse in a Christian role.

12. The standard reference point is F. T. Prince, *The Italian Element in Milton's Verse* (Oxford: Clarendon Press, 1954).

13. The source was an exceptionally famous fifteenth-century picture book of speculations on the symbolic meaning of the Egyptian hieroglyphics, all of which are simply made up. See George S. Boas, trans., *The Hieroglyphics of Horapollo* (1950; repr., Princeton, N.J.: Princeton University Press, 1993). By the seventeenth century, speculative reading of hieroglyphics had reached baroque proportions in Athanasius Kircher's encyclopedic *Oedipus Aegytiacus* (Rome, 1652–1654).

14. I venture to say more about the irony of Milton's Latin funereal poems in my introduction to *Milton's Latin Poems*, trans. David Slavitt (Baltimore, Md.: Johns Hopkins University Press, 2011), vii–xxx.

On *"L'Allegro"* and *"Il Penseroso"*

1. Helen Vendler, *Our Secret Discipline: Yeats and Lyric Form* (Cambridge, Mass.: Harvard University Press, 2007), 160.

2. Plato, *Cratylus*, 402a–b.

3. "The Phases of the Moon," lines 16 and 19, in Daniel Albright, ed., *The Poems* (London: Dent, 1990).

4. James Joyce, *Ulysses* (London: Bodley Head, 1967), 45.

5. Milton would have known the Greek hellenistic poem by "Musaeus," entitled "Hero and Leander," but would not have supposed it to have been composed by the shadowy, legendary poet of that name.

On the Work Not Called Comus

1. For the sake of clarity, I follow *OED* in spelling the Jacobean and Caroline courtly dramatic genre *masque*, rather than the slightly misleading *mask*, or *maske*, both of which spellings Milton used and some modern critics and editors have begun to favor. Milton's *A Masque* has 1,023 lines. Epitaphium *Damonis*, the longest poetical work between the masque and *Paradise Lost*, has 219 lines." On the Morning of Christ's Nativity," the longest work before the masque, has 244 lines. If we take "L'Allegro" and "Il Penseroso" as one work of 328 lines, then Milton's masque is 1.8 times as long as these two poems combined.

The textual witnesses are (1) Milton's working manuscript, in the Trinity manuscript; (2) the Bridgewater manuscript, which is the closest to the acted version, this being a presentation copy in a scribal hand, presented to the Earl of Bridgewater; (3) the stand-alone volume published by Henry Lawes in 1637, hereafter *1637*, in which Milton remains anonymous; (4) the definitive text, in *Poems of Mr. John Milton*, hereafter *Poems 1645*, dated 1645 but published in January 1646. As for the text of *A Masque* published in 1673, in *Poems upon Several Occasions by Mr. John Milton*, it appeared in the year before the poet's death, when he had been blind for twenty years. This text has a few substantive changes, none of which is authorial and all of which are worse. The definitive edition for study of the three early witnesses is S. E. Sprott, ed., *A Maske: The Earlier Versions* (Toronto: University of Toronto Press, 1973).

Of interest for the original performance, see Lady Alix Egerton, *Milton's "Comus": Being the Bridgewater Manuscript* (London: Dent, 1910); Stephen Orgel, *The Jonsonian Masque* (Cambridge, Mass.: Harvard University Press, 1965); and Stephen Orgel, ed., *Ben Jonson: The Complete Masques* (New Haven, Conn.: Yale University Press, 1969), 1–2, an excellent condensed account of the masque; John Demaray, *Milton and the Masque Tradition: The Early Poems, Arcades and "Comus"* (Cambridge, Mass.: Harvard University Press, 1968); John S. Diekhoff, ed., *A Maske at Ludlow: Essays on Milton's "Comus"* (Cleveland, Ohio: Case Western Reserve, 1968); David Lindley, *The Court Masque* (Manchester: Manchester University Press, 1984); David Bevington and Peter Holbrook, *The Politics of the Stuart Court Masque* (Cambridge: Cambridge University Press, 1998); Cedric Brown, *John Milton's Aristocratic Entertainments* (Cambridge: Cambridge University Press, 1985); Stephen Orgel and Roy Strong, *Inigo Jones: The Theatre of the Stuart Court* (London: Sotheby Parke Bernet, 1998). Especially to be recommended is Jerzy Limon, *The Masque of Stuart Culture* (Newark, N.J.: University of Delaware Press, 1990), for the methodological clarity with which it distinguishes between the literary masque and the masque-in-performance (8).

We have the names of about ninety masques, half of which have survived in some form (Limon, *The Masque of Stuart Culture*, 18). For a good selection of masques and an excellent introduction to the genre, see David Lindley, ed., *Court Masques: Jacobean and Caroline Entertainments, 1605–1640* (Oxford: Clarendon Press, 1995). For ritualistic and anthropological implications in *A Masque*, see Richard Halpern, "Puritanism and Maenadism in *A Mask*," in *Rewriting the Renaissance: The Discourses of Sexual Difference in Early Modern Europe*, ed. Margaret W. Ferguson, Maureen Quilligan, and Nancy J. Vickers (Chicago: University of Chicago Press, 1986), 88–105; William Shullenberger, *Lady in the Labyrinth: Milton's "Comus" as Initiation* (London: Associated University Presses, 2008); and Ann Baynes Coiro, "'A Thousand Fantasies': The Lady and the *Maske*," in *The Oxford Handbook of Milton*, ed. Nicholas McDowell and Nigel Smith (Oxford: Oxford University Press, 209), 89–111.

2. *A Masque* is on signatures continuous with the *Poems 1645*, however. The *Poemata* is on independent signatures and is therefore a separate volume, although bound and issued with *Poems 1645*.

3. John Middendorf and Stephen Fix, eds., *The Lives of the Poets*, vol. 1, *The Yale Edition of the Works of Samuel Johnson XXI* (New Haven, Conn.: Yale University Press, 2010), 180.

4. Angus Fletcher, *The Transcendental Masque: An Essay on Milton's* Comus (Ithaca, N.Y.: Cornell University Press, 1971), 243–44. For "the politics of the vanishing point," see 79–86.

5. The phrase *wide Atlantic* is from canceled lines from the Trinity manuscript, in Barbara Kiefer Lewalski and Estelle Haan, eds., *The Shorter Poems*, vol. 3, *The Complete Works of John Milton* (Oxford: Oxford University Press, 2012), 300.

6. Ibid., 331–32.

7. Ibid., 300.

8. Gordon Campbell and Thomas N. Corns, *John Milton: Life, Work, and Thought* (Oxford: Oxford University Press, 2008), 84. See John Creaser, "Milton's *Comus:* The Irrelevance of the Castlehaven Scandal," *Notes and Queries* 31 (1984): 307–17.

9. See Jacques Derrida, *De La Grammatologie* (Paris: Minuit, 1967), on the continual affirmation within the frame of Western metaphysics of the priority of speech to writing—priority in time as well as in authority—as an *arché*. In Christian theology, the priority is grounded in the Word or *logos* of John's gospel, borrowed from the *logos* or "reason principle" of Greek philosophy. In Derrida's *La Dissémination* (Paris: Seuil, 1972), especially "La Pharmacie de Platon" (originally published in 1968, 69–198), the discussion is carried back to Plato's condemnation of writing in the *Phaedrus*. Derrida proposes to reverse this seemingly commonsensical but actually tendentious hierarchy by placing writing before speech, parodying the Greek *arché* with the term *archi-écriture*, "original and originative writing." Most literary works are presented as phonic enunciations merely recorded, or represented, in writing. But we know the act of writing a poem is prior to and the cause of this *effect* of an original speaking. My argument concerning *A Masque* is that the event of an actual performance, a dramatic enunciation, strongly increases this illusion that the speaking—the "original" performance—is of prior authority artistically to any subsequent text (Bridgewater manuscript, *1637, Poems 1645*) when in truth the performance was merely one draft of the finished work of art, which begins and ends with a text, Trinity manuscript and *Poems 1645*.

10. Gordon Campbell and Thomas N. Corns, *John Milton: Life, Work, and Thought* (Oxford: Oxford University Press, 2008), 78–79. Barbara K. Lewalski, *The Life of John Milton: A Critical Biography* (Oxford: Blackwell, 2000), 63–64 and 76–81. See also Cedric Brown, *Milton's Aristocratic Entertainments* (Cambridge: Cambridge University Press, 1985), 26–40; M. S. Berkowitz, "An Earl's Michelmas in Wales: Some Thoughts on the Original Presentation of *Comus*," *Milton Quarterly* 13 (1979): 122–25.

11. Lewalski and Haan, *Shorter Poems*, 330–31 and 360.

12. For "declamatory airs" in masques of the period, see John Cunningham, "Appendix E. Henry Lawes' Music for the songs in *A Mask*," in Lewalski and Haan, *Shorter Poems*, 587–88. Cunningham discusses Lawes's art of accommodating speech patterns to the melodic line in formal songs, such as the Echo song. It seems likely more verses of *A Masque* than we might suppose, and especially those delivered by Lawes, were half sung, half spoken, which is why I have proposed Schonberg's term *Sprechstimme*, adopted by Alban Berg in *Wozzek*. The epilogue is not a declamatory air in the sense Cunningham means. But Milton clearly thought the epilogue could be sung. When Milton writes that the *daemon "sings or*

says," instead of one or the other, he may have meant something in between the two alternatives.

13. John Creaser, "The Original of Sabrina?," *Milton Quarterly* 46 (2012): 15–20.

14. Lewalski and Haan, *Shorter Poems*, 360.

15. *Earth's green* would become *green earth's* in *1637*. See Sprott, *A Maske*.

16. Bridgewater manuscript. Lewalski and Haan, *Shorter Poems*, 360. See Sprott, *A Maske*; Bridgewater manuscript, left column, 181, 183, and 185. The Trinity manuscript has the same stage direction, struck out along with a draft of the longer epilogue (left column, 180). Before the final, long version of the epilogue in the Trinity manuscript, in a passage developed after the performance but before 1637, the direction reads, *"The Daemon sings or says"* (see Lewalski and Haan, *Shorter Poems*, 332; Sprott, *A Maske*, 184, left column).

17. The Trinity manuscript has "of hyacinth," a genitive plural, in lower case. It is clear Milton intends the flowers, not the youth after whom they were named.

18. Spenser, *Faerie Queene*, 3.4.29–50. Cupid and Psyche are also mentioned in this passage, confirming Milton's indebtedness to it. For Renaissance interpretations of the myth, see James G. Frazer, *Adonis, Attis, Osiris: Studies in Oriental Religions*, 3rd ed. (London: Macmillan, 1966), 1:30; George Sandys, *Ovid's Metamorphosis Englished, Mythologized, and Represented in Figures*, ed. Karl K. Hulley and Stanley T. Vandersall, foreword by Douglas Bush (1632; repr., Lincoln: University of Nebraska Press, 1970), 492–94; and Natalis Comes, *Mythologiae* (Venice, 1581), 5:16. See *Natale Conti's "Mythologiae*," trans. John Mulryan and Steven Brown (Tempe, Ariz.: ACMRS, 2006), 437–41.

19. R. A. Foakes, ed., *Lectures 1808–1819, on Literature*, vol. 5 (in two parts), *The Collected Works of Samuel Taylor Coleridge* (Princeton, N.J.: Princeton University Press, 1987), 2:409–10.

20. Sprott, *A Maske*, 45.

21. Ibid., 82, 88, and 89.

22. *Iliad*, 1.423; *Odyssey*, 1.23.

23. Martin Heidegger, "The Origin of the Work of Art," in *Poetry, Language, Thought*, trans. Albert Hofstadter (New York: Harper and Row, 1971), 49; and, from the original, "Ursprung des Kunstwerkes," in *Holzwege* (1950; repr., Frankfurt: Klostermann, 1980), 35. The verb *ragen*, translated as "jut," could be rendered "towers up" and is associated with mountains.

24. Egerton, *Milton's "Comus*," 30.

25. See Theodore W. Adorno, *Aesthetic Theory*, trans. Robert Hullot-Kentor, ed. Gretel Adorno and Rolf Tiedemann (Minneapolis: University of Minneapolis Press, 1997), 81, in which phenomena such as fireworks are apparitions that have certain qualities of art—as a masque does—but are liberated from the obligation to endure, and hence from the obligation to be art.

On Engagement in A Masque

1. For the Hesperides, the daughters of Hesperus—the evening star—who tend the golden apples on the guarded tree, see Hesiod, *Theogony*, line 215. As Carey notes for lines 980–1 (in his text, which is a line shorter at this point), Milton speaks of Hesperus's *gardens*, in the plural (line 981), because in Pliny

these gardens were several islands in the western ocean. But Renaissance tradition tended to conflate them with Elysium. Milton clearly means one place, as the canceled lines of the Trinity manuscript show, in which the stream of ocean flows around a single island: "and round the verge / And sacred limits of this blisful isle / The jealous Ocean that old river winds / his far-extended arms" (S. E. Sprott, *A Maske: The Earlier Versions* (Toronto: University of Toronto Press, 1973), 46.

2. For *dynamis* "potential," see Aristotle, *Metaphysics*, 1046a.

3. David Knowles, *The Evolution of Medieval Thought* (New York: Vintage, 1962), 79. Charles Norris Cochrane, *Christianity and Classical Culture: A Study of Thought and Action from Augustus to Augustine* (Oxford: Clarendon, 1940), 398. Hopes for Christ's imminent return and the end of the world were fading already in the later first century. See Diarmaid MacCulloch, *A History of Christianity: The First Three Thousand Years* (London: Allen Lane, 2009), 118.

4. Andrew Marvell, *An Horatian Ode upon Cromwell's Return from Ireland*, in *The Poems of Andrew Marvell*, ed. Nigel Smith (London: Pearson/Longman, 2003), 276.

5. The best place to follow Milton's revisions of this passage in the Trinity manuscript is in the invaluable edition of Sprott, *A Maske*, 44, 46, 180, 182, 184.

6. Apuleius *Metamorphoses*, book 6, paragraph 24, lines 282–84.

7. Coleridge's fanciful Greek etymology, αἷμα+οἶνος, "blood wine," making the plant a symbol of the Eucharist, is ingenious but improbable, given Milton's respect for good Greek. See Earl Leslie Griggs, ed., *Collected Letters* (Oxford: Clarendon, 1956), 2:866–67. More likely is the nineteenth-century editor Thomas Keightley's suggestion in a note on the line that the word refers to *Haemonia*, another name for Thessaly in northern Greece, famous for magic. Thomas Keightley, ed., *The Poems of John Milton*, 2 vols. (London: Chapman and Hall, 1859). The *OED* etymology of *Haemony* is Greek αἷμον, "skillful," or αἱμώνιος, "bloodred." The color red is no help, and αἷμον in the *Iliad* (5.49) means "wily or skilled," referring to a hunter, which is also no help. For an account of the many theories associated with this word, see *Variorum* (II. 3: 932–38). *Haemonia* "Thessaly" seems to have been the primary association in Milton's mind, followed by the Roman god *Haemon*, as in "L'Allegro" (line 125). As for his description of the plant (lines 634–35), it recalls Sappho's mountain hyacinth carelessly trodden on by the shepherd, so that the purple flower is crushed on the ground, an image culled by Milton from Demetrius's *De Elocutione*. For the verses attributed to Sappho, see Edgar Lobel and Denys Page, eds., *Poetarum Lesbiorum Fragmenta* (Oxford: Clarendon, 1955), 87. The reference was discovered, and Milton's familiarity with *De Elocutione* shown, by Scott Elledge, "Milton, Sappho and Demetrius," *Modern Language Notes*58 (1943): 552–53. Cited in A. S. P. Woodhouse and D. Bush, *The Minor English Poems*, vol. 2 of *A Variorum Commentary on the Poems of John Milton*, gen. ed. Merritt Y. Hughes (New York: Columbia University Press, 1972), 930–38.

8. This is the, in my view correct argument of Stanley Fish's *How Milton Works* (Cambridge, Mass.: Harvard University Press, 2001).

On "Lycidas" as Primitive Art

1. Barbara K. Lewalski, *The Life of John Milton: A Critical Biography* (Oxford: Blackwell, 2000), 81–82. Pattison is quoted in A. S. P. Woodhouse and Douglas Bush's *Variorum Commentary on the Poems of John Milton*, vol. 2, part 2, *The Minor*

English Poems (New York: Columbia University Press, 1972), 568, as is Ruskin (674). Ruskin is quoted in full in Scott Elledge, ed., *Milton's "Lycidas": Edited to Serve as an Introduction to Criticism* (New York: Harper and Row, 1966), 237–44. Almost half a century ago, in a foreword to C. A. Patrides's *Milton's "Lycidas": The Tradition and the Poem* (Columbia: University of Missouri Press, 1963), M. H. Abrams called "Lycidas" "the greatest, and at any rate the most often discussed, of all lyric poems," and Patrides placed it "among the foremost productions of the human mind." In 1983, when the second, revised edition of Patrides appeared, twenty years after the first, Abrams called *Lycidas* "the lyric of lyrics," and a "standing challenge" to anyone intending to make a mark on the tradition of English literary criticism. Certainly they tried: in the second edition of his collection, Patrides speaks with only a little exaggeration of a "veritable explosion" of scholarship on the poem in the intervening twenty years (x, xi, xiv, xvii, and 345). Woodhouse and Bush's *Variorum* appeared in 1972, almost exactly halfway between Patrides's two editions. Woodhouse and Bush survey the critical tradition to date, from Samuel Johnson's strictures on Milton's use of the pastoral form to the beginning of modern criticism of Milton in 1930, with E. M. W. Tillyard's *Milton* (566 and 572–73). Following Emile Legouis, Tillyard says the poem is about Milton, not Edward King. Woodhouse and Bush date the beginning of modern scholarship on the poem from James Holly Hanford's groundbreaking survey of the pastoral tradition, "The Pastoral Elegy and Milton's 'Lycidas,'" *PMLA* 25 (1910): 403–47. After Tillyard, Woodhouse and Bush summarize no less than sixty critics, most of them prominent figures in their day. My own view is that modern criticism of "Lycidas" stems from Arthur Barker's standard account of its three-part structure in "The Pattern of Milton's *Nativity Ode*," *University of Toronto Quarterly* 10 (1941): 171–72; A. S. P. Woodhouse's "Milton's Pastoral Monodies," in *Studies in Honour of Gilbert Norwood*, ed. M. E. White (Toronto: University of Toronto Press, 1952), 261–78; and M. H. Abrams's "Five Types of 'Lycidas,'" in Patrides, *Milton's "Lycidas."* In Abrams, "Lycidas" is for the first time treated as a proving ground for different approaches to the reading of poetry: "the necessary, though not sufficient condition for a competent reader of poetry remains what it has always been—a keen eye for the obvious" (Patrides, *Milton's "Lycidas,"* 235). An essay just missed by the second Patrides edition is Paul Alpers, "'Lycidas' and Modern Criticism," *English Literary History* 49 (1982): 468–96. See also Alpers, *What Is Pastoral?* (Chicago: University of Chicago Press, 1996), 93–112. Alpers responds to the final essay in Patrides in Stanley E. Fish, "'Lycidas': A Poem Finally Anonymous," in *Glyph: Johns Hopkins Textual Studies 8*, ed. Walter B. Michaels (Baltimore: Johns Hopkins University Press, 1981), 319–40.

The argument for a prophetic and visionary Milton, a forerunner of Blake, is moved in Joseph A. Wittreich's *Visionary Poetics: Milton's Tradition and His Legacy* (San Marino, Calif.: Huntington Library, 1979). For a magisterial political reading of Lycidas, see Mary Ann Radzinowicz, *Toward Samson Agonistes: The Growth of Milton's Mind* (Princeton, N.J.: Princeton University Press, 1978), 119–26. See also Radzinowicz's "The Politics of *Paradise Lost*," in *Politics of Discourse: The Literature and History of Seventeenth-Century England*, ed. Kevin Sharpe and Stephen N. Zwicker (Berkeley: University of California Press, 1987), 204–29.

2. The first critic to see the importance of different time frames in *Lycidas* was Lowry Nelson, Jr., in "Milton's *Lycidas*," in Nelson, *Baroque Lyric Poetry* (New Haven, Conn.: Yale University Press, 1961), 64–76.

3. "Concepts of death involving ships and boats often accompany the sun cult." Erik Nylén, *Stones, Ships, and Symbols: The Picture Stones of Gotland from the Viking Age and Before* (Stockholm: Gidlunds, 1988), 22. See also John Livingston Lowes, *The Road to Xanadu: A Study in the Ways of the Imagination* (Boston: Houghton Mifflin, 1927), 274–80 and 558–65.

4. Too much credence has been given to F. T. Prince's assertion of the influence of the Italian *canzone*, in *The Italian Element in Milton's Verse* (1954; repr., Oxford: Clarendon, 1962), 71–88. Prince does indeed cite the *canzone*, but as only one among several verse forms in Italian Renaissance eclogues; Prince cautions "that there is no exact parallel in Italian literature to the pattern of Milton's poem" (88 and 71). In fact, the only relevant comparison with the *canzone* is the use of a short line in the middle of the stanza—the "key" or *chiave*—rhyming with a preceding line: the rhyme turns us back, and the brevity of the line propels us forward (86–87). The comparison of Milton's final stanza in *ottava rima* with the *commiato* of the *canzone*, with which, says Prince, the final stanza "undoubtedly corresponds in its own way" (73 and 84), is illusory. Like the purloined letter, the model for Milton's stanza in "Lycidas" and for his use of the syncopating short line elsewhere is in plain view, in Edmund Spenser's *Epithalamion*. Among the many influences that went in to the making of the improvisational brilliance of the verse of "Lycidas," Pindar should be counted. See Stella P. Revard, *Milton and the Tangles of Neaera's Hair: The Making of the 1645 Poems* (Columbia: University of Missouri Press, 1997), 131–56.

5. Patrides, *Milton's"Lycidas,"* xvii.

6. *Childe Harold's Pilgrimage*, in *Poetical Works*, ed. Frederick Page, revised by John D. Jump (Oxford: Oxford University Press, 1970), 2.57; Mikhail Lermontov, *A Hero of Our Time*, trans. Paul Foote (London: Penguin, 1966); Laurence Kelly, *Lermontov: Tragedy in the Caucasus* (1978; repr., London: Tauris Parke, 2003); Leo Tolstoy, *Hadji Murad*, trans. Aylmer Maude (New York: Modern Library, 2003).

7. James Joyce, *Ulysses* (London: Bodley Head, 1967), 63.

8. Theocritus, *Idylls*, 7.68. Hesiod, *Works and Days*, 41. *Odyssey*, 11.539: "meadow of asphodels" ἀσφοδελὸν λειμῶνα. See the note on this line by W. B. Stanford, ed., *The Odyssey of Homer*, 2nd ed. (London: Macmillan, 1959).

9. Mircea Eliade, *Shamanism: Archaic Techniques of Ecstasy*, trans. Willard R. Trask, Bollingen Series 76 (Princeton, N.J.: Princeton University Press, 1964), 63 and 435, for the skeleton as transcendent. For a discussion of Greek and Roman burial rites involving partial cremation to preserve the bones, rendering them "dried up" or skeletos, at once preserving the body and freeing the vapory psychê, "soul," and the moist thumos, the vital powers associated with the viscera, see Richard Broxton Onians, *The Origins of European Thought about the Body, the Mind, the Soul, the World, Time, and Fate* (Cambridge: Cambridge University Press, 1951), 261–64. Other indispensable studies are E. R. Dodds, *The Greeks and the Irrational* (Berkeley: University of California Press, 1951), especially the chapters "The Blessings of Madness" (64–101) and "The Greek Shamans and the Origins of Puritanism" (135–78); John Block Friedman, *Orpheus in the Middle Ages* (Cambridge, Mass.: Harvard University Press, 1970); and M. L. West, *The Orphic Poems* (Oxford: Clarendon Press, 1983).

10. *Measure for Measure*, 3.1.126. For suffering caused by the psychological absence of purgatory in Protestant culture, see Stephen Greenblatt, *Hamlet in Purgatory* (Princeton, N.J.: Princeton University Press, 2001).

11. The *glory* in "singing in their glory" (line 180) refers to the curious passage in 1 Corinthians 15:40–43, in which Paul speaks of the different "glories" of earthly and heavenly bodies, and of the differences of "glory" between one star and another. In biblical Greek "glory" is *doxa*, which means something very different from what it meant in the classical period, opinon, as opposed to knowledge. *Doxa* now means "reputation, honor" and even "splendor." The honor and reputation in question is that accorded to different bodies in Heaven, by the angels and ultimately by God. For Paul, this honor or *doxa*, which is how one is seen from without, is also a metaphysical condition, a state of ontological transformation. A body with glory is totally different in being from the same body without glory. Paul is driving at the difference between human bodies on earth and in Heaven, after the resurrection: "So also is the resurrection of the dead. It is sewn in corruption; it is raised in incorruption: It is sown in dishonor *(en atimia)*; it is raised in glory *(en doxê)*" (15:42–44). The body is sown in earth as corruptible and subject to change. But at the resurrection the body is raised in glory and splendor. It is a new ontic condition for the body, but it is constituted phenomenologically as a way of being seen, of appearing, as the opposition with "unglory" *(atimia)* shows. Glory is reputation, and in this sense, at least for Milton—but I think for early Christians, too—glory has the luster of heroic honor, the *timê* won by epic heroes. We should note that it is not the angels but rather the "saints"—that is, resurrected and glorified human beings—who "entertain" Lycidas in Heaven, that is, hold him among themselves (Fr. *entretenir*) as they sing in their state of glory. This sense of glory, as a transfigured state of being worthy of praise, is significant for the conclusion of "Mansus," in which Milton imagines himself in the future, having gone to an Olympian Heaven of poetic achievement, applauding himself. Applause for literary accomplishment is the decorous, classical counterpart of the Christian mystery of glorification.

12. Although the word looks like "image," it is dialect term for songs related to *aeidô*, "to sing, chant," and has no etymological relation to seeing or images. The common translation of *eidullia* as "little pictures" is an error. See J. M. Edmonds, ed., *The Greek Bucolic Poets Loeb Classical Library* (Cambridge, Mass.: Harvard University Press, 1928), xix–xx.

13. Ibid., xxv.

14. For the bees of the Hyblaean mountains in Sicily, see Virgil, *Eclogues*, 1.54.

15. For the height of Oromedon, the association of the crowing cock with Apollonius of Rhodes, and of the Chian nightingale with Homer, I follow the notes of Edmonds in *Greek Bucolic Poets*, 95 and 97.

16. Ovid, *Metamorphoses*, 5.572–641. Pausanias, *Description of Greece*, 5.7.2–3. See Pausanias's *Description of Greece*, trans. with commentary, J. G. Frazer, 6 vols. (1897; repr., New York: Biblio and Tannen, 1965), 1:245. For the legends of cups and sacred offal traveling to Sicily in the stream Alpheus, see 3:483.

17. Jacopo Sannazaro, "Ecloga V," in *Arcadia, L'Arcadie*, ed. Francesco Erspamer, trans. Gérard Marino (Paris: Belles Lettres, 2004), 79–81. The relation of this eclogue to *Lycidas* is well known, and interesting on more points than the repetition of the word *other*. See Prince, *The Italian Element in Milton's Verse*, 76.

18. Samuel Johnson, "Milton," in *The Lives of the Poets*, ed. Stephen Fix (New Haven, Conn.: Yale University Press, 2010), 1:176. In his "Life of Cowley," which

precedes the life of Milton, Johnson comments on the wonder occasioned by Cowley's "learned puerilities": "this comedy is of the pastoral kind, which requires no acquaintance with the living world, and therefore the time at which it was composed adds little to the wonders of Cowley's minority" (7–8).

19. Charles Baudelaire, "Perte d'auréole," in *Petits poèmes en prose (Le Spleen de Paris)*, ed. Pierre-Louis Rey (Paris: Pocket, 1995), 130.

20. Charles Baudelaire, "Le Cygne," in *Les Fleurs du Mal*, ed. Antoine Adam (Paris: Garnier, 1959), 141–42, lines 17–23.

21. For an exemplary reading, see Balachandra Rajan, *"Lycidas:* The Shattering of the Leaves," in Patrides, *Milton's "Lycidas,"* 267–80, from chapter 4 of *The Lofty Rhyme: A Study of Milton's Major Poetry* (London: Routledge and Kegan Paul, 1970).

22. W. G. Madsen, "The Voice of Michael in 'Lycidas,'" *SEL* 3 (1963): 1–7; repeated with elaboration in *From Shadowy Types to Truth* (New Haven, Conn.: Yale University Press, 1968), 6–17.

23. John Creaser, "Dolphins in 'Lycidas'," *Review of English Studies* 36 (1985): 236–43. Creaser shows how no specific dolphin myth fits the context and purpose of Milton's dolphins, but the general view of the dolphin as *philanthropos* ("the friend to man") included wafting to shore bodies drowned in the sea. For the frequent image of dolphins on ancient sarcophagi, see Creaser, "Dolphins in 'Lycidas,'" 241, with citations. See also Marie-Claire Anne Beaulieu, "The Sea as a Two-Way Passage between Life and Death in Greek Mythology" (PhD diss., University of Texas at Austin, 2008), 9 and 77–106.

24. Pierre Encrevé and Albert Pacquement, ed., *Pierre Soulages* (Paris: Centre Pompidou, 2009).

25. Peter Sacks, *The English Elegy: Studies in the Genre from Spenser to Yeats* (Baltimore: Johns Hopkins University Press, 1985), 115.

26. C. S. Jerram, *The "Lycidas" and Epitaphium Damonis of Milton* (London, 1874), 84, note on line 166.

27. Wallace Stevens, *The Collected Poems of Wallace Stevens* (New York: Knopf, 1974), 304.

On the Interstitial Latin Poems and an English Fragment

1. "Fix Here," in *Milton: The Complete Shorter Poems*, ed. John Carey, 2nd ed. (Edinburgh Gate, Harlow: Longman, Pearson: 2007), 257 and n.

2. S. M. Oberhelman and John Mulryan, "Milton's Use of Classical Meters in the 'Sylvarum Liber'," *Modern Philology* 81 (1983): 131–45.

3. Richard Fanshawe's brilliant English translation of this epic poem would not be published until 1655. But Milton may have heard of it or seen it. Even without Portuguese he would have been able to make much of it out, because Camões's diction is highly Latinate. See *The Poems and Translations of Sir Richard Fanshawe*, 2 vols., ed. Peter Davidson (Oxford: Clarendon: 1997–1999). *The Lusiad, or, Portugals historicall poem* is in volume 1.

4. Diodati was studying theology in Geneva in 1630, the birthplace of his father, a protestant exile from Italy, and of his uncle Giovanni, the famous Protestant theologian whom Milton would meet. Gordon Campbell, "Diodati, Charles (1609/10–1638)," *Oxford Dictionary of National Biography* (Oxford University

Press, 2004). Diodati's family was originally from Lucca and it is not impossible he did travel to Italy at some point during his studies. But this seems to me doubtful. He soon returned to England and a brief medical career. See Barbara Lewalski, *The Life of John Milton: A Critical Biography* (Oxford: Blackwell, 2000), 38.

5. E. M. W. Tillyard, *Milton*, ed. Phyllis B. Tillyard, rev. ed. (New York: Collier, 1967), 144. "Not that the style is predominantly Pindaric: the ode is a mixture of stateliness and of half-humorous and urbane elegance" (146).

6. The volume might be called *three* books in one, because in it *A Masque Presented at Ludlow Castle, 1634*, has its own title page and front matter, but the masque is on signatures continuous with the rest of the English poems, which it follows. "Lycidas" is placed before it. From the point of view of the printing house, the book is double. From the point of view of its presentation, the book is triple. For critical discussion of the volume, see Stella Purce Revard, *Milton and the Tangles of Neaera's Hair: The Making of the 1645 Poems* (Columbia: University of Missouri Press, 1997).

7. Lewalski, *The Life of John Milton*, 206–8.

On the Sonnets and Shorter Poems of the Political Period

1. See *Milton: The Complete Shorter Poems*, ed. John Carey, 2nd ed. (Edinburgh Gate, Harlow: Longman, Pearson: 2007), 341–42.

2. Arthur Barker, *Milton and the Puritan Dilemma, 1641–1660* (Toronto: University of Toronto Press, 1942), 111.

3. Carey, ed., *Shorter Poems*, 308–9. Masson, *Life*, 3:283.

4. Horace, *Satires*, book 10, satire 10, lines 14–15.

5. See Ramie Targoff, *Posthumous Love: Eros and the Afterlife in Renaissance England* (Chicago: University of Chicago Press, 2014).

6. Carey, ed., *Shorter Poems*, 328.

7. *YP* 2.566.

8. (*Columbia*, 6:262). When he wrote his *Observations*, Milton could not have foreseen what havoc Cromwell's army was soon to wreak in Ireland but, given his characterization of the Irish, he probably accepted it as necessary. Most Englishmen did. See Lewalski, *Life*, 244. See Thomas Corns, "Milton's *Observations upon the Articles of Peace*: Ireland under English Eyes," in *Politics, Poetics, and Hermeneutics in Milton's Prose*, ed. David Loewenstein and James Grantham Turner (Cambridge: Cambridge University Press, 1990), 123–34.

9. The Greek original of *reficiam* is ἀναπαύσω, "I will give you rest," as the Authorized (KJV) Version has it. The word is repeated as a substantive in the following verse, ἀνάπαυσιν, and this is followed in the Authorized Version: "ye shall find rest unto your souls." The Latin text, however, has *restoration* at first—*ego reficiam vos*—and *rest* after: "*invenietis requiem animabus vestris.*"

10. Stewart Perowne, *The Life and Times of Herod the Great* (London: Hodder and Stoughton, 1956), 129–35.

11. See Mary Ann Radzinowicz, *Milton's Epic and the Book of Psalms* (Princeton: Princeton University Press, 1989), 5.

On the Romantics and the Principles of Milton

1. I shall be concerned in this chapter with the men among the major Romantics who were in varying degrees preoccupied with Milton: William Blake, William Wordsworth, Samuel Taylor Coleridge, George Gordon Lord Byron, John Keats, and Percy Bysshe Shelley. I am aware that the term *Romantics* can, has been, and should be expanded. *Paradise Lost* plays a large role in Mary Shelley's *Frankenstein*, in which the monster achieves human awareness—and awareness of his nonhumanity—by reading Milton's epic and comparing himself with Adam and with Satan. Milton's Satan and Shelley's monster are hostile to their respective creators. But Mary Shelley, like Felicia Hemans, seems to have an untroubled relation to Milton, in contrast with the agonistic and imitative one suffered by the male Romantic poets. (See Bate and Bloom, below.) Indeed, women authors appear to have been impatient with the awe in which Milton was held. As Mary Wollstonecraft said, "I am sick of hearing of the sublimity of Milton." "Thoughts on the Education of Daughters," in *Posthumous Works of the Author of "A Vindication of the Rights of Women,"* ed. William Godwin (London: J. Johnson, 1798), 4:21; cited in Joseph Anthony Wittreich, "Miltonic Romanticism," in *The Oxford Handbook of Milton*, ed. Nicholas McDowell and Nigel Smith (Oxford: Oxford University Press, 2009), 693. Of all the romantics, Wollstonecraft's character and temperament seem to me closest to Milton's. Anyone interested in the problem of Milton's relation to the Romantics will owe an immense debt of gratitude to Joseph Anthony Wittreich, whose *The Romantics on Milton: Formal Essays and Critical Asides* (Cleveland: Case Western Reserve University Press, 1970) is referred to hereafter as *Wittreich*. Wittreich covers the six major Romantic poets, but he also surveys Milton's vital presence in Romantic criticism—criticism by Wordsworth and Coleridge, but also by Charles Lamb, Walter Savage Landor, William Hazlitt, Leigh Hunt and Thomas De Quincey.

2. See René Wellek, *The Rise of English Literary History* (Chapel Hill: University of North Carolina Press, 1941).

3. Northrop Frye, *A Study of English Romanticism* (New York: Random House, 1968), p. 16. Ian Balfour, *The Rhetoric of Romantic Prophecy* (Stanford: Stanford University Press, 2002), 183.

4. Wittreich, "Miltonic Romanticism," 704. See also *Angel of Apocalypse: Blake's Idea of Milton* (Madison: University of Wisconsin Press, 1975); and Joseph Anthony Wittreich, ed., *Milton and the Line of Vision* (Madison: University of Wisconsin Press, 1975).

5. See Wittreich's discussion, in "Miltonic Romanticism," of the radical William Godwin's effort at "wrestling Milton down, reconstituting his vision," but only as a way of "furthering his revelations" (688).

6. Edward Said, *Orientalism* (New York: Pantheon, 1978).

7. Andrew Warren, *The Orient and the Young Romantics* (Cambridge: Cambridge University Press, 2014), 182–86; see especially the chapter on Shelley, "The Sandy Desert of Politics: The Orient and Solitude in *The Revolt of Islam*" (185–230). Similar scenes are played out among oriental lovers in Tasso, one of Milton's models, although they are awakened to the knowledge of Christ.

8. Georg Wilhelm Friedrich Hegel, *Lectures on the Philosophy of History*, trans. H. B. Nisbet (Cambridge: Cambridge University Press, 1975), 54.

9. Percy Bysshe Shelley, *The Poems of Shelley*, vol. 2, ed. Kevin Everest and Geoffrey Matthews (Harlow, England: Longman/Pearson, 2000), 474.

10. John Toland, *The Life of John Milton* (1698), in *The Early Lives of Milton*, ed. Helen Darbishire (1932; repr., New York: Barnes and Noble, 1965), 180.

11. Walter Jackson Bate, *The Burden of the Past and the English Poet* (Cambridge, Mass.: Harvard University Press, 1970); Harold Bloom, *The Anxiety of Influence: A Theory of Poetry* (New York: Oxford University Press, 1973).

12. See Charles Mahoney, *Romantics and Renegades: the Poetics of Political Reaction* (New York: Palgrave, 2003).

13. Review of Comus, *Examiner*, June 11, 1815. P. P. Howe, ed., *The Complete Works of William Hazlitt* (London: Dent, 1930), 5:233. Hazlitt was just as savage with that other political apostate, Coleridge, especially for the snobbery, conservatism, and absurdity of his *The Statesman's Manual*.

14. Leigh Hunt, *The Examiner*, February 18, 1816. In *The Examiner*, photographic reprint, introduced by Yasuo Deguchi, vols. 6–10, 1813–1817 (London: Pickering and Chatto, 1997), 9:98–99. For the importance of *The Examiner*, see Charles Mahoney's review of these volumes, in *Romantic Circles* 2, no. 1 (1998).

15. *Don Juan*, dedication, stanza 10, line 76. Frederick Page, ed., *Poetical Works*, revised by John D. Jump (Oxford: Oxford University Press, 1970).

16. C. M. Bowra, *From Virgil to Milton* (London: Macmillan, 1945), 246.

17. Andrew Marvell, "On Mr. Milton's *Paradise Lost*," in *The Poems of Andrew Marvell*, ed. Nigel Smith (London: Pearson/Longman, 2003), 180–84.

18. James Kinsley, ed., *The Poems and Fables of John Dryden* (London: Oxford University Press, 1962), 424.

19. Editors and critics of Milton, with few exceptions, long held the view that the poet prevaricated between the old Ptolemaic system and the modern one. But Milton never prevaricates, and he puts the Ptolemaic spheres in his Paradise of Fools (see *PL*, 3.481–84 and notes). John Leonard has traced this longstanding error in Milton scholarship and restored one of epochal effects of Milton's *Paradise Lost*, the poem's extraordinary apprehension of space. See his final chapter, "The Universe," in vol. 2 of *Faithful Labourers: A Reception History of "Paradise Lost," 1667–1970* (Oxford: Oxford University Press, 2013), 705–820. See also Angus Fletcher, *Time, Space, and Motion in the Age of Shakespeare* (Cambridge, Mass.: Harvard University Press, 2007).

20. To J. H. Reynolds, Letter 76, April 9, 1818, *The Letters of John Keats*, vol. 1, ed. Hyder Rollins (Cambridge, Mass.: Harvard University Press, 1958), 268. Keats proposed to "gorge wonders" during the second, canceled trip to Scotland. It was of the first trip that Keats told Benjamin Bailey he expected to "identify finer scenes, load me with grander mountains, and strengthen more my reach in poetry." See Walter Jackson Bate, *John Keats* (Cambridge, Mass.: Harvard University Press, 1964), 357–68, and Helen Vendler, *The Odes of John Keats* (Cambridge, Mass.: Harvard University Press), 226.

21. *Jerusalem*, plate 3, "To the Public." G. E. Bentley Jr., ed., *William Blake's Writings*, vol. 1, *Engraved and Etched Writings* (Oxford: Clarendon Press, 1978), 419. Further references to Blake are to this edition.

22. Erich Auerbach, "Odysseus' Scar," in *Mimesis: The Representation of Reality in Western Literature*, trans. Willard R. Trask; intro. for this ed. by Edward W. Said (1953; repr., Princeton, N.J.: Princeton University Press, 2003), 4: "to represent phenomena in a fully externalized form, visible and palpable in all their parts, and completely fixed in their spatial and temporal relations."

23. To Peter Heimbach, November 8, 1656. *Columbia*, 12:82.

24. See John Livingston Lowes, *The Road to Xanadu: A Study in the Ways of the Imagination* (Boston: Houghton Mifflin, 1927), 312–23 passim, for Coleridge's delight in narratives of travel and exploration.

25. Wordsworth, *The Prelude* (1805), book 1, line 335. Nicolas Halmi, ed., *Wordsworth's Poetry and Prose* (New York: Norton, 2014).

26. Percy Bysshe Shelley, *The Poems of Shelley*, vol. 2, ed. Kevin Everest and Geoffrey Matthews (Harlow, England: Longman/Pearson, 2000), 472. See Danielle St. Hilaire, *Satan's Poetry: Fallenness and Poetic Tradition in "Paradise Lost"* (Pittsburgh: Duquesne University Press, 2012).

27. On Satan as the product of Milton's talent and originality, see Tobias Gregory, *From Many Gods to One: Divine Action in the Renaissance Epic* (Chicago: University of Chicago Press, 2006), 96–97; and Armand Himy, *John Milton, 1608–1674* (Paris: Fayard, 2003), 475, who, after mentioning the classical and biblical elements that went into the construction of Satan, adds (I translate) that "a properly and uniquely Miltonic crown is placed on these various borrowings, and gives them an undeniable reality."

28. "What is a Poet? To whom does he address himself? And what language is to be expected from him? He is a man speaking to men." "Preface to *Lyrical Ballads*, Second Edition (1802)," in Halmi, *Wordsworth's Poetry and Prose*, 85. See Stephen Gill, ed., *William Wordsworth* (Oxford: Oxford University Press, 1984), 603. For Romantic *improvisatori*, see Angela Esterhammer, *Romanticism and Improvisation, 1750–1850* (Cambridge: Cambridge University Press, 2008).

29. These phrases and the ones shortly to follow are from Milton's polemical defense of the measure of *Paradise Lost*, "The Verse," which was added to a later issue (the fourth, 1668) of the first edition (1667), in response to complaints that the poem, as the publisher expressed it, "rhymes not." See *PL*, p. 2, note.

30. *The Poems of Shelley*, vol. 2, ed. Kevin Everest and Geoffrey Matthews (Harlow, England: Longman/Pearson, 2000), 42. The poem in this edition is titled *Laon and Cynthia; Or, The Revolution of the Golden City: A Vision of the Nineteenth Century, In the Stanza of Spenser*.

31. Keats, Letter 193, to J. H. Reynolds, September 21, 1819: "I have given up Hyperion—there were too many Miltonic inversions in it—Miltonic verse cannot be written but in an artful or rather artist's humour. I wish to give myself up to other sensations. English ought to be kept up." Keats also mentions with distaste the appearance every now and then in *Hyperion* of "a Miltonic intonation" that he himself is unable to detect (167). In Letter 199, to George and Georgiana Keats, September 24, 1819, Keats repeats much of this and adds he has "lately stood on my guard against Milton [because] Life to him would be death to me" (212). Hyder Edward Rollins, ed., *The Letters of John Keats: 1814–1821* (Cambridge, Mass.: Harvard University Press, 1958), vol. 2. "Miltonic inversions" are the least of Keats's problems with Milton in *Hyperion* and its revision, *The Fall of Hyperion*. The experiment is too closely modeled on the first two books of *Paradise Lost*, especially

the "great consult" of devils (*PL*, 1.798), imitated in the harangues of Keats's titans, and it is doubtful Keats had any clear conception where he would take the story from there. The words of Keats's Saturn could equally be his own: "I am gone / Away from my own bosom: I have left / My strong identity, my real self" (lines 112–14). Even so, the *Hyperion* poems are a most impressive experiment. They show Keats composing with massive sculptural power, abandoning the sentimentality of *Endymion* for what he called "a more naked and grecian manner" (Rollins, *Letters*, 1:207). See Ian Jack, *Keats and the Mirror of Art* (Oxford: Clarendon Press, 1967), 161–62, and John Keats, *Complete Poems*, 2nd ed., ed. Jack Stillinger (Cambridge, Mass.: Harvard University Press, 1982), 361–73.

32. "Observations Upon an Article in Blackwood's Magazine," in *The Complete Works of Lord Byron*, ed. John Galt (Paris: Baudry's European Library, 1835), 715.

33. Letter to James Hogg, March 24, 1814. *Selected Letters*, ed. Leslie A. Marchand (1973; repr., Cambridge, Mass.: Harvard University Press, 1982), 100.

34. *Don Juan*, canto 1, stanza 205. *Wittreich*, 517.

35. *The Prelude* (1805), book 3, lines 294–306. As an undergraduate in the 1620s Milton did not have "apartments" at Christ's College, nor is it probable he had a room to himself. Tradition has him in a dormitory adjoining the gate.

36. *The Prelude* (1805), book 3, lines 284–88. Halmi, *Wordsworth's Poetry and Prose*, 202 and note 5.

37. *Wittreich*, 119.

38. *The Charles Lamb Bulletin*, issues 97–104 (London: Charles Lamb Society, 1973), 14.

39. The phrase *republican austerity* is from a letter to Walter Savage Landor, April 20, 1822. The other quotations are from a letter to an unknown correspondent, November 1802; see *Wittreich*, 134 and 110.

40. "London, 1802," in Halmi, *Wordsworth's Poetry and Prose*. In 1820 Wordsworth changed the reflexive pronoun of *thy heart* from *itself* to *herself*.

41. *The Excursion*, 1.249; and 7.534–36; cited in *Wittreich*, 103 and 112.

42. *The Prelude* (1805), book 13, lines 31–73; Halmi, *Wordsworth's Poetry and Prose*, 366–67. In the 1850 *Prelude* Wordsworth hews more closely still to Milton's words.

43. For an account of *The Excursion* and its relation to *The Prelude* and *The Recluse*, see Halmi, *Wordsworth's Poetry and Prose*, 440–43. Halmi's notes on the "preface" to the *Excursion* pick up the more salient borrowings from and allusions to Milton.

44. See Simon Jarvis, *Wordsworth's Philosophic Song* (Cambridge: Cambridge University Press, 2007). I cite this brilliant study not as support for the view I have expressed—that an aspiration to philosophic truth put Wordsworth on the wrong path—since Jarvis takes nearly the opposite view: that despite himself, a philosophical value attaches to Wordsworth's poetry. I am far from opposing such a claim. But I think Wordsworth's philosophic song is successful when he is not thinking of either of two things: (1) philosophy; (2) Milton.

45. Halmi, *Wordsworth's Poetry and Prose*; *The Excursion*, "preface," lines 1–41.

46. "Of the Measure, in which the following Poem is written," *Jerusalem*, plate 3, paragraph 3.

47. *The Poems of Shelley*, vol. 2, ed. Kevin Everest and Geoffrey Matthews (Harlow, England: Longman/Pearson, 2000), 474.

48. To John Murray, November 3, 1821 (Marchand, *Byron's Letters and Journals*, 9:53).

49. Thomas Medwin, *Journal of the Conversations of Lord Byron: Noted during a Residence with His Lordship at Pisa, in the Years 1821 and 1822*, a New Edition (London, 1824), 243.

50. Shelley's remarks are from *On the Devil and Devils*, in *Wittreich*, 534–35. Charles Baudelaire, *"Fusées,"* in *Oeuvres complètes*, ed. Claude Pichois (Paris: Gallimard, 1975), 1:657–58: "des besoins spirituels, des ambitions ténébreusement refoulées—l'idée d'une puissance grondante, et sans emploi—quelquefois l'idée d'une insensibilté vengeresse (car le type idéal du Dandy n'est pas a negligé dans ce sujet) . . . et enfin (pour que j'aie le courage d'avouer jusqu'à quel point je me sens moderne en esthétique), le *Malheur* . . . le plus parfait type de Beauté virile est *Satan*—à la manière de Milton" ("Strange spiritual needs, ambitions that have been obscurely denied—the idea of a growling, rumbling power, but without employment—sometimes the notion of a vengeful callousness (for in this subject the ideal type of the Dandy is not to be neglected) . . . and finally (so that I might have the courage to avow to what extent I feel myself to be modern in aesthetics) *Misfortune* . . . the most perfect type of virile Beauty is *Satan*—in the style of Milton"). See Himy, *John Milton*, 480–81. Chateaubriand's translation of Milton's description of Satan—"un excès de gloire obscurcie"—illustrates Baudelaire's point. Quoted by Pichois (1480).

51. William Empson, *Milton's God*, 2nd ed. (London: Chatto and Windus, 1965), 14–21.

52. Shelley, *The Poems of Shelley*, vol. 2, ed. Kevin Everest and Geoffrey Matthews (Harlow, England: Longman/Pearson, 2000), 472–73.

53. *Wittreich*, 535.

54. *The Poems of Shelley*, vol. 2, ed. Kevin Everest and Geoffrey Matthews (Harlow, England: Longman/Pearson, 2000), 472. David Loewenstein observes that "Shelley was by no means an unqualified Satanist," *Paradise Lost* (Cambridge: Cambridge University Press, 1993), 134. I would say he was not a Satanist at all, which is why he invented Prometheus.

55. *The Poems of Shelley*, vol. 2, ed. Kevin Everest and Geoffrey Matthews (Harlow, England: Longman/Pearson, 2000), 473.

56. Northrop Frye, "The Case against Locke," in *Fearful Symmetry: A Study of William Blake*, ed. Nicholas Halmi, vol. 14, *The Collected Works of Northrop Frye* (Toronto: University of Toronto Press, 2004), 11–36.

57. *Europe*, plate 1, entire page. The title, "The Ancient of Days," appears in another version. See *William Blake's Writings, Europe*, plate 1, 204 and 222. The phrase and image are from the throne vision in Daniel 7:9: "I beheld till the thrones were cast down, and the Ancient of Days did sit, whose garment was white as snow, and the hair of his head like the pure wool: his throne was like the fiery flame, and his wheels as burning fire."

58. *The Marriage of Heaven and Hell*, plate 6, paragraph 22, page 80.

59. Ibid., paragraphs 11 and 12, page 78.

60. Ibid., plates 5–6, paragraphs 13–16 and 21–22, pages 79–80.

61. *Milton*, plate 14, lines 47–50. I have benefited from Armand Himy's fine chapter on Blake's *Milton*, "Une Quête de soi: *Milton*," in *William Blake: Peintre et Poète* (Paris: Fayard, 2008), 187–216.

62. See Stephen Fallon, *Milton among the Philosophers: Poetry and Materialism in "Paradise Lost"* (Ithaca, N.Y.: Cornell University Press, 1991); and John Rogers, *The Matter of Revolution: Science, Poetry, and Politics in the Age of Milton* (Ithaca, N.Y.: Cornell University Press, 1996).

63. *Milton*, plate 2, line 8, page 318.

64. *Milton*, plate 12, lines 28–32, page 344.

On History in Paradise Lost

1. For an excellent account of Milton during this period, see Frank Kermode, "Milton in Old Age," *An Appetite for Poetry* (Cambridge, Mass.: Harvard University Press, 1989), 59–78. Kermode's supposition that Milton's act of submission (assuming he had to make one to be released from prison) was "a violation of his own purity" causing permanent trauma (77) strikes me as attaching too much psychological importance to such an act, if it took place.

2. *The Tenure of Kings and Magistrates* (*YP*, 3:206–7): "the king or magistrate holds his authority of the people." "We may from hence with ease and force of argument determine what a tyrant is and what the people may do against him" (212). "Lawless king" (257). "No man who knows aught can be so stupid to deny that all men naturally were born free, being the image and resemblance of God himself, and were by privilege above all the creatures born to command and not to obey; and that they lived so. Till from the root of Adam's transgression falling among themselves to do wrong and violence and foreseeing that such courses must needs tend to the destruction of them all, they agreed by common league to bind each other from mutual injury, and jointly to defend themselves against any that gave disturbance and opposition to such agreement" (*YP* 3:198–99).

3. "They who seek nothing but their own just liberty have always the right to win it and to keep it, whenever they have the power, be the voices never so numerous that oppose it"; see *The Ready and Easy Way to Establish a Free Commonwealth*, 2nd ed. (April 1–10, 1660), (*YP*, 7 rev. ed., 455). This passage does not occur in the first edition of the tract (February 23–29, 1660), in which Milton does not feel he is speaking to a minority, and in which he is warning the entire nation of the irreversibility of submission: "besides the loss of all their blood and treasure spent to no purpose . . . they never be able to regain what they now have purchased and may enjoy, or to free themselves from any yoke imposed on them" (*YP*, 7, rev. ed., 378).

4. "He began about 2 years before the K. came in, and finished about 3 years after the K's Restauracion"; see John Aubrey, "Minutes of the Life of Mr. John Milton," in *The Early Lives of Milton*, ed. Helen Darbishire (London: Constable, 1932), 13. Whether we may regard the English Revolution as coming to its true end in 1688 instead of 1660, or 1658, is a question for the theorists of revolution. The history books give exact dates for when revolutions begin and end. The reality is far more complex, and always a matter of interpretation. See Crane Brinton's, *The Anatomy of Revolution*, 2nd ed. (New York: Vintage, 1965), 86 and 226–27.

5. David Masson, *The Life of John Milton, Narrated in Connexion with the Political, Eccleasiastical, and Literary History of his Time* (1881; repr., Glouscester, Mass.: Peter Smith, 1965), 6: 500–509. For the stones of the collapsing church

breaking the vaults where the paper was stored, see 508. Barbara K. Lewalski, *The Life of John Milton* (Oxford: Blackwell, 2000), 451–53.

6. John Dryden, *Annus Mirabilis*, lines 21–24. *Poems and Fables*, ed. James Kinsley (Oxford: Oxford University Press, 1962).

7. Jonathan Richardson Sr., "Explanatory Notes and Remarks on Milton's *Paradise Lost*," in Helen Darbishire, *The Early Lives of Milton* (1932; repr., New York: Barnes and Noble, 1965), 295.

8. Edmund Waller, "On the Foregoing Divine Poems," lines 13–18, in *The Poetical Works of Edmund Waller and Sir John Denham*, ed. George Gilfillan (Edinburgh: Nichol, 1857), 200.

9. Sir John Denham, "Cooper's Hill," lines 189–92, in *Poetical Works of Edmund Waller and Sir John Denham*, 221.

10. John Dryden, *Astraea Redux*, lines 87–92. *Poems and Fables*, ed. James Kinsley.

11. Masson, *Life of John Milton*, 6.620–30. The contract survives. More recently scholars, accustomed, perhaps, to remunerations paid for academic studies, have argued Milton was reasonably paid for a work of genius that was a decade in the making and a lifetime in preparation.

12. See David Quint, *Epic and Empire: Politics and Generic Form from Virgil to Milton* (Princeton, N.J.: Princeton University Press, 1993), 269 and 316; David Norbrook, *Writing the English Republic: Poetry, Rhetoric and Politics*, 1627–1660 (Cambridge: Cambridge University Press, 1999), 438 and 493; Barbara K. Lewalski, *The Life of John Milton: A Critical Biography* (Oxford: Blackwell, 2000), 448 and 460; Phillip J. Donnelly, "Poetic Justice: Plato's *Republic* in *Paradise Lost* (1667)," in *"Paradise Lost: A Poem Written in Ten Books": Essays on the 1667 First Edition*, ed. Michael Lieb and John T. Shawcross (Pittsburgh: Duquesne University Press, 2007), 159–81; and Achsah Guibbory, "Milton's 1667 *Paradise Lost* in Its Historical and Literary Contexts," in Lieb and Shawcross, *"Paradise Lost,"* 79–95.

13. *"Mansus,"* lines 78–84; *"Epitaphium Damonis,"* lines 162–170. I discuss the limitations for Milton of Renaissance theories of the epic in "Milton's Choice of Subject," in *Delirious Milton: The Fate of the Poet in Modernity* (Cambridge, Mass.: Harvard University Press, 2006), 133–35.

14. Milad Doueihi, *Le Paradis terrestre: mythes et philosophies* (Paris: Seuil, 2006), 190. Doueihi points out the great difference between Utopia and Paradise: one includes history and the other does not. Doueihi gives a remarkable account of the various ways Paradise was conceived and materialized in seventeenth-century European culture. It had philosophical interest. Jane Marie Todd, trans., *The Earthly Paradise* (Cambridge, Mass.: Harvard University Press, 2009).

15. See R. G. Moyles, *The Text of "Paradise Lost": A Study in Editorial Procedure* (Toronto: University of Toronto Press, 1985).

16. Samuel Johnson, "Life of Milton," ed. Stephen Fix, vol. 1, *The Lives of the Poets*, gen. ed. John H. Middendorf, in *The Collected Works of Samuel Johnson XXI* (New Haven, Conn.: Yale University Press, 2010), 182–83 and 205.

17. For the argument that the volume containing *Paradise Regained* and *Samson Agonistes*, printed by John Starkey, is internally fashioned in all respects by the radical circles in the late 1660s, see Laura Lunger Knoppers, ed., *The 1671 Poems "Paradise Regain'd" and "Samson Agonistes,"* vol. II, *The Complete Works of John Milton* (Oxford: Oxford University Press, 2008), xxxi–l.

18. See Barbara Lewalski, *Milton's Brief Epic: The Genre, Meaning and Art of Milton's "Paradise Regained"* (Providence, R.I.: Brown University Press, 1966).

19. For review of the most recent discussions of the date of *Samson Agonistes*, see Knoppers, *The 1671 Poems*, lxxxviii–xcviii. Knoppers concludes *Samson Agonistes* is Milton's final work. For a date in the early 1660s, that is, immediately after the Restoration and responding to the shock of that event, see, for example, Christopher Hill, "*Samson Agonistes* Again," *Literature and History* 1, no. 1 (1990): 24–39. For a less conclusive account of the date, see Archie Burnett, "Date," in *Samson Agonistes*, vol. 3, *A Variorum Commentary on the Poems of John Milton*, ed. Stephen B. Dobranski and Paul J. Klemp (Pittsburgh: Duquesne University Press, 2009), 1–7. See also John Carey, ed., *John Milton, Complete Shorter Poems*, rev. 2nd ed. (London: Pearson/Longman, 2007), 349–50. The best discussion of the date of *Samson Agonistes*, concluding it is Milton's final work, remains that of Mary Ann Radzinowicz, *Toward Samson Agonistes: The Growth of Milton's Mind* (Princeton, N.J.: Princeton University Press, 1978), 387–407.

20. Milton was commonly reported to have large passages of Homer by heart. For the importance of Virgil, see David Quint, *Inside "Paradise Lost": Reading the Designs of Milton's Epic* (Princeton, N.J.: Princeton University Press, 2014).

21. Roger Ascham, *The Schoolmaster*, ed. R. J. Schoeck (Toronto: Dent, 1966), 67. *Areopagitica:* "our sage and serious poet Spenser, whom I dare be known to think a better teacher than Scotus or Aquinas" (*YP*, 2:516).

22. That pollution was a recognized problem in the seventeenth century is documented by Ken Hiltner, *What Else Is Pastoral? Renaissance Literature and the Environment* (Ithaca, N.Y.: Cornell University Press, 2011).

23. *City of God*, 13.14. See R. A. Markus, "*Saeculum*": *History and Society in the Theology of Saint Augustine* (Cambridge: Cambridge University Press, 1970), 10.

24. *The Ready and Easy Way to Establish a Free Commonwealth*, 1st ed. (February 23–26, 1660) (*YP*, 7:363). The sentence is enlarged in the second expanded edition of *The Ready and Easy Way* (published April 1–10, 1660) (*YP*, 7:428), when events were tending more certainly to "readmitting kingship in this nation" and "returning to bondage" (*YP*, 7:405 and 407), thus "making vain and viler than dirt the blood of so many thousand faithful and valiant Englishmen who left us in this liberty, bought with their lives" (*YP*, 7:423–24). Other memorable phrases include: "their necks yoked with these tigers of Bacchus" (*YP*, 7:452–53); "the Jews to return back to Egypt to worship their idol queen"; "monarchizing our government"; "what I have spoken is the language of that which is not called amiss *the good old cause*" (*YP*, 7:452–53); "though I were sure I should have spoken only to trees and stones, and had none to cry to, but with the prophet, *O earth, earth, earth!* to tell the very soil itself what her perverse inhabitants are deaf to" (*YP*, 7:462–63); "the last words of our expiring liberty"; "some perhaps whom God may raise of these stones to become children of reviving liberty and may reclaim, though they seem now choosing them a captain back for Egypt, to bethink themselves a little and consider whither they are rushing" (*YP*, 7:463).

25. For a theoretically acute discussion of Milton, Homer, and influence, see Gregory Machacek, *Milton and Homer: "Written to Aftertimes"* (Pittsburgh: Duquesne University Press, 2011).

26. *Reason of Church Government* (*YP*, 1:813).

27. *Iliad*, 12.243: "εἷς οἰωνὸς ἄριστος ἀμύνεσθαι περὶ πάτρης."

28. Luís de Camões, *Os Lusiadas*, ed. Frank Pierce (1973; repr., Oxford: Clarendon Press, 1981). Sir Richard Fanshawe, trans. *The Lusiad; or, Portugal's Historical Poem* (London, 1655), in vol. 2 of *The Poems and Translations of Sir Richard Fanshawe*, ed. Peter Davidson (Oxford: Clarendon Press, 1999).

29. Andrew Fichter, *Poets Historical: Dynastic Epic in the Renaissance* (New Haven, Conn.: Yale University Press, 1982).

30. Stanley Fish, *How Milton Works* (Cambridge, Mass.: Harvard University Press, 2001), 494, refers to places in *Paradise Lost* "when the ownership of the poem is itself an issue."

31. Bernard of Clairvaux *Apologia* (1124), in which he attacks the art decorating monastic cloisters—on the column capitals—as a distraction of the mind from reading and a violation of nature, by putting several heads on one body, and so on, making beauty a deformity and deformity beautiful *(deformis formositas ac formosa deformitas)*. See Erwin Panofsky, "Abbot Suger of Saint Denis," in *Meaning in the Visual Arts* (New York: Doubleday, 1955), 132–33.

32. See Fish, *How Milton Works*, 496–98.

On the Origin in Paradise Lost

1. On potential, see Leland de la Durantaye, *Giorgio Agamben: A Critical Introduction* (Stanford: Stanford University Press).

2. Jean-Louis Vieillard-Baron, *Hegel, Penseur du Politique* (Paris: Félin, 2006), 133–35. Hegel's opposition, which is key to the *Logic*, of *Wirklichkeit* and *Realität*, presents two kinds of reality, the first containing reflection, the second not, the first philosophical and ideal, the second empirical and positivistic. The Garden of Eden that Milton destroys is presented as empirical fact. The Garden of Eden Milton calls "a paradise within" (*PL*, 587) is universal and ideal, and transcendently true, a revelation of the interior or essence of history. But this universal ideal is not merely abstract but rather exists by subsuming the finite and factual paradise. The difference may be seen by comparing the universal archetype of man in Milton's *"De Idea Platonica"* with Adam in *Paradise Lost*. The first is an abstract universal, disengaged from the world, the second a finite universal. See G. F. W. Hegel, *Vorlesungen über die Geschichte der Philosophie*, part 1, *Einleitung*, vol. 6 in *Vorlesungen, Ausgewälte Nachschriften und Manuskripte* (Hamburg: Hamburg, Meiner, 1994), 24.

3. I discuss Heidegger's politics and the notion of *care* in *Allegory and Violence* (Ithaca, N.Y.: Cornell University Press, 1996). There is of course a large bibliography on Heidegger and *place*, as also on the late concept that replaces it, "event," *Ereignis*, especially in *Contributions to Philosophy: from enowning*, trans. Parvis Emad and Kenneth Maly (Bloomington: Indiana University Press, 1999). Useful discussions may be found in James K. Lyon, *Paul Celan and Martin Heidegger: An Unresolved Conversation, 1951–1970* (Baltimore: Johns Hopkins University Press, 2006), 122–34; and Jeff Malpas, *Heidegger and the Thinking of Place: Explorations in the Topology of Being* (Cambridge, Mass.: MIT Press, 2012), 46–47.

4. Micea Eliade, *The Sacred and the Profane: On the Nature of Religion* (New York: Harcourt Brace, 1959). Despite his subtitle, Eliade's point about space is that some places are "sacred" to us in a passionate but secular sense, and other places

are "profane" or indifferent to us. Eliade is secularizing a religious point of view, but he is also "secularizing" the Heideggerean mystique of place.

5. Friedrich Hölderlin, *Der Rhein*, 4:46–47. Michael Hamburger, ed., trans., *Poems and Fragments* (Cambridge: Cambridge University Press, 1980), 410.

6. Martin Heidegger makes this point in his commentary on "The Rhine." *Les Hymnes de Hölderlin: "La Germanie" et "Le Rhin,"* ed. Susanne Ziegler, trans. François Fédier and Julien Hervier (Paris: Gallimard, 1988), 188. Originally *Hölderlins Hymnen "Germanien" und "Der Rhein"* (Frankfurt: Klostermann, 1980).

7. See also, for contrast, the short but complex description of Satan's flight path, avoiding detection by avoiding the advancing line of the light (*PL*, 9.63–66).

8. Edward Young, *Conjectures on Original Composition, in a Letter of the Author to Sir Charles Grandison*, 2nd ed. (London, 1759), 20. For excerpts and an account of the work's importance, see Russell Noyes, ed., *English Romantic Poetry and Prose* (1956; repr., Oxford: Oxford University Press, 1967), 21.

9. Nicholas von Maltzahn, *Milton's History of Britain: Republican Historiography in the English Revolution* (Oxford: Clarendon Press, 1991), 92–99.

10. See, e.g., J. N. Spuhler, "Somatic Paths to Culture," and S. L. Washburn, "Speculations on the Interrelations of the History of Tools and Biological Evolution," in *The Evolution of Man's Capacity for Culture*, ed. J. N. Spuhler (Detroit: Wayne State University Press, 1965), 1–133, and 21–31.

11. Andrew Marvell, "On Mr. Milton's *Paradise Lost*," line 5, in *The Poems of Andrew Marvell*, ed. Nigel Smith (London: Pearson/Longman, 2003), 182.

12. *Of Education* (*YP*, 2:405).

13. Theodore W. Adorno, *Beethoven: The Philosophy of Music*, ed. Rolf Tiedemann, trans. Edmund Jephcott (Stanford, Calif.: Stanford University Press, 1998), 142.

14. For dramas that would have inspired *Paradise Lost*, see Douglas Bush, *John Milton: A Sketch of his Life and Writings* (London: Weidenfeld and Nicolson, 1964), 143. For the possibility, according to Voltaire, of Milton's having attended in Milan a performance of the *dramma per musica* entitled *L'Adamo*, by Giovanni Battista Andreini, see William Riley Parker, *Milton: A Biography* (Oxford: Clarendon, 1968), 2:830n60. In Rome, Milton did attend, in February 1637, a lavish musical production, with sets by Bernini, at the Palazzo Barberini, and with an audience of thirty-five hundred, probably *Chi soffra spera*, a comic opera by Cardinal Giulio Rospigliosi, later to be Pope Clement IX. See Barbara K. Lewalski, *The Life of John Milton: A Critical Biography* (London: Blackwell, 2000), 100. Milton was in Venice not long after the first public opera houses were opened (1637) and Claudio Monteverdi, though in his seventies and near the end of his life, was at the height of his powers.

15. *Iliad*, 1.3–4.

16. Adam and Eve have taken their way through Eden because Eden is the large country in which the garden paradise is situated, on the top of a high mountain. After their exile from the garden paradise, when they are led "down the cliff . . . To the subjected plain" (*PL*, 12.639–40), Adam and Eve are still in Eden, but no longer in the garden. Sixteenth- and seventeenth-century maps of the Near East show Eden as a large territory. Abraham Ortelius, *Theatri orbis terrarum parergon* (1624); the map in this work entitled *Geographia sacra* shows Eden in a large region at the headwaters of the Euphrates. See Alessandro Scafi, *Il Para-*

diso in terra: mappe del giardino dell'Eden (Milan: Mondadori, 2007). Original English text published in 2006.

17. *Areopagitica* (*YP*, 2:514). Milton's striking image may have been called forth by the twins Argante and Ollyphant in *The Faerie Queene*, who copulate in the womb and are born "in that monstrous wise" (3.7.48).

18. *The Ready and Easy Way to Establish a Free Commonwealth*, 2nd ed. (*YP*, 7:428). Christopher Hill, *The Experience of Defeat: Milton and Some Contemporaries* (New York: Viking, 1984).

19. Horace, *Ars Poetica*, line 147. Horace actually says "from the double egg": *nec gemino bellum Troianum orditur ab ovo* ("nor orders the tale of the Trojan war from the double egg").

20. See the discussion of *materia prima*, in *De Doctrina Christiana*, 1:286–89; from chapter 7, "De creatione." See Gordon Teskey, "God's Body: Concept and Metaphor," in *Delirious Milton* (Cambridge, Mass.: Harvard University Press, 2006), 85–106.

21. H. R. MacCallum, "Milton and Figurative Interpretation of the Bible," *University of Toronto Quarterly* 31 (1962): 397–415. MacCallum points out, among other things, the inaccuracy of applying a term for a fourth-century heresy, *Arianism*, to the view of a seventeenth-century poet, whose Christology had more complex and recent formative influences. For a full discussion of the relationship of creatures and sons to God, see MacCallum's *Milton and the Sons of God: The Divine Image in Milton's Epic Poetry* (Toronto: University of Toronto Press, 1986). If *Arianism* means only that the Son is not equal to or co-eternal with the Father, then of course Milton is an Arian; I happen to think the term entails more than that. If *Trinitarian* means the three persons of the godhead are co-equal and one as well as three, as in the notorious Johannine Comma (1 John 5: 7–8), which Milton knew to be a later insertion into the Bible, then Milton is not a Trinitarian. But I still think it is possible to describe him as a heterodox Trinitarian because he believed in three persons in the godhead. In short, I would urge a stricter interpretation of the term *Arian*, because the term is historical, and a looser interpretation of the word *Trinitarian*, because it is not necessary for Miltonists to conform with orthodox Christian belief. For an expert, orthodox discussion of Milton's theology, see William Poole, "Theology," in *Milton in Context*, ed. Stephen B. Dobranski (Cambridge: Cambridge University Press, 2010), 477–78.

On the Verse of Paradise Lost

1. Vladimir Majakovskij, cited in Roman Jakobson, *Language in Literature*. ed., trans., Krystyna Pomorska and Stephen Rudy (Cambridge, Mass.: Harvard University Press, 1987), 274. Mao Zedong, *"Talks at the Yan'an Conference on Literature and Art": A Translation of the 1943 Text with Commentary by Bonnie S. McDougall* (Ann Arbor: Center for Chinese Studies, University of Michigan Press, 1980). In short, writers should be on the side of the workers and the masses; they should shun bourgeois, psychological writing, which merely sympathizes with the oppressor class; and they should study Marxism in order to create works that will provide leadership to the masses in the struggle.

2. Sir Philip Sidney, *Defence Poesie, the Prose Works of Sir Philip Sidney* (Cambridge: Cambridge University Press, 1968), 3:10–11.

3. William Hazlitt, "My First Acquaintance with Poets," *Liberal* 3 (1823), in P. P. Howe, ed., *The Complete Works of William Hazlitt* (London: Dent, 1930–1934), 17:119. See Roger Gilbert, *Walks in the World: Representation and Experience in Modern American Poetry* (Princeton, N.J.: Princeton University Press, 1991), 10–12.

4. Philip Larkin, "Cut Grass," in *Collected Poems*, ed. Anthony Thwaite (New York: Farrar, Straus, Giroux, 1989), 183. First published in *High Windows* (New York: Farrar, Straus, Giroux, 1974).

5. Jacques Derrida, *De la grammatologie* (Paris: Minuit, 1967), 13n4, citing I. J. Gelb, *A Study of Writing: The Foundations of Grammatology* (Chicago: University of Chicago Press, 1952). Gelb's subtitle was dropped in the reprint of 1963. See *Faerie Queene*, 3.12. 47 (canceled stanza): "But now my teme begins to faint and fayle, / . . . Therefore I will their sweatie yokes assoyle / At this same furrowes end, till a new day."

6. See Craig MacDonald, "The Nastawgan: Traditional Routes of Travel in the Temagami District," in *Nastawgan: The Canadian North by Canoe and Showshoe*, ed. Bruce W. Hodgins and Margaret Hobbs (Toronto: Betelgeuse Books, 1987), 183–87.

7. For the frequent use of accusative pronouns at the beginning of lines in oral formulaic verse, see Milman Parry, *The Making of Homeric Verse*, ed. Adam Parry (Oxford: Oxford University Press, 1971), 10–16.

8. *Iliad*, 2.484–93; *Aeneid*, 7.641–46. That divine simplicity of Homer's— *divina illa simplicitas*—is Macrobius's phrase. R. D. Williams, *The Aeneid of Virgil* (London: Macmillan, 1973), 641n213. *Saturnalia* 5.15.16.

9. See Jason Rosenblatt, *Renaissance England's Chief Rabbi: John Selden* (New York: Oxford University Press, 2006).

10. For an interesting discussion of these words, see Daniel Shore, *Milton and the Art of Rhetoric* (Cambridge: Cambridge University Press, 2012), 95.

11. Ingrid Basso, "The 'Enormous Scepticism' of European Development: Kierkegaard's Unpolitical Christianity," in *Kierkegaard and the Renaissance and Modern Traditions* (Burlington, Vt.: Ashgate, 2009), 109.

12. Edward Phillips, "The Life of Mr. John Milton" (1694), in *The Early Lives of Milton*, ed. Helen Darbishire (London: Constable, 1932), 72–73.

13. A. J. A. Waldock, *"Paradise Lost" and Its Critics* (Cambridge: Cambridge University Press, 1947), 77–78.

14. Stanley Fish, in *Surprised by Sin: The Reader in "Paradise Lost"* (1968; repr., Cambridge, Mass.: Harvard University Press, 1998).

15. Matthew Arnold, *Essays Religious and Mixed*, ed. R. H. Super (Ann Arbor: University of Michigan Press, 1972), 183.

16. M. H. Abrams, *The Fourth Dimension of a Poem, and Other Essays* (New York: W. W. Norton, 2012). I believe it was in one of several of his talks while this book was being written that Abrams mentioned faint neurological signals being sent to the organs of speech, even when we read silently. I have been unable to find this exact point in the book, concerning "the activity of enunciating the great variety of speech-sounds that constitute the words of a poem" (2).

17. I take the terms *hot* and *cool* from Marshall McLuhan, *Understanding Media* (New York: McGraw-Hill, 1964).

18. A. R. Ammons, *Tape for the Turn of the Year* (1965; repr., New York: W. W. Norton, 1994); *Garbage* (New York: W. W. Norton, 1993); *Glare* (New York: W. W. Norton, 1997).

19. Jorie Graham, "Positive Feedback Loop (June 2007)," in *Sea Change* (New York: HarperCollins, 2008), 42.

20. Verlaine, *"Art Poétique,"* line 21, from *Jadis and Naguère: poésies* (Paris, 1884), in *Oeuvres poétique complètes,* ed. Y.-G Le Dantec, rev. ed. Jacques Borel (Paris: Gallimard, 1962), 327.

21. John Milton, *History of Britain* (*YP,* 5:15). Accounts of the Trojan tradition in late antiquity and the Middle Ages, and in the early modern world up to Goethe, may be found in, respectively, Hermann Dunger, *Die Sage vom tro-janischen Kriege in den Bearbeitungen des Mittelalters und ihre antiken Quellen* (Dresden, 1869); Georg Finsler, *Homer in der Neuzeit von Dante bis Goethe: Italien, Frankreich, England, Deutschland* (Leipzig: Teubner, 1912). For the Renaissance ac-ceptance of stories about Troy supposedly told by "Dictys Cretensis" and "Dares Phrygius," who fought on either side, see Douglas Bush, *Mythology and the Renais-sance Tradition in English Poetry* (1932; repr., New York: W. W. Norton, 1963). Spenser lays special emphasis on the Trojan origin of the English "Britons," of whom his queen is a supposed descendant.

22. John Dryden, "Preface to *Fables Ancient and Modern,*" in *The Poems and Fables of John Dryden,* ed. James Kinsley (London: Oxford University Press, 1962), 521.

On the Sublime in Paradise Lost

1. Samuel Johnson, "Life of Milton," ed. Stephen Fix, vol. 1, *The Lives of the Poets,* gen. ed. John H. Middendorf, in *The Collected Works of Samuel Johnson XXI* (New Haven, Conn.: Yale University Press, 2010), 189–90.

2. For a darker interpretation of what appears as Longinus's exuberant gener-osity, see Anne Carson, "On the Sublime in Longinus and Antonioni," in *Decre-ation: Opera, Essays, Poetry* (New York: Knopf, 2005), 45. Cited by Emma Gilby, "The Seventeenth-Century Sublime: Boileau and Poussin," in The Art of the Sublime, ed. Nigel Llewellyn and Christine Riding, January 2013, www.tate.org.uk /art/research-publications/the-sublime/emma-gilby-the-seventeenth-century -sublime-boileau-and-poussin.

3. J. E. B. Spencer, "Longinus in English Criticism: Influences before Milton," *Review of English Studies,* n.s. 8, no. 30 (1957): 137.

4. Edmund Burke, *A Philosophical Inquiry into the Origin of our Ideas of the Beau-tiful and the Sublime,* ed. Adam Phillips (Oxford: Oxford University Press, 1990). Immanuel Kant, *Kritik der Urteilskraft* (1790), *Critique of Judgment,* trans. James Creed Meredith, rev. Nicholas Walker (Oxford: Oxford University Press, 2007), 76. See book 2, sections 23–29, paragraphs 244–64. Influential modern discussions include Samuel Holt Monk, *The Sublime: A Study of Critical Theories in XVIII-Century England,* 2nd ed. (Ann Arbor: University of Michigan Press, 1960); Thomas Weiskel, *The Romantic Sublime: Studies in the Structure and Psychology of Transcen-dence* (Baltimore: Johns Hopkins University Press, 1976); Neil Hertz, *The End of the Line: Essays on Psychoanalysis and the Sublime* (New York: Columbia University Press, 1985), esp. 49–50, an unusually clear account of Kant on the sublime; Steven Knapp, *Personification and the Sublime: Milton to Coleridge* (Cambridge, Mass.: Har-vard University Press, 1985); John H. Zammito, *The Genesis of Kant's "Critique of Judgment"* (Chicago: University of Chicago Press, 1992), 263–69; Timothy Bahti, "The (Un)Natural Language of the Sublime in Wordsworth's *Prelude,*" in *A Com-panion to Romantic Poetry,* ed. Charles Mahoney (Malden, Mass.: Wiley-Blackwell,

2011), 483–502; and Ian Balfour, "The Matter of Genre in the Romantic Sublime," in *A Companion to Romantic Poetry*, ed. Mahoney, 503–20.

5. See Sanford Budick, *Milton and Kant* (Cambridge: Harvard University Press, 2010), 18 et passim. There are many reasons to compare Milton and Kant, as Budick's book shows, because both are centrally concerned with human freedom. Budick has much to say throughout about the series of steps in the *Critique of Judgment* moving from outward perception of grandeur to inward reason.

6. *Iliad*, 5. 772.

7. *The Prelude*, in *Wordsworth's Poetry and Prose*, ed. Nicholas Halmi (New York: Norton, 2014), 177n2.

8. Ibid., 1:421–24.

9. Ibid., 177n2.

10. See Barbara Lewalski, *The Life of John Milton: A Critical Biography* (Malden, Mass.: Wiley-Blackwell, 2000), 89–109.

11. Neil Hertz, "A Reading of Longinus," in *The End of the Line: Essays on Psychoanalysis and the Sublime*, 4 and 14; and "The Notion of Blockage in the Literature of the Sublime," 40–60.

12. *The Prelude*, 7.616–17. The passage is discussed in Hertz, *End of the Line*, 59–60.

13. Erwin Panofsky, "Et in Arcadia Ego: Poussin and the Elegiac Tradition," in *Meaning in the Visual Arts* (1955; repr., Chicago: University of Chicago Press, 1982), 300.

14. See 2 Corinthians 12:9–10. J. M. French, ed., *The Life Records of John Milton 4* (New Brunswick, N.J.: Rutgers University Press, 1949–58), 118–19. For the Greek motto and Christopher Arnold, in whose autograph book Milton wrote it in 1651, less than a year before he became totally blind, see David Masson, *The Life of John Milton: Narrated in Connexion with the Political, Ecclesiastical, and Literary History of His Time* (1881; repr., Gloucester, Mass.: Peter Smith, 1965), 4:352–53. Milton has been thinking about weakness for some time. Twelve years before, when he was in Geneva, he wrote in the album of Camillo Cerdogni (January 10, 1639) the final two lines of *A Masque*—"if Vertue feeble were / Heaven itself would stoop to her." He was then moved to add another text, one adapted from Horace, suggesting firmness of mind and connected, intriguingly, with space: *coelum non animum muto dum trans mare curro* ("when I run over sea, I change my skies but not my mind"). Horace is condemning pointless travel in a fine phrase, "strenuous inertia," and says that those who rush over the sea are no wiser for doing so, changing merely their skies, but not improving their minds: *"caelum non animum mutant qui trans mare currunt"* (*Epistles*, 1.1.27).

15. Johnson, "Life of Milton," *The Lives of the Poets*, vol. 1, ed. Stephen Fix, The Yale Edition of the Works of Samuel Johnson 21 (New Haven: Yale University Press, 2010), 202.

On Temptation in Paradise Lost

1. In the Christian tradition, it is God the Son—the Word (John 1:1)—who creates the world and Adam and Eve. It is also the Son who judges Adam and Eve in the garden, after the Fall, anticipating his judgment of all people at the Apocalypse. In the same tradition the serpent who tempts Adam and Eve is Satan in

disguise. In fact Satan is a late-appearing figure in the Jewish Septuagint, the Christian Old Testament. Of course, neither the Son nor Satan makes any appearance in the folktale narrative of Genesis 3. God creates Adam and Eve and judges them, and the serpent is *phronimôtatos*, "more subtle than any beast of the field which the Lord God had made" (3:1). At the time of the Authorized Version (1611), the word *subtle* means "tricky" or *rusé* (as in the French version of the Jerusalem Bible). The Latin Vulgate and Luther's German Bibles follow this sense: the serpent is *callidior cunctis animantibus terrae* and *listiger als alle Tiere auf dem Feld*.

2. The first sin is the most atrocious (*atrocissimum*) because the most comprehensive, a transgression of the entire law, "for under this head what did man not perpetrate?" *De Doctrina Christiana*, chapter 11, "*De Lapsu primorum parentum et de peccato*" ("On the Fall of the First Parents and on Sin"), 2:412–13.

3. This well-known phrase is from Bernard Williams's, "Persons, Character and Morality," in *Moral Luck* (Cambridge: Cambridge University Press, 1981), 18.

4. *Iliad*, 16.46–47.

5. *Iliad*, 16.833.

6. "Once in three weeks or a month he would drop into the society of some young sparks of his acquaintance . . . with these gentlemen he would so far make bold with his body as now and then to keep a gaudy day." Milton's nephew Edward Phillips wrote this in his biography of the poet, published in 1694. Helen Darbishire, ed., *The Early Lives of Milton* (London: Constable, 1932), 62.

7. Marlowe, *Hero and Leander*, in *Marlowe's Poems*, ed. L. C. Martin (London: Methuen, 1931): "like to a bold sharp sophister" (197), and "One is no number" (255).

8. "*Elenchus autem est redargutio sive vera sive falsa*," that is, "a refutation, true or false." *Art of Logic*, 2.4, in *The Works of John Milton*, ed. Frank Allen Patterson et al., 18 vols. in 21 (New York: Columbia University Press, 1931–1938), 2:374–75.

9. Dante Alighieri, *La Divina Commedia*, ed. Giorgio Petrocchi (Turin: Einaudi, 1975), *Purgatorio*, 28.49–51.

10. C. S. Lewis, *Preface to "Paradise Lost"* (1942; repr., New York: Oxford University Press, 1961), 127: "What would have happened if . . . Adam had . . . interceded with God on her behalf, we are not told. The reason we are not told is that Milton does not know: he says cautiously that the situation '*seemd* remediless'" (919).

11. "The Nun's Priest's Tale," 3163–66, in *The Works of Geoffrey Chaucer*, ed. F. N. Robinson, 2nd ed. (Boston: Houghton Mifflin, 1957).

12. This point is developed at more length in my *Allegory and Violence* (Ithaca, N.Y.: Cornell University Press, 1996). See also Joseph Campana, *The Pain of Reformation: Spenser, Vulnerability, and the Ethics of Masculinity* (New York: Fordham University Press, 2012).

13. The inversion of one hierarchy within an entire system—for example, that of acoustic speech (*phonê*) over the written sign (*graphê*)—is a theme in the many writings of Jacques Derrida, especially *De la grammatologie* (Paris: Minuit, 1967), 201–2 and 444.

On the End in Paradise Lost

1. Aristotle, *Poetics*, ed. D. W. Lucas (1968; repr., Oxford: Clarendon, 1972), 1452a12: "Of plots there are those that are simple (*haploi*) and those that are complex (*peplegmenoi*)." Johnson writes, "It is only by a blind confidence in the reputation

of Milton that a drama can be praised in which the intermediate parts have neither cause nor consequences, neither hasten nor retard the catastrophe." Samuel Johnson, "Life of Milton," ed. Stephen Fix, vol. 1, *Lives of the Poets*, gen. ed. John H. Middendorf, in *The Collected Works of Samuel Johnson XXI* (New Haven, Conn.: Yale University Press, 2010), 1:201.

2. The Greek noun *schêma*, "form, shape, figure," generally means the outward appearance of something, its arrangement and outline, like the harness of a horse, or a dance figure, or a certain carriage and manner, as opposed to the inward *form* of something, its *eidos*, in the Aristotelian sense. The verbal form, *schêmatizô*, *schêmatizein*, has the active sense of molding, shaping, arranging, and improvising. There is a subjective element to such "schematizing," a sense of the word Kant had in mind for the *schemata*. In medieval Latin *schêma* was rendered as *figura*. *Schêma* is related to *echein*, "to have, to grasp," and to *epochê*, a holding against or holding together (also, a retention, a stoppage, a suspension). The Indo-European root word (*segh-) suggests "conquering" and "holding." This sense appears in the cognate, German word *Sieg* ("victory"). See *OED* "scheme" and Liddell and Scott σχῆμα.

3. In the ten-book *Paradise Lost* published in 1667, the present books, 11 and 12, formed one book, thus leaving two books after the Fall. It seems to me not unlikely Milton was following the *Iliad* and the *Odyssey*, both of which have two books following their crises. Milton would not have known the division of the Homeric epics into books is the later invention of the Alexandrian editors, whose work was published after Milton's death. But the Alexandrian divisions are intelligent and follow real divisions in these poems.

4. *Iliad*, 14.346–51: "Whereupon in his arms the son of Kronos clasped his wife. / Beneath them the god Earth caused fresh grass to grow / dewy lotus, crocus and hyacinth / densely packed and yet yielding, such that the ground was far below. / The two of them lay down there, and around them they drew a cloud / beautiful and golden."

5. *Oedipus Tyrannus*, lines 1295–96. Before Oedipus, who has stabbed out his eyes, returns to the stage, the messenger says, "You shall soon look upon a sight / which even he who abhors it must pity." I have slightly modified Jebb's translation.

6. Euripides, *Electra*, 1282–83. "Ζεὺς δ᾽, ὡς ἔρις γένοιτο καὶ φόνος βροτῶν, / εἴδωλον Ἑλένης ἐξέπεμψ᾽ ἐς Ἴλιον."

7. These remarks are inspired by the discussion of frames in Jacques Derrida, *La Vérité en peinture* (Paris: Flammarion, 1978).

8. This famous phrase is from Augustine's Confessions (7.10.13–17), where he finds himself "far from you [God] in a region of unlikeness" ("*et inveni longe me esse a te in regio dissimilitudinis*"). See Brian Stock, *Augustine the Reader: Meditation, Self-Knowledge, and the Ethics of Interpretation* (Cambridge, Mass.: Harvard University Press, 1996), 72 and 332n266.

9. *Iliad*, 2.486.

10. "If, at that sight, repugnance overpowers compassion, the spell has been imperfect; if all other feelings are absorbed in the profound pathos of the situation, then Sophocles has triumphed." Richard Claverhouse Jebb, "Introduction," in *Sophocles: The Plays and Fragments*, vol. 1, *The Oedipus Tyrannus* (1883; repr., Cambridge: Cambridge University Press, 2010), lii.

11. Genesis 2:8. Seventeenth-century maps such as Abraham Ortelius's *Geographica sacra* (1624) generally show Eden as a large country on the upper

Euphrates—sometimes stretching between the Euphrates and the Tigris—in which the Paradise would be one location. Sir Walter Raleigh devotes several chapters to "the seat of paradise" and its difference from the surrounding country around the upper Euphrates. See *The History of the World*, in *The Works of Walter Raleigh* (New York: Burt Franklin, 1829), vol. 2, chap. 3, sec. 12, p. 109. For Raleigh's maps of the country of Eden surrounding the island of paradise, see Alessandro Scafi, *Il Paradiso in terra: mappe del giardino dell'Eden* (Milan: Mondadori, 2007), 250–51. There is an English version I have been unable to obtain, *Mapping Paradise: A History of Heaven on Earth* (London: British Library, 2006). Some maps of the period show Eden between the Euphrates and the Tigris, near the Persian Gulf, in the marshlands near Nashiriyah and ancient Ur. A small park, Janat Adan, is still regarded as the site. Bruce Feiler, *Where God Was Born* (New York: HarperCollins, 2005), 153.

12. F. S. Boas and Arthur Lovejoy, *Primitivism and Related Ideas in Antiquity* (Baltimore, Md.: Johns Hopkins University Press, 1935). Of interest for the rarer, anthropological tradition of hard primitivism before Vico are the hunting scenes of Piero di Cosimo in the Metropolitan Museum, New York, and *The Forest Fire*, in the Ashmolean Museum, Oxford.

13. Cited from Wikipedia (I have slightly altered the text as there quoted), under "Siphonaptera" and, for Swift and de Morgan, "Ad Infinitum."

14. "The Hell assigned to the rebellious spirits is described as not less local than the residence of man. It is placed in some distant part of space, separated from the regions of harmony and order by a chaotic waste and an unoccupied vacuity. But Sin and Death worked up a 'mole of aggregated soil' cemented with asphaltus, a work too bulky for ideal architects." Johnson, "Life of Milton," 3:198.

15. *Allegory and Violence* (Ithaca, N.Y.: Cornell University Press, 1996), 42–43.

16. I discuss these frescoes in the Palais de la porte dorée in "The Ideology of Primitive Art," in *Reading Allegory Otherwise*, ed. Brenda Machosky (Stanford, Calif.: Stanford University Press, 2010), 119–41.

17. The Orcagna fresco was detached from the wall and remounted. It is now in the Museo dell'Opera di Santa Croce. The detail is superbly reproduced in Millard Meiss, The *Great Age of Fresco* (New York: Brazillier, 1970), 95. See also Joachim Poeschke, *Italian Frescoes: The Age of Giotto 1280–1400* (New York: Abbeville, 2005), 324–25, figs. 84–86; and Alastair Smart, *The Dawn of Italian Painting, 1250–1400* (Ithaca, N.Y.: Cornell University Press, 1978), 61 and fig. 149. For the cultural context of such representations, see Millard Meiss, *Painting in Florence and Siena after the Black Death* (1951; repr., Princeton, N.J.: Princeton University Press, 1978).

18. Ruth 1:16: "Intreat me not to leave thee, or to return from following after thee: for whither thou goest, I will go; and where thou lodgest, I will lodge: thy people shall be my people, and thy God my God"; Numbers 12:6: "I the Lord will make myself known to him in a vision, and will speak unto him in a dream"; *Iliad*, 1.63: "for a dream also is from Zeus"; *Iliad*, 6.429–30: "Hector, you are both father and noble mother to me / You are my brother, as well as my young husband"; and Virgil, *Eclogues*, 3.52: *in me mora non erit ulla*, "in me there shall be no delay."

On Late Style in Paradise Regained *and* Samson Agonistes

1. In John's gospel, Jesus refers three times to "the prince of this world," in 12:31; 14:30; and 16:11. But Satan is not involved in any action. See Luke 10:18 and Isaiah 14:12.

2. The sonnet to Vane was published previously, in George Sikes's *Life and Death of Sir Henry Vane* (1662). Milton had sent the sonnet to Vane in July 1652. See John Carey, ed., *Complete Shorter Poems*, rev. 2nd ed. (London: Pearson/ Longman, 2007), 329. Milton's nephew Edward Phillips published the sonnets in 1694 with his translation of Milton's *Letters of State* and his life of Milton. See Douglas Bush, *John Milton: A Sketch of his Life and Writings* (1964; repr., London: Weidenfeld and Nicolson, 1965), 203. For a fuller narrative account of these years, see Barbara Lewalski, *The Life of John Milton: A Critical Biography* (Oxford and Malden, Mass.: Blackwell, 2000), 489–510. For the publication of the minor poems, see also David Masson, *The Life of John Milton, narrated in connexion with the Political, Ecclesiastical, and Literary History of his Time*, vol. 6 (1881; repr., Gloucester, Mass: Peter Smith, 1965), 687–90. See also 684–86 for Masson's account of the content and publication circumstances of Milton's Ramist text on logic.

3. Edward LeCompte notes that the expression "old age," which appears four times in *Samson Agonistes*, is used nowhere else in Milton's poetry. See *John Milton: "'Paradise Lost,'" "'Samson Agonistes,'" "'Lycidas'"* (New York: New American Library, 1961), *SA* line 1487, n.

4. Edward Phillips, "The Life of Mr. John Milton," (1694), in *The Early Lives of Milton*, ed. Helen Darbishire (London: Constable, 1932), 75.

5. Thomas Ellwood, *The History of the Life of Thomas Ellwood* (London: J. Sowle, 1714), 233–34.

6. Edward Said, *Late Style: Music and Literature against the Grain*, ed. Michael Wood (New York: Pantheon, 2006); Peter Szondi, "Der andere Pfeil: Zur Entstehungsgeschichte des humnischen Spätstils," in *Hölderlin-Studien, mit einem Traktat über philologische Erkenntnis* (1967; repr., Frankfurt am Main: Suhrkamp, 1970), 37–61; "The Other Arrow: On the Genesis of the Late Hymnic Style," in *On Textual Understanding and Other Essays*, trans. Harvey Mendelsohn, forward by Michael Hays, Theory and History of Literature 15 (Minneapolis: University of Minnesota Press, 1986), 23–42; Theodore Wiesengrund Adorno, *Beethoven: The Philosophy of Music*, trans. Edmund Jephcott (Stanford: Stanford University Press, 1998), first published as *Beethoven: Philosophie der Musik*, ed. Rolf Tiedemann, in *Theodore W. Adorno Nachgelassene Schriften 1* (Frankfurt am Main: Suhrkamp, 1993), 180–233. Adorno's general indebtedness to Walter Benjamin's notion of allegory as mortification is apparent throughout, notably on how musical ornament withers and grows numb under the "saturnine gaze" (139)—*unter dem saturninischen Blick* (199)—of the aged artist. For criticism of late style as a general concept, see Linda Hutcheon and Michael Hutcheon, "Late Style(s): The Ageism of the Singular," *Arcade* 2014 http://arcade.stanford.edu; and Robert Kastenbaum, whom the Hutcheons cite: "late style is essentially an illusion that has been propagated on a sentimental basis and which ignores the variety of processes and contexts in which creative works are produced late in life," *Gerontologist* 25 (October 1985): 252. See also Michael Spitzer, *Music as Philosophy: Adorno and Beethoven's Late Style* (Bloomington: University of Indiana Press, 2006), 213–14.

7. Arnold Schoenberg, *The Structural Functions of Harmony* (New York: Norton, 1969), 91; cited in Wikipedia.

8. On the popularity in the Renaissance of the genre of the brief epic, see Barbara Lewalski, *Milton's Brief Epic* (Providence, R.I.: Brown University Press, 1966).

9. For the Bible in *Paradise Lost* and *Paradise Regained*, see Mary Ann Radzinowicz, "How Milton Read the Bible: The Case of *Paradise Regained*," in *The Cambridge Companion to Milton*, ed. Dennis Danielson (Cambridge: Cambridge University Press, 1989), 207–23.

10. Balachandra Rajan, "To Which Is Added *Samson Agonistes*," in *The Prison and the Pinnacle: Papers to Commemorate the Tercentary of "Paradise Regained" and "Samson Agonistes*," ed. Balachandra Rajan (Toronto: University of Toronto Press, 1973), 82–110.

11. This work, falsely attributed to Saint Gregory Nazianzen, is not entirely composed of verses from elsewhere, as in a true cento. About one-third of it is, almost all from Euripides. See *Christus patiens, tragoedia christiana*, ed. J. G. Brambs (Leipzig: Teubner, 1885). In modern times it has proven to be invaluable for recovering the text of Euripides. See the textual commentary in Euripides, *Bacchae*, ed. E. R. Dodds (1960; repr., Oxford: Clarendon Press, 1977).

12. See E. M. W. Tillyard, *Milton*, ed. Phillis B. Tillyard (New York: Macmillan, 1967), 291–92, in which the very favorable views of *Samson Agonistes* by specialists, notably the great Sophocles scholar, Sir Richard Claverhouse Jebb, are summarized.

13. Northrop Frye, *The Return of Eden: Five Essays on Milton's Epics* (Toronto: University of Toronto Press, 1965), 133. The title of Frye's chapter on *Paradise Regained* brings out the latent political sense of the poem: "Revolt in the Desert," 118–43.

14. Prefatory note to *Samson Agonistes*: ""Of That Sort of Dramatic Poem Which Is Called Tragedy." Compare *Reason of Church Government* (*YP*, 1:816–17): "to allay the perturbations of the mind and set the affections in right tune."

15. John Creaser, "Fear of Change: Closed Minds and Open Forms in Milton," *Milton Quarterly* 43 (2008): 177.

16. Horace, *The Odes*, ed. Kenneth Quinn (1980; repr., London: Macmillan, 1985), 3.4.65.

17. The other notable classical model, after Sophocles's *Oedipus at Colonus*, is Aeschylus's *Prometheus Bound*. Prometheus, unlike Samson, can keep a secret. Denys Page, ed., *Prometheus Bound*, *Aeschyli Septem quae Supersunt Tragoedias* (Oxford: Clarendon, 1972), lines 520–25.

18. Frank Kermode, "Milton in Old Age," in *An Appetite for Poetry* (Cambridge, Mass.: Harvard University Press, 1989), 63–64.

19. David Norbrook, *Writing the English Republic* (Cambridge: Cambridge University Press, 1999), 357–78.

20. Especially in end-stopped lines, the stressed final syllable of the penultimate foot tends to separate off and join with the last foot to form the cretic. In Fellini's *La Strada* Giulietta Masina with a drumroll announces the appearance of the strong man: "*è arrivato ZAM—pan—O!*" In English, an example of this rhythm is "WATCH your STEP!" although a better example may the termination of certain threats, such as "SMACK your HEAD!" In the final chorus, nine out of thirteen

lines have this termination. In the choruses of *Samson Agonistes*, the similar but more complicated choriambic termination (long short short long) also appears for pugnacious effect. The claims made by critics for the modern effects of free verse in *Samson Agonistes* strike me as exaggerated. But Milton does seem a little to shift his metrical attention to the end of the line instead of the entire row, and this practice does reflect the less rigorous, distributed rhythms of modern poetry.

21. John Aubrey, "Minutes of the Life of Mr. John Milton," in *The Early Lives of Milton*, ed. Helen Darbishire (London: Constable, 1934), 6. There is a tradition dating from the eighteenth century that James, Duke of York, the future King James II (reigned 1685–1688), visited Milton some time in 1663 and asked him if he did not think his blindness a judgment of God on him for "what he had written against the late king, his father." To which Milton is said to have replied *to this effect* (that is, not in these exact words): "If your Highness thinks that the calamities which befall us here are indications of the wrath of Heaven, in what manner are we to account for the fate of the King your father? The displeasure of Heaven must, upon this supposition, have been much greater against him than against me: for I have lost only my eyes, but he lost his head." The authority for the story is dubious and the style of the response is that of second-rank eighteenth-century prose, without Milton's terse and pointed wit. But the opposition, "**lost** my **eyes . . . lost** his **head**" sounds like Milton. See J. Milton French, ed., *Life Records of John Milton* (New Brunswick, N.J.: Rutgers University Press, 1949–1958), 4:314–15, and William Riley Parker, *Milton: A Biography* (Oxford: Clarendon, 1968), 1:579–80 and 2:1146n55.

22. Aeschylus *Agamemnon*, lines 1381–1383: "ὡς μήτε φεύγειν μήτ' ἀμύνεσθαι μόρον, / ἄπειρον ἀμφιβλήστρον, ὥσπερ ἰχθύων, / περιστιχίζω, πλοῦτον εἵματος κακόν." Denys Page, ed., *Aeschyli Septem quae supersunt tragoedias*, ed. Denys Page (Oxford: Clarendon, 1972).

23. Kenneth Quinn, ed., *The Odes*, ed. Kenneth Quinn (1980; repr., London: Macmillan, 1985), 3.24.6.

24. Richard Claverhouse Jebb, ed. and trans., *Oedipus Tyrannus* (1883; repr., Cambridge: Cambridge University Press, 2010), 1295–96: "Soon thou shalt behold a sight (θέαμα) / such as even one who abhors it must pity" (1295–96). Later, the chorus says it is at once repelled by the sight of Oedipus and drawn to him, such is the shuddering by which the chorus is seized—τοίαν φρίκην παρέχεις μοι—(1306). Milton appears to translate this moment from the end of *Oedipus* to the beginning of *Samson Agonistes*, with the first appearance of his chorus.

25. Also of interest: "**spec**ular **mount**" (*PR*, 4.236, a choriambic); "*walks and shades*" (*PR*, 4.243); "Ilisssus **rolls**" (*PR*, 4.249); "Irassa **strove**" (*PR*, 4.564); "**Ar**taxerxes **throne**" (*PR*, 4.271).

26. Northrop Frye points out the obvious but, for Milton, central ethical point that anything Satan offers is bad not inherently but because Satan offers it: "Later in his career he shows no hesitation in providing miraculous food." Angela Esterhammer, ed., *Northrop Frye on Milton and Blake*, Collected Works of Northrop Frye 16 (Toronto: University of Toronto Press, 2005), 124. True. But Milton intends us to think further into the matter. The things Satan offers—from bread for the poor to political liberty and classical learning—cannot be lightly dismissed.

They are offered because they have real worth. By contrast, what Comus offers the Lady in *A Masque* is worthless.

27. Another route went a longer way around, east of the Jordan River, to avoid Samaria. I imagine Jesus did not take it.

Appendix II

1. "He began about two years before the king came in, and finished about three years after the king's restoration." John Aubrey, "Minutes of the Life of Mr. John Milton," in *The Early Lives of Milton*, ed. Helen Darbishire (1932; repr., New York: Barnes and Noble, 1965), 13. I have regularized Aubrey's spelling and shorthand abbreviations.

2. *The History of the Life of Thomas Ellwood* (London, 1714), 233. See Gordon Campbell, *A Milton Chronology* (London: Macmillan, 1997), 202–3.

Index